and Psalms Proverbs in two Versions with Commentary

and Psalms Proverbs in two Versions with Commentary

PRODUCED FOR

MOODY MONTHLY

THE IVERSEN-NORMAN ASSOCIATES

NEW YORK 1973

Foreword

Psalms and Proverbs are without question the two most frequently quoted legacies from the Old Testament. Christians of every generation have found them to be a unique source of inspiration and encouragement for daily living. Perhaps this is because they are the divine record of the human soul's outpouring in the face of trials and experiences common to all human existence.

In Psalms, man is reaching Godward. David, Moses, Asaph, and others told of their deepest needs, griefs, and joys to God in songs and poetry. In these expressions we can learn much concerning a right relationship with God.

The reverse is true of Proverbs: God is reaching manward. He gives us instruction about our relations with other men. Proverbs provides a concise practical theology—a bedrock of basic principles for Christian living.

Christ's summation of the ten commandments clearly relates one's love for God and his love for his neighbor. Jesus said, "Thou shalt love the Lord thy God with all thy heart, and with all thy soul, and with all thy mind. This is the first and great commandment. And the second is like unto it, Thou shalt love thy neighbor as thyself." (Matthew 22:37-39) Certainly these two basic commandments form the motivation for proper Christian action and thought. A careful study of Psalms and Proverbs will help you to put into practice Christ's "love principle."

In this volume, we have attempted to make such a study easier by placing on the same page the time-honored King James Version with the most-readable modern translation of today, The Living Bible. On each facing page, we have placed the corresponding text from the Wycliff Bible Commentary—described by many evangelicals as the best one-volume commentary available—and have also left space for your own personal notes.

This parallel arrangement will enable you to compare at a glance the classic English, contemporary terminology, and the meaning as set forth by leading scholars through geographical and historical notes and cross-references to other passages. Most important to you is the way God has spoken to *you* through Psalms and Proverbs. A permanent record of this is formed as you write down your own commentary, notes, and outlines.

You have many blessed hours ahead as you employ this book in your exploration of Psalms and Proverbs.

THE IVERSEN-NORMAN ASSOCIATES

THE PSALMS

INTRODUCTION

Nature. Among all the books of antiquity, none has made such a powerful appeal to the human heart as *The Psalms.* In no other book of the Bible can one find such varieties of religious experience. Here the heart of Israel is laid bare in manifold expressions of faith, for Israel knew experientially the truth of God's revelation. In the various psalms Israel's insights of former days are united with worship and thus given permanence. The experience of individuals is here linked with the corporate life of Israel. Hence, in the Book of Psalms there is a universal quality which can come only from the combined expression of the spiritual experiences of men in many periods of history and in a variety of circumstances of life. Each man was motivated by his desire to respond to the living God. All were united by their inherent desire to respond by means of their deepest emotions. Every type of religious experience is reflected in the crucible of daily life and projected upon the life of the believer today. There is thus in the Psalms a timelessness which makes this book equally applicable to every age of history.

The term "Psalms" comes from the LXX, which applies the title *Psalmoi* to the collection. One of the major Biblical manuscripts, the Codex Alexandrinus, furnishes the designation "Psalter" by using the Greek word *Psâlterion.* However, the Hebrew Bible uses the designation *Tehillîm,* which means "Praises." In Rabbinical literature this same idea was carried over in the term *Sēper Tehillîm,* meaning "Book of Praises." In both the Hebrew and Greek terms there is the root meaning of playing instrumental music. In time the word took on the meaning of singing to a musical accompaniment, a feature of Israelite worship made popular by the singing of the Levitical choirs. Many of the psalms give evidence of their use by choirs and worshipers as hymns, while others are not suited to such use. However, the collection as a whole attests to the deepest and most passionate yearning of corporate Israel at worship before God.

Titles and Authorship. One of the first things noticed about a particular psalm is the title it bears. How to arrive at a proper interpretation of these titles is one of the most vexing problems posed by this book. At times, authorship is emphasized in the titles, at other times, relationship. The occasion of the psalm's composition is sometimes pointed out. Certain titles make reference to the designated use of a psalm for public worship. Other titles indicate the desired musical effect or setting. Still others describe the basic character of the psalm as (1) a hymn to be sung with musical accompaniment (*mizmôr*), (2) a song (*shîr*), (3) an anthem (*maśkîl*), or (4) a lamentation (*miktām*).

All but thirty-four of the psalms bear some type of title as a superscription. The thirty-four psalms without titles are referred to as the Jewish "orphans." Among the titled psalms, seventy-three use the inscription *le Dāwid.* This is rendered as "A Psalm of David" in the AV, RV, ASV, and RSV. However, the Hebrew usage may indicate "belonging to David," "connected with David," "concerning David," "for David," "dedicated to David," "in the style of David," or "by David." By no means must these titles be required always to indicate authorship, whether referring to David or others. The LXX adds David's name to fifteen psalms not so designated in the Hebrew. In addition to the seventy-three referred to David (eighty-eight in the LXX), twelve are connected with Asaph, twelve with the Sons of Korah, two with Solomon, one with Ethan, and one with Moses.

Although these titles are not a part of the original text, they are based upon relatively ancient tradition. A comparison between the Masoretic Text and the LXX indicates that the titles antedate the LXX, for some of the musical directions were already unintelligible to the Greek translators, and the titles had not become fixed. Though the superscriptions are not a part of the original text, they are worthy of consideration, for they represent man's first effort to write an introduction to the Psalter.

Structure. Though the book of Psalms may appear to lack a plan, it is not without definite order. While it lacks organi-

1

zation in terms of subject matter, it follows a much more obvious system of organization. It is divided into five sections, representing various collections brought together. According to the *Midrash on the Psalms*, an ancient Jewish commentary, this fivefold division was made to correspond to the five books of the Law. Thus there may have been an original purpose among the editors of the psalm collections to parallel this fivefold response of the people to the fivefold summons by God.

Further evidence of a plan is the presence of a doxology at the end of each of the five books. Psalms 41, 72, 89, 106, and 150 include doxologies for each of the five books. Indeed, Psalm 150 is an over-all doxology, while Psalm 1 is a general introduction to the Psalter. Psalms 2, 42, 73, 90, and 107 serve as introductions to their respective books.

This careful organization gives evidence that the final edition of the entire collection was designed to fit into the scheme of Jewish worship. There is an amazing correlation between the first four books of Law and the first four divisions in Psalms. Since the worshiper in Palestinian Judaism completed the reading of the Pentateuch every three years, it is very probable that the use of the Psalms was scheduled to correspond. According to ancient tradition, it appears that eight portions of the Law were assigned to the Sabbaths in a two-month period, along with suitable portions from the Prophets. N. H. Snaith (*Hymns of the Temple*, p. 18) has shown that successive psalms may well have been used in similar fashion. He has calculated that the book of Exodus was started on the 42nd Sabbath, Leviticus was reached on the 73rd, Numbers by the 90th, and Deuteronomy on the 117th. These Sabbaths correspond exactly with the first chapters in each of the five books of the Psalter. No psalm could be more fitting than Psalm 1 to introduce the forthcoming three-year "meditation upon the Law." Psalm 23, for example, would accompany the reading of the story of Jacob at Bethel.

Collection and Growth. The present organization of the Psalter is the result of a process of growth. Long before the book of Psalms took its present form, minor collections were in circulation. And gradually these smaller collections were added together.

Within the present fivefold arrangement, the bounds of certain smaller collections are still discernible. In addition to the Davidic collections, there are certain groupings assigned to the Sons of Korah and Asaph. In Psalm 72:20, it is stated that "the prayers of David are ended," though other psalms follow which are ascribed to David. Other smaller collections include the Psalms of Ascents and the Hallelujah Psalms. Certain sections also show a decided preference for either *Yahweh* or *Elohim*, pointing toward early existence in specialized collections. The following collections may well have circulated separately, to be later united:

Psalms 3 – 41. A Davidic collection with doxology and preference for *Yahweh* (272 occurrences compared with 15 for *Elōhim*).

Psalms 51 – 72. A Davidic collection with doxology and preference for *Elōhim* (208 occurrences compared with 48 for *Yahweh*).

Psalms 50, 73 – 83. Levitical guild collection ascribed to Asaph.

Psalms 42 – 49. Levitical guild collection attributed to the Sons of Korah.

Psalms 90 – 99. Sabbath Psalms closely connected with regular Sabbath worship.

Psalms 113 – 118. Hallel of Egypt Psalms, connected in worship with the Passover Feast (cf. Ps 136).

Psalms 120 – 134. Songs of Ascents or Degrees, probably sung by the pilgrims journeying to the Temple.

Psalms 146 – 150. Hallelujah Psalms sung at festivals.

T. H. Robinson (*The Poetry of the Old Testament*) and others have suggested that a threefold division preceded the final fivefold form. These three books, 1-41, 42-89, 90-150, may well have been redivided into the present form to make them correspond to the divisions of the Law. Whether this theory can be proved or not, a proper understanding of the composite nature of the book of Psalms is essential. Through the gradual process of collection, rearrangement, and revision, God preserved this treasure of Israel's response to his revelation.

Dating. A precise system of dating for the book of Psalms is impossible. Those responsible for the final edition of the Psalter, as well as previous collectors, endeavored to provide a hymnbook for their own generation. In times of stress and difficulty, they sought to revive the vigor of the past to serve the needs of their own day. The process of revision and adaptation makes many of the psalms appear to be later than they were in their original form. N. H. Snaith (*Twentieth Century Bible Commentary*, p. 235) says: "Few Psalms are either pre-exilic or wholly post-exilic. Some Psalms may contain elements varying in date by more than a thousand years." Some scholars have followed Duhm in making the majority of the psalms originate in Maccabean times. However, the trend today among such scholars as Gunkel, Snaith, Patterson, Oesterley, and others is toward earlier dates. The phrase, "The Hymn and Prayer Book of the Second Temple," may still be applied to the over-all collection because of the final editing after the Exile. Yet much of the Psalter is pre-Exilic, with some elements originally pre-Davidic. This recognition of early and late material makes the book of Psalms even more valuable as a record of the entire history of Israel's response to God as his Chosen People.

While it is important in interpretation to know the exact historical background and date of a passage, it is less imperative in the Psalms than in other Old Testament sections. Because of the universality of its truth, the book suffers less from lack of this knowledge than may be expected. Its timeless message makes it applicable in the pre-Exilic period, the post-Exilic period, and in our present age. However, this timelessness should not keep us from discovering the historical background wherever possible. Literary style, historical allusions, language, theological ideas, and other internal evidences should be examined, because any passage gains in reality when the background is properly understood. Even though such gains in reality are desirable, dogmatism in assigning authors, dates, and circumstances is out of place because of the timeless message of the book. It must be remembered that history has a way of repeating itself again and again.

Poetic Form. The Hebrews have given to the world a heritage of simple and childlike poetic expression. Their poetic utterances came from the heart rather than from a desire for artful excellence. Since Hebrew is a pictorial language, every word is graphic and vivid. The verbal roots portray visible action, while the usage provides room for strong imagination. There is in the language an intense emotional quality well fitted to display burning religious passion.

Although Hebrew poetry lacks rhyme and is weak in metrical system, it has compensatory features. Instead of these basic fundamentals of English verse, Hebrew employs two main distinguishing characteristics—accentual stress (rhythm) and parallelism. According to F. C. Eiselen (*The Psalms and Other Sacred Writings*), rhythm is "the harmonious repetition of fixed sound relations." An accentual pattern of two, three, or four beats to the line makes possible this harmonious repetition. Several unaccented syllables between the beats make a regulation of short and long syllables. This form of regulation depends upon rhythm within clauses and rhythmical balance between clauses. The result is a simple but pleasing rise and fall of the voice which can express animated spirit, calm assurance, excitement, lamentation, or other emotional qualities.

The second main distinguishing characteristic of Hebrew poetry is the balance of form and sense called *parallelism*. The poet states an idea; then he reinforces it by means of repetition, variation, or contrast. Three major types of parallelism are found throughout the Psalter:

1. Synonymous. The second line repeats the first in slightly different words (cf. Ps 1:2).
2. Antithetic. The second line shows sharp contrast with the first (cf. Ps 1:6).
3. Synthetic. The second line completes the first by supplementing the original thought (cf. Ps 7:1).

Three lesser types help to add richness and variety to Hebrew expression:

1. Introverted. The second line is parallel to the third and the first to the fourth (cf. Ps 30:8-10; 137:5,6).
2. Climactic. The second line completes the first by bringing the thought to a climax (cf. Ps 29:1,2).
3. Emblematic. The second line continues the thought of the first by raising it to a higher realm or using a simile (cf. Ps 1:4).

There are other factors which explain the effectiveness of parallelism. At the heart of the matter is the reader's expectation and satisfaction. The first line should always raise a sense of expectation, while the succeeding lines should satisfy that expectation. The poet can gain variety by changing the degree of expectation raised or the method of satisfying it by using contrast to show the unexpected. The parallelism is sometimes complete, sometimes incomplete, with one element missing; and at other times there is a compensatory element added to bring a better sense of satisfaction. Not only parallelism but patterned rhythm produces this expectation-satisfaction sensation. G. B. Gray (*The Forms of Hebrew Poetry*, 1915) has given names to the two basic types of rhythm. "Balancing rhythm" produces a certain satisfaction because the number of accentual stresses is equal (3:3 or 2:2). "Echoing rhythm" produces a different sensation by giving the second line fewer stresses than the first (3:2). The most frequently used form of the latter is the *Quinah* metre, used in laments and dirges.

In addition to parallelism and rhythm, two other elements affect Hebrew poetry. These are not distinguishing characteristics, for they are present in all poetry. The first is the emotional quality which produces a *heightened expression*. Special power-packed words or phrases can produce this effect. The use of a profuse number of gutturals can display harshness. Sharp sibilants can express victory or grief over defeat. Onomatopoetic words can easily suggest the message. The second element is the *mnemonic value* of the poem, which helps the reader to remember it. Rather than using rhyme, the psalmist occasionally employed an acrostic arrangement. Each line or a set number of lines would begin with successive letters of the Hebrew alphabet. Psalm 119 is an excellent example, as each line in an eight-line section begins with the same letter. All twenty-two letters of the Hebrew alphabet are used in successive sections. Such an artificial device made it easier for people to commit these psalms to memory. Actually, only eight or nine psalms are so constructed in their entirety. Each of these is proverbial in nature and would suffer from some detachment of thought if it were not for this alphabetical arrangement.

In basic style Hebrew poetry is vastly different from modern poetry. However, the Hebrew pattern has close affinity with that of the Near East. There are numerous similarities in style between the poetry of Israel and that of Egypt and Mesopotamia. Yet the most marked similarities are evident in a comparison of Hebrew psalms and Ugarit poems. The poetry of Ugarit is basically the Canaanite-Syrian type. Canaan and Syria were in close contact with Israel throughout pre-Exilic history. The main similarities concern metaphors, phrases, rhythm,

and parellelism—all matters of literary style and phraseology. Religiously and theologically, the differences outweigh all the similarities.

Classification. Any cursory comparison of the poems in the Psalter reveals that they have not been grouped by subject matter. The subjects, covered or alluded to, run the gamut of human experience. Although the various topics are too numerous to list, five dominant themes can be recognized:

1. Realization of God's presence.
2. Recognition of a need for thanksgiving.
3. Personal communion with God.
4. Remembrance of God's part in history.
5. Sense of deliverance from enemies.

There have been many attempts to classify the psalms according to a preconceived standard. Mowinckel and others have centered on the *content*, developing elaborate topical subdivisions. Others have attempted to uncover the basic *mood* of the author of each psalm. Still other authors have relied upon the *type* of each psalm as a criterion for classification. This began simply as a threefold division into hymns of praise, prayers, and songs of faith. Recently Gunkel has done valuable work in further identifying these types or categories. His basic premise is that the psalms were originally cult songs used in the worship of Israel. He thus classifies each according to the "regular recurring formulae" of each particular type. Gunkel recognizes five main types as follows:

1. Hymns of Praise
2. National Laments
3. Royal Psalms (including Messianic Psalms)
4. Individual Laments
5. Thanksgivings of the Individual

To these he adds a number of minor types represented by a few psalms each:

6. Songs of Pilgrimage
7. Thanksgivings of the Nation
8. Wisdom Poems
9. Torah Liturgies
10. Mixed Types

These categories represent the final and latest scheme by Gunkel (cf. N. H. Snaith in *Twentieth Century Bible Commentary*, p. 235 ff.). Previously, Gunkel had included other minor types, such as: "Blessings and Curses," and "Prophetic Psalms" (cf. John Patterson, *The Praises of Israel*, p. 32). We may add to these classifications the category of Messianic Psalms.

As tempting as it is to discover a system of classification, there is a certain indefiniteness about the Psalter which defies absolute classification. This lack of definiteness is caused by the timeless and universal characteristics of the collection. Actually, each method of classification gives a different view of the Psalms, making possible an understanding of the many facets available.

Abiding Value. The Psalter is first a living testimony to Israel's faith. The individual psalms give evidence of the thought and feeling of countless Hebrew worshipers. They echo the aspirations and hopes of men and women in every era of Israel's history. They reflect the hardships and struggles of God's people. They show the pilgrimage from doubt to certainty in these critical centuries of God's leading. They point always toward the conquest of despair by means of faith in the living God. The history of Israel would be lacking indeed without these evidences of faith's response to God's revelation.

Secondly, the Psalms form an important background for Jesus' ministry. He learned them in his Jewish home at his devotions. At his baptism, his mission was stated in the words of a psalm. On the cross, a psalm came to his mind in his last moments there. The Psalms are quoted more frequently in the New Testament than any other book of the Old Testament. There are about a hundred direct references or allusions to the Psalter in the New Testament. Phrases and verses are carried over to explain the character and message of Jesus as the Messiah.

In the third place, the book of Psalms has proved to be an indispensable source of devotional material. Christians around the world have been aided in their personal approach to God in worship. Psalm 51 voices the thoughts of the repentant sinner. Psalm 32 shows what joy a forgiven man can experience. Psalm 23 expresses the sense of trust common to all children of God. Psalm 103 pours forth the praise of God which every believer should express. Other psalms satisfy basic devotional needs, enriching the personal experience of any seeking person.

Finally, the Psalter has become the hymnbook of the ages. No other book of hymns has been used so long by so many people. It is read, chanted, or sung every day of the year. Samuel Terrien says of it: "No other book of hymns and prayers has been used for so long a time and by so many diverse men and women" *(The Psalms and Their Meaning for Today,* p. vii). In an age of informality, the Psalms provide an indispensable language for worship. In the words of Luther's "A Mighty Fortress Is Our God," Watts' "Jesus Shall Reign," and his "O God, Our Help in Ages Past," the message of the Psalter sounds around the earth.

OUTLINE

The present organization of the book clearly indicates its own appropriate outline:

Book I. Psalms 1–41.
Book II. Psalms 42–72.
Book III. Psalms 73–89.
Book IV. Psalms 90–106.
Book V. Psalms 107–150.

The Book of
PSALMS

King James Version

Living Bible

PSALM 1

BLESSED *is* the man that walketh not in the counsel of the ungodly, nor standeth in the way of sinners, nor sitteth in the seat of the scornful. ² But his delight *is* in the law of the Lord; and in his law doth he meditate day and night.

³ And he shall be like a tree planted by the rivers of water, that bringeth forth his fruit in his season; his leaf also shall not wither; and whatsoever he doeth shall prosper.

⁴ The ungodly *are* not so: but *are* like the chaff which the wind driveth away. ⁵ Therefore the ungodly shall not stand in the judgment, nor sinners in the congregation of the righteous.

⁶ For the Lord knoweth the way of the righteous: but the way of the ungodly shall perish.

1 OH, THE JOYS of those who do not follow evil men's advice, who do not hang around with sinners, scoffing at the things of God: ² But they delight in doing everything God wants them to, and day and night are always meditating on his laws and thinking about ways to follow him more closely.

³ They are like trees along a river bank bearing luscious fruit each season without fail. Their leaves shall never wither, and all they do shall prosper.

⁴ But for sinners, what a different story! They blow away like chaff before the wind. ⁵ They are not safe on Judgment Day; they shall not stand among the godly.

⁶ For the Lord watches over all the plans and paths of godly men, but the paths of the godless lead to doom.

COMMENTARY

BOOK I. Psalms 1–41

The first book in the fivefold division of the Book of Psalms appears to have been once in a separate Davidic collection. The name Lord, Hebrew *Yahweh,* occurs 272 times, while the more general *'Elōhim* is found only 15 times. The psalms are varied in content, but the moral teaching is simple and direct. Evident throughout this division is a positive faith in the justice of God. Psalm 1 serves as an introduction to the entire Psalter, while Psalm 2 introduces the collection in Book I. The fact that some manuscripts list Psalm 3 as the first psalm makes the introductory character of 1 and 2 more apparent. It is further possible that 1 and 2 were originally joined as one psalm, beginning and ending with "Blessed." All except 1, 2, 10, and 33 are connected with David in the title annotations.

Psalm 1. The Two Ways of Life

This psalm presents in sharp contrast two extremes—the truly righteous way of life and the basically wicked way. The contrast introduces in a didactic manner the two categories of men to be described throughout the Psalter. The psalmist continues the antithesis by showing the present and future destinies of each group.

1-3. The Way of the Godly Man. **Blessed is the man.** The Psalter opens with a strong interjection, *O the happinesses of the man* who follows God's plan. The verbs, **walketh, standeth, sitteth,** describe the characteristic steps of the wicked which the righteous avoid: accepting the principles of the wicked, participating in the practices of outright sinners, and finally joining with those who openly mock. Note the threefold parallel between the three verbs and their modifying clauses. The shift is then made from the negative refusal to the positive delight. Such a man meditates or muses constantly on God's teaching. As a result, he becomes more and more like a "transplanted tree," with roots in eternal realities. Constant vitality is assured and ultimate success is certain because he has put his trust firmly in God.

4-6. The Way of the Ungodly Man. **The ungodly are not so.** An abrupt change now occurs with the words **not so.** The sharp contrast is intensified by the use of this frequent term for the wicked, which stands as the exact antithesis of the term, **the righteous.** Unlike the firmly established tree, the ungodly is swept away by the wind. The picture is that of a threshing floor on a hill-top, where the wind clears away the chaff and leaves the grain. In parallel construction, the two classes (**ungodly** and **sinners**) are promised no part in the vindicated company of the righteous. While God *regards* or concerns himself with the way of the righteous, the wicked merely drift on to ultimate destruction.

NOTES

PSALM 2

WHY do the heathen rage, and the people imagine a vain thing? ² The kings of the earth set themselves, and the rulers take counsel together, against the Lord, and against his anointed, *saying,* ³ Let us break their bands asunder, and cast away their cords from us.

⁴ He that sitteth in the heavens shall laugh: the Lord shall have them in derision. ⁵ Then shall he speak unto them in his wrath, and vex them in his sore displeasure.

⁶ Yet have I set my king upon my holy hill of Zion.

⁷ I will declare the decree: the Lord hath said unto me, Thou *art* my Son; this day have I begotten thee. ⁸ Ask of me, and I shall give *thee* the heathen *for* thine inheritance, and the uttermost parts of the earth *for* thy possession. ⁹ Thou shalt break them with a rod of iron; thou shalt dash them in pieces like a potter's vessel.

¹⁰ Be wise now therefore, O ye kings: be instructed, ye judges of the earth. ¹¹ Serve the Lord with fear, and rejoice with trembling. ¹² Kiss the Son, lest he be angry, and ye perish *from* the way, when his wrath is kindled but a little. Blessed *are* all they that put their trust in him.

2 WHAT FOOLS THE nations are to rage against the Lord! How strange that men should try to outwit God! ² For a summit conference of the nations has been called to plot against the Lord and his Messiah, Christ the King. ³ "Come, let us break his chains," they say, "and free ourselves from all this slavery to God."

⁴ But God in heaven merely laughs! He is amused by all their puny plans. ⁵ And then in fierce fury he rebukes them and fills them with fear.

⁶ For the Lord declares, "This is the King of my choice, and I have enthroned him in Jerusalem, my holy city."

⁷ His chosen one replies, "I will reveal the everlasting purposes of God, for the Lord has said to me, 'You are my Son. This is your Coronation Day. Today I am giving you your glory.'" ⁸ "Only ask, and I will give you all the nations of the world. ⁹ Rule them with an iron rod; smash them like clay pots!"

¹⁰ O kings and rulers of the earth, listen while there is time. ¹¹ Serve the Lord with reverent fear; rejoice with trembling. ¹² Fall down before his Son and kiss his feet before his anger is roused and you perish. I am warning you—his wrath will soon begin. But oh, the joys of those who put their trust in him!

Psalm 2. The Victory of God's Messiah

This is basically a royal psalm, with highly dramatic qualities and great poetical power. Included in its structure is an oracle of the Lord which has occasioned various interpretations. Gunkel connects it with a festival celebrating the coronation of a Judean king. If such was the original setting, the psalm has been thoroughly adapted to wider Messianic hopes. Even as Psalm 1 deals with the two ways for an individual's life, Psalm 2 sets forth the two ways for nations and peoples.

1-3. The Rebellion of the Nations. **Why?** In prophetic style, the psalmist begins with two rhetorical questions. The point of the questions is to demonstrate the absurdity of those who would rebel against the decree of the Almighty. Their rebellion against God's people and king is regarded as an attack against God himself. Basically, this antagonism is aimed at Jehovah's rulership through his **anointed** (one).

4-6. The Answer of God. **He . . . shall laugh . . . . then shall he speak.** A bold anthropomorphism draws a sharp contrast between the worried little kings and the supreme Ruler who puts them **in derision** (root idea, "to stammer"). His laughter changes quickly to burning anger as he informs these rebellious ones that he has already installed his king with full divine approval.

7-9. The Plan for the Anointed. **The Lord hath said.** The oracle by God's anointed is declared as God's decree. The declaration, **Thou art my Son,** parallels the "my king" of God's answer. The phrase is applied to Jesus at his baptism (Mk 1:11). The term, **begotten,** is part of an Oriental formula for adoption used in the Code of Hammurabi. Note that two promises are given to God's anointed —dominion and victory. Although the psalmist probably thought of the **Son** as the chosen ruler (II Sam 7:14), in the light of the NT we see the Messiah as truly the Son of God.

10-12. The Admonition to the Kings. **Be wise . . . be instructed.** The choice is laid before the kings, along with the admonition to be wise and straighten up in making their decision. The choice of wisdom goes beyond mere acceptance of the decree. They are to serve the Lord with the awe and reverence due him. The kissing of royal feet and hands was a symbol of homage. Even as the way of the wicked shall perish in Psalm 1, so shall the way of those who refuse to do homage.

NOTES

PSALM 3

A Psalm of David, when he fled from Absalom his son

LORD, how are they increased that trouble me! many *are* they that rise up against me. ² Many *there be* which say of my soul, *There is* no help for him in God. Se-lah. ³ But thou, O Lord, *art* a shield for me; my glory, and the lifter up of mine head.

⁴ I cried unto the Lord with my voice, and he heard me out of his holy hill. Se-lah. ⁵ I laid me down and slept; I awaked; for the Lord sustained me. ⁶ I will not be afraid of ten thousands of people, that have set *themselves* against me round about. ⁷ Arise, O Lord; save me, O my God: for thou hast smitten all mine enemies *upon* the cheek bone; thou hast broken the teeth of the ungodly.

⁸ Salvation *belongeth* unto the Lord: thy blessing *is* upon thy people. Se-lah.

PSALM 4

To the chief Musician on Neginoth, A Psalm of David

HEAR me when I call, O God of my righteousness: thou hast enlarged me *when I was* in distress; have mercy upon me, and hear my prayer.

² O ye sons of men, how long *will ye turn* my glory into shame? *how long* will ye love vanity, *and* seek after leasing? Se-lah.

³ But know that the Lord hath set apart him that is godly for himself: the Lord will hear when I call unto him. ⁴ Stand in awe, and sin not: commune with your own heart upon your bed, and be still. Se-lah. ⁵ Offer the sacrifices of righteousness, and put your trust in the Lord.

A Psalm of David when he fled from his son Absalom

3 O LORD, SO many are against me. So many seek to harm me. I have so many enemies. ² So many say that God will never help me. ³ But Lord, you are my shield, my glory, and my only hope. You alone can lift my head, now bowed in shame.

⁴ I cried out to the Lord, and he heard me from his Temple in Jerusalem. ⁵ Then I lay down and slept and woke up safely, for the Lord was watching over me. ⁶ And now, although ten thousand enemies surround me on every side, I am not afraid. ⁷ I will cry to him, "Arise, O Lord! Save me, O my God!" And he will slap them in the face, insulting them and breaking off their teeth.

⁸ For salvation comes from God. What joys he gives to all his people.

4 O GOD, YOU have declared me perfect in your eyes; you have always cared for me in my distress; now hear me as I call again. Have mercy on me. Hear my prayer.

² The Lord God asks, "Sons of men, will you forever turn my glory into shame by worshiping these silly idols, when every claim that's made for them is false?"

³ Mark this well: The Lord has set apart the redeemed for himself. Therefore he will listen to me and answer when I call to him. ⁴ Stand before the Lord in awe, and do not sin against him. Lie quietly upon your bed in silent meditation. ⁵ Put your trust in the Lord, and offer him pleasing sacrifices.

Psalm 3. A Morning Prayer of Confidence

The basic characteristics of an individual lament are exhibited in this psalm, the sequel to which is found in Psalm 4, where a sense of relief is evident. Because of the expression of sublime trust in God's protection, this psalm has been a favorite of many people facing peril. Verse 5 clearly identifies it as a morning prayer.

1,2. The Psalmist's Plight. **They . . . that trouble me.** The enemies of the psalmist are becoming more numerous than they have ever been before. Physically, he is in grave danger. And besides, his spirit is weighed down by his adversaries' taunts to the effect that he. is beyond the help of God. These disheartening comments are similar to those directed toward Job (Job 2:11-13).

3,4. His Helper. **But Thou, O Lord.** In the midst of his troubles he remembers again that God is **a shield** to protect him, **my glory** to restore his dignity, and **the lifter up of my head** to give him new courage. The verbs in verse 4 should be frequentative: *Whenever I call, He answers!*

5,6. His Confidence. **I laid me down and slept.** The knowledge that God is his helper and protector makes this sleep possible. Upon awaking, he realizes that it is God who has sustained him. With his confidence increased by this experience, he is certain that no number of foes can make him afraid.

7,8. His Prayer. **Arise, O Lord.** The power and deliverance of God are invoked by this petition, as the psalmist seeks active intervention. He is either recalling what God has done on previous occasions or using a prophetic perfect. The latter foresees an end as clearly certain and so speaks of it as complete already. The last verse adapts the psalm to public worship, and may indicate a lack of selfishness in the whole private prayer.

Psalm 4. An Evening Prayer of Relief

The circumstances surrounding this psalm are similar to those of Psalm 3. However, here the lament becomes a song of trust to express the psalmist's relief. The serenity of tone throughout is the result of an experience of God's help in the past. Even as God gave rest in the previous experience (Ps 3), there is assurance that he will provide that same peaceful rest again. Verse 8 connects this song with evening prayer.

1. Urgent Appeal to God. **Answer me . . . be gracious . . . hear my prayer** (RSV). There is here a threefold request to God, who has proved himself to be righteous and capable of deliverance. Past experience leads the psalmist to believe that God will again meet his deepest needs.

2-5. Wise Counsel for Fellowmen. **O ye sons of men.** These men had slandered the reputation of the psalmist; they had loved vain schemes, and thrived on falsehood. In quietness they should meditate on their needs and sin not. They should speak to their own consciences and be silent. Even as the psalmist calls, "O God of my righteousness" (v. 1), he demands this same righteous motive in their sacrifices. The logical parallel is that of trust in the One to whom they offer these sacrifices.

NOTES

11

⁶ *There be* many that say, Who will shew us *any* good? Lord, lift thou up the light of thy countenance upon us. ⁷ Thou hast put gladness in my heart, more than in the time *that* their corn and their wine increased. ⁸ I will both lay me down in peace, and sleep: for thou, Lord, only makest me dwell in safety.

PSALM 5

To the chief Musician upon Nehiloth, A Psalm of David

GIVE ear to my words, O Lord, consider my meditation. ² Hearken unto the voice of my cry, my King, and my God: for unto thee will I pray. ³ My voice shalt thou hear in the morning, ·O Lord; in the morning will I direct *my prayer* unto thee, and will look up.

⁴ For thou *art* not a God that hath pleasure in wickedness: neither shall evil dwell with thee. ⁵ The foolish shall not stand in thy sight: thou hatest all workers of iniquity. ⁶ Thou shalt destroy them that speak leasing: the Lord will abhor the bloody and deceitful man.

⁷ But as for me, I will come *into* thy house in the multitude of thy mercy: *and* in thy fear will I worship toward thy holy temple.

⁸ Lead me, O Lord, in thy righteousness because of mine enemies; make thy way straight before my face. ⁹ For *there is* no faithfulness in their mouth; their inward part *is* very wickedness; their throat *is* an open sepulchre; they flatter with their tongue. ¹⁰ Destroy thou them, O God; let them fall by their own counsels; cast them out in the multitude of their transgressions; for they have rebelled against thee.

¹¹ But let all those that put their trust in thee rejoice: let them ever shout for joy, because thou defendest them: let them also that love thy name be joyful in thee. ¹² For thou, Lord, wilt bless the righteous; with favour wilt thou compass him as *with* a shield.

⁶ Many say that God will never help us. Prove them wrong, O Lord, by letting the light of your face shine down upon us. ⁷ Yes, the gladness you have given me is far greater than their joys at harvest time as they gaze at their bountiful crops. ⁸ I will lie down in peace and sleep, for though I am alone, O Lord, you will keep me safe.

5 O LORD, HEAR me praying; listen to my plea, O God my King, for I will never pray to anyone but you. ³ Each morning I will look to you in heaven and lay my requests before you, praying earnestly.

⁴ I know you get no pleasure from wickedness and cannot tolerate the slightest sin. ⁵ Therefore proud sinners will not survive your searching gaze, for how you hate their evil deeds. ⁶ You will destroy them for their lies; how you abhor all murder and deception.

⁷ But as for me, I will come into your Temple protected by your mercy and your love; I will worship you with deepest awe.

⁸ Lord, lead me as you promised me you would; otherwise my enemies will conquer me. Tell me clearly what to do, which way to turn. ⁹ For they cannot speak one truthful word. Their hearts are filled to the brim with wickedness. Their suggestions are full of the stench of sin and death. Their tongues are filled with flatteries to gain their wicked ends. ¹⁰ O God, hold them responsible. Catch them in their own traps; let them fall beneath the weight of their own transgressions, for they rebel against you.

¹¹ But make everyone rejoice who puts his trust in you. Keep them shouting for joy because you are defending them. Fill all who love you with your happiness. ¹² For you bless the godly man, O Lord; you protect him with your shield of love.

6-8. Serene Trust in God. Thou hast put gladness in my heart. Many individuals were discontented and pessimistic, lacking the gladness which the psalmist knew. In contrast to these pessimists, the author knows that God's help in the time of need causes more gladness than bumper crops. He closes with the picture of peaceful sleep possible to one who knows God's care by personal experience.

Psalm 5. A Morning Prayer, Preparatory to Worship

There is in this psalm an atmosphere of strife between the righteous and the wicked, such as is frequently found in the Psalter. The situation is similar to that of Psalms 3 and 4 in that in both there are dangerous foes all about. The psalm may have been used by the priests in their preparation for morning sacrifice or by the individual as he prepared for worship.

1-3. An Invocation to God. Give ear . . . consider . . . hearken. The preparation for worship must always include the individual's cry to God. Not only his words but his meditation (lit., *whispering*) is a part of this invocation. In parallel form, the time is specified, probably connecting the speaker's prayer with the morning sacrifice.

4-9. A Lesson in Contrast. Wickedness . . . worship. There is a double contrast in these verses: the attitudes of the righteous and wicked toward sin and worship are contrasted, as well as the different responses of God toward the two groups. The psalmist recognizes that God cannot tolerate sin nor sojourn with the evil man. Therefore, God will not allow the **foolish** (lit., *arrogant*) to stand in his presence. He considers the **workers of iniquity** detestable. The end destined for those **that speak lies (ASV)** is utter destruction, and **the bloodthirsty and deceitful man (ASV)** is an abomination that God abhors. While these wicked men deal in treachery, the psalmist prostrates himself before God, praying for divine guidance.

10-12. A Prayer for Retribution. Destroy thou them. The prayer continues with a plea for justice upon these enemies. As those who rebel against God, they must be held guilty, allowed to fall, and cast down completely. In contrast to the threefold fate of the wicked ones, those who trust in God share in unending joy. They are to **rejoice**, to **shout for joy**, and to **exult in God.**

NOTES

13

PSALM 6

To the chief Musician on Neginoth upon Sheminith, A Psalm of David

O LORD rebuke me not in thine anger, neither chasten me in thy hot displeasure. ² Have mercy upon me, O Lord; for I *am* weak: O Lord, heal me; for my bones are vexed. ³ My soul is also sore vexed: but thou, O Lord, how long?

⁴ Return, O Lord, deliver my soul: oh save me for thy mercies' sake. ⁵ For in death *there is* no remembrance of thee: in the grave who shall give thee thanks? ⁶ I am weary with my groaning; all the night make I my bed to swim; I water my couch with my tears. ⁷ Mine eye is consumed because of grief; it waxeth old because of all mine enemies.

⁸ Depart from me, all ye workers of iniquity; for the Lord hath heard the voice of my weeping. ⁹ The Lord hath heard my supplication; the Lord will receive my prayer. ¹⁰ Let all mine enemies be ashamed and sore vexed: let them return *and* be ashamed suddenly.

PSALM 7

Shiggaion of David, which he sang unto the Lord, concerning the words of Cush the Benjamite

O LORD my God, in thee do I put my trust: save me from all them that persecute me, and deliver me: ² Lest he tear my soul like a lion, rending *it* in pieces, while *there is* none to deliver. ³ O Lord my God, if I have done this; if there be iniquity in my hands; ⁴ If I have rewarded evil unto him that was at peace with me; (yea, I have delivered him that without cause is mine enemy:) ⁵ Let the enemy persecute my soul, and take *it;* yea, let him tread down my life upon the earth, and lay mine honour in the dust. Se-lah.

⁶ Arise, O Lord, in thine anger, lift up thyself because of the rage of mine enemies: and awake for me *to* the judgment *that* thou hast commanded. ⁷ So shall the congregation of the people compass thee about: for their sakes therefore return thou on high. ⁸ The Lord shall judge the people: judge me, O Lord, according to my righteousness,

6 NO, LORD! DON'T punish me in the heat of your anger. ² Pity me, O Lord, for I am weak. Heal me, for my body is sick, ³ and I am upset and disturbed. My mind is filled with apprehension and with gloom. Oh, restore me soon.

⁴ Come, O Lord, and make me well. In your kindness save me. ⁵ For if I die I cannot give you glory by praising you before my friends. ⁶ I am worn out with pain; every night my pillow is wet with tears. ⁷ My eyes are growing old and dim with grief because of all my enemies.

⁸ Go, leave me now, you men of evil deeds, for the Lord has heard my weeping ⁹ and my pleading. He will answer all my prayers. ¹⁰ All my enemies shall be suddenly dishonored, terror-stricken, and disgraced. God will turn them back in shame.

7 I AM DEPENDING on you, O Lord my God, to save me from my persecutors. ² Don't let them pounce upon me as a lion would and maul me and drag me away with no one to rescue me. ³ It would be different, Lord, if I were doing evil things— ⁴ if I were paying back evil for good or unjustly attacking those I dislike. ⁵ Then it would be right for you to let my enemies destroy me, crush me to the ground, and trample my life in the dust.

⁶ But Lord! Arise in anger against the anger of my enemies. Awake! Demand justice for me, Lord! ⁷,⁸ Gather all peoples before you; sit high above them, judging their sins. But justify me publicly; establish

Psalm 6. A Cry for Relief

Here is a vivid picture of a man in dire distress because of a severe illness. Although the psalmist refers to his enemies, he is primarily crying out for relief from his malady. His mention of divine wrath shows that he conceives of his suffering as resulting from sin. While used among Christians as one of the seven Penitential Psalms, this may have been a penitential liturgy in the temple worship as well.

1,2a. Prayer for Cessation of Punishment. **Rebuke me not . . . neither chasten . . . have mercy.** These expressions show a recognition of the disciplinary side of suffering. The writer does not deny his guilt, not claim innocence. His punishment must cease before his emaciated body can be restored. All he can do is cast himself on the mercy of God.

2b-5. Prayer for Recovery. **Heal me . . . deliver my soul . . . save me.** The sufferer clearly realizes that deliverance must come from without, for he is thoroughly inadequate. He bases his plea upon the seriousness of his suffering, the mercy of God, and the fact that God will lose his thanksgiving if he goes to Sheol.

6,7. Description of His Condition. **Groaning . . . tears . . . grief.** The nature of his illness is somewhat obscured by the characteristic Oriental expressions. However, there can be no doubt that his grief is real and his suffering intense. Like Job, he has to endure the insults of his enemies in addition to his wretchedness.

8-10. Answered Prayers. **The Lord hath heard.** Twice the psalmist uses this phrase to indicate that a new era has arrived. He predicts that all his enemies shall turn back because God has taken command.

Psalm 7. A Prayer for Justice

Like many other psalms, this is first of all the lament of an individual. There is an element of self-righteousness in the psalmist's appeal. This may be due to the nature of the religious strife which occasioned the bitter persecution. However, there are corporate aspects which point to the possibility that several psalms have been combined into this one. If the individual is taken as representative of the nation, the unity of the psalm is preserved.

1,2. Prayer for Deliverance. **Save me . . . deliver me.** This appeal is based upon the speaker's personal trust in God.

The fierce attack of the enemy also appears to be personal, as indicated by **my soul.**

3-5. Protestation of Innocence. **O Lord . . . if I have.** The author was certain that he was not deserving of his persecution. He was willing to put the protest in the form of an oath and an offer to accept any deserved reward for punishment.

6-8. Prayer for Judgment. **Arise, O Lord.** A bold figure of waking God is used to point up the necessity of immediate judgment. There is here a combination of personal vindication and the eschatological idea of a world judgment.

NOTES

and according to mine integrity *that is* in me. ⁹ Oh let the wickedness of the wicked come to an end; but establish the just: for the righteous God trieth the hearts and reins.

¹⁰ My defence *is* of God, which saveth the upright in heart.

¹¹ God judgeth the righteous, and God is angry *with the wicked* every day. ¹² If he turn not, he will whet his sword; he hath bent his bow, and made it ready.

¹³ He hath also prepared for him the instruments of death; he ordaineth his arrows against the persecutors.

¹⁴ Behold, he travaileth with iniquity, and hath conceived mischief, and brought forth falsehood. ¹⁵ He made a pit, and digged it, and is fallen into the ditch *which* he made. ¹⁶ His mischief shall return upon his own head, and his violent dealing shall come down upon his own pate.

¹⁷ I will praise the Lord according to his righteousness: and will sing praise to the name of the Lord most high.

PSALM 8

To the chief Musician upon Gittith, A Psalm of David

O Lord our Lord, how excellent *is* thy name in all the earth! who hast set thy glory above the heavens. ² Out of the mouth of babes and sucklings hast thou ordained strength because of thine enemies, that thou mightest still the enemy and the avenger.

³ When I consider thy heavens, the work of thy fingers, the moon and the stars, which thou hast ordained; ⁴ What is man, that thou art mindful of him? and the son of man, that thou visitest him? ⁵ For thou hast made him a little lower than the angels, and hast crowned him with glory and honour.

⁶ Thou madest him to have dominion over the works of thy hands: thou hast put all *things* under his feet: ⁷ All sheep and oxen, yea, and the beasts of the field; ⁸ The fowl of the air, and the fish of the sea, *and whatsoever* passeth through the paths of the seas. ⁹ O Lord our Lord, how excellent *is* thy name in all the earth!

my honor and truth before them all. ⁹ End all wickedness, O Lord, and bless all who truly worship God; for you, the righteous God, look deep within the hearts of men and examine all their motives and their thoughts.

¹⁰ God is my shield; he will defend me. He saves those whose hearts and lives are true and right.

¹¹ God is a judge who is perfectly fair, and he is angry with the wicked every day. ¹² Unless they repent, he will sharpen his sword and slay them.

He has bent and strung his bow ¹³ and fitted it with deadly arrows made from shafts of fire.

¹⁴ The wicked man conceives an evil plot, labors with its dark details, and brings to birth his treachery and lies; ¹⁵ let him fall into his own trap. ¹⁶ May the violence he plans for others boomerang upon himself; let him die.

¹⁷ Oh, how grateful and thankful I am to the Lord because he is so good. I will sing praise to the name of the Lord who is above all lords.

8 O Lord our God, the majesty and glory of your name fills all the earth and overflows the heavens. ² You have taught the little children to praise you perfectly. May their example shame and silence your enemies!

³ When I look up into the night skies and see the work of your fingers—the moon and the stars you have made— ⁴ I cannot understand how you can bother with mere puny man, to pay any attention to him! ⁵ And yet you have made him only a little lower than the angels, and placed a crown of glory and honor upon his head.

⁶ You have put him in charge of everything you made; everything is put under his authority: ⁷ all sheep and oxen, and wild animals too, ⁸ the birds and fish, and all the life in the sea. ⁹ O Jehovah, our Lord, the majesty and glory of your name fills the earth.

9-13. Confidence in the Righteous Judge. The righteous God trieth the hearts and reins. The outcome is assured by the very nature of God. The upright are preserved, while the wicked suffer God's wrath every day. God's action of judgment upon the unrepentant is figuratively stated in terms of earthly combat.

14-16. Nature of the Wicked. Iniquity . . . mischief . . . falsehood. These words characterize the adversary, who has fallen by his own devices. He is covering himself with the shroud of his evil desires.

17. Concluding Vow. I will praise. This characteristic doxology illustrates the assurance of the psalmist that the cause of righteousness will triumph.

Psalm 8. Man's Dignity and God's Glory

This psalm is a hymn which reaches a height of majesty seldom realized by finite man. There is a development of thought from the grandeur of God's throne in heaven to the lowest beasts of the earth. Man is pictured at the center of God's creation. The poem is artistically set inside a refrain at the beginning and end. This refrain acts as a beautiful introduction and conclusion. The questions of Psalm 8 are cited in Heb 2:6ff. in describing the humiliation and exaltation of Christ.

1,2. The Glory of God. How excellent thy name. The introduction carefully identifies that "name" as **Jehovah, our Lord** (*'Adôn*). "Magnificent" or "majestic" would be a better translation than **excellent.** The phrase **babes and sucklings** may be a figure of man in his weakness. The sincere praise of these "babes" is set in sharp contrast to the scheming of God's enemies.

3,4. Man in Contrast. When I consider thy heavens . . . what is man? The night scene calls forth this praise of God's glory in the heavens. When man (*'enôsh,* frail man) is compared with all of the expanse above, how insignificant he seems. He is truly just the son of mankind (*'ādām,* generic man).

5,6. The Place of Man. Little lower than the angels. This would be better translated "little lower than divine" or "little less than divinity." Three things designate man's position: his relation to divinity, his dignity (glory and honor), and his dominion.

7,8. Illustrations of Man's Dominion. All sheep . . . oxen . . . beasts . . . fowl . . . fish. These lesser forms of life illustrate "all things" of the previous verse.

The creatures of earth, air, and sea are included in this obvious reference to the creation story of Genesis 1.

9. Doxology. How excellent is thy name. The refrain calls man back to the majesty of God lest he become absorbed in thoughts of personal grandeur. Man has dignity, but God alone is majestic.

NOTES

17

PSALM 9

To the chief Musician upon Muth-labben, A Psalm of David

I WILL praise *thee,* O Lord, with my whole heart; I will shew forth all thy marvellous works. ² I will be glad and rejoice in thee: I will sing praise to thy name, O thou most High.

³ When mine enemies are turned back, they shall fall and perish at thy presence. ⁴ For thou hast maintained my right and my cause; thou satest in the throne judging right. ⁵ Thou hast rebuked the heathen, thou hast destroyed the wicked, thou hast put out their name for ever and ever. ⁶ O thou enemy, destructions are come to a perpetual end: and thou hast destroyed cities; their memorial is perished with them.

⁷ But the Lord shall endure for ever: he hath prepared his throne for judgment. ⁸ And he shall judge the world in righteousness, he shall minister judgment to the people in uprightness. ⁹ The Lord also will be a refuge for the oppressed, a refuge in times of trouble. ¹⁰ And they that know thy name will put their trust in thee: for thou, Lord, hast not forsaken them that seek thee.

¹¹ Sing praises to the Lord, which dwelleth in Zion: declare among the people his doings. ¹² When he maketh inquisition for blood, he remembereth them: he forgetteth not the cry of the humble.

¹³ Have mercy upon me, O Lord; consider my trouble *which I suffer* of them that hate me, thou that liftest me up from the gates of death: ¹⁴ That I may shew forth all thy praise in the gates of the daughter of Zion: I will rejoice in thy salvation.

¹⁵ The heathen are sunk down in the pit *that* they made: in the net which they hid is their own foot taken. ¹⁶ The Lord is known *by* the judgment *which* he executeth: the wicked is snared in the work of his own hands. Hig-ga-ion. Se-lah.

¹⁷ The wicked shall be turned into hell, *and* all the nations that forget God. ¹⁸ For the needy shall not always be forgotten: the expectation of the poor shall *not* perish for ever.

9 O LORD, I will praise you with all my heart, and tell everyone about the marvelous things you do. ² I will be glad, yes, filled with joy because of you. I will sing your praises, O Lord God above all gods.

³ My enemies will fall back and perish in your presence; ⁴ you have vindicated me; you have endorsed my work, declaring from your throne that it is good. ⁵ You have rebuked the nations and destroyed the wicked, blotting out their names forever and ever. ⁶ O enemies of mine, you are doomed forever. The Lord will destroy your cities; even the memory of them will disappear.

⁷,⁸ But the Lord lives on forever; he sits upon his throne to judge justly the nations of the world. ⁹ All who are oppressed may come to him. He is a refuge for them in their times of trouble. ¹⁰ All those who know your mercy, Lord, will count on you for help. For you have never yet forsaken those who trust in you.

¹¹ Oh, sing out your praises to the God who lives in Jerusalem. Tell the world about his unforgettable deeds. ¹² He who avenges murder has an open ear to those who cry to him for justice. He does not ignore the prayers of men in trouble when they call to him for help.

¹³ And now, O Lord, have mercy on me; see how I suffer at the hands of those who hate me. Lord, snatch me back from the jaws of death. ¹⁴ Save me, so that I can praise you publicly before all the people at Jerusalem's gates and rejoice that you have rescued me.

¹⁵ The nations fall into the pitfalls they have dug for others; the trap they set has snapped on them. ¹⁶ The Lord is famous for the way he punishes the wicked in their own snares!

¹⁷ The wicked shall be sent away to hell; this is the fate of all the nations forgetting the Lord. ¹⁸ For the needs of the needy shall not be ignored forever; the hopes of the poor shall not always be crushed.

Psalm 9. Praise for Destruction of the Enemy

Evidently this psalm was originally joined to Ps 10, as shown in certain Hebrew manuscripts, the LXX, the Vulgate, and in another Latin version by Jerome. The two psalms form an acrostic using the letters of the Hebrew alphabet. The presence of *selāh* at the end of Ps 9 and the lack of a title on Ps 10 bear this out. The first psalm is highly national, while the second is strongly personal.

1-3. The Reason for Thanksgiving. 1 will praise . . . shew forth . . . be glad . . . rejoice . . . sing. All of this is wholehearted thanksgiving because the psalmist's enemies have been condemned by God. Sitting on his throne, God has passed judgment so that there is no doubt about the outcome.

4-8. A Vision of Final Judgment. He shall judge the world in righteousness. This is an eschatological picture of the final judgment, visualized as present. Mowinckel believes this to be a psalm used at the Feast of Tabernacles in a symbolical enthronement celebration.

9-12. The Exhortation to Praise. Sing praises. Since God will bless those that trust him, the psalmist seeks those who will join him in sincere praise. The natural sequel to praising God's name is to declare his doings.

13,14. An Appeal for God's Favor. Have mercy upon me. In the midst of national appeal a personal note is inserted. This lament is unusual within an expression of thanksgiving, but it may be natural for one expressing such sincere gratitude.

15-20. The Certainty of Judgment. The Lord is known *by* the judgment. The idea, previously introduced, of a world judgment to come is continued, as the writer declares that doom will surely overtake the wicked. The psalmist adds a request that nations may be brought to realize that they are only men!

¹⁹ Arise, O Lord; let not man prevail: let the heathen be judged in thy sight. ²⁰ Put them in fear, O Lord: *that* the nations may know themselves *to be but* men. Se-lah.

PSALM 10

WHY standest thou afar off, O Lord? *why* hidest thou *thyself* in times of trouble?

² The wicked in *his* pride doth persecute the poor: let them be taken in the devices that they have imagined. ³ For the wicked boasteth of his heart's desire, and blesseth the covetous, *whom* the Lord abhorreth.

⁴ The wicked, through the pride of his countenance, will not seek *after God:* God *is* not in all his thoughts. ⁵ His ways are always grievous; thy judgments *are* far above out of his sight: *as for* all his enemies, he puffeth at them. ⁶ He hath said in his heart, I shall not be moved: for *I shall* never *be* in adversity.

⁷ His mouth is full of cursing and deceit and fraud: under his tongue *is* michief and vanity. ⁸ He sitteth in the lurking places of the villages: in the secret places doth he murder the innocent: his eyes are privily set against the poor. ⁹ He lieth in wait secretly as a lion in his den: he lieth in wait to catch the poor: he doth catch the poor, when he draweth him into his net. ¹⁰ He croucheth, *and* humbleth himself, that the poor may fall by his strong ones. ¹¹ He hath said in his heart, God hath forgotten: he hideth his face; he will never see *it.*

¹² Arise, O Lord; O God, lift up thine hand: forget not the humble. ¹³ Wherefore doth the wicked contemn God? he hath said in his heart, Thou wilt not require *it.* ¹⁴ Thou hast seen *it;* for thou beholdest mischief and spite, to requite *it* with thy hand: the poor committeth himself unto thee; thou art the helper of the fatherless. ¹⁵ Break thou the arm of the wicked and the evil *man:* seek out his wickedness *till* thou find none.

¹⁶ The Lord *is* King for ever and ever: the heathen are perished out of his land.

¹⁹ O Lord, arise and judge and punish the nations; don't let them conquer you! ²⁰ Make them tremble in fear; put the nations in their place until at last they know they are but puny men.

10 LORD, WHY ARE you standing aloof and far away? Why do you hide when I need you the most?

² Come and deal with all these proud and wicked men who viciously persecute the poor. Pour upon these men the evil they planned for others! ³ For these men brag of all their evil lusts; they revile God and congratulate those the Lord abhors, whose only goal in life is money.

⁴ These wicked men, so proud and haughty, seem to think that God is dead. They wouldn't think of looking for him! ⁵ Yet there is success in everything they do, and their enemies fall before them. They do not see your punishment awaiting them. ⁶ They boast that neither God nor man can ever keep them down—somehow they'll find a way!

⁷ Their mouths are full of profanity and lies and fraud. They are always boasting of their evil plans. ⁸ They lurk in dark alleys of the city and murder passersby. ⁹ Like lions they crouch silently, waiting to pounce upon the poor. Like hunters they catch their victims in their traps. ¹⁰ The unfortunate are overwhelmed by their superior strength and fall beneath their blows. ¹¹ "God isn't watching," they say to themselves; "he'll never know!"

¹² O Lord, arise! O God, crush them! Don't forget the poor or anyone else in need. ¹³ Why do you let the wicked get away with this contempt for God? For they think that God will never call them to account. ¹⁴ Lord, you see what they are doing. You have noted each evil act. You know what trouble and grief they have caused. Now punish them. O Lord, the poor man trusts himself to you; you are known as the helper of the helpless. ¹⁵ Break the arms of these wicked men. Go after them until the last of them is destroyed.

¹⁶ The Lord is King forever and forever. Those who follow other gods shall be swept from his land.

Psalm 10. A Plea for Action

While this psalm has literary and textual affinity with the preceding one, the mood here is entirely different. The enemy is no longer the wicked of the nations but the wicked within Israel. The calamity has been caused by the misuse of power on the part of ungodly men of power. The mood is one of lament rather than of thanksgiving.

1,2. The Statement of the Plea. **Why . . . Why?** The frequent question beginning with "why" always describes a situation of frustration and forsakenness. The psalmist shows his own impatience and despair. After all, the persecution of the poor by the proud wicked leaders has reached an unbearable limit. His plea is that the wicked may reap what they have sown.

3-11. The Basis of the Problem. **The wicked boasteth.** This long list of grievances begins with the pride mentioned in the previous verses. The singular is used collectively of the many in Israel who have given no thought to God. Each condition is ethically oriented to Israel's way of life, and the whole passage reminds one of the writings of Isaiah, Micah, and Jeremiah.

12-18. The Call for Intervention. **Arise, O Lord . . . lift up thine hand.** This intense appeal for direct action by God is followed by arguments to strengthen the force of the appeal. The faith of the psalmist does not waver as he concludes that the Lord is King forever.

THE SOVEREIGNTY OF GOD . . .

21

¹⁷ Lord, thou hast heard the desire of the humble: thou wilt prepare their heart, thou wilt cause thine ear to hear: ¹⁸ To judge the fatherless and the oppressed, that the man of the earth may no more oppress.

PSALM 11

To the chief Musician, A Psalm *of David.*

IN the Lord put I my trust: how say ye to my soul, Flee *as* a bird to your mountain? ² For, lo, the wicked bend *their* bow, they make ready their arrow upon the string, that they may privily shoot at the upright in heart. ³ If the foundations be destroyed, what can the righteous do?

⁴ The Lord *is* in his holy temple, the Lord's throne *is* in heaven: his eyes behold, his eyelids try, the children of men. ⁵ The Lord trieth the righteous: but the wicked and him that loveth violence his soul hateth. ⁶ Upon the wicked he shall rain snares, fire and brimstone, and an horrible tempest: *this shall be* the portion of their cup.

⁷ For the righteous Lord loveth righteousness; his countenance doth behold the upright.

PSALM 12

To the chief Musician upon Sheminith, A Psalm of David

HELP, Lord; for the godly man ceaseth; for the faithful fail from among the children of men. ² They speak vanity every one with his neighbour: *with* flattering lips *and* with a double heart do they speak.

³ The Lord shall cut off all flattering lips, *and* the tongue that speaketh proud things: ⁴ Who have said, With our tongue will we prevail; our lips *are* our own: who *is* lord over us? ⁵ For the oppression of the poor, for the sighing of the needy, now will I arise, saith the Lord; I will set *him* in safety *from him that* puffeth at him. ⁶ The words of the Lord *are* pure words; *as* silver tried in a furnace of earth, purified seven

¹⁷ Lord, you know the hopes of humble people. Surely you will hear their cries and comfort their hearts by helping them. ¹⁸ You will be with the orphans and all who are oppressed, so that mere earthly man will terrify them no longer.

11 HOW DARE YOU tell me, "Flee to the mountains for safety," when I am trusting in the Lord? ² For the wicked have strung their bows, drawn their arrows tight against the bowstrings, and aimed from ambush at the people of God. ³ "Law and order have collapsed," we are told. "What can the righteous do but flee?"

⁴ But the Lord is still in his holy temple; he still rules from heaven. He closely watches everything that happens here on earth. ⁵ He puts the righteous and the wicked to the test; he hates those loving violence. ⁶ He will rain down fire and brimstone on the wicked and scorch them with his burning wind.

⁷ For God is good, and he loves goodness; the godly shall see his face.

12 LORD! HELP! GODLY men are fast disappearing. Where in all the world can dependable men be found? ² Everyone deceives and flatters and lies. There is no sincerity left.

³,⁴ But the Lord will not deal gently with people who act like that; he will destroy those proud liars who say, "We will lie to our hearts' content. Our lips are our own; who can stop us?" ⁵ The Lord replies, "I will arise and defend the oppressed, the poor, the needy. I will rescue them as they have longed for me to do." ⁶ The Lord's promise is sure. He speaks no careless word; all he says is purest truth, like silver seven times refined. ⁷ O Lord, we know that you will forever preserve your own from the reach of evil men, ⁸ although they prowl on every side and vileness is praised throughout the land.

Psalm 11. The Assurance of Faith

A grave peril confronts the psalmist as enemies seek his life. His desperate situation gives rise to deep thought and noble expression of his confidence in the Lord. His words of assurance flow in a poem of true lyric quality. The circumstances are strikingly similar to those of several episodes in David's life.

1,2. Faith versus Expediency. Trust or flee. The advice of well-meaning friends is to take the way of expediency. "Flee to the mountain, where there are plenty of hiding places," is the worldly idea of how to find safety. Even in the face of the drawn bow of the enemy, the speaker affirms that his trust is in the Lord. Instead of taking the easy way out, he will take the way of faith.

3-7. The Foundation of Faith. If the foundation be destroyed. The psalmist knows that fleeing would only undermine his basic faith. After all, God is in his holy temple, his throne is established in heaven, and his eyes behold what goes on down here. Therefore, the punishment of God shall come upon the wicked even as it did upon Sodom, while the upright shall behold God's face.

Psalm 12. A Prayer for the Faithful

This psalm depicts another dark hour of persecution, when society is falling apart. While lamenting a situation in which lying and falsehood prevail, the author is likewise expressing his utmost confidence in God, who is still worshiped by the faithful minority. Gunkel treats this psalm in a liturgical sense, making it corporate. Whatever the final usage, there could well have been an original individualistic basis for its composition.

1-4. The Prayer of the Faithful. Help, Lord. The writer is speaking for the faithful, godly men who have been abused by the loudmouthed ones who speak idle flattery and indulge in double talk. Like Elijah, the psalmist speaks of himself as the only one left who has not joined these braggarts.

5. The Answer of God. Saith the Lord. This verse takes the form of an oracle from the Lord answering the sincere prayer of the faithful. God promises his help, which will result in complete safety.

6-8. The Response of the Worshiper. Pure words. In contrast to the talk of the loudmouthed ones, God's words are as pure as the finest silver. What he has promised, he will perform. His trust-

times. 7 Thou shalt keep them, O Lord, thou shalt preserve them from this generation for ever. 8 The wicked walk on every side, when the vilest men are exalted.

times refined. 7 O Lord, we know that you will forever preserve your own from the reach of evil men, 8 although they prowl on every side and vileness is praised throughout the land.

PSALM 13

To the chief Musician, A Psalm of David

How long wilt thou forget me, O Lord? for ever? how long wilt thou hide thy face from me? 2 How long shall I take counsel in my soul, *having* sorrow in my heart daily? how long shall mine enemy be exalted over me? 3 Consider *and* hear me, O Lord my God: lighten mine eyes, lest I sleep the *sleep of* death; 4 Lest mine enemy say, I have prevailed against him; *and* those that trouble me rejoice when I am moved.

5 But I have trusted in thy mercy; my heart shall rejoice in thy salvation. 6 I will sing unto the Lord, because he hath dealt bountifully with me.

13 HOW LONG WILL you forget me, Lord? Forever? How long will you look the other way when I am in need? 2 How long must I be hiding daily anguish in my heart? How long shall my enemy have the upper hand? 3 Answer me, O Lord my God; give me light in my darkness lest I die. 4 Don't let my enemies say, "We have conquered him!" Don't let them gloat that I am down.

5 But I will always trust in you and in your mercy and shall rejoice in your salvation. 6 I will sing to the Lord because he has blessed me so richly.

PSALM 14

To the chief Musician, A Psalm *of David*

THE fool hath said in his heart, *There is* no God. They are corrupt, they have done abominable works, *there is* none that doeth good.

2 The Lord looked down from heaven upon the children of men, to see if there were any that did understand, *and* seek God. 3 They are all gone aside, they are *all* together become filthy: *there is* none that doeth good, no, not one. 4 Have all the workers of iniquity no knowledge? who eat up my people *as* they eat bread, and call not upon the Lord.

5 There were they in great fear: for God *is* in the generation of the righteous. 6 Ye have shamed the counsel of the poor, because the Lord *is* his refuge. 7 Oh that the salvation of Israel *were come* out of Zion! when the Lord bringeth back the captivity of his people, Jacob shall rejoice, *and* Israel shall be glad.

14 THAT MAN IS a fool who says to himself, "There is no God!" Anyone who talks like that is warped and evil and cannot really be a good person at all.

2 The Lord looks down from heaven on all mankind to see if there are any who are wise, who want to please God. 3 But no, all have strayed away; all are rotten with sin. Not one is good, not one! 4 They eat my people like bread and wouldn't think of praying! Don't they really know any better?

5 Terror shall grip them, for God is with those who love him. 6 He is the refuge of the poor and humble when evildoers are oppressing them. 7 Oh, that the time of their rescue were already here, that God would come from Zion now to save his people. What gladness when the Lord has rescued Israel!

worthiness is assured and proclaimed as a response of worship.

Psalm 13. From Doubt to Trust

Expressed in this brief psalm are the deepest longings of a troubled soul. Although a personal enemy is behind the scenes, the psalmist is wrestling with his own doubts as to God's divine activity on his behalf. Since sickness is not alluded to, the problem is probably mental, very likely fear. In its structure this psalm is an excellent example of the lament of an individual, being carefully divided into three brief stanzas of two verses each.

1,2. His Problem of Doubt. How long . . . ? The fourfold repetition of this phrase clearly shows the writer's intense suffering. He is wearied by his enemy but even more distressed by God's seeming unconcern. He feels God-forsaken in the time of his greatest need.

3,4. His Prayer for Assistance. Consider . . . hear . . . lighten mine eyes. In the midst of doubt and dejection, he prays for God to understand his problem and bring back the brightness in his eyes. Not only does he fear physical death, but he knows how his enemies, in their godlessness, will boast concerning the downfall of a friend of God.

5,6. His Relief in Trust. But I have trusted. Although no spoken answer is recorded, a real relief comes over this troubled soul. His trust is based upon God's loving-kindness, his rejoicing upon God's salvation, his singing upon God's bountiful care. He has found true peace by utter trust in God.

Psalm 14. Judgment for Denying God

Here we have a good example to show how the Psalter developed. Except for minor textual variations (esp. v. 6) it is identical with Psalm 53. Since the latter is from a later collection and substitutes *Elohim* for *Yahweh*, Psalm 14 is considered to be the earlier form. In both psalms the speaker views the depraved condition of men with the true prophetic spirit.

1-3. The Depravity of the Fool. No God. The use of the word *fool (nābāl)* indicates not a theoretical atheist but a practical atheist, who lives as if there were no god. For all practical purposes God does not enter into his thinking. The words **corrupt, abominable,** and **filthy** all point to the depravity of such an individual, who is clearly pictured as typical of Israel in this age.

4-6. The Corruption of the Priesthood. **No knowledge.** These who lack knowledge of God are perhaps the priests, who eat the shewbread and should call upon God. Instead they are becoming **workers of iniquity** (cf. Hos 1:4-6). Instead of leading God's people, they devour them. The **generation of the righteous** obviously refers to **my people,** while **the poor** have a special place of refuge in God.

7. The Hope of Deliverance. **Oh that . . . !** This appended prayer may have been added for liturgical purposes. Or it may express the psalmist's one glimmer of hope in this dark period. To bring **back the captivity** may mean simply to "restore the fortunes." Regardless of when this verse was composed, it serves as a fitting conclusion.

NOTES

PSALM 15

A Psalm of David

LORD, who shall abide in thy tabernacle? who shall dwell in thy holy hill? ² He that walketh uprightly, and worketh righteousness, and speaketh the truth in his heart. ³ *He that* backbiteth not with his tongue, nor doeth evil to his neighbour, nor taketh up a reproach against his neighbour. ⁴ In whose eyes a vile person is contemned; but he honoureth them that fear the Lord. *He that* sweareth to *his own* hurt, and changeth not. ⁵ *He that* putteth not out his money to usury, nor taketh reward against the innocent. He that doeth these *things* shall never be moved.

PSALM 16

Michtam of David

PRESERVE me, O God: for in thee do I put my trust. ² *O my soul,* thou hast said unto the Lord, Thou *art* my Lord: my goodness *extendeth* not to thee; ³ *But* to the saints that *are* in the earth, and *to* the excellent, in whom *is* all my delight. ⁴ Their sorrows shall be multiplied *that* hasten *after* another *god:* their drink offerings of blood will I not offer, nor take up their names into my lips. ⁵ The Lord *is* the portion of mine inheritance and of my cup: thou maintainest my lot. ⁶ The lines are fallen unto me in pleasant *places;* yea, I have a goodly heritage. ⁷ I will bless the Lord, who hath given me counsel: my reins also instruct me in the night seasons. ⁸ I have set the Lord always before me: because *he is* at my right hand, I shall not be moved. ⁹ Therefore my heart is glad, and my glory rejoiceth: my flesh also shall rest in hope. ¹⁰ For thou wilt not leave my soul in hell; neither wilt thou suffer thine Holy One to see corruption. ¹¹ Thou wilt shew me the path of life: in thy presence *is* fulness of joy; at thy right hand *there are* pleasures for evermore.

15 LORD, WHO MAY go and find refuge and shelter in your tabernacle up on your holy hill? ² Anyone who leads a blameless life and is truly sincere. ³ Anyone who refuses to slander others, does not listen to gossip, never harms his neighbor, ⁴ speaks out against sin, criticizes those committing it, commends the faithful followers of the Lord, keeps a promise even if it ruins him, ⁵ does not crush his debtors with high interest rates, and refuses to testify against the innocent despite the bribes offered him— such a man shall stand firm forever.

16 SAVE ME, O God, because I have come to you for refuge. ² I said to him, "You are my Lord; I have no other help but yours." ³ I want the company of the godly men and women in the land; they are the true nobility. ⁴ Those choosing other gods shall all be filled with sorrow; I will not offer the sacrifices they do or even speak the names of their gods.

⁵ The Lord himself is my inheritance, my prize. He is my food and drink, my highest joy! He guards all that is mine. ⁶ He sees that I am given pleasant brooks and meadows as my share! What a wonderful inheritance! ⁷ I will bless the Lord who counsels me; he gives me wisdom in the night. He tells me what to do.

⁸ I am always thinking of the Lord; and because he is so near, I never need to stumble or to fall. ⁹ Heart, body, and soul are filled with joy. ¹⁰ For you will not leave me among the dead; you will not allow your beloved one to rot in the grave. ¹¹ You have let me experience the joys of life and the exquisite pleasures of your own eternal presence.

Psalm 15. The Guest of God

This Wisdom psalm is a commentary on man's duty to God and to his fellow-man as set forth in Deut 6:5 and Lev 19:18. It deals with the moral and ethical qualifications which admit a worshiper to the presence of God. The early custom of challenging the fitness of a worshiper may be reflected here. Perhaps the priest asked the questions in verse 1, the worshiper responded with an answer such as is given here, and the priest closed the challenge with the final promise of verse 5b. Some interpreters refer the question to the worshiper, with the answer and promise as the usual reply of the priests to the worshipers entering the Temple. The former seems preferable.

1. The Pertinent Question. **Lord, who . . . ?** The person who is to come into God's presence must face squarely this twofold question. The practice of pitching tents on Mount Moriah may have been allowed to pilgrims in certain periods of Israel's history. However, the parallel questions emphasize that God's standard must be met if a man is to be God's guest.

2-5b. The Acceptable Answer. **He that.** The matters of integrity and righteousness relate to man's duty to God, while truthfulness and the remaining virtues refer to man's duty toward his neighbor. By combining the similar **uprightness** and **integrity** (AV, *righteousness*), it is possible to discover an ethical decalogue in the phrases of this section.

5c. The Priestly Promise. **He that doeth.** The one who meets God's standard must be one who **doeth these things.** Such a person not only knows what God expects of his guest, but puts these principles into practice. The note of stability gives a proper climax to the psalm.

Psalm 16. The Joy of Loyalty

This song of trust is a wholehearted profession of the joy that comes from faithfulness and loyalty. The author lived in a day when apostasy and idolatry were extensive. Against this background he contrasts his supreme happiness with the plight of those who have slipped into idolatry. His great hope amplifies his present trust in God. The psalm is ascribed to David by Peter (Acts 2:25) and by Paul (Acts 13:35,36) when they refer to its prophecy of Messiah's resurrection.

1-4. Joy in Service. **Preserve me, O God.** This prayer is not for deliverance from an enemy but for the continuance of the happiness he has already found. His delight is in the saints, while his trust is in God. Contrasted with this is the state of multiplied sorrows which is the lot of those who have sought other gods.

5-8. Joy in Faith. **Inheritance . . . lot . . . lines.** These figures all refer to the allotment of land by lots whereby the Levites received no specific apportionment. Along with the figure of the writer's cup of happiness, these add up to a truly **goodly** heritage because God is his choicest possession. His stability is based upon God's constant leadership.

9-11. Joy in Hope. **Therefore.** On the basis of his present joy, the psalmist uses phrase after phrase to show the basis of his joyous hope. His **heart, liver** (rather than *glory*), and **flesh** all respond to the thrill of this hope. Verse 10a does not present a clear-cut reference to an afterlife, because the first phrase can be better translated, "For thou wilt not abandon my soul to Sheol"; but verse 10b must refer to someone other than the psalmist in saying, "Neither wilt thou allow thine Holy One to undergo corruption." Verse 11 points to a continuance of the happy life which he has already come to know in the presence of the Lord.

NOTES

PSALM 17

A Prayer of David

HEAR the right, O Lord, attend unto my cry, give ear unto my prayer, *that goeth* not out of feigned lips. ² Let my sentence come forth from thy presence; let thine eyes behold the things that are equal. ³ Thou hast proved mine heart; thou hast visited *me* in the night; thou hast tried me, *and* shalt find nothing; I am purposed *that* my mouth shall not transgress. ⁴ Concerning the works of men, by the word of thy lips I have kept *me from* the paths of the destroyer. ⁵ Hold up my goings in thy paths, *that* my footsteps slip not.

⁶ I have called upon thee, for thou wilt hear me, O God: incline thine ear unto me, *and hear* my speech. ⁷ Shew thy marvellous lovingkindness, O thou that savest by thy right hand them which put their trust *in thee* from those that rise up *against them.* ⁸ Keep me as the apple of the eye, hide me under the shadow of thy wings,

⁹ From the wicked that oppress me, *from* my deadly enemies, *who* compass me about. ¹⁰ They are inclosed in their own fat: with their mouth they speak proudly. ¹¹ They have now compassed us in our steps: they have set their eyes bowing down to the earth; ¹² Like as a lion *that* is greedy of his prey, and as it were a young lion lurking in secret places.

¹³ Arise, O Lord, disappoint him, cast him down: deliver my soul from the wicked, *which is* thy sword: ¹⁴ From men *which are* thy hand, O Lord, from men of the world, *which have* their portion in *this* life, and whose belly thou fillest with thy hid *treasure:* they are full of children, and leave the rest of their *substance* to their babes.

¹⁵ As for me, I will behold thy face in righteousness: I shall be satisfied, when I awake, with thy likeness.

17 I AM PLEADING for your help, O Lord; for I have been honest and have done what is right, and you must listen to my earnest cry! ² Publicly acquit me, Lord, for you are always fair. ³ You have tested me and seen that I am good. You have come even in the night and found nothing amiss and know that I have told the truth. ⁴ I have followed your commands and have not gone along with cruel and evil men. ⁵ My feet have not slipped from your paths.

⁶ Why am I praying like this? Because I know you will answer me, O God! Yes, listen as I pray. ⁷ Show me your strong love in wonderful ways, O Savior of all those seeking your help against their foes. ⁸ Protect me as you would the pupil of your eye; hide me in the shadow of your wings as you hover over me.

⁹ My enemies encircle me with murder in their eyes. ¹⁰ They are pitiless and arrogant. Listen to their boasting. ¹¹ They close in upon me and are ready to throw me to the ground. ¹² They are like lions eager to tear me apart, like young lions hiding and waiting their chance.

¹³,¹⁴ Lord, arise and stand against them. Push them back! Come and save me from these men of the world whose only concern is earthly gain—these men whom you have filled with your treasures so that their children and grandchildren are rich and prosperous.

¹⁵ But as for me, my contentment is not in wealth but in seeing you and knowing all is well between us. And when I awake in heaven, I will be fully satisfied, for I will see you face to face.

Psalm 17. The Vindication of the Righteous

The psalmist here laments his unjust treatment at the hands of his enemies. The cause of his problem is not known, only that he is innocent of the charges brought against him. God is clearly his last court of appeal, his only hope. His absolute confidence in God is shown throughout, but especially in the final verse.

1-5. An Appeal for Justice. Hear the right. The psalmist prays first that God will **hear, attend,** and **give ear** to his side of the case, which he presents, he declares, with lips free of deceit. His cry is only for a just sentence from the One who knows his innocence. God has **proved, visited,** and **tried** him, and will continue to find him guiltless.

6-12. An Appeal for Mercy. Shew thy marvelous lovingkindness. The speaker repeats his cry, this time with direct reference to his enemies. He requests that God will demonstrate his loving-kindness, keep him safe, and hide him from those who rise up against him. He describes his enemies in terms that point up the contrast between them and himself.

13-15. An Appeal for Deliverance. Deliver my soul. The next step is naturally the actual deliverance of this sufferer and the attendant destruction of the wicked enemy. The psalmist calls for decisive action to **disappoint** and **cast down** the enemy in open vindication of himself. **When I awake** may refer to the next morning after this experience or to a vision of God beyond the sleep of death.

PSALM 18

To the chief Musician, A Psalm of David, the servant of the Lord, who spake unto the Lord the words of this song in the day that the Lord delivered him from the hand of all his enemies, and from the hand of Saul: And he said,

I WILL love thee, O Lord, my strength.

² The Lord *is* my rock, and my fortress, and my deliverer; my God, my strength, in whom I will trust; my buckler, and the horn of my salvation, *and* my high tower. ³ I will call upon the Lord, *who is worthy* to be praised: so shall I be saved from mine enemies.

⁴ The sorrows of death compassed me, and the floods of ungodly men made me afraid. ⁵ The sorrows of hell compassed me about: the snares of death prevented me.

⁶ In my distress I called upon the Lord, and cried unto my God: he heard my voice out of his temple, and my cry came before him, *even* into his ears. ⁷ Then the earth shook and trembled; the foundations also of the hills moved and were shaken, because he was wroth. ⁸ There went up a smoke out of his nostrils, and fire out of his mouth devoured: coals were kindled by it. ⁹ He bowed the heavens also, and came down: and darkness *was* under his feet. ¹⁰ And he rode upon a cherub, and did fly: yea, he did fly upon the wings of the wind. ¹¹ He made darkness his secret place; his pavilion round about him *were* dark waters *and* thick clouds of the skies. ¹² At the brightness *that was* before him his thick clouds passed, hail *stones* and coals of fire.

¹³ The Lord also thundered in the heavens, and the Highest gave his voice; hail *stones* and coals of fire. ¹⁴ Yea, he sent out his arrows, and scattered them; and he shot out lightnings, and discomfited them. ¹⁵ Then the channels of waters were seen, and the foundations of the world were discovered at thy rebuke, O Lord, at the blast of the breath of thy nostrils.

¹⁶ He sent from above, he took me, he drew me out of many waters. ¹⁷ He delivered me from my strong enemy, and from them which hated me: for they were too strong for me.

This song of David was written at a time when the Lord had delivered him from his many enemies, including Saul.

18 LORD, HOW I love you! For you have done such tremendous things for me. ² The Lord is my fort where I can enter and be safe; no one can follow me in and slay me. He is a rugged mountain where I hide; he is my Savior, a rock where none can reach me, and a tower of safety. He is my shield. He is like the strong horn of a mighty fighting bull. ³ All I need to do is cry to him—oh, praise the Lord—and I am saved from all my enemies!

⁴ Death bound me with chains, and the floods of ungodliness mounted a massive attack against me. ⁵ Trapped and helpless, I struggled against the ropes that drew me on to death.

⁶ In my distress I screamed to the Lord for his help. And he heard me from heaven; my cry reached his ears. ⁷ Then the earth rocked and reeled, and mountains shook and trembled. How they quaked! For he was angry. ⁸ Fierce flames leaped from his mouth, setting fire to the earth; smoke blew from his nostrils. ⁹ He bent the heavens down and came to my defense; thick darkness was beneath his feet. ¹⁰ Mounted on the cherubim, he sped swiftly to my aid with wings of wind. ¹¹ He enshrouded himself with darkness, veiling his approach with dense clouds dark as murky waters. ¹² Suddenly the brilliance of his presence broke through the clouds with lightning and a mighty storm of hail.

¹³ The Lord thundered in the heavens; the God above all gods has spoken—oh, the hailstones; oh, the fire! ¹⁴ He flashed his fearful arrows of lightning and routed all my enemies. See how they run! ¹⁵ Then at your command, O Lord, the sea receded from the shore. At the blast of your breath the depths were laid bare.

¹⁶ He reached down from heaven and took me and drew me out of my great trials. He rescued me from deep waters. ¹⁷ He delivered me from my strong enemy, from those who hated me—I who was helpless in their hands.

18 They prevented me in the day of my calamity: but the Lord was my stay. 19 He brought me forth also into a large place; he delivered me, because he delighted in me. 20 The Lord rewarded me according to my righteousness; according to the cleanness of my hands hath he recompensed me. 21 For I have kept the ways of the Lord, and have not wickedly departed from my God. 22 For all his judgments *were* before me, and I did not put away his statutes from me. 23 I was also upright before him, and I kept myself from mine iniquity. 24 Therefore hath the Lord recompensed me according to my righteousness, according to the cleanness of my hands in his eyesight.

25 With the merciful thou wilt shew thyself merciful; with an upright man thou wilt shew thyself upright; 26 With the pure thou wilt shew thyself pure; and with the froward thou wilt shew thyself froward. 27 For thou wilt save the afflicted people; but wilt bring down high looks. 28 For thou wilt light my candle: the Lord my God will enlighten my darkness. 29 For by thee I have run through a troop; and by my God have I leaped over a wall.

30 *As for* God, his way *is* perfect: the word of the Lord is tried: he *is* a buckler to all those that trust in him. 31 For who *is* God save the Lord? or who *is* a rock save our God?

32 *It is* God that girdeth me with strength, and maketh my way perfect. 33 He maketh my feet like hinds' *feet,* and setteth me upon my high places. 34 He teacheth my hands to war, so that a bow of steel is broken by mine arms.

35 Thou hast also given me the shield of thy salvation: and thy right hand hath holden me up, and thy gentleness hath made me great. 36 Thou hast enlarged my steps under me, that my feet did not slip. 37 I have pursued mine enemies, and overtaken them: neither did I turn again till they were consumed. 38 I have wounded them that they were not able to rise: they are fallen under my feet. 39 For thou hast girded me with strength unto the battle: thou hast subdued under me those that rose up

18 On the day when I was weakest, they attacked. But the Lord held me steady. 19 He led me to a place of safety, for he delights in me. 20 The Lord rewarded me for doing right and being pure. 21 For I have followed his commands and have not sinned by turning back from following him. 22 I kept close watch on all his laws; I did not refuse a single one. 23 I did my best to keep them all, holding myself back from doing wrong. 24 And so the Lord has paid me with his blessings, for I have done what is right, and I am pure of heart. This he knows, for he watches my every step.

25 Lord, how merciful you are to those who are merciful. And you do not punish those who run from evil. 26 You give blessings to the pure but pain to those who leave your paths. 27 You deliver the humble but condemn the proud and haughty ones. 28 You have turned on my light! The Lord my God has made my darkness turn to light. 29 Now in your strength I can scale any wall, attack any troop.

30 What a God he is! How perfect in every way! All his promises prove true. He is a shield for everyone who hides behind him. 31 For who is God except our Lord? Who but he is as a rock?

32 He fills me with strength and protects me wherever I go. 33 He gives me the sure-footedness of a mountain goat upon the crags. He leads me safely along the top of the cliffs. 34 He prepares me for battle and gives me strength to draw an iron bow!

35 You have given me your salvation as my shield. Your right hand, O Lord, supports me; your gentleness has made me great. 36 You have made wide steps beneath my feet so that I need never slip. 37 I chased my enemies; I caught up with them and did not turn back until all were conquered. 38 I pinned them to the ground; all were helpless before me. I placed my feet upon their necks. 39 For you have armed me with strong armor for the battle. My enemies quail before me and fall defeated at my feet.

against me. 40 Thou hast also given me the necks of mine enemies; that I might destroy them that hate me. 41 They cried, *but there was* none to save *them: even* unto the Lord, but he answered them not. 42 Then did I beat them small as the dust before the wind: I did cast them out as the dirt in the streets. 43 Thou hast delivered me from the strivings of the people; *and* thou hast made me the head of the heathen: a people *whom* I have not known shall serve me. 44 As soon as they hear of me, they shall obey me: the strangers shall submit themselves unto me. 45 The strangers shall fade away, and be afraid out of their close places.

46 The Lord liveth; and blessed *be* my rock; and let the God of my salvation be exalted. 47 *It is* God that avengeth me, and subdueth the people under me.

48 He delivereth me from mine enemies: yea, thou liftest me up above those that rise up against me: thou hast delivered me from the violent man. 49 Therefore will I give thanks unto thee, O Lord, among the heathen, and sing praises unto thy name. 50 Great deliverance giveth he to his king; and sheweth mercy to his anointed, to David, and to his seed for evermore.

PSALM 19

To the chief Musician, A Psalm of David

THE heavens declare the glory of God; and the firmament sheweth his handywork. 2 Day unto day uttereth speech, and night unto night sheweth knowledge. 3 *There is* no speech nor language, *where* their voice is not heard. 4 Their line is gone out through all the earth, and their words to the end of the world. In them hath he set a tabernacle for the sun, 5 Which *is* as a bridegroom coming out of his chamber, *and* rejoiceth as a strong man to run a race. 6 His going forth *is* from the end of the heaven, and his circuit unto the ends of it: and there is nothing hid from the heat thereof.

40 You made them turn and run; I destroyed all who hated me. 41 They shouted for help but no one dared to rescue them; they cried to the Lord, but he refused to answer them. 42 So I crushed them fine as dust and cast them to the wind. I threw them away like sweepings from the floor. 43,44,45 You gave me victory in every battle. The nations came and served me. Even those I didn't know before come now and bow before me. Foreigners who have never seen me submit instantly. They come trembling from their strongholds.

46 God is alive! Praise him who is the great rock of protection. 47 He is the God who pays back those who harm me and subdues the nations before me.

48 He rescues me from my enemies; he holds me safely out of their reach and saves me from these powerful opponents. 49 For this, O Lord, I will praise you among the nations. 50 Many times you have miraculously rescued me, the king you appointed. You have been loving and kind to me and will be to my descendants.

19 THE HEAVENS ARE telling the glory of God; they are a marvelous display of his craftsmanship. 2 Day and night they keep on telling about God. 3,4 Without a sound or word, silent in the skies, their message reaches out to all the world. The sun lives in the heavens where God placed it 5 and moves out across the skies as radiant as a bridegroom going to his wedding, or as joyous as an athlete looking forward to a race! 6 The sun crosses the heavens from end to end, and nothing can hide from its heat.

46-50. A Concluding Hymn of Praise. **Let the God of my salvation be exalted.** All honor and praise is due unto God alone.

Psalm 19. God's Glory Above and Within

This psalm is clearly divided into two distinct sections, which suggests that it may be a composite of two poems. The first section (vv. 1-6) uses a general Semitic name for God *('Ēl)*, while the second uses the special covenant name *(Yahweh)*. In subject matter, style, and form the two sections differ. However, the union has been skillfully made; the psalmist's exaltation of the revelation of nature is fused with his exaltation of the law of God into one glorious hymn of praise.

1-6. The Testimony of the Heavens. **The heavens . . . the firmament . . . the sun.** Each of these has its part in making known the mystery of God's glory. In constant revelation by day and by night the expanse of the heavens reveals the excellence of God's creative work. The sun appears as the greatest member of the heavenly choir, running its appointed course of witness. While similar figures abound in Akkadian literature describing the sun-god Shamash (ANET, pp. 91, 116, 179, 387-389), the psalmist clearly regards the sun as an agent of God in revealing His glory.

7 The law of the Lord *is* perfect, converting the soul: the testimony of the Lord *is* sure, making wise the simple. 8 The statutes of the Lord *are* right, rejoicing the heart: the commandment of the Lord *is* pure, enlightening the eyes. 9 The fear of the Lord *is* clean, enduring for ever: the judgments of the Lord *are* true *and* righteous altogether. 10 More to be desired *are they* than gold, yea, than much fine gold: sweeter also than honey and the honeycomb. 11 Moreover by them is thy servant warned: *and* in keeping of them *there is* great reward.

12 Who can understand *his* errors? cleanse thou me from secret *faults.* 13 Keep back thy servant also from presumptuous *sins;* let them not have dominion over me: then shall I be upright, and I shall be innocent from the great transgression.

14 Let the words of my mouth, and the meditation of my heart, be acceptable in thy sight, O Lord, my strength, and my redeemer.

7,8 God's laws are perfect. They protect us, make us wise, and give us joy and light. 9 God's laws are pure, eternal, just. 10 They are more desirable than gold. They are sweeter than honey dripping from a honeycomb. 11 For they warn us away from harm and give success to those who obey them.

12 But how can I ever know what sins are lurking in my heart? Cleanse me from these hidden faults. 13 And keep me from deliberate wrongs; help me to stop doing them. Only then can I be free of guilt and innocent of some great crime.

14 May my spoken words and unspoken thoughts be pleasing even to you, O Lord my Rock and my Redeemer.

PSALM 20

To the chief Musician, A Psalm of David

THE Lord hear thee in the day of trouble; the name of the God of Jacob defend thee; 2 Send thee help from the sanctuary, and strengthen thee out of Zion; 3 Remember all thy offerings, and accept thy burnt sacrifice; Se-lah. 4 Grant thee according to thine own heart, and fulfil all thy counsel. 5 We will rejoice in thy salvation, and in the name of our God we will set up *our* banners: the Lord fulfil all thy petitions.

6 Now know I that the Lord saveth his anointed; he will hear him from his holy heaven with the saving strength of his right hand. 7 Some *trust* in chariots, and some in horses: but we will remember the name of the Lord our God. 8 They are brought down and fallen: but we are risen, and stand upright.

9 Save, Lord: let the king hear us when we call.

20 IN YOUR DAY of trouble, may the Lord be with you! May the God of Jacob keep you from all harm. 2 May he send you aid from his sanctuary in Zion. 3 May he remember with pleasure the gifts you have given him, your sacrifices and burnt offerings. 4 May he grant you your heart's desire and fulfill all your plans. 5 May there be shouts of joy when we hear the news of your victory, flags flying with praise to God for all that he has done for you. May he answer all your prayers!

6 "God save the king"—I know he does! He hears me from highest heaven and sends great victories. 7 Some nations boast of armies and of weaponry, but our boast is in the Lord our God. 8 Those nations will collapse and perish; we will arise to stand firm and sure!

9 Give victory to our king, O Lord; oh, hear our prayer.

7-10. The Testimony of the Torah. The law of the Lord. The psalmist here uses six names to describe the whole of God's inner revelation. The word *tôrâ* (law) embodies more than a written list of precepts; it includes all of God's teaching. Using adjectives and participial phrases, the psalmist describes the excellence of God's revelation, which surpasses even gold or honey.

11-14. The Personal Application. Cleanse thou me. The moral teaching of God, which serves as a warning, can lead a person to the desired reward. Meditating upon God's teaching acts as a mirror to make visible the inner man. Therefore, the psalmist closes by requesting the strength to overcome all types of sin and be found acceptable.

Psalm 20. Supplication for Victory

In both structure and content this royal psalm is very closely linked with Psalm 21. The latter acts as a sequel of thanksgiving for answered prayer. The king is the central figure, while his victory occupies the attention of his subjects. It may well have been arranged for antiphonal singing, with the congregation or the Levitical choir acting as a chorus in verses 1-5 and 9. A priest or Levite may have voiced the words of assurance in verses 6-8. Complete confidence in God is expressed throughout.

1-5. A Prayer for the King. The Lord hear thee. Although the prayer is addressed *to* the king, it is also an act of intercession *for* the king. This describes a vital step in the preparation for battle, as the king presented his sacrifices to the Lord and received the assurance of God's blessing.

6-8. An Oracle of Assurance. Now know I. After an interval, possibly the time during which the sacrifices were offered, the speaker's response of confidence issues in the form of a prophetic oracle. The use of the prophetic perfect tense gives the necessary divine assurance to the king and worshipers. The army is now prepared to go forth in the **name of the Lord.**

9. Closing Chorus. Save, Lord . . . This is more literally stated in the LXX as *O Lord, save the King and answer us when we call.* It may have been sung by the whole congregation or by the Levitical choir.

NOTES

PSALM 21

To the chief Musician, A Psalm of David

THE king shall joy in thy strength, O Lord; and in thy salvation how greatly shall he rejoice! ² Thou hast given him his heart's desire, and hast not withholden the request of his lips. Se-lah.

³ For thou preventest him with the blessings of goodness: thou settest a crown of pure gold on his head. ⁴ He asked life of thee, *and* thou gavest *it* him, *even* length of days for ever and ever. ⁵ His glory *is* great in thy salvation: honour and majesty hast thou laid upon him. ⁶ For thou hast made him most blessed for ever: thou hast made him exceeding glad with thy countenance. ⁷ For the king trusteth in the Lord, and through the mercy of the most High he shall not be moved.

⁸ Thine hand shall find out all thine enemies: thy right hand shall find out those that hate thee. ⁹ Thou shalt make them as a fiery oven in the time of thine anger: the Lord shall swallow them up in his wrath, and the fire shall devour them. ¹⁰ Their fruit shalt thou destroy from the earth, and their seed from among the children of men. ¹¹ For they intended evil against thee: they imagined a mischievous device, *which* they are not able *to perform.* ¹² Therefore shalt thou make them turn their back, *when* thou shalt make ready *thine arrows* upon thy strings against the face of them.

¹³ Be thou exalted, Lord, in thine own strength: *so* will we sing and praise thy power.

21 HOW THE KING rejoices in your strength, O Lord! How he exults in your salvation. ² For you have given him his heart's desire, everything he asks you for!

³ You welcomed him to the throne with success and prosperity. You set a kingly crown of purest gold upon his head. ⁴ He asked for a long, good life, and you have granted his request; the days of his life stretch on and on forever. ⁵ You have given him fame and honor. You have clothed him with splendor and majesty. ⁶ You have endowed him with eternal happiness. You have given him the unquenchable joy of your presence. ⁷ And because the king trusts in the Lord, he will never stumble, never fall; for he depends upon the steadfast love of the God who is above all gods.

⁸ Your hand, O Lord, will find your enemies, all who hate you. ⁹,¹⁰ When you appear, they will be destroyed in the fierce fire of your presence. The Lord will destroy them and their children. ¹¹ For these men plot against you, Lord, but they cannot possibly succeed. ¹² They will turn and flee when they see your arrows aimed straight at them.

¹³ Accept our praise, O Lord, for all your glorious power. We will write songs to celebrate your mighty acts!

PSALM 22

To the chief Musician upon Aijeleth Shahar, A Psalm of David.

MY God, my God, why hast thou forsaken me? *why art thou so* far from helping me, *and from* the words of my roaring? ² O my God, I cry in the day-time, but thou hearest not; and in the night season, and am not silent. ³ But thou *art* holy, *O thou* that inhabitest the

22 MY GOD, MY God, why have you forsaken me? Why do you refuse to help me or even to listen to my groans? ² Day and night I keep on weeping, crying for your help, but there is no reply— ³,⁴ for *you are holy.*

38

Psalm 21. Thanksgiving for Victory

This royal psalm acts as the natural sequel to Psalm 20, since supplication becomes thanksgiving because of the recent victory. The same antiphonal arrangement may have been used in its adaptation for temple worship. Some commentators have suggested that the occasion was the birthday (cf. v. 4) or the coronation of a king (cf. v. 3).

1-7. Thanksgiving for Answered Prayer. **The king shall joy.** The congregation or temple choir addresses a prayer of gratitude to God for his signal victory. Each verse contributes to the list of things which God has done for and through the king. All of these blessings are directly related to the king's utter trust in God.

8-12. Confidence in the Future. **Thine hand shall.** The words are now addressed directly to the king but still in an attitude of worship. The thanksgiving is continued in terms of anticipated victories until finally all enemies will be destroyed.

13. Closing Doxology. **Be thou exalted.** Again the chorus joins in a final expression of heart-felt gratitude and united praise, returning to the picture of strength in verse 1.

Psalm 22. Triumph in Suffering

This psalm is the first of those sometimes called Passion Psalms. The use of the opening cry by Christ on the cross and the amazing phraseology of verses 6-8 and 13-18 have made this psalm especially important to Christians. There is within the psalm a strange mixture of praise and complaint. There is no reference to sin as the cause of the trouble, no plea of innocence, no claim of righteousness, and no vengeance. Therefore the words are peculiarly appropriate of the suffering Messiah, although in their primary meaning they are based on some experience of the psalmist.

1-18. His Personal Suffering. **My God, my God, why . . . ?** This initial appeal is stated in a question of only four words in the Hebrew (*'Ēlî 'Ēlî lāmâ 'ăzabtāni*). These words were quoted by Jesus on the cross in Aramaic. Note that the

praises of Israel. ⁴ Our fathers trusted in thee: they trusted, and thou didst deliver them. ⁵ They cried unto thee, and were delivered: they trusted in thee, and were not confounded.

⁶ But I *am* a worm, and no man; a reproach of men, and despised of the people. ⁷ All they that see me laugh me to scorn: they shoot out the lip, they shake the head, *saying,* ⁸ He trusted on the Lord *that* he would deliver him: let him deliver him, seeing he delighted in him.

⁹ But thou *art* he that took me out of the womb: thou didst make me hope *when I was* upon my mother's breasts. ¹⁰ I was cast upon thee from the womb: thou *art* my God from my mother's belly. ¹¹ Be not far from me; for trouble *is* near; for *there is* none to help.

¹² Many bulls have compassed me: strong *bulls* of Ba-shan have beset me round. ¹³ They gaped upon me *with* their mouths, *as* a ravening and a roaring lion. ¹⁴ I am poured out like water, and all my bones are out of joint: my heart is like wax; it is melted in the midst of my bowels. ¹⁵ My strength is dried up like a potsherd; and my tongue cleaveth to my jaws; and thou hast brought me into the dust of death. ¹⁶ For dogs have compassed me: the assembly of the wicked have inclosed me: they pierced my hands and my feet. ¹⁷ I may tell all my bones: they look *and* stare upon me. ¹⁸ They part my garments among them, and cast lots upon my vesture.

¹⁹ But be not thou far from me, O Lord: O my strength, haste thee to help me. ²⁰ Deliver my soul from the sword; my darling from the power of the dog. ²¹ Save me from the lion's mouth: for thou hast heard me from the horns of the unicorns.

²² I will declare thy name unto my brethren: in the midst of the congregation will I praise thee. ²³ Ye that fear the Lord, praise him; all ye the seed of Jacob, glorify him; and fear him, all ye the seed of Israel. ²⁴ For he hath not despised nor abhorred the affliction of the afflicted; neither hath he hid his face from him; but when he cried unto him, he heard.

The praises of our fathers surrounded your throne; they trusted you and you delivered them. ⁵ You heard their cries for help and saved them; they were never disappointed when they sought your aid.

⁶ But I am a worm, not a man, scorned and despised by my own people and by all mankind. ⁷ Everyone who sees me mocks and sneers and shrugs. ⁸ "Is this the one who rolled his burden on the Lord?" they laugh. "Is this the one who claims the Lord delights in him? We'll believe it when we see God rescue him!"

⁹,¹⁰,¹¹ Lord, how you have helped me before! You took me safely from my mother's womb and brought me through the years of infancy. I have depended upon you since birth; you have always been my God. Don't leave me now, for trouble is near and no one else can possibly help.

¹² I am surrounded by fearsome enemies, strong as the giant bulls from Bashan. ¹³ They come at me with open jaws, like roaring lions attacking their prey. ¹⁴ My strength has drained away like water, and all my bones are out of joint. My heart melts like wax; ¹⁵ my strength has dried up like sun-baked clay; my tongue sticks to my mouth, for you have laid me in the dust of death. ¹⁶ The enemy, this gang of evil men, circles me like a pack of dogs; they have pierced my hands and feet. ¹⁷ I can count every bone in my body. See these men of evil gloat and stare; ¹⁸ they divide my clothes among themselves by a toss of the dice.

¹⁹ O Lord, don't stay away. O God my Strength, hurry to my aid. ²⁰ Rescue me from death; spare my precious life from all these evil men. ²¹ Save me from these lions' jaws and from the horns of these wild oxen. Yes, God will answer me and rescue me.

²² I will praise you to all my brothers; I will stand up before the congregation and testify of the wonderful things you have done. ²³ "Praise the Lord, each one of you who fears him," I will say. "Each of you must fear and reverence his name. Let all Israel sing his praises, ²⁴ for he has not despised my cries of deep despair; he has not turned and walked away. When I cried to him, he heard and came."

psalmist does not lose faith even while describing his intense suffering and persecution. He feels forsaken by God but knows that God is near. After recalling the trust of his forefathers and their deliverance, he describes the contemptuous action by his enemies.

19-21. His Plea for Deliverance. **Be not thou far from me.** This idea occurs for the third time in an open plea for God's aid. **Haste thee to help, deliver,** and **save** all point to the urgency of his need.

22-26. His Public Thanksgiving. **I will declare.** This vow forms a transition from his description of suffering to his expression of praise. His desire is now to acknowledge publicly his dependence upon God and to proclaim his own personal deliverance.

25 My praise *shall be* of thee in the great congregation: I will pay my vows before them that fear him. 26 The meek shall eat and be satisfied: they shall praise the Lord that seek him: your heart shall live for ever. 27 All the ends of the world shall remember and turn unto the Lord: and all the kindreds of the nations shall worship before thee.

28 For the kingdom *is* the Lord's: and he *is* the governor among the nations. 29 All *they that be* fat upon earth shall eat and worship: all they that go down to the dust shall bow before him: and none can keep alive his own soul. 30 A seed shall serve him; it shall be accounted to the Lord for a generation. 31 They shall come, and shall declare his righteousness unto a people that shall be born, that he hath done *this.*

PSALM 23

A Psalm of David

THE Lord *is* my shepherd; I shall not want.

2 He maketh me to lie down in green pastures: he leadeth me beside the still waters. 3 He restoreth my soul: he leadeth me in the paths of righteousness for his name's sake.

4 Yea, though I walk through the valley of the shadow of death, I will fear no evil: for thou *art* with me; thy rod and thy staff they comfort me.

5 Thou preparest a table before me in the presence of mine enemies: thou anointest my head with oil; my cup runneth over.

6 Surely goodness and mercy shall follow me all the days of my life: and I will dwell in the house of the Lord for ever.

25 Yes, I will stand and praise you before all the people. I will publicly fulfill my vows in the presence of all who reverence your name. 26 The poor shall eat and be satisfied; all who seek the Lord shall find him and shall praise his name. Their hearts shall rejoice with everlasting joy. 27 The whole earth shall see it and return to the Lord; the people of every nation shall worship him. 28 For the Lord is King and rules the nations. 29 Both proud and humble together, all who are mortal—born to die—shall worship him. 30 Our children too shall serve him, for they shall hear from us about the wonders of the Lord; 31 generations yet unborn shall hear of all the miracles he did for us.

23 BECAUSE THE LORD is my Shepherd, I have everything I need!

2,3 He lets me rest in the meadow grass and leads me beside the quiet streams. He restores my failing health. He helps me do what honors him the most.

4 Even when walking through the dark valley of death I will not be afraid, for you are close beside me, guarding, guiding all the way.

5 You provide delicious food for me in the presence of my enemies. You have welcomed me as your guest; blessings overflow!

6 Your goodness and unfailing kindness shall be with me all of my life, and afterwards I will live with you forever in your home.

27-31. His Joyful Anticipation. All the ends of the world. In hope, the psalmist sees the circle widen to include all mankind and future generations. His personal hope encompasses the nation and then the world. In accord with the highest hope of Israel, the turning of mankind to God in worship (cf. Isa 40:7; Phil 2:10) is based upon *what he* (the Lord) *has done.*

Psalm 23. My Shepherd

As a song of trust, this psalm has no peer. It is impossible to estimate its effect upon man through the centuries. Grief, sadness, and doubt have been driven away by this strong affirmation of faith. Peace, contentment, and trust have been the blessings upon those who have come to share the psalmist's sublime confidence. While the language is simple and the meaning clear, no one has been able to exhaust the message of the poem or improve upon its quiet beauty.

1-4. God as the Personal Shepherd. The Lord is my shepherd. A long experience of trusting God lies behind these words. The rich corporate relation of Israel to God is appropriated as an individual realization. The picture of a faithful shepherd is the epitome of tender care and continuing watchfulness. The sheep instinctively trust the shepherd to provide for the morrow. The most distinctive feature of this extended metaphor is the wise leading of the shepherd. He leads into rest and reviving, into the struggles of life, and through the dangerous places. The shepherd thus provides for the needs of life and protects from the fear of danger.

5-6. God as the Gracious Host. Thou preparest a table. The writer introduces a secondary metaphor to further express his trust. The scene changes to show the psalmist as the guest of honor at God's house, enjoying the warm hospitality characteristic of the East. He is under God's protection. His head is anointed with perfumed oil. His every need is completely satisfied. On the basis of this trust, every moment of his life will be filled with God's richest blessings. The greatest blessing will be an intimate fellowship with God through continued worship of Him.

NOTES

4. YOU ARE CLOSE BY
HE MAKETH ME TO FEEL SECURE.

HE LEADETH ME IN PATHS OF SERVICE.

PSALM 24

A Psalm of David

THE earth *is* the Lord's, and the fulness thereof; the world, and they that dwell therein. ² For he hath founded it upon the seas, and established it upon the floods.

³ Who shall ascend into the hill of the Lord? or who shall stand in his holy place? ⁴ He that hath clean hands, and a pure heart; who hath not lifted up his soul unto vanity, nor sworn deceitfully. ⁵ He shall receive the blessing from the Lord, and righteousness from the God of his salvation. ⁶ This *is* the generation of them that seek him, that seek thy face, O Jacob. Se-lah.

⁷ Lift up your heads, O ye gates; and be ye lift up, ye everlasting doors; and the King of glory shall come in. ⁸ Who *is* this King of glory? The Lord strong and mighty, the Lord mighty in battle. ⁹ Lift up your heads, O ye gates; even lift *them* up, ye everlasting doors; and the King of glory shall come in.

¹⁰ Who is this King of glory? The Lord of hosts, he *is* the King of glory. Se-lah.

24 THE EARTH BELONGS to God! Everything in all the world is his! ² He is the one who pushed the oceans back to let dry land appear.

³ Who may climb the mountain of the Lord and enter where he lives? Who may stand before the Lord? ⁴ Only those with pure hands and hearts, who do not practice dishonesty and lying. ⁵ They will receive God's own goodness as their blessing from him, planted in their lives by God himself, their Savior. ⁶ These are the ones who are allowed to stand before the Lord and worship the God of Jacob.

⁷ Open up, O ancient gates, and let the King of Glory in. ⁸ Who is this King of Glory? The Lord, strong and mighty, invincible in battle. ⁹ Yes, open wide the gates and let the King of Glory in.

¹⁰ Who is this King of Glory? The Commander of all of heaven's armies!

PSALM 25

A Psalm *of David*

UNTO thee, O Lord, do I lift up my soul. ² O my God, I trust in thee: let me not be ashamed, let not mine enemies triumph over me. ³ Yea, let none that wait on thee be ashamed: let them be ashamed which transgress without cause.

⁴ Shew me thy ways, O Lord; teach me thy paths. ⁵ Lead me in thy truth, and teach me: for thou *art* the God of my salvation; on thee do I wait all the day. ⁶ Remember, O Lord, thy tender mercies and thy lovingkindnesses; for they *have been* ever of old. ⁷ Remember not the sins of my youth, nor my transgressions: according to thy mercy remember thou me for thy goodness' sake, O Lord.

25 TO YOU, O Lord, I pray. ² Don't fail me, Lord, for I am trusting you. Don't let my enemies succeed. Don't give them victory over me. ³ None who have faith in God will ever be disgraced for trusting him. But all who harm the innocent shall be defeated.

⁴ Show me the path where I should go, O Lord; point out the right road for me to walk. ⁵ Lead me; teach me; for you are the God who gives me salvation. I have no hope except in you. ⁶,⁷ Overlook my youthful sins, O Lord! Look at me instead through eyes of mercy and forgiveness, through eyes of everlasting love and kindness.

Psalm 24. An Inaugural Anthem

This is one of the most majestic and stately hymns of the entire Psalter. Because of several abrupt changes in subject matter, many have judged that this psalm is made up of selections from three poems originally independent (vv. 1,2; 3-6; 7-10). While this may be so, the psalm is now an appropriate unit. The occasion has been associated with the Feast of Tabernacles, an annual New Year's festival, the dedication of the Temple, and the bringing of the ark to Jerusalem. It is very likely that this psalm, like many others, was used antiphonally.

1,2. The Processional Chorus. **The earth is the Lord's.** This emphasis upon the sovereignty of God over the habitable earth and all creatures is worthy caution against limiting God to one city or one temple. These words were probably sung on many occasions by groups approaching the city of Jerusalem.

3-6. The Prerequisites of Worship. **Who shall ascend . . . shall stand?** A recognition of the Creator. God as sovereign over all the earth must not be approached lightly. The moral requirements for approaching God are carefully set forth by questions similar to those of Psalm 15. The same high standards of ethical conduct are demanded, with special emphasis upon the character of the worship. The questions and answers were probably chanted by priests or Levites, while verse 6 may have been used as a chorus.

7-10. The Divine Entrance. **Lift up your heads, O ye gates.** The lintels or tops of the portals are pictured as being too low for the divine king to enter. **The King of glory shall come in.** The summons to the gatekeepers symbolizes the truth that the presence of God is to be evident. Then the challenge to identify this King is chanted by another group or by an individual on the city wall. The powerful answer may well have been the response of the congregation clearly identifying this King as the Lord. After the second summons and challenge, the response rings clear — **The Lord of hosts** (*Yahweh Ṣ^ebā'ôt*), **He is the King of glory.**

Psalm 25. An Acrostic Prayer for Help

This psalm, the supplication of an individual, uses the letters of the Hebrew alphabet as a framework. It is difficult to recognize here a logical order of thought because of the necessity of beginning each verse with a subsequent letter of the alphabet. There are only three places in our present text (vv. 2,5,18) where the acrostic breaks down. The style is simple, straightforward, prayerful, and humble.

1-7. A Prayer for Protection. **Unto thee, O Lord.** The basis of this petition for protection is the psalmist's simple trust in God. Though his enemies have not triumphed over him, they are a constant threat. He appeals to God's mercy and loving-kindness, which have been revealed in history.

NOTES

8 Good and upright *is* the Lord: therefore will he teach sinners in the way. 9 The meek will he guide in judgment: and the meek will he teach his way. 10 All the paths of the Lord *are* mercy and truth unto such as keep his covenant and his testimonies.

11 For thy name's sake, O Lord, pardon mine iniquity; for it *is* great.

12 What man *is* he that feareth the Lord? him shall he teach in the way *that* he shall choose.

13 His soul shall dwell at ease; and his seed shall inherit the earth.

14 The secret of the Lord *is* with them that fear him; and he will shew them his covenant.

15 Mine eyes *are* ever toward the Lord; for he shall pluck my feet out of the net. 16 Turn thee unto me, and have mercy upon me; for I *am* desolate and afflicted. 17 The troubles of my heart are enlarged: *O* bring thou me out of my distresses. 18 Look upon mine affliction and my pain; and forgive all my sins. 19 Consider mine enemies; for they are many; and they hate me with cruel hatred. 20 O keep my soul, and deliver me: let me ·not be ashamed; for I put my trust in thee.

21 Let integrity and uprightness preserve me; for I wait on thee. 22 Redeem Israel, O God, out of all his troubles.

PSALM 26

A Psalm *of David*

JUDGE me, O Lord; for I have walked in mine integrity: I have trusted also in the Lord; *therefore* I shall not slide. 2 Examine me, O Lord, and prove me; try my reins and my heart. 3 For thy lovingkindness *is* before mine eyes: and I have walked in thy truth. 4 I have not sat with vain persons, neither will I go in with dissemblers. 5 I have hated the congregation of evil doers; and will not sit with the wicked. 6 I will wash mine hands in innocency: so will I compass thine altar, O Lord: 7 That I may publish with the voice of thanksgiving, and tell of all thy wondrous works.

8 Lord, I have loved the habitation of thy house, and the place where thine honour dwelleth.

8 The Lord is good and glad to teach the proper path to all who go astray; 9 he will teach the ways that are right and best to those who humbly turn to him. 10 And when we obey him, every path he guides us on is fragrant with his lovingkindness and his truth.

11 But Lord, my sins! How many they are. Oh, pardon them for the honor of your name.

12 Where is the man who fears the Lord? God will teach him how to choose the best.

13 He shall live within God's circle of blessing, and his children shall inherit the earth.

14 Friendship with God is reserved for those who reverence him. With them alone he shares the secrets of his promises.

15 My eyes are ever looking to the Lord for help, for he alone can rescue me. 16 Come, Lord, and show me your mercy, for I am helpless, overwhelmed, in deep distress; 17 my problems go from bad to worse. Oh, save me from them all! 18 See my sorrows; feel my pain; forgive my sins. 19 See how many enemies I have and how viciously they hate me! 20 Save me from them! Deliver my life from their power! Oh, let it never be said that I trusted you in vain!

21 Assign me Godliness and Integrity as my bodyguards, for I expect you to protect me 22 and to ransom Israel from all her troubles.

26 DISMISS ALL THE charges against me, Lord, for I have tried to keep your laws and have trusted you without wavering. 2 Cross-examine me, O Lord, and see that this is so; test my motives and affections too. 3 For I have taken your lovingkindness and your truth as my ideals. 4 I do not have fellowship with tricky, two-faced men; they are false and hypocritical. 5 I hate the sinners' hangouts and refuse to enter them. 6 I wash my hands to prove my innocence and come before your altar, 7 singing a song of thanksgiving and telling about your miracles.

8 Lord, I love your home, this shrine where the brilliant, dazzling splendor of your presence lives.

8-10. A Meditation upon the Character of God. Good and upright is the Lord. These and other characteristics of God are discerned from his response in history. Because of his justice, righteousness, loving-kindness, and truth, he will guide and teach men in these same paths.

11-14. A Meditation upon Man's Relation to God. The secret of the Lord. After a brief prayer for pardon, the psalmist reflects on the secret of man's proper relation to God. This he discovers to be the fear of the Lord — that reverential and trustful relation referred to frequently in Proverbs.

15-22. A Prayer for Deliverance. Turn thee unto me. Using graphic verbs (**pluck, turn, bring, look, forgive, consider, keep, preserve**), the writer prays for God to deliver him. A fitting conclusion to the psalm is found in the broadened view of verse 22, where God is petitioned to **redeem** the nation as well as the speaker himself. If this verse is taken as an integral part of the original psalm, it forms a climax for the thought. If, however, it is taken as an addition, it serves **to** adapt the psalm for corporate use.

Psalm 26. A Worshiper's Prayer

That there was conflict between religious groups in Israel is evident from this lament. Some commentators suggest that a pestilence is involved in the background. However that may be, the psalmist's protests regarding his integrity point to a society in which the ungodly have ascendancy. This psalm, although more individual than corporate, could well be used by a pious group in the time of affliction.

1-7. A Protest of Innocence. Judge me, O Lord. The psalmist is so sure of his integrity that he seeks divine judgment; he asks that God examine, prove, and try him. He claims to have walked in the truth, to have avoided any contact with renegade Jews, and to have participated regularly in worship. All of this stands in sharp contrast to the conduct of his enemies.

⁹ Gather not my soul with sinners, nor my life with bloody men: ¹⁰ In whose hands *is* mischief, and their right hand is full of bribes.

¹¹ But as for me, I will walk in mine integrity: redeem me, and be merciful unto me.

¹² My foot standeth in an even place: in the congregations will I bless the Lord.

PSALM 27

A Psalm *of David*

THE Lord *is* my light and my salvation; whom shall I fear? the Lord *is* the strength of my life; of whom shall I be afraid? ² When the wicked, *even* mine enemies and my foes, came upon me to eat up my flesh, they stumbled and fell. ³ Though an host should encamp against me, my heart shall not fear: though war should rise against me, in this *will* I *be* confident.

⁴ One *thing* have I desired of the Lord, that will I seek after; that I may dwell in the house of the Lord all the days of my life, to behold the beauty of the Lord, and to enquire in his temple. ⁵ For in the time of trouble he shall hide me in his pavilion: in the secret of his tabernacle shall he hide me; he shall set me up upon a rock. ⁶ And now shall mine head be lifted up above mine enemies round about me: therefore will I offer in his tabernacle sacrifices of joy; I will sing, yea, I will sing praises unto the Lord. ⁷ Hear, O Lord, *when* I cry with my voice: have mercy also upon me, and answer me.

⁸ *When thou saidst,* Seek ye my face; my heart said unto thee, Thy face, Lord, will I seek.

⁹ Hide not thy face *far* from me; put not thy servant away in anger: thou hast been my help; leave me not, neither forsake me, O God of my salvation. ¹⁰ When my father and my mother forsake me, then the Lord will take me up.

¹¹ Teach me thy way, O Lord, and lead me in a plain path, because of mine enemies. ¹² Deliver me not over unto the will of mine enemies: for false witnesses are risen up against me, and such as

⁹,¹⁰ Don't treat me as a common sinner or murderer who plots against the innocent and demands bribes.

¹¹ No, I am not like that, O Lord; I try to walk a straight and narrow path of doing what is right; therefore in mercy save me.

¹² I publicly praise the Lord for keeping me from slipping and falling.

27 THE LORD IS my light and my salvation; whom shall I fear? ² When evil men come to destroy me, they will stumble and fall! ³ Yes, though a mighty army marches against me, my heart shall know no fear! I am confident that God will save me.

⁴ The one thing I want from God, the thing I seek most of all, is the privilege of meditating in his Temple, living in his presence every day of my life, delighting in his incomparable perfections and glory. ⁵ There I'll be when troubles come. He will hide me. He will set me on a high rock ⁶ out of reach of all my enemies. Then I will bring him sacrifices and sing his praises with much joy. ⁷ Listen to my pleading, Lord! Be merciful and send the help I need.

⁸ My heart has heard you say, "Come and talk with me, O my people." And my heart responds, "Lord, I am coming."

⁹ Oh, do not hide yourself when I am trying to find you. Do not angrily reject your servant. You have been my help in all my trials before; don't leave me now. Don't forsake me, O God of my salvation. ¹⁰ For if my father and mother should abandon me, you would welcome and comfort me.

¹¹ Tell me what to do, O Lord, and make it plain because I am surrounded by waiting enemies. ¹² Don't let them get me, Lord! Don't let me fall into their hands! For they accuse me of things I never did, and all the

8-12. A Prayer for Vindication. Gather not my soul with sinners. His plea is not that he may avoid death, but that he may avoid being grouped with the ungodly, whom he has so carefully avoided in life. In this prayer for special treatment, he prays for God to **redeem** and **be merciful** to him because he is going to continue to walk in integrity, stand firmly, and bless the Lord publicly.

Psalm 27. A Song of Trust

The marked contrast between verses 1-6 and 7-14 has led most commentators to designate this psalm as a composite. Both the content and the spirit of these sections are vastly different. The mood changes from joyful confidence to anxious fear. However, two elements tie together these dissimilar parts — similar enemies and trust in God.

1-3. Unconditional Trust. The Lord is my light and my salvation. These exultant words introduce a scene of serenity. Nowhere else in the OT is the Lord referred to as my light. Because the psalmist has found God as **light, salvation,** and **strength,** there is no cause for fear or terror. His serenity is not conditioned by outward circumstances but is unconditional.

4-6. Life's Greatest Desire. One thing have I desired. The one thing desired cannot be equated with the Temple, as many commentators suggest. It must refer to a basis for the three-part wish. That basis or common denominator is most likely the presence of the Lord, which the psalmist desires and seeks. The realization of this presence comes from dwelling in God's house, beholding his beauty, and inquiring in his Temple. This same presence results in safety in the time of trouble.

7-14. A Cry of Anxious Fear. Hear, O Lord. These words shift the mood entirely from triumph to deep distress as they introduce a new situation and occasion. Even though the psalmist has been forsaken and rejected, his trust does not fail. From the depths of despair, he calls himself back to the patience required in waiting for God to work out his will.

NOTES

= UNCONDITIONAL LOVE.

breathe out cruelty. ¹³ *I had fainted, un-less I had believed to see the goodness of the Lord in the land of the living.*

¹⁴ Wait on the Lord: be of good courage, and he shall strengthen thine heart: wait, I say, on the Lord.

PSALM 28

A Psalm *of David*

UNTO thee will I cry, O Lord my rock; be not silent to me: lest, *if* thou be silent to me, I become like them that go down into the pit. ² Hear the voice of my supplications, when I cry unto thee, when I lift up my hands toward thy holy oracle.

³ Draw me not away with the wicked, and with the workers of iniquity, which speak peace to their neighbours, but mischief *is* in their hearts. ⁴ Give them according to their deeds, and according to the wickedness of their endeavours: give them after the work of their hands; render to them their desert. ⁵ Because they regard not the works of the Lord, nor the operation of his hands, he shall destroy them, and not build them up.

⁶ Blessed *be* the Lord, because he hath heard the voice of my supplications. ⁷ The Lord *is* my strength and my shield; my heart trusted in him, and I am helped: therefore my heart greatly rejoiceth; and with my song will I praise him. ⁸ The Lord *is* their strength, and he *is* the saving strength of his anointed.

⁹ Save thy people, and bless thine inheritance: feed them also, and lift them up for ever.

PSALM 29

A Psalm *of David*

GIVE unto the Lord, O ye mighty, give unto the Lord glory and strength. ² Give unto the Lord the glory due unto his name; worship the Lord in the beauty of holiness.

³ The voice of the Lord *is* upon the waters: the God of glory thundereth: the Lord *is* upon many waters. ⁴ The voice of the Lord *is* powerful; the voice

while are plotting cruelty. ¹³ I am expecting the Lord to rescue me again, so that once again I will see his goodness to me here in the land of the living.

¹⁴ Don't be impatient. Wait for the Lord, and he will come and save you! Be brave, stouthearted and courageous. Yes, wait and he will help you.

MCH : GOD WILL NEVER FAIL YOU!

28 I PLEAD WITH you to help me, Lord, for you are my Rock of safety. If you refuse to answer me, I might as well give up and die. ² Lord, I lift my hands to heaven and implore your help. Oh, listen to my cry.

³ Don't punish me with all the wicked ones who speak so sweetly to their neighbors while planning to murder them. ⁴ Give them the punishment they so richly deserve! Measure it out to them in proportion to their wickedness; pay them back for all their evil deeds. ⁵ They care nothing for God or what he has done or what he has made; therefore God will dismantle them like old buildings, never to be rebuilt again.

⁶ Oh, praise the Lord, for he has listened to my pleadings! ⁷ He is my strength, my shield from every danger. I trusted in him, and he helped me. Joy rises in my heart until I burst out in songs of praise to him. ⁸ The Lord protects his people and gives victory to his anointed king.

⁹ Defend your people, Lord; defend and bless your chosen ones. Lead them like a shepherd and carry them forever in your arms.

29 PRAISE THE LORD, you angels of his; praise his glory and his strength. ² Praise him for his majestic glory, the glory of his name. Come before him clothed in sacred garments.

³ The voice of the Lord echoes from the clouds. The God of glory thunders through the skies. ⁴ So powerful is his voice; so full

Psalm 28. An Answered Prayer

This psalm, like many other laments, deals with the strife between those of traditional faith and those affected by alien influences. The psalmist is deeply afraid he will suffer the fate which must overtake his wicked antagonists. That he views his prayer as answered is obvious from the change in verse 6.

1,2. Appeal To Be Heard. Be not silent. . . . Hear. The psalmist appeals to God both to hear him and to answer. To a Hebrew, the lack of an answer often seemed to indicate that God would not hear the petition. The urgent nature of the speaker's cry is emphasized by his fear that he will die if God does not answer.

3-5. Prayer for Intervention. Draw me not away. . . . Give them according to their deeds. His first prayer is for protection against his godless foes. However, his emphasis quickly changes to a plea for retribution upon these enemies.

6,7. Thanksgiving for Answered Prayer. **Blessed be the Lord.** The cause of this outburst of praise is to be understood as God's response to the appeal of verses 1 and 2. This thanksgiving may have been added later by the psalmist. Or it may be the expression of an inner confidence that God has truly heard and is no longer silent.

8,9. Application for the Nation. The Lord their strength. The fact that God is the psalmist's strength finds application for the nation and the king. This may well be a later addition designed to adapt the individual's expression of faith for corporate worship.

Psalm 29. God's Glory in the Storm

In awe-inspiring poetry, this hymn of praise points to the thunderstorm as another evidence of God's glory. Notes of assurance are constantly intermingled with the phrases descriptive of God's omnipotence. Seldom does any psalmist exhibit more graphic poetical power than the one who wrote this nature psalm. The close parallels in terminology with Canaanite poems from 1400—1300 B.C. discovered at Ugarit in Syria indicate that this psalm is at least as old as David, but the psalmist is careful to recognize Yahweh alone as the true God.

1,2. The Call to Worship. Worship the Lord. The whole heavenly host is exhorted to **ascribe unto the Lord glory and strength.** This worship is to be accomplished **in holy array** (RSV; rather than *in the beauty of holiness,* AV). Many commentators believe that in using the term $b^e n\hat{e}$ '$\bar{e}lim$ (AV, *O ye mighty*), which might be translated as "sons of God," the author is summoning the angels. But others believe that the people of Israel, as the sons of God, are being addressed (cf. Deut 14:1; Ps 82:6).

3-9. The Seven fold Voice. The voice of the Lord. Seven times this phrase is used to express the thunder of the storm.

NOTES

of the Lord *is* full of majesty. ⁵ The voice of the Lord breaketh the cedars; yea, the Lord breaketh the cedars of Lebanon. ⁶ He maketh them also to skip like a calf; Lebanon and Sir-i-on like a young unicorn. ⁷ The voice of the Lord divideth the flames of fire. ⁸ The voice of the Lord shaketh the wilderness; the Lord shaketh the wilderness of Ka-desh. ⁹ The voice of the Lord maketh the hinds to calve, and discovereth the forests: and in his temple doth every one speak of *his* glory.

¹⁰ The Lord sitteth upon the flood; yea, the Lord sitteth King for ever. ¹¹ The Lord will give strength unto his people; the Lord will bless his people with peace.

of majesty. ⁵,⁶ It breaks down the cedars. It splits the giant trees of Lebanon. It shakes Mount Lebanon and Mount Sirion. They leap and skip before him like young calves! ⁷ The voice of the Lord thunders through the lightning. ⁸ It resounds through the deserts and shakes the wilderness of Kadesh. ⁹ The voice of the Lord spins and topples the mighty oaks. It strips the forests bare. They whirl and sway beneath the blast. But in his temple all are praising, "Glory, glory to the Lord."

¹⁰ At the Flood, the Lord showed his control of all creation. Now he continues to unveil his power. ¹¹ He will give his people strength. He will bless them with peace.

PSALM 30

A Psalm and *Song* at *the dedication of the house of David*

I WILL extol thee, O Lord; for thou hast lifted me up, and hast not made my foes to rejoice over me. ² O Lord my God, I cried unto thee, and thou hast healed me. ³ O Lord, thou hast brought up my soul from the grave: thou hast kept me alive, that I should not go down to the pit.

⁴ Sing unto the Lord, O ye saints of his, and give thanks at the remembrance of his holiness. ⁵ For his anger *endureth but* a moment; in his favour *is* life: weeping may endure for a night, but joy *cometh* in the morning.

⁶ And in my prosperity I said, I shall never be moved. ⁷ Lord, by thy favour thou hast made my mountain to stand strong: thou didst hide thy face, *and* I was troubled. ⁸ I cried to thee, O Lord; and unto the Lord I made supplication. ⁹ What profit *is there* in my blood, when I go down to the pit? Shall the dust praise thee? shall it declare thy truth? ¹⁰ Hear, O Lord, and have mercy upon me: Lord, be thou my helper. ¹¹ Thou hast turned for me my mourning into dancing: thou hast put off my sackcloth, and girded me with gladness; ¹² To the end that *my* glory may sing praise to thee, and not be silent. O Lord my God, I will give thanks unto thee for ever.

30 I WILL PRAISE you, Lord, for you have saved me from my enemies. You refuse to let them triumph over me. ² O Lord my God, I pleaded with you, and you gave me my health again. ³ You brought me back from the brink of the grave, from death itself, and here I am alive!

⁴ Oh, sing to him you saints of his; give thanks to his holy name. ⁵ His anger lasts a moment; his favor lasts for life! Weeping may go on all night, but in the morning there is joy.

⁶,⁷ In my prosperity I said, "This is forever; nothing can stop me now! The Lord has shown me his favor. He has made me steady as a mountain." Then, Lord, you turned your face away from me and cut off your river of blessings. Suddenly my courage was gone; I was terrified and panic-stricken. ⁸ I cried to you, O Lord; oh, how I pled: ⁹ "What will you gain, O Lord, from killing me? How can I praise you then to all my friends? How can my dust in the grave speak out and tell the world about your faithfulness? ¹⁰ Hear me, Lord; oh, have pity and help me." ¹¹ Then he turned my sorrow into joy! He took away my clothes of mourning and gave me gay and festive garments to rejoice in ¹² so that I might sing glad praises to the Lord instead of lying in silence in the grave. O Lord my God, I will keep on thanking you forever!

It is not God's anger but his majestic power which makes the storm move. It begins out over the Mediterranean Sea with power and majesty. It then moves in over the mountains to the north of Palestine and over the wilderness to the south. The description of the effect upon trees, mountains, wilderness, and animals is followed by the chorus of "glory" which comes from man's worship.

10,11. Conclusion. **The Lord will bless.** While God sits over all in **glory** (v. 9), he grants to his people the two things they most need — **strength** and **peace.**

Psalm 30. Praise for God's Healing

This psalm relates the experience of one who has just escaped death by being delivered from a serious illness. His remarkable recovery produces joyful thanksgiving and causes him to reflect on the lessons he has gained from his suffering.

1-3. Praise for Recovery. **I will extol thee, O Lord.** The psalmist's object is, clearly, to exalt the Lord because he has been saved from Sheol and the grave. He gives full credit to God for his deliverance. There are, however, foes in the background who rejoice to see a righteous man suffer.

4,5. A Call to Remembrance. **Sing . . . give thanks.** Because of his personal experience with God, the psalmist calls on **the saints** to join him in praise. These are the like-minded ones who are bound to the Lord in covenant relation. They are urged to give thanks **to the memorial of his holiness.** The phrase **in his favor is life** may also be translated *his favor is for a lifetime.* This rendering contrasts the moment of God's wrath with a lifetime of his favor.

6-10. Suffering in Retrospect. **I shall never be moved.** Prior to his sickness, he had boasted, in a spirit of self-sufficiency. His pride collapsed with the crush of illness. However, the sickness had the effect of opening his eyes to his dependence upon God, so that he cried for mercy and healing.

11,12. Renewed Praise. **I will give thanks unto thee for ever.** No longer silent, the psalmist wants everyone to know of the change in his life — from mourning to dancing, from sackcloth to gladness, from silence to praise.

PSALM 31

To the chief Musician, A Psalm of David

In thee, O Lord, do I put my trust; let me never be ashamed: deliver me in thy righteousness. ² Bow down thine ear to me; deliver me speedily: be thou my strong rock, for an house of defence to save me. ³ For thou *art* my rock and my fortress; therefore for thy name's sake lead me, and guide me. ⁴ Pull me out of the net that they have laid privily for me: for thou *art* my strength. ⁵ Into thine hand I commit my spirit: thou hast redeemed me, O Lord God of truth.

⁶ I have hated them that regard lying vanities: but I trust in the Lord. ⁷ I will be glad and rejoice in thy mercy: for thou hast considered my trouble; thou hast known my soul in adversities; ⁸ And hast not shut me up into the hand of the enemy: thou hast set my feet in a large room.

⁹ Have mercy upon me, O Lord, for I am in trouble: mine eye is consumed with grief, *yea* my soul and my belly. ¹⁰ For my life is spent with grief, and my years with sighing: my strength faileth because of mine iniquity, and my bones are consumed. ¹¹ I was a reproach among all mine enemies, but especially among my neighbours, and a fear to mine acquaintance: they that did see me without fled from me. ¹² I am forgotten as a dead man out of mind: I am like a broken vessel. ¹³ For I have heard the slander of many: fear *was* on every side: while they took counsel together against me, they devised to take away my life.

¹⁴ But I trusted in thee, O Lord: I said, Thou *art* my God. ¹⁵ My times *are* in thy hand: deliver me from the hand of mine enemies, and from them that persecute me. ¹⁶ Make thy face to shine upon thy servant: save me for thy mercies' sake. ¹⁷ Let me not be ashamed, O Lord; for I have called upon thee: let the wicked be ashamed, *and* let them be silent in the grave. ¹⁸ Let the lying lips be put to silence; which speak grievous things proudly and contemptuously against the righteous.

31 LORD, I TRUST in you alone. Don't let my enemies defeat me. Rescue me because you are the God who always does what is right. ² Answer quickly when I cry to you; bend low and hear my whispered plea. Be for me a great Rock of safety from my foes. ³ Yes, you are my Rock and my fortress; honor your name by leading me out of this peril. ⁴ Pull me from the trap my enemies have set for me. For you alone are strong enough. ⁵,⁶ Into your hand I commit my spirit.

You have rescued me, O God who keeps his promises. I worship only you; how you hate all those who worship idols, those imitation gods. ⁷ I am radiant with joy because of your mercy, for you have listened to my troubles and have seen the crisis in my soul. ⁸ You have not handed me over to my enemy, but have given me open ground in which to maneuver.

⁹,¹⁰ O Lord, have mercy on me in my anguish. My eyes are red from weeping; my health is broken from sorrow. I am pining away with grief; my years are shortened, drained away because of sadness. My sins have sapped my strength; I stoop with sorrow and with shame. ¹¹ I am scorned by all my enemies and even more by my neighbors and friends. They dread meeting me and look the other way when I go by. ¹² I am forgotten like a dead man, like a broken and discarded pot. ¹³ I heard the lies about me, the slanders of my enemies. Everywhere I looked I was afraid, for they were plotting against my life.

¹⁴,¹⁵ But I was trusting you, O Lord. I said, "You alone are my God; my times are in your hands. Rescue me from those who hunt me down relentlessly. ¹⁶ Let your favor shine again upon your servant; save me just because you are so kind! ¹⁷ Don't disgrace me, Lord, by not replying when I call to you for aid. But let the wicked be shamed by what they trust in; let them lie silently in their graves, ¹⁸ their lying lips quieted at last—the lips of these arrogant men who are accusing honest men of evil deeds."

Psalm 31. A Prayer of Surrender

Here, again, is the strong complaint of an individual against the unmerciful treatment of his enemies. The general nature of his sufferings (esp. vv. 1-8) makes this psalm the voice of many worshipers through the centuries. The seeming change in tone in verse 9 and the fact that relief has already come have led many commentators to suggest composite authorship. However, the latter section seems to describe an intensified problem on the part of the same author.

1-8. A Trustful Appeal. In thee . . . my trust. It is in God that the psalmist has taken refuge. Upon this basis he can appeal in faith for deliverance and security. Jesus' use of verse 5 on the cross has made this entire psalm sacred and memorable.

9-18. An Intensified Appeal. Have mercy upon me. While the preceding verses describe the mercies of the past, these verses set forth the extreme need of the present. This section has several striking parallels with the experiences of Jeremiah. The psalmist has become a **reproach** and **a fear** to his friends. He is a forgotten man who is cast away as a broken vessel. In this state of loneliness and despair, his only friend is God, and his only hope is surrender to God's mercy.

¹⁹ *Oh* how great *is* thy goodness, which thou hast laid up for them that fear thee; *which* thou hast wrought for them that trust in thee before the sons of men!

²⁰ Thou shalt hide them in the secret of thy presence from the pride of man: thou shalt keep them secretly in a pavilion from the strife of tongues. ²¹ Blessed *be* the Lord: for he hath shewed me his marvellous kindness in a strong city. ²² For I said in my haste, I am cut off from before thine eyes: nevertheless thou heardest the voice of my supplications when I cried unto thee.

²³ O love the Lord, all ye his saints: *for* the Lord preserveth the faithful, and plentifully rewardeth the proud doer. ²⁴ Be of good courage, and he shall strengthen your heart, all ye that hope in the Lord.

¹⁹ Oh, how great is your goodness to those who publicly declare that you will rescue them. For you have stored up great blessings for those who trust and reverence you.

²⁰ Hide your loved ones in the shelter of your presence, safe beneath your hand, safe from all conspiring men. ²¹ Blessed is the Lord, for he has shown me that his never-failing love protects me like the walls of a fort! ²² I spoke too hastily when I said, "The Lord has deserted me," for you listened to my plea and answered me.

²³ Oh, love the Lord, all of you who are his people; for the Lord protects those who are loyal to him, but harshly punishes all who haughtily reject him. ²⁴ So cheer up! Take courage if you are depending on the Lord.

PSALM 32

A Psalm *of David, Maschil*

BLESSED *is he whose* transgression *is* forgiven, *whose* sin *is* covered. ² Blessed *is* the man unto whom the Lord imputeth not iniquity, and in whose spirit *there is* no guile.

³ When I kept silence, my bones waxed old through my roaring all the day long. ⁴ For day and night thy hand was heavy upon me: my moisture is turned into the drought of summer. Se-lah. ⁵ I acknowledged my sin unto thee, and mine iniquity have I not hid. I said, I will confess my transgressions unto the Lord; and thou forgavest the iniquity of my sin. Se-lah.

⁶ For this shall every one that is godly pray unto thee in a time when thou mayest be found: surely in the floods of great waters they shall not come nigh unto him.

⁷ Thou *art* my hiding place; thou shalt preserve me from trouble; thou shalt compass me about with songs of deliverance. Se-lah. ⁸ I will instruct thee and teach thee in the way which thou shalt go: I will guide thee with mine eye. ⁹ Be ye not as the horse, *or* as the mule, *which* have no understanding: whose mouth must be held in with bit and bridle, lest they come near unto thee.

32 WHAT HAPPINESS FOR those whose guilt has been forgiven! What joys when sins are covered over! What relief for those who have confessed their sins and God has cleared their record.

³ There was a time when I wouldn't admit what a sinner I was. But my dishonesty made me miserable and filled my days with frustration. ⁴ All day and all night your hand was heavy on me. My strength evaporated like water on a sunny day ⁵ until I finally admitted all my sins to you and stopped trying to hide them. I said to myself, "I will confess them to the Lord." And you forgave me! All my guilt is gone.

⁶ Now I say that each believer should confess his sins to God when he is aware of them, while there is time to be forgiven. Judgment will not touch him if he does.

⁷ You are my hiding place from every storm of life; you even keep me from getting into trouble! You surround me with songs of victory. ⁸ I will instruct you (says the Lord) and guide you along the best pathway for your life; I will advise you and watch your progress. ⁹ Don't be like a senseless horse or mule that has to have a bit in its mouth to keep it in line!

19-24. A Spirit of Gratitude. Oh how great is thy goodness. The recollection of past mercies and the assurance of continuing help calls forth words of praise and blessing. This trust in God prompts him to exhort others to **love** the Lord and **be of good courage.**

Psalm 32. The Joy of Forgiveness

The psalmist, in this second one of the seven Penitential Psalms, clearly speaks of his own personal experience. There is only a secondary sense in which the application may be made corporate. The true nature of sin is forcibly realized while the joyous freedom of pardon is a past and present reality. The didactic purpose of the psalmist indicates that the poem has affinity with the Wisdom psalms.

1,2. The Blessedness of Forgiveness. Blessed. Literally, *O how happy.* Joy comes to the sinner because God has completely pardoned him. Note the four words for sin: **transgression** means willful disobedience or rebellion; **sin** refers to missing the mark or aim; **iniquity** implies twistedness or perversity; **guile** suggests self-deception in this context. Each of these is an aspect of moral offense and is cared for in God's mercy and forgiveness.

3,4. The Burden of Guilt. When I kept silence. His previous silence was actually a refusal to acknowledge his sin before God. Whether sickness was involved or not, the psalmist recognized that God's chastening was being felt. There was no relief, day or night, as long as he refused to confess his sin before the Lord.

5. The Relief of Confession. I acknowledged . . . thou forgavest. This was undoubtedly a process rather than an instantaneous act. He first began to acknowledge, did not hide, and finally said, "I will confess." Note the emphatic position of **thou** as the writer shifts the emphasis to what God does.

6-11. The Wisdom of Experience. For this. Because of the availability of God's forgiveness, the psalmist exhorts men to pray in like manner. On the basis of his own profound experience, he becomes an instructor, a teacher, and a guide, using the language of a sage. Verse 8 seems to be a quotation from one of the songs of deliverance mentioned in verse 7, so that it is God who guides and instructs the believer.

NOTES

10 Many sorrows *shall be* to the wicked: but he that trusteth in the Lord, mercy shall compass him about. 11 Be glad in the Lord, and rejoice, ye righteous: and shout for joy, all *ye that are* upright in heart.

10 Many sorrows come to the wicked, but abiding love surrounds those who trust in the Lord. 11 So rejoice in him, all those who are his, and shout for joy, all those who try to obey him.

PSALM 33

REJOICE in the Lord, O ye righteous; *for* praise is comely for the upright. 2 Praise the Lord with harp: sing unto him with the psaltery *and* an instrument of ten strings. 3 Sing unto him a new song; play skilfully with a loud noise.

4 For the word of the Lord *is* right; and all his works *are done* in truth. 5 He loveth righteousness and judgment: the earth is full of the goodness of the Lord. 6 By the word of the Lord were the heavens made; and all the host of them by the breath of his mouth. 7 He gathereth the waters of the sea together as an heap: he layeth up the depth in storehouses.

8 Let all the earth fear the Lord: let all the inhabitants of the world stand in awe of him. 9 For he spake, and it was *done;* he commanded, and it stood fast. 10 The Lord bringeth the counsel of the heathen to nought: he maketh the devices of the people of none effect. 11 The counsel of the Lord standeth for ever, the thoughts of his heart to all generations.

12 Blessed *is* the nation whose God *is* the Lord: *and* the people *whom* he hath chosen for his own inheritance. 13 The Lord looketh from heaven; he beholdeth all the sons of men. 14 From the place of his habitation he looketh upon all the inhabitants of the earth. 15 He fashioneth their hearts alike; he considereth all their works.

16 There is no king saved by the multitude of an host: a mighty man is not delivered by much strength. 17 An horse *is* a vain thing for safety: neither shall he deliver *any* by his great strength. 18 Behold, the eye of the Lord *is* upon them that fear him, upon them that hope in his mercy; 19 To deliver their soul from death, and to keep them alive in famine. 20 Our soul waiteth for the Lord: he *is* our help and our shield.

33 LET ALL THE joys of the godly well up in praise to the Lord, for it is right to praise him. 2 Play joyous melodies of praise upon the lyre and on the harp. 3 Compose new songs of praise to him, accompanied skillfully on the harp; sing joyfully.

4 For all God's words are right, and everything he does is worthy of our trust. 5 He loves whatever is just and good; the earth is filled with his tender love. 6 He merely spoke, and the heavens were formed, and all the galaxies of stars. 7 He made the oceans, pouring them into his vast reservoirs.

8 Let everyone in all the world—men, women and children—fear the Lord and stand in awe of him. 9 For when he but spoke, the world began! It appeared at his command! 10 And with a breath he can scatter the plans of all the nations who oppose him, 11 but his own plan stands forever. His intentions are the same for every generation.

12 Blessed is the nation whose God is the Lord, whose people he has chosen as his own. 13,14,15 The Lord gazes down upon mankind from heaven where he lives. He has made their hearts and closely watches everything they do.

16,17 The best-equipped army cannot save a king—for great strength is not enough to save anyone. A war horse is a poor risk for winning victories—it is strong but it cannot save.

18,19 But the eyes of the Lord are watching over those who fear him, who rely upon his steady love. He will keep them from death even in times of famine! 20 We depend upon the Lord alone to save us. Only he can

Psalm 33. A Call to Congregational Worship

This psalm corresponds to the nationalistic psalms of Book V. At first glance it appears to be out of place in Book I, but it is placed here as an answer to the invitation .of verse 11 in the preceding psalm. The answer translates the personal experience into a national hymn of thanksgiving. The presence of twenty-two verses suggests a relation to the Hebrew alphabet, although there is no acrostic arrangement.

1-3. The Call to Worship. **Rejoice . . . praise . . . sing . . . play.** The response of the righteous takes the form of public worship. The nature of the accompaniment to be used, as to kinds of instruments and intensity of sound, is clearly stated. The occasion demands a new song or a fresh composition.

4-9. Praise of the Lord's Word. **The word of the Lord.** The actual praise begins with a listing of God's moral attributes as evidenced in history. **Uprightness, faithfulness, righteousness, justice,** and **lovingkindness** all describe him. Praise continues as the writer describes the creative power of God's word. The word is thus viewed as an expression of the Lord's thought, will, and action.

10-12. Praise of the Lord's Counsel. **The counsel of the Lord standeth for ever.** In contrast to the futile counsel of the heathen, God has chosen and guided his chosen people.

13-19. Praise of the Lord's Watchfulness. **The Lord looketh.** God looks, beholds, and considers all that men think or plan. He understands the plots of evil men and his all-seeing eye recognizes the needs of his people.

20-22. The Final Chorus of Praise. **Our soul waiteth.** The rejoicing of the entire psalm is based upon the waiting, trusting, and hoping of the assembled worshipers.

21 For our heart shall rejoice in him, because we have trusted in his holy name. 22 Let thy mercy, O Lord, be upon us, according as we hope in thee.

PSALM 34

A Psalm *of David, when he changed his behaviour before Abimelech; who drove him away, and he departed*

I WILL bless the Lord at all times: his praise *shall* continually *be* in my mouth. 2 My soul shall make her boast in the Lord: the humble shall hear *thereof,* and be glad. 3 O magnify the Lord with me, and let us exalt his name together.

4 I sought the Lord, and he heard me, and delivered me from all my fears. 5 They looked unto him, and were lightened: and their faces were not ashamed. 6 This poor man cried, and the Lord heard *him,* and saved him out of all his troubles. 7 The angel of the Lord encampeth round about them that fear him, and delivereth them.

8 O taste and see that the Lord *is* good: blessed *is* the man *that* trusteth in him. 9 O fear the Lord, ye his saints: for *there is* no want to them that fear him. 10 The young lions do lack, and suffer hunger: but they that seek the Lord shall not want any good *thing.*

11 Come, ye children, hearken unto me: I will teach you the fear of the Lord. 12 What man *is he that* desireth life, *and* loveth *many* days, that he may see good? 13 Keep thy tongue from evil, and thy lips from speaking guile. 14 Depart from evil, and do good; seek peace, and pursue it.

15 The eyes of the Lord *are* upon the righteous, and his ears *are open* unto their cry. 16 The face of the Lord *is* against them that do evil, to cut off the remembrance of them from the earth. 17 *The righteous* cry, and the Lord heareth, and delivereth them out of all their troubles.

18 The Lord *is* nigh unto them that are of a broken heart; and saveth such as be of a contrite spirit. 19 Many *are* the afflictions of the righteous: but the Lord delivereth him out of them all. 20 He keepeth all his bones: not one of them is broken.

help us; he protects us like a shield. 21 No wonder we are happy in the Lord! For we are trusting him. We trust his holy name. 22 Yes, Lord, let your constant love surround us, for our hopes are in you alone.

34 I WILL PRAISE the Lord no matter what happens. I will constantly speak of his glories and grace. 2 I will boast of all his kindness to me. Let all who are discouraged take heart. 3 Let us praise the Lord together, and exalt his name.

4 For I cried to him and he answered me! He freed me from all my fears. 5 Others too were radiant at what he did for them. Theirs was no downcast look of rejection! 6 This poor man cried to the Lord—and the Lord heard him and saved him out of his troubles. 7 For the Angel of the Lord guards and rescues all who reverence him.

8 Oh, put God to the test and see how kind he is! See for yourself the way his mercies shower down on all who trust in him. 9 If you belong to the Lord, reverence him; for everyone who does this has everything he needs. 10 Even strong young lions sometimes go hungry, but those of us who reverence the Lord will never lack any good thing.

11 Sons and daughters, come and listen and let me teach you the importance of trusting and fearing the Lord. 12 Do you want a long, good life? 13 Then watch your tongue! Keep your lips from lying. 14 Turn from all known sin and spend your time in doing good. Try to live in peace with everyone; work hard at it.

15 For the eyes of the Lord are intently watching all who live good lives, and he gives attention when they cry to him. 16 But the Lord has made up his mind to wipe out even the memory of evil men from the earth. 17 Yes, the Lord hears the good man when he calls to him for help, and saves him out of all his troubles.

18 The Lord is close to those whose hearts are breaking; he rescues those who are humbly sorry for their sins. 19 The good man does not escape all troubles—he has them too. But the Lord helps him in each and every one. 20 God even protects him from accidents.

Psalm 34. The Goodness of the Lord

This song of praise is an acrostic, similar in structure to Psalm 25. It is indeed striking that both psalms omit the letter *Waw* and add an extra *Pe* at the end. In regard to content, both are songs of thanksgiving, similar in thought to the book of Proverbs.

1-3. His Invitation to Praise. O magnify the Lord with me. The resolution to praise God continually is the basis for seeking others to magnify and exalt the Lord. This invitation is directed toward those who are humble and teachable.

4-6. His Testimony of Deliverance. I sought . . . he heard . . . and delivered. Out of his firsthand experience, the psalmist illustrates the basis for this sincere praise. Following the LXX and various manuscripts and versions, verse 5 would be better translated, **Look upon me and be lightened, and your faces will not be ashamed.**

7-10. His Assurance of Blessing. O taste and see. The only way that others can know the blessings is by putting God to the test. The psalmist says, "Try him and see." The true blessings come only to those who **trust, fear,** and **seek** the Lord.

11-22. His Lesson for Disciples. Come, ye children . . . I will teach you. His experiential knowledge has given him the right to teach others. Those addressed as children are again the humble and teachable disciples of any age. The style is the didactic question and answer method of the wise men. The theme is retribution as interpreted by orthodox Judaism.

21 Evil shall slay the wicked: and they that hate the righteous shall be desolate. 22 The Lord redeemeth the soul of his servants: and none of them that trust in him shall be desolate.

PSALM 35

A Psalm *of David*

PLEAD *my cause,* O Lord, with them that strive with me: fight against them that fight against me. 2 Take hold of shield and buckler, and stand up for mine help. 3 Draw out also the spear, and stop *the way* against them that persecute me: say unto my soul, I *am* thy salvation. 4 Let them be confounded and put to shame that seek after my soul: let them be turned back and brought to confusion that devise my hurt. 5 Let them be as chaff before the wind: and let the angel of the Lord chase *them.* 6 Let their way be dark and slippery: and let the angel of the Lord persecute them. 7 For without cause have they hid for me their net *in* a pit, *which* without cause they have digged for my soul. 8 Let destruction come upon him at unawares; and let his net that he hath hid catch himself: into that very destruction let him fall.

9 And my soul shall be joyful in the Lord: it shall rejoice in his salvation. 10 All my bones shall say, Lord, who *is* like unto thee, which deliverest the poor from him that is too strong for him, yea, the poor and the needy from him that spoileth him?

11 False witnesses did rise up; they laid to my charge *things* that I knew not. 12 They rewarded me evil for good *to* the spoiling of my soul. 13 But as for me, when they were sick, my clothing *was* sackcloth: I humbled my soul with fasting; and my prayer returned into mine own bosom. 14 I behaved myself as though *he had been* my friend *or* brother: I bowed down heavily, as one that mourneth *for his* mother. 15 But in mine adversity they rejoiced, and gathered themselves together: *yea,* the abjects gathered themselves together against me, and I knew *it* not; they did tear *me,* and ceased not: 16 With hypocritical mockers in feasts, they gnashed upon me with their teeth.

21 Calamity will surely overtake the wicked; heavy penalties are meted out to those who hate the good. 22 But as for those who serve the Lord, he will redeem them; everyone who takes refuge in him will be freely pardoned.

35 O LORD, FIGHT those fighting me; declare war on them for their attacks on me. 2 Put on your armor, take your shield and protect me by standing in front. 3 Lift your spear in my defense, for my pursuers are getting very close. Let me hear you say that you will save me from them. 4 Dishonor those who are trying to kill me. Turn them back and confuse them, 5 Blow them away like chaff in the wind—wind sent by the Angel of the Lord. 6 Make their path dark and slippery before them, with the Angel of the Lord pursuing them. 7 For though I did them no wrong, yet they laid a trap for me and dug a pitfall in my path. 8 Let them be overtaken by sudden ruin, caught in their own net, and destroyed.

9 But I will rejoice in the Lord. He shall rescue me! 10 From the bottom of my heart praise rises to him. Where is his equal in all of heaven and earth? Who else protects the weak and helpless from the strong, and the poor and needy from those who would rob them?

11 These evil men swear to a lie. They accuse me of things I have never even heard about. 12 I do them good, but they return me harm. I am sinking down to death. 13 When they were ill, I mourned before the Lord in sackcloth, asking him to make them well; I refused to eat; I prayed for them with utmost earnestness, but God did not listen. 14 I went about sadly as though it were my mother, friend or brother who was sick and nearing death. 15 But now that I am in trouble they are glad; they come together in meetings filled with slander against me—I didn't even know some of those who were there. 16 For they gather with the worthless fellows of the town and spend their time cursing me.

¹⁷ Lord, how long wilt thou look on? rescue my soul from their destructions, my darling from the lions. ¹⁸ I will give thee thanks in the great congregation: I will praise thee among much people.

¹⁹ Let not them that are mine enemies wrongfully rejoice over me: *neither* let them wink with the eye that hate me without a cause. ²⁰ For they speak not peace: but they devise deceitful matters against *them that are* quiet in the land. ²¹ Yea, they opened their mouth wide against me, *and* said, Aha, aha, our eye hath seen *it*. ²² *This* thou hast seen, O Lord: keep not silence: O Lord, be not far from me.

²³ Stir up thyself, and awake to my judgment, *even* unto my cause, my God and my Lord. ²⁴ Judge me, O Lord my God, according to thy righteousness; and let them not rejoice over me. ²⁵ Let them not say in their hearts, Ah, so would we have it: let them not say, We have swallowed him up. ²⁶ Let them be ashamed and brought to confusion together that rejoice at mine hurt: let them be clothed with shame and dishonour that magnify *themselves* against me. ²⁷ Let them shout for joy, and be glad, that favour my righteous cause: yea, let them say continually, Let the Lord be magnified, which hath pleasure in the prosperity of his servant. ²⁸ And my tongue shall speak of thy righteousness *and* of thy praise all the day long.

¹⁷ Lord, how long will you stand there, doing nothing? Act now and rescue me, for I have but one life and these young lions are out to get it. ¹⁸ Save me, and I will thank you publicly before the entire congregation, before the largest crowd I can find.

¹⁹ Don't give victory to those who fight me without any reason! Don't let them rejoice at my fall—let them die. ²⁰ They don't talk of peace and doing good, but of plots against innocent men who are minding their own business. ²¹ They shout that they have seen *me* doing wrong! "Aha!" they say. "With our own eyes we saw him do it." ²² Lord, you know all about it. Don't stay silent! Don't desert me now!

²³ Rise up, O Lord my God; vindicate me. ²⁴ Declare me "not guilty," for you are just. Don't let my enemies rejoice over me in my troubles. ²⁵ Don't let them say, "Aha! Our dearest wish against him will soon be fulfilled!" and, "At last we have him!" ²⁶ Shame them; let these who boast against me and who rejoice at my troubles be themselves overcome by misfortune that strips them bare of everything they own. Bare them to dishonor. ²⁷ But give great joy to all who wish me well. Let them shout with delight, "Great is the Lord who enjoys helping his child!" ²⁸ And I will tell everyone how great and good you are; I will praise you all day long.

PSALM 36

To the chief Musician, A Psalm of David the servant of the Lord

THE transgression of the wicked saith within my heart, *that there is* no fear of God before his eyes. ² For he flattereth himself in his own eyes, until his iniquity be found to be hateful. ³ The words of his mouth *are* iniquity and deceit: he hath left off to be wise, *and* to do good. ⁴ He deviseth mischief upon his bed; he setteth himself in a way *that is* not good; he abhorreth not evil.

⁵ Thy mercy, O Lord, *is* in the heavens; *and* thy faithfulness *reacheth* unto the clouds. ⁶ Thy righteousness *is* like the great mountains; thy judgments *are* a great deep: O Lord, thou preservest

36 SIN LURKS DEEP in the hearts of the wicked, forever urging them on to evil deeds. They have no fear of God to hold them back. ² Instead, in their conceit, they think they can hide their evil deeds and not get caught. ³ Everything they say is crooked and deceitful; they are no longer wise and good. ⁴ They lie awake at night to hatch their evil plots, instead of planning how to keep away from wrong.

⁵ Your steadfast love, O Lord, is as great as all the heavens. Your faithfulness reaches beyond the clouds. ⁶ Your justice is as solid as God's mountains. Your decisions are as full of wisdom as the oceans are with water. You are concerned for men and animals

19-28. The Second Appeal for Judgment. Judge me, O Lord. The psalmist pleads first that his enemies may no longer taunt him or speak evil of him. Then he appeals for a final judgment on the case so that his enemies will receive the treatment of shame and dishonor which they afforded him. Once again he closes the cycle with a vow of thanksgiving.

Psalm 36. A Lesson in Contrast

Two sharply defined pictures, one of godlessness and the other of godliness are presented here. The style varies with the contrast in themes. The psalmist uses rough poetic form and language to describe evil, and smooth form and beautiful language for the description of God. Although some commentators suggest that two poems have been joined together in this psalm, that is neither clear nor necessary. The language and thought of the conclusion in verses 10-12 revert to the pattern of the first section.

1-4. The Hideousness of Evil. No fear of God. This appears to be the substance of an oracle which describes in essence the evil enemy of the psalmist. The manuscripts and versions differ as to whether the oracle is directed to the heart of the psalmist or to that of the wicked man. There is also a question as to the subject of **flattereth** in verse 2. It may be the wicked man, transgression, or God. The first seems to be preferable if the oracle is designed to reach the heart of the psalmist, while the second possibility fits best if verse 1 refers to the heart of the wicked. The obvious fruits of denying God are stated in verses 3,4.

5-9. The Gloriousness of God. Thy mercy . . . thy faithfulness . . . thy righteousness . . . thy judgments . . . thy lovingkindness . . . thy light. In a beautiful and melodious flow of words, these various attributes of God are likened to

NOTES

man and beast. ⁷ How excellent *is* thy lovingkindness, O God! therefore the children of men put their trust under the shadow of thy wings. ⁸ They shall be abundantly satisfied with the fatness of thy house; and thou shalt make them drink of the river of thy pleasures.

⁹ For with thee *is* the fountain of life: in thy light shall we see light. ¹⁰ O continue thy lovingkindness unto them that know thee; and thy righteousness to the upright in heart.

¹¹ Let not the foot of pride come against me, and let not the hand of the wicked remove me. ¹² There are the workers of iniquity fallen: they are cast down, and shall not be able to rise.

PSALM 37

A Psalm *of David*

FRET not thyself because of evildoers, neither be thou envious against the workers of iniquity. ² For they shall soon be cut down like the grass, and wither as the green herb. ³ Trust in the Lord, and do good; *so* shalt thou dwell in the land, and verily thou shalt be fed.

⁴ Delight thyself also in the Lord; and he shall give thee the desires of thine heart. ⁵ Commit thy way unto the Lord; trust also in him; and he shall bring *it* to pass. ⁶ And he shall bring forth thy righteousness as the light, and thy judgment as the noonday.

⁷ Rest in the Lord, and wait patiently for him: fret not thyself because of him who prospereth in his way, because of the man who bringeth wicked devices to pass.

⁸ Cease from anger, and forsake wrath: fret not thyself in any wise to do evil. ⁹ For evildoers shall be cut off: but those that wait upon the Lord, they shall inherit the earth. ¹⁰ For yet a little while, and the wicked *shall* not *be*: yea, thou shalt diligently consider his place, and it *shall* not *be*. ¹¹ But the meek shall inherit the earth; and shall delight themselves in the abundance of peace.

¹² The wicked plotteth against the just, and gnasheth upon him with his teeth. ¹³ The Lord shall laugh at him: for he seeth that his day is coming. ¹⁴ The wicked have drawn out the sword, and have bent their bow, to cast

alike. ⁷ How precious is your constant love, O God! All humanity takes refuge in the shadow of your wings. ⁸ You feed them with blessings from your own table and let them drink from your rivers of delight.

⁹ For you are the Fountain of life; our light is from your Light. ¹⁰ Pour out your unfailing love on those who know you! Never stop giving your salvation to those who long to do your will.

¹¹ Don't let these proud men trample me. Don't let their wicked hands push me around. ¹² Look! They have fallen. They are thrown down and will not rise again.

37 NEVER ENVY THE wicked! ² Soon they fade away like grass and disappear. ³ Trust in the Lord instead. Be kind and good to others; then you will live safely here in the land and prosper, feeding in safety.

⁴ Be delighted with the Lord. Then he will give you all your heart's desires. ⁵ Commit everything you do to the Lord. Trust him to help you do it and he will! ⁶ Your innocence will be clear to everyone. He will vindicate you with the blazing light of justice shining down as from the noonday sun.

⁷ Rest in the Lord; wait patiently for him to act. Don't be envious of evil men who prosper.

⁸ Stop your anger! Turn off your wrath. Don't fret and worry—it only leads to harm. ⁹ For the wicked shall be destroyed, but those who trust the Lord shall be given every blessing. ¹⁰ Only a little while and the wicked shall disappear. You will look for them in vain. ¹¹ But all who humble themselves before the Lord shall be given every blessing, and shall have wonderful peace.

¹²,¹³ The Lord is laughing at those who plot against the godly, for he knows their judgment day is coming. ¹⁴ Evil men take

different phenomena of nature and then to human experience. In addition, God is spoken of as "the fountain of life." Every aspect of God's glory is spiritually oriented to produce one of the most spiritual pictures of God in the Psalter.

10-12. The Triumph of Love. **O continue thy lovingkindness.** After a brief prayer for the continuance of God's dealings with the righteous, the psalmist envisions the actual overthrow of the wicked.

Psalm 37. A Vindication of Providence

This psalm is related to the Wisdom literature by its distinctively didactic character. The major problem for the psalmist is the inconsistency connected with the prosperity of the wicked. Although tempted to doubt God's goodness, the author quiets his own mind and his hearers' by appealing to patience and trust. The organization is alphabetic, similar in many ways to the acrostic in Psalms 9 and 10.

1-11. Counsel for the Wise. **Fret not thyself because of evildoers.** The opening verse sets forth the basic maxim for a mature outlook: Don't fret or be envious about those who seem to prosper though wicked. Instead, the wise man will **trust, delight in, commit** himself **unto, rest in,** and **wait patiently for** the Lord. Herein is the positive cure for indignation and envy.

12-20. Doom for the Wicked. **His day is coming.** In the preceding passage the scene was set for this proclamation of woe by the declaration that the wicked have just **a little while** (v. 10). The various calamities are carefully catalogued.

down the poor and needy, *and* to slay such as be of upright conversation. ¹⁵ Their sword shall enter into their own heart, and their bows shall be broken.

¹⁶ A little that a righteous man hath *is* better than the riches of many wicked. ¹⁷ For the arms of the wicked shall be broken: but the Lord upholdeth the righteous.

¹⁸ The Lord knoweth the days of the upright: and their inheritance shall be for ever. ¹⁹ They shall not be ashamed in the evil time: and in the days of famine they shall be satisfied. ²⁰ But the wicked shall perish, and the enemies of the Lord *shall be* as the fat of lambs: they shall consume; into smoke shall they consume away. ²¹ The wicked borroweth, and payeth not again: but the righteous sheweth mercy, and giveth. ²² For *such as be* blessed of him shall inherit the earth; and *they that be* cursed of him shall be cut off.

²³ The steps of a *good* man are ordered by the Lord: and he delighteth in his way. ²⁴ Though he fall, he shall not be utterly cast down: for the Lord upholdeth *him with* his hand.

²⁵ I have been young, and *now* am old; yet have I not seen the righteous forsaken, nor his seed begging bread. ²⁶ *He is* ever merciful, and lendeth; and his seed *is* blessed.

²⁷ Depart from evil, and do good; and dwell for evermore. ²⁸ For the Lord loveth judgment, and forsaketh not his saints; they are preserved for ever: but the seed of the wicked shall be cut off.

²⁹ The righteous shall inherit the land, and dwell therein for ever. ³⁰ The mouth of the righteous speaketh wisdom, and his tongue talketh of judgment. ³¹ The law of his God *is* in his heart; none of his steps shall slide.

³² The wicked watcheth the righteous, and seeketh to slay him. ³³ The Lord will not leave him in his hand, nor condemn him when he is judged.

³⁴ Wait on the Lord, and keep his way, and he shall exalt thee to inherit the land: when the wicked are cut off, thou shall see *it*. ³⁵ I have seen the wicked in great power, and spreading himself like a green bay tree. ³⁶ Yet he passed away, and, lo, he *was* not: yea, I sought him, but he could not be found.

aim to slay the poor; they are ready to butcher those who do right. ¹⁵ But their swords will be plunged into their own hearts and all their weapons will be broken.

¹⁶ It is better to have little and be godly than to own an evil man's wealth; ¹⁷ for the strength of evil men shall be broken, but the Lord takes care of those he has forgiven.

¹⁸ Day by day the Lord observes the good deeds done by godly men, and gives them eternal rewards. ¹⁹ He cares for them when times are hard; even in famine, they will have enough. ²⁰ But evil men shall perish. These enemies of God will wither like grass, and disappear like smoke. ²¹ Evil men borrow and "cannot pay it back"! But the good man returns what he owes with some extra besides. ²² Those blessed by the Lord shall inherit the earth, but those cursed by him shall die.

²³ The steps of good men are directed by the Lord. He delights in each step they take. ²⁴ If they fall it isn't fatal, for the Lord holds them with his hand.

²⁵ I have been young and now I am old. And in all my years I have never seen the Lord forsake a man who loves him; nor have I seen the children of the godly go hungry. ²⁶ Instead, the godly are able to be generous with their gifts and loans to others, and their children are a blessing.

²⁷ So if you want an eternal home, leave your evil, low-down ways and live good lives. ²⁸ For the Lord loves justice and fairness; he will never abandon his people. They will be kept safe forever; but all who love wickedness shall perish.

²⁹ The godly shall be firmly planted in the land, and live there forever. ³⁰,³¹ The godly man is a good counselor because he is just and fair and knows right from wrong.

³² Evil men spy on the godly, waiting for an excuse to accuse them and then demanding their death. ³³ But the Lord will not let these evil men succeed, nor let the godly be condemned when they are brought before the judge.

³⁴ Don't be impatient for the Lord to act! Keep traveling steadily along his pathway and in due season he will honor you with every blessing, and you will see the wicked destroyed. ³⁵,³⁶ I myself have seen it happen: a proud and evil man, towering like a cedar of Lebanon, but when I looked again, he was gone! I searched but could not find him!

21-31. Reward for the Righteous. **Shall inherit the earth.** The **meek** (v. 11), the **blessed** (v. 22), and the **righteous** (v. 29) are the terms applied to the recipients of the promised reward. The personal illustration in verse 25 is a unique departure from the formalized style of the psalm as a whole.

32-40. Contrasts of Retribution. **When the wicked are cut off, thou shalt see it.** While the wicked now watch for an opportunity to trap the righteous, in the future the righteous will have their chance to watch. The end of the upright is **peace,** but the end of the wicked is destruction.

NOTES

37 Mark the perfect *man,* and behold the upright: for the end of *that* man *is* peace. 38 But the transgressors shall be destroyed together: the end of the wicked shall be cut off.

39 But the salvation of the righteous *is* of the Lord: *he is* their strength in the time of trouble. 40 And the Lord shall help them, and deliver them: he shall deliver them from the wicked, and save them, because they trust in him.

PSALM 38

A Psalm of David, to bring to remembrance

O Lord, rebuke me not in thy wrath: neither chasten me in thy hot displeasure. 2 For thine arrows stick fast in me, and thy hand presseth me sore. 3 *There is* no soundness in my flesh because of thine anger; neither *is there any* rest in my bones because of my sin. 4 For mine iniquities are gone over mine head: as an heavy burden they are too heavy for me. 5 My wounds stink *and* are corrupt because of my foolishness. 6 I am troubled; I am bowed down greatly; I go mourning all the day long. 7 For my loins are filled with a loathsome *disease:* and *there is* no soundness in my flesh. 8 I am feeble and sore broken: I have roared by reason of the disquietness of my heart.

9 Lord, all my desire *is* before thee; and my groaning is not hid from thee. 10 My heart panteth, my strength faileth me: as for the light of mine eyes, it also is gone from me. 11 My lovers and my friends stand aloof from my sore; and my kinsmen stand afar off.

12 They also that seek after my life lay snares *for me:* and they that seek my hurt speak mischievous things, and imagine deceits all the day long. 13 But I, as a deaf *man,* heard not; and *I was* as a dumb man *that* openeth not his mouth. 14 Thus I was as a man that heareth not, and in whose mouth *are* no reproofs. 15 For in thee, O Lord, do I hope: thou wilt hear, O Lord my God. 16 For I said, *Hear me,* lest *otherwise* they should rejoice over me: when my foot slippeth, they magnify *themselves* against me.

37 But the good man—what a different story! For the good man—the blameless, the upright, the man of peace—he has a wonderful future ahead of him. For him there is a happy ending. 38 But evil men shall be destroyed, and their posterity shall be cut off.

39 The Lord saves the godly! He is their salvation and their refuge when trouble comes. 40 Because they trust in him, he helps them and delivers them from the plots of evil men.

38 O Lord, don't punish me while you are angry! 2 Your arrows have struck deep; your blows are crushing me. 3,4 Because of your anger my body is sick, my health is broken beneath my sins. They are like a flood, higher than my head; they are a burden too heavy to bear. 5,6 My wounds are festering and full of pus. Because of my sins I am bent and racked with pain. My days are filled with anguish. 7 My loins burn with inflammation and my whole body is diseased. 8 I am exhausted and crushed; I groan in despair.

9 Lord, you know how I long for my health once more. You hear my every sigh. 10 My heart beats wildly, my strength fails, and I am going blind. 11 My loved ones and friends stay away, fearing my disease. Even my own family stands at a distance.

12 Meanwhile my enemies are trying to kill me. They plot my ruin and spend all their waking hours planning treachery. 13,14 But I am deaf to all their threats; I am silent before them as a man who cannot speak. I have nothing to say. 15 For I am waiting for you, O Lord my God. Come and protect me. 16 Put an end to their arrogance, these who gloat when I am cast down!

Psalm 38. The Lamentation of a Sufferer

Although this psalm is a personal lament, it is also classed as one of the seven Penitential Psalms. The writer complains of a serious bodily affliction aggravated by mental anguish and the desertion of loved ones. He accepts the fact that his suffering is merited retribution for his sins. Forsaken and dejected, he looks to God as his last and only hope.

1-8. The Suffering of Sin. No soundness in my flesh because of thine anger. The psalmist does not contend with God or claim innocence. He pleads for mercy, that his burden may be lightened. His suffering is clearly **because of my sin.** The seriousness of his ailment is indicated by the description of a skin disease comparable to that of Job.

9-14. The Suffering of Persecution. **Stand aloof . . . lay snares . . . speak mischievous things.** These words describe the treatment of his former friends. His **loved ones, friends,** and **kinsmen** all keep their distance. His enemies take advantage of his distress and weakened condition. This phase of his suffering is also similar to Job's circumstances in that friends desert him or fail to sympathize properly with him.

15-22. The Hope of Deliverance. **For in thee, O Lord, do I hope.** The author has not attempted to refute his enemies because his hope is in God alone. After repeating his confession of sin, he voices again his petition for mercy.

¹⁷ For I *am* ready to halt, and my sorrow *is* continually before me. ¹⁸ For I will declare mine iniquity; I will be sorry for my sin. ¹⁹ But mine enemies *are* lively, *and* they are strong: and they that hate me wrongfully are multiplied. ²⁰ They also that render evil for good are mine adversaries; because I follow *the thing that* good *is.*

²¹ Forsake me not, O Lord: O my God, be not far from me. ²² Make haste to help me, O Lord my salvation.

PSALM 39

To the chief Musician, even *to Jeduthun, A Psalm of David*

I SAID, I will take heed to my ways, that I sin not with my tongue: I will keep my mouth with a bridle, while the wicked is before me. ² I was dumb with silence, I held my peace, *even* from good; and my sorrow was stirred. ³ My heart was hot within me, while I was musing the fire burned: *then* spake I with my tongue, ⁴ Lord, make me to know mine end, and the measure of my days, what it *is: that* I may know how frail I *am.* ⁵ Behold, thou hast made my days *as* an handbreadth; and mine age *is* as nothing before thee: verily every man at his best state *is* altogether vanity. Se-lah. ⁶ Surely every man walketh in a vain shew: surely they are disquieted in vain: he heapeth up *riches,* and knoweth not who shall gather them. ⁷ And now, Lord, what wait I for? my hope *is* in thee.

⁸ Deliver me from all my transgressions: make me not the reproach of the foolish.

⁹ I was dumb, I opened not my mouth; because thou didst *it.*

¹⁰ Remove thy stroke away from me: I am consumed by the blow of thine hand. ¹¹ When thou with rebukes dost correct man for iniquity, thou makest his beauty to consume away like a moth: surely every man *is* vanity. Se-lah.

¹² Hear my prayer, O Lord, and give ear unto my cry; hold not thy peace at my tears: for I *am* a stranger with thee, *and* a sojourner, as all my fathers *were.*

¹³ O spare me, that I may recover strength, before I go hence, and be no more.

¹⁷ How constantly I find myself upon the verge of sin; this source of sorrow always stares me in the face. ¹⁸ I confess my sins; I am sorry for what I have done. ¹⁹ But my enemies persecute with vigor, and continue to hate me—though I have done nothing against them to deserve it. ²⁰ They repay me evil for good and hate me for standing for the right.

²¹ Don't leave me, Lord; don't go away! ²² Come quickly! Help me, O my Savior.

39 I SAID TO myself, I'm going to quit complaining! I'll keep quiet, especially when the ungodly are around me. ²,³ But as I stood there silently the turmoil within me grew to the bursting point. The more I mused, the hotter the fires inside. Then at last I spoke, and pled with God: ⁴ Lord, help me to realize how brief my time on earth will be. Help me to know that I am here for but a moment more. ⁵,⁶ My life is no longer than my hand! My whole lifetime is but a moment to you. Proud man! Frail as breath! A shadow! And all his busy rushing ends in nothing. He heaps up riches for someone else to spend. ⁷ And so, Lord, my only hope is in you.

⁸ Save me from being overpowered by my sins, for even fools will mock me then.

⁹ Lord, I am speechless before you. I will not open my mouth to speak one word of complaint, for my punishment is from you.

¹⁰ Lord, don't hit me anymore—I am exhausted beneath your hand. ¹¹ When you punish a man for his sins, he is destroyed, for he is as fragile as a moth-infested cloth; yes, man is frail as breath.

¹² Hear my prayer, O Lord; listen to my cry! Don't sit back, unmindful of my tears. For I am your guest. I am a traveler passing through the earth, as all my fathers were.

¹³ Spare me, Lord! Let me recover and be filled with happiness again before my death.

Psalm 39. An Appeal for Strength

This appears to be a sequel to the preceding psalm. However, the author need not be the same in each case, since it is the arrangement of the psalms within the collection that gives this continuity. Although penitential in character, this poem has not been included among the seven Penitential Psalms. There are certain affinities to the experience of Job in the suffering of the psalmist as well as a parallel to the book of Ecclesiastes in the view of life.

1-3. A Resolve of Self-control. I will keep my mouth. Because of the stroke of God mentioned in verse 10, the psalmist is sorely tempted to complain against God. Like Job, he must restrain the temptation to charge God with foolishness. The presence of the wicked suggests an outside source of temptation and the possibility of doing great harm to the cause of the righteous by public complaining.

4-6. A Prayer for Understanding. Lord, make me to know. The object of his prayer is knowledge to enable him to understand the frailty and vanity of life. He gives vent to his feelings and thoughts concerning the vanity of human aims. He hopes to be led back to a quiet confidence in God which will dispel these vain thoughts.

7-13. A Request for Mercy. And now, Lord. . . . Deliver me. On the basis of his present hope in God, he can ask that God will **deliver, remove thy stroke, hear,** and **spare.** In tone, these requests are quite different from his former thoughts. His recognition and confession of his sins has given a sense of humility not possible previously.

NOTES

PSALM 40

To the chief Musician, A Psalm of David

I WAITED patiently for the Lord; and he inclined unto me, and heard my cry. ² He brought me up also out of an horrible pit, out of the miry clay, and set my feet upon a rock, *and* established my goings. ³ And he hath put a new song in my mouth, *even* praise unto our God: many shall see *it,* and fear, and shall trust in the Lord. ⁴ Blessed *is* that man that maketh the Lord his trust, and respecteth not the proud, nor such as turn aside to lies.

⁵ Many, O Lord my God, *are* thy wonderful works *which* thou hast done, and thy thoughts *which are* to us-ward: they cannot be reckoned up in order unto thee: *if* I would declare and speak *of them,* they are more than can be numbered.

⁶ Sacrifice and offering thou didst not desire; mine ears hast thou opened: burnt offering and sin offering hast thou not required. ⁷ Then said I, Lo, I come: in the volume of the book *it is* written of me, ⁸ I delight to do thy will, O my God: yea, thy law *is* within my heart.

⁹ I have preached righteousness in the great congregation: lo, I have not refrained my lips, O Lord, thou knowest. ¹⁰ I have not hid thy righteousness within my heart; I have declared thy faithfulness and thy salvation: I have not concealed thy lovingkindness and thy truth from the great congregation.

¹¹ Withhold not thou thy tender mercies from me, O Lord: let thy lovingkindness and thy truth continually preserve me. ¹² For innumerable evils have compassed me about: mine iniquities have taken hold upon me, so that I am not able to look up; they are more than the hairs of mine head: therefore my heart faileth me.

¹³ Be pleased, O Lord, to deliver me: O Lord, make haste to help me. ¹⁴ Let them be ashamed and confounded together that seek after my soul to destroy it; let them be driven backward and put to shame that wish me evil. ¹⁵ Let them be desolate for a reward of their shame that say unto me, Aha, aha.

40 I WAITED PATIENTLY for God to help me; then he listened and heard my cry. ² He lifted me out of the pit of despair, out from the bog and the mire, and set my feet on a hard, firm path and steadied me as I walked along. ³ He has given me a new song to sing, of praises to our God. Now many will hear of the glorious things he did for me, and stand in awe before the Lord, and put their trust in him. ⁴ Many blessings are given to those who trust the Lord, and have no confidence in those who are proud, or who trust in idols.

⁵ O Lord my God, many and many a time you have done great miracles for us, and we are ever in your thoughts. Who else can do such glorious things? No one else can be compared with you. There isn't time to tell of all your wonderful deeds.

⁶ It isn't sacrifices and offerings which you really want from your people. Burnt animals bring no special joy to your heart. But you have accepted the offer of my lifelong service. ⁷ Then I said, "See, I have come, just as all the prophets foretold. ⁸ And I delight to do your will, my God, for your law is written upon my heart!"

⁹ I have told everyone the Good News that you forgive men's sins. I have not been timid about it, as you well know, O Lord. ¹⁰ I have not kept this Good News hidden in my heart, but have proclaimed your lovingkindness and truth to all the congregation.

¹¹ O Lord, don't hold back your tender mercies from me! My only hope is in your love and faithfulness. ¹² Otherwise I perish, for problems far too big for me to solve are piled higher than my head. Meanwhile my sins, too many to count, have all caught up with me and I am ashamed to look up. My heart quails within me.

¹³ Please, Lord, rescue me! Quick! Come and help me! ¹⁴,¹⁵ Confuse them! Turn them around and send them sprawling—all these who are trying to destroy me. Disgrace these scoffers with their utter failure!

Psalm 40. A New Song of Praise

Here is yet another good illustration of the method of compiling which has produced our present Psalter. A reading of the psalm soon shows the sudden change from praise for answered prayer to petition for immediate deliverance, verse 12. That a new psalm begins here is verified by the use of verses 13-17 as Psalm 70. Although the latter may have drawn from this psalm in its present form, the separate identity of verse 12 is obvious.

1-3. An Experience of Answered Prayer. **I waited . . . he inclined . . . and heard.** After a period of waiting, the psalmist was rescued from great trouble. The problem may have been illness or another situation where death seemed imminent. This experience has given him a new song which will inspire trust in God.

4,5. The Theme of the Song. **Many . . . thy wonderful works.** Although the psalm begins like Psalm 1 with a beatitude, the theme of God's goodness is uppermost in the psalmist's praise. His wonderful deeds and thoughts are too great to be described and too numerous to be counted.

6-11. The Response to the New Song. **I delight to do thy will.** It is the new song and the experience behind it that leads the psalmist to look beyond the sacrificial system. The four basic sacrifices and offerings of verse 6 are unacceptable to present true gratitude and praise. The depth of the writer's experience is shown in his open proclamation of the nature and work of the Lord. The author of Hebrews quotes these words as applicable to Christ (Heb 10:5-7).

12-17. The Petition for Deliverance. **Make haste to help me.** Verse 12 appears to be a connecting link to join these two poems and to serve as an introduction to the appeal for help. Almost every phrase in this section is found in other psalms as well as in Psalm 70. This use of other sources stands in sharp contrast to the originality of verses 1-11. However, the great need of the psalmist is no less real. After pleading for immediate attention, he requests that his enemies **be ashamed, confounded, driven backward, put to shame,** and **desolate.** He further requests that seekers of God may rightly rejoice and magnify the Lord. Realizing his own inadequacy, he is confident that God considers him and will prove to be his helper and deliverer.

75

16 Let all those that seek thee rejoice and be glad in thee: let such as love thy salvation say continually, The Lord be magnified.

17 But I *am* poor and needy; *yet* the Lord thinketh upon me: thou *art* my help and my deliverer; make no tarrying, O my God.

PSALM 41

To the chief Musician, A Psalm of David

BLESSED *is* he that considereth the poor: the Lord will deliver him in time of trouble. 2 The Lord will preserve him, and keep him alive; *and* he shall be blessed upon the earth: and thou wilt not deliver him unto the will of his enemies. 3 The Lord will strengthen him upon the bed of languishing: thou wilt make all his bed in his sickness.

4 I said, Lord, be merciful unto me: heal my soul; for I have sinned against thee. 5 Mine enemies speak evil of me, When shall he die, and his name perish? 6 And if he come to see *me,* he speaketh vanity: his heart gathereth iniquity to itself; *when* he goeth abroad, he telleth *it.* 7 All that hate me whisper together against me: against me do they devise my hurt. 8 An evil disease, *say they,* cleaveth fast unto him: and *now* that he lieth he shall rise up no more.

9 Yea, mine own familiar friend, in whom I trusted, which did eat of my bread, hath lifted up *his* heel against me. 10 But thou, O Lord, be merciful unto me, and raise me up, that I may requite them. 11 By this I know that thou favourest me, because mine enemy doth not triumph over me. 12 And as for me, thou upholdest me in mine integrity, and settest me before thy face for ever.

13 Blessed *be* the Lord God of Israel from everlasting, and to everlasting. Amen, and Amen.

PSALM 42

To the chief Musician, Maschil, for the sons of Korah

As the hart panteth after the water brooks, so panteth my soul after thee, O God. 2 My soul thirsteth for God, for

16 But may the joy of the Lord be given to everyone who loves him and his salvation. May they constantly exclaim, "How great God is!"

17 I am poor and needy, yet the Lord is thinking about me right now! O my God, you are my helper. You are my Savior; come quickly, and save me. Please don't delay!

41 GOD BLESSES THOSE who are kind to the poor. He helps them out of their troubles. 2 He protects them and keeps them alive; he publicly honors them and destroys the power of their enemies. 3 He nurses them when they are sick, and soothes their pains and worries.

4 "O Lord," I prayed, "be kind and heal me, for I have confessed my sins." 5 But my enemies say, "May he soon die and be forgotten!" 6 They act so friendly when they come to visit me while I am sick; but all the time they hate me and are glad that I am lying there upon my bed of pain. And when they leave, they laugh and mock. 7 They whisper together about what they will do when I am dead. 8 "It's fatal, whatever it is," they say. "He'll never get out of that bed!"

9 Even my best friend has turned against me—a man I completely trusted; how often we ate together. 10 Lord, don't you desert me! Be gracious, Lord, and make me well again so I can pay them back! 11 I know you are pleased with me because you haven't let my enemies triumph over me. 12 You have preserved me because I was honest; you have admitted me forever to your presence.

13 Bless the Lord, the God of Israel, who exists from everlasting ages past—and on into everlasting eternity ahead. Amen and amen!

42 AS THE DEER pants for water, so I long for you, O God. 2 I thirst for

Psalm 41. Thanksgiving for Healing and Vindication

An individual who has just recovered from a serious illness here expresses his thanksgiving. It is not pure thanksgiving in that he is influenced by the Wisdom school in the opening verses and reverts to a lament in describing his desperate situation. However, the danger is now past and recovery is assured.

1-3. Meditation upon God's Deliverance. **Blessed is he that considereth the poor.** This beatitude corresponds to the "Blessed are the merciful" of the Sermon on the Mount. Such a man is delivered, preserved, blessed, and strengthened by God. The psalmist recognizes himself as an illustration of his case in point.

4-9. Prayer for Restoration. **I said, Lord . . . heal.** His appeal includes a plea for mercy and for actual healing. Note that a confession of sin makes the prayer complete. His enemies have taken great delight in viewing his afflictions. Even a close friend has turned on him, as Judas Iscariot betrayed his Master and Friend (cf. Jn 13:18; Acts 1:16).

10-12. Prayer for Vengeance. **Raise me up, that I may requite them.** This is not a prayer that God will punish those who took advantage of him. He asks for strength to do it himself! It is only through such a victory that he can feel sure of God's favor.

13. Benediction. **Blessed be the Lord.** This subscript marks the close of Book I of the Psalter.

BOOK II. Psalms 42–72

The second book in the fivefold division of the Psalms appears to be a part of a larger collection, i.e., Psalms 42–83, which uses the name '*Elōhim* instead of *Yahweh* for the most part. The former is used 164 times and the latter only 30 times in Book II. Within the larger collection, several smaller collections are observable: one connected with the Levitical family called the Sons of Korah; one associated with David; and one referring to Asaph. Besides these collections Book II also includes one anonymous psalm and one ascribed to Solomon.

Psalms 42, 43. Longing for God

Here are two poems so closely connected in content and style as to defy separation. The occurrence of the same refrain in 42:5; 42:11; and 43:5, the fact that Psalm 43 is without a title, and the

internal form of the two psalms all point to one original composition. The division probably was made after the Elohistic collection, 42–83, began to be circulated. The psalmist is despondent because he cannot make his usual pilgrimages to the Temple. He seems to live in the northern section of Palestine, where he is constantly taunted by enemies who do not share his longings for God. The entire poem is one of great poetic beauty, constantly mingling longing and hope.

42:1-5. The Nature of His Longing. **My soul thirsteth for God.** Even as the hind (not *hart*) cannot disguise her thirst, neither can the psalmist hide his passion for **the living God.** His heathen enemies taunt him with remarks about the in-

NOTES

the living God: when shall I come and appear before God? ³ My tears have been my meat day and night, while they continually say unto me, Where *is* thy God?

⁴ When I remember these *things,* I pour out my soul in me: for I had gone with the multitude, I went with them to the house of God, with the voice of joy and praise, with a multitude that kept holyday. ⁵ Why art thou cast down, O my soul? and *why* art thou disquieted in me? hope thou in God: for I shall yet praise him *for* the help of his countenance. ⁶ O my God, my soul is cast down within me: therefore will I remember thee from the land of Jordan, and of the Her-mon-ites, from the hill Mi-zar. ⁷ Deep calleth unto deep at the noise of thy waterspouts: all thy waves and thy billows are gone over me.

⁸ *Yet* the Lord will command his lovingkindness in the daytime, and in the night his song *shall be* with me, *and* my prayer unto the God of my life.

⁹ I will say unto God my rock, Why hast thou forgotten me? why go I mourning because of the oppression of the enemy? ¹⁰ As with a sword in my bones, mine enemies reproach me; while they say daily unto me, Where *is* thy God? ¹¹ Why art thou cast down, O my soul? and why art thou disquieted within me? hope thou in God: for I shall yet praise him, *who is* the health of my countenance, and my God.

PSALM 43

JUDGE me, O God, and plead my cause against an ungodly nation: O deliver me from the deceitful and unjust man. ² For thou *art* the God of my strength: why dost thou cast me off? why go I mourning because of the oppression of the enemy?

³ O send out thy light and thy truth: let them lead me; let them bring me unto thy holy hill, and to thy tabernacles. ⁴ Then will I go unto the altar of God, unto God my exceeding joy: yea, upon the harp will I praise thee, O God my God. ⁵ Why art thou cast down, O my soul? and why art thou disquieted within me? hope in God: for I shall yet praise him, *who is* the health of my countenance, and my God.

God, the living God. Where can I find him to come and stand before him? ³ Day and night I weep for his help, and all the while my enemies taunt me. "Where is this God of yours?" they scoff.

⁴,⁵ Take courage, my soul! Do you remember those times (but how could you ever forget them!) when you led a great procession to the Temple on festival days, singing with joy, praising the Lord? Why then be downcast? Why be discouraged and sad? Hope in God! I shall yet praise him again. Yes, I shall again praise him for his help. ⁶ Yet I am standing here depressed and gloomy, but I will meditate upon your kindness to this lovely land where the Jordan River flows and where Mount Hermon and Mount Mizar stand. ⁷ All your waves and billows have gone over me, and floods of sorrow pour upon me like a thundering cataract.

⁸ Yet day by day the Lord also pours out his steadfast love upon me, and through the night I sing his songs and pray to God who gives me life.

⁹ "O God my Rock," I cry, "why have you forsaken me? Why must I suffer these attacks from my enemies?" ¹⁰ Their taunts pierce me like a fatal wound; again and again they scoff, "Where is that God of yours?" ¹¹ But O my soul, don't be discouraged. Don't be upset. Expect God to act! For I know that I shall again have plenty of reason to praise him for all that he will do. He is my help! He is my God!

43 O GOD, DEFEND me from the charges of these merciless, deceitful men. ² For you are God, my only place of refuge. Why have you tossed me aside? Why must I mourn at the oppression of my enemies?

³ Oh, send out your light and your truth—let them lead me. Let them lead me to your Temple on your holy mountain, Zion. ⁴ There I will go to the altar of God my exceeding joy, and praise him with my harp. O God—my God! ⁵ O my soul, why be so gloomy and discouraged? Trust in God! I shall again praise him for his wondrous help; he will make me smile again, *for he is my God!*

difference of his God. The hardest thing
for him to endure is the remembrance
of the days when he was able to lead
pilgrimages to the great festivals. The
refrain in verse 5 is the beautiful formula of trust with which he allays his de-
spondency.

**42:6-11. The Depths of His Despair.
Deep calleth unto deep.** Again the psalmist becomes downcast and voices despair,
which is more plaintive than before. Although he attempts to pray and recall
how measureless is God's loving-kindness,
he still feels forsaken. Mixed with his
longing for the Temple is his remembrance of the constant barbs of his enemies. He gains renewed strength by repeating his formula for inner peace.

**43:1-5. The Prayer for His Restora-
tion. Judge me, O God, and plead my
cause.** Despairing again, the psalmist
lays his case before God. Two desires
alternate here – the desire for freedom
from persecution and the desire to go
to the Temple. **Light** and **truth** are the
personified forces which he requests to
lead him even as he has led pilgrims in
the past. The repetition of the refrain
echoes a confident hope that God will
answer his prayer.

NOTES

PSALM 44

To the chief Musician for the sons of Korah, Maschil

WE have heard with our ears, O God, our fathers have told us, *what* work thou didst in their days, in the times of old. ² *How* thou didst drive out the heathen with thy hand, and plantedst them; *how* thou didst afflict the people, and cast them out. ³ For they got not the land in possession by their own sword, neither did their own arm save them: but thy right hand, and thine arm, and the light of thy countenance, because thou hadst a favour unto them.

⁴ Thou art my King, O God: command deliverances for Jacob. ⁵ Through thee will we push down our enemies: through thy name will we tread them under that rise up against us. ⁶ For I will not trust in my bow, neither shall my sword save me. ⁷ But thou hast saved us from our enemies, and hast put them to shame that hated us.

⁸ In God we boast all the day long, and praise thy name for ever. Se-lah. ⁹ But thou hast cast off, and put us to shame; and goest not forth with our armies. ¹⁰ Thou makest us to turn back from the enemy: and they which hate us spoil for themselves. ¹¹ Thou hast given us like sheep *appointed* for meat; and hast scattered us among the heathen. ¹² Thou sellest thy people for nought, and dost not increase *thy wealth* by their price. ¹³ Thou makest us a reproach to our neighbours, a scorn and a derision to them that are round about us. ¹⁴ Thou makest us a byword among the heathen, a shaking of the head among the people. ¹⁵ My confusion *is* continually before me, and the shame of my face hath covered me, ¹⁶ For the voice of him that reproacheth and blasphemeth; by reason of the enemy and avenger.

¹⁷ All this is come upon us; yet have we not forgotten thee, neither have we dealt falsely in thy covenant. ¹⁸ Our heart is not turned back, neither have our steps declined from thy way; ¹⁹ Though thou hast sore broken us in the place of dragons, and covered us with the shadow of death. ²⁰ If we have forgotten the name of our God, or stretched out our hands to a strange god;

44 O GOD, WE have heard of the glorious miracles you did in the days of long ago. Our forefathers have told us how you drove the heathen nations from this land and gave it all to us, spreading Israel from one end of the country to the other. ³ They did not conquer by their own strength and skill, but by your mighty power and because you smiled upon them and favored them.

⁴ You are my King and my God. Decree victories for your people. ⁵ For it is only by your power and through your name that we tread down our enemies; ⁶ I do not trust my weapons. They could never save me. ⁷ Only you can give us the victory over those who hate us.

⁸ My constant boast is God. I can never thank you enough! ⁹ And yet for a time, O Lord, you have tossed us aside in dishonor, and have not helped us in our battles. ¹⁰ You have actually fought against us and defeated us before our foes. Our enemies have invaded our land and pillaged the countryside. ¹¹ You have treated us like sheep in a slaughter pen, and scattered us among the nations. ¹² You sold us for a pittance. You valued us at nothing at all. ¹³ The neighboring nations laugh and mock at us because of all the evil you have sent. ¹⁴ You have made the word "Jew" a byword of contempt and shame among the nations, disliked by all. ^{15,16} I am constantly despised, mocked, taunted and cursed by my vengeful enemies.

¹⁷ And all this has happened, Lord, despite our loyalty to you. We have not violated your covenant. ¹⁸ Our hearts have not deserted you! We have not left your path by a single step. ¹⁹ If we had, we could understand your punishing us in the barren wilderness and sending us into darkness and death. ²⁰ If we had turned away from worshiping our God, and were worshiping

Psalm 44. A Plea for Justice

NOTES

This psalm, national in scope, is permeated with a deep sense of self-justification. The serious calamity alluded to and the attendant humiliation are not viewed as resulting from sin but are taken as ground for rebuking God. The spirit of disrespectful rebuke is found nowhere else in the Psalter. No other psalm makes such claims of national fidelity to God. There is presented here another side of Israel's heart life. The abiding value lies in the emphasis upon God's power to help.

1-3. The Blessings of the Past. **We have heard.** By oral tradition, as well as in the sacred Scriptures read publicly at the religious festivals, the mighty deeds of God in times of old have been preserved. This sense of history is frequently seen because God is best known by what he has done.

4-8. The Assurance of the Present. **In God we boast.** It is by God that all victories are possible. The personal illustration of the bow and sword amplifies the argument of the psalmist.

9-16. The Abandonment of Israel. **But thou hast cast off.** Their only hope does not go out into battle with them. God is thus blamed for their recent defeat. The psalmist uses cutting sarcasm in saying that God made a bad bargain in selling his people to the enemy for nothing.

17-22. The Claim of Faithfulness. **Yet have we not forgotten thee.** The claim is repeated over and over that the nation has remained faithful. At no time in Israel's history was this literally true. The psalmist must have in mind a comparative fidelity based on generalities.

²¹ Shall not God search this out? for he knoweth the secrets of the heart. ²² Yea, for thy sake are we killed all the day long; we are counted as sheep for the slaughter.

²³ Awake, why sleepest thou, O Lord? arise, cast *us* not off for ever. ²⁴ Wherefore hidest thou thy face, *and* forgettest our affliction and our oppression? ²⁵ For our soul is bowed down to the dust: our belly cleaveth unto the earth. ²⁶ Arise for our help, and redeem us for thy mercies' sake.

PSALM 45

To the chief Musician upon Shoshannim, for the sons of Korah, Maschil, A Song of loves

My heart is inditing a good matter: I speak of the things which I have made touching the king: my tongue *is* the pen of a ready writer.

² Thou art fairer than the children of men: grace is poured into thy lips: therefore God hath blessed thee for ever. ³ Gird thy sword upon *thy* thigh, O *most* mighty, with thy glory and thy majesty. ⁴ And in thy majesty ride prosperously because of truth and meekness *and* righteousness; and thy right hand shall teach thee terrible things. ⁵ Thine arrows *are* sharp in the heart of the king's enemies; *whereby* the people fall under thee. ⁶ Thy throne, O God, *is* for ever and ever: the sceptre of thy kingdom *is* a right sceptre. ⁷ Thou lovest righteousness, and hatest wickedness: therefore God, thy God, hath anointed thee with the oil of gladness above thy fellows.

⁸ All thy garments *smell* of myrrh, and aloes, *and* cassia, out of the ivory palaces, whereby they have made thee glad. ⁹ Kings' daughters *were* among thy honourable women: upon thy right hand did stand the queen in gold of O-phir. ¹⁰ Hearken, O daughter, and consider, and incline thine ear; forget also thine own people, and thy father's house; ¹¹ So shall the king greatly desire thy beauty: for he *is* thy Lord; and worship thou him. ¹² And the daughter of Tyre *shall be there* with a gift; *even* the rich among the people shall intreat thy favour.

idols, ²¹ would God not know it? Yes, he knows the secrets of every heart. ²² But that is not our case. For we are facing death threats constantly because of serving you! We are like sheep awaiting slaughter.

²³ Waken! Rouse yourself! Don't sleep, O Lord! Are we cast off forever? ²⁴ Why do you look the other way? Why do you ignore our sorrows and oppression? ²⁵ We lie face downward in the dust. ²⁶ Rise up, O Lord, and come and help us. Save us by your constant love.

45 MY HEART IS overflowing with a beautiful thought! I will write a lovely poem to the King, for I am as full of words as the speediest writer pouring out his story.

² You are the fairest of all;
Your words are filled with grace;
God himself is blessing you forever.
³ Arm yourself, O Mighty One,
So glorious, so majestic!
⁴ And in your majesty
Go on to victory,
Defending truth, humility, and justice.
Go forth to awe-inspiring deeds!
⁵ Your arrows are sharp
In your enemies' hearts;
They fall before you.
⁶ Your throne, O God, endures forever.
Justice is your royal scepter.
⁷ You love what is good
And hate what is wrong.
Therefore God, your God,
Has given you more gladness
Than anyone else.

⁸ Your robes are perfumed with myrrh, aloes and cassia. In your inlaid palaces of ivory, lovely music is being played for your enjoyment. ⁹ Kings' daughters are among your concubines. Standing beside you is the queen, wearing jewelry of finest gold from Ophir. ^{10,11} "I advise you, O daughter, not to fret about your parents in your homeland far away. Your royal husband delights in your beauty. Reverence him, for he is your lord. ¹² The people of Tyre, the richest people of our day, will shower you with gifts and entreat your favors."

23-26. The Request for Justice. **Awake . . . cast us not off for ever.** The concept of God sleeping on the job is out of place, even in poetical expression. This is similar to the sarcastic words of Elijah on Mount Carmel concerning Baal. However, the psalm closes with the request that God **redeem us for thy mercies' sake.**

Psalm 45. The Marriage of a King

This is one of several royal psalms which relate to many phases of kingly life. Its secular nature is at once recognized. However, the event is idealized and spiritualized by a court attendant who is obviously moved by this solemn occasion. The hopelessness of identifying the king or the period in history gives a more idealized significance to it. Later Jewish interpreters made it Messianic, as did early Christian writers (cf. Heb 1:8, 9).

1. Dedication of the Song. **Touching the king.** Because his heart is overflowing, the psalmist dedicates this song of his own composition to the king.

2-9. Eulogy of the Groom. **Thou art fairer.** His appearance is handsome; his speech is graceful; his bearing is majestic; his rule is righteous; his military might is powerful; his spiritual choices are right; his garments and court are regal. If verse 6a refers to a human king, it might be translated, **Thy throne is like God's.** In Heb 1:8,9 the words are applied to Christ, in accord with the literal sense, "Thy throne, O God."

10-12. Advice to the Bride. **Hearken, O daughter.** Fatherly advice is appropriate for a young princess, to help her find her proper place in the royal family. She must be submissive to the king as well as loyal to his people.

13 The king's daughter *is* all glorious within: her clothing *is* of wrought gold. 14 She shall be brought unto the king in raiment of needlework: the virgins her companions that follow her shall be brought unto thee. 15 With gladness and rejoicing shall they be brought: they shall enter into the king's palace. 16 Instead of thy fathers shall be thy children, whom thou mayest make princes in all the earth.

17 I will make thy name to be remembered in all generations: therefore shall the people praise thee for ever and ever.

13 The bride, a princess, waits within her chamber, robed in beautiful clothing woven with gold. 14 Lovely she is, led beside her maids of honor to the king! 15 What a joyful, glad procession as they enter in the palace gates! 16 "Your sons will some day be kings like their father. They shall sit on thrones around the world!

17 "I will cause your name to be honored in all generations; the nations of the earth will praise you forever."

PSALM 46

To the chief Musician for the sons of Korah, A Song upon Alamoth

GOD *is* our refuge and strength, a very present help in trouble. 2 Therefore will not we fear, though the earth be removed, and though the mountains be carried into the midst of the sea; 3 *Though* the waters thereof roar *and* be troubled, *though* the mountains shake with the swelling thereof. Se-lah.

4 *There is* a river, the streams whereof shall make glad the city of God, the holy *place* of the tabernacles of the most High. 5 God *is* in the midst of her; she shall not be moved: God shall help her, *and that* right early. 6 The heathen raged, the kingdoms were moved: he uttered his voice, the earth melted.

7 The Lord of hosts *is* with us; the God of Jacob *is* our refuge. Se-lah.

8 Come, behold the works of the Lord, what desolations he hath made in the earth. 9 He maketh wars to cease unto the end of the earth; he breaketh the bow, and cutteth the spear in sunder; he burneth the chariot in the fire. 10 Be still, and know that I *am* God: I will be exalted among the heathen, I will be exalted in the earth.

11 The Lord of hosts *is* with us; the God of Jacob *is* our refuge. Se-lah.

46 GOD IS OUR refuge and strength, a tested help in times of trouble. 2 And so we need not fear even if the world blows up, and the mountains crumble into the sea. 3 Let the oceans roar and foam; let the mountains tremble!

4 There is a river of joy flowing through the City of our God—the sacred home of the God above all gods. 5 God himself is living in that City; therefore it stands unmoved despite the turmoil everywhere. He will not delay his help. 6 The nations rant and rave in anger—but when God speaks, the earth melts in submission and kingdoms totter into ruin.

7 The Commander of the armies of heaven is here among us. He, the God of Jacob, has come to rescue us. 8 Come, see the glorious things that our God does, how he brings ruin upon the world, 9 and causes wars to end throughout the earth, breaking and burning every weapon. 10 "Stand Silent! Know that I am God! I will be honored by every nation in the world!"

11 The Commander of the heavenly armies is here among *us!* He, the God of Jacob, has come to rescue *us!*

13-15. Entrance of the Bride. She shall be brought unto the king. The bride is not described in detail; but, instead, emphasis is placed on the scene of the processional march. Her clothing and attendants are fitting for the occasion.

16,17. Anticipation for the Marriage. Thy children . . . thy name. Two wishes are set forth as assured results. There will be princes to bless this union and carry on his name. The psalmist promises to make that name to be remembered for all generations. The name represents the character, reputation, nature, and attributes of a person.

Psalm 46. A Mighty Fortress

This and the next two psalms form a trilogy of praise. The likelihood that the same historical situation provided the background for all three has caused much speculation as to the event itself. Although some great deliverance seems to be understood, the particular occasion cannot be identified. The pronounced apocalyptic elements are used by the psalmist to encourage the people in their current crisis.

1-3. Our Refuge. God . . . our refuge and strength. These words express the dominant theme of the psalm, a theme which inspired Luther to write "A Mighty Fortress Is Our God." The idea of a world-wide catastrophe was drawn from the writings of the prophets. It furnishes the background for assuring the people that God will be present whatever the outward circumstances. The refrain found in verses 7 and 11 may originally have appeared also between verses 3 and 4.

4-7. Our Deliverer. God shall help her. In contrast to troubled waters, there is a life-giving river which supplies Jerusalem, for God is in her midst (cf. Ezk 47). Again, in the picture of the final battle of the ages, reference is made to the apocalyptic view. Deliverance is certain because the **Lord of hosts is with us.**

8-11. Our Peace. He maketh wars to cease. The outcome of the apocalyptic battle is triumph and the end of warfare. The beautiful phrase, **Be still, and know that I am God,** carries the idea of refraining from vain strivings and lack of confidence. The refrain is repeated in order to show the triumph of this confidence in God.

PSALM 47

To the chief Musician, A Psalm for the sons of Korah

O CLAP your hands, all ye people; shout unto God with the voice of triumph. ² For the Lord most high *is* terrible; *he is* a great King over all the earth. ³ He shall subdue the people under us, and the nations under our feet. ⁴ He shall choose our inheritance for us, the excellency of Jacob whom he loved. Se-lah.

⁵ God is gone up with a shout, the Lord with the sound of a trumpet. ⁶ Sing praises to God, sing praises: sing praises unto our King, sing praises. ⁷ For God *is* the King of all the earth: sing ye praises with understanding. ⁸ God reigneth over the heathen: God sitteth upon the throne of his holiness. ⁹ The princes of the people are gathered together, *even* the people of the God of Abraham: for the shields of the earth *belong* unto God: he is greatly exalted.

PSALM 48

A Song and Psalm for the sons of Korah

GREAT *is* the Lord, and greatly to be praised in the city of our God, *in* the mountain of his holiness. ² Beautiful for situation, the joy of the whole earth, *is* mount Zion, *on* the sides of the north, the city of the great King.

³ God is known in her palaces for a refuge. ⁴ For, lo, the kings were assembled, they passed by together. ⁵ They saw *it, and* so they marvelled; they were troubled, *and* hasted away. ⁶ Fear took hold upon them there, *and* pain, as of a woman in travail. ⁷ Thou breakest the ships of Tarshish with an east wind. ⁸ As we have heard, so have we seen in the city of the Lord of hosts, in the city of our God: God will establish it for ever. Se-lah.

⁹ We have thought of thy lovingkindness, O God, in the midst of thy temple. ¹⁰ According to thy name, O God, so *is* thy praise unto the ends of the earth: thy right hand is full of righteousness. ¹¹ Let mount Zion rejoice, let the daughters of Judah be glad, because of thy

47 COME, EVERYONE, AND clap for joy! Shout triumphant praises to the Lord! ² For the Lord, the God above all gods, is awesome beyond words; he is the great King of all the earth. ³ He subdues the nations before us, ⁴ and will personally select his choicest blessings for his Jewish people —the very best for those he loves.

⁵ God has ascended with a mighty shout, with trumpets blaring. ⁶,⁷ Sing out your praises to our God, our King. Yes, sing your highest praises to our King, the King of all the earth. Sing thoughtful praises! ⁸ He reigns above the nations, sitting on his holy throne. ⁹ The Gentile rulers of the world have joined with us in praising him— praising the God of Abraham—for the battle shields of all the armies of the world are his trophies. He is highly honored everywhere.

48 HOW GREAT IS the Lord! How much we should praise him. He lives upon Mount Zion in Jerusalem. ² What a glorious sight! See Mount Zion rising north of the city high above the plains for all to see— Mount Zion, joy of all the earth, the residence of the great King.

³ God himself is the defender of Jerusalem. ⁴ The kings of the earth have arrived together to inspect the city. ⁵ They marvel at the sight and hurry home again, ⁶ afraid of what they have seen; they are filled with panic like a woman in travail! ⁷ For God destroys the mightiest warships with a breath of wind. ⁸ We have heard of the city's glory—the city of our God, the Commander of the armies of heaven. And now we see it for ourselves! God has established Jerusalem forever.

⁹ Lord, here in your Temple we meditate upon your kindness and your love. ¹⁰ Your name is known throughout the earth, O God. You are praised everywhere for the salvation you have scattered throughout the world. ¹¹ O Jerusalem, rejoice! O people of Judah, rejoice! For God will see to

Psalm 47. A Victorious King

This second psalm in the trilogy that expresses confidence in God amplifies the thought expressed in 46:10 and 48:2. According to the Talmud, Psalm 47 was used in later Judaism on the Jewish New Year's Day. As a result of the work of Mowinckel, many commentators regard Psalms 47, 93, 95–100 as celebrating the enthronement of Yahweh as the King of all the earth. There is no direct evidence that such a festival took place in pre-Exilic days. But these psalms become more meaningful when viewed against the background of such a celebration. In its prophetic aspect this psalm finds its fulfillment in the future reign of Christ on earth.

1-4. The Call for Rejoicing. O clap your hands . . . shout. In an eschatological vein, all peoples are called upon to rejoice. The description of the divine sovereignty introduced in Psalm 46 reaches a new height here. The psalmist, like the prophets, here envisions the action of the future as occurring in the present. He sees all nations subdued, while Israel stands in a unique relation to God because of her inheritance.

5-9. The Call for Praise. Sing praises. There is a slight shift here from jubilant rejoicing to more formal praise. The cue for the shift to praise is seen in verse 5. The future victory of the Lord is again set forth as present in order to give confidence in its absolute certainty.

Psalm 48. A Holy City

The trilogy begun in Psalm 46 with emphasis on confidence in God is here concluded with a similar note of confidence. The concepts of God as Refuge in Psalm 46 and of God as King in 46 and 47 are both incorporated in this psalm. The eschatological features are continued here but in lesser degree. The fact that there is some historical background for the trilogy becomes more apparent. The psalm was undoubtedly used in connection with a prominent festival as first-time pilgrims were shown the city.

1-8. City of Our God. The city of our God. The two themes within this section — the greatness of God and the glory of his city, complement one another. Not only is the Lord great, he is the **great King** and exceedingly worthy to be praised. The close connection of this psalm with the preceding ones suggests that perhaps it is the apocalyptic

Jerusalem as the center of the Messianic kingdom that is described. However, it is possible that the siege by Sennacherib in 701 B.C. is referred to in verses 4-8 (cf. Isa 37:33-37).

9-14. Praise of Our God. For this God is our God. While the psalm begins with praise "in the city of our God," it is raised to praise **unto the ends of the earth** in verse 10. After the worship in the Temple was concluded, the pilgrims undoubtedly joined in joyful procession around the city. Each sacred place reminded them that God would guide them even as he had guided their fathers.

NOTES

judgments. 12 Walk about Zion, and go round about her: tell the towers thereof. 13 Mark ye well her bulwarks, consider her palaces; that ye may tell it to the generation following.

14 For this God is our God for ever and ever: he will be our guide even unto death.

PSALM 49

To the chief Musician, A Psalm for the sons of Korah

HEAR this, all ye people; give ear, all ye inhabitants of the world: 2 Both low and high, rich and poor, together. 3 My mouth shall speak of wisdom; and the meditation of my heart *shall be* of understanding.

4 I will incline mine ear to a parable: I will open my dark saying upon the harp. 5 Wherefore should I fear in the days of evil, *when* the iniquity of my heels shall compass me about? 6 They that trust in their wealth, and boast themselves in the multitude of their riches; 7 None *of them* can by any means redeem his brother, nor give to God a ransom for him: 8 (For the redemption of their soul *is* precious, and it ceaseth for ever:) 9 That he should still live for ever, *and* not see corruption.

10 For he seeth *that* wise men die, likewise the fool and the brutish person perish, and leave their wealth to others. 11 Their inward thought *is, that* their houses *shall continue* for ever, *and* their dwelling places to all generations; they call *their* lands after their own names. 12 Nevertheless man *being* in honour abideth not: he is like the beasts *that* perish. 13 This their way *is* their folly: yet their posterity approve their sayings. Se-lah.

14 Like sheep they are laid in the grave; death shall feed on them; and the upright shall have dominion over them in the morning; and their beauty shall consume in the grave from their dwelling.

15 But God will redeem my soul from the power of the grave: for he shall receive me. Se-lah. 16 Be not thou afraid when one is made rich, when the glory of his house is increased; 17 For when

it that you are finally treated fairly. 12 Go, inspect the city! Walk around and count her many towers! 13 Note her walls and tour her palaces, so that you can tell your children.

14 For this great God is our God forever and ever. He will be our guide until we die.

49 LISTEN, EVERYONE! HIGH and low, rich and poor, all around the world— listen to my words, 3 for they are wise and filled with insight.

4 I will tell in song accompanied by harps the answer to one of life's most perplexing problems: 5 *There is no need to fear when times of trouble come,* even though surrounded by enemies! 6 They trust in their wealth and boast about how rich they are, 7 yet not one of them, though rich as kings, can ransom his own brother from the penalty of sin! For God's forgiveness does not come that way. 8,9 For a soul is far too precious to be ransomed by mere earthly wealth. There is not enough of it in all the earth to buy eternal life for just one soul, to keep it out of hell.

10 Rich man! Proud man! Wise man! You must die like all the rest! You have no greater lease on life than foolish, stupid men. You must leave your wealth to others. 11 You name your estates after yourselves as though your lands could be forever yours, and you could live on them eternally. 12 But man with all his pomp must die like any animal. 13 Such is the folly of these men, though after they die they will be quoted as having great wisdom.

14 Death is the shepherd of all mankind. And "in the morning" those who are evil will be the slaves of those who are good. For the power of their wealth is gone when they die; they cannot take it with them.

15 But as for me, God will redeem my soul from the power of death, for he will receive me. 16 So do not be dismayed when evil men grow rich and build their lovely homes. 17 For when they die they carry

Psalm 49. The Folly of Earthly Wealth

Psalm 49 is a moral lesson designed for all peoples. There is an avowed didactic purpose throughout, in keeping with the purpose of Wisdom writers. Never does the psalmist address God, and only twice does he mention Him by name. His purpose is to present a meditation on the riddle of life.

1-4. Call to Attention. Hear . . . give ear. The call is not restricted to any class or nationality. It is universal in scope; the psalmist is speaking to mankind. He uses four words frequently employed by the Wisdom school: **wisdom, understanding, parable,** and **dark saying.** His use of the harp to accompany his words is interesting, because this was not the usual practice in instruction of this sort.

5-12. Wealth and the Present Life. **Wherefore should I fear.** The psalmist deals in a different way with the age-old problem of the prosperity of the wicked. He says, Why worry? With this premise he goes on to discuss the problem with a confident rather than a pessimistic attitude. He never accuses God of injustice, but continually points to the fate of those who trust in their wealth. All must come to the end of life and all must leave their wealth behind. Following the LXX, 11a reads better: **Their graves are their houses forever.** Verse 12 is a refrain, emphasizing that man without discernment will go the way of all beasts.

13-20. Wealth and the Fate of Man. **Like sheep they are laid in the grave.** Those who trust in their wealth and honor will share a common fate. They will be led into Sheol by the shepherd, Death. Verse 15 is one of the clearest evidences of a hint of immortality in the OT. This is not a general promise but a prediction regarding the personal fate of the psalmist in contrast to that of the wicked man of wealth. **He shall take me.** The same verb is used here as is employed to describe the special cases of Enoch and Elijah. The refrain of verse 12 is used again as a closing thought.

he dieth he shall carry nothing away: his glory shall not descend after him. ¹⁸ Though while he lived he blessed his soul: and *men* will praise thee, when thou doest well to thyself. ¹⁹ He shall go to the generation of his fathers; they shall never see light.

²⁰ Man *that is* in honour, and understandeth not, is like the beasts *that* perish.

PSALM 50

A Psalm of Asaph

THE mighty God, *even* the Lord, hath spoken, and called the earth from the rising of the sun unto the going down thereof. ² Out of Zion, the perfection of beauty, God hath shined. ³ Our God shall come, and shall not keep silence: a fire shall devour before him, and it shall be very tempestuous round about him. ⁴ He shall call to the heavens from above, and to the earth, that he may judge his people. ⁵ Gather my saints together unto me; those that have made a covenant with me by sacrifice. ⁶And the heavens shall declare his righteousness: for God *is* judge himself. Se-lah.

⁷ Hear, O my people, and I will speak; O Israel, and I will testify against thee: I *am* God, *even* thy God. ⁸ I will not reprove thee for thy sacrifices or thy burnt offerings, *to have been* continually before me. ⁹ I will take no bullock out of thy house, *nor* he goats out of thy folds. ¹⁰ For every beast of the forest *is* mine, *and* the cattle upon a thousand hills. ¹¹ I know all the fowls of the mountains: and the wild beasts of the field *are* mine. ¹² If I were hungry, I would not tell thee: for the world *is* mine, and the fulness thereof. ¹³ Will I eat the flesh of bulls, or drink the blood of goats? ¹⁴ Offer unto God thanksgiving; and pay thy vows unto the most High: ¹⁵ And call upon me in the day of trouble: I will deliver thee, and thou shalt glorify me.

¹⁶ But unto the wicked God saith, What hast thou to do to declare my statutes, or *that* thou shouldest take my covenant in thy mouth? ¹⁷ Seeing thou hatest instruction, and casteth my words behind thee. ¹⁸ When thou sawest

nothing with them! Their honors will not follow them. ¹⁸ Though a man calls himself happy all through his life—and the world loudly applauds success— ¹⁹ yet in the end he dies like everyone else, and enters eternal darkness.

²⁰ For man with all his pomp must die like any animal.

50 THE MIGHTY GOD, the Lord, has summoned all mankind from east to west! ² God's glory-light shines from the beautiful Temple on Mount Zion. ³ He comes with the noise of thunder, surrounded by devastating fire; a great storm rages round about him. ⁴ He has come to judge his people. To heaven and earth he shouts, ⁵ "Gather together my own people who by their sacrifice upon my altar have promised to obey me." ⁶ God will judge them with complete fairness, for all heaven declares that he is just.

⁷ O my people, listen! For I am your God. Listen! Here are my charges against you: ⁸ I have no complaint about the sacrifices you bring to my altar, for you bring them regularly. ⁹ But it isn't sacrificial bullocks and goats that I really want from you. ¹⁰,¹¹ For all the animals of field and forest are mine! The cattle on a thousand hills! And all the birds upon the mountains! ¹² If I were hungry, I would not mention it to you—for all the world is mine, and everything in it. ¹³ No, I don't need your sacrifices of flesh and blood. ¹⁴,¹⁵ What I want from you is your true thanks; I want your promises fulfilled. *I want you to trust me in your times of trouble, so I can rescue you, and you can give me glory.*

¹⁶ But God says to evil men: Recite my laws no longer, and stop claiming my promises, ¹⁷ for you have refused my discipline, disregarding my laws. ¹⁸ You see a thief and

Psalm 50. The Nature of True Worship

This didactic psalm is closer to the prophetic tradition than to the Wisdom emphasis. The opening utterance of God, the emphasis upon spiritual religion, and the straightforward denunciation of the wicked point to a prophetic background. Acceptable worship and social morality are the two dominant themes. These correspond to the two main divisions of the Ten Commandments — man's relation to God and man's relation to his neighbor.

1-6. The Summons by the Judge. The mighty God . . . hath spoken. In a prophetic theophany, God comes to gather and judge Israel. This manifestation takes place out of Zion rather than out of Mount Sinai. Notice that the judgment is to be upon **his people**, although other peoples are to listen. In fact, heaven and earth are to act as silent witnesses.

7-15. The Message to the Worshiper. Hear, O my people. God is speaking to the formalistic worshiper and the one who trusts ritual. The judgment is not upon sacrifice as such but upon the wrong motives involved. It is made clear that God is not dependent upon the sacrifice of his people. He most desires heartfelt thanksgiving, proper payment of vows, and sincere prayer.

16-23. The Message of the Wicked. But unto the wicked, God saith. This judgment is upon the hypocrites within Israel who claim to keep the law of God in outward observance, but use the keeping of the law as justification for their evil deeds. Even though God has kept silence by delaying punishment, the time of reproof has come.

a thief, then thou consentedst with him, and hast been partaker with adulterers. [19] Thou givest thy mouth to evil, and thy tongue frameth deceit. [20] Thou sittest *and* speakest against thy brother; thou slanderest thine own mother's son. [21] These *things* hast thou done, and I kept silence; thou thoughtest that I was altogether *such an one* as thyself: *but* I will reprove thee, and set *them* in order before thine eyes. [22] Now consider this, ye that forget God, lest I tear *you* in pieces, and *there be* none to deliver. [23] Whoso offereth praise glorifieth me: and to him that ordereth *his* conversation *aright* will I shew the salvation of God.

help him, and spend your time with evil and immoral men. [19] You curse and lie, and vile language streams from your mouths. [20] You slander your own brother. [21] I remained silent—you thought I didn't care—but now your time of punishment has come, and I list all the above charges against you. [22] This is the last chance for all of you who have forgotten God, before I tear you apart—and no one can help you then.

[23] But true praise is a worthy sacrifice; this really honors me. Those who walk my paths will receive salvation from the Lord.

PSALM 51

To the chief Musician, A Psalm of David, when Nathan the prophet came unto him, after he had gone in to Bathsheba

Have mercy upon me, O God, according to thy lovingkindness: according unto the multitude of thy tender mercies blot out my transgressions. [2] Wash me thoroughly from mine iniquity, and cleanse me from my sin. [3] For I acknowledge my transgressions: and my sin *is* ever before me. [4] Against thee, thee only, have I sinned, and done *this* evil in thy sight: that thou mightest be justified when thou speakest, *and* be clear when thou judgest. [5] Behold, I was shapen in iniquity; and in sin did my mother conceive me. [6] Behold, thou desirest truth in the inward parts: and in the hidden *part* thou shalt make me to know wisdom.

[7] Purge me with hyssop, and I shall be clean: wash me, and I shall be whiter than snow. [8] Make me to hear joy and gladness; *that* the bones *which* thou hast broken may rejoice. [9] Hide thy face from my sins, and blot out all mine iniquities. [10] Create in me a clean heart, O God; and renew a right spirit within me. [11] Cast me not away from thy presence; and take not thy holy spirit from me. [12] Restore unto me the joy of thy salvation; and uphold me *with thy* free

Written after Nathan the prophet had come to inform David of God's judgment against him because of his adultery with Bathsheba, and his murder of Uriah, her husband.

51 O LOVING AND kind God, have mercy. Have pity upon me and take away the awful stain of my transgressions. [2] Oh, wash me, cleanse me from this guilt. Let me be pure again. [3] For I admit my shameful deed—it haunts me day and night. [4] It is against you and you alone I sinned, and did this terrible thing. You saw it all, and your sentence against me is just. [5] But I was born a sinner, yes, from the moment my mother conceived me. [6] You deserve honesty from the heart; yes, utter sincerity and truthfulness. Oh, give me this wisdom.

[7] Sprinkle me with the cleansing blood and I shall be clean again. Wash me and I shall be whiter than snow. [8] And after you have punished me, give me back my joy again. [9] Don't keep looking at my sins—erase them from your sight. [10] Create in me a new, clean heart, O God, filled with clean thoughts and right desires. [11] Don't toss me aside, banished forever from your presence. Don't take your Holy Spirit from me. [12] Restore to me again the joy of your salvation,

Psalm 51. A Cry for Forgiveness

This is the fourth and most profound of the Penitential Psalms. The depth of individual experience, the sense of sin, and the plea for forgiveness are unsurpassed in any other psalm. This is the first psalm in another collection bearing David's name, Psalms 51–70. Opinion is greatly divided as to the occasion suggested by this confession. To some it has a corporate significance; to some it arises from the well-known experience of David; to others it describes a worshiper who goes to the Temple for pardon and cleansing. The addition of verses 18 and 19 seems to adapt a purely individual plea to the requirements of corporate worship. Whether David composed the poem or not, his experience seems to have occasioned it.

1,2. A Cry for Mercy. **Have mercy on me, O God.** The psalmist neither pleads innocence nor shifts the blame to someone else. Since he knows that he does not deserve forgiveness, he pleads first for mercy, based on God's loving-kindness. In line with this mercy, he asks that his transgressions or **rebellions** be wiped out and his iniquity or **twistedness** be washed away.

3-6. A Confession of Sin. **For I acknowledge my transgressions.** Here the psalmist emphasizes the fact that he knows and is constantly aware of his sin, and acknowledges that his sin is more than sin against man. At the same time he recognizes the universal tendency toward sin but does not excuse himself on this basis. The depth of his confession is apparent in his desire to open up the inward and hidden parts of his being.

7-12. A Plea for Cleansing. **Purge me . . . wash me.** The verbs are extremely significant in carrying forward the plea. The psalmist begins (vv. 7-9) by asking for external cleansing. Purging with hyssop and washing are related to ritual acts. With the plea for a newly created heart and a renewed steadfast spirit, his emphasis shifts to inward cleansing.

spirit. [13] *Then* will I teach transgressors thy ways; and sinners shall be converted unto thee. [14] Deliver me from bloodguiltiness, O God, thou God of my salvation: *and* my tongue shall sing aloud of thy righteousness. [15] O Lord, open thou my lips; and my mouth shall shew forth thy praise.

[16] For thou desirest not sacrifice; else would I give *it:* thou delightest not in burnt offering. [17] The sacrifices of God *are* a broken spirit: a broken and a contrite heart, O God, thou wilt not despise.

[18] Do good in thy good pleasure unto Zion: build thou the walls of Jerusalem. [19] Then shalt thou be pleased with the sacrifices of righteousness, with burnt offering and whole burnt offering: then shall they offer bullocks upon thine altar.

PSALM 52

To the chief Musician, Maschil, A Psalm of David, when Doeg the Edomite came and told Saul, and said unto him, David is come to the house of Ahimelech

WHY boastest thou thyself in mischief, O mighty man? the goodness of God *endureth* continually. [2] Thy tongue deviseth mischiefs; like a sharp razor, working deceitfully. [3] Thou lovest evil more than good; *and* lying rather than to speak righteousness. Se-lah. [4] Thou lovest all devouring words, O *thou* deceitful tongue.

[5] God shall likewise destroy thee for ever, he shall take thee away, and pluck thee out of *thy* dwelling place, and root thee out of the land of the living. Se-lah. [6] The righteous also shall see, and fear, and shall laugh at him: [7] Lo, *this is* the man *that* made not God his strength; but trusted in the abundance of his riches, *and* strengthened himself in his wickedness.

[8] But I *am* like a green olive tree in the house of God: I trust in the mercy of God for ever and ever. [9] I will praise thee for ever, because thou hast done *it:* and I will wait on thy name; for *it is* good before thy saints.

and make me willing to obey you. [13] Then I will teach your ways to other sinners, and they—guilty like me—will repent and return to you. [14,15] Don't sentence me to death. O my God, you alone can rescue me. Then I will sing of your forgiveness, for my lips will be unsealed—oh, how I will praise you.

[16] You don't want penance; if you did, how gladly I would do it! You aren't interested in offerings burned before you on the altar. [17] It is a broken spirit you want —remorse and penitence. A broken and a contrite heart, O God, you will not ignore.

[18] And Lord, don't punish Israel for my sins—help your people and protect Jerusalem.

[19] And when my heart is right, then you will rejoice in the good that I do and in the bullocks I bring to sacrifice upon your altar.

Written by David to protest against his enemy Doeg (1 Samuel 22), who later slaughtered eighty-five priests and their families.

52 YOU CALL YOURSELF a *hero,* do you? You *boast* about this evil deed of yours against God's people. [2] You are sharp as a tack in plotting your evil tricks. [3] How you love wickedness—far more than good! And lying more than truth! [4] You love to slander—you love to say anything that will do harm, O man with the lying tongue.

[5] But God will strike you down and pull you from your home, and drag you away from the land of the living. [6] The followers of God will see it happen. They will watch in awe. Then they will laugh and say, [7] "See what happens to those who despise God and trust in their wealth, and become ever more bold in their wickedness."

[8] But I am like a sheltered olive tree protected by the Lord himself. I trust in the mercy of God forever and ever. [9] O Lord, I will praise you forever and ever for your punishment. And I will wait for your mercies—for everyone knows what a merciful God you are.

13-17. A Vow of Consecration. Then will I teach. This vow to testify to others gives evidence of the writer's pardon and changed nature. The psalmist's view of sacrifice is essentially prophetic and very similar to that of the author of Psalm 50. His sense of sin and guilt requires more than burnt offerings; hence he offers his broken spirit and contrite heart.

18,19. A Prayer for Restoration. Do good . . . build . . . then. This emphasis upon works as a means of making sacrifices acceptable appears to be a liturgical addition by a priestly writer or editor.

Psalm 52. The Fate of an Arrogant Sinner

In this individual lament, presented in the direct manner of the prophets, there is no appeal for God's help, only confidence that God will bring a retributive fate. Although a particular individual is addressed throughout, a class of men may be referred to, with the prophet as the example of a righteous man.

1-4. The Character of the Opponent. Thou lovest evil. This denunciation is directed toward an arrogant tyrant whose tongue seems to be his weapon. His greed, treachery, and falsehood all stem from this razor-like tongue.

5-7. The Retribution of God. God shall likewise destroy thee. This is the pronouncement of the psalmist, still directed toward the arrogant tyrant. The destruction is described in verse 5 in three stages—God will *snatch, tear away,* and *uproot* (RSV). Although these verbs are rendered as a prayer in the LXX (*May God destroy,* etc.), the future usage seems better, since the psalmist is certain that the righteous will observe this destruction.

8,9. The Trust of the Psalmist. I trust in the mercy of God. While the tyrant trusts in his riches, the psalmist has the stability of absolute trust in God. The green olive tree may have stood in the temple courtyard, or the psalmist may be emphasizing his strength in the Lord with two figures — like a **green olive tree** and in the **house of God.**

NOTES

PSALM 53

To the chief Musician upon Mahalath, Maschil, A Psalm of David

THE fool hath said in his heart, *There is* no God. Corrupt are they, and have done abominable iniquity: *there is* none that doeth good.

² God looked down from heaven upon the children of men, to see if there were *any* that did understand, that did seek God. ³ Every one of them is gone back: they are altogether become filthy; *there is* none that doeth good, no, not one. ⁴ Have the workers of iniquity no knowledge? who eat up my people *as* they eat bread: they have not called upon God. ⁵ There were they in great fear, *where* no fear was: for God hath scattered the bones of him that encampeth *against* thee: thou hast put *them* to shame, because God hath despised them.

⁶ Oh that the salvation of Israel *were* come out of Zion! When God bringeth back the captivity of his people, Jacob shall rejoice, *and* Israel shall be glad.

53 ONLY A FOOL would say to himself, "There is no God." And why does he say it? Because of his wicked heart, his dark and evil deeds. His life is corroded with sin.

² God looks down from heaven, searching among all mankind to see if there is a single one who does right and really seeks for God. ³ But all have turned their backs on him; they are filthy with sin—corrupt and rotten through and through. Not one is good, not one! ⁴ How can this be? Can't they understand anything? For they devour my people like bread and refuse to come to God. ⁵ But soon unheard-of terror will fall on them. God will scatter the bones of these, your enemies. They are doomed, for God has rejected them.

⁶ Oh, that God would come from Zion now and save Israel! Only when the Lord himself restores them can they ever be really happy again.

PSALM 54

To the chief Musician on Neginoth, Maschil, A Psalm of David, when the Ziphims came and said to Saul, Doth not David hide himself with us?

SAVE me, O God, by thy name, and judge me by thy strength. ² Hear my prayer, O God; give ear to the words of my mouth. ³ For strangers are risen up against me, and oppressors seek after my soul: they have not set God before them. Se-lah.

⁴ Behold, God *is* mine helper: the Lord *is* with them that uphold my soul. ⁵ He shall reward evil unto mine enemies: cut them off in thy truth. ⁶ I will freely sacrifice unto thee: I will praise thy name, O Lord; for *it is* good.

⁷ For he hath delivered me out of all trouble: and mine eye hath seen *his desire* upon mine enemies.

Written by David at the time the men of Ziph tried to betray him to Saul.

54 COME WITH GREAT power, O God, and save me! Defend me with your might! ² Oh, listen to my prayer. ³ For violent men have risen against me—ruthless men who care nothing for God are seeking my life.

⁴ But God is my helper. He is a friend of mine! ⁵ He will cause the evil deeds of my enemies to boomerang upon them. Do as you promised and put an end to these wicked men, O God. ⁶ Gladly I bring my sacrifices to you; I will praise your name, O Lord, for it is good.

⁷ God has rescued me from all my trouble, and triumphed over my enemies.

Psalm 53. The Judgment for Denying God

NOTES

This psalm is actually another version of Psalm 14. The only significant change is that the content of 14:5,6 is here strengthened and compressed into one verse. It is possible that both of these psalms are adapted versions of an original poem. However, 53 may be simply a version of 14, adapted for some historical crisis. (For outline and comments, see on Ps 14.)

Psalm 54. A Prayer for Assistance

Though this is the appeal of a troubled man, in the characteristic form of an individual lament, the language and content are so general as to make it adaptable for the needs of any who are oppressed by godless men.

1-3. Prayer in a Perilous Situation. **Save me, O God.** This appeal for help is based upon God's revealed character (his **name**) and his revealed power (his **strength**). The adversaries are called **strangers** *(zārîm)* according to the Masoretic Text, while certain manuscripts designate them as proud or insolent men *(zādîm)*. Psalm 86:14 seems to quote verse 3 of this psalm, using the latter spelling. The most important characteristic of these men, however, is their utter disregard of God.

4-7. Praise for an Assured Deliverance. **I will praise . . . for he hath delivered.** Since the psalmist has complete confidence in God as his helper, he is sure that God will give suitable punishment to his enemies. His certainty is such that he can vow to give a freewill offering and promise to praise the name of *Jehovah.*

PSALM 55

To the chief Musician on Neginoth, Maschil, A Psalm *of David*

GIVE ear to my prayer, O God; and hide not thyself from my supplication. ² Attend unto me, and hear me: I mourn in my complaint, and make a noise;

³ Because of the voice of the enemy, because of the oppression of the wicked: for they cast iniquity upon me, and in wrath they hate me. ⁴ My heart is sore pained within me: and the terrors of death are fallen upon me. ⁵ Fearfulness and trembling are come upon me, and horror hath overwhelmed me. ⁶ And I said, Oh that I had wings like a dove! *for then* would I fly away, and be at rest. ⁷ Lo, *then* would I wander far off, *and* remain in the wilderness. Se-lah. ⁸ I would hasten my escape from the windy storm *and* tempest.

⁹ Destroy, O Lord, *and* divide their tongues: for I have seen violence and strife in the city. ¹⁰ Day and night they go about it upon the walls thereof: mischief also and sorrow *are* in the midst of it. ¹¹ Wickedness *is* in the midst thereof: deceit and guile depart not from her streets.

¹² For *it was* not an enemy *that* reproached me; then I could have borne *it:* neither *was it* he that hated me *that* did magnify *himself* against me; then I would have hid myself from him: ¹³ But *it was* thou, a man mine equal, my guide, and mine acquaintance. ¹⁴ We took sweet counsel together, *and* walked unto the house of God in company.

¹⁵ Let death seize upon them, *and* let them go down quick into hell: for wickedness *is* in their dwellings, *and* among them. ¹⁶ As for me, I will call upon God; and the Lord shall save me. ¹⁷ Evening, and morning, and at noon, will I pray, and cry aloud: and he shall hear my voice. ¹⁸ He hath delivered my soul in peace from the battle *that was* against me: for there were many with me. ¹⁹ God shall hear, and afflict them, even he that abideth of old. Se-lah. Because they have no changes, therefore they fear not God.

WAIT FOR

55 LISTEN TO MY prayer, O God; don't hide yourself when I cry to you. ² Hear me, Lord! Listen to me! For I groan and weep beneath my burden of woe.

³ My enemies shout against me and threaten me with death. They surround me with terror and plot to kill me. Their fury and hatred rise to engulf me. ⁴ My heart is in anguish within me. Stark fear overpowers me. ⁵ Trembling and horror overwhelm me. ⁶ Oh, for wings like a dove, to fly away and rest! ⁷ I would fly to the far off deserts and stay there. ⁸ I would flee to some refuge from all this storm.

⁹ O Lord, make these enemies begin to quarrel among themselves—destroy them with their own violence and strife. ¹⁰ Though they patrol their walls night and day against invaders, their real problem is internal—wickedness and dishonesty are entrenched in the heart of the city. ¹¹ There is murder and robbery there, and cheating in the markets and wherever you look.

¹² It was not an enemy who taunted me—then I could have borne it; I could have hidden and escaped. ¹³ But it was you, a man like myself, my companion and my friend. ¹⁴ What fellowship we had, what wonderful discussions as we walked together to the Temple of the Lord on holy days.

¹⁵ Let death seize them and cut them down in their prime, for there is sin in their homes, and they are polluted to the depths of their souls. ¹⁶ But I will call upon the Lord to save me—and he will. ¹⁷ I will pray morning, noon, and night, pleading aloud with God; and he will hear and answer. ¹⁸ Though the tide of battle runs strongly against me, for so many are fighting me, yet he will rescue me. ¹⁹ God himself—God from everlasting ages past—will answer them! For they refuse to fear him or even honor his commands.

Psalm 55. A Protest Against the Wicked

Basically this is a lament of an individual oppressed by enemies and deserted by friends. However, some commentators consider that the original lament has been adapted for a national situation. Indeed, many scholars believe that two poems have been combined into one psalm. Verses 12-14, 18b-21, and 23 are most in question. However, no agreement can be reached as to which verses were once a separate poem.

1-8. Complaint of the Psalmist. **I mourn in my complaint.** In keeping with the form of a poetic lament, the writer appeals for God's attention to his restless condition. He is slandered, oppressed, mistreated, and hated. The constant threat to his life causes pain, fear, trembling, and horror. In words of lyric beauty, he expresses his desire to fly away to the wilderness, where he may be able to escape persecution.

9-15. Denunciation of the Wicked. **Destroy O Lord, divide their tongues.** This section opens and closes with a plea for vengeance. The division of tongues is reminiscent of God's judgment upon the builders of the Tower of Babel (Gen 11:5-9). **Violence, strife, mischief,** and **sorrow** are all descriptive of the wickedness inside the city walls. The thing hardest to bear, the psalmist finds, is the treachery of a close friend who had worshiped with him.

16-23. Confidence Through Prayer. **Evening . . . morning . . . noon.** His persistence in prayer is rewarded by personal peace and by confidence in the affliction of his adversaries. The confu-

20 He hath put forth his hands against such as be at peace with him: he hath broken his covenant. 21 *The words* of his mouth were smoother than butter, but war *was* in his heart: his words were softer than oil, yet *were* they drawn swords.

22 Cast thy burden upon the Lord, and he shall sustain thee: he shall never suffer the righteous to be moved. 23 But thou, O God, shalt bring them down into the pit of destruction: bloody and deceitful men shall not live out half their days; but I will trust in thee.

PSALM 56

To the chief Musician upon Jonath–elem–rechokim, Michtam of David, when the Philistines took him in Gath

BE merciful unto me, O God: for man would swallow me up; he fighting daily oppresseth me. 2 Mine enemies would daily swallow *me* up: for *they be* many that fight against me, O thou most High.

3 What time I am afraid, I will trust in thee. 4 In God I will praise his word, in God I have put my trust; I will not fear what flesh can do unto me. 5 Every day they wrest my words: all their thoughts *are* against me for evil. 6 They gather themselves together, they hide themselves, they mark my steps, when they wait for my soul. 7 Shall they escape by iniquity? in *thine* anger cast down the people, O God.

8 Thou tellest my wanderings: put thou my tears into thy bottle: *are they* not in thy book?

9 When I cry *unto thee,* then shall mine enemies turn back: this I know; for God *is* for me. 10 In God will I praise *his* word: in the Lord will I praise *his* word. 11 In God have I put my trust: I will not be afraid what man can do unto me. 12 Thy vows *are* upon me, O God: I will render praises unto thee. 13 For thou hast delivered my soul from death: *wilt* not *thou deliver* my feet from falling, that I may walk before God in the light of the living?

20 This friend of mine betrayed me—I who was at peace with him. He broke his promises. 21 His words were oily smooth, but in his heart was war. His words were sweet, but underneath were daggers.

22 Give your burdens to the Lord. He will carry them. He will not permit the godly to slip or fall. 23 He will send my enemies to the pit of destruction. Murderers and liars will not live out half their days. But I am trusting you to save me.

56 LORD, HAVE MERCY on me; all day long the enemy troops press in. So many are proud to fight against me; how they long to conquer me.

3,4 But when I am afraid, I will put my confidence in you. Yes, I will trust the promises of God. And since I am trusting him, what can mere man do to me? 5 They are always twisting what I say. All their thoughts are how to harm me. 6 They meet together to perfect their plans; they hide beside the trail, listening for my steps, waiting to kill me. 7 They expect to get away with it. Don't let them, Lord. In anger cast them to the ground.

8 You have seen me tossing and turning through the night. You have collected all my tears and preserved them in your bottle! You have recorded every one in your book.

9 The very day I call for help, the tide of battle turns. My enemies flee! This one thing I *know: God is for me!* 10,11 I am trusting God—oh, praise his promises! I am not afraid of anything mere man can do to me! Yes, praise his promises. 12 I will surely do what I have promised, Lord, and thank you for your help. 13 For you have saved me from death and my feet from slipping, so that I can walk before the Lord in the land of the living.

sion between singular and plural has suggested to some interpreters that verses 20,21 should follow verses 12-14, or form a separate original poem. However, the intensity of wrath may have caused the psalmist to shift from the group to his chief foe without clear transition. The trust of verse 22 brings the assurance of the closing verse.

Psalm 56. The Triumph of Faith

Here, again, an individual voices his lament over his treatment by his enemies. The distress of the psalmist, prompted by the malicious plots of crafty men, makes fear inevitable. However, his trust in God overcomes all fear.

1-4. The Plea for Help. Be merciful unto me. This plea is often repeated by the devout worshiper in Israel. It seems that the psalmist's enemies are warriors rather than religious antagonists. They trample him under foot. Yet, the inevitable fear is conquered by trust in God.

5-11. The Appeal for Vengeance. In anger cast down the people, O God. After describing the treachery of his enemies, the psalmist calls for divine aid. He has conquered fear, but God must conquer the oppressors lest they escape judgment. The writer is certain that God will answer his prayers and give vengeance. This assurance leads into a repetition of the expression of trust, a kind of refrain, found in verse 4.

12,13. The Vows of Victory. Thy vows are upon me. Since victory has already come or is envisioned as assured, the psalmist recalls his obligation of praise and thanksgiving. Perhaps he vowed a vow during his trouble. Since God has fulfilled his part in delivering from oppression and death, the rest is up to the psalmist.

PSALM 57

To the chief Musician, Al–taschith, Michtam of David, when he fled from Saul in the cave

BE merciful unto me, O God, be merciful unto me: for my soul trusteth in thee: yea, in the shadow of thy wings will I make my refuge, until *these* calamities be overpast. ² I will cry unto God most high; unto God that performeth *all things* for me. ³ He shall send from heaven, and save me *from* the reproach of him that would swallow me up. Se-lah. God shall send forth his mercy and his truth. ⁴ My soul *is* among lions: *and* I lie *even among* them that are set on fire, *even* the sons of men, whose teeth *are* spears and arrows, and their tongue a sharp sword. ⁵ Be thou exalted, O God, above the heavens; *let* thy glory *be* above all the earth. ⁶ They have prepared a net for my steps; my soul is bowed down: they have digged a pit before me, into the midst whereof they are fallen *themselves*. Se-lah. ⁷ My heart is fixed, O God, my heart is fixed: I will sing and give praise. ⁸ Awake up, my glory; awake, psaltery and harp: I *myself* will awake early. ⁹ I will praise thee, O Lord, among the people: I will sing unto thee among the nations. ¹⁰ For thy mercy *is* great unto the heavens, and thy truth unto the clouds.

¹¹ Be thou exalted, O God, above the heavens: *let* thy glory *be* above all the earth.

PSALM 58

To the chief Musician, Al–taschith, Michtam of David

Do ye indeed speak righteousness, O congregation? do ye judge uprightly, O ye sons of men? ² Yea, in heart ye work wickedness; ye weigh the violence of your hands in the earth. ³ The wicked are estranged from the womb: they go astray as soon as they be born, speaking lies. ⁴ Their poison *is* like the poison of a serpent: *they are* like the deaf adder *that* stoppeth her ear; ⁵ Which will not hearken to the voice of charmers, charming never so wisely.

57 O GOD, HAVE pity, for I am trusting you! I will hide beneath the shadow of your wings until this storm is past. ² I will cry to the God of heaven who does such wonders for me. ³ He will send down help from heaven to save me, because of his love and his faithfulness. He will rescue me from these liars who are so intent upon destroying me. ⁴ I am surrounded by fierce lions— hotheads whose teeth are sharp as spears and arrows. Their tongues are like swords. ⁵ Lord, be exalted above the highest heavens! Show your glory high above the earth. ⁶ My enemies have set a trap for me. Frantic fear grips me. They have dug a pitfall in my path. But look! They themselves have fallen into it!

⁷ O God, my heart is quiet and confident. No wonder I can sing your praises! ⁸ Rouse yourself, my soul! Arise, O harp and lyre! Let us greet the dawn with song! ⁹ I will thank you publicly throughout the land. I will sing your praises among the nations. ¹⁰ Your kindness and love are as vast as the heavens. Your faithfulness is higher than the skies.

¹¹ Yes, be exalted, O God, above the heavens. May your glory shine throughout the earth.

58 JUSTICE? YOU HIGH and mighty politicians don't even know the meaning of the word! Fairness? Which of you has any left? Not one! All your dealings are crooked: you give "justice" in exchange for bribes. ³ These men are born sinners, lying from their earliest words! ⁴,⁵ They are poisonous as deadly snakes, cobras that close their ears to the most expert of charmers.

Psalm 57. A Prayer for Protection

The same person who wrote Psalm 56 may possibly have also written this lament of an individual. In spirit, content, style, and situation the two psalms are similar. Both begin with the same appeal and both use a striking refrain as a division of structure. Verses 7-11 of this psalm form a striking hymn that is repeated in Psalm 108. It is possible that two poems were united to fashion this psalm in its present form.

1-5. A Prayer for Protection. **Be merciful to me, O God.** The psalmist's request is not for vengeance or destruction but for God's watchcare and mercy. Since his trust in God is so implicit, he is taking refuge in the confidence that God's mercy and truth will suffice.

6-11. A Resolution of Thanksgiving. **My heart is fixed . . . I will sing and give praise.** After a brief reminder of his present situation and the assurance that his enemies will suffer self-destruction, the psalmist makes his steadfast resolution. His praise is universal and it arises from the two grounds of confidence named in verse 3 – God's mercy and his truth. The psalm closes with the prayerful refrain exalting the universal sovereignty of God.

Psalm 58. A Protest Against Injustice

This is the lament of an individual indignant over the lack of justice in the world. He sees tyranny and oppression as the rule in society rather than the exception. He is especially concerned with the perversion of justice by earthly rulers or judges. It is difficult, however, to determine whether he refers to the leaders of Israel or to foreign rulers (cf. Ps 82).

1-5. A World of Injustice. **In heart ye work wickedness.** The whole problem of injustice in the affairs of men is here recognized as due to innate wickedness. The term translated congregation (*'ēlem*) in verse 1 is obscure. Some commentators read instead – *O ye gods* (*'ēlîm*), and find here an expression of sarcasm directed at the unjust judges. This emendation parallels Psalm 82 but is not supported by the MSS or LXX. In verses 3-5 direct reference is made to these wicked men as innately wicked and untamable.

⁶ Break their teeth, O God, in their mouth: break out the great teeth of the young lions, O Lord. ⁷ Let them melt away as waters *which* run continually: *when* he bendeth *his bow to shoot* his arrows, let them be as cut in pieces. ⁸ As a snail *which* melteth, let *every one of them* pass away: *like* the untimely birth of a woman, *that* they may not see the sun. ⁹ Before your pots can feel the thorns, he shall take them away as with a whirlwind, both living, and in *his* wrath.

¹⁰ The righteous shall rejoice when he seeth the vengeance: he shall wash his feet in the blood of the wicked. ¹¹ So that a man shall say, Verily *there is* a reward for the righteous; verily he is a God that judgeth in the earth.

⁶ O God, break off their fangs. Tear out the teeth of these young lions, Lord. ⁷ Let them disappear like water into thirsty ground. Make their weapons useless in their hands. ⁸ Let them be as snails that dissolve into slime; and as those who die at birth, who never see the sun. ⁹ God will sweep away both old and young. He will destroy them more quickly than a cooking pot can feel the blazing fire of thorns beneath it.

¹⁰ The godly shall rejoice in the triumph of right; they shall walk the blood-stained fields of slaughtered, wicked men. ¹¹ Then at last everyone will know that good is rewarded, and that there is a God who judges justly here on earth.

PSALM 59

To the chief Musician, Al–taschith, Michtam of David; when Saul sent, and they watched the house to kill him

DELIVER me from mine enemies, O my God: defend me from them that rise up against me. ² Deliver me from the workers of iniquity, and save me from bloody men. ³ For, lo, they lie in wait for my soul: the mighty are gathered against me; not *for* my transgression, nor *for* my sin, O Lord. ⁴ They run and prepare themselves without *my* fault: awake to help me, and behold. ⁵ Thou therefore, O Lord God of hosts, the God of Israel, awake to visit all the heathen: be not merciful to any wicked transgressors. Se-lah. ⁶ They return at evening: they make a noise like a dog, and go round about the city. ⁷ Behold, they belch out with their mouth: swords *are* in their lips: for who, *say they*, doth hear? ⁸ But thou, O Lord, shalt laugh at them; thou shalt have all the heathen in derision.

⁹ *Because of* his strength will I wait upon thee: for God *is* my defence. ¹⁰ The God of my mercy shall prevent me: God shall let me see *my desire* upon mine enemies. ¹¹ Slay them not, lest my people forget: scatter them by thy power; and bring them down, O Lord our shield. ¹² *For* the sin of their mouth *and* the words of their lips let them even be taken in their pride: and for cursing and lying *which* they speak.

Written by David at the time King Saul set guards at his home to capture and kill him. 1 Samuel 19:11

59 O MY GOD, save me from my enemies. Protect me from these who have come to destroy me. ² Preserve me from these criminals, these murderers. ³ They lurk in ambush for my life. Strong men are out there waiting. And not, O Lord, because I've done them wrong. ⁴ Yet they prepare to kill me. Lord, waken! See what is happening! Help me! ⁵ (And O Jehovah, God of heaven's armies, God of Israel, arise and punish the heathen nations surrounding us.) Do not spare these evil, treacherous men. ⁶ At evening they come to spy, slinking around like dogs that prowl the city. ⁷ I hear them shouting insults and cursing God, for "No one will hear us," they think. ⁸ Lord, laugh at them! (And scoff at these surrounding nations too.)

⁹ O God my Strength! I will sing your praises, for you are my place of safety. ¹⁰ My God is changeless in his love for me and he will come and help me. He will let me see my wish come true upon my enemies. ¹¹ Don't kill them—for my people soon forget such lessons—but stagger them with your power and bring them to their knees. Bring them to the dust, O Lord our shield. ¹²,¹³ They are proud, cursing liars. Angrily

6-11. A Call for Vengeance. Break their teeth, O God. With blistering language the psalmist creates a series of brief metaphors dealing with lions' teeth, streams, a snail, miscarriage, and thorns. Each of these is spoken as an imprecation against his unjust enemies. Thus there is here a sevenfold curse in the form of prayer. Verses 10,11 show the confidence of the psalmist in realistic terms. He feels sure that the righteous, whom he represents, will see and rejoice in the utter destruction of these unjust enemies.

Psalm 59. A Prayer for Rescue

Though this psalm is basically the lament of an individual, it has overtones which adapt it to national use as well. There are points of similarity with Psalms 55 and 58. The picture of oppression is again dominant, as is the vindictive attitude of the writer. Contrary to the normal pattern of an individual lament, refrains are evident. Verses 6,13, although not completely identical, act as a recurrent thought. Verses 9,10 are likewise repeated in similar thought pattern in verse 17.

1-5. Prayer for Protection. Deliver me . . . defend me . . . Deliver me . . . save me. The seriousness of the psalmist's plight is evident in this fourfold outcry. After describing his enemies' activity and pleading innocence, the psalmist pleads that God will rise up against the **heathen,** i.e., the *nations.* The reference to punishing the nations seems to apply the experience to a national emergency.

6-9. Defiance of the Enemy. They make a noise like a dog. The sharp words and taunts remind the psalmist of scavenger dogs searching for food at night. However, he is confident that God will laugh the enemy to scorn and come to his defense.

10-13. Plea for Vengeance. Slay them not . . . scatter them. Because of his trust that God will *meet* (AV, **prevent**) him, he prays for a gradual punishment upon his enemies. He does not want them destroyed immediately but rather made an

13 Consume *them* in wrath, consume *them,* that they *may* not *be:* and let them know that God ruleth in Jacob unto the ends of the earth. Se-lah. 14 And at evening let them return; *and* let them make a noise like a dog, and go round about the city. 15 Let them wander up and down for meat, and grudge if they be not satisfied.

16 But I will sing of thy power; yea, I will sing aloud of thy mercy in the morning: for thou hast been my defence and refuge in the day of my trouble. 17 Unto thee, O my strength, will I sing: for God *is* my defence, *and* the God of my mercy.

destroy them. Wipe them out. (And let the nations find out too that God rules in Israel and will reign throughout the world.) 14,15 Let these evil men slink back at evening, and prowl the city all night before they are satisfied, howling like dogs and searching for food.

16 But as for me, I will sing each morning about your power and mercy. For you have been my high tower of refuge, a place of safety in the day of my distress. 17 O my Strength, to you I sing my praises; for you are my high tower of safety, my God of mercy.

PSALM 60

To the chief Musician upon Shushan— eduth, Michtam of David, to teach; when he strove with Aram—naharaim and with Aram—zobah, when Joab re— turned, and smote of Edom in the valley of salt twelve thousand

O GOD, thou hast cast us off, thou hast scattered us, thou hast been dis— pleased; O turn thyself to us again. 2 Thou hast made the earth to tremble; thou hast broken it: heal the breaches thereof; for it shaketh. 3 Thou hast shewed thy people hard things: thou hast made us to drink the wine of aston— ishment.

4 Thou hast given a banner to them that fear thee, that it may be displayed because of the truth. Se-lah. 5 That thy beloved may be delivered; save *with* thy right hand, and hear me. 6 God hath spoken in his holiness; I will rejoice, I will divide She-chem, and mete out the valley of Suc-coth. 7 Gilead *is* mine, and Ma-nas-seh *is* mine; E-phra-im also *is* the strength of mine head; Judah *is* my lawgiver; 8 Moab *is* my washpot; over Edom will I cast out my shoe: Philistia, triumph thou because of me.

9 Who will bring me *into* the strong city? who will lead me into Edom? 10 *Wilt* not thou, O God, *which* hadst cast us off? and *thou,* O God, *which* didst not go out with our armies? 11 Give us help from trouble: for vain *is* the help of man.

12 Through God we shall do valiantly: for he *it is that* shall tread down our enemies.

Written by David at the time he was at war with Syria, with the outcome still uncertain; this was when Joab, captain of his forces, slaughtered 12,000 men of Edom in the Val— ley of Salt.

60 O GOD, YOU have rejected us and bro— ken our defenses; you have become angry and deserted us. Lord, restore us again to your favor. 2 You have caused this nation to tremble in fear; you have torn it apart. Lord, heal it now, for it is shaken to its depths. 3 You have been very hard on us and made us reel beneath your blows.

4,5 But you have given us a banner to rally to; all who love truth will rally to it; then you can deliver your beloved people. Use your strong right arm to rescue us. 6,7 God has promised to help us. He has vowed it by his holiness! No wonder I exult! "Shechem, Succoth, Gilead, Manasseh— still are mine!" he says. "Judah shall con— tinue to produce kings, and Ephraim great warriors. 8 Moab shall become my lowly servant, and Edom my slave. And I will shout in triumph over the Philistines."

9,10 Who will bring me in triumph into Edom's strong cities? God will! He who cast us off! He who abandoned us to our foes! 11 Yes, Lord, help us against our enemies, for man's help is useless.

12 With God's help we shall do mighty things, for he will trample down our foes.

example to the people. The shift to con-sume them in verse 13 shows his ulti-mate desire for them.

14-17. Contrasts of Fate. **Let them make a noise . . . But I will sing.** Verse 7 is repeated to set up this vivid con-trast. While the wicked search in vain all night like scavenger dogs, the psalm-ist vows that he will sing aloud in the morning. Verses 9,10 serve as a basis for the closing refrain of assurance.

Psalm 60. A Plea for Ultimate Victory

Because of the evident disaster facing the nation, and because of the frequent plurals, this psalm should be classed as a national lament. Public complaint is voiced at the beginning and at the end of the psalm, and a separate oracle of God is placed in the middle. The psalm ends on a note of confidence. Verses 6-12 are repeated by the author of Psalm 108.

1-5. A Dire Circumstance. **O God, thou hast cast us off.** The situation is worse than mere military defeat and dis-aster, because it is interpreted as God's forsaking his people. The seeming dis-pleasure of God is graphically described as causing earthquakes and making the people reel as if from drunkenness. The conclusion is drawn that God has given them his banner but led them into de-feat. The plea of verse 5 is transitional, introducing the promise of God.

6-8. A Prophetic Oracle. **God hath spoken.** The answer is expressed in terms of a previous promise by God. The refer-ences to widespread geographical areas seem to express God's universal power and ownership rather than describe a historical situation.

9-12. A Confident Hope. **Through God we shall do valiantly.** Although public complaint continues in spite of the heart-ening oracle, hope begins to emerge. God is their only hope to win the battle. The plea for help brings with it an as-surance of ultimate victory.

PSALM 61

To the chief Musician upon Neginah,
A Psalm *of David*

HEAR my cry, O God; attend unto my prayer. ² From the end of the earth will I cry unto thee, when my heart is overwhelmed: lead me to the rock *that* is higher than I. ³ For thou hast been a shelter for me, *and* a strong tower from the enemy. ⁴ I will abide in thy tabernacle for ever: I will trust in the covert of thy wings. Se-lah. ⁵ For thou, O God, hast heard my vows: thou hast given *me* the heritage of those that fear thy name.

⁶ Thou wilt prolong the king's life: *and* his years as many generations. ⁷ He shall abide before God for ever: O prepare mercy and truth, *which* may preserve him. ⁸ So will I sing praise unto thy name for ever, that I may daily perform my vows.

61 O GOD, LISTEN to me! Hear my prayer! ² For wherever I am, though far away at the ends of the earth, I will cry to you for help. When my heart is faint and overwhelmed, lead me to the mighty, towering Rock of safety. ³ For you are my refuge, a high tower where my enemies can never reach me. ⁴ I shall live forever in your tabernacle; oh, to be safe beneath the shelter of your wings! ⁵ For you have heard my vows, O God, to praise you every day, and you have given me the blessings you reserve for those who reverence your name.

⁶ You will give me added years of life, as rich and full as those of many generations, all packed into one. ⁷ And I shall live before the Lord forever. Oh, send your lovingkindness and truth to guard and watch over me, ⁸ and I will praise your name continually, fulfilling my vow of praising you each day.

PSALM 62

To the chief Musician, to Jeduthun, A Psalm of David

TRULY my soul waiteth upon God: from him *cometh* my salvation. ² He only *is* my rock and my salvation; *he is* my defence; I shall not be greatly moved.

³ How long will ye imagine mischief against a man? ye shall be slain all of you: as a bowing wall *shall ye be, and as* a tottering fence. ⁴ They only consult to cast *him* down from his excellency: they delight in lies: they bless with their mouth, but they curse inwardly. Se-lah. ⁵ My soul, wait thou only upon God; for my expectation *is* from him. ⁶ He only *is* my rock and my salvation: *he is* my defence; I shall not be moved.

⁷ In God *is* my salvation and my glory: the rock of my strength, *and* my refuge, *is* in God. ⁸ Trust in him at all times; ye people, pour out your heart before him: God *is* a refuge for us. Se-lah. ⁹ Surely men of low degree *are* vanity, *and* men of high degree *are* a lie: to be laid in the balance, they *are* altogether *lighter* than vanity.

¹⁰ Trust not in oppression, and become not vain in robbery: if riches increase, set not your heart *upon them.*

62 I STAND SILENTLY before the Lord, waiting for him to rescue me. For salvation comes from him alone. ² Yes, he alone is my Rock, my rescuer, defense and fortress. Why then should I be tense with fear when troubles come?

³,⁴ But what is this? They pick on me at a time when my throne is tottering; they plot my death and use lies and deceit to try to force me from the throne. They are so friendly to my face while cursing in their hearts! ⁵ But I stand silently before the Lord, waiting for him to rescue me. For salvation comes from him alone. ⁶ Yes, he alone is my Rock, my rescuer, defense and fortress—why then should I be tense with fear when troubles come?

⁷ My protection and success come from God alone. He is my refuge, a Rock where no enemy can reach me. ⁸ O my people, trust him all the time. Pour out your longings before him, for he can help! ⁹ The greatest of men, or the lowest—both alike are nothing in his sight. They weigh less than air on scales.

¹⁰,¹¹ Don't become rich by extortion and robbery. And don't let the rich men be

Psalm 61. Prayer for a King

This psalm is the earnest lamentation and appeal of one who is away from Jerusalem. **The end of the earth** need not refer to a remote area, because the distance is magnified by the yearning to be back home. Although an enforced exile may be the lot of the psalmist, it is not required by this phrase.

1-4. A Petition for Personal Restoration. **Hear my cry, O God.** In despair the psalmist pleads for the sense of God's presence and protection. He desires to experience the safety of a rock that is too high for him to climb without God's help. Because of God's past blessings, he finds assurance for the present and hope for the future.

5-8. A Prayer for Royal Blessing. **Thou . . . hast heard.** The writer expresses deep confidence that his prayer for the welfare of the reigning king will be answered. Verses 6,7 can be viewed as a statement of his previous prayer or translated as a present request — **Prolong the king's life. . . .** Note that the writer prays for three things — for prolonged life, for an extended reign, and for the blessings of mercy and truth. His confidence that God will answer makes him determine to pay daily vows of thanksgiving.

Psalm 62. An Unshakable Faith

There is an element of lamentation in the opening verses of this outstanding song of passive trust, and a didactic purpose in the closing verses. However, the dominant note of trust and confidence is evident throughout. The author is a man of authority whose position is threatened. Though his opponents are from various walks of life, he views them all as utterly worthless.

1-4. The Only Salvation. **From him my salvation.** The key to the serene confidence is probably tied up with the Hebrew particle, *'ak*, which occurs six times in this brief psalm, three times as the first word of a stanza. The particle may be translated "surely," "but," "alone," or better, "only." *Only* for God does he wait, while *only* God is his rock, salvation, and defense. His persecutors are scheming against him all the time.

5-8. The Only Hope. **My expectation from him.** The words of verses 1 and 2 are slightly altered to form an introduction to this stanza. The writer calls himself to calm remembrance of the key to his peace. Again it is *only* God upon whom he waits and in whom he trusts. In this stillness of humble resignation he adds hope or expectation to the certainty of salvation.

9-12. The Only Strength. **Strength belongeth unto God.** Although he begins the stanza with the same Hebrew particle, *'ak*, it is not until verse 12 that he presents the basis of this phase of his inner peace. His enemies trust in oppression, robbery, and riches, but he has received the twice-spoken oracle describing God as the only strength and mercy worth having.

NOTES

11 God hath spoken once; twice have I heard this; that power *belongeth* unto God. 12 Also unto thee, O Lord, *belongeth* mercy: for thou renderest to every man according to his work.

PSALM 63

A Psalm of David, when he was in the wilderness of Judah

O GOD, thou *art* my God; early will I seek thee: my soul thirsteth for thee, my flesh longeth for thee in a dry and thirsty land, where no water is; 2 To see thy power and thy glory, so *as* I have seen thee in the sanctuary. 3 Because thy lovingkindness *is* better than life, my lips shall praise thee. 4 Thus will I bless thee while I live: I will lift up my hands in thy name. 5 My soul shall be satisfied as *with* marrow and fatness; and my mouth shall praise *thee* with joyful lips:

6 When I remember thee upon my bed, *and* meditate on thee in the *night* watches. 7 Because thou hast been my help, therefore in the shadow of thy wings will I rejoice. 8 My soul followeth hard after thee: thy right hand upholdeth me. 9 But those *that* seek my soul, to destroy *it,* shall go into the lower parts of the earth. 10 They shall fall by the sword: they shall be a portion for foxes. 11 But the king shall rejoice in God; every one that sweareth by him shall glory: but the mouth of them that speak lies shall be stopped.

PSALM 64

To the chief Musician, A Psalm of David

HEAR my voice, O God, in my prayer: preserve my life from fear of the enemy. 2 Hide me from the secret counsel of the wicked; from the insurrection of the workers of iniquity: 3 Who whet their tongue like a sword, *and* bend *their bows to shoot* their arrows, *even* bitter words: 4 That they may shoot in secret at the perfect: suddenly do they shoot at him, and fear not. 5 They encourage themselves *in* an evil matter: they commune of laying snares privily; they say, Who shall see

proud. 12 He is loving and kind and rewards each one of us according to the work we do for him.

A Psalm of David when he was hiding in the wilderness of Judea.

63 O GOD, MY God! How I search for you! How I thirst for you in this parched and weary land where there is no water. How I long to find you! 2 How I wish I could go into your sanctuary to see your strength and glory, 3 for your love and kindness are better to me than life itself. How I praise you! 4 I will bless you as long as I live, lifting up my hands to you in prayer. 5 At last I shall be fully satisfied; I will praise you with great joy.

6 I lie awake at night thinking of you— 7 of how much you have helped me—and how I rejoice through the night beneath the protecting shadow of your wings. 8 I follow close behind you, protected by your strong right arm. 9 But those plotting to destroy me shall go down to the depths of hell. 10 They are doomed to die by the sword, to become the food of jackals. 11 But I will rejoice in God. All who trust in him exult, while liars shall be silenced.

64 LORD, LISTEN TO my complaint: Oh, preserve my life from the conspiracy of these wicked men, these gangs of criminals. 3 They cut me down with sharpened tongues; they aim their bitter words like arrows straight at my heart. 4 They shoot from ambush at the innocent. Suddenly the deed is done, yet they are not afraid. 5 They encourage each other to do evil. They meet in secret to set their traps. "He will never

Psalm 63. A Thirst for God

Like the preceding psalm, this is a song of trust, based upon a close relation to God. The psalmist is obviously in exile or banished from his home. His deep desire to share in public worship is partially satisfied by his fellowship with God in meditation. This song is an excellent example of the highest type of personal and spiritual worship in Israel.

1-4. Longing for God. My soul thirsteth . . . my flesh longeth. After positively identifying his life with God, the psalmist expresses his deepest desire. The whole of his being yearns for communion with God. His life is as dry as a thirsty desert without this fellowship. God's loving-kindness is more important to him than existence itself and causes life-long praise.

5-8. Remembering Past Mercies. When I remember thee. Recalling his experiences of worship, he likens the soul satisfaction of nightly meditation to **the marrow and fatness** of the sacrifices. In the stillness of the three night watches, he praises and rejoices because God has been near as his Helper.

9-11. Hoping for Retribution. They shall fall. The enemies of the psalmist here come into view for the first time. This is not an imprecatory prayer against them, but a quiet confidence that righteous retribution will result. The speaker feels sure that they will die by the sword, their bodies will lie unburied for jackals to eat, and they will find themselves in Sheol.

Psalm 64. An Appeal for Assistance

The familiar plea for help is heard again in this individual lament. The plight of the psalmist is desperate, although there is no reference here to physical harm. His enemies scheme and slander secretly rather than coming out in open opposition. After enumerating and describing their wicked deeds, the psalmist expresses his certainty that God will judge them rightly.

1-6. The Petition for Protection. Hear my voice . . . preserve my life. The appeal begins with the request that God will hear his **complaint** (not *prayer*) and will act to give him protection from fear. He describes the machinations of his conspiring enemies in a series of metaphors normally used to portray the hunting of wild animals.

them? [6] They search out iniquities; they accomplish a diligent search: both the inward *thought* of every one *of them,* and the heart, *is* deep.

[7] But God shall shoot at them *with* an arrow; suddenly shall they be wounded. [8] So they shall make their own tongue to fall upon themselves: all that see them shall flee away. [9] And all men shall fear, and shall declare the work of God; for they shall wisely consider of his doing. [10] The righteous shall be glad in the Lord, and shall trust in him; and all the upright in heart shall glory.

PSALM 65

To the chief Musician, A Psalm and *Song of David*

PRAISE waiteth for thee, O God, in Sion: and unto thee shall the vow be performed. [2] O thou that hearest prayer, unto thee shall all flesh come. [3] Iniquities prevail against me: *as for* our transgressions, thou shalt purge them away. [4] Blessed *is the man whom* thou choosest, and causest to approach *unto thee, that* he may dwell in thy courts: we shall be satisfied with the goodness of thy house, *even* of thy holy temple. [5] *By* terrible things in righteousness wilt thou answer us, O God of our salvation; *who art* the confidence of all the ends of the earth, and of them that are afar off *upon* the sea:

[6] Which by his strength setteth fast the mountains; *being* girded with power: [7] Which stilleth the noise of the seas, the noise of their waves, and the tumult of the people. [8] They also that dwell in the uttermost parts are afraid at thy tokens: thou makest the outgoings of the morning and evening to rejoice. [9] Thou visitest the earth, and waterest it: thou greatly enrichest it with the river of God, *which* is full of water: thou preparest them corn, when thou hast so provided for it. [10] Thou waterest the ridges thereof abundantly: thou settlest the furrows thereof: thou makest it soft with showers: thou blessest the springing thereof. [11] Thou crownest the year with thy goodness; and thy paths drop fatness. [12] They drop *upon* the pastures of the wilderness: and the

notice them here," they say. [6] They keep a sharp lookout for opportunities of crime. They spend long hours with all their endless evil thoughts and plans.

[7] But God himself will shoot them down. Suddenly his arrow will pierce them. [8] They will stagger backward, destroyed by those they spoke against. All who see it happening will scoff at them. [9] Then everyone shall stand in awe and confess the greatness of the miracles of God; at last they will realize what amazing things he does. [10] And the godly shall rejoice in the Lord, and trust and praise him.

65 O GOD IN Zion, we wait before you in silent praise, and thus fulfill our vow. And because you answer prayer, all mankind will come to you with their requests. [3] Though sins fill our hearts, you forgive them all. [4] How greatly to be envied are those you have chosen to come and live with you within the holy tabernacle courts! What joys await us among all the good things there. [5] With dread deeds and awesome power you will defend us from our enemies, O God who saves us. You are the only hope of all mankind throughout the world and far away upon the sea.

[6] He formed the mountains by his mighty strength. [7] He quiets the raging oceans and all the world's clamor. [8] In the farthest corners of the earth the glorious acts of God shall startle everyone. The dawn and sunset shout for joy! [9] He waters the earth to make it fertile. The rivers of God will not run dry! He prepares the earth for his people and sends them rich harvests of grain. [10] He waters the furrows with abundant rain. Showers soften the earth, melting the clods and causing seeds to sprout across the land. [11,12] Then he crowns it all with green, lush pastures in the wilder-

7-10. The Certainty of Judgment. But God. The change is swift and abrupt to a statement of prophetic authority. The psalmist declares that the evil deeds of the enemies shall turn back on them. Then men will recognize the hand of God at work. The sorrow of heart finally turns to gladness when the writer considers the fate of the righteous.

Psalm 65. A Hymn of Thanksgiving

As a thanksgiving psalm this is a remarkable review of God's gracious dealings with the children of men. A spirit of universalism breaks the bounds of narrow nationalism in Israel. This hymn was closely connected with a thanksgiving festival at the Temple, either composed for or inspired by such an occasion.

1-4. Praise for God's Favor. Praise waiteth for thee. As evidenced by the ancient versions, this can better be rendered *praise is seemly* or *fitting.* Praise is voiced for God's answer to prayer, his forgiveness of sin, and his spiritual favor. The universal note is strong in that **all flesh** is included.

5-8. Praise for God's Power. By terrible things in righteousness. God's deeds are pictured as awe-inspiring and righteous, even to men at the ends of the earth. His dominion in creation and his power to still storms are but two illustrations of his sovereignty over the earth.

9-13. Praise for God's Harvest. Thou visitest the earth, and waterest it. The aforementioned praise leads up to the primary praise because of the harvest season. It is clearly God who watered the earth, prepared the seed, and made ready the soil. All this brought about a record harvest — **Thou crownest the year.** There is such happiness that the hills, pastures, and valleys join in the rejoicing.

NOTES

113

little hills rejoice on every side. ¹³ The pastures are clothed with flocks; the valleys also are covered over with corn; they shout for joy, they also sing.

ness; hillsides blossom with joy. ¹³ The pastures are filled with flocks of sheep, and the valleys are carpeted with grain. All the world shouts with joy, and sings.

PSALM 66

To the chief Musician, A Song or Psalm
MAKE a joyful noise unto God, all ye lands: ² Sing forth the honour of his name: make his praise glorious.

³ Say unto God, How terrible *art thou in* thy works! through the greatness of thy power shall thine enemies submit themselves unto thee. ⁴ All the earth shall worship thee, and shall sing unto thee; they shall sing *to* thy name. Se-lah.
⁵ Come and see the works of God: *he is* terrible *in his* doing toward the children of men. ⁶ He turned the sea into dry *land:* they went through the flood on foot: there did we rejoice in him.

⁷ He ruleth by his power for ever; his eyes behold the nations: let not the rebellious exalt themselves. Se-lah.

⁸ O bless our God, ye people, and make the voice of his praise to be heard: ⁹ Which holdeth our soul in life, and suffereth not our feet to be moved. ¹⁰ For thou, O God, hast proved us: thou hast tried us, as silver is tried. ¹¹ Thou broughtest us into the net; thou laidst affliction upon our loins. ¹² Thou hast caused men to ride over our heads; we went through fire and through water: but thou broughtest us out into a wealthy *place.*

¹³ I will go into thy house with burnt offerings: I will pay thee my vows, ¹⁴ Which my lips have uttered, and my mouth hath spoken, when I was in trouble. ¹⁵ I will offer unto thee burnt sacrifices of fatlings, with the incense of rams; I will offer bullocks with goats. Se-lah.

¹⁶ Come *and* hear, all ye that fear God, and I will declare what he hath done for my soul. ¹⁷ I cried unto him with my mouth, and he was extolled with my tongue. ¹⁸ If I regard iniquity in my heart, the Lord will not hear *me:* ¹⁹ *But* verily God hath heard *me;* he hath attended to the voice of my prayer.

²⁰ Blessed *be* God, which hath not turned away my prayer, nor his mercy from me.

66 SING TO THE Lord, all the earth! ² Sing of his glorious name! Tell the world how wonderful he is.

³ How awe-inspiring are your deeds, O God! How great your power! No wonder your enemies surrender! ⁴ All the earth shall worship you and sing of your glories. ⁵ Come, see the glorious things God has done. What marvelous miracles happen to his people! ⁶ He made a dry road through the sea for them. They went across on foot. What excitement and joy there was that day!

⁷ Because of his great power he rules forever. He watches every movement of the nations. O rebel lands, he will deflate your pride.

⁸ Let everyone bless God and sing his praises, ⁹ for he holds our lives in his hands. And he holds our feet to the path. ¹⁰ You have purified us with fire, O Lord, like silver in a crucible. ¹¹ You captured us in your net and laid great burdens on our backs. ¹² You sent troops to ride across our broken bodies. We went through fire and flood. But in the end, you brought us into wealth and great abundance.

¹³ Now I have come to your Temple with burnt offerings to pay my vows. ¹⁴ For when I was in trouble I promised you many offerings. ¹⁵ That is why I am bringing you these fat he-goats, rams and calves. The smoke of their sacrifice shall rise before you.

¹⁶ Come and hear, all of you who reverence the Lord, and I will tell you what he did for me: ¹⁷ For I cried to him for help, with praises ready on my tongue. ¹⁸ He would not have listened if I had not confessed my sins. ¹⁹ But he listened! He heard my prayer! He paid attention to it!

²⁰ Blessed be God who didn't turn away when I was praying, and didn't refuse me his kindness and love.

Psalm 66. A Song of Deliverance

Psalm 66 is both nationalistic and individualistic in its presentation of thanksgiving. Verses 1-12 relate to the nation but also reach out to the world, while verses 13-20 refer to the personal life of the psalmist. Some commentators see here two distinct psalms which have been joined. However, the corporate experience of the nation forms an excellent background for the individual experience of the author.

1-4. The Call for Praise. **Make a joyful noise . . . make his praise glorious.** The psalmist takes in the whole world in one sweep as he sounds the call and gives the proper words for the expression of true praise.

5-12. The Testimony of History. **Come and see.** The events of the exodus from Egypt and Israel's early history were awe-inspiring enough to call forth the praise of God by the peoples of the earth. More recent evidences of deliverance are also included to justify this universal call to praise.

13-20. The Experience of the Psalmist. **Come and hear.** Those who fear God are called to witness the payment of the writer's vow in the Temple. His offerings and sacrifices are supplemented by his public testimony of what God has done for him.

PSALM 67

To the chief Musician on Neginoth, A Psalm or *Song*

GOD be merciful unto us, and bless us; *and* cause his face to shine upon us; Se-lah.

² That thy way may be known upon earth, thy saving health among all nations. ³ Let the people praise thee, O God; let all the people praise thee. ⁴ O let the nations be glad and sing for joy: for thou shalt judge the people righteously, and govern the nations upon earth. Se-lah. ⁵ Let the people praise thee, O God; let all the people praise thee. ⁶ *Then* shall the earth yield her increase; *and* God, *even* our own God, shall bless us. ⁷ God shall bless us; and all the ends of the earth shall fear him.

67 O GOD, IN mercy bless us; let your face beam with joy as you look down at us.

² Send us around the world with the news of your saving power and your eternal plan for all mankind. ³ How everyone throughout the earth will praise the Lord! ⁴ How glad the nations will be, singing for joy because you are their King and will give true justice to their people! ⁵ Praise God, O world! May all the peoples of the earth give thanks to you. ⁶,⁷ For the earth has yielded abundant harvests. God, even our own God, will bless us. And peoples from remotest lands will worship him.

PSALM 68

To the chief Musician, A Psalm or *Song of David*

LET God arise, let his enemies be scattered: let them also that hate him flee before him. ² As smoke is driven away, *so* drive *them* away: as wax melteth before the fire, *so* let the wicked perish at the presence of God.

³ But let the righteous be glad; let them rejoice before God: yea, let them exceedingly rejoice. ⁴ Sing unto God, sing praises to his name: extol him that rideth upon the heavens by his name JAH, and rejoice before him. ⁵ A father of the fatherless, and a judge of the widows, *is* God in his holy habitation. ⁶ God setteth the solitary in families: he bringeth out those which are bound with chains: but the rebellious dwell in a dry *land*.

⁷ O God, when thou wentest forth before thy people, when thou didst march through the wilderness; Se-lah: ⁸ The earth shook, the heavens also dropped at the presence of God: *even* Si-nai itself *was moved* at the presence of God, the God of Israel. ⁹ Thou, O God, didst send a plentiful rain, whereby thou didst confirm thine inheritance, when it was weary. ¹⁰ Thy congregation hath dwelt therein: thou, O God, hast prepared of thy goodness for the poor.

68 ARISE, O GOD, and scatter all your enemies! Chase them away! ² Drive them off like smoke before the wind; melt them like wax in fire! So let the wicked perish at the presence of God.

³ But may the godly man exult. May he rejoice and be merry. ⁴ Sing praises to the Lord! Raise your voice in song to him who rides upon the clouds! Jehovah is his name —oh, rejoice in his presence. ⁵ He is a father to the fatherless; he gives justice to the widows, for he is holy. ⁶ He gives families to the lonely, and releases prisoners from jail, singing with joy! But for rebels there is famine and distress.

⁷ O God, when you led your people through the wilderness, ⁸ the earth trembled and the heavens shook. Mount Sinai quailed before you—the God of Israel. ⁹,¹⁰ You sent abundant rain upon your land, O God, to refresh it in its weariness! There your people lived, for you gave them this home when they were destitute.

Psalm 67. Hymn for a Harvest Festival

This brief psalm of thanksgiving is remarkable for its beauty, its simplicity, and its world outlook. The occasion for its use is probably to be seen in verse 6, where the climax is expressed in terms of harvest thanksgiving. The hymn may well have been a part of the music for the Feast of Pentecost or the Feast of Tabernacles.

1,2. The Purpose in God's Blessings. That thy way may be known. The familiar priestly blessing of Num 6:24-26 is adapted for use in the first person in order to present the basis of Israel's greater mission. God's gracious dealings are viewed as the means by which all people are led to turn to God. Israel is to be the witness by which the knowledge of God is spread abroad.

3,4. The Call for Universal Praise. Let the people praise thee. The refrain in verses 3 and 5 appears to be introductory, because of the presence of the *selâ* at the end of verse 4 and because of the general thought development. This call for joyful praise is based upon God's vindication and guidance of the nations. This is a striking universalistic note.

5-7. The Hope of Continued Blessing. God shall bless us. The psalmist repeats the meaningful refrain to correspond to the introductory pleas of verses 1 and 3. The declaration that the earth has yielded its increase (RSV) appears to be an obvious connection of the psalm with the joyous harvest festivals. Verse 7 amplifies the thought of verse 1 expressing hope for God's continued blessing in order that Israel's mission may be completed.

Psalm 68. God's Victorious March

This psalm is composed of such diverse elements as to defy classification. Verses 1-18 are basically an ode, while verses 19-35 resemble more closely a hymn. Several commentators have recognized a great number of forms, classifying it as a medley of songs and hymns. The dominant theme appears to be God's march as victor both past, present, and future. The background of the material is to be seen in the totality of Israel's history, rather than in a specific deliverance.

1-6. God's Appearance as Leader. Let God arise. This may be a plea or a reference to his appearance ("God ariseth!"). The basis for this language is found in the ancient signal for lifting up the ark (cf. Num 10:35). The righteous are to rejoice at his appearance while the wicked will melt away.

7-18. God's March As Deliverer. When thou didst march through the wilderness. The picture is still that of a leader out in front of his people, delivering them by special acts of mercy. The march begins with the deliverance from Egypt and ends with God dwelling in Zion. Cf. Eph 4:8ff., where Paul applies verse 18 to the ministry of the risen Christ.

NOTES

11 The Lord gave the word: great *was* the company of those that published *it*. 12 Kings of armies did flee apace: and she that tarried at home divided the spoil. 13 Though ye have lien among the pots, *yet shall ye be as* the wings of a dove covered with silver, and her feathers with yellow gold. 14 When the Almighty scattered kings in it, it was *white* as snow in Sal-mon.

15 The hill of God *is as* the hill of Ba-shan; an high hill *as* the hill of Ba-shan. 16 Why leap ye, ye high hills? *this is* the hill *which* God desireth to dwell in; yea, the Lord will dwell *in it* for ever. 17 The chariots of God *are* twenty thousand, *even* thousands of angels: the Lord *is* among them, *as in* Si-nai in the holy *place*. 18 Thou hast ascended on high, thou hast led captivity captive: thou hast received gifts for men; yea, *for* the rebellious also, that the Lord God might dwell *among them*.

19 Blessed *be* the Lord, *who* daily loadeth us *with benefits, even* the God of our salvation. Se-lah.

20 *He that is* our God *is* the God of salvation; and unto God the Lord *belong* the issues from death. 21 But God shall wound the head of his enemies, *and* the hairy scalp of such an one as goeth on still in his trespasses. 22 The Lord said, I will bring again from Ba-shan, I will bring *my people* again from the depths of the sea: 23 That thy foot may be dipped in the blood of *thine* enemies, *and* the tongue of thy dogs in the same.

24 They have seen thy goings, O God; *even* the goings of my God, my King, in the sanctuary. 25 The singers went before, the players on instruments *followed* after; among *them were* the damsels playing with timbrels. 26 Bless ye God in the congregations, *even* the Lord, from the fountain of Israel. 27 There *is* little Benjamin *with* their ruler, the princes of Judah *and* their council, the princes of Zeb-u-lun, *and* the princes of Naph-ta-li. 28 Thy God hath commanded thy strength: strengthen, O God, that which thou hast wrought for us.

29 Because of thy temple at Jerusalem shall kings bring presents unto thee.

11,12,13 The Lord speaks. The enemy flees. The women at home cry out the happy news: "The armies that came to destroy us have fled!" Now all the women of Israel are dividing the booty. See them sparkle with jewels of silver and gold, covered all over as wings cover doves! 14 God scattered their enemies like snowflakes melting in the forests of Zalmon.

15,16 O mighty mountains in Bashan! O splendid many-peaked ranges! Well may you look with envy at Mount Zion, the mount where God has chosen to live forever. 17 Surrounded by unnumbered chariots, the Lord moves on from Mount Sinai and comes to his holy temple high upon Mount Zion. 18 He ascends the heights, leading many captives in his train. He receives gifts for men, even those who once were rebels. God will live among us here.

19 What a glorious Lord! He who daily bears our burdens also gives us our salvation.

20 He frees us! He rescues us from death. 21 But he will crush his enemies, for they refuse to leave their guilty, stubborn ways. 22 The Lord says, "Come," to all his people's enemies; they are hiding on Mount Hermon's highest slopes and deep within the sea! 23 His people must destroy them. Cover your feet with their blood; dogs will eat them.

24 The procession of God my King moves onward to the sanctuary— 25 singers in front, musicians behind, girls playing the timbrels in between. 26 Let all the people of Israel praise the Lord, who is Israel's fountain. 27 The little tribe of Benjamin leads the way. The princes and elders of Judah, and the princes of Zebulun and Naphtali are right behind. 28 Summon your might; display your strength, O God, for you have done such mighty things for us.

29 The kings of the earth are bringing their gifts to your temple in Jerusalem.

30 Rebuke the company of spearmen, the multitude of the bulls, with the calves of the people, *till every one* submit himself with pieces of silver: scatter thou the people *that* delight in war. 31 Princes shall come out of Egypt; E-thi-o-pi-a shall soon stretch out her hands unto God. 32 Sing unto God, ye kingdoms of the earth; O sing praises unto the Lord; Se-lah: 33 To him that rideth upon the heavens of heavens, *which were* of old; lo, he doth send out his voice, *and that* a mighty voice.

34 Ascribe ye strength unto God: his excellency *is* over Israel, and his strength *is* in the clouds. 35 O God, *thou art* terrible out of thy holy places: the God of Israel *is* he that giveth strength and power unto *his* people. Blessed *be* God.

30 Rebuke our enemies, O Lord. Bring them—submissive, tax in hand. Scatter all who delight in war. 31 Egypt will send gifts of precious metals. Ethiopia will stretch out her hands to God in adoration. 32 Sing to the Lord, O kingdoms of the earth—sing praises to the Lord, 33 to him who rides upon the ancient heavens, whose mighty voice thunders from the sky.

34 Power belongs to God! His majesty shines down on Israel; his strength is mighty in the heavens. 35 What awe we feel, kneeling here before him in the sanctuary. The God of Israel gives strength and mighty power to his people. Blessed be God!

PSALM 69

To the chief Musician upon Shoshannim, A Psalm of David

SAVE me, O God; for the waters are come in unto *my* soul. 2 I sink in deep mire, where *there is* no standing: I am come into deep waters, where the floods overflow me. 3 I am weary of my crying: my throat is dried: mine eyes fail while I wait for my God. 4 They that hate me without a cause are more than the hairs of mine head: they that would destroy me, *being* mine enemies wrongfully, are mighty: then I restored *that* which I took not away.

5 O God, thou knowest my foolishness; and my sins are not hid from thee. 6 Let not them that wait on thee, O Lord God of hosts, be ashamed for my sake: let not those that seek thee be confounded for my sake, O God of Israel. 7 Because for thy sake I have borne reproach; shame hath covered my face. 8 I am become a stranger unto my brethren, and an alien unto my mother's children. 9 For the zeal of thine house hath eaten me up; and the reproaches of them that reproached thee are fallen upon me. 10 When I wept, *and chastened* my soul with fasting, that was to my reproach. 11 I made sackcloth also my garment; and I became a proverb to them. 12 They that sit in the gate speak against me; and I *was* the song of the drunk-

69 SAVE ME, O my God. The floods have risen. Deeper and deeper I sink in the mire; the waters rise around me. 3 I have wept until I am exhausted; my throat is dry and hoarse; my eyes are swollen with weeping, waiting for my God to act. 4 I cannot even count all those who hate me without cause. They are influential men, these who plot to kill me though I am innocent. They demand that I be punished for what I didn't do.

5 O God, you know so well how stupid I am, and you know all my sins. 6 O Lord God of the armies of heaven, don't let me be a stumbling block to those who trust in you. O God of Israel, don't let me cause them to be confused, 7 though I am mocked and cursed and shamed for your sake. 8 Even my own brothers pretend they don't know me! 9 My zeal for God and his work burns hot within me. And because I advocate your cause, your enemies insult me even as they insult you. 10 How they scoff and mock me when I mourn and fast before the Lord! 11 How they talk about me when I wear sackcloth to show my humiliation and sorrow for my sins! 12 I am the talk of the town and the song of the drunkards.

God. God is called upon to command his strength in a final act of power. After the assertion of ultimate victory, all the nations are called upon to exalt God as Lord through praise.

Psalm 69. A Prayer for Retribution

An individual in the depths of despair and agony here laments his case. His persecution is viewed as a result of his religious convictions. With fervor he pleads for retribution upon his persecutors. Because of his worried state of mind, his mood changes often. However, his despair becomes triumph and his complaint becomes praise after he voices his innermost feelings.

1-6. The Basic Complaint. Save me. . . . I sink in deep mire. After crying out for help in one brief phrase, the psalmist describes his plight. The words **waters, mire, deep waters,** and **floods** are all used to show the extreme nature of his trouble. His enemies are numerous, hateful, and powerful. He is greatly concerned that his reproach not injure other devout men who look to him as an example.

7-12. The Underlying Cause. Because for thy sake. It is because of his loyalty, faithfulness, and zeal that he has suffered. He appears to have fought against the liberal and popular forms of religious expression in his day. For all this, he has become the laughing-stock of the community and the jest of the drunkards.

121

ards. [13] But as for me, my prayer *is* unto thee, O Lord, *in* an acceptable time: O God, in the multitude of thy mercy hear me, in the truth of thy salvation. [14] Deliver me out of the mire, and let me not sink: let me be delivered from them that hate me, and out of the deep waters.

[15] Let not the waterflood overflow me, neither let the deep swallow me up, and let not the pit shut her mouth upon me. [16] Hear me, O Lord; for thy lovingkindness *is* good: turn unto me according to the multitude of thy tender mercies. [17] And hide not thy face from thy servant; for I am in trouble: hear me speedily. [18] Draw nigh unto my soul, *and* redeem it: deliver me because of mine enemies. [19] Thou hast known my reproach, and my shame, and my dishonour: mine adversaries *are* all before thee.

[20] Reproach hath broken my heart; and I am full of heaviness: and I looked *for some* to take pity, but *there was* none; and for comforters, but I found none. [21] They gave me also gall for my meat; and in my thirst they gave me vinegar to drink. [22] Let their table become a snare before them: and *that which should have been* for *their* welfare, *let it become* a trap. [23] Let their eyes be darkened, that they see not; and make their loins continually to shake. [24] Pour out thine indignation upon them, and let thy wrathful anger take hold of them. [25] Let their habitation be desolate; *and* let none dwell in their tents. [26] For they persecute *him* whom thou hast smitten; and they talk to the grief of those whom thou hast wounded. [27] Add iniquity unto their iniquity: and let them not come into thy righteousness. [28] Let them be blotted out of the book of the living, and not be written with the righteous.

[29] But I *am* poor and sorrowful: let thy salvation, O God, set me up on high. [30] I will praise the name of God with a song, and will magnify him with thanksgiving. [31] *This* also shall please the Lord better than an ox *or* bullock that hath horns and hoofs. [32] The humble shall see *this, and* be glad: and your heart shall live that seek God. [33] For the Lord heareth the poor, and despiseth not his prisoners.

[13] But I keep right on praying to you, Lord. For now is the time—you are bending down to hear! You are ready with a plentiful supply of love and kindness. Now answer my prayer and rescue me as you promised. [14] Pull me out of this mire. Don't let me sink in. Rescue me from those who hate me, and from these deep waters I am in.

[15] Don't let the floods overwhelm me, or the ocean swallow me; save me from the pit that threatens me. [16] O Jehovah, answer my prayers, for your lovingkindness is wonderful; your mercy is so plentiful, so tender and so kind. [17] Don't hide from me, for I am in deep trouble. Quick! Come and save me. [18] Come, Lord, and rescue me. Ransom me from all my enemies. [19] You know how they talk about me, and how they so shamefully dishonor me. You see them all and know what each has said.

[20] Their contempt has broken my heart; my spirit is heavy within me. If even one would show some pity, if even one would comfort me! [21] For food they gave me poison; for my awful thirst they offered me vinegar. [22] Let their joys turn to ashes and their peace disappear; [23] let darkness, blindness and great feebleness be theirs. [24] Pour out your fury upon them; consume them with the fierceness of your anger. [25] Let their homes be desolate and abandoned. [26] For they persecute the one you have smitten, and scoff at the pain of the one you have pierced. [27] Pile their sins high and do not overlook them. [28] Let these men be blotted from the list of the living; do not give them the joys of life with the righteous.

[29] But rescue me, O God, from my poverty and pain. [30] Then I will praise God with my singing! My thanks will be his praise— [31] that will please him more than sacrificing a bullock or an ox. [32] The humble shall see their God at work for them. No wonder they will be so glad! All who seek for God shall live in joy. [33] For Jehovah hears the cries of his needy ones, and does not look the other way.

13-18. The Intensified Appeal. My prayer is unto thee. In terse and rapid pleas, he asks for deliverance and vindication. His previous complaint is repeated but becomes secondary to his request for immediate assistance.

19-28. The Bitter Imprecation. Pour out thine indignation upon them. Each of these requests for retribution is based upon God's entering into the bitter indignation of the psalmist. These are God's enemies as well as his. The fierce climax is reached in the plea that they be completely obliterated from the book of the living (cf. Ex 32:32; Phil 4:3; Rev 13:8; 20:15). The Gospel writers may well have had verse 21 in mind as they depicted the passion of Christ (Mt 27: 34; Mk 15:23; Jn 19:29).

29-36. The Assured Deliverance. Let thy salvation, O God, set me on high. The vow of thanksgiving which follows seems to presuppose an answer to this request for deliverance. It is interesting to note that the psalmist's views on sacrifice may account for some of his oppo-

NOTES

34 Let the heaven and earth praise him, the seas, and every thing that moveth therein. 35 For God will save Zion, and will build the cities of Judah: that they may dwell there, and have it in possession. 36 The seed also of his servants shall inherit it: and they that love his name shall dwell therein.

34 Praise him, all heaven and earth! Praise him, all the seas and everything in them! 35 For God will save Jerusalem; he rebuilds the cities of Judah. His people shall live in them and not be dispossessed. 36 Their children shall inherit the land; all who love his name shall live there safely.

PSALM 70

To the chief Musician, A Psalm *of David, to bring to remembrance*

MAKE *haste,* O God, to deliver me; make haste to help me, O Lord. 2 Let them be ashamed and confounded that seek after my soul: let them be turned backward, and put to confusion, that desire my hurt. 3 Let them be turned back for a reward of their shame that say, Aha, aha. 4 Let all those that seek thee rejoice and be glad in thee: and let such as love thy salvation say continually, Let God be magnified. 5 But I *am* poor and needy: make haste unto me, O God: thou *art* my help and my deliverer; O Lord, make no tarrying.

70 RESCUE ME, O God! Lord, hurry to my aid! 2,3 They are after my life, and delight in hurting me. Confuse them! Shame them! Stop them! Don't let them keep on mocking me! 4 But fill the followers of God with joy. Let those who love your salvation exclaim, "What a wonderful God he is!" 5 But I am in deep trouble. Rush to my aid, for only you can help and save me. O Lord, don't delay.

PSALM 71

IN thee, O Lord, do I put my trust: let me never be put to confusion. 2 Deliver me in thy righteousness, and cause me to escape: incline thine ear unto me, and save me. 3 Be thou my strong habitation, whereunto I may continually resort: thou hast given commandment to save me; for thou *art* my rock and my fortress. 4 Deliver me, O my God, out of the hand of the wicked, out of the hand of the unrighteous and cruel man. 5 For thou *art* my hope, O Lord God: *thou art* my trust from my youth. 6 By thee have I been holden up from the womb: thou art he that took me out of my mother's bowels: my praise *shall be* continually of thee. 7 I am as a wonder unto many; but thou *art* my strong refuge. 8 Let my mouth be filled *with* thy praise *and with* thy honour all the day.

9 Cast me not off in the time of old age; forsake me not when my strength faileth. 10 For mine enemies speak against me; and they that lay wait for my soul take counsel together, 11 Saying, God hath forsaken him: persecute

71 LORD, YOU ARE my refuge! Don't let me down! 2 Save me from my enemies, for you are just! Rescue me! Bend down your ear and listen to my plea and save me. 3 Be to me a great protecting Rock, where I am always welcome, safe from all attacks. For you have issued the order to save me. 4 Rescue me, O God, from these unjust and cruel men. 5 O Lord, you alone are my hope; I've trusted you from childhood. 6 Yes, you have been with me from birth and have helped me constantly—no wonder I am always praising you! 7 My success—at which so many stand amazed—is because you are my mighty protector. 8 All day long I'll praise and honor you, O God, for all that you have done for me.

9 And now, in my old age, don't set me aside. Don't forsake me now when my strength is failing. 10 My enemies are whispering, 11 "God has forsaken him! Now we

sition. The psalm closes on a note of
intense praise as heaven and earth are
invited to join in the chorus.

Psalm 70. A Cry for Immediate Help

This psalm is an individual lament
which also occurs as part of Psalm 40.
Here the name for God has been changed
from *Yahweh* to *Elohim,* and some slight
variations in wording are evident. Its
presence as a separate psalm may indicate that it was found in both of the
basic collections already mentioned, or
that it was detached from Psalm 40 for
liturgical use in the Temple. (Cf. Ps
40:13-17 for added notes.)

Psalm 71. The Confidence of
an Aged Saint

Here is the lament of an individual
who has suffered great adversity in his
many years upon earth. Persecutions,
sickness, calamities, and trials have
added gray hairs to his head. Yet he
has maintained his close relation to God
since childhood. His appeal for help once
more is based upon the blessings of past
experience. His desire is to live long
enough to teach the present generation
something of what life has taught him.

1-3. His Confidence in God. **In thee,
O Lord, do I put my trust.** These words
are drawn by the psalmist from Psalm
31 as an expression of his deep confidence in God. He knows God to be his
refuge and **rock of safety.**

4-13. His Appeal for Deliverance. **Deliver me, O my God.** Although his enemies are quick to take advantage of his
weakness, God has **stayed** or *braced* him
since birth (cf. Ps 22:9,10). These enemies, who believe that God has forsaken
him, are rebuffed for their wrong interpretation of his affliction. His appeal is
based solely on his trust in God's power
and willingness to deliver him.

and take him; for *there is* none to deliver *him*. ¹² O God, be not far from me: O my God, make haste for my help. ¹³ Let them be confounded *and* consumed that are adversaries to my soul; let them be covered *with* reproach and dishonour that seek my hurt. ¹⁴ But I will hope continually, and will yet praise thee more and more. ¹⁵ My mouth shall shew forth thy righteousness *and* thy salvation all the day; for I know not the numbers *thereof*. ¹⁶ I will go in the strength of the Lord God: I will make mention of thy righteousness, *even* of thine only. ¹⁷ O God, thou hast taught me from my youth: and hitherto have I declared thy wondrous works. ¹⁸ Now also when I am old and greyheaded, O God, forsake me not; until I have shewed thy strength unto *this* generation, *and* thy power to every one *that* is to come. ¹⁹ Thy righteousness also, O God, *is* very high, who hast done great things: O God, who *is* like unto thee! ²⁰ *Thou,* which hast shewed me great and sore troubles, shalt quicken me again, and shalt bring me up again from the depths of the earth. ²¹ Thou shalt increase my greatness, and comfort me on every side. ²² I will also praise thee with the psaltery, *even* thy truth, O my God: unto thee will I sing with the harp, O thou Holy One of Israel. ²³ My lips shall greatly rejoice when I sing unto thee; and my soul, which thou hast redeemed. ²⁴ My tongue also shall talk of thy righteousness all the day long: for they are confounded, for they are brought unto shame, that seek my hurt.

can get him. There is no one to help him now!" ¹² O God, don't stay away! Come quickly! Help! ¹³ Destroy them! Cover them with failure and disgrace—these enemies of mine. ¹⁴ I will keep on expecting you to help me. I praise you more and more. ¹⁵ I cannot count the times when you have faithfully rescued me from danger. I will tell everyone how good you are, and of your constant, daily care. ¹⁶ I walk in the strength of the Lord God. I tell everyone that you alone are just and good. ¹⁷ O God, you have helped me from my earliest childhood—and I have constantly testified to others of the wonderful things you do. ¹⁸ And now that I am old and gray, don't forsake me. Give me time to tell this new generation (and their children too) about all your mighty miracles. ¹⁹ Your power and goodness, Lord, reach to the highest heavens. You have done such wonderful things. Where is there another God like you? ²⁰ You have let me sink down deep in desperate problems. But you will bring me back to life again, up from the depths of the earth. ²¹ You will give me greater honor than before, and turn again and comfort me.

²² I will praise you with music, telling of your faithfulness to all your promises, O Holy One of Israel. ²³ I will shout and sing your praises for redeeming me. ²⁴ I will talk to others all day long about your justice and your goodness. For all who tried to hurt me have been disgraced and dishonored.

PSALM 72

A Psalm *for* Solomon

GIVE the king thy judgments, O God, and thy righteousness unto the king's son. ² He shall judge thy people with righteousness, and thy poor with judgment. ³ The mountains shall bring peace to the people, and the little hills, by righteousness. ⁴ He shall judge the poor of the people, he shall save the children of the needy, and shall break in pieces the oppressor. ⁵ They shall fear thee as long as the sun and moon endure, throughout all generations.

72 O GOD, HELP the king to judge as you would, and help his son to walk in godliness. ² Help him to give justice to your people, even to the poor. ³ May the mountains and hills flourish in prosperity because of his good reign. ⁴ Help him to defend the poor and needy and to crush their oppressors. ⁵ May the poor and needy revere you constantly, as long as sun and moon continue in the skies! Yes, forever!

NOTES

14-16. His Hope in God. **But I will hope continually.** The turning point of the psalm is seen here, as appeal changes to hope and praise. The past gives way to the future.

17-21. His Testimony of Revelation. **Thou hast taught me.** On the basis of God's special teaching, he has been able to teach others. Now he asks for more time in order to show forth God's strength, power, and righteousness (vv. 18,19).

22-24. His Vow of Praise. **I will also praise thee.** The psalmist promises to praise with voice, instruments, lips, tongue, and his whole being. He is inwardly assured that he will be vindicated even as he requested (v. 13).

Psalm 72. Blessings on the King

This is the prayer of a loyal subject who desires God's richest blessing upon a young king. All of the hopes of the nation rest on this king, who is God's representative. The description was inspired by Solomon's reign or accession, but it may have been applied to more than one king in its historic use. There is throughout a picture of an ideal king, and thus the psalm has Messianic significance.

1-7. Prayer for Justice and Righteousness. **Give the king thy judgments, O God.** This prayer begins rightly with a plea for the two most important royal characteristics — justice and righteousness. It is on the basis of God's judgment that the king can act justly. The phrase, **the king's son,** probably refers to the new king as young, and parallels the first line of the verse. The verbs translated as futures may express prophetic confidence or be better rendered as prayers, i.e., *may he judge* or *let him judge.*

⁶ He shall come down like rain upon the mown grass: as showers *that* water the earth. ⁷ In his days shall the righteous flourish; and abundance of peace so long as the moon endureth. ⁸ He shall have dominion also from sea to sea, and from the river unto the ends of the earth. ⁹ They that dwell in the wilderness shall bow before him; and his enemies shall lick the dust. ¹⁰ The kings of Tarshish and of the isles shall bring presents: the kings of She-ba and Se-ba shall offer gifts. ¹¹ Yea, all kings shall fall down before him: all nations shall serve him.

¹² For he shall deliver the needy when he crieth; the poor also, and *him* that hath no helper. ¹³ He shall spare the poor and needy, and shall save the souls of the needy. ¹⁴ He shall redeem their soul from deceit and violence: and precious shall their blood be in his sight.

¹⁵ And he shall live, and to him shall be given of the gold of She-ba: prayer also shall be made for him continually; *and* daily shall he be praised. ¹⁶ There shall be an handful of corn in the earth upon the top of the mountains; the fruit thereof shall shake like Lebanon: and *they* of the city shall flourish like grass of the earth. ¹⁷ His name shall endure for ever: his name shall be continued as long as the sun: and *men* shall be blessed in him: all nations shall call him blessed.

¹⁸ Blessed *be* the Lord God, the God of Israel, who only doeth wondrous things. ¹⁹ And blessed *be* his glorious name for ever: and let the whole earth be filled *with* his glory; Amen, and Amen.

²⁰ The prayers of David the son of Jesse are ended.

⁶ May the reign of this son of mine be as gentle and fruitful as the springtime rains upon the grass—like showers that water the earth! ⁷ May all good men flourish in his reign, with abundance of peace to the end of time. ⁸ Let him reign from sea to sea, and from the Euphrates River to the ends of the earth. ⁹ The desert nomads shall bow before him; his enemies shall fall face downward in the dust. ¹⁰ Kings along the Mediterranean coast—the kings of Tarshish and the islands—and those from Sheba and from Seba—all will bring their gifts. ¹¹ Yes, kings from everywhere! All will bow before him! All will serve him!

¹² He will take care of the helpless and poor when they cry to him; for they have no one else to defend them. ¹³ He feels pity for the weak and needy, and will rescue them. ¹⁴ He will save them from oppression and from violence, for their lives are precious to him.

¹⁵ And he shall live; and to him will be given the gold of Sheba, and there will be constant praise for him. His people will bless him all day long. ¹⁶ Bless us with abundant crops throughout the land, even on the highland plains; may there be fruit like that of Lebanon; may the cities be as full of people as the fields are of grass. ¹⁷ His name will be honored forever; it will continue as the sun; and all will be blessed in him; all nations will praise him.

¹⁸ Blessed be Jehovah God, the God of Israel, who only does wonderful things! ¹⁹ Blessed be his glorious name forever! Let the whole earth be filled with his glory. Amen, and amen!

²⁰ (This ends the psalms of David, son of Jesse.)

PSALM 73

A Psalm of Ascph

TRULY God *is* good to Israel, *even* to such as are of a clean heart. ² But as for me, my feet were almost gone; my steps had well nigh slipped. ³ For I was envious at the foolish, *when* I saw the prosperity of the wicked. ⁴ For *there are* no bands in their death: but their strength *is* firm. ⁵ They *are* not in trouble *as other* men; neither are they

73 HOW GOOD GOD is to Israel—to those whose hearts are pure. ² But as for me, I came *so* close to the edge of the cliff! My feet were slipping and I was almost gone. ³ For I was envious of the prosperity of the proud and wicked. ⁴ Yes, all through life their road is smooth! They grow sleek and fat. ⁵ They aren't always in trouble and plagued with problems like everyone else,

8-14. Prayer for Dominion and Peace. He shall have dominion. Again this plea may better be translated, *May he have dominion.* On the basis of the king's justice, righteousness, and dominion, there will be peace for his subjects. The verbs in verses 12-14 are properly indicatives ("he spares . . . saves . . . redeems," etc.), and mark out the public rewards arising from his ideal characteristics.

15-17. Prayer for Fame and Blessing. His name shall endure . . . and men shall be blessed in him. This section is also a prayer, better rendered *may he live* and *may his name endure.* The psalmist prays that the king's fame (his name) may endure long after he has died, even among the other nations which he rules.

18-20. Doxology of Praise, and Conclusion. Blessed be the Lord God. These verses were added as a concluding doxology to Book II of the Psalter. Verse 20 is an editorial note which originally separated the preceding collection from the psalms connected with Asaph, which follow. A number of the manuscripts do not include verse 20 here.

BOOK III. Psalms 73—89

The third major division in the Psalter, which is much shorter than the previous two books, includes only seventeen psalms. The first eleven are connected with the name of Asaph, who was one of the chief musicians under David's rule. The other two chief musicians of David were Heman and Ethan, each of whom is connected with a psalm in this book. One psalm is referred to David, while the remaining four psalms are associated with the sons of Korah. Again it is not necessary to attribute authorship to those connected with these titles. Just as the sons of Korah formed a Levitical guild, so Asaph's sons continued to occupy places of musical leadership.

Psalm 73. The Trial of Faith

Here is yet another approach to the problem of the prosperity of the wicked. Although the psalmist is troubled by his own suffering, he is more perplexed by the lack of punishment of the wicked. This psalm goes deeper into the problem than do Psalms 37 and 49, and the author finds peace in spiritual fellowship with God. It may be classified as a song of trust, with overtones that link it with the Wisdom writers. The didactic purpose is evident throughout,

but it is interwoven with the confession of a man whose faith has been sorely tested.

1. His Conclusion. Truly God is good. The psalmist states first the confident conclusion which came from his supreme test of faith. He uses the Hebrew particle *'ak,* which can be translated in many ways — "now," "truly," "surely," "only," "after all." Here and in verses 13 and 18 it is probably best translated *surely.*

2-12. His Problem. I saw the prosperity of the wicked. Contrasted with the writer's general conclusion is his pilgrimage in the valley of doubt, introduced by the emphatic **as for me.** He was in danger of complete apostasy because of his envy toward prosperous wicked men.

NOTES

plagued like *other* men. 6 Therefore pride compasseth them about as a chain; violence covereth them *as* a garment. 7 Their eyes stand out with fatness: they have more than heart could wish. 8 They are corrupt, and speak wickedly *concerning* oppression: they speak loftily. 9 They set their mouth against the heavens, and their tongue walketh through the earth.

10 Therefore his people return hither: and waters of a full *cup* are wrung out to them. 11 And they say, How doth God know? and is there knowledge in the most High? 12 Behold, these *are* the ungodly, who prosper in the world; they increase *in* riches.

13 Verily I have cleansed my heart *in* vain, and washed my hands in innocency. 14 For all the day long have I been plagued, and chastened every morning. 15 If I say, I will speak thus; behold, I should offend *against* the generation of thy children. 16 When I thought to know this, it *was* too painful for me; 17 Until I went into the sanctuary of God; *then* understood I their end. 18 Surely thou didst set them in slippery places: thou castedst them down into destruction. 19 How are they *brought* into desolation, as in a moment! they are utterly consumed with terrors. 20 As a dream when *one* awaketh; *so,* O Lord, when thou awakest, thou shalt despise their image.

21 Thus my heart was grieved, and I was pricked in my reins. 22 So foolish *was* I, and ignorant: I was *as* a beast before thee. 23 Nevertheless I *am* continually with thee: thou hast holden *me* by my right hand. 24 Thou shalt guide me with thy counsel, and afterward receive me *to* glory. 25 Whom have I in heaven *but thee?* and *there is* none upon earth *that* I desire beside thee. 26 My flesh and my heart faileth: *but* God *is* the strength of my heart, and my portion for ever.

27 For, lo, they that are far from thee shall perish: thou hast destroyed all them that go a whoring from thee.

28 But *it is* good for me to draw near to God: I have put my trust in the Lord God, that I may declare all thy works.

6 so their pride sparkles like a jeweled necklace, and their clothing is woven of cruelty! 7 These fat cats have everything their hearts could ever wish for! 8 They scoff at God and threaten his people. How proudly they speak! 9 They boast against the very heavens, and their words strut through the earth.

10 And so God's people are dismayed and confused, and drink it all in. 11 "Does God realize what is going on?" they ask. 12 "Look at these men of arrogance; they never have to lift a finger—theirs is a life of ease; and all the time their riches multiply."

13 Have I been wasting my time? Why take the trouble to be pure? 14 All I get out of it is trouble and woe—every day and all day long! 15 If I had really said that, I would have been a traitor to your people. 16 Yet it is so hard to explain it—this prosperity of those who hate the Lord. 17 Then one day I went into God's sanctuary to meditate, and thought about the future of these evil men. 18 What a slippery path they are on— suddenly God will send them sliding over the edge of the cliff and down to their destruction: 19 an instant end to all their happiness, an eternity of terror. 20 Their present life is only a dream! They will awaken to the truth as one awakens from a dream of things that never really were!

21 When I saw this, what turmoil filled my heart! 22 I saw myself so stupid and so ignorant; I must seem like an animal to you, O God. 23 But even so, you love me! You are holding my right hand! 24 You will keep on guiding me all my life with your wisdom and counsel; and afterwards receive me into the glories of heaven! 25 Whom have I in heaven but you? And I desire no one on earth as much as you! 26 My health fails; my spirits droop, yet God remains! He is the strength of my heart; he is mine forever!

27 But those refusing to worship God will perish, for he destroys those serving other gods.

28 But as for me, I get as close to him as I can! I have chosen him and I will tell everyone about the wonderful ways he rescues me.

PSALM 74

Maschil of Asaph

O GOD, why hast thou cast *us* off for ever? *why* doth thine anger smoke against the sheep of thy pasture? ² Remember thy congregation, *which* thou hast purchased of old; the rod of thine inheritance, *which* thou hast redeemed; this mount Zion, wherein thou hast dwelt.

³ Lift up thy feet unto the perpetual desolations; *even* all *that* the enemy hath done wickedly in the sanctuary. ⁴ Thine enemies roar in the midst of thy congregations; they set up their ensigns *for* signs. ⁵ *A man* was famous according as he had lifted up axes upon the thick trees. ⁶ But now they break down the carved work thereof at once with axes and hammers. ⁷ They have cast fire into thy sanctuary, they have defiled *by casting down* the dwelling place of thy name to the ground. ⁸ They said in their hearts, Let us destroy them together: they have burned up all the synagogues of God in the land.

⁹ We see not our signs: *there is* no more any prophet: neither *is there* among us any that knoweth how long. ¹⁰ O God, how long shall the adversary reproach? shall the enemy blaspheme thy name for ever? ¹¹ Why withdrawest thou thy hand, even thy right hand? pluck *it* out of thy bosom.

¹² For God *is* my King of old, working salvation in the midst of the earth. ¹³ Thou didst divide the sea by thy strength: thou brakest the heads of the dragons in the waters. ¹⁴ Thou brakest the heads of leviathan in pieces, *and* gavest him *to be* meat to the people inhabiting the wilderness. ¹⁵ Thou didst cleave the fountain and the flood: thou driedst up mighty rivers. ¹⁶ The day *is* thine, the night also *is* thine: thou hast prepared the light and the sun. ¹⁷ Thou hast set all the borders of the earth: thou hast made summer and winter. ¹⁸ Remember this, *that* the enemy hath reproached, O Lord, and *that* the foolish people have blasphemed thy name. ¹⁹ O deliver not the soul of thy turtledove unto the multitude *of the wicked:* forget not the congregation of thy poor

74 O GOD, WHY have you cast us away forever? Why is your anger hot against us—the sheep of your own pasture? ² Remember that we are your people—the ones you chose in ancient times from slavery and made the choicest of your possessions. You chose Jerusalem as your home on earth!

³ Walk through the awful ruins of the city, and see what the enemy has done to your sanctuary. ⁴ There they shouted their battle cry and erected their idols to flaunt their victory. ⁵,⁶ Everything lies in shambles like a forest chopped to the ground. They came with their axes and sledgehammers and smashed and chopped the carved paneling, ⁷ and set the sanctuary on fire, and razed it to the ground—your sanctuary, Lord. ⁸ "Let's wipe out every trace of God," they said, and went through the entire country burning down the assembly places where we worshiped you.

⁹,¹⁰ There is nothing left to show that we are your people. The prophets are gone, and who can say when it all will end? How long, O God, will you allow our enemies to dishonor your name? Will you let them get away with this forever? ¹¹ Why do you delay? Why hold back your power? Unleash your fist and give them a final blow.

¹² God is my King from ages past; you have been actively helping me everywhere throughout the land. ¹³,¹⁴ You divided the Red Sea with your strength; you crushed the sea-god's heads! You gave him to the desert tribes to eat! ¹⁵ At your command the springs burst forth to give your people water; and then you dried a path for them across the ever-flowing Jordan. ¹⁶ Day and night alike belong to you; you made the starlight and the sun. ¹⁷ All nature is within your hands; you make the summer and the winter too. ¹⁸ Lord, see how these enemies scoff at you. O Jehovah, an arrogant nation has blasphemed your name.

¹⁹ O Lord, save me! Protect your turtledove from the hawks. Save your beloved

Psalm 74. An Appeal for Vindication

This psalm is the expression of national lament by Israel in the wake of extreme disaster. The feeling is widespread that God has forsaken and forgotten his people. The destruction of the city and the Temple suggests the occasion of the Babylonian conquest. This is the only time known when the Temple was burned to the ground. The conditions are similar to those described in the book of Lamentations.

1-3. The Nation's Appeal. Remember thy congregation. The psalmist voices the basic appeal to God to remember His relationship of love with Israel. Even though the Divine wrath is evident in the present tragedy, it is incomprehensible to the psalmist that the Lord, as Israel's Shepherd, could forsake His sheep. Therefore, he pleads for God to take the giant steps necessary to redeem His people.

4-11. The Nation's Plight. Thine enemies roar. Instead of being filled with rejoicing worshipers, the temple area is filled with roaring enemies. In place of the emblems of the tribes, the standards of the enemy are seen. The patient, quiet work by which the Temple was built has been nullified by the ruthless axes and hammers of the invaders. The questions introduced by **how long** and **Why** express the heightened nature of the lament, and relate the basic appeal to the specific disaster.

12-17. The Nation's King. For God is my King of old. It is Israel's supreme King whose power is pictured here. Using symbolic language and descriptive terminology drawn from the mythology of the Canaanites, the psalmist insists that it is God who has won the mighty victories of the past. While the figures of speech are derived from ancient creation stories, the psalmist is applying them to God's displays of power in the Exodus and the wilderness wanderings.

for ever. 20 Have respect unto the covenant: for the dark places of the earth are full of the habitations of cruelty. 21 O let not the oppressed return ashamed: let the poor and needy praise thy name. 22 Arise, O God, plead thine own cause: remember how the foolish man reproacheth thee daily. 23 Forget not the voice of thine enemies: the tumult of those that rise up against thee increaseth continually.

people from these beasts. 20 Remember your promise! For the land is full of darkness and cruel men. 21 O Lord, don't let your downtrodden people be constantly insulted. Give cause for these poor and needy ones to praise your name! 22 Arise, O God, and state your case against our enemies. Remember the insults these rebels have hurled against you all day long. 23 Don't overlook the cursing of these enemies of yours; it grows louder and louder.

PSALM 75

To the chief Musician, Al–taschith, A Psalm or *Song of Asaph*

UNTO thee, O God, do we give thanks, *unto thee* do we give thanks: for *that* thy name is near thy wondrous works declare.

2 When I shall receive the congregation I will judge uprightly. 3 The earth and all the inhabitants thereof are dissolved: I bear up the pillars of it. Se-lah.

4 I said unto the fools, Deal not foolishly: and to the wicked, Lift not up the horn: 5 Lift not up your horn on high: speak *not with* a stiff neck. 6 For promotion *cometh* neither from the east, nor from the west, nor from the south. 7 But God *is* the judge: he putteth down one, and setteth up another. 8 For in the hand of the Lord *there is* a cup, and the wine is red; it is full of mixture; and he poureth out of the same: but the dregs thereof, all the wicked of the earth shall wring *them* out, *and* drink *them*. 9 But I will declare for ever; I will sing praises to the God of Jacob. 10 All the horns of the wicked also will I cut off; *but* the horns of the righteous shall be exalted.

75 HOW WE THANK you, Lord! Your mighty miracles give proof that you care.

2 "Yes," the Lord replies, "and when I am ready, I will punish the wicked! 3 Though the earth shakes and all its people live in turmoil, yet its pillars are firm, for I have set them in place!"

4 I warned the proud to cease their arrogance! I told the wicked to lower their insolent gaze, 5 and to stop being stubborn and proud. 6,7 For promotion and power come from nowhere on earth, but only from God. He promotes one and deposes another. 8 In Jehovah's hand there is a cup of pale and sparkling wine. It is his judgment, poured out upon the wicked of the earth. They must drain that cup to the dregs. 9 But as for me, I shall forever declare the praises of the God of Jacob. 10 "I will cut off the strength of evil men," says the Lord, "and increase the power of good men in their place."

PSALM 76

To the chief Musician on Neginoth, A Psalm or *Song of Asaph*

IN Judah *is* God known: his name *is* great in Israel. 2 In Sa-lem also is his tabernacle, and his dwelling place in Zion. 3 There brake he the arrows of the bow, the shield, and the sword, and the battle. Se-lah.

76 GOD'S REPUTATION IS very great in Judah and in Israel. 2 His home is in Jerusalem. He lives upon Mount Zion. 3 There he breaks the weapons of our enemies.

18-23. The Nation's Prayer. Arise, O God, plead thine own cause. The former appeal is raised to a higher level with this impassioned plea. This is not merely Israel's cause, but God's cause as well. Therefore, the psalmist prays that God will watch over His defenseless people, remember the covenant of love, and keep an eye on the roaring enemies.

Psalm 75. The Gratitude of the Nation

While the opening of this psalm is an expression of national thanksgiving, and the conclusion is related to an individual, the central portion is difficult to classify. Some commentators suggest that verse 1 has been added to an individual's prayer for victory in order to adapt the psalm for public worship. Although this may have been the case, the psalm exhibits careful poetic arrangement as well as definite progression of thought.

1. The Invocation of Israel. Unto thee . . . we give thanks. Behind this terse statement of gratitude there appears to lie an actual, historical deliverance. The reality of a recent manifestation of power gives confidence that God's revealed nature (his **name**) is close at hand.

2,3. The Response of God. I will judge uprightly. This oracle from God gives the basis for the pronouncements which follow. It is at **the appointed time** (v. 2; mō'ēd, not "the congregation," AV) when God will take his place on the judgment seat. His control of the universe assures that the judgment will be sure.

4-8. The Warning of the Psalmist. I say unto the arrogant . . . to the wicked. The arrogant and wicked are reminded that power to **lift high** is not found in the east, west, or south. God alone can **lift up** or **put down** (v. 7, ASV) for he it is who executes judgment and causes the wicked to drink the cup of his wrath (Ps 11:6; Rev 14:10).

9,10. The Triumph of the Righteous. But I will declare for ever. Speaking as Israel's representative, the psalmist vows endless praise. With these vows comes the assurance that the arrogant will fall from their self-elevation, while the righteous will gain their rightful place.

Psalm 76. A Song of Victory

This song is closely related to Psalms 46, 48, and 75 in its celebration of a military victory. Many commentators seek the common background for these four pieces in the defeat of the Assyrians in 701 b.c. Even though some historical event may have inspired the original poem, the present psalm seems to have been adapted for temple worship.

1-3. The Fame of God. In Judah . . . in Israel . . . in Salem . . . in Zion. The reputation of God has been spread far and wide because of his victories. Jerusalem is the center of his fame because his battle headquarters are located there.

NOTES

⁴ Thou *art* more glorious *and* excellent than the mountains of prey. ⁵ The stouthearted are spoiled, they have slept their sleep: and none of the men of might have found their hands. ⁶ At thy rebuke, O God of Jacob, both the chariot and horse are cast into a dead sleep. ⁷ Thou, *even* thou, *art* to be feared: and who may stand in thy sight when once thou art angry? ⁸ Thou didst cause judgment to be heard from heaven; the earth feared, and was still, ⁹ When God arose to judgment, to save all the meek of the earth. Se-lah. ¹⁰ Surely the wrath of man shall praise thee: the remainder of wrath shalt thou restrain.

¹¹ Vow, and pay unto the Lord your God: let all that be round about him bring presents unto him that ought to be feared. ¹² He shall cut off the spirit of princes: *he is* terrible to the kings of the earth.

⁴ The everlasting mountains cannot compare with you in glory! ⁵ The mightiest of our enemies are conquered. They lie before us in the sleep of death; not one can lift a hand against us. ⁶ When you rebuked them, God of Jacob, steeds and riders fell. ⁷ No wonder you are greatly feared! Who can stand before an angry God? ⁸ You pronounce sentence on them from heaven; the earth trembles and stands silently before you. ⁹ You stand up to punish the evil-doers and to defend the meek of the earth. ¹⁰ Man's futile wrath will bring you glory. You will use it as an ornament!

¹¹ Fulfill all your vows that you have made to Jehovah your God. Let everyone bring him presents. He should be reverenced and feared, ¹² for he cuts down princes and does awesome things to the kings of the earth.

PSALM 77

To the chief Musician, to Jeduthun, A Psalm of Asaph

I CRIED unto God with my voice, *even* unto God with my voice; and he gave ear unto me. ² In the day of my trouble I sought the Lord: my sore ran in the night, and ceased not: my soul refused to be comforted. ³ I remembered God, and was troubled: I complained, and my spirit was overwhelmed. Se-lah. ⁴ Thou holdest mine eyes waking: I am so troubled that I cannot speak.

⁵ I have considered the days of old, the years of ancient times. ⁶ I call to remembrance my song in the night: I commune with mine own heart: and my spirit made diligent search. ⁷ Will the Lord cast off for ever? and will he be favourable no more? ⁸ Is his mercy clean gone for ever? doth *his* promise fail for evermore? ⁹ Hath God forgotten to be gracious? hath he in anger shut up his tender mercies? Se-lah. ¹⁰ And I said, This *is* my infirmity: *but I will remember* the years of the right hand of the most High. ¹¹ I will remember the works of the Lord: surely I will remember thy wonders of old. ¹² I will meditate also of all thy work, and talk of thy doings.

77 I CRY TO the Lord; I call and call to him. Oh, that he would listen. ² I am in deep trouble and I need his help so badly. All night long I pray, lifting my hands to heaven, pleading. There can be no joy for me until he acts. ³ I think of God and moan, overwhelmed with longing for his help. ⁴ I cannot sleep until you act. I am too distressed even to pray!

⁵ I keep thinking of the good old days of the past, long since ended. ⁶ Then my nights were filled with joyous songs. I search my soul and meditate upon the difference now. ⁷ Has the Lord rejected me forever? Will he never again be favorable? ⁸ Is his lovingkindness gone forever? Has his promise failed? ⁹ Has he forgotten to be kind to one so undeserving? Has he slammed the door in anger on his love? ¹⁰ And I said: This is my fate, that the blessings of God have changed to hate. ¹¹ I recall the many miracles he did for me so long ago. ¹² Those wonderful deeds are constantly in my thoughts. I cannot stop thinking about them.

4-6. The Might of God. Thou art more glorious. The Lord has proved himself in battle to be mightier than all his foes. He easily conquers the **stouthearted** and the **men of might.** He is glorious and majestic, more majestic even than **the everlasting mountains** (cf. LXX).

7-9. The Judgment of God. Thou, even thou, art to be feared. The thought goes beyond the battle scene as God takes his seat in heaven. He is the judge **to be feared,** who strikes man with terror. All of the earth stands still as the Lord saves the oppressed peoples, of whom Israel is representative.

10-12. The Homage Due God. Vow, and pay unto the Lord your God. This call for praise and offerings is based upon the bold assertion that the Lord can turn even man's most dangerous passion into a means of glory. The last ounce of his enemies' wrath can only add to God's glory, as he girds it upon himself (ASV; not *restrain,* AV).

Psalm 77. Remembering God's Works

Lament is intermingled with praise in this psalm. The opening verses (1-9) are the lamentations of an individual, who may represent the nation in affliction. The later verses (10-20) are words of praise which clearly complement the opening section. Verses 16-19 express a different mood and exhibit a different style and rhythm from the rest of the psalm.

1-3. His Perplexity of Spirit. I cried unto the Lord . . . my spirit was overwhelmed. Between these clauses the psalmist's deep anguish and anxiety are graphically portrayed. His outstretched hand (not **sore,** AV) sought God, but found no comfort. His meditations and musings only overwhelmed his spirit.

4-9. His Search for Answers. My spirit made diligent search. Worry and anxiety still ruled his life so that he could not sleep. He counted the days of the past, instead of sheep. Finally, he voiced the six questions that puzzled as well as troubled him. He could not understand why a God of mercy and compassion should remain silent and inactive.

10-15. His Solution in History. I will remember the works of the Lord. Recalling the wonders of God in past days brings hope for the psalmist. God has proved himself to be one who does glorious deeds; he has shown his strength, and has redeemed the children of Israel.

13 Thy way, O God, *is* in the sanctuary: who *is* so great a God as *our* God? 14 Thou *art* the God that doest wonders: thou hast declared thy strength among the people.

15 Thou hast with *thine* arm redeemed thy people, the sons of Jacob and Joseph. Se-lah. 16 The waters saw thee, O God, the waters saw thee; they were afraid: the depths also were troubled. 17 The clouds poured out water: the skies sent out a sound: thine arrows also went abroad. 18 The voice of thy thunder *was* in the heaven: the lightnings lightened the world: the earth trembled and shook.

19 Thy way *is* in the sea, and thy path in the great waters, and thy footsteps are not known. 20 Thou leddest thy people like a flock by the hand of Moses and Aaron.

PSALM 78

Maschil of Asaph

GIVE ear, O my people, *to* my law: incline your ears to the words of my mouth. 2 I will open my mouth in a parable: I will utter dark sayings of old: 3 Which we have heard and known, and our fathers have told us. 4 We will not hide *them* from their children, shewing to the generation to come the praises of the Lord, and his strength, and his wonderful works that he hath done. 5 For he established a testimony in Jacob, and appointed a law in Israel, which he commanded our fathers, that they should make them known to their children: 6 That the generation to come might know *them, even* the children *which* should be born; *who* should arise and declare *them* to their children: 7 That they might set their hope in God, and not forget the works of God, but keep his commandments: 8 And might not be as their fathers, a stubborn and rebellious generation; a generation *that* set not their heart aright, and whose spirit was not stedfast with God.

9 The children of E-phra-im, *being* armed, *and* carrying bows, turned back in the day of battle. 10 They kept not the covenant of God, and refused to walk in his law; 11 And forgat his works, and his wonders that he had shewed

13 O God, your ways are holy. Where is there any other as mighty as you? 14 You are the God of miracles and wonders! You still demonstrate your awesome power.

15 You have redeemed us who are the sons of Jacob and of Joseph by your might. 16 When the Red Sea saw you, how it feared! It trembled to its depths! 17 The clouds poured down their rain, the thunder rolled and crackled in the sky. Your lightning flashed. 18 There was thunder in the whirlwind; the lightning lighted up the world! The earth trembled and shook.

19 Your road led by a pathway through the sea—a pathway no one knew was there! 20 You led your people along that road like a flock of sheep, with Moses and Aaron as their shepherds.

78 O MY PEOPLE, listen to my teaching. Open your ears to what I am saying. 2,3 For I will show you lessons from our history, stories handed down to us from former generations. 4 I will reveal these truths to you so that you can describe these glorious deeds of Jehovah to your children, and tell them about the mighty miracles he did. 5 For he gave his laws to Israel, and commanded our fathers to teach them to their children, 6 so that they in turn could teach their children too. Thus his laws pass down from generation to generation. 7 In this way each generation has been able to obey his laws and to set its hope anew on God and not forget his glorious miracles. 8 Thus they did not need to be as their fathers were—stubborn, rebellious, unfaithful, refusing to give their hearts to God.

9 The people of Ephraim, though fully armed, turned their backs and fled when the day of battle came, 10 because they didn't obey his laws. They refused to follow his ways. 11,12 And they forgot about the wonderful miracles God had done for them, and

The unspoken request is that God may so act again.

16-19. His Confidence in God's Power. The waters saw thee . . . they were afraid. These verses, which act as a hymn within a hymn, differ greatly in mood and form from the rest of the poem. Although the dominant note of this section is God's power over nature in general, the position of the passage, between verses 15 and 20, relates it to the deliverance at the Red Sea.

20. His Assurance of God's Leadership. Thou leddest thy people. This verse voices again the thought of verse 15, with the forceful implication that God can do it again.

Psalm 78. Wisdom from History

Here is a good example of the didactic purposes of the Wisdom writers. God's wonderful acts of deliverance, blessing, and guidance are recalled to serve as a lesson for the psalmist's generation. The teaching is directed toward the inhabitants of Judah, illustrating God's choice of Jerusalem and the Davidic line as recipients of his promises instead of the tribe of Ephraim, which disqualified itself by rebellion (vv. 9-11,57,60,67,68).

1-11. The Warnings of the Past. I will utter dark sayings of old. The didactic purpose of the psalmist is clearly stated. A general statement stressing the responsibility of the 'fathers' to teach the children, and the danger of apostasy serves as an introduction to the many illustrations from history which follow.

them. 12 Marvellous things did he in the sight of their fathers, in the land of Egypt, *in* the field of Zo-an. 13 He divided the sea, and caused them to pass through; and he made the waters to stand as an heap. 14 In the daytime also he led them with a cloud, and all the night with a light of fire. 15 He clave the rocks in the wilderness, and gave *them* drink as *out of* the great depths. 16 He brought streams also out of the rock, and caused waters to run down like rivers. 17 And they sinned yet more against him by provoking the most High in the wilderness. 18 And they tempted God in their heart by asking meat for their lust. 19 Yea, they spake against God; they said, Can God furnish a table in the wilderness? 20 Behold, he smote the rock, that the waters gushed out, and the streams overflowed; can he give bread also? can he provide flesh for his people? 21 Therefore the Lord heard *this,* and was wroth; so a fire was kindled against Jacob; and anger also came up against Israel; 22 Because they believed not in God, and trusted not in his salvation: 23 Though he had commanded the clouds from above, and opened the doors of heaven, 24 And had rained down manna upon them to eat, and had given them of the corn of heaven. 25 Man did eat angels' food: he sent them meat to the full.

26 He caused an east wind to blow in the heaven: and by his power he brought in the south wind. 27 He rained flesh also upon them as dust, and feathered fowls like as the sand of the sea: 28 And he let *it* fall in the midst of their camp, round about their habitations. 29 So they did eat, and were well filled: for he gave them their own desire; 30 They were not estranged from their lust. But while their meat *was* yet in their mouths, 31 The wrath of God came upon them, and slew the fattest of them, and smote down the chosen *men* of Israel. 32 For all this they sinned still, and believed not for his wondrous works. 33 Therefore their days did he consume in vanity, and their years in trouble.

34 When he slew them, then they sought him: and they returned and enquired early after God. 35 And they remembered that God *was* their rock,

for their fathers in Egypt. 13 For he divided the sea before them and led them through! The water stood banked up along both sides of them! 14 In the daytime he led them by a cloud, and at night by a pillar of fire. 15 He split open the rocks in the wilderness to give them plenty of water, as though gushing from a spring. 16 Streams poured from the rock, flowing like a river! 17 Yet they kept on with their rebellion, sinning against the God who is above all gods. 18 They murmured and complained, demanding other food than God was giving them. 19,20 They even spoke against God himself. "Why can't he give us decent food as well as water?" they grumbled. 21 Jehovah heard them and was angry; the fire of his wrath burned against Israel, 22 because they didn't believe in God or trust in him to care for them, 23 even though he commanded the skies to open—he opened the windows of heaven— 24 and rained down manna for their food. He gave them bread from heaven! 25 They ate angel's food! He gave them all that they could hold.

26 And he led forth the east wind and guided the south wind by his mighty power. 27 He rained down birds as thick as dust, clouds of them like sands along the shore! 28 He caused the birds to fall to the ground among the tents. 29 The people ate their fill. He gave them what they asked for. 30 But they had hardly finished eating, and the meat was yet in their mouths, 31 when the anger of the Lord rose against them and killed the finest of Israel's young men. 32 Yet even so the people kept on sinning and refused to believe in miracles. 33 So he cut their lives short and gave them years of terror and disaster.

34 Then at last, when he had ruined them, they walked awhile behind him; how earnestly they turned around and followed him! 35 Then they remembered that God was their Rock—that their Savior was the

12-39. The Experiences of the Wilderness. Marvelous things did he. . . . and they sinned yet more. The works of God are described in detail: the crossing of the sea, the guidance of the cloud and the pillar of fire, the provision of water, manna, and quails. Even in the face of these constant blessings, the people kept on sinning and tempting God. But in spite of their sin, God demonstrated his compassion and understanding by forgiving them.

NOTES

and the high God their redeemer. [36] Nevertheless they did flatter him with their mouth, and they lied unto him with their tongues. [37] For their heart was not right with him, neither were they stedfast in his covenant. [38] But he, *being* full of compassion, forgave *their* iniquity, and destroyed *them* not: yea, many a time turned he his anger away, and did not stir up all his wrath. [39] For he remembered that they *were but* flesh; a wind that passeth away, and cometh not again.

[40] How oft did they provoke him in the wilderness, *and* grieve him in the desert! [41] Yea, they turned back and tempted God, and limited the Holy One of Israel. [42] They remembered not his hand, *nor* the day when he delivered them from the enemy. [43] How he had wrought his signs in Egypt, and his wonders in the field of Zo-an: [44] And had turned their rivers into blood; and their floods that they could not drink. [45] He sent divers sorts of flies among them, which devoured them; and frogs, which destroyed them.

[46] He gave also their increase unto the caterpiller, and their labour unto the locust. [47] He destroyed their vines with hail, and their sycomore trees with frost. [48] He gave up their cattle also to the hail, and their flocks to hot thunderbolts. [49] He cast upon them the fierceness of his anger, wrath, and indignation, and trouble, by sending evil angels *among them.* [50] He made a way to his anger; he spared not their soul from death, but gave their life over to the pestilence; [51] And smote all the firstborn in Egypt; the chief of *their* strength in the tabernacles of Ham:

[52] But made his own people to go forth like sheep, and guided them in the wilderness like a flock. [53] And he led them on safely, so that they feared not: but the sea overwhelmed their enemies. [54] And he brought them to the border of his sanctuary, *even to* this mountain, *which* his right hand had purchased. [55] He cast out the heathen also before them, and divided them an inheritance by line, and made the tribes of Israel to dwell in their tents.

[56] Yet they tempted and provoked the most high God, and kept not his

God above all gods. [36] But it was only with their words they followed him, not with their hearts; [37] their hearts were far away. They did not keep their promises. [38] Yet he was merciful and forgave their sins and didn't destroy them all. Many and many a time he held back his anger. [39] For he remembered that they were merely mortal men, gone in a moment like a breath of wind.

[40] Oh, how often they rebelled against him in those desert years and grieved his heart. [41] Again and again they turned away and tempted God to kill them, and limited the Holy One of Israel from giving them his blessings. [42] They forgot his power and love, and how he had rescued them from their enemies; [43] they forgot the plagues he sent upon the Egyptians in Tanis — [44] how he turned their rivers into blood, so that no one could drink, [45] and how he sent vast swarms of flies to fill the land, and how the frogs had covered all of Egypt!

[46] He gave their crops to caterpillars. Their harvest was consumed by locusts. [47] He destroyed their grapevines and their sycamores with hail. [48] Their cattle died in the fields, mortally wounded by iceballs from heaven. Their sheep were killed by lightning. [49] He loosed on them the fierceness of his anger, sending sorrow and trouble. He dispatched against them a band of destroying angels. [50] He gave free course to his anger and did not spare the Egyptians' lives, but handed them over to plagues and sickness. [51] Then he killed the eldest son in each Egyptian family—he who was the beginning of its strength and joy.

[52] But he led forth his own people like a flock, guiding them safely through the wilderness. [53] He kept them safe, so they were not afraid. But the Sea closed in upon their enemies and overwhelmed them. [54] He brought them to the border of his land of blessing, to this land of hills he made for them. [55] He drove out the nations occupying the land, and gave each tribe of Israel its apportioned place as its home.

[56] Yet though he did all this for them, they still rebelled against the God above all gods, and refused to follow his commands.

testimonies: ⁵⁷ But turned back, and dealt unfaithfully like their fathers: they were turned aside like a deceitful bow. ⁵⁸ For they provoked him to anger with their high places, and moved him to jealousy with their graven images.

⁵⁹ When God heard *this,* he was wroth, and greatly abhorred Israel: ⁶⁰ So that he forsook the tabernacle of Shi-loh, the tent *which* he placed among men; ⁶¹ And delivered his strength into captivity, and his glory into the enemy's hand. ⁶² He gave his people over also unto the sword; and was wroth with his inheritance. ⁶³ The fire consumed their young men; and their maidens were not given to marriage. ⁶⁴ Their priests fell by the sword; and their widows made no lamentation. ⁶⁵ Then the Lord awaked as one out of sleep, *and* like a mighty man that shouteth by reason of wine. ⁶⁶ And he smote his enemies in the hinder parts: he put them to a perpetual reproach. ⁶⁷ Moreover he refused the tabernacle of Joseph, and chose not the tribe of E-phra-im: ⁶⁸ But chose the tribe of Judah, the mount Zion which he loved. ⁶⁹ And he built his sanctuary like high *palaces,* like the earth which he hath established for ever. ⁷⁰ He chose David also his servant, and took him from the sheepfolds: ⁷¹ From following the ewes great with young he brought him to feed Jacob his people, and Israel his inheritance. ⁷² So he fed them according to the integrity of his heart; and guided them by the skilfulness of his hands.

PSALM 79

A Psalm of Asaph

O God, the heathen are come into thine inheritance; thy holy temple have they defiled; they have laid Jerusalem on heaps. ² The dead bodies of thy servants have they given *to be* meat unto the fowls of the heaven, the flesh of thy saints unto the beasts of the earth. ³ Their blood have they shed like water round about Jerusalem; and *there was* none to bury *them.* ⁴ We are become a reproach to our neighbours, a scorn and derision to them that are round about us.

⁵⁷ They turned back from entering the Promised Land and disobeyed as their fathers had. Like a crooked arrow, they missed the target of God's will. ⁵⁸ They made him angry by erecting idols and altars to other gods.

⁵⁹ When God saw their deeds, his wrath was strong and he despised his people. ⁶⁰ Then he abandoned his Tabernacle at Shiloh, where he had lived among mankind, ⁶¹ and allowed his Ark to be captured; he surrendered his glory into enemy hands. ⁶² He caused his people to be butchered because his anger was intense. ⁶³ Their young men were killed by fire and their girls died before they were old enough to sing their wedding songs. ⁶⁴ The priests were slaughtered and their widows died before they could even begin their lament. ⁶⁵ Then the Lord rose up as though awakening from sleep, and like a mighty man aroused by wine, ⁶⁶ he routed his enemies and drove them back and sent them to eternal shame. ⁶⁷ But he rejected Joseph's family, the tribe of Ephraim, ⁶⁸ and chose the tribe of Judah —and Mount Zion which he loved. ⁶⁹ There he built his towering temple, solid and enduring as the heavens and the earth. ⁷⁰ He chose his servant David, taking him from feeding sheep, ⁷¹,⁷² and from following the ewes with lambs; God presented David to his people as their shepherd and he cared for them with a true heart and skillful hands.

79 O God, your land has been conquered by the heathen nations. Your Temple is defiled and Jerusalem is a heap of ruins. ² The bodies of your people lie exposed— food for birds and animals. ³ The enemy has butchered the entire population of Jerusalem; blood has flowed like water. No one is left even to bury them. ⁴ The nations all around us scoff. They heap contempt on us.

56-72. The Choices of God for Israel. He forsook . . . awaked . . . chose. The subjection of Israel during the period of the Judges is pointed out as evidence of abandonment by God. Then, in bold language, the psalmist suggests that the Lord awoke to the need of Israel. The rejection of the northern tribes brought the assurance of God's choice of Judah. The establishment of Jerusalem as Israel's center of worship and David as king marked the southern tribes as undisputed leaders of God's people.

Psalm 79. A Prayer for Vengeance

This psalm is the collective lament of the community of Jerusalem in a time of national disaster. The description of the defiling of the Temple and the devastation of the city points to a serious destruction, such as the Babylonian conquest in 586 B.C. There is here close affinity to the background of Psalm 74, where the Babylonian destruction seems most appropriate. The Jews have long connected these two poems for use on the fast day which commemorates the two destructions of Jerusalem, in 586 B.C. and in A.D. 70.

1-4. The Grief in Jerusalem. The heathen are come. The city of Jerusalem is described as being in a real state of emergency. Gentiles have desecrated the Temple, laid the city in ruins, and left the dead unburied. All of this devastation and slaughter has resulted in scorn and ridicule on the part of Israel's Gentile neighbors.

NOTES

⁵ How long, Lord? wilt thou be angry for ever? shall thy jealousy burn like fire? ⁶ Pour out thy wrath upon the heathen that have not known thee, and upon the kingdoms that have not called upon thy name. ⁷ For they have devoured Jacob, and laid waste his dwelling place. ⁸ O remember not against us former iniquities: let thy tender mercies speedily prevent us: for we are brought very low. ⁹ Help us, O God of our salvation, for the glory of thy name: and deliver us, and purge away our sins, for thy name's sake. ¹⁰ Wherefore should the heathen say, Where *is* their God? let him be known among the heathen in our sight *by* the revenging of the blood of thy servants *which is* shed. ¹¹ Let the sighing of the prisoner come before thee; according to the greatness of thy power preserve thou those that are appointed to die; ¹² And render unto our neighbours sevenfold into their bosom their reproach, wherewith they have reproached thee, O Lord.

¹³ So we thy people and sheep of thy pasture will give thee thanks for ever: we will shew forth thy praise to all generations.

⁵ O Jehovah, how long will you be angry with us? Forever? Will your jealousy burn till every hope is gone? ⁶ Pour out your wrath upon the godless nations, not on us! And on kingdoms that refuse to pray, that will not call upon your name! ⁷ For they have destroyed your people Israel, invading every home. ⁸ Oh, do not hold us guilty for our former sins! Let your tenderhearted mercies meet our needs, for we are brought low to the dust. ⁹ Help us, God of our salvation! Help us for the honor of your name. Oh, save us and forgive our sins. ¹⁰ Why should the heathen nations be allowed to scoff, "Where is their God?" Publicly avenge this slaughter of your people! ¹¹ Listen to the sighing of the prisoners and those condemned to die. Demonstrate the greatness of your power by saving them. ¹² O Lord, take sevenfold vengeance on these nations scorning you.

¹³ Then we your people, the sheep of your pasture, will thank you forever and forever, praising your greatness from generation to generation.

PSALM 80

To the chief Musician upon Shoshannim–Eduth, A Psalm of Asaph

GIVE ear, O Shepherd of Israel, thou that leadest Joseph like a flock; thou that dwellest *between* the cherubims, shine forth. ² Before E-phra-im and Benjamin and Ma-nas-seh stir up thy strength, and come *and* save us.

³ Turn us again, O God, and cause thy face to shine; and we shall be saved. ⁴ O Lord God of hosts, how long wilt though be angry against the prayer of thy people? ⁵ Thou feedest them with the bread of tears; and givest them tears to drink in great measure. ⁶ Thou makest us a strife unto our neighbours: and our enemies laugh among themselves.

⁷ Turn us again, O God of hosts, and cause thy face to shine; and we shall be saved. ⁸ Thou hast brought a vine out of Egypt: thou hast cast out the heathen, and planted it. ⁹ Thou preparedst *room* before it, and didst cause

80 O SHEPHERD OF Israel who leads Israel like a flock; O God enthroned above the cherubim, bend down your ear and listen as I plead. Display your power and radiant glory. ² Let Ephraim, Benjamin and Manasseh see you rouse yourself and use your mighty power to rescue us.

³ Turn us again to yourself, O God. Look down on us in joy and love; only then shall we be saved. ⁴ O Jehovah, God of heaven's armies, how long will you be angry and reject our prayers? ⁵ You have fed us with sorrow and tears, ⁶ and have made us the scorn of the neighboring nations. They laugh among themselves.

⁷ Turn us again to yourself, O God of Hosts. Look down on us in joy and love; only then shall we be saved. ⁸ You brought us from Egypt as though we were a tender vine and drove away the heathen from your land and planted us. ⁹ You cleared the ground and tilled the soil and we took root

5-8. The Plea for Mercy. How long, Lord? This frequent cry of the distressed is followed quickly by the second question, "Will it be forever?" The bitter hurt of the psalmist is evident in his begging God to wreak vengeance on the godless even before he asks Him to extend His **tender mercies** to His people.

9-12. The Prayer for Help. Help . . . deliver . . . purge . . . for thy name's sake. The psalmist not only recognizes his forefathers' sin but confesses the sin of his own generation. He stresses not selfish desire, but the glory of God's name. After all, God's name has been abused in the defilement of the Temple and in the derision by the heathen. The psalmist calls upon God to pay them back seven fold for their scoffing.

13. The Vow of Praise. We will show forth thy praise. If God will answer the prayer for help, his people will fulfill a double vow. They determine to praise God by giving continual thanks and by publicly declaring his praise.

Psalm 80. A Plea for Restoration

Here is another expression of national lament in a time of distress. The psalmist has sincere interest in the Northern Kingdom either as an outsider or as an inhabitant of that area. The former is probably the case, for the distress appears to be associated with the Exile. The irregular recurrence of a refrain, in verses 3,7, and 19, with an abbreviated form in verse 14, makes the structure of the psalm difficult to explain.

1-3. The Cry to the Shepherd. Give ear, O Shepherd of Israel. Although the phrase, **Shepherd of Israel**, is not used elsewhere in the OT, the figure occurs frequently. The three tribes, Ephraim, Benjamin, and Manasseh, were all descended from Rachel and represent the Northern Kingdom. The cry is designed to call God into action to restore his people.

4-7. The Plight of the Flock. Thou feedest them with the bread of tears. As in Psalms 74 and 79, the psalmist cries out, **How long . . . ?** He wants to know how much longer God is going to keep on fuming in anger. Although the Lord is not mentioned as shepherd in these verses, the metaphor is continued in the reference to his feeding them with tears.

8-13. The Nurture of the Vine. Thou hast brought a vine out of Egypt. Another metaphor is used here to show how God nurtured his chosen people. After transplanting the vine from Egypt

it to take deep root, and it filled the land. 10 The hills were covered with the shadow of it, and the boughs thereof *were like* the goodly cedars. 11 She sent out her boughs unto the sea, and her branches unto the river. 12 Why hast thou *then* broken down her hedges, so that all they which pass by the way do pluck her? 13 The boar out of the wood doth waste it, and the wild beast of the field doth devour it.

14 Return, we beseech thee, O God of hosts: look down from heaven, and behold, and visit this vine; 15 And the vineyard which thy right hand hath planted, and the branch *that* thou madest strong for thyself. 16 *It is* burned with fire, *it is* cut down: they perish at the rebuke of thy countenance. 17 Let thy hand be upon the man of thy right hand, upon the son of man *whom* thou madest strong for thyself. 18 So will not we go back from thee: quicken us, and we will call upon thy name.

19 Turn us again, O Lord God of hosts, cause thy face to shine; and we shall be saved.

and filled the land. 10 The mountains were covered with our shadow; we were like the mighty cedar trees, 11 covering the entire land from the Mediterranean Sea to the Euphrates River. 12 But now you have broken down our walls, leaving us without protection. 13 The boar from the forest roots around us, and the wild animals feed on us.

14 Come back, we beg of you, O God of the armies of heaven, and bless us. Look down from heaven and see our plight and care for this your vine! 15 Protect what you yourself have planted, this son you have raised for yourself. 16 For we are chopped and burned by our enemies. May they perish at your frown. 17 Strengthen the man you love, the son of your choice, 18 and we will never forsake you again. Revive us to trust in you.

19 Turn us again to yourself, O God of the armies of heaven. Look down on us, your face aglow with joy and love—only then shall we be saved.

PSALM 81

To the chief Musician upon Gittith, A Psalm of Asaph

SING aloud unto God our strength: make a joyful noise unto the God of Jacob.

2 Take a psalm, and bring hither the timbrel, the pleasant harp with the psaltery. 3 Blow up the trumpet in the new moon, in the time appointed, on our solemn feast day. 4 For this *was* a statute for Israel, *and* a law of the God of Jacob. 5 This he ordained in Joseph *for* a testimony, when he went out through the land of Egypt: *where* I heard a language *that* I understood not. 6 I removed his shoulder from the burden: his hands were delivered from the pots. 7 Thou calledst in trouble, and I delivered thee; I answered thee in the secret place of thunder: I proved thee at the waters of Mer-i-bah. Se-lah. 8 Hear, O my people, and I will testify unto thee: O Israel, if thou wilt harken unto me; 9 There shall no strange god be in thee; neither shalt thou worship any strange god. 10 I *am* the Lord thy

81 THE LORD MAKES us strong! Sing praises! Sing to Israel's God!

2 Sing, accompanied by drums; pluck the sweet lyre and harp. 3 Sound the trumpet! Come to the joyous celebrations at full moon, new moon and all the other holidays. 4 For God has given us these times of joy; they are scheduled in the laws of Israel. 5 He gave them as reminders of his war against Egypt where we were slaves on foreign soil.

I heard an unknown voice that said, 6 "Now I will relieve your shoulder of its burden; I will free your hands from their heavy tasks." 7 He said, "You cried to me in trouble and I saved you; I answered from Mount Sinai where the thunder hides. I tested your faith at Meribah, when you complained there was no water. 8 Listen to me, O my people, while I give you stern warnings. O Israel, if you will only listen! 9 *You must never worship any other god*, nor ever have an idol in your home. 10 For it

to Canaan, the Lord caused it to cover the hills and spread out from the Mediterranean to the Euphrates. With verse 12, the past nurture is compared with the present rejection. The vine has been ravaged by man and beast as they have passed by:

14-19. The Appeal to the Husbandman. Return . . . and visit this vine. Since God planted and cared for the vine, he should continue to look down on it and visit it. It is God's wrath which has caused the vine to be burned, and hence the people are in danger of annihilation. If God will revive and restore his people, they will worship him. The last occurrence of the refrain is heightened by the use of the covenant name for God. **The man of thy right hand.** The psalmist prays for help for God's people Israel, depicted as the man of God's right hand. Ultimately, of course, the Messiah became the fulfillment of this prayer (cf. the use of the phrase, "Son of man," in the Gospels, and references to Christ as being at the right hand of the Majesty on high – Heb 1:3; 8:1; 10:12; Acts 7:56).

Psalm 81. A Warning from Experience

A hymn of praise opens this psalm, and a prophetic utterance concludes it. The abrupt change at the end of verse 5 has suggested to many commentators that fragments of two psalms are joined together here. However, this view is not imperative, for a solemn festival would be a logical time for such a recital of God's relation to Israel. The special term for festival, the blowing of the trumpet, the references to the new moon and to the full moon probably give the poem double reference to the Feast of Trumpets and the Feast of Tabernacles.

1-5. A Festival Summons. Sing . . . make a joyful noise. This call is a graphic picture of the opening ritual for a great festival. The call was probably vocalized by a priest, who summoned the people to join their voices in joyful singing, the Levitical choir to share with psalms and instruments, and the priests to sound the horns. The **time appointed** in verse 3 is better translated *full moon*.

6-10. A Divine Testimony. I removed his shoulder from the burden. In terse statements, the deliverances of the Exodus are recounted by a prophet who acts as God's spokesman. Since God has always satisfied the needs of Israel, He promises to continue to fill their mouths if only they will open them in complete trust.

NOTES

God, which brought thee out of the land of Egypt: open thy mouth wide, and I will fill it. ¹¹ But my people would not hearken to my voice; and Israel would none of me. ¹² So I gave them up unto their own hearts' lust: *and* they walked in their own counsels.

¹³ Oh that my people had hearkened unto me, *and* Israel had walked in my ways! ¹⁴ I should soon have subdued their enemies, and turned my hand against their adversaries. ¹⁵ The haters of the Lord should have submitted themselves unto him: but their time should have endured for ever. ¹⁶ He should have fed them also with the finest of the wheat: and with honey out of the rock should I have satisfied thee.

PSALM 82

A Psalm of Asaph

God standeth in the congregation of the mighty; he judgeth among the gods. ² How long will ye judge unjustly, and accept the persons of the wicked? Se-lah. ³ Defend the poor and fatherless: do justice to the afflicted and needy. ⁴ Deliver the poor and needy: rid *them* out of the hand of the wicked. ⁵ They know not, neither will they understand; they walk on in darkness: all the foundations of the earth are out of course. ⁶ I have said, Ye *are* gods; and all of you *are* children of the most High. ⁷ But ye shall die like men, and fall like one of the princes.

⁸ Arise, O God, judge the earth: for thou shalt inherit all nations.

PSALM 83

A Song or *Psalm of Asaph*

Keep not thou silence, O God: hold not thy peace, and be not still, O God. ² For, lo, thine enemies make a tumult: and they that hate thee have lifted up the head. ³ They have taken crafty counsel against thy people, and consulted against thy hidden ones. ⁴ They have said, Come, and let us cut them off from *being* a nation; that the name of Israel may be no more in remembrance. ⁵ For they have consulted together with one consent: they are con-

was I, Jehovah your God, who brought you out of the land of Egypt. Only test me! Open your mouth wide and see if I won't fill it. You will receive every blessing you can use! ¹¹ But no, my people won't listen. Israel doesn't want me around. ¹² So I am letting them go their blind and stubborn way, living according to their own desires.

¹³ But oh, that my people would listen to me! Oh, that Israel would follow me, walking in my paths! ¹⁴ How quickly then I would subdue her enemies! How soon my hands would be upon her foes! ¹⁵ Those who hate the Lord would cringe before him; their desolation would last forever. ¹⁶ But he would feed you with the choicest foods. He would satisfy you with honey for the taking.

82 GOD STANDS UP to open heaven's court. He pronounces judgment on the judges. ² How long will you judges refuse to listen to the evidence? How long will you shower special favors on the wicked? ³ Give fair judgment to the poor man, the afflicted, the fatherless, the destitute. ⁴ Rescue the poor and needy from the grasp of evil men. ⁵ But you are so foolish and so ignorant! Because you are in darkness, all the foundations of society are shaken to the core. ⁶ I have called you all "gods" and "sons of the Most High." ⁷ But in death you are mere men. You will fall as any prince—for all must die.

⁸ Stand up, O God, and judge the earth. For all of it belongs to you. All nations are in your hands.

83 O GOD, DON'T sit idly by, silent and inactive when we pray. Answer us! Deliver us!

² Don't you hear the tumult and commotion of your enemies? Don't you see what they are doing, these proud men who hate the Lord? ³ They are full of craftiness and plot against your people, laying plans to slay your precious ones. ⁴ Come, they say, and let us wipe out Israel as a nation—we will destroy the very memory of her existence. ⁵ This was their unanimous decision at their summit conference—they signed a treaty to ally themselves against Almighty

11-16. A Divine Lament. But my people would not hearken. The prophetic utterance continues as a lament over Israel's ingratitude. The cry of verse 13 intensifies the grief of the lament. How different things would have been if only Israel had walked in God's ways! Then she would have had victory and blessings instead of defeat and misery.

Psalm 82. The Final Authority

A scene of judgment upon injustice is set forth in this didactic poem. The proper interpretation of the entire psalm rests on the identity of the second *'Ĕlôhîm* in verse 1. Some commentators translate it literally as *gods* and relate it to a concept of subordinate gods in a heavenly council. Others translate it *angels* and connect it with a less polytheistic concept. Still other interpreters translate it as *judges* and make it refer to the unjust men in authority. The last interpretation seems preferable.

1. The Supreme Judge. God standeth . . . he judgeth. The scene is a vision of the assembly over which God presides. This may be identified with the nation of Israel (cf. Neh 13:1, where we find the synonymous phrase, *qᵉhal ha'elohîm*). Thus God takes his stand in his nation and judges among the human judges appointed over Israel.

2-4. The Corrupt Judges. How long will ye judge unjustly. The arraignment involves the assembled judges of the nation; the indictment concerns the unjust decisions they have pronounced. The basic problem involves the judges' favoring influential men in the courts. These unjust authorities are admonished to cease their partiality, do justice, and defend the oppressed.

5-7. The Just Sentence. Ye shall die . . . and fall. Since these judges lack understanding, the essential quality of justice, judgment is unavoidable. They were given god-like functions as judges, but now they must fall like all men who pervert justice.

8. The Sovereign Judge. Arise, O God, judge the earth. The psalm closes with an appeal to God to complete his work as the Sovereign Judge of all nations. He must take possession as well as pass judgment before true justice can endure.

Psalm 83. Judgment upon the Nations

Psalm 83 is a typical national lament in a time of great danger. Since the enemies of Israel are automatically the enemies of God, the name of God (Yahweh) is at stake. The occasion cannot be identified with certainty, because at no period in Israel's history has such a confederation of nations existed. The psalm may refer to an event unrecorded elsewhere in Israel's history, or it may list tribal groups which merely gave moral support in a time of crisis.

1-8. An Appeal for Action. Keep not thou silence, O God. In the Hebrew this is a strong plea for activity, repeated in a threefold manner. God's silence must be broken because these nations are his enemies as well. They are making a loud noise about their conspiracy to blot out the name of Israel. Most of these peoples named were nomadic tribes dwelling south and east of Israel. Philistia and Tyre are exceptions; they occupied territory west and north respectively. The majority of these were traditional foes of Israel.

NOTES

federate against thee: ⁶ The tabernacles of Edom, and the Ish-ma-el-ites; of Moab, and the Ha-gar-enes; ⁷ Ge-bal, and Ammon, and Am-a-lek; the Philistines with the inhabitants of Tyre; ⁸ Assur also is joined with them: they have holpen the children of Lot. Se-lah.

⁹ Do unto them as *unto* the Mid-i-an-ites; as *to* Sis-e-ra, as *to* Ja-bin, at the brook of Ki-son: ¹⁰ *Which* perished at En-dor: they became *as* dung for the earth. ¹¹ Make their nobles like O-reb, and like Ze-eb: yea, all their princes as Ze-bah, and as Zal-mun-na: ¹² Who said, Let us take to ourselves the houses of God in possession.

¹³ O my God, make them like a wheel; as the stubble before the wind. ¹⁴ As the fire burneth a wood, and as the flame setteth the mountains on fire; ¹⁵ So persecute them with thy tempest, and make them afraid with thy storm. ¹⁶ Fill their faces with shame; that they may seek thy name, O Lord. ¹⁷ Let them be confounded and troubled for ever; yea, let them be put to shame, and perish: ¹⁸ That *men* may know that thou, whose name alone *is* JE-HO-VAH, *art* the most high over all the earth.

PSALM 84

To the chief Musician upon Gittith, A Psalm for the sons of Korah

How amiable *are* thy tabernacles, O Lord of hosts!

² My soul longeth, yea, even fainteth for the courts of the Lord: my heart and my flesh crieth out for the living God. ³ Yea, the sparrow hath found an house, and the swallow a nest for herself, where she may lay her young, *even* thine altars, O Lord of hosts, my King, and my God. ⁴ Blessed *are* they that dwell in thy house: they will be still praising thee. Se-lah.

⁵ Blessed *is* the man whose strength *is* in thee; in whose heart *are* the ways *of them.* ⁶ *Who* passing through the valley of Ba-ca make it a well; the rain also filleth the pools. ⁷ They go from strength to strength, *every one of them* in Zion appeareth before God.

God— ⁶ these Ishmaelites and Edomites and Moabites and Hagrites; ⁷ people from the lands of Gebal, Ammon, Amalek, Philistia and Tyre; ⁸ Assyria has joined them too, and is allied with the descendants of Lot.

⁹ Do to them as once you did to Midian, or as you did to Sisera and Jabin at the river Kishon, ¹⁰ and as you did to your enemies at Endor, whose decaying corpses fertilized the soil. ¹¹ Make their mighty nobles die as Oreb did, and Zeeb; let all their princes die like Zebah and Zalmunna, ¹² who said, "Let us seize for our own use these pasture-lands of God!"

¹³ O my God, blow them away like dust; like chaff before the wind— ¹⁴ as a forest fire that roars across a mountain. ¹⁵ Chase them with your fiery storms, tempests and tornados. ¹⁶ Utterly disgrace them until they recognize your power and name, O Lord. ¹⁷ Make them failures in everything they do; let them be ashamed and terrified ¹⁸ until they learn that you alone, Jehovah, are the God above all gods in supreme charge of all the earth.

84 HOW LOVELY IS your Temple, O Lord of the armies of heaven.

² I long, yes, faint with longing to be able to enter your courtyard and come near to the Living God. ³ Even the sparrows and swallows are welcome to come and nest among your altars and there have their young, O Lord of heaven's armies, my King and my God! ⁴ How happy are those who can live in your Temple, singing your praises.

⁵ Happy are those who are strong in the Lord, who want above all else to follow your steps. ⁶ When they walk through the Valley of Weeping it will become a place of springs where pools of blessing and refreshment collect after rains! ⁷ They will grow constantly in strength and each of them is invited to meet with the Lord in Zion.

9-18. A Prayer for Vengeance. Do unto them. In a blistering imprecation the psalmist appeals for the utter destruction of these would-be foes. He uses the defeat of the Canaanites and Midianites as an illustration of the type of destruction he desires. The severity of his prayer is lessened in verses 16-18 when he inserts a moral basis of conversion and expresses a desire that others may learn from their destruction.

Psalm 84. A Joyful Pilgrimage

This is the song of a pilgrim whose goal is almost reached. There is throughout a sense of peace and communion which transcends the ritual and other outward features of worship. While the poem reflects the sentiments of pilgrims of any age, it appears to come from the period of the monarchy at a time when the Temple was still standing.

1-4. The Longing for God's House. My soul longeth, yea, even fainteth. After exclaiming, **How lovely are thy dwelling places**, the psalmist shares his intense longings, which are about to be satisfied. His whole being yearns for fellowship with God. He envies the birds that live in the temple precincts. He recognizes how fortunate are those servants who live within the temple buildings.

5-8. The Pilgrimage to God's House. Blessed is the man whose strength is in thee. The happiness of the permanent dweller is reflected in the pilgrim. He has a special sense of God's strength and has **in his heart the highway** to Zion. As he passes through the waterless valley, where only balsam trees can grow, a change takes place. The parched valley is transformed into a place of springs as the pilgrim receives and transmits the blessings of God.

8 O Lord God of hosts, hear my prayer: give ear, O God of Jacob. Selah. 9 Behold, O God our shield, and look upon the face of thine anointed.

10 For a day in thy courts *is* better than a thousand. I had rather be a doorkeeper in the house of my God, than to dwell in the tents of wickedness. 11 For the Lord God *is* a sun and shield: the Lord will give grace and glory: no good *thing* will he withhold from them that walk uprightly. 12 O Lord of hosts, blessed *is* the man that trusteth in thee.

PSALM 85

To the chief Musician, A Psalm for the sons of Korah

Lord, thou hast been favourable unto thy land: thou hast brought back the captivity of Jacob. 2 Thou hast forgiven the iniquity of thy people, thou hast covered all their sin. Se-lah. 3 Thou hast taken away all thy wrath: thou hast turned *thyself* from the fierceness of thine anger.

4 Turn us, O God of our salvation, and cause thine anger toward us to cease. 5 Wilt thou be angry with us for ever? wilt thou draw out thine anger to all generations? 6 Wilt thou not revive us again: that thy people may rejoice in thee? 7 Shew us thy mercy, O Lord, and grant us thy salvation.

8 I will hear what God the Lord will speak: for he will speak peace unto his people, and to his saints: but let them not turn again to folly. 9 Surely his salvation *is* nigh them that fear him; that glory may dwell in our land.

10 Mercy and truth are met together; righteousness and peace have kissed *each other*. 11 Truth shall spring out of the earth; and righteousness shall look down from heaven.

12 Yea, the Lord shall give *that which is* good; and our land shall yield her increase. 13 Righteousness shall go before him; and shall set *us* in the way of his steps.

8 O Jehovah, God of the heavenly armies, hear my prayer! Listen, God of Israel. 9 O God, our Defender and our Shield, have mercy on the one you have anointed as your king.

10 A single day spent in your Temple is better than a thousand anywhere else! I would rather be a doorman of the Temple of my God than live in palaces of wickedness. 11 For Jehovah God is our Light and our Protector. He gives us grace and glory. No good thing will he withhold from those who walk along his paths.

12 O Lord of the armies of heaven, blessed are those who trust in you.

85 Lord, you have poured out amazing blessings on this land! You have restored the fortunes of Israel, 2 and forgiven the sins of your people—yes, covered over each one, 3 so that all your wrath, your blazing anger, is now ended.

4 Now bring us back to loving you, O Lord, so that your anger will never need rise against us again. 5 (Or will you be always angry—on and on to distant generations?) 6 Oh, revive us! Then your people can rejoice in you again. 7 Pour out your love and kindness on us, Lord, and grant us your salvation.

8 I am listening carefully to all the Lord is saying—for he speaks peace to his people, his saints, if they will only stop their sinning. 9 Surely his salvation is near to those who reverence him; our land will be filled with his glory.

10 Mercy and truth have met together. Grim justice and peace have kissed! 11 Truth rises from the earth and righteousness smiles down from heaven.

12 Yes, the Lord pours down his blessings on the land and it yields its bountiful crops. 13 Justice goes before him to make a pathway for his steps.

9-12. The Joy of Worship in God's House. For a day in thy courts is better than a thousand. After breathing a short prayer for God's anointed king, the psalmist describes the joy of joining others in the service of worship. One day in the place of worship, he feels, would be worth more than a thousand days anywhere else. He would rather be the humblest servant in the Temple, or get no further than the door, than have a permanent place where wickedness abounds. **A sun and shield.** God, like the chief heavenly body in the physical realm, is the sole source of all our spiritual power, energy, and light. He is our protection, and He bestows needed grace in this life and glory in the life to come. **Blessed,** or *happy.* Happiness is again emphasized for the one who has taken refuge in God through spiritual worship.

Psalm 85. A Cry for Pardon

Though basically a national lament, this psalm has a strong prophetic element as well. The first section (vv. 1-3) appears to refer to the return from captivity, but these verses are idealized beyond the known situation of those days. The psalmist uses this ideal picture to show the sharp contrast with the present and the assurance for the future.

1-3. The Ideal of Forgiveness. Lord, thou hast been favourable. The pictures of God's favor, restoration, forgiveness, and cessation from wrath set forth the ideal of a perfect relation to God. The verbs in these verses, although translated as past tenses, are probably prophetic perfects, indicating that the psalmist views the events they forecast as certain of fulfillment.

4-7. The Reality of the Present. Turn us . . . cause thine anger toward us to cease. The present situation stands in bold relief when viewed in relation to the prophetic ideal. God's anger is still evident and appears to be unending. The psalmist appeals to God to **restore, revive, show** loving-kindness, and **grant** deliverance.

8-13. The Answer of Hope. I will hear what God the Lord will speak. In prophetic fashion the psalmist pauses to hear God's message in answer to the prayer of the people. He is certain that it will be a message of peace. By means of vivid personifications, he describes how real is God's salvation. The union of God's **mercy** or covenant love and our **truth** or faithfulness, of His **righteousness** and our **peace** of heart, of **earth** and **heaven** are certain when God and men meet. As a result of this encounter, God will provide for men's needs and lead them in right paths. For us today, the meeting-place can only be at the foot of the cross.

NOTES

PSALM 86

A Prayer of David

Bow down thine ear, O Lord, hear me: for I *am* poor and needy. ² Preserve my soul; for I *am* holy: O thou my God, save thy servant that trusteth in thee. ³ Be merciful unto me, O Lord: for I cry unto thee daily. ⁴ Rejoice the soul of thy servant: for unto thee, O Lord, do I lift up my soul. ⁵ For thou, Lord, *art* good, and ready to forgive; and plenteous in mercy unto all them that call upon thee. ⁶ Give ear, O Lord, unto my prayer; and attend to the voice of my supplications. ⁷ In the day of my trouble I will call upon thee: for thou wilt answer me.

⁸ Among the gods *there is* none like unto thee, O Lord; neither *are there any works* like unto thy works. ⁹ All nations whom thou hast made shall come and worship before thee, O Lord; and shall glorify thy name. ¹⁰ For thou *art* great, and doest wondrous things: thou *art* God alone.

¹¹ Teach me thy way, O Lord; I will walk in thy truth: unite my heart to fear thy name. ¹² I will praise thee, O Lord my God, with all my heart: and I will glorify thy name for evermore. ¹³ For great *is* thy mercy toward me: and thou hast delivered my soul from the lowest hell.

¹⁴ O God, the proud are risen against me, and the assemblies of violent *men* have sought after my soul; and have not set thee before them. ¹⁵ But thou, O Lord, *art* a God full of compassion, and gracious, longsuffering, and plenteous in mercy and truth. ¹⁶ O turn unto me, and have mercy upon me; give thy strength unto thy servant, and save the son of thine handmaid. ¹⁷ Shew me a token for good; that they which hate me may see *it,* and be ashamed: because thou, Lord, hast holpen me, and comforted me.

PSALM 87

A Psalm or Song for the sons of Korah

His foundation *is* in the holy mountains. ² The Lord loveth the gates of Zion more than all the dwellings of Jacob.

86 BEND DOWN AND hear my prayer, O Lord, and answer me, for I am deep in trouble.

² Protect me from death, for I try to follow all your laws. Save me, for I am serving you and trusting you. ³ Be merciful, O Lord, for I am looking up to you in constant hope. ⁴ Give me happiness, O Lord, for I worship only you. ⁵ O Lord, you are so good and kind, so ready to forgive; so full of mercy for all who ask your aid.

⁶ Listen closely to my prayer, O God. Hear my urgent cry. ⁷ I will call to you whenever trouble strikes, and you will help me.

⁸ Where among the heathen gods is there a god like you? Where are their miracles? ⁹ All the nations—and you made each one—will come and bow before you, Lord, and praise your great and holy name. ¹⁰ For you are great, and do great miracles. You alone are God.

¹¹ Tell me where you want me to go and I will go there. May every fiber of my being unite in reverence to your name. ¹² With all my heart I will praise you. I will give glory to your name forever, ¹³ for you love me so much! You are constantly so kind! You have rescued me from deepest hell.

¹⁴ O God, proud and insolent men defy me; violent, godless men are trying to kill me. ¹⁵ But you are merciful and gentle, Lord, slow in getting angry, full of constant lovingkindness and of truth; ¹⁶ so look down in pity and grant strength to your servant and save me. ¹⁷ Send me a sign of your favor. When those who hate me see it they will lose face because you help and comfort me.

87 HIGH ON HIS holy mountain stands Jerusalem, the city of God, the city he loves more than any other!

Psalm 86. A Prayer for God's Favor

In Psalm 86 we recognize the sincere prayer of an individual who is in personal distress. The general nature of his distress makes the message apply to any person in trouble. It is this lack of specific detail that has led several commentators to view the psalm as corporate rather than individual. While this is basically a personal meditation, the author at times identifies himself with his community.

1-5. A General Plea for Help. Bow down . . . hear me. In general terms the psalmist sets forth his needs. Each plea carries with it the reason why God should answer it. He cries for God to **hear** because of his needy condition, to **keep** because of his pious nature, to **save** because of his continual prayer, and to **gladden** because of his sincere devotions. His faith is based upon the fact that God is a "forgiver," who shows mercy and pardons.

6-10. A Confident Hope in a Response. Give ear . . . for thou wilt answer me. The majesty and power of God make this confidence possible. While the other nations have their own gods, none of them can do the mighty works of the Lord. His greatness will eventually cause these nations to worship Him who is God alone.

11-17. A Prayer for Guidance and Protection. Teach me . . . unite my heart. It is God's teaching that will enable the psalmist to walk in truth. He desires unity of purpose that he may worthily praise and glorify the name of the Lord. With the humility of a slave or a handmaid's son, he asks for God's merciful protection and requests some sign of divine favor toward him.

Psalm 87. The City of God

The psalmist sings a song in praise of Zion as the center of worship for the world. The abrupt, terse style, which identifies the psalm with prophetic oracles, also renders several phrases obscure and difficult. The pronounced universalism points to the author's contact with the major prophets. The mention of Egypt and Babylon together as world powers suggests the period of the Exile as the occasion of composition of the poem.

1-3. The Glories of Zion. Glorious things are spoken of thee. These glories include the facts that God himself found-

157

³ Glorious things are spoken of thee, O city of God. Se-lah. ⁴ I will make mention of Rahab and Babylon to them that know me: behold Philistia, and Tyre, with E-thi-o-pi-a; this *man* was born there. ⁵ And of Zibn it shall be said, This and that man was born in her: and the highest himself shall establish her. ⁶ The Lord shall count, when he writeth up the people, *that* this *man* was born there. Se-lah. ⁷ As well the singers as the players on instruments *shall be there:* all my springs *are* in thee.

³ O city of God, what wondrous tales are told of you! ⁴ Nowadays when I mention among my friends the names of Egypt and Babylonia, Philistia and Tyre, or even distant Ethiopia, someone boasts that he was born in one or another of those countries. ⁵ But someday the highest honor will be to be a native of Jerusalem! For the God above all gods will personally bless this city. ⁶ When he registers her citizens he will place a checkmark beside the names of those who were born here. ⁷ And in the festivals they'll sing, "All my heart is in Jerusalem."

PSALM 88

A Song or *Psalm for the sons of Korah, to the chief Musician upon Mahalath Leannoth, Maschil of Heman the Ezrahite*

O LORD God of my salvation, I have cried day *and* night before thee: ² Let my prayer come before thee: incline thine ear unto my cry; ³ For my soul is full of troubles: and my life draweth nigh unto the grave. ⁴ I am counted with them that go down into the pit: I am as a man *that hath* no strength: ⁵ Free among the dead, like the slain that lie in the grave, whom thou rememberest no more: and they are cut off from thy hand.

⁶ Thou hast laid me in the lowest pit, in darkness, in the deeps. ⁷ Thy wrath lieth hard upon me, and thou hast afflicted *me* with all thy waves. Se-lah. ⁸ Thou hast put away mine acquaintance far from me; thou hast made me an abomination unto them: *I am* shut up, and I cannot come forth. ⁹ Mine eye mourneth by reason of affliction: Lord, I have called daily upon thee, I have stretched out my hands unto thee.

¹⁰ Wilt thou shew wonders to the dead? shall the dead arise *and* praise thee? Se-lah. ¹¹ Shall thy lovingkindness be declared in the grave? *or* thy faithfulness in destruction? ¹² Shall thy wonders be known in the dark? and thy righteousness in the land of forgetfulness?

88 O JEHOVAH, GOD of my salvation, I have wept before you day and night. ² Now hear my prayers; oh, listen to my cry, ³ for my life is full of troubles, and death draws near. ⁴ They say my life is ebbing out—a hopeless case. ⁵ They have left me here to die, like those slain on battlefields, from whom your mercies are removed.

⁶ You have thrust me down to the darkest depths. ⁷ Your wrath lies heavy on me; wave after wave engulfs me. ⁸ You have made my friends to loathe me, and they have gone away. I am in a trap with no way out. ⁹ My eyes grow dim with weeping. Each day I beg your help; O Lord, I reach my pleading hands to you for mercy.

¹⁰ Soon it will be too late! Of what use are your miracles when I am in the grave? How can I praise you then? ¹¹ Can those in the grave declare your lovingkindness? Can they proclaim your faithfulness? ¹² Can the darkness speak of your miracles? Can anyone in the Land of Forgetfulness talk about your help?

ed Zion, that he chose her in preference to every other place where Israelites dwell, and that she is in reality the **city of God.** Further glorious things are referred to in the verses which follow.

4-6. The Citizens of Zion. **This man was born there.** These words act as a refrain in this prophetic utterance. The Egyptians (**Rahab**), the Babylonians, the Philistines, the Phoenicians (**Tyre**), and the Ethiopians are all to become citizens of Zion. The certainty of this edict is assured by God's registering them in his census of the nations as "born in Zion." The concept of the future Jerusalem as the mother of all peoples is developed in Isa 60; 66:7-13,20,23; and referred to in Gal 4:26 and Heb 12:22.

7. The Rejoicing in Zion. **All my springs are in thee.** The musicians are instructed to sing, **All my fountains are in thee. Thee** is feminine, referring to Zion. The psalmist exults in addressing the sacred city as the mother or cradle of Israel's future generations. For *ma'yān,* "springs," in the sense of wife or mother, the source of offspring, see Prov 5:16; Song 4:12,15; Isa 48:1.

Psalm 88. The Darkness of Despair

This lament and prayer of an individual completely engulfed in gloom and despair ends without an answer or even a glimmer of hope. Although some interpreters view the psalm as a corporate sequel to portions of the book of Lamentations, the personal aspects are too intense for such a national interpretation. The psalmist cannot be located in history, but this does not affect the interpretation, for his suffering has a timeless quality.

1,2. His Appeal. **Let my prayer come before thee.** In the midst of his suffering he demonstrates his faith by this direct appeal to the **Lord God of my salvation.** This is not his first plea to God but the continuation of a prayer which begins in the day and runs on into the night.

3-8. His Complaint. **My life draweth nigh unto the grave.** His trouble is so serious that he is as good as dead. Nothing is left for him but the grave and Sheol. His most descriptive term for Sheol is **the pit** (v. 4), a place of darkness where the dead are cut off from God's hand. He seems to feel that the Lord no longer remembers him, since he is counted with the dead.

9-12. His Urgency. **Lord, I have called daily upon thee.** He is certain that he

159

13 But unto thee have I cried, O Lord; and in the morning shall my prayer prevent thee. 14 Lord, why castest thou off my soul? *why* hidest thou thy face from me? 15 I *am* afflicted and ready to die from *my* youth up: *while* I suffer thy terrors I am distracted. 16 Thy fierce wrath goeth over me; thy terrors have cut me off. 17 They came round about me daily like water; they compassed me about together. 18 Lover and friend hast thou put far from me, *and* mine acquaintance into darkness.

PSALM 89

Maschil of Ethan the Ezrahite

I WILL sing of the mercies of the Lord for ever: with my mouth will I make known thy faithfulness to all generations. 2 For I have said, Mercy shall be built up for ever: thy faithfulness shalt thou establish in the very heavens.

3 I have made a covenant with my chosen, I have sworn unto David my servant, 4 Thy seed will I establish for ever, and build up thy throne to all generations. Se-lah.

5 And the heavens shall praise thy wonders, O Lord: thy faithfulness also in the congregation of the saints. 6 For who in the heaven can be compared unto the Lord? *who* among the sons of the mighty can be likened unto the Lord? 7 God is greatly to be feared in the assembly of the saints, and to be had in reverence of all *them that are* about him. 8 O Lord God of hosts, who *is* a strong Lord like unto thee? or to thy faithfulness round about thee?

9 Thou rulest the raging of the sea: when the waves thereof arise, thou stillest them. 10 Thou hast broken Rahab in pieces, as one that is slain; thou hast scattered thine enemies with thy strong arm. 11 The heavens *are* thine, the earth also *is* thine: *as for* the world and the fulness thereof, thou hast founded them. 12 The north and the south thou hast created them: Ta-bor and Her-mon shall rejoice in thy name. 13 Thou hast a mighty arm: strong is thy hand, *and* high is thy right hand.

13 O Lord, I plead for my life and will keep on pleading day by day. 14 O Jehovah, why have you thrown my life away? Why are you turning your face from me, and looking the other way? 15 From my youth I have been sickly and ready to die. I stand helpless before your terrors. 16 Your fierce wrath has overwhelmed me. Your terrors have cut me off. 17 They flow around me all day long. 18 Lover, friend, acquaintance —all are gone. There is only darkness everywhere.

89 FOREVER AND EVER I will sing about the tender kindness of the Lord! Young and old shall hear about your blessings. 2 Your love and kindness are forever; your truth is as enduring as the heavens.

3,4 The Lord God says, "I have made a solemn agreement with my chosen servant David. I have taken an oath to establish his descendants as kings forever on his throne, from now until eternity!"

5 All heaven shall praise your miracles, O Lord; myriads of angels will praise you for your faithfulness. 6 For who in all of heaven can be compared with God? What mightiest angel is anything like him? 7 The highest of angelic powers stand in dread and awe of him. Who is as revered as he by those surrounding him? 8 O Jehovah, Commander of the heavenly armies, where is there any other Mighty One like you? Faithfulness is your very character.

9 You rule the oceans when their waves arise in fearful storms; you speak, and they lie still. 10 You have cut haughty Egypt to pieces. Your enemies are scattered by your awesome power. 11 The heavens are yours, the world, everything—for you created them all. 12 You created north and south! Mount Tabor and Mount Hermon rejoice to be signed by your name as their maker! 13 Strong is your arm! Strong is your hand! Your right hand is lifted high in glorious strength.

will pass beyond God's help when he actually goes to Sheol. Therefore, God must act immediately if He is going to show His wonders, loving-kindness, faithfulness, and righteousness.

13-18. His Desperation. But unto thee have I cried. His petition becomes more impassioned with each outcry. Now in a spirit of desperation, he asks the ever-recurring question, **Why . . . ?** Having prayed continually for relief since his youth, only one conclusion is left: "It is all the result of God's wrath." He makes no further request, but leaves his burden with the Lord. How different is the NT hope in life with Christ beyond the grave (cf. Phil 1:21,23; II Cor 5:1-8).

Psalm 89. An Appeal to God's Promises

This psalm is basically a lament by an individual who speaks for the nation. The actual lament is prefaced by a lengthy introduction, which consists of a hymn of praise and an oracle. These divergent elements have suggested to some commentators that this piece is a composite of two or three original poems. While it is possible that the author incorporated existing poems, the subject matter is arranged in a logical manner. The hymn and oracle both present the basis for the lament.

1-4. God's Limitless Loving-kindness. Mercies . . . faithfulness . . . covenant. In this beautiful introduction the psalmist presents the themes which he will develop. The Lord has shown his *loving-kindness* (v. 1, ASV) in his acts of deliverance. His **faithfulness** is the guarantee of his continued loving-kindness. His **covenant** gives binding power to these important attributes.

5-18. God's Incomparable Faithfulness. For who in the heaven can be compared unto the Lord? The incomparableness of God both in heaven and among his saints within Israel is set forth as a plea to God and a comfort to the people. The reference to Rahab (v. 10) employs a term from an ancient Near Eastern legend to speak of God's victory over Egypt at the Red Sea (cf. Job 9:13; Ps 74:13-15; 87:4; I Sam 30:7; Isa 51:9,10). The other allusions are used here to intensify the picture of God's power in creation, his victory over all opposition, and his dominion over heaven and earth.

14 Justice and judgment *are* the habitation of thy throne: mercy and truth shall go before thy face. 15 Blessed *is* the people that know the joyful sound: they shall walk, O Lord, in the light of thy countenance. 16 In thy name shall they rejoice all the day: and in thy righteousness shall they be exalted. 17 For thou *art* the glory of their strength: and in thy favour our horn shall be exalted. 18 For the Lord *is* our defence; and the Holy One of Israel *is* our king.

19 Then thou spakest in vision to thy holy one, and saidst, I have laid help upon *one that is* mighty; I have exalted *one* chosen out of the people. 20 I have found David my servant; with my holy oil have I anointed him: 21 With whom my hand shall be established: mine arm also shall strengthen him. 22 The enemy shall not exact upon him; nor the son of wickedness afflict him. 23 And I will beat down his foes before his face, and plague them that hate him. 24 But my faithfulness and my mercy *shall be* with him: and in my name shall his horn be exalted. 25 I will set his hand also in the sea, and his right hand in the rivers. 26 He shall cry unto me, Thou *art* my father, my God, and the rock of my salvation.

27 Also I will make him *my* first-born, higher than the kings of the earth. 28 My mercy will I keep for him for evermore, and my covenant shall stand fast with him. 29 His seed also will I make *to endure* for ever, and his throne as the days of heaven. 30 If his children forsake my law, and walk not in my judgments; 31 If they break my statutes, and keep not my commandments; 32 Then will I visit their transgression with the rod, and their iniquity with stripes. 33 Nevertheless my lovingkindness will I not utterly take from him, nor suffer my faithfulness to fail. 34 My covenant will I not break, nor alter the thing that is gone out of my lips. 35 Once have I sworn by my holiness that I will not lie unto David. 36 His seed shall endure for ever, and his throne as the sun before me. 37 It shall be established for ever as the moon, and *as* a faithful witness in heaven. Se-lah.

14,15 Your throne is founded on two strong pillars—the one is Justice and the other Righteousness. Mercy and Truth walk before you as your attendants. Blessed are those who hear the joyful blast of the trumpet, for they shall walk in the light of your presence. 16 They rejoice all day long in your wonderful reputation and in your perfect righteousness. 17 You are their strength. What glory! Our power is based on your favor! 18 Yes, our protection is from the Lord himself and he, the Holy One of Israel, has given us our king.

19 In a vision you spoke to your prophet and said, "I have chosen a splendid young man from the common people to be the king— 20 he is my servant David! I have anointed him with my holy oil. 21 I will steady him and make him strong. 22 His enemies shall not outwit him, nor shall the wicked overpower him. 23 I will beat down his adversaries before him, and destroy those who hate him. 24 I will protect and bless him constantly and surround him with my love; he will be great because of me. 25 He will hold sway from the Euphrates River to the Mediterranean Sea. 26 And he will cry to me, 'You are my Father, my God, and my Rock of Salvation.'

27 "I will treat him as my firstborn son, and make him the mightiest king in all the earth. 28 I will love him forever, and be kind to him always; my covenant with him will never end. 29 He will always have an heir; his throne will be as endless as the days of heaven. 30,31,32 If his children forsake my laws and don't obey them, then I will punish them, 33 but I will never completely take away my lovingkindness from them, nor let my promise fail. 34 No, I will not break my covenant; I will not take back one word of what I said. 35,36 For I have sworn to David (and a holy God can never lie), that his dynasty will go on forever, and his throne will continue to the end of time. 37 It shall be eternal as the moon, my faithful witness in the sky!"

19-37. God's Sworn Promise. Then thou spakest in vision. The motif of the covenant with David now becomes central, though it is still connected with God's loving-kindness and faithfulness (cf. vv. 24,28,33). The psalmist first deals with the divine promise to David. The former promise to the nation as God's firstborn in his estimation (Ex 4:22) is now focused on the king; the epithet of verse 27 is extended to all the Davidic succession, culminating in Jesus, God's anointed one (Messiah). Then the emphasis is shifted in verse 29 to the working out of the promise through the seed of David. While he appeals to God's sworn testimony that the covenant will stand, he recognizes that punishment must come upon David's seed for their unfaithfulness (vv. 30-32).

NOTES

38 But thou hast cast off and abhorred, thou hast been wroth with thine anointed. 39 Thou hast made void the covenant of thy servant: thou hast profaned his crown *by casting it* to the ground. 40 Thou hast broken down all his hedges; thou hast brought his strong holds to ruin. 41 All that pass by the way spoil him: he is a reproach to his neighbours. 42 Thou hast set up the right hand of his adversaries; thou hast made all his enemies to rejoice. 43 Thou hast also turned the edge of his sword, and hast not made him to stand in the battle. 44 Thou hast made his glory to cease, and cast his throne down to the ground. 45 The days of his youth hast thou shortened: thou hast covered him with shame. Se-lah.

46 How long, Lord? wilt thou hide thyself for ever? shall thy wrath burn like fire? 47 Remember how short my time is: wherefore hast thou made all men in vain? 48 What man *is he that* liveth, and shall not see death? shall he deliver his soul from the hand of the grave? Se-lah.

49 Lord, where *are* thy former lovingkindnesses, *which* thou swarest unto David in thy truth? 50 Remember, Lord, the reproach of thy servants; *how* I do bear in my bosom *the reproach of* all the mighty people; 51 Wherewith thine enemies have reproached, O Lord; wherewith they have reproached the footsteps of thine anointed.

52 Blessed *be* the Lord for evermore. Amen, and Amen.

38 Then why cast me off, rejected? Why be so angry with the one you chose as king? 39 Have you renounced your covenant with him? For you have thrown his crown in the dust. 40 You have broken down the walls protecting him and laid in ruins every fort defending him. 41 Everyone who comes along has robbed him while his neighbors mock. 42 You have strengthened his enemies against him and made them rejoice. 43 You have struck down his sword and refused to help him in battle. 44 You have ended his splendor and overturned his throne. 45 You have made him old before his time and publicly disgraced him.

46 O Jehovah, how long will this go on? Will you hide yourself from me forever? How long will your wrath burn like fire? 47 Oh, remember how short you have made man's lifespan. Is it an empty, futile life you give the sons of men? 48 No man can live forever. All will die. Who can rescue his life from the power of the grave?

49 Lord, where is the love you used to have for me? Where is your kindness that you promised to David with a faithful pledge? 50 Lord, see how all the people are despising me. 51 Your enemies joke about me, the one you anointed as their king.

52 And yet—blessed be the Lord forever! Amen and amen!

PSALM 90

A Prayer of Moses the man of God

LORD, thou hast been our dwelling place in all generations. 2 Before the mountains were brought forth, or ever thou hadst formed the earth and the world, even from everlasting to everlasting, thou *art* God.

3 Thou turnest man to destruction; and sayest, Return, ye children of men. 4 For a thousand years in thy sight *are but* as yesterday when it is past, and *as* a watch in the night. 5 Thou carriest them away as with a flood; they are *as* a sleep: in the morning *they are* like grass *which* groweth up. 6 In the morn-

A prayer of Moses, the man of God.

90 LORD, THROUGH ALL the generations you have been our home! 2 Before the mountains were created, before the earth was formed, you are God without beginning or end.

3 You speak, and man turns back to dust. 4 A thousand years are but as yesterday to you! They are like a single hour! 5,6 We glide along the tides of time as swiftly as a racing river, and vanish as quickly as a dream. We are like grass that is green in the morning but mowed down and withered

**38-51. God's Shattered Covenant. But
thou hast cast off and abhorred.** The
emphatic **But thou** marks a sharp contrast between the promises of God and
the present situation. The covenant has
been made void, the city walls are
broken down, the land is spoiled, the
battle lost, and the throne cast down.
The shortening of the king's youth may
refer to Jehoiachin, who was only eighteen when carried away captive. After
setting forth the present plight of the
nation, the psalmist turns to his appeal in
verse 46. The transitoriness of human
life, God's power to save, and his former
loving-kindness are all linked to the covenant with David as reasons for immediate restoration. While no hope is expressed, the enthusiasm of the former
sections would suggest a positive expectation of hope.

52. Closing Benediction. **Blessed be
the Lord for evermore.** This benediction
is not a part of the psalm itself, but a
doxology added as a formal close to
Book III.

BOOK IV. Psalms 90—106

The fourth major division in the Psalter is actually a part of a larger collection embracing Psalms 90—150. The
break at Psalm 106 seems to be made
for convenience, since the same dominant thought continues in Psalm 107.
While the psalms in Book I were primarily personal and those in Books II
and III were generally national, the remainder of the Psalter is basically liturgical. The emphasis is upon the worship
of God's people as they offer their thanksgiving and praise in a form suitable for
temple worship. The covenant name for
God, *Yahweh,* predominates. It occurs
in every psalm in Book IV and is absent from only two in Book V.

Psalm 90. Our Help in Ages Past

Although this may well be the meditation of an individual, its purpose is
clearly to voice the petition of a corporate group. The author looks back on a
long period of history to arrive at his
concept of God's wrath. In view of man's
frailty and brevity, he pleads for restoration to God's favor.

1-6. Man's Life Contrasted with God's
Eternity. **Lord, thou hast been our
dwelling place.** The psalmist begins by
citing his confidence in God's everlasting nature (cf. Deut 33:27). Truly **all
generations** have found this to be true.

The Lord is immortal; man is mortal.
The Lord is above time; man is ever
time-conscious. The Lord is from everlasting to everlasting; man, like grass,
is short-lived. The similes of verses 4-6
emphasize not merely the brevity or
frailty of life, but man's dependence upon the Eternal. Man is surely at God's
disposal, returning to dust at His command and being swept away as by a
flood.

NOTES

ing it flourisheth, and groweth up; in the evening it is cut down, and withereth. ⁷ For we are consumed by thine anger, and by thy wrath are we troubled. ⁸ Thou hast set our iniquities before thee, our secret *sins* in the light of thy countenance. ⁹ For all our days are passed away in thy wrath: we spend our years as a tale *that is told.*

¹⁰ The days of our years *are* threescore years and ten; and if by reason of strength *they be* fourscore years, yet *is* their strength labour and sorrow; for it is soon cut off, and we fly away. ¹¹ Who knoweth the power of thine anger? even according to thy fear, *so is* thy wrath.

¹² So teach *us* to number our days, that we may apply *our* hearts unto wisdom.

¹³ Return, O Lord, how long? and let it repent thee concerning thy servants. ¹⁴ O satisfy us early with thy mercy; that we may rejoice and be glad all our days. ¹⁵ Make us glad according to the days *wherein* thou hast afflicted us, *and* the years *wherein* we have seen evil. ¹⁶ Let thy work appear unto thy servants, and thy glory unto their children. ¹⁷ And let the beauty of the Lord our God be upon us: and establish thou the work of our hands upon us; yea, the work of our hands establish thou it.

PSALM 91

He that dwelleth in the secret place of the most High shall abide under the shadow of the Almighty.

² I will say of the Lord, *He is* my refuge and my fortress: my God; in him will I trust. ³ Surely he shall deliver thee from the snare of the fowler, *and* from the noisome pestilence. ⁴ He shall cover thee with his feathers, and under his wings shalt thou trust: his truth *shall be thy* shield and buckler. ⁵ Thou shalt not be afraid for the terror by night; *nor* for the arrow *that* flieth by day; ⁶ *Nor* for the pestilence *that* walketh in darkness; *nor* for the destruction *that* wasteth at noonday.

⁷ A thousand shall fall at thy side, and ten thousand at thy right hand; *but* it shall not come nigh thee. ⁸ Only with thine eyes shalt thou behold and see the reward of the wicked. ⁹ Because thou

before the evening shadows fall. ⁷ We die beneath your anger; we are overwhelmed by your wrath. ⁸ You spread out our sins before you—our secret sins—and see them all. ⁹ No wonder the years are long and heavy here beneath your wrath. All our days are filled with sighing.

¹⁰ Seventy years are given us! And some may even live to eighty. But even the best of these years are often emptiness and pain; soon they disappear, and we are gone. ¹¹ Who can realize the terrors of your anger? Which of us can fear you as he should?

¹² Teach us to number our days and recognize how few they are; help us to spend them as we should.

¹³ O Jehovah, come and bless us! How long will you delay? Turn away your anger from us. ¹⁴ Satisfy us in our earliest youth with your lovingkindness, giving us constant joy to the end of our lives. ¹⁵ Give us gladness in proportion to our former misery! Replace the evil years with good. ¹⁶ Let us see your miracles again; let our children see glorious things, the kind you used to do, ¹⁷ and let the Lord our God favor us and give us success.

91 WE LIVE WITHIN the shadow of the Almighty, sheltered by the God who is above all gods.

² This I declare, that he alone is my refuge, my place of safety; he is my God, and I am trusting him. ³ For he rescues you from every trap, and protects you from the fatal plague. ⁴ He will shield you with his wings! They will shelter you. His faithful promises are your armor. ⁵ Now you don't need to be afraid of the dark any more, nor fear the dangers of the day; ⁶ nor dread the plagues of darkness, nor disasters in the morning.

⁷ Though a thousand fall at my side, though ten thousand are dying around me, the evil will not touch me. ⁸ I will see how the wicked are punished but I will not share it. ⁹ For Jehovah is my refuge! I choose the

7-12. Man Consumed by God's Wrath. For we are consumed by thine anger. The psalmist now interprets the reason for man's transitory nature and his suffering. He realizes from history and personal experience that God's face is as the light of the sun in its power to probe into the depths of man's being. Compared with God's timelessness, a lifetime of seventy or eighty years seems pitifully short. Furthermore, this span of years is filled with sorrow and suffering. Out of this pessimistic view of life comes the plaintive cry for teaching and wisdom to help a man discern the true meaning of life.

13-17. Man Seeking for God's Favor. Return, O Lord . . . satisfy us. The appeal introduced in verse 12 is continued throughout the poem. The writer desires God to grant his people happiness in proportion to the suffering they have endured under His wrath. The psalm closes with a plea that God's loveliness or graciousness (his **beauty**) may be the basis of the Lord's preparing and establishing (cf. Eph 2:10) all the daily tasks ahead (viz., **the work of our hands**; cf. Deut 2:7; 14:29; 16:15; 24:19).

Psalm 91. The Security of Trust

In this companion poem to Psalm 90 the psalmist sings a noble song of trust, but he has a didactic purpose as well. The prophetic oracle at the close adds a note of authority to the confidence expressed throughout. The depth of trust and the quiet confidence suggest that this is the meditation of an individual. However, its possible use as an antiphonal song adapts it for congregational use.

1,2. Divine Protection. He is my refuge and my fortress. The writer opens with a powerful presentation of his theme — the security of the one who trusts completely in God. **The secret place** may better be translated *the shelter,* which meaning better parallels the concept of *the shadow.*

3-8. Divine Providence. Surely he shall deliver thee . . . cover thee. The basic idea of protection is expanded to include many acts of providential care as well as active deliverance. Because of the references to pestilence and disease, many commentators treat the entire psalm as a polemic against the use of magic formulae for warding off demons. Indeed, the Talmud suggests that the psalm be used in the case of demonic attacks. The **terror by night** may refer to the night demon Lilith, while the **arrow . . . by day** may describe the devices of the wicked demons. The **pestilence . . . in darkness** may have affinity with the demon Namtar, while the **destruction . . . at noonday** may refer to a one-eyed demon also mentioned in Rabbinical tradition. Even if these ideas were absent from the author's thoughts, they were very much a part of the psalm in its actual Jewish use. The **snare of the fowler** is a reference to traps set by adversaries (cf. Ps 124:7). **Noisome pestilence** is literally, *death of destructions,* perhaps referring to a violent death. The psalmist was conscious of God's care amid the varied circumstances of life.

9-13. Divine Reward. Because thou

NOTES

hast made the Lord, *which is* my refuge, *even* the most High, thy habitation; ¹⁰ There shall no evil befall thee, neither shall any plague come nigh thy dwelling. ¹¹ For he shall give his angels charge over thee, to keep thee in all thy ways. ¹² They shall bear thee up in *their* hands, lest thou dash thy foot against a stone. ¹³ Thou shalt tread upon the lion and adder: the young lion and the dragon shalt thou trample under feet.

¹⁴ Because he hath set his love upon me, therefore will I deliver him: I will set him on high, because he hath known my name. ¹⁵ He shall call upon me, and I will answer him: I *will be* with him in trouble; I will deliver him, and honour him. ¹⁶ With long life will I satisfy him, and shew him my salvation.

PSALM 92

A Psalm or *Song for the sabbath day*

It *is a* good *thing* to give thanks unto the Lord, and to sing praises unto thy name, O most High:

² To shew forth thy lovingkindness in the morning, and thy faithfulness every night, ³ Upon an instrument of ten strings, and upon the psaltery; upon the harp with a solemn sound. ⁴ For thou, Lord, hast made me glad through thy work: I will triumph in the works of thy hands.

⁵ O Lord, how great are thy works! *and* thy thoughts are very deep. ⁶ A brutish man knoweth not; neither doth a fool understand this. ⁷ When the wicked spring as the grass, and when all the workers of iniquity do flourish; *it is* that they shall be destroyed for ever: ⁸ But thou, Lord, *art most* high for evermore. ⁹ For, lo, thine enemies, O Lord, for, lo, thine enemies shall perish; all the workers of iniquity shall be scattered.

¹⁰ But my horn shalt thou exalt like *the horn of* an unicorn: I shall be anointed with fresh oil. ¹¹ Mine eye also shall see *my desire* on mine enemies, *and* mine ears shall hear *my desire* of the wicked that rise up against me. ¹² The righteous shall flourish like the palm tree: he shall grow like a cedar in Lebanon. ¹³ Those that be planted in the house of the Lord shall

God above all gods to shelter me. ¹⁰ How then can evil overtake me or any plague come near? ¹¹ For he orders his angels to protect you wherever you go. ¹² They will steady you with their hands to keep you from stumbling against the rocks on the trail. ¹³ You can safely meet a lion or step on poisonous snakes, yes, even trample them beneath your feet!

¹⁴ For the Lord says, "Because he loves me, I will rescue him; I will make him great because he trusts in my name. ¹⁵ When he calls on me I will answer; I will be with him in trouble, and rescue him and honor him. ¹⁶ I will satisfy him with a full life and give him my salvation."

A song to sing on the Lord's Day

92 It is good to say, "Thank you" to the Lord, to sing praises to the God who is above all gods.

² Every morning tell him, "Thank you for your kindness," and every evening rejoice in all his faithfulness. ³ Sing his praises, accompanied by music from the harp and lute and lyre. ⁴ You have done so much for me, O Lord. No wonder I am glad! I sing for joy.

⁵ O Lord, what miracles you do! And how deep are your thoughts! ⁶ Unthinking people do not understand them! No fool can comprehend this: ⁷ that although the wicked flourish like weeds, there is only eternal destruction ahead of them. ⁸ But the Lord continues forever, exalted in the heavens, ⁹ while his enemies—all evil-doers— shall be scattered.

¹⁰ But you have made me as strong as a wild bull. How refreshed I am by your blessings! ¹¹ I have heard the doom of my enemies announced and seen them destroyed. ¹² But the godly shall flourish like palm trees, and grow tall as the cedars of Lebanon. ¹³ For they are transplanted into the Lord's own garden, and are under his per-

hast made the Lord . . . thy habitation.
The psalmist, reverting to his main
theme, carries forward the idea of reward alluded to in verse 8. The man
of faith is assured that God will send
guardian angels to protect him from
plagues and stumbling. Satan quoted
these words in tempting Jesus (Mt 4:6;
Lk 4:10). According to the Talmud,
every man has two ministering angels
beside him during his entire life.

14-16. Divine Promise. Because he
hath set his love upon me. The authority
behind the idea of reward is heightened
by the oracle from God. The promise
includes the blessings of deliverance, exaltation, answer to prayer, long life, and
victory. These blessings and more are
promised to the one who has come to
love and trust God.

Psalm 92. A Hymn of Gratitude

An individual with great confidence
in the righteous judgment of God here
expresses his thanksgiving. His confidence
goes beyond theory or formal theology,
for it is derived from personal experience. The use of the psalm as a hymn
for the weekly observance of the Sabbath is attested by ancient Jewish
sources. The notation in verse 3 of the
instruments to be used shows that it
was probably designed for corporate
worship.

1-4. The Delight of Praise. It is a
good thing to give thanks . . . to sing
praises. The psalmist expresses his personal delight in the services of the Temple. After enumerating the instruments
involved, he clearly sets forth the basis
of public praise. It is God's wondrous
works that make the worshipers glad.

5-8. The Sovereignty of God. O Lord,
how great are thy works. The sovereign,
sublime nature of God as expressed in
his works and his thoughts is set in contrast to the lack of comprehension of the
fool and the brutish man. In comparison
to the sure destruction of these men
who lack perception and understanding,
God stands immovable on high for evermore.

9-15. The Certainty of Judgment.
Thine enemies shall perish. . . . but my
horn shalt thou exalt. The writer's enemies are again viewed as God's enemies,
too. The psalmist is certain that God will
bring true retribution, for he feels at one
with the Lord, that he is inseparable
from the vindicating triumph of God's
righteous cause. He closes with a beau-

flourish in the courts of our God. ¹⁴ They shall still bring forth fruit in old age; they shall be fat and flourishing; ¹⁵ To shew that the Lord *is* upright: *he is* my rock, and *there is* no unrighteousness in him.

PSALM 93

THE Lord reigneth, he is clothed with majesty; the Lord is clothed with strength, *wherewith* he hath girded himself: the world also is stablished, that it cannot be moved.

² Thy throne *is* established of old: thou *art* from everlasting. ³ The floods have lifted up, O Lord, the floods have lifted up their voice; the floods lift up their waves. ⁴ The Lord on high *is* mightier than the noise of many waters, *yea, than* the mighty waves of the sea. ⁵ Thy testimonies are very sure: holiness becometh thine house, O Lord, for ever.

PSALM 94

O LORD God, to whom vengeance belongeth; O God, to whom vengeance belongeth, shew thyself. ² Lift up thyself, thou judge of the earth: render a reward to the proud. ³ Lord, how long shall the wicked, how long shall the wicked triumph? ⁴ *How long* shall they utter *and* speak hard things? *and* all the workers of iniquity boast themselves? ⁵ They break in pieces thy people, O Lord, and afflict thine heritage. ⁶ They slay the widow and the stranger, and murder the fatherless. ⁷ Yet they say, The Lord shall not see, neither shall the God of Jacob regard *it*.

⁸ Understand, ye brutish among the people: and *ye* fools, when will ye be wise? ⁹ He that planted the ear, shall he not hear? he that formed the eye, shall he not see? ¹⁰ He that chastiseth the heathen, shall not he correct? he that teacheth man knowledge, *shall not he know?*

¹¹ The Lord knoweth the thoughts of man, that they *are* vanity. ¹² Blessed *is* the man whom thou chastenest, O Lord, and teachest him out of thy law; ¹³ That thou mayest give him rest from the days of adversity, until the pit be digged for

sonal care. ¹⁴ Even in old age they will still produce fruit and be vital and green. ¹⁵ This honors the Lord, and exhibits his faithful care. He is my shelter. There is nothing but goodness in him!

93 JEHOVAH IS KING! He is robed in majesty and strength. The world is his throne.

O Lord, you have reigned from prehistoric times, from the everlasting past. ³ The mighty oceans thunder your praise. ⁴ You are mightier than all the breakers pounding on the seashores of the world! ⁵ Your royal decrees cannot be changed. Holiness is forever the keynote of your reign.

94 LORD GOD, TO whom vengeance belongs, let your glory shine out. Arise and judge the earth; sentence the proud to the penalties they deserve. ³ Lord, how long shall the wicked be allowed to triumph and exult? ⁴ Hear their insolence! See their arrogance! How these men of evil boast! ⁵ See them oppressing your people, O Lord, afflicting those you love. ⁶·⁷ They murder widows, immigrants, and orphans, for "The Lord isn't looking," they say, "and besides, he doesn't care."

⁸ Fools! ⁹ Is God deaf and blind—he who makes ears and eyes? ¹⁰ He punishes the nations—won't he also punish you? He knows everything—doesn't he also know what you are doing?

¹¹ The Lord is fully aware of how limited and futile the thoughts of mankind are, ¹²·¹³ so he helps us by punishing us. This makes us follow his paths, and gives us respite from our enemies while God traps

tiful description of the happy lot of the righteous, who are transplanted into the household of the Lord (v. 13). Following the pattern of antiquity, he gloats over this certain destruction, but returns quickly to a description of the happy lot of the righteous.

Psalm 93. The Everlasting King

The emphasis upon the enthronement of Yahweh as King gives this psalm close affinity with Psalms 47 and 96–99. For this reason, these six poems are usually called Royal Psalms or Enthronement Psalms. Mowinckel and others have done extensive research in an attempt to reconstruct an actual enthronement ceremony in connection with the New Year's celebration. These psalms would take on increased meaning and significance if it could be shown that they were used in such a ceremony. However, positive evidence of such a practice is indeed slight.

1,2. God's Kingship. **The Lord reigneth.** These opening words can better be translated, *Yahweh is King* or *has become king.* He has robed himself with majesty, has girded himself with strength, and is ready for action. The psalmist hastens to state that the Lord's rulership is not a new thing, but has been **established of old** (cf. Jud 8:23), while God himself is **from everlasting.**

3,4. God's Might. **Mightier than the noise of many waters.** It is God's might that assures the permanence and immutability of his rule. Raging storms and pounding waves cannot shake his everlasting throne. The Lord's supremacy in creation is probably alluded to here, as well as his victory over heathen powers.

5. God's Government. **Thy testimonies are very sure.** God's kingship and might are evidenced by his moral laws or decrees. Permanence and immutability characterize the holiness God imparts to his house.

Psalm 94. A Plea for Vengeance

Although this lament embraces the whole community, it is pervaded by a deep personal element. Some writers consider the psalm to be composite, but there is little justification for denying its basic unity. Its position between two joyous psalms sets it out in sharper contrast. While it is possible that foreign oppressors are in view, the author is mainly concerned over those leaders in Israel who oppress the righteous.

1-7. The Judge Sought. **Shew thyself. . . . lift up thyself.** The psalmist appeals to the Lord as the God of **vengeance** and **judge of the earth,** as the One having the power to punish and the right to effect retribution. The big question is not whether God can avenge wrongs done, but **how long** it will be before he brings about justice.

8-11. The Unwise Rebuked. **Understand, ye brutish . . . ye fools.** These two epithets classify the oppressors as cruel and lacking in common sense. The direct address (v. 8) drives home the point that God is aware of all that goes on in the world.

12-15. The Righteous Vindicated. **Blessed is the man.** Happy is the man who is educated by God. He will have strength for the difficult days and assurance of ultimate vindication.

NOTES

the wicked. ¹⁴ For the Lord will not cast off his people, neither will he forsake his inheritance. ¹⁵ But judgment shall return unto righteousness: and all the upright in heart shall follow it.

¹⁶ Who will rise up for me against the evildoers? *or* who will stand up for me against the workers of iniquity? ¹⁷ Unless the Lord *had been* my help, my soul had almost dwelt in silence. ¹⁸ When I said, My foot slippeth; thy mercy, O Lord, held me up.

¹⁹ In the multitude of my thoughts within me thy comforts delight my soul. ²⁰ Shall the throne of iniquity have fellowship with thee, which frameth mischief by a law? ²¹ They gather themselves together against the soul of the righteous, and condemn the innocent blood. ²² But the Lord is my defence; and my God *is* the rock of my refuge. ²³ And he shall bring upon them their own iniquity, and shall cut them off in their own wickedness; *yea,* the Lord our God shall cut them off.

them and destroys them. ¹⁴ The Lord will not forsake his people, for they are his prize. ¹⁵ Judgment will again be just and all the upright will rejoice.

¹⁶ Who will protect me from the wicked? Who will be my shield? ¹⁷ I would have died unless the Lord had helped me. ¹⁸ I screamed, "I'm slipping, Lord!" and he was kind and saved me.

¹⁹ Lord, when doubts fill my mind, when my heart is in turmoil, quiet me and give me renewed hope and cheer. ²⁰ Will you permit a corrupt government to rule under your protection—a government permitting wrong to defeat right? ^{21,22} Do you approve of those who condemn the innocent to death? No! The Lord my God is my fortress—the mighty Rock where I can hide. ²³ God has made the sins of evil men to boomerang upon them! He will destroy them by their own plans. Jehovah our God will cut them off.

PSALM 95

O COME, let us sing unto the Lord: let us make a joyful noise to the rock of our salvation.

² Let us come before his presence with thanksgiving, and make a joyful noise unto him with psalms. ³ For the Lord *is* a great God, and a great King above all gods. ⁴ In his hand *are* the deep places of the earth: the strength of the hills *is* his also. ⁵ The sea *is* his, and he made it: and his hands formed the dry *land.* ⁶ O come, let us worship and bow down: let us kneel before the Lord our maker. ⁷ For he *is* our God; and we *are* the people of his pasture, and the sheep of his hand. To day if ye will hear his voice,

⁸ Harden not your heart, as in the provocation, *and* as *in* the day of temptation in the wilderness: ⁹ When your fathers tempted me, proved me, and saw my work. ¹⁰ Forty years long was I grieved with *this* generation, and said, It *is* a people that do err in their heart, and they have not known my ways: ¹¹ Unto whom I sware in my wrath that they should not enter into my rest.

95 OH, COME, LET us sing to the Lord! Give a joyous shout in honor of the Rock of our salvation!

² Come before him with thankful hearts. Let us sing him psalms of praise. ³ For the Lord is a great God, the great King of all gods. ⁴ He controls the formation of the depths of the earth and the mightiest mountains; all are his. ⁵ He made the sea and formed the land; they too are his. ⁶ Come, kneel before the Lord our Maker, ⁷ for he is our God. We are his sheep and he is our Shepherd. Oh, that you would hear him calling you today and come to him!

⁸ Don't harden your hearts as Israel did in the wilderness at Meribah and Massah. ⁹ For there your fathers doubted me, though they had seen so many of my miracles before. My patience was severely tried by their complaints. ¹⁰ "For forty years I watched them in disgust," the Lord God says. "They were a nation whose thoughts and heart were far away from me. They refused to accept my laws. ¹¹ Therefore in mighty wrath I swore that they would never enter the Promised Land, the place of rest I planned for them."

16-23. The Judgment Realized. Who will rise up for me against the evildoers? From his experience with God, the psalmist answers his own question: God will surely give the vengeance he seeks (cf. v. 1).

Psalm 95. A Call to Worship

This psalm combines a hymn and a prophetic oracle for group worship. The latter section has the distinctly didactic purpose of reminding the worshipers of their forebears' failures, lest they fall into the same errors. The hymn section was undoubtedly designed as a processional to be sung as the congregation gathered for Sabbath worship. Along with the other psalms in this group (95–100), it seems to have been composed for use in the services of the Second Temple.

1,2. The Call Announced. O come, let us sing. This summons was probably sounded by a Levitical choir as the procession to the Temple began. The happy worshipers quickly joined in by making a joyful noise of praise in exuberant Oriental style.

3-5. The Lord Described. A great God, and a great King. The basis for the summons of verses 1 and 2 is declared in true hymn style. The greatness of Yahweh as King and Creator and Shepherd is beautifully expressed. The menace of foreign beliefs makes necessary a clear statement of the nature of God as a preparation for worship.

6,7. The Call Repeated. O come, let us worship. The processional has now reached the temple gates. The joyful singing gives way to the more solemn acts of worship, such as bowing down and kneeling before God. The emphasis upon God's sovereignty over his cosmic creation gives way to a reminder to the worshipers of his special relation to Israel.

8-11. The Warning Voiced. Harden not your heart. The reminder of Israel's sin in wilderness days serves as a warning to those waiting to enter the Temple. God's **rest** refers historically to entrance into the Promised Land, which was denied to those who doubted. Here the worshipers are exhorted to keep their hearts tender before the Lord lest he reject them also.

PSALM 96

O SING unto the Lord a new song: sing unto the Lord, all the earth. ² Sing unto the Lord, bless his name; shew forth his salvation from day to day.

³ Declare his glory among the heathen, his wonders among all people. ⁴ For the Lord *is* great, and greatly to be praised: he *is* to be feared above all gods. ⁵ For all the gods of the nations *are* idols: but the Lord made the heavens. ⁶ Honour and majesty *are* before him: strength and beauty *are* in his sanctuary.

⁷ Give unto the Lord, O ye kindreds of the people, give unto the Lord glory and strength. ⁸ Give unto the Lord the glory *due unto* his name: bring an offering, and come into his courts. ⁹ O worship the Lord in the beauty of holiness: fear before him, all the earth. ¹⁰ Say among the heathen *that* the Lord reigneth: the world also shall be established that it shall not be moved: he shall judge the people righteously.

¹¹ Let the heavens rejoice, and let the earth be glad; let the sea roar, and the fulness thereof. ¹² Let the field be joyful, and all that *is* therein: then shall all the trees of the wood rejoice ¹³ Before the Lord: for he cometh, for he cometh to judge the earth: he shall judge the world with righteousness, and the people with his truth.

96 SING A NEW song to the Lord! Sing it everywhere around the world! ² Sing out his praises! Bless his name. Each day tell someone that he saves.

³ Publish his glorious acts throughout the earth. Tell everyone about the amazing things he does. ⁴ For the Lord is great beyond description, and greatly to be praised. Worship only him among the gods! ⁵ For the gods of other nations are merely idols, but our God made the heavens! ⁶ Honor and majesty surround him; strength and beauty are in his Temple.

⁷ O nations of the world, confess that God alone is glorious and strong. ⁸ Give him the glory he deserves! Bring your offering and come to worship him. ⁹ Worship the Lord with the beauty of holy lives. Let the earth tremble before him. ¹⁰ Tell the nations that Jehovah reigns! He rules the world. His power can never be overthrown. He will judge all nations fairly.

¹¹ Let the heavens be glad, the earth rejoice; let the vastness of the roaring seas demonstrate his glory. ¹² Praise him for the growing fields, for they display his greatness. Let the trees of the forest rustle with praise. ¹³ For the Lord is coming to judge the earth; he will judge the nations fairly and with truth!

PSALM 97

THE Lord reigneth; let the earth rejoice; let the multitude of isles be glad *thereof.*

² Clouds and darkness *are* round about him: righteousness and judgement *are* the habitation of his throne. ³ A fire goeth before him, and burneth up his enemies round about. ⁴ His lightnings enlightened the world: the earth saw, and trembled. ⁵ The hills melted like wax at the presence of the Lord, at the presence of the Lord of the whole earth. ⁶ The heavens declare his righteousness, and all the people see his glory.

⁷ Confounded be all they that serve graven images, that boast themselves of idols: worship him, all *ye* gods. ⁸ Zion

97 JEHOVAH IS KING! Let all the earth rejoice! Tell the farthest islands to be glad.

² Clouds and darkness surround him. Righteousness and justice are the foundation of his throne. ³ Fire goes forth before him and burns up all his foes. ⁴ His lightning flashes out across the world. The earth sees and trembles. ⁵ The mountains melt like wax before the Lord of all the earth. ⁶ The heavens declare his perfect righteousness; every nation sees his glory.

⁷ Let those who worship idols be disgraced—all who brag about their worthless gods—for every god must bow to him! ⁸,⁹ Jerusalem and all the cities of Judah have

Psalm 96. The Glory of God

Here is a hymn of praise which closes on an eschatological note. The striking universalism running throughout demonstrates the enlarged outlook of the exiles as they returned from captivity. The LXX identifies the occasion as the time "when the house was being built after the captivity." The frequent quoting of other psalms (9,29,33,40,48,95,98,105), the universalism, and the concept of the "nothingness" of the gods all tend to confirm the LXX designation of the occasion.

1-3. Israel's Mission of Praise. O sing . . . declare his glory among the heathen. A new song was needed to express praise for Israel's deliverance from captivity. The people are exhorted to sing unto God and bless him, making known his salvation with new outbursts of praise every day.

4-6. God's Glorious Nature. Great, and greatly to be praised. As in the previous psalm, the people are exhorted to praise God, because the great God is worthy of great praise. **Honour . . . majesty . . . strength . . . beauty,** though here personified, are still related in thought to God's characteristics.

7-9. Mankind's Duty of Praise. Ye kindreds of the people. In keeping with Israel's universal mission, all the nations are called to praise God. They are invited to give due praise, bring their offering, enter the sacred precincts, and worship God. Note that they must worship in the proper attire — **holy array** (RSV), and in the proper attitude — **fear** or *reverence*.

10-13. God's Righteous Rule. The Lord reigneth. The literal translation of this phrase is: *Yahweh is King* or *is become King*. Perhaps this refers to a ceremonial enthronement which may have been a part of the New Year's celebration. However, the main emphasis is eschatological; God is pictured as King of the nations and Judge of the earth.

Psalm 97. The Sovereignty of God

In this hymn of praise the theocratic principle of God's kingship is acclaimed. An eschatological note predominates in the first half of the psalm, which is then applied to the people. The entire hymn may have been designed as a commentary on the last verse of the preceding psalm, or it may have been placed in its present position because of the close relationship in thought. Though almost every phrase that appears here had already been used by other writers, the skill of this psalmist in weaving the phrases together is evident throughout.

1-6. The Manifestation of the King. The Lord reigneth. Again the idea is, "*Yahweh is become King.*" All those who will benefit are called to rejoice in the truth of this eschatological dominion. Mystery and awesome majesty characterize the King's coming. However, the righteousness of God's government undergirds all of this awesome display of power.

7-12. The Effect upon Mankind. Confounded. . . . glad. The manifestation of God as King makes evident a sharp contrast. Those who worship idols are put to shame, while the worshipers of the Lord are made glad. With this contrast in mind, the conclusion follows that Israel has a distinct duty to God. Those who rejoice at the coming of the King must even now love the Lord, hate evil, rejoice, and give thanks.

NOTES

heard, and was glad; and the daughters of Judah rejoiced because of thy judgments, O Lord. ⁹ For thou, Lord, *art* high above all the earth: thou art exalted far above all gods.

¹⁰ Ye that love the Lord, hate evil: he preserveth the souls of his saints; he delivereth them out of the hand of the wicked. ¹¹ Light is sown for the righteous, and gladness for the upright in heart. ¹² Rejoice in the Lord, ye righteous; and give thanks at the remembrance of his holiness.

heard of your justice, Lord, and are glad that you reign in majesty over the entire earth and are far greater than these other gods.

¹⁰ The Lord loves those who hate evil; he protects the lives of his people, and rescues them from the wicked. ¹¹ Light is sown for the godly and joy for the good. ¹² May all who are godly be happy in the Lord and crown him, our holy God.

PSALM 98

A Psalm

O SING unto the Lord a new song; for he hath done marvellous things: his right hand, and his holy arm, hath gotten him the victory. ² The Lord hath made known his salvation: his righteousness hath he openly shewed in the sight of the heathen. ³ He hath remembered his mercy and his truth toward the house of Israel: all the ends of the earth have seen the salvation of our God. ⁴ Make a joyful noise unto the Lord, all the earth: make a loud noise, and rejoice, and sing praise.

⁵ Sing unto the Lord with the harp; with the harp, and the voice of a psalm. ⁶ With trumpets and sound of cornets make a joyful noise before the Lord, the King. ⁷ Let the sea roar, and the fulness thereof; the world, and they that dwell therein.

⁸ Let the floods clap *their* hands: let the hills be joyful together ⁹ Before the Lord; for he cometh to judge the earth: with righteousness shall he judge the world, and the people with equity.

98 SING A NEW song to the Lord telling about his mighty deeds! For he has won a mighty victory by his power and holiness. ²,³ He has announced this victory and revealed it to every nation by fulfilling his promise to be kind to Israel. The whole earth has seen God's salvation of his people. ⁴ That is why the earth breaks out in praise to God, and sings for utter joy!

⁵ Sing your praise accompanied by music from the harp. ⁶ Let the cornets and trumpets shout! Make a joyful symphony before the Lord, the King! ⁷ Let the sea in all its vastness roar with praise! Let the earth and all those living on it shout, "Glory to the Lord."

⁸,⁹ Let the waves clap their hands in glee, and the hills sing out their songs of joy before the Lord, for he is coming to judge the world with perfect justice.

PSALM 99

THE Lord reigneth; let the people tremble: he sitteth *between* the cherubims; let the earth be moved.

² The Lord *is* great in Zion; and he *is* high above all the people. ³ Let them praise thy great and terrible name; *for* it *is* holy.

99 JEHOVAH IS KING! Let the nations tremble! He is enthroned upon the cherubim. Let the whole earth shake.

² Jehovah sits in majesty in Zion, supreme above all rulers of the earth. ³ Let them reverence your great and holy name.

Psalm 98. Praise by All Nature

Psalm 98, a hymn of praise, echoes the thoughts of many other psalmists. It is an integral part of the collection that emphasizes God's kingship (Ps 95–99). The reference to God as **the King** in verse 6 and the eschatological note in the concluding verses connect it with the preceding psalms. All nature is here summoned to join in acclaiming God's praise.

1-3. Praise to the Deliverer. **O sing unto the Lord a new song.** This new song, although drawn from previous sources, is occasioned by some recent deliverance. God has done marvelous things, won the victory, and brought deliverance. All of this is based upon the declaration of his righteousness to the nations and the remembrance of his mercy and truth to Israel.

4-6. Praise to the King. **Make a joyful noise unto the Lord. . . . the King.** Since all the earth has seen how God has delivered Israel, all men are called to join with the Israelites in worshiping him. This is a call for universal participation, in keeping with the broad outlook of Isaiah 40–66.

7-9 Praise to the Judge. **Let the sea roar. . . . for he cometh to judge the earth.** Although this stanza continues the appeal of the preceding stanza, a new element is here introduced. God the King comes as the Judge of the earth. Since all creation is to be judged, all created things must join in praise. The psalm closes with the prediction that the judgment will be characterized by **righteousness** and **equity.**

Psalm 99. The Holiness of God

The emphasis in this hymn of praise is on the sublime nature of God, expressed by his holiness. While the hymn is based upon the concept of God's kingship, there is less of the eschatological in this than in the four preceding psalms. The refrain in verses 3,5, and 9 expresses strongly the distinctive teaching on God's holiness.

1-3. The Holy God is Sovereign. **The Lord reigneth.** Again the translation should be: *Yahweh is King* or *is become King*. God is pictured as enthroned upon the mercy seat, between the cherubim, the place of his earthly manifestation in the Temple. He is also represented as taking his place upon his earthly throne in Zion, a concept that relates this psalm explicitly to an enthronement celebration.

NOTES

4 The king's strength also loveth judgment; thou dost establish equity, thou executest judgment and righteousness in Jacob. 5 Exalt ye the Lord our God, and worship at his footstool; *for* he *is* holy.

6 Moses and Aaron among his priests, and Samuel among them that call upon his name; they called upon the Lord, and he answered them. 7 He spake unto them in the cloudy pillar: they kept his testimonies, and the ordinance *that* he gave them. 8 Thou answeredst them, O Lord our God: thou wast a God that forgavest them, though thou tookest vengeance of their inventions.

9 Exalt the Lord our God, and worship at his holy hill; for the Lord our God *is* holy.

4 This mighty King is determined to give justice. Fairness is the touchstone of everything he does. He gives justice throughout Israel. 5 Exalt the Lord our holy God! Bow low before his feet.

6 When Moses and Aaron and Samuel, his prophet, cried to him for help, he answered them. 7 He spoke to them from the pillar of cloud and they followed his instructions. 8 O Jehovah our God! You answered them and forgave their sins, yet punished them when they went wrong.

9 Exalt the Lord our God, and worship at his holy mountain in Jerusalem, for he is holy.

PSALM 100

A Psalm of praise

MAKE a joyful noise unto the Lord, all ye lands. 2 Serve the Lord with gladness: come before his presence with singing.

3 Know ye that the Lord he *is* God: *it is* he *that* hath made us, and not we ourselves; *we are* his people, and the sheep of his pasture. 4 Enter into his gates with thanksgiving, *and* into his courts with praise: be thankful unto him, *and* bless his name. 5 For the Lord *is* good; his mercy *is* everlasting; and his truth *endureth* to all generations.

100 SHOUT WITH JOY before the Lord, O earth! 2 Obey him gladly; come before him, singing with joy.

3 Try to realize what this means—the Lord is God! He made us—we are his people, the sheep of his pasture.

4 Go through his open gates with great thanksgiving; enter his courts with praise. Give thanks to him and bless his name. 5 For the Lord is always good. He is always loving and kind, and his faithfulness goes on and on to each succeeding generation.

Such a manifestation of the Eternal causes trembling of man and nature, but issues in praise to His name.

4,5. The Holy God is Righteous. **Judgment . . . equity . . . righteousness.** Not only is God sovereign in his rule of the world; he is righteous in his judgment of men. He does not wield his power in an arbitrary way but according to his just and righteous nature. Again, this righteousness is summed up in the words of the refrain, **Holy is he** (ASV).

6,9. The Holy God is Faithful. **They called . . . he answered.** Moses, Aaron, and Samuel are cited as great intercessors of the past. This is the only place in the OT where Moses is classed as a priest, although he did perform some priestly functions and had access to the Tabernacle. While God answered the prayers of these spiritual giants for Israel, he still found it necessary to punish his people for their persistent evil-doing. The final call for exaltation and worship is occasioned by the Lord's faithfulness and is based upon his holiness.

Psalm 100. The Essentials of Worship

A double call to worship characterizes this brief but eloquent hymn of praise. The psalm was undoubtedly used as a processional hymn and appears to have been written for this purpose. Verses 3 and 5 give a concise statement of the doctrine of Judaism.

1-3. A Joyful Procession. **Make a joyful noise unto the Lord.** This first call to worship may well have been rendered by a choir outside the Temple precincts. Prime essential for such worship is a knowledge of God; that is, a recognition that the Lord is God, Creator, and Shepherd of his people Israel. And this knowledge leads to joyful praise, gladness, and singing.

4,5. A Thankful Entry. **Enter into his gates with thanksgiving.** This second call to worship may well have been the invitation by a choir within the Temple precincts. The worshipers, approaching the gates, were invited to continue their worship by entering the gates and then the courts. The further essentials of worship are thanksgiving, praise, prayer, and additional knowledge of God's character. The Lord's attributes of goodness, love, and faithfulness must be recognized by worshipers in any period of time.

PSALM 101

A Psalm of David

I WILL sing of mercy and judgment: unto thee, O Lord, will I sing.

2 I will behave myself wisely in a perfect way. O when wilt thou come unto me? I will walk within my house with a perfect heart.

3 I will set no wicked thing before mine eyes: I hate the work of them that turn aside; *it* shall not cleave to me. 4 A froward heart shall depart from me: I will not know a wicked *person.* 5 Whoso privily slandereth his neighbour, him will I cut off: him that hath an high look and a proud heart will not I suffer. 6 Mine eyes *shall be* upon the faithful of the land, that they may dwell with me: he that walketh in a perfect way, he shall serve me. 7 He that worketh deceit shall not dwell within my house: he that telleth lies shall not tarry in my sight. 8 I will early destroy all the wicked of the land; that I may cut off all wicked doers from the city of the Lord.

101 I WILL SING about your loving-kindness and your justice, Lord. I will sing your praises!

2 I will try to walk a blameless path, but how I need your help, especially in my own home, where I long to act as I should.

3 Help me to refuse the low and vulgar things; help me to abhor all crooked deals of every kind, to have no part in them. 4 I will reject all selfishness and stay away from every evil. 5 I will not tolerate anyone who secretly slanders his neighbors; I will not permit conceit and pride. 6 I will make the godly of the land my heroes, and invite them to my home. Only those who are truly good shall be my servants. 7 But I will not allow those who deceive and lie to stay in my house. 8 My daily task will be to ferret out criminals and free the city of God from their grip.

PSALM 102

A Prayer of the afflicted, when he is overwhelmed, and poureth out his complaint before the Lord

HEAR my prayer, O Lord, and let my cry come unto thee.

2 Hide not thy face from me in the day *when* I am in trouble; incline thine ear unto me: in the day *when* I call answer me speedily. 3 For my days are consumed like smoke, and my bones are burned as an hearth. 4 My heart is smitten, and withered like grass; so that I forget to eat my bread. 5 By reason of the voice of my groaning my bones cleave to my skin. 6 I am like a pelican of the wilderness: I am like an owl of the desert. 7 I watch, and am as a sparrow alone upon the house top.

8 Mine enemies reproach me all the day; *and* they that are mad against me are sworn against me. 9 For I have eaten ashes like bread, and mingled my drink with weeping, 10 Because of thine indignation and thy wrath: for thou hast lifted me up, and cast me down. 11 My days *are* like a shadow that declineth; and I am withered like grass. 12 But thou, O Lord, shalt endure for ever; and

A prayer when overwhelmed with trouble.

102 LORD, HEAR MY prayer! Listen to my plea!

2 Don't turn away from me in this time of my distress. Bend down your ear and give me speedy answers, 3,4 for my days disappear like smoke. My health is broken and my heart is sick; it is trampled like grass and is withered. My food is tasteless, and I have lost my appetite. 5 I am reduced to skin and bones because of all my groaning and despair. 6 I am like a vulture in a far-off wilderness, or like an owl alone in the desert. 7 I lie awake, lonely as a solitary sparrow on the roof.

8 My enemies taunt me day after day and curse at me. 9,10 I eat ashes instead of bread. My tears run down into my drink because of your anger against me, because of your wrath. For you have rejected me and thrown me out. 11 My life is passing swiftly as the evening shadows. I am withering like grass, 12 while you, Lord, are a famous King forever. Your fame will endure to every generation.

Psalm 101. A Royal Code of Ethics

This is best classified as a royal psalm, since it is a declaration of principles by which a ruler intends to rule. These principles, or resolutions, are expressed in the form of promises to God, and therefore addressed to him. Though no king is mentioned in the body of the psalm, the nobility of expression certainly fits the personality and character of David. As an ideal for kingship, it could have been used by many rulers in Israel, whatever the occasion of its composition.

1-4. Personal Resolutions. I will sing of mercy and judgment. The guiding principles of mercy and judgment form the basis for the resolutions. After declaring his determination to choose the way of uprightness or integrity, the speaker voices his longing for closer fellowship with God. He resolves to abstain from wickedness and apostasy. Not only does he hate the work of apostates, but he promises to refuse to know, or entertain any evil thought (v. 4).

5-8. Official Intentions. Whoso privily slandereth . . . him will I cut off. In keeping with the guiding principles of mercy and judgment, the speaker sets forth his intentions as to what kind of people he will show favor and what kind he will shun or destroy. Only the faithful and those who walk in integrity will know his favor. Slanderers and wicked-doers he will destroy, and he will deny his favor to the proud, to the deceitful, and to liars. In so doing he will cleanse the royal court, the royal city – Jerusalem, and the entire land.

Psalm 102. A Prayer for Help

Though basically the lament of an individual, this psalm has a corporate element as well. For this reason, commentators are divided as to its original intent. A distinctly personal appeal is followed by a plea for the nation. Then the psalmist reverts to his own problem again, facing it in the light of his assured hope for the nation.

1-11. The Suffering of the Psalmist. Hear my prayer, O Lord. The psalmist's deep sense of urgency makes this cry especially poignant. He needs an answer immediately. He is suffering from a disease that has produced mental anxiety, and his enemies have taken advantage of his condition. All of this suffering, he believes, is due to God's wrath.

12-22. The Restoration of the Nation. But thou, O Lord, shalt endure for ever.

thy remembrance unto all generations.
13 Thou shalt arise, *and* have mercy upon Zion: for the time to favour her, yea, the set time, is come. 14 For thy servants take pleasure in her stones, and favour the dust thereof. 15 So the heathen shall fear the name of the Lord, and all the kings of the earth thy glory. 16 When the Lord shall build up Zion, he shall appear in his glory.

17 He will regard the prayer of the destitute, and not despise their prayer. 18 This shall be written for the generation to come: and the people which shall be created shall praise the Lord. 19 For he hath looked down from the height of his sanctuary; from heaven did the Lord behold the earth; 20 To hear the groaning of the prisoner; to loose those that are appointed to death; 21 To declare the name of the Lord in Zion, and his praise in Jerusalem; 22 When the people are gathered together, and the kingdoms, to serve the Lord.

23 He weakened my strength in the way; he shortened my days. 24 I said, O my God, take me not away in the midst of my days: thy years *are* throughout all generations. 25 Of old hast thou laid the foundation of the earth: and the heavens *are* the work of thy hands. 26 They shall perish, but thou shalt endure: yea, all of them shall wax old like a garment; as a vesture shalt thou change them, and they shall be changed: 27 But thou *art* the same, and thy years shall have no end.

28 The children of thy servants shall continue, and their seed shall be established before thee.

13 I know that you will come and have mercy on Jerusalem—and now is the time to pity her—the time you promised help. 14 For your people love every stone in her walls and feel sympathy for every grain of dust in her streets. 15 Now let the nations and their rulers tremble before the Lord, before his glory. 16 For Jehovah will rebuild Jerusalem! He will appear in his glory!

17 He will listen to the prayers of the destitute, for he is never too busy to heed their requests. 18 I am recording this so that future generations will also praise the Lord for all that he has done. And a people that shall be created shall praise the Lord. 19 Tell them that God looked down from his temple in heaven, 20 and heard the groans of his people in slavery—they were children of death—and released them, 21,22 so that multitudes would stream to the Temple in Jerusalem to praise him, and his praises were sung throughout the city; and many rulers throughout the earth came to worship him.

23 He has cut me down in middle life, shortening my days. 24 But I cried to him, "O God, you live forever and forever! Don't let me die half through my years! 25 In ages past you laid the foundations of the earth, and made the heavens with your hands! 26 They shall perish, but you go on forever. They will grow old, like worn-out clothing, and you will change them like a man putting on a new shirt and throwing away the old one! 27 But you yourself never grow old. You are forever, and your years never end.

28 But our families will continue; generation after generation will be preserved by your protection.

PSALM 103

A Psalm *of David*

BLESS the Lord, O my soul: and all that is within me, *bless* his holy name. 2 Bless the Lord, O my soul, and forget not all his benefits: 3 Who forgiveth all thine iniquities; who healeth all thy diseases; 4 Who redeemeth thy life from destruction; who crowneth thee with lovingkindness and tender mercies; 5 Who satisfieth thy mouth with good *things; so that* thy

103 I BLESS THE holy name of God with all my heart. 2 Yes, I will bless the Lord and not forget the glorious things he does for me.

3 He forgives all my sins. He heals me. 4 He ransoms me from hell. He surrounds me with lovingkindness and tender mercies. 5 He fills my life with good things! My youth

In contrast to the psalmist's transitory nature (v. 11), God endures. It is upon this truth that Zion's restoration is based. The suggestion of some that this section is a separate psalm inserted by the compiler is not warranted. It is evident that the solution of the speaker's problem is intimately tied in with the solution of that of his nation (cf. vv. 12,26,27).

23-28. The Assurance of the Psalmist. They shall perish, but thou shalt endure. Though the speaker reverts to his suffering and weakness, he gains assurance from his nation's hope in the Lord. Even when the entire creation has passed away, God will endure. Verses 25-27 are referred to Christ the Lord in Heb 1:10-12 (cf. Heb 13:8). In the meantime, His eternity guarantees deliverance and permanence for the psalmist's people.

Psalm 103. A Hymn of Thankful Praise

This hymn of praise is without a peer in all the world's literature. It appears to be the expression of an individual, though some commentators find here a corporate voice. The psalmist seeks first to stir his own spirit to offer praise and thanksgiving to God, then the spirits of others. His words are untouched by sorrow, complaint, or sadness. The manner of expression and the depth of insight are remarkable for one living prior to the coming of Christ.

1-5. Praise for Personal Blessings. Bless the Lord, O my soul. The psalmist first addresses an exhortation to himself. In the term translated **soul** (*nepesh*) as well as in the parallel expression — **all that is within me**, he refers to his entire being. He now stirs his inner self to remembrance as he counts his many blessings. Note the strength in the verbs — forgives, heals, redeems, crowns, satisfies, and renews.

youth is renewed like the eagle's. ⁶ The Lord executeth righteousness and judgment for all that are oppressed. ⁷ <u>He made known his ways unto Moses, his acts unto the children of Israel.</u>

⁸ The Lord *is* merciful and gracious, slow to anger, and plenteous in mercy. ⁹ He will not always chide: neither will he keep *his anger* for ever. ¹⁰ He hath not dealt with us after our sins; nor rewarded us according to our iniquities. ¹¹ For as the heaven is high above the earth, *so* great is his mercy toward them that fear him. ¹² As far as the east is from the west, *so* far hath he removed our transgressions from us. ¹³ Like as a father pitieth *his* children, *so* the Lord pitieth them that fear him. ¹⁴ For he knoweth our frame; he remembereth that we *are* dust. ¹⁵ *As for* man, his days *are* as grass; as a flower of the field, so he flourisheth. ¹⁶ For the wind passeth over it, and it is gone; and the place thereof shall know it no more.

¹⁷ But the mercy of the Lord *is* from everlasting to everlasting upon them that fear him, and his righteousness unto children's children; ¹⁸ To such as keep his covenant, and to those that remember his commandments to do them.

¹⁹ The Lord hath prepared his throne in the heavens; and his kingdom ruleth over all. ²⁰ Bless the Lord, ye his angels, that excel in strength, that do his commandments, hearkening unto the voice of his word. ²¹ Bless ye the Lord, all *ye* his hosts; *ye* ministers of his, that do his pleasure. ²² Bless the Lord, all his works in all places of his dominion: bless the Lord, O my soul.

PSALM 104

BLESS the Lord, O my soul. O Lord my God, thou art very great; thou art clothed with honour and majesty. ² Who coverest *thyself* with light as *with* a garment: who stretchest out the heavens like a curtain: ³ Who layeth the beams of his chambers in the waters: who maketh the clouds his chariot: who walketh upon the wings of the wind: ⁴ Who maketh his angels spirits; his ministers a flaming fire:

is renewed like the eagle's! ⁶ He gives justice to all who are treated unfairly. ⁷ He revealed his will and nature to Moses and the people of Israel.

⁸ He is merciful and tender toward those who don't deserve it; he is slow to get angry and full of kindness and love. ⁹ He never bears a grudge, nor remains angry forever. ¹⁰ He has not punished us as we deserve for all our sins, ¹¹ for his mercy toward those who fear and honor him is as great as the height of the heavens above the earth. ¹² He has removed our sins as far away from us as the east is from the west. ¹³ He is like a father to us, tender and sympathetic to those who reverence him. ¹⁴ For he knows we are but dust, ¹⁵ and that our days are few and brief, like grass, like flowers, ¹⁶ blown by the wind and gone forever.

¹⁷,¹⁸ But the lovingkindness of the Lord is from everlasting to everlasting, to those who reverence him; his salvation is to children's children of those who are faithful to his covenant and remember to obey him!

¹⁹ The Lord has made the heavens his throne; from there he rules over everything there is. ²⁰ Bless the Lord, you mighty angels of his who carry out his orders, listening for each of his commands. ²¹ Yes, bless the Lord, you armies of his angels who serve him constantly.

²² Let everything everywhere bless the Lord. And how I bless him too!

104 ¹ I BLESS THE Lord: O Lord my God, how great you are! You are robed with honor and with majesty and light! You stretched out the starry curtain of the heavens, ³ and hollowed out the surface of the earth to form the seas. The clouds are his chariots. He rides upon the wings of the wind. ⁴ The angels are his messengers—his servants of fire!

6-10. Praise for National Blessings. The Lord executeth righteousness and judgment. God is not only righteous and just in himself, but he actively engages in acts of righteousness and justice for oppressed peoples. Just as the Lord has crowned the psalmist with **lovingkindness** (*ḥesed,* v. 4), he has proved himself in Israel's history to be **plenteous in loving kindness.** This is best seen in his being slow to anger and in his punishing his people less severely than they deserve.

11-14. Praise for Forgiving Love. So great is his mercy. Adding illustration to illustration, the psalmist seeks to convey an adequate description of God's loving-kindness. He does not know how far it is from earth to heaven, but he knows that even that vastness could not contain God's mercy. He does not know how far east is from west, but he knows that God's love has removed our sins even farther. The most beautiful and intimate illustration is that of God as the Father who has compassion upon man in his weakness and frailty.

15-18. Praise for Eternal Love. From everlasting to everlasting. The continuance of God's loving-kindness stands in the sharpest contrast possible to man's transitoriness. The extension of this loving-kindness to man is conditioned by man's responding to the covenant and commands of God in a proper attitude of fear or reverence.

19-22. Call for Universal Praise. Bless the Lord, ye his angels. . . . hosts . . . ministers. After stating the principle of divine kingship, the psalmist calls for praise by the chorus of the whole universe. The purpose of the praise is to declare **all his works in all places,** both in heaven and on earth. The psalmist closes by taking his place in the anthem of the ages.

Psalm 104. The Creative Power of God

Here is a hymn of praise similar in certain respects to the preceding one. The opening and concluding phrases of the two psalms are almost identical, setting forth an attitude of thanksgiving and praise. While the previous hymn emphasized God's relation to history, this one pictures God's relation to creation. It offers interesting parallels to Persian, Babylonian, and Egyptian thought (cf. "Hymn to Aten," ANET, pp. 369-371). Even more important are the parallels with Genesis 1 and Job 38—41.

1-4. God's Greatness in Creation. Thou art very great. After calling his whole being to praise, the psalmist pictures the

185

⁵ *Who* laid the foundations of the earth, *that* it should not be removed for ever. ⁶ Thou coveredst it with the deep as *with* a garment: the waters stood above the mountains. ⁷ At thy rebuke they fled; at the voice of thy thunder they hasted away. ⁸ They go up by the mountains; they go down by the valleys unto the place which thou hast founded for them. ⁹ Thou hast set a bound that they may not pass over; that they turn not again to cover the earth.

¹⁰ He sendeth the springs into the valleys, *which* run among the hills. ¹¹ They give drink to every beast of the field: the wild asses quench their thirst. ¹² By them shall the fowls of the heaven have their habitation, *which* sing among the branches. ¹³ He watereth the hills from his chambers: the earth is satisfied with the fruit of thy works. ¹⁴ He causeth the grass to grow for the cattle, and herb for the service of man: that he may bring forth food out of the earth; ¹⁵ And wine *that* maketh glad the heart of man, *and* oil to make *his* face to shine, and bread *which* strengtheneth man's heart. ¹⁶ The trees of the Lord are full *of sap;* the cedars of Lebanon, which he hath planted; ¹⁷ Where the birds make their nests: *as for* the stork, the fir trees *are* her house. ¹⁸ The high hills *are* a refuge for the wild goats; *and* the rocks for the conies.

¹⁹ He appointed the moon for seasons: the sun knoweth his going down. ²⁰ Thou makest darkness and it is night: wherein all the beasts of the forest do creep *forth*. ²¹ The young lions roar after their prey, and seek their meat from God. ²² The sun ariseth, they gather themselves together, and lay them down in their dens. ²³ Man goeth forth unto his work and to his labour until the evening. ²⁴ O Lord, how manifold are thy works! in wisdom hast thou made them all: the earth is full of thy riches.

²⁵ *So is* this great and wide sea, wherein *are* things creeping innumerable, both small and great beasts. ²⁶ There go the ships: *there is* that leviathan, *whom* thou hast made to play therein. ²⁷ These wait all upon thee; that thou mayest give *them* their meat in due season. ²⁸ *That* thou givest them

⁵ You bound the world together so that it would never fall apart. ⁶ You clothed the earth with floods of waters covering up the mountains. ⁷,⁸ You spoke, and at the sound of your shout the water collected into its vast ocean beds, and mountains rose and valleys sank to the levels you decreed. ⁹ And then you set a boundary for the seas, so that they would never again cover the earth.

¹⁰ He placed springs in the valleys, and streams that gush from the mountains. ¹¹ They give water for all the animals to drink. There the wild donkeys quench their thirst, ¹² and the birds nest beside the streams and sing among the branches of the trees. ¹³ He sends rain upon the mountains and fills the earth with fruit. ¹⁴ The tender grass grows up at his command to feed the cattle, and there are fruit trees, vegetables and grain for man to cultivate, ¹⁵ and wine to make him glad, and olive oil as lotion for his skin, and bread to give him strength. ¹⁶ The Lord planted the cedars of Lebanon. They are tall and flourishing. ¹⁷ There the birds make their nests, the storks in the firs. ¹⁸ High in the mountains are pastures for the wild goats, and rock-badgers burrow in among the rocks and find protection there.

¹⁹ He assigned the moon to mark the months, and the sun to mark the days. ²⁰ He sends the night and darkness, when all the forest folk come out. ²¹ Then the young lions roar for their food, but they are dependent on the Lord. ²² At dawn they slink back into their dens to rest, ²³ and men go off to work until the evening shadows fall again. ²⁴ O Lord, what a variety you have made! And in wisdom you have made them all! The earth is full of your riches.

²⁵ There before me lies the mighty ocean, teeming with life of every kind, both great and small. ²⁶ And look! See the ships! And over there, the whale you made to play in the sea. ²⁷ Every one of these depends on you to give them daily food. ²⁸ You supply

Lord as clothed in the wonderful majesty of his creation. Light appears as his robe; the heavens are spread out as a canopy; his abode is supported by pillars; clouds, wind, and angels are created for his use.

5-9. God's Formation of the Earth. **The foundations of the earth.** The Near Eastern concepts of cosmology are evident here as well as throughout the psalm. The earth is firmly established *upon her bases* (AV marg.) or pillars (v. 5); the mountains and valleys are formed; the seas are divided and fixed as to their bounds.

10-18. God's Provision for His Creatures. **He sendeth the springs.** One of the greatest needs in ancient Palestine was an adequate supply of water. The psalmist praises God for making provision for springs and rain so that all forms of life, animal and vegetable, may be sustained. He praises Him, too, for the blessings of food, wine, oil, trees, hills, and rocks.

19-23. God's Ordering of the Heavens. **The moon . . . the sun.** These two celestial bodies are singled out for attention because they are indispensable in the ordering of seasons and days. While the wild animals thrive on darkness, man's labor is mainly accomplished in the hours of daylight.

24-30. God's Providence. **In wisdom hast thou made them all.** The psalmist pauses to marvel at the Divine wisdom displayed in all God's wondrous creations. The marvels of the sea and the mystery of life are pointed out as illustrations of God's providence.

they gather: thou openest thine hand, they are filled with good.

²⁹ Thou hidest thy face, they are troubled: thou takest away their breath, they die, and return to their dust. ³⁰ Thou sendest forth thy spirit, they are created: and thou renewest the face of the earth. ³¹ The glory of the Lord shall endure for ever: the Lord shall rejoice in his works. ³² He looketh on the earth, and it trembleth: he toucheth the hills, and they smoke.

³³ I will sing unto the Lord as long as I live: I will sing praise to my God while I have my being. ³⁴ My meditation of him shall be sweet: I will be glad in the Lord. ³⁵ Let the sinners be consumed out of the earth, and let the wicked be no more. Bless thou the Lord, O my soul. Praise ye the Lord.

PSALM 105

O GIVE thanks unto the Lord; call upon his name: make known his deeds among the people. ² Sing unto him, sing psalms unto him: talk ye of all his wondrous works. ³ Glory ye in his holy name: let the heart of them rejoice that seek the Lord.

⁴ Seek the Lord, and his strength: seek his face evermore.

⁵ Remember his marvellous works that he hath done; his wonders, and the judgments of his mouth; ⁶ O ye seed of Abraham his servant, ye children of Jacob his chosen. ⁷ He *is* the Lord our God: his judgments *are* in all the earth. ⁸ He hath remembered his covenant for ever, the word *which* he commanded to a thousand generations. ⁹ Which *covenant* he made with Abraham, and his oath unto Isaac; ¹⁰ And confirmed the same unto Jacob for a law, *and* to Israel *for* an everlasting covenant: ¹¹ Saying, Unto thee will I give the land of Canaan, the lot of your inheritance: ¹² When they were *but* a few men in number; yea, very few, and strangers in it. ¹³ When they went from one nation to another, from *one* kingdom to another people; ¹⁴ He suffered no man to do them wrong: yea, he reproved kings for their sakes; ¹⁵ *Saying,* Touch not mine anointed, and do my prophets no harm.

it, and they gather it. You open wide your hand to feed them and they are satisfied with all your bountiful provision.

²⁹ But if you turn away from them, then all is lost. And when you gather up their breath, they die and turn again to dust. ³⁰ Then you send your Spirit, and new life is born to replenish all the living of the earth. ³¹ Praise God forever! How he must rejoice in all his work! ³² The earth trembles at his glance; the mountains burst into flame at his touch.

³³ I will sing to the Lord as long as I live. I will praise God to my last breath! ³⁴ May he be pleased by all these thoughts about him, for he is the source of all my joy. ³⁵ Let all sinners perish—all who refuse to praise him. But I will praise him. Hallelujah!

105 THANK THE LORD for all the glorious things he does; proclaim them to the nations. ² Sing his praises and tell everyone about his miracles. ³ Glory in the Lord; O worshipers of God, rejoice.

⁴ Search for him and for his strength, and keep on searching!

⁵,⁶ Think of the mighty deeds he did for us, his chosen ones—descendants of God's servant Abraham, and of Jacob. Remember how he destroyed our enemies. ⁷ He is the Lord our God. His goodness is seen everywhere throughout the land. ⁸,⁹ Though a thousand generations pass he never forgets his promise, his covenant with Abraham and Isaac, ¹⁰,¹¹ and confirmed with Jacob. This is his never-ending treaty with the people of Israel: *"I will give you the land of Canaan as your inheritance."* ¹² He said this when they were but few in number, very few, and were only visitors in Canaan. ¹³ Later they were dispersed among the nations, and were driven from one kingdom to another; ¹⁴ but through it all he would not let one thing be done to them apart from his decision. He destroyed many a king who tried! ¹⁵ "Touch not these chosen ones of mine," he warned, "and do not hurt my prophets."

31-35. God's Glory in Praise. The glory of the Lord shall endure for ever. The psalmist vows that he will sing praise to God as long as he has life. His desire that evil be eradicated is in keeping with his concept of the goodness of God's creation (cf. Gen 1).

Psalm 105. The Wonders of the Past

Again the psalmist sings a hymn of praise, this time emphasizing the wondrous acts of God within the covenant relation. Psalms 105 and 106 are companion pieces in that history is searched in both. In the former, God's acts are emphasized; in the latter, Israel's acts of disobedience are recited. Both poems show affinity with Psalm 78, in which the two themes are interwoven.

1-6. The Call for Thanksgiving. Give thanks . . . call . . . sing . . . talk . . . glory . . . rejoice. . . . seek. . . . remember. The psalmist's detailed instructions reveal what it means to praise the Lord. It is clear that the hymn was designed for congregational use.

7-15. The Covenant with the Patriarchs. He hath remembered his covenant. The special feature of the covenant singled out is the promise that Canaan was to be Israel's inheritance. The rest of the psalm demonstrates the working out of this aspect of the covenant. Note the unusual use of **mine anointed ones** and **my prophets** to refer to the patriarchs.

16 Moreover he called for a famine upon the land: he brake the whole staff of bread. 17 He sent a man before them, *even* Joseph, *who* was sold for a servant: 18 Whose feet they hurt with fetters: he was laid in iron: 19 Until the time that his word came: the word of the Lord tried him. 20 The king sent and loosed him; *even* the ruler of the people, and let him go free. 21 He made him lord of his house, and ruler of all his substance: 22 To bind his princes at his pleasure; and teach his senators wisdom.

23 Israel also came into Egypt; and Jacob sojourned in the land of Ham. 24 And he increased his people greatly; and made them stronger than their enemies. 25 He turned their heart to hate his people, to deal subtilly with his servants.

26 He sent Moses his servant; *and* Aaron whom he had chosen. 27 They shewed his signs among them, and wonders in the land of Ham. 28 He sent darkness, and made it dark; and they rebelled not against his word. 29 He turned their waters into blood, and slew their fish. 30 Their land brought forth frogs in abundance, in the chambers of their kings. 31 He spake, and there came divers sorts of flies, *and* lice in all their coasts. 32 He gave them hail for rain, *and* flaming fire in their land. 33 He smote their vines also and their fig trees; and brake the trees of their coasts. 34 He spake, and the locusts came, and caterpillers, and that without number, 35 And did eat up all the herbs in their land, and devoured the fruit of their ground. 36 He smote also all the firstborn in their land, the chief of all their strength. 37 He brought them forth also with silver and gold: and *there was* not one feeble *person* among their tribes. 38 Egypt was glad when they departed: for the fear of them fell upon them.

39 He spread a cloud for a covering; and fire to give light in the night. 40 *The people* asked, and he brought quails, and satisfied them with the bread of heaven. 41 He opened the rock, and the waters gushed out; they ran in the dry places *like* a river. 42 For he remembered his holy promise, *and* Abraham his servant.

16 He called for a famine on the land of Canaan, cutting off its food supply. 17 Then he sent Joseph as a slave to Egypt to save his people from starvation. 18 There in prison they hurt his feet with fetters, and placed his neck in an iron collar, 19 until God's time finally came—how God tested his patience! 20 Then the king sent for him and set him free. 21 He was put in charge of all the king's possessions. 22 At his pleasure he could imprison the king's aides and teach the king's advisors.

23 Then Jacob (Israel) arrived in Egypt and lived there with his sons. 24 In the years that followed, the people of Israel multiplied explosively, until they were a greater nation than their rulers. 25 At that point God turned the Egyptians against the Israelis; they hated and enslaved them.

26 But God sent Moses as his representative, and Aaron with him, 27 to call down miracles of terror upon the land of Egypt. 28 They followed his instructions and he sent thick darkness through the land, 29 and turned the nation's water into blood, poisoning the fish. 30 Then frogs invaded in enormous numbers; they were found even in the king's private rooms. 31 When Moses spoke, the flies and other insects swarmed in vast clouds from one end of Egypt to the other. 32 Instead of rain he sent down murderous hail, and lightning flashes overwhelmed the nation. 33 Their grape vines and fig trees were ruined; all the trees lay broken on the ground. 34 He spoke, and hordes of locusts came, 35 and ate up everything green, destroying all the crops. 36 Then he killed the oldest child in each Egyptian home, their pride and joy— 37 and brought his people safely out from Egypt, loaded with silver and gold; there were no sick and feeble folk among them then. 38 Egypt was glad when they were gone, for the dread of them was great.

39 He spread out a cloud above them to shield them from the burning sun, and gave them a pillar of flame at night to give them light. 40 They asked for meat and he sent them quail, and gave them manna—bread from heaven. 41 He opened up a rock, and water gushed out to form a river through the dry and barren land; 42 for he remembered his sacred promises to Abraham his servant.

16-25. The Experiences of the Sojourn. **Moreover he called for a famine.** Also unusual is this reference to God as the direct cause of the famine that brought Israel's family into Egypt. The psalmist is primarily emphasizing God's part in all that occurred: He called a famine, sent a man (Joseph), tried him, allowed him to be raised to power, increased his people, and stirred up hatred for Israel among the Egyptians. In keeping with general OT thought, the psalmist ignores secondary causes.

26-38. The Deliverance from Egypt. **He sent Moses . . . Aaron.** The writer places special emphasis upon the plagues as signs of God's power. He moves the ninth plague to the head of the list, inverts the order of the third and fourth, and omits the fifth and sixth.

39-45. The Realization of the Promise. **For he remembered his holy promise.** After recalling how God guided Israel in the wilderness, the psalmist draws his conclusion: Each of God's wondrous acts was brought about because the Lord remembered and kept his promise, first given to Abraham. The climax comes in

NOTES

43 And he brought forth his people with joy, *and* his chosen with gladness: 44 And gave them the lands of the heathen: and they inherited the labour of the people; 45 That they might observe his statutes, and keep his laws. Praise ye the Lord.

PSALM 106

PRAISE ye the Lord. O give thanks unto the Lord; for *he is* good: for his mercy *endureth* for ever. 2 Who can utter the mighty acts of the Lord? *who* can shew forth all his praise?

3 Blessed *are* they that keep judgment, *and* he that doeth righteousness at all times.

4 Remember me, O Lord, with the favour *that thou bearest unto* thy people: O visit me with thy salvation; 5 That I may see the good of thy chosen, that I may rejoice in the gladness of thy nation, that I may glory with thine inheritance.

6 We have sinned with our fathers, we have committed iniquity, we have done wickedly. 7 Our fathers understood not thy wonders in Egypt; they remembered not the multitude of thy mercies; but provoked *him* at the sea, *even* at the Red sea. 8 Nevertheless he saved them for his name's sake, that he might make his mighty power to be known. 9 He rebuked the Red sea also, and it was dried up: so he led them through the depths, as through the wilderness. 10 And he saved them from the hand of him that hated *them,* and redeemed them from the hand of the enemy. 11 And the waters covered their enemies: there was not one of them left. 12 Then believed they his words; they sang his praise.

13 They soon forgat his works; they waited not for his counsel: 14 But lusted exceedingly in the wilderness, and tempted God in the desert. 15 And he gave them their request; but sent leanness into their soul. 16 They envied Moses also in the camp, *and* Aaron the saint of the Lord. 17 The earth opened and swallowed up Da-than, and covered the company of A-bi-ram. 18 And a fire was kindled in their company; the flame burned up the wicked. 19 They made a

43 So he brought his chosen ones singing into the Promised Land. 44 He gave them the lands of the Gentiles, complete with their growing crops; they ate what others planted. 45 This was done to make them faithful and obedient to his laws. Hallelujah!

106 HALLELUJAH! THANK YOU, Lord! How good you are! Your love for us continues on forever. 2 Who can ever list the glorious miracles of God? Who can ever praise him half enough?

3 Happiness comes to those who are fair to others and are always just and good.

4 Remember me too, O Lord, while you are blessing and saving your people. 5 Let me share in your chosen ones' prosperity and rejoice in all their joys, and receive the glory you give to them.

6 Both we and our fathers have sinned so much. 7 They weren't impressed by the wonder of your miracles in Egypt, and soon forgot your many acts of kindness to them. Instead they rebelled against you at the Red Sea. 8 Even so you saved them—to defend the honor of your name and demonstrate your power to all the world. 9 You commanded the Red Sea to divide, forming a dry road across its bottom. Yes, as dry as any desert! 10 Thus you rescued them from their enemies. 11 Then the water returned and covered the road and drowned their foes; not one survived.

12 Then at last his people believed him. Then they finally sang his praise.

13 Yet how quickly they forgot again! They wouldn't wait for him to act, 14 but demanded better food, testing God's patience to the breaking point. 15 So he gave them their demands, but sent them leanness in their souls. 16 They were envious of Moses; yes, and Aaron, too, the man anointed by God as his priest. 17 Because of this the earth opened and swallowed Dathan, Abiram and his friends; 18 and fire fell from heaven to consume these wicked men. 19,20 For they preferred a statue of an ox that

the fulfillment of the promise that Canaan, **the lands of the nations** (AV, *heathen*), with all the fruits of previous labor, should belong to Israel

Psalm 106. The Long-suffering Nature of God

The continuous rebellion of Israel is emphasized in this sequel to Psalm 105. While beginning as a hymn (vv. 1-5), the poem continues as a national lament or confession. The sadness of the lament section is offset, to a certain degree, by the picture of God's long-suffering mercy in dealing with his people.

1-6. Praise and Confession. Praise . . . give thanks. . . . we have sinned. In hymnic fashion the author issues a call to praise, followed by an expression of beatitude, a personal prayer, and a confession of national sin. Note that the present generation is included along with the past generations.

7-33. Murmuring and Disobedience. Our fathers understood not. Here, as frequently in the Psalms, the Exodus and the period of wandering through the wilderness provide illustrations of the way the children of Israel misunderstood God. They murmured for food (vv. 13-15); they rebelled against Moses and Aaron (vv. 16-18); they apostatized in

calf in Ho-reb, and worshipped the molten image. 20 Thus they changed their glory into the similitude of an ox that eateth grass. 21 They forgat God their saviour, which had done great things in Egypt; 22 Wondrous works in the land of Ham, *and* terrible things by the Red sea. 23 Therefore he said that he would destroy them, had not Moses his chosen stood before him in the breach, to turn away his wrath, lest he should destroy *them*.

24 Yea, they despised the pleasant land, they believed not his word: 25 But murmured in their tents, *and* hearkened not unto the voice of the Lord. 26 Therefore he lifted up his hand against them, to overthrow them in the wilderness: 27 To overthrow their seed also among the nations, and to scatter them in the lands. 28 They joined themselves also unto Ba-al–pe-or, and ate the sacrifices of the dead. 29 Thus they provoked *him* to anger with their inventions: and the plague brake in upon them. 30 Then stood up Phin-e-has, and executed judgment: and *so* the plague was stayed. 31 And that was counted unto him for righteousness unto all generations for evermore.

32 They angered *him* also at the waters of strife, so that it went ill with Moses for their sakes: 33 Because they provoked his spirit, so that he spake unadvisedly with his lips. 34 They did not destroy the nations, concerning whom the Lord commanded them: 35 But were mingled among the heathen, and learned their works. 36 And they served their idols: which were a snare unto them. 37 Yea, they sacrificed their sons and their daughters unto devils, 38 And shed innocent blood, *even* the blood of their sons and of their daughters, whom they sacrificed unto the idols of Canaan: and the land was polluted with blood. 39 Thus were they defiled with their own works, and went a whoring with their own inventions. 40 Therefore was the wrath of the Lord kindled against his people, insomuch that he abhorred his own inheritance. 41 And he gave them into the hand of the heathen; and they that hated them ruled over them. 42 Their enemies also oppressed them, and they were brought into subjection under their hand.

eats grass, to the glorious presence of God himself. 21,22 Thus they despised their Savior who had done such mighty miracles in Egypt and at the Sea. 23 So the Lord declared he would destroy them. But Moses, his chosen one, stepped into the breach between the people and their God and begged him to turn from his wrath, and not destroy them.

24 They refused to enter the Promised Land, for they wouldn't believe his solemn oath to care for them. 25 Instead, they pouted in their tents and mourned and despised his command. 26 Therefore he swore that he would kill them in the wilderness 27 and send their children away to distant lands as exiles. 28 Then our fathers joined the worshipers of Baal at Peor and even offered sacrifices to the dead! 29 With all these things they angered him—and so a plague broke out upon them 30 and continued until Phineas executed those whose sins had caused the plague to start. 31 (For this good deed Phineas will be remembered forever.)

32 At Meribah, too, Israel angered God, causing Moses serious trouble, 33 for he became angry and spoke foolishly. 34 Nor did Israel destroy the nations in the land as God had told them to, 35 but mingled in among the heathen and learned their evil ways, 36 sacrificing to their idols, and were led away from God. 37,38 They even sacrificed their little children to the demons—the idols of Canaan—shedding innocent blood and polluting the land with murder. 39 Their evil deeds defiled them, for their love of idols was adultery in the sight of God. 40 That is why Jehovah's anger burned against his people, and he abhorred them. 41,42 That is why he let the heathen nations crush them. They were ruled by those who hated them and oppressed by their enemies.

making a golden calf (vv. 19-23); they refused to accept God's leadership in the incident of the spies (vv. 24-27); they joined in Moabite worship (vv. 28-31); and they involved Moses in their murmuring at Meribah (vv. 32,33).

34-36. Backsliding and Unfaithfulness. **Thus were they defiled with their own works.** In contrast to God's faithfulness, shown by the mighty works he performed in Israel's behalf, his people repeatedly proved unfaithful after entering Canaan. Mingling with the inhabitants, they learned new modes of sin. Not only did they serve idols, but they joined in the abomination of human sacrifice. God's compassion notwithstanding, punishment was repeatedly necessary.

NOTES

43 Many times did he deliver them; but they provoked *him* with their counsel, and were brought low for their iniquity. 44 Nevertheless he regarded their affliction, when he heard their cry: 45 And he remembered for them his covenant, and repented according to the multitude of his mercies. 46 He made them also to be pitied of all those that carried them captives.

47 Save us, O Lord our God, and gather us from among the heathen, to give thanks unto thy holy name, *and* to triumph in thy praise.

48 Blessed *be* the Lord God of Israel from everlasting to everlasting: and let all the people say, Amen. Praise ye the Lord.

43 Again and again he delivered them from their slavery, but they continued to rebel against him, and were finally destroyed by their sin. 44 Yet, even so, he listened to their cries and heeded their distress; 45 he remembered his promises to them and relented because of his great love, 46 and caused even their enemies who captured them to pity them.

47 O Lord God, save us! Regather us from the nations so we can thank your holy name and rejoice and praise you.

48 Blessed be the Lord, the God of Israel, from everlasting to everlasting. Let all the people say, "Amen!" Hallelujah!

PSALM 107

O GIVE thanks unto the Lord, for *he is* good: for his mercy *endureth* for ever. 2 Let the redeemed of the Lord say *so,* whom he hath redeemed from the hand of the enemy;

3 And gathered them out of the lands, from the east, and from the west, from the north, and from the south. 4 They wandered in the wilderness in a solitary way; they found no city to dwell in. 5 Hungry and thirsty, their soul fainted in them. 6 Then they cried unto the Lord in their trouble, *and* he delivered them out of their distresses. 7 And he led them forth by the right way, that they might go to a city of habitation. 8 Oh that *men* would praise the Lord *for* his goodness, and *for* his wonderful works to the children of men! 9 For he satisfieth the longing soul, and filleth the hungry soul with goodness.

10 Such as sit in darkness and in the shadow of death, *being* bound in affliction and iron; 11 Because they rebelled against the words of God, and contemned the counsel of the most High: 12 Therefore he brought down their heart with labour; they fell down and *there was* none to help. 13 Then they cried unto the Lord in their trouble, *and* he saved them out of their distresses. 14 He brought them out of darkness and the shadow of death, and brake their bands in sunder. 15 Oh that *men* would praise the Lord *for* his goodness,

107 SAY "THANK YOU" to the Lord for being so good, for always being so loving and kind. 2 Has the Lord redeemed you? Then speak out! Tell others he has saved you from your enemies.

3 He brought the exiles back from the farthest corners of the earth. 4 They were wandering homeless in the desert, 5 hungry and thirsty and faint. 6 "Lord, help!" they cried, and he did! 7 He led them straight to safety and a place to live. 8 Oh, that these men would praise the Lord for his lovingkindness, and for all of his wonderful deeds! 9 For he satisfies the thirsty soul and fills the hungry soul with good.

10 Who are these who sit in darkness, in the shadow of death, crushed by misery and slavery? 11 They rebelled against the Lord, scorning him who is the God above all gods. 12 That is why he broke them with hard labor; they fell and none could help them rise again. 13 Then they cried to the Lord in their troubles, and he rescued them! 14 He led them from the darkness and shadow of death and snapped their chains. 15 Oh, that these men would praise the Lord for his

47,48. Prayer and Doxology. Save us. . . . Blessed be the Lord. The lengthy confession leads to a request for mercy and restoration. The doxology appears to be an integral part of the psalm, while also serving as a concluding doxology for Book IV.

BOOK V. Psalms 107–150

The fifth book in the fivefold division includes several smaller collections or groups of psalms. The Psalms of Ascents (120–134) and the Hallelujah Psalms (111–113, 115–117, 146–150) are evidently the nucleus around which the other psalms were grouped together. Prior to the fivefold division, there was probably a threefold arrangement in which Books IV and V were one large collection. An over-all liturgical purpose is evident throughout, resulting in a deep sense of public worship, which culminates in the closing words of Psalm 150: "Let everything that hath breath praise the Lord. Hallelujah!"

Psalm 107. The Song of the Redeemed

Psalms 105,106, and 107 constitute a trilogy of praise and thanksgiving, in spite of the book division here. The different character of verses 33-42 has suggested to many that this passage was added later. The differences in content and style make this suggestion plausible although not mandatory.

1-3. The Call to Thanksgiving. O give thanks unto the Lord. The recipients of this call are **the redeemed of the Lord.** Isaiah 62:12 uses this term to apply to the captives returning from Babylon, but a wider usage of the term may well be meant.

4-32. The Reasons for Thanksgiving. They wandered. . . . cried unto the Lord. . . . and he led them forth. The psalmist uses four vivid illustrations of God's deliverances to reinforce his call to thanksgiving. After each incident he repeats the call in the form of an interjection. This fourfold refrain keeps central the theme of thanksgiving. God's care over lost travelers (vv. 4-9), over captives (vv. 10-16), over the sick (vv. 17-22), and over seafarers (vv. 23-32) calls for thankful remembrance. In each instance, the author describes the helpless condition of those in trouble, their cry to God, and the deliverance He gives.

and *for* his wonderful works to the children of men! [16] For he hath broken the gates of brass, and cut the bars of iron in sunder.

[17] Fools because of their transgression, and because of their iniquities, are afflicted. [18] Their soul abhorreth all manner of meat; and they draw near unto the gates of death. [19] Then they cry unto the Lord in their trouble, *and* he saveth them out of their distresses. [20] He sent his word, and healed them, and delivered *them* from their destructions. [21] Oh that *men* would praise the Lord *for* his goodness, and *for* his wonderful works to the children of men! [22] And let them sacrifice the sacrifices of thanksgiving, and declare his works with rejoicing.

[23] They that go down to the sea in ships, that do business in great waters; [24] These see the works of the Lord, and his wonders in the deep. [25] For he commandeth, and raiseth the stormy wind, which lifteth up the waves thereof. [26] They mount up to the heaven, they go down again to the depths: their soul is melted because of trouble. [27] They reel to and fro, and stagger like a drunken man, and are at their wit's end. [28] Then they cry unto the Lord in their trouble, and he bringeth them out of their distresses. [29] He maketh the storm a calm, so that the waves thereof are still. [30] Then are they glad because they be quiet; so he bringeth them unto their desired haven. [31] Oh that *men* would praise the Lord *for* his goodness, and *for* his wonderful works to the children of men! [32] Let them exalt him also in the congregation of the people, and praise him in the assembly of the elders.

[33] He turneth rivers into a wilderness, and the watersprings into dry ground; [34] A fruitful land into barrenness, for the wickedness of them that dwell therein. [35] He turneth the wilderness into a standing water, and dry ground into watersprings. [36] And there he maketh the hungry to dwell, that they may prepare a city for habitation; [37] And sow the fields, and plant vineyards, which may yield fruits of increase. [38] He blesseth them also, so that they are multiplied greatly; and suffereth not their cattle to decrease.

lovingkindness and for all of his wonderful deeds! [16] For he broke down their prison gates of brass and cut apart their iron bars.

[17] Others, the fools, were ill because of their sinful ways. [18] Their appetites were gone and death was near. [19] Then they cried to the Lord in their troubles, and he helped them and delivered them. [20] He spoke, and they were healed—snatched from the door of death. [21] Oh, that these men would praise the Lord for his lovingkindness and for all of his wonderful deeds! [22] Let them tell him "Thank you" as their sacrifice, and sing about his glorious deeds.

[23] And then there are the sailors sailing the seven seas, plying the trade routes of the world. [24] They, too, observe the power of God in action. [25] He calls to the storm winds; the waves rise high. [26] Their ships are tossed to the heavens and sink again to the depths; the sailors cringe in terror. [27] They reel and stagger like drunkards and are at their wit's end. [28] Then they cry to the Lord in their trouble, and he saves them. [29] He calms the storm and stills the waves. [30] What a blessing is that stillness, as he brings them safely into harbor! [31] Oh, that these men would praise the Lord for his lovingkindness and for all of his wonderful deeds! [32] Let them praise him publicly before the congregation, and before the leaders of the nation.

[33] He dries up rivers, [34] and turns the good land of the wicked into deserts of salt. [35] Again, he turns deserts into fertile, watered valleys. [36] He brings the hungry to settle there and build their cities, [37] to sow their fields and plant their vineyards, and reap their bumper crops! [38] How he blesses them! They raise big families there, and many cattle.

33-42. The Providence of God. **He turneth rivers into a wilderness. . . . wilderness into a standing water.** These verses describe the blessings and curses apparent in God's rule of nature and mankind. They may serve as a general conclusion drawn from the more particular situations described in verses 4-32. However, the illustrations given are quite different from those of previous passages. This fact, plus the lack of any note of thanksgiving, the didactic purpose, the emphasis upon wisdom in the closing verse, and the lack of any refrain, certainly suggests that these verses were designed for a separate occasion.

³⁹ Again, they are minished and brought low through oppression, affliction, and sorrow. ⁴⁰ He poureth contempt upon princes, and causeth them to wander in the wilderness, *where there is no way.* ⁴¹ Yet setteth he the poor on high from affliction, and maketh *him* families like a flock. ⁴² The righteous shall see *it*, and rejoice: and all iniquity shall stop her mouth.

⁴³ Whoso *is* wise, and will observe these *things*, even they shall understand the lovingkindness of the Lord.

³⁹ But others become poor through oppression, trouble and sorrow. ⁴⁰ For God pours contempt upon the haughty and causes princes to wander among ruins; ⁴¹ but he rescues the poor who are godly and gives them many children and much prosperity. ⁴² Good men everywhere will see it and be glad, while evil men are stricken silent.

⁴³ Listen, if you are wise, to what I am saying. Think about the lovingkindness of the Lord!

PSALM 108

A Song or Psalm of David

O God, my heart is fixed: I will sing and give praise, even with my glory.

² Awake, psaltery and harp: I *myself* will awake early. ³ I will praise thee, O Lord, among the people: and I will sing praises unto thee among the nations. ⁴ For thy mercy *is* great above the heavens: and thy truth *reacheth* unto the clouds. ⁵ Be thou exalted, O God, above the heavens: and thy glory above all the earth; ⁶ That thy beloved may be delivered: save *with* thy right hand, and answer me.

⁷ God hath spoken in his holiness; I will rejoice, I will divide She-chem, and mete out the valley of Suc-coth. ⁸ Gilead *is* mine; Ma-nas-seh *is* mine; E-phra-im also *is* the strength of mine head; Judah *is* my lawgiver; ⁹ Moab *is* my washpot; over Edom will I cast out my shoe; over Philistia will I triumph.

¹⁰ Who will bring me into the strong city? who will lead me into Edom?

¹¹ *Wilt* not *thou*, O God, *who* hast cast us off? and wilt not thou, O God, go forth with our hosts? ¹² Give us help from trouble: for vain *is* the help of man. ¹³ Through God we shall do valiantly: for he *it is that* shall tread down our enemies.

108 O God, my heart is ready to praise you! I will sing and rejoice before you.

² Wake up, O harp and lyre! We will meet the dawn with song. ³ I will praise you everywhere around the world, in every nation. ⁴ For your lovingkindness is great beyond measure, high as the heavens. Your faithfulness reaches the skies. ⁵ His glory is far more vast than the heavens. It towers above the earth. ⁶ Hear the cry of your beloved child—come with mighty power and rescue me.

⁷ God has given sacred promises; no wonder I exult! He has promised to give us all the land of Shechem, and also Succoth Valley. ⁸ "Gilead is mine to give to you," he says, "and Manasseh as well; the land of Ephraim is the helmet on my head. Judah is my scepter. ⁹ But Moab and Edom are despised; and I will shout in triumph over the Philistines."

¹⁰ Who but God can give me strength to conquer these fortified cities? Who else can lead me into Edom?

¹¹ Lord, have you thrown us away? Have you deserted our army? ¹² Oh, help us fight against our enemies, for men are useless allies. ¹³ But with the help of God we shall do mighty acts of valor. For he treads down our foes.

PSALM 109

To the chief Musician, A Psalm of David

Hold not thy peace, O God of my praise; ² For the mouth of the wicked and the mouth of the deceitful are

109 O God of my praise, don't stand silent and aloof ² while the wicked

Psalm 108. A Prayer for God's Help

In this psalm are combined a hymn and a lament, both of which are found in other psalms. Verses 1-5 occur also in Ps 57:7-11, while verses 6-13 are found in Ps 60:5-12 with only minor variations. Since the divine name *Yahweh* is used in verse 3 rather than the *'Adōnāy* of Psalm 57, the present psalmist undoubtedly drew his material from the two earlier works. Perhaps the combination was formed to meet the needs of a new historical situation. (Cf. the previously mentioned psalms for further comments.)

Psalm 109. A Plea for Vengeance

Contrary to the views of some commentators, this psalm is clearly the lament of an individual rather than the voice of the nation. The personal character of the thought and expression is too strong for corporate significance. The imprecations in verses 9-20 make the poem unadaptable for worship purposes. The theory of some interpreters that these imprecations are the taunts of the psalmist's enemies is not convincing. There is a *righteous* indignation against evil (cf. Mt 23:13ff.); and the psalmist was assured that his foes were enemies of God.

1-5. His Appeal for Help. **Hold not thy peace.** In one terse statement the writer makes his appeal, and immediately he begins to voice his complaint. His enemies have been extremely vocal, while God has been silent. They have slandered him unjustly **with a lying tongue.** They have rewarded his love and goodness with hatred and evil.

NOTES

opened against me: they have spoken against me with a lying tongue. ³ They compassed me about also with words of hatred; and fought against me without *a* cause. ⁴ For my love they are my adversaries: but I *give myself unto* prayer. ⁵ And they have rewarded me evil for good, and hatred for my love.

⁶ Set thou a wicked man over him: and let Satan stand at his right hand. ⁷ When he shall be judged, let him be condemned: and let his prayer become sin. ⁸ Let his days be few; *and* let another take his office. ⁹ Let his children be fatherless, and his wife a widow. ¹⁰ Let his children be continually vagabonds, and beg: let them seek *their* bread also out of their desolate places. ¹¹ Let the extortioner catch all that he hath; and let the strangers spoil his labour. ¹² Let there be none to extend mercy unto him: neither let there be any to favour his fatherless children. ¹³ Let his posterity be cut off; *and* in the generation following let their name be blotted out. ¹⁴ Let the iniquity of his fathers be remembered with the Lord; and let not the sin of his mother be blotted out. ¹⁵ Let them be before the Lord continually, that he may cut off the memory of them from the earth.

¹⁶ Because that he remembered not to shew mercy, but persecuted the poor and needy man, that he might even slay the broken in heart. ¹⁷ As he loved cursing, so let it come unto him: as he delighted not in blessing, so let it be far from him. ¹⁸ As he clothed himself with cursing like as with his garment, so let it come into his bowels like water, and like oil into his bones.

¹⁹ Let it be unto him as the garment *which* covereth him, and for a girdle wherewith he is girded continually. ³⁰ *Let* this *be* the reward of mine adversaries from the Lord, and of them that speak evil against my soul.

²¹ But do thou for me, O God the Lord, for thy name's sake: because thy mercy *is* good, deliver thou me.

²² For I *am* poor and needy, and my heart is wounded within me. ²³ I am gone like the shadow when it declineth: I am tossed up and down as the locust. ²⁴ My knees are weak through fasting; and my flesh faileth of fatness. ²⁵ I be-

slander me and tell their lies. ³ They have no reason to hate and fight me, yet they do! ⁴ I love them, but even while I am praying for them, they are trying to destroy me. ⁵ They return evil for good, and hatred for love.

⁶ Show him how it feels! Let lies be told about him, and bring him to court before an unfair judge. ⁷ When his case is called for judgment, let him be pronounced guilty. Count his prayers as sins. ⁸ Let his years be few and brief; let others step forward to replace him. ⁹,¹⁰ May his children become fatherless and his wife a widow; may they be evicted from the ruins of their home. ¹¹ May creditors seize his entire estate and strangers take all he has earned. ¹²,¹³ Let no one be kind to him; let no one pity his fatherless children. May they die. May his family name be blotted out in a single generation. ¹⁴ Punish the sins of his father and mother. Don't overlook them. ¹⁵ Think constantly about the evil things he has done, and cut off his name from the memory of man.

¹⁶ For he refused all kindness to others, and persecuted those in need, and hounded brokenhearted ones to death. ¹⁷ He loved to curse others; now you curse him. He never blessed others; now don't you bless him. ¹⁸ Cursing is as much a part of him as his clothing, or as the water he drinks, or the rich food he eats.

¹⁹ Now may those curses return and cling to him like his clothing or his belt. ²⁰ This is the Lord's punishment upon my enemies who tell lies about me and threaten me with death.

²¹ But as for me, O Lord, deal with me as your child, as one who bears your name! Because you are so kind, O Lord, deliver me.

²²,²³ I am slipping down the hill to death; I am shaken off from life as easily as a man brushes a grasshopper from his arm. ²⁴ My knees are weak from fasting and I am skin and bones. ²⁵ I am a symbol of failure to all

6-20. His Plea for Retribution. Let him be condemned. The psalmist envisions a law court in which a wicked man is to be judged. The speaker sets forth the details of the sentence which the accused deserves. At the death of the accused someone else will take his office, and many difficulties will beset his wife and children. Worse than the speaker's desire for the death of his enemy is his wish that his enemy's family may come to an end and the father's name be forgotten within one generation. In verse 20, all of the speaker's adversaries are included in the foregoing imprecations.

21-31. His Prayer for Deliverance. But do thou for me . . . deliver thou me. The psalmist prays that God will have mercy upon him in his sick and needy condition, and vindicate him, so that his enemies may realize that God's hand has delivered him. After another outburst of imprecation, he closes with the confident promise that he will have opportunity to praise God for answered prayer.

NOTES

came also a reproach unto them: *when* they looked upon me they shaked their heads.

²⁶ Help me, O Lord my God: O save me according to thy mercy: ²⁷ That they may know that this *is* thy hand; *that* thou, Lord, hast done it. ²⁸ Let them curse, but bless thou: when they arise, let them be ashamed; but let thy servant rejoice.

²⁹ Let mine adversaries be clothed with shame, and let them cover themselves with their own confusion, as with a mantle. ³⁰ I will greatly praise the Lord with my mouth; yea, I will praise him among the multitude. ³¹ For he shall stand at the right hand of the poor, to save *him* from those that condemn his soul.

PSALM 110

A Psalm of David

THE Lord said unto my Lord, Sit thou at my right hand, until I make thine enemies thy footstool.

² The Lord shall send the rod of thy strength out of Zion: rule thou in the midst of thine enemies. ³ Thy people *shall be* willing in the day of thy power, in the beauties of holiness from the womb of the morning: thou hast the dew of thy youth. ⁴ The Lord hath sworn, and will not repent, Thou *art* a priest for ever after the order of Mel-chiz-e-dek. ⁵ The Lord at thy right hand shall strike through kings in the day of his wrath. ⁶ He shall judge among the heathen, he shall fill *the places* with the dead bodies; he shall wound the heads over many countries. ⁷ He shall drink of the brook in the way: therefore shall he lift up the head.

PSALM 111

PRAISE ye the Lord. I will praise the Lord with *my* whole heart, in the assembly of the upright, and *in* the congregation. ² The works of the Lord *are* great, sought out of all them that have pleasure therein. ³ His work *is* honourable and glorious: and his righteousness endureth for ever.

mankind; when they see me they shake their heads.

²⁶ Help me, O Lord my God! Save me because you are loving and kind. ²⁷ Do it publicly, so all will see that you yourself have done it. ²⁸ Then let them curse me if they like—I won't mind that if you are blessing me! For then all their efforts to destroy me will fail, and I shall go right on rejoicing!

²⁹ Make them fail in everything they do. Clothe them with disgrace. ³⁰ But I will give repeated thanks to the Lord, praising him to everyone. ³¹ For he stands beside the poor and hungry to save them from their enemies.

110 JEHOVAH SAID TO my Lord the Messiah, "Rule as my regent—I will subdue your enemies and make them bow low before you."

² Jehovah has established your throne in Jerusalem to rule over your enemies. ³ In that day of your power your people shall come to you willingly, dressed in holy altar robes. And your strength shall be renewed day by day like morning dew. ⁴ Jehovah has taken oath, and will not rescind his vow, that you are a priest forever like Melchizedek. ⁵ God stands beside you to protect you. He will strike down many kings in the day of his anger. ⁶ He will punish the nations, and fill them with their dead. He will crush many heads. ⁷ But he himself shall be refreshed from springs along the way.

111 HALLELUJAH! I WANT to express publicly before his people my heart-felt thanks to God for his mighty miracles. All who are thankful should ponder them with me. ³ For his miracles demonstrate his honor, majesty, and eternal goodness.

Psalm 110. The Promise of Victory and Dominion

This is properly a royal psalm with Messianic overtones throughout. The psalmist is uttering a divine oracle with the authority of a prophet. He addresses the oracle to his king and gives him assurance of victory. Men from Abraham to Simon of Maccabean times have been suggested as the historical recipient of the message. Yet Jesus' use of verse 1 clearly authorizes our finding here a wider significance than the primary meaning of the psalm in OT history (cf. Mt 22:41-45).

1-4. The Oracle of the Lord. **The Lord said.** The term used is a prophetic formula, "Oracle of the Lord." It is nowhere else employed in the Psalter, but it is frequently used by the prophets. While some commentators limit the extent of the oracle to verse 1, it seems better to extend it through verse 4. The Messianic king is commanded to occupy the position of highest honor and share the divine rule until his enemies are completely vanquished (cf. Josh 10:24; I Kgs 5:3). The term *footstool* is used by David (I Chr 28:2). The king rules from Zion, and all foes are submissive to him. The oracle is addressed to **my Lord** (*'Adōni*), a title of respect used for a king or superior. This king is to be honored and protected by divine blessing. His rule is to be universal. His subjects are to be willing volunteers. All of this is made certain by the use of a prophetic oath declaring the king's priesthood by divine appointment. The Messianic ruler serves a priestly as well as a royal office. In this he is likened to Melchizedek, the priest-king of Salem (Gen 14:18), whose ministry typified that of Jesus (cf. Heb 6:20−7:24).

5-7. The Victory of the Priest-King. **The Lord at thy right hand.** The scene changes now to the battlefield, where the Lord at Yahweh's right hand will shatter all his foes. The vivid language and the prophetic perfect tenses are designed to show clearly the completeness of the victory. The subject changes in verse 7 to the anointed king, whose head will be lifted in triumph. The frequent NT application of this psalm to Christ gives it special importance for the Christian interpreter.

Psalm 111. God's Wonderful Works

Here is a hymn of praise carefully designed as an acrostic poem. The twenty-two short lines begin with successive letters of the Hebrew alphabet. While this serves as an excellent mnemonic device, it greatly restricts the choice of words for a given line. This hymn is closely connected with Psalm 112 in form, language, and subject-matter. The two psalms are introductory to the *Hallēl* collection, which properly begins with Psalm 113.

1. The Annunciation of Praise. **I will praise the Lord.** The psalmist declares his intention to praise God **with a whole heart** as an act of public worship. This probably signifies that the message was delivered in the temple services by a solo voice.

2-4. The Greatness of God's Works. **The works of the Lord are great. . . . honourable and glorious.** The author thus describes God's works in general, then speaks of the Lord's eternal righteousness, his graciousness, and his compassion, attributes revealed most fully in his

NOTES

205

4 He hath made his wonderful works to be remembered: the Lord *is* gracious and full of compassion. 5 He hath given meat unto them that fear him: he will ever be mindful of his covenant. 6 He hath shewed his people the power of his works, that he may give them the heritage of the heathen. 7 The works of his hands *are* verity and judgment; all his commandments *are* sure. 8 They stand fast for ever and ever, *and are* done in truth and uprightness. 9 He sent redemption unto his people: he hath commanded his covenant for ever: holy and reverend *is* his name.

10 The fear of the Lord *is* the beginning of wisdom: a good understanding have all they that do *his commandments:* his praise endureth for ever.

PSALM 112

PRAISE ye the Lord. Blessed *is* the man *that* feareth the Lord, *that* delighteth greatly in his commandments.

2 His seed shall be mighty upon earth: the generation of the upright shall be blessed. 3 Wealth and riches *shall be* in his house: and his righteousness endureth for ever. 4 Unto the upright there ariseth light in the darkness: *he is* gracious, and full of compassion, and righteous. 5 A good man sheweth favour, and lendeth: he will guide his affairs with discretion.

6 Surely he shall not be moved for ever: the righteous shall be in everlasting remembrance. 7 He shall not be afraid of evil tidings: his heart is fixed, trusting in the Lord. 8 His heart *is* established, he shall not be afraid, until he see *his desire* upon his enemies. 9 He hath dispersed, he hath given to the poor; his righteousness endureth for ever; his horn shall be exalted with honour.

10 The wicked shall see *it,* and be grieved; he shall gnash with his teeth, and melt away: the desire of the wicked shall perish.

4 Who can forget the wonders he performs—deeds of mercy and of grace? 5 He gives food to those who trust him; he never forgets his promises. 6 He has shown his great power to his people by giving them the land of Israel, though it was the home of many nations living there. 7 All he does is just and good, and all his laws are right, 8 for they are formed from truth and goodness, and stand firm forever. 9 He has paid a full ransom for his people; now they are always free to come to Jehovah (what a holy, awe-inspiring name that is).

10 How can men be wise? The only way to begin is by reverence for God. For growth in wisdom comes from obeying his laws. Praise his name forever.

112 PRAISE THE LORD! For all who fear God and trust in him are blessed beyond expression. Yes, happy is the man who delights in doing his commands.

2 His children shall be honored everywhere, for good men's sons have a special heritage. 3 He himself shall be wealthy, and his good deeds will never be forgotten. 4 When darkness overtakes him, light will come bursting in. He is kind and merciful— 5 and all goes well for the generous man who conducts his business fairly.

6 Such a man will not be overthrown by evil circumstances. God's constant care of him will make a deep impression on all who see it. 7 He does not fear bad news, nor live in dread of what may happen. For he is settled in his mind that Jehovah will take care of him. 8 That is why he is not afraid, but can calmly face his foes. 9 He gives generously to those in need. His deeds will never be forgotten. He shall have influence and honor.

10 Evil-minded men will be infuriated when they see all this; they will gnash their teeth in anger and slink away, their hopes thwarted.

mighty acts. Note that man responds to evidences of God at work by seeking for further evidences and by remembering those works already performed.

5-9. The Verity of God's Care. The works of his hands are verity and judgment. God's provision of manna and quail demonstrated that he was mindful of the covenant. His works in the conquest of Canaan showed his intention to fulfill his covenant promise to Abraham. The verity of God's works is made known by his faithfulness.

10. The Beginning of Wisdom. The fear of the Lord. The psalm closes with a familiar maxim of the Wisdom writers. This kind of **fear** is best understood as *reverence* and *awe* that pervade every area of life. It is the beginning of true religion in that insight and understanding follow. It is also the consummation, for it is never replaced in true religious expression.

Psalm 112. Portrait of a Righteous Man

The concluding thought of Psalm 111 is more fully developed here, in keeping with the emphasis of the Wisdom literature. While 111 declares God's wonderful works, 112 describes the righteous man who has learned what it means to fear God. In its acrostic construction as well as in its subject-matter, this didactic psalm is a companion to the preceding one.

1-3. His Blessedness. Blessed is the man. In language reminiscent of Ps 1:1, the happiness of the God-fearer is set forth. A man who fears the Lord naturally finds delight in keeping the divine commandments. His children become heirs of his spiritual and material blessings. Note that the phrase, **his righteousness endureth for ever,** is applied to God in the preceding psalm.

4-6. His Character. Gracious, and full of compassion, and righteous. These terms are also used in Psalm 111 in the author's description of God. This is an application of the eternal truth that a devout man becomes more and more like the object of his worship. His prosperity will be lasting and his name long remembered because of his godly character.

7-10. His Permanence. His heart is fixed. His utter trust in God has given a sense of stability that the wicked cannot know. The truth that **his righteousness endureth for ever** here stands in sharp contrast to the fate of the wicked.

PSALM 113

PRAISE ye the Lord. Praise, O ye servants of the Lord, praise the name of the Lord. ² Blessed be the name of the Lord from this time forth and for evermore. ³ From the rising of the sun unto the going down of the same the Lord's name *is* to be praised. ⁴ The Lord *is* high above all nations, *and* his glory above the heavens.

⁵ Who *is* like unto the Lord our God, who dwelleth on high, ⁶ Who humbleth *himself* to behold *the things that are* in heaven, and in the earth! ⁷ He raiseth up the poor out of the dust, *and* lifteth the needy out of the dunghill; ⁸ That he may set *him* with princes, *even* with the princes of his people. ⁹ He maketh the barren woman to keep house, *and to be* a joyful mother of children. Praise ye the Lord.

113 HALLELUJAH! O SERVANTS of Jehovah, praise his name. ² Blessed is his name forever and forever. ³ Praise him from sunrise to sunset! ⁴ For he is high above the nations; his glory is far greater than the heavens.

⁵ Who can be compared with God enthroned on high? ⁶ Far below him are the heavens and the earth; he stoops to look, ⁷ and lifts the poor from the dirt, and the hungry from the garbage dump, ⁸ and sets them among princes! ⁹ He gives children to the childless wife, so that she becomes a happy mother.

Hallelujah! Praise the Lord.

PSALM 114

WHEN Israel went out of Egypt, the house of Jacob from a people of strange language; ² Judah was his sanctuary, *and* Israel his dominion.

114 LONG AGO WHEN the Israelis escaped from Egypt, from that land of foreign tongue, ² then the lands of Judah and of Israel became God's new home and kingdom.

Psalm 113. The Condescension of God

This hymn of praise is the first psalm in a collection known in the Talmud as "The Hallel of Egypt." The designation comes from the repeated use of the Hebrew exclamation *Hallelujah* (**Praise ye the Lord**), and from the reference to the Exodus in 114:1. This collection (113–118) was included in the worship of Judaism on festival occasions.

1-3. Praise to His Name. Praise the name of the Lord. The psalmist opens with an appeal to the servants or worshipers of the Lord. By **name** the writer means not a mere appellation, but the character of God's revealed nature and the manifestations of his person. Note that the praise is to be both unending (v. 2) and universal (v. 3).

4-6. Praise for His Incomparableness. Who is like unto the Lord? The incomparable nature of the Lord is pictured in the twofold aspects of his transcendence and his immanence. These two aspects are not set in contrast but treated as complementary. While supreme over the nations of the earth and the hosts of the heavens, God humbles himself to consider the needs of mankind.

7-9. Illustrations of His Condescension. He raiseth up the poor. The element of God's condescension, set forth by the psalmist in verse 6, deserves further illustration. The **poor**, the **needy**, and the **barren woman** are singled out as beneficiaries of God's special providence. These instances are cited as representative of all God's generous deeds toward the children of men.

Psalm 114. The Wonder of the Exodus

The power of Hebrew poetry at its best is illustrated by this lyric. The terse expression, the dramatic vividness, the excellent parallelism, and the imaginative exaggeration mark the psalm as a poetic masterpiece. The arrangement of the material into four stanzas of two verses each adds balance to the poem's heightened expression. The final "Hallelujah" of Psalm 113 undoubtedly once stood at the beginning of this psalm, as attested by the LXX.

1,2. The Birth of Israel. When Israel went out of Egypt. In concise language, the psalmist presents his theme as the Exodus and the subsequent settlement in Canaan. God brought His people out of a land of strange language into their home. The parallel reference to Judah

and Israel points to a time when the Temple was the center of worship and the northern area was considered a part of God's dominion.

NOTES

3 The sea saw *it,* and fled: Jordan was driven back. 4 The mountains skipped like rams, *and* the little hills like lambs. 5 What *ailed* thee, O thou sea, that thou fleddest? thou Jordan, *that* thou wast driven back? 6 Ye mountains, *that* ye skipped like rams; *and* ye little hills, like lambs?

7 Tremble, thou earth, at the presence of the Lord, at the presence of the God of Jacob; 8 Which turned the rock *into* a standing water, the flint into a fountain of waters.

PSALM 115

Not unto us, O Lord, not unto us, but unto thy name give glory, for thy mercy, *and* for thy truth's sake. 2 Wherefore should the heathen say, Where *is* now their God?

3 But our God *is* in the heavens: he hath done whatsoever he hath pleased. 4 Their idols *are* silver and gold, the work of men's hands. 5 They have mouths, but they speak not: eyes have they, but they see not: 6 They have ears, but they hear not: noses have they, but they smell not: 7 They have hands, but they handle not: feet have they, but they walk not: neither speak they through their throat. 8 They that make them are like unto them; *so is* every one that trusteth in them.

9 O Israel, trust thou in the Lord: he *is* their help and their shield. 10 O house of Aaron, trust in the Lord: he *is* their help and their shield. 11 Ye that fear the Lord, trust in the Lord: he *is* their help and their shield.

12 The Lord hath been mindful of us; he will bless *us;* he will bless the house of Israel; he will bless the house of Aaron. 13 He will bless them that fear the Lord, *both* small and great.

14 The Lord shall increase you more and more, you and your children. 15 Ye *are* blessed of the Lord which made heaven and earth. 16 The heaven, *even* the heavens, *are* the Lord's: but the earth hath he given to the children of men.

17 The dead praise not the Lord, neither any that go down into silence. 18 But we will bless the Lord from this time forth and for evermore. Praise the Lord.

3 The Red Sea saw them coming and quickly broke apart before them. The Jordan River opened up a path for them to cross. 4 The mountains skipped like rams, the little hills like lambs! 5 What's wrong, Red Sea, that made you cut yourself in two? What happened, Jordan River, to your waters? Why were they held back? 6 Why, mountains, did you skip like rams? Why, little hills, like lambs?

7 Tremble, O earth, at the presence of the Lord, the God of Jacob. 8 For he caused gushing streams to burst from flinty rock.

115 GLORIFY YOUR NAME, not ours, O Lord! Cause everyone to praise your lovingkindness and your truth. 2 Why let the nations say, "Their God is dead!"

3 For he is in the heavens, and does as he wishes. 4 Their gods are merely man-made things of silver and gold. 5 They can't talk or see, despite their eyes and mouths! 6 Nor can they hear, nor smell, 7 nor use their hands or feet! Nor speak! 8 And those who make and worship them are just as foolish as their idols are.

9 O Israel, trust the Lord! He is your helper. He is your shield. 10 O priests of Aaron, trust the Lord! He is your helper; he is your shield. 11 All of you, his people, trust in him. He is your helper; he is your shield.

12 Jehovah is constantly thinking about us and he will surely bless us. He will bless the people of Israel and the priests of Aaron, 13 and all, both great and small, who reverence him.

14 May the Lord richly bless both you and your children. 15 Yes, Jehovah who made heaven and earth will personally bless you! 16 The heavens belong to the Lord, but he has given the earth to all mankind.

17 The dead cannot sing praises to Jehovah here on earth, 18 but we can! We praise him forever! Hallelujah! Praise the Lord!

3-6. The Effect upon Nature. **The sea saw it, and fled.** With poetic imagination, the psalmist describes the effect of God's works on nature. The **sea,** the **Jordan,** the **mountains,** and the **hills** were witnesses to his power in overcoming all obstacles that threatened to hinder the progress of Israel. The statements of verses 3,4 become Why? questions in verses 5,6. The answers are clearly implied in the further emphasis upon the awesomeness of God's power.

7,8. The Admonition to Nature. **Tremble, thou earth.** The recognition of God's wondrous acts and the effect of his presence should make all creation tremble. The conclusion to be drawn is that, even as God brought forth water in the wilderness, he will provide for the needs of his people.

Psalm 115. Glory to His Name

This psalm is basically a hymn of praise designed for use in the temple worship. The presence of a complaint (vv. 1,2) does not nullify the hymnic qualities, but gives a historical basis for its original composition. That it was used in the worship of the feast celebrations is known from various sources. In fact, Psalms 115—118 were sung at the conclusion of the Passover meal, just before the worshipers returned to their homes. The hymn appears to have been designed originally for antiphonal use.

1-8. A Contrast of Power. **Our God. . . . their idols.** The burden of the psalm is seen in the question by Israel's Gentile enemies, **Where is now their God?** In appealing for help, the psalmist does not seek glory for his nation but recognition by the heathen of the glory due to the name of Yahweh. The impotent idols and their feeble worshipers stand in sharp contrast to God's power and glory.

9-11. An Exhortation to Trust. **O Israel, trust thou in the Lord.** This threefold appeal for trust was probably voiced by a priest; and very likely a choral response followed each appeal. The nation, the priests, and the devoted Godfearers are all addressed in turn.

12-15. An Assurance of Blessing. **The Lord hath been mindful of us.** Remembrance of God's previous blessings gives assurance for the present and the future. Note that blessing is assured for each of the groups singled out in the previous exhortation.

16-18. A Chorus of Praise. **We will bless the Lord . . . for evermore.** The Lord who created both the heavens and the earth has reserved the heavens for his domain. To man he has given the earth and the right to praise him here and now. In the thinking of most writers, death ends the opportunity for further worship. Hence the urgency of the exhortation, **Praise ye the Lord.**

NOTES

PSALM 116

I LOVE the Lord, because he hath heard my voice *and* my supplications. ² Because he hath inclined his ear unto me, therefore will I call upon *him* as long as I live. ³ The sorrows of death compassed me, and the pains of hell gat hold upon me: I found trouble and sorrow. ⁴ Then called I upon the name of the Lord; O Lord, I beseech thee, deliver my soul. ⁵ Gracious *is* the Lord, and righteous; yea, our God *is* merciful. ⁶ The Lord preserveth the simple: I was brought low, and he helped me. ⁷ Return unto thy rest, O my soul; for the Lord hath dealt bountifully with thee. ⁸ For thou hast delivered my soul from death, mine eyes from tears, *and* my feet from falling. ⁹ I will walk before the Lord in the land of the living. ¹⁰ I believed, therefore have I spoken: I was greatly afflicted: ¹¹ I said in my haste, All men *are* liars. ¹² What shall I render unto the Lord *for* all his benefits toward me? ¹³ I will take the cup of salvation, and call upon the name of the Lord. ¹⁴ I will pay my vows unto the Lord now in the presence of all his people. ¹⁵ Precious in the sight of the Lord *is* the death of his saints. ¹⁶ O Lord, truly I *am* thy servant; I *am* thy servant, *and* the son of thine handmaid: thou hast loosed my bonds. ¹⁷ I will offer to thee the sacrifice of thanksgiving, and will call upon the name of the Lord. ¹⁸ I will pay my vows unto the Lord now in the presence of all his people, ¹⁹ In the courts of the Lord's house, in the midst of thee, O Jerusalem. Praise ye the Lord.

PSALM 117

O PRAISE the Lord, all ye nations: praise him, all ye people. ² For his merciful kindness is great toward us: and the truth of the Lord *endureth* for ever. Praise ye the Lord.

116 I LOVE THE Lord because he hears my prayers and answers them. ² Because he bends down and listens, I will pray as long as I breathe!

³ Death stared me in the face—I was frightened and sad. ⁴ Then I cried, "Lord, save me!" ⁵ How kind he is! How good he is! So merciful, this God of ours! ⁶ The Lord protects the simple and the childlike; I was facing death and then he saved me. ⁷ Now I can relax. For the Lord has done this wonderful miracle for me. ⁸ He has saved me from death, my eyes from tears, my feet from stumbling. ⁹ I shall live! Yes, in his presence—here on earth!

¹⁰,¹¹ In my discouragement I thought, "They are lying when they say I will recover." ¹² But now what can I offer Jehovah for all he has done for me? ¹³ I will bring him an offering of wine and praise his name for saving me. ¹⁴ I will publicly bring him the sacrifice I vowed I would. ¹⁵ His loved ones are very precious to him and he does not lightly let them die.

¹⁶ O Lord, you have freed me from my bonds and I will serve you forever. ¹⁷ I will worship you and offer you a sacrifice of thanksgiving. ¹⁸,¹⁹ Here in the courts of the Temple in Jerusalem, before all the people, I will pay everything I vowed to the Lord. Praise the Lord.

117 PRAISE THE LORD, all nations everywhere. Praise him, all the peoples of the earth. ² For he loves us very dearly, and his truth endures. Praise the Lord.

Psalm 116. A Song of Personal Thanksgiving

This hymn of thanksgiving is strikingly personal from beginning to end. Its use in this Hallel collection in connection with the main feasts probably indicates that it was associated with the payment of individual vows. The LXX divides this psalm into two separate poems, making a division after verse 9. The presence of frequent Aramaic expressions points to a post-Exilic setting.

1-11. Praise for Deliverance. **I love the Lord, because . . .** Out of the depths of trouble and sickness the psalmist called and the Lord answered. From this experience of answered prayer, he came to know God as **gracious, righteous,** and **merciful.** He now knows by experience that God preserves, helps, deals bountifully, and delivers. In the midst of his exultation he recalls that previously he had clung to his faith even when he had said, "I am greatly afflicted" (v. 10). In his consternation or alarm (haste, AV) he had said, "All men are liars," i.e., deceitful for not fulfilling their promised help. His quoting of Ps 31:22 in verse 11 probably indicates that now he has learned to rely on God in the face of human frailty.

12-19. Expressions of Gratitude. **What shall I render unto the Lord?** The speaker's realization of God's blessings gives birth to his desire for more concrete expression of gratitude. He promises to offer a drink offering (**take the cup of salvation**), worship (**call upon the name of the Lord**), pay vows, and offer a thanksgiving sacrifice. This is not the usual order of such sacrifices and offerings. The psalmist's humility and sense of dedication are seen in verse 16. As a servant, yea a trusted servant (**son of thine handmaid**), he expresses his dependence upon God.

Psalm 117. A Shout of Praise

This is the shortest hymn of praise recorded in the Psalter. In some MSS it is attached to the preceding poem and in other MSS to the following one. However, both the Hebrew Text and the LXX treat it as an entity. The two verses contain a complete act of praise. The first verse, employing strict parallelism of form, sets forth a universal call to praise. The second verse, which is in similar form, completes the call by expressing the reasons for rendering praise. Truly universal, the call includes all nations and all peoples. The concept of God is equally lofty, as his mercy and truth are singled out for mention.

NOTES

PSALM 118

O GIVE thanks unto the Lord; for *he is* good: because his mercy *endureth* for ever.

[2] Let Israel now say, that his mercy *endureth* for ever. [3] Let the house of Aaron now say, that his mercy *endureth* for ever. [4] Let them now that fear the Lord say, that his mercy *endureth* for ever.

[5] I called upon the Lord in distress: the Lord answered me, *and set me* in a large place. [6] The Lord *is* on my side; I will not fear: what can man do unto me? [7] The Lord taketh my part with them that help me: therefore shall I see *my desire* upon them that hate me.

[8] *It is* better to trust in the Lord than to put confidence in man. [9] *It is* better to trust in the Lord than to put confidence in princes.

[10] All nations compassed me about: but in the name of the Lord will I destroy them. [11] They compassed me about; yea, they compassed me about: but in the name of the Lord I will destroy them. [12] They compassed me about like bees; they are quenched as the fire of thorns: for in the name of the Lord I will destroy them. [13] Thou hast thrust sore at me that I might fall: but the Lord helped me. [14] The Lord *is* my strength and song, and is become my salvation. [15] The voice of rejoicing and salvation *is* in the tabernacles of the righteous: the right hand of the Lord doeth valiantly. [16] The right hand of the Lord is exalted: the right hand of the Lord doeth valiantly. [17] I shall not die, but live, and declare the works of the Lord. [18] The Lord hath chastened me sore: but he hath not given me over unto death.

[19] Open to me the gates of righteousness: I will go into them, *and* I will praise the Lord: [20] This gate of the Lord, into which the righteous shall enter. [21] I will praise thee: for thou hast heard me, and art become my salvation.

[22] The stone *which* the builders refused is become the head *stone* of the corner. [23] This is the Lord's doing; *it is* marvellous in our eyes. [24] This *is* the day *which* the Lord hath made; we will rejoice and be glad in it. [25] Save now, I beseech thee, O Lord: O Lord, I beseech

118 OH, THANK THE Lord, for he's so good! His lovingkindness is forever.

[2] Let the congregation of Israel praise him with these same words: "His lovingkindness is forever." [3] And let the priests of Aaron chant, "His lovingkindness is forever." [4] Let the Gentile converts chant, "His lovingkindness is forever."

[5] In my distress I prayed to the Lord and he answered me and rescued me. [6] He is for me! How can I be afraid? What can mere man do to me? [7] The Lord is on my side, he will help me. Let those who hate me beware.

[8] It is better to trust the Lord than to put confidence in men. [9] It is better to take refuge in him than in the mightiest king!

[10] Though all the nations of the world attack me, I will march out behind his banner and destroy them. [11] Yes, they surround and attack me; but with his flag flying above me I will cut them off. [12] They swarm around me like bees; they blaze against me like a roaring flame. Yet beneath his flag I shall destroy them. [13] You did your best to kill me, O my enemy, but the Lord helped me. [14] He is my strength and song in the heat of battle, and now he has given me the victory. [15,16] Songs of joy at the news of our rescue are sung in the homes of the godly. The strong arm of the Lord has done glorious things! [17] I shall not die, but live to tell of all his deeds. [18] The Lord has punished me, but not handed me over to death.

[19] Open the gates of the Temple —I will go in and give him my thanks. [20] Those gates are the way into the presence of the Lord, and the godly enter there. [21] O Lord, thank you so much for answering my prayer and saving me.

[22] The stone rejected by the builders has now become the capstone of the arch! [23] This is the Lord's doing, and it is marvelous to see! [24] This is the day the Lord has made. We will rejoice and be glad in it. [25] O Lord, please help us. Save us. Give us suc-

Psalm 118. Thanksgiving for Deliverance

As a processional and a jubilant expression of thanksgiving, this song of praise serves as a fitting conclusion to the Hallel collection. Clearly designed for antiphonal use, it employs solo voices, choruses, and congregational refrains. Verses 5-21 are quite individualistic in content, suggesting that verses 1-4 and 22 ff. were added to adapt the original psalm for collective use.

1-4. The Invocation to Praise. **O give thanks unto the Lord.** This call to thanksgiving and praise was the signal for beginning the procession to the Temple. The leader or priest presented the call, while a chorus or the congregation answered with the refrain. Note that the same threefold division is found in Ps 115:9-11 (Israel, house of Aaron, and God-fearers), while the refrain comes from Psalm 136.

5-21. The Deliverance of God. **I called . . . the Lord answered me.** The theme throughout this passage is one of rejoicing that God has given deliverance and victory. In actual use, this passage, because of its individualized nature, called for a solo voice. The single voice represented the personified nation in general and the assembled worshipers in particular. With verses 19-21, the procession had undoubtedly reached the temple gates and was demanding entrance.

22-29. The Application for Worship. **This is the Lord's doing.** These verses abound in words well known from their NT application. Verse 22, describing the chief cornerstone, was probably a proverb of that day referring to Israel, rejected by the great empire-builders as unworthy to fit into their plans. But the divine mission of Israel became focused and fulfilled in its greatest representative, the Messiah. Thus Jesus appropriated its imagery for his own ministry (cf. Mt 21:42; Mk 12:10; Lk 20:17; Acts 4:11; Eph 2:20; I Pet 2:7). The priestly bene-

thee, send now prosperity. ²⁶ Blessed *be* he that cometh in the name of the Lord: we have blessed you out of the house of the Lord.

²⁷ God *is* the Lord, which hath shewed us light: bind the sacrifice with cords, *even* unto the horns of the altar. ²⁸ Thou *art* my God, and I will praise thee: *thou art* my God, I will exalt thee. ²⁹ O give thanks unto the Lord; for *he is* good: for his mercy *endureth* for ever.

PSALM 119

ALEPH

BLESSED *are* the undefiled in the way, who walk in the law of the Lord. ² Blessed *are* they that keep his testimonies, *and that* seek him with the whole heart. ³ They also do no iniquity: they walk in his ways. ⁴ Thou hast commanded *us* to keep thy precepts diligently. ⁵ O that my ways were directed to keep thy statutes! ⁶ Then shall I not be ashamed, when I have respect unto all thy commandments.

⁷ I will praise thee with uprightness of heart, when I shall have learned thy righteous judgments. ⁸ I will keep thy statutes: O forsake me not utterly.

BETH

⁹ Wherewithal shall a young man cleanse his way? by taking heed *thereto* according to thy word. ¹⁰ With my whole heart have I sought thee: O let me not wander from thy commandments. ¹¹ Thy word have I hid in mine heart, that I might not sin against thee.

¹² Blessed *art* thou, O Lord: teach me thy statutes. ¹³ With my lips have I declared all the judgments of thy mouth. ¹⁴ I have rejoiced in the way of thy testimonies, as *much as* in all riches. ¹⁵ I will meditate in thy precepts, and have respect unto thy ways. ¹⁶ I will delight myself in thy statutes: I will not forget thy word.

GIMEL

¹⁷ Deal bountifully with thy servant, *that* I may live, and keep thy word. ¹⁸ Open thou mine eyes, that I may behold wondrous things out of thy law. ¹⁹ I am a stranger in the earth: hide not

cess. ²⁶ Blessed is the one who is coming, the one sent by the Lord. We bless you from the Temple.

²⁷,²⁸ Jehovah God is our light. I present to him my sacrifice upon the altar, for you are my God, and I shall give you this thanks and this praise. ²⁹ Oh, give thanks to the Lord, for he is so good! For his lovingkindness is forever.

119 HAPPY ARE ALL who perfectly follow the laws of God. ² Happy are all who search for God, and always do his will, ³ rejecting compromise with evil, and walking only in his paths. ⁴ You have given us your laws to obey— ⁵ oh, how I want to follow them consistently. ⁶ Then I will not be disgraced, for I will have a clean record.

⁷ After you have corrected me I will thank you by living as I should! ⁸ I *will* obey! Oh, don't forsake me and let me slip back into sin again.

⁹ How can a young man stay pure? By reading your Word and following its rules. ¹⁰ I have tried my best to find you—don't let me wander off from your instructions. ¹¹ I have thought much about your words, and stored them in my heart so that they would hold me back from sin.

¹² Blessed Lord, teach me your rules. ¹³ I have recited your laws, ¹⁴ and rejoiced in them more than in riches. ¹⁵ I will meditate upon them and give them my full respect. ¹⁶ I will delight in them and not forget them.

¹⁷ Bless me with life so that I can continue to obey you. ¹⁸ Open my eyes to see wonderful things in your Word. ¹⁹ I am but a pilgrim here on earth: how I need a map

diction of verse 26 found expression six times in the Gospels because of its distinct application to the mission of Christ.

Psalm 119. The Torah of the Lord

Essentially a didactic poem, this psalm takes the form of a personal testimony. Although the poem contains allusions to persecution and shows certain characteristics of laments, its main purpose is to glorify the *Tôrâ* (God's law or teaching). The psalmist directs almost every verse to God, using many forms of petition. At the same time, he uses some synonym for the law in all but seven verses. The synonyms are: law, testimonies, precepts, judgments, commandments, statutes, sayings, word, way, and path. Possibly in employing ten terms to describe God's Torah, he was following the lead of Ps 19:7-9, where six such synonyms for the *law* are used.

The acrostic principle is highly developed in this psalm, employing all twenty-two letters of the Hebrew alphabet. Each stanza is composed of eight lines, which begin with the letter characteristic of that stanza. This artificial yet artistic arrangement makes for a certain monotony in the great repetition of words and phrases. However, this mechanical monotony is overcome by the intensity of the psalmist's own devotion to God's teachings.

1-8. The Blessing of Obedience. Blessed . . . who walk in the law of the Lord. The theme of the psalm is here set forth clearly. Note that most of the ten synonyms for the law are used in this first strophe.

9-16. The Way of Cleansing. Wherewithal shall a young man cleanse his way? The question and answer are in keeping with the emphasis of the Wisdom writers. The answer to the problems of youth in any period of history is to heed God's Word by meditating on it (v. 15) and committing it to memory (v. 11) and by testifying concerning it to others (v. 13).

17-24. The Delight of Experience. Thy testimonies are my delight. This delight is based upon his past experience with God in times of persecution. A note of sorrow and desire runs through this strophe, but the section ends in delight.

I MEDITATION & PRAYER
II MEMORIZATION
III SHARING

thy commandments from me. ²⁰ My soul breaketh for the longing *that it hath* unto thy judgments at all times.

²¹ Thou hast rebuked the proud *that are* cursed, which do err from thy commandments. ²² Remove from me reproach and contempt; for I have kept thy testimonies. ²³ Princes also did sit *and* speak against me: *but* thy servant did meditate in thy statutes. ²⁴ Thy testimonies also *are* my delight *and* my counsellors.

DALETH

²⁵ My soul cleaveth unto the dust: quicken thou me according to thy word. ²⁶ I have declared my ways, and thou heardest me: teach me thy statutes. ²⁷ Make me to understand the way of thy precepts: so shall I talk of thy wondrous works.

²⁸ My soul melteth for heaviness: strengthen thou me according unto thy word. ²⁹ Remove from me the way of lying: and grant me thy law graciously. ³⁰ I have chosen the way of truth: thy judgments have I laid *before me.* ³¹ I have stuck into thy testimonies: O Lord, put me not to shame. ³² I will run the way of thy commandments, when thou shalt enlarge my heart.

HE

³³ Teach me, O Lord, the way of thy statutes; and I shall keep it *unto* the end. ³⁴ Give me understanding, and I shall keep thy law; yea, I shall observe it with *my* whole heart. ³⁵ Make me to go in the path of thy commandments; for therein do I delight.

³⁶ Incline my heart unto thy testimonies, and not to covetousness. ³⁷ Turn away mine eyes from beholding vanity; *and* quicken thou me in thy way. ³⁸ Stablish thy word unto thy servant, who *is devoted* to thy fear.

³⁹ Turn away my reproach which I fear: for thy judgments *are* good. ⁴⁰ Behold, I have longed after thy precepts: quicken me in thy righteousness.

VAU

⁴¹ Let thy mercies come also unto me, O Lord, *even* thy salvation, according to thy word. ⁴² So shall I have wherewith to answer him that reproacheth me: for I trust in thy word.

—and your commands are my chart and guide. ²⁰ I long for your instructions more than I can tell.

²¹ You rebuke those cursed proud ones who refuse your commands— ²² don't let them scorn me for obeying you. ²³ For even princes sit and talk against me, but I will continue in your plans. ²⁴ Your laws are both my light and my counselors.

²⁵ I am completely discouraged—I lie in the dust. Revive me by your Word. ²⁶ I told you my plans and you replied. Now give me your instructions. ²⁷ Make me understand what you want; for then I shall see your miracles.

²⁸ I weep with grief; my heart is heavy with sorrow; encourage and cheer me with your words. ²⁹,³⁰ Keep me far from every wrong; help me, undeserving as I am, to obey your laws, for I have chosen to do right. ³¹ I cling to your commands and follow them as closely as I can. Lord, don't let me make a mess of things. ³² If you will only help me to want your will, then I will follow your laws even more closely.

³³,³⁴ Just tell me what to do and I will do it, Lord. As long as I live I'll wholeheartedly obey. ³⁵ Make me walk along the right paths for I know how delightful they really are.

³⁶ Help me to prefer obedience to making money! ³⁷ Turn me away from wanting any other plan than yours. Revive my heart toward you. ³⁸ Reassure me that your promises are for me, for I trust and revere you.

³⁹ How I dread being mocked for obeying, for your laws are right and good. ⁴⁰,⁴¹,⁴² I long to obey them! Therefore in fairness renew my life, for this was your promise—yes, Lord, to save me! Now spare me by your kindness and your love. Then I will have an answer for those who taunt me, for I trust your promises.

25-32. The Strength in Understanding. **Quicken. . . . teach. . . . make me to understand.** The peril confronting the psalmist makes him call for strength and comfort. He realizes that the quickening he desires comes from an understanding of God's teachings.

33-40. The Need for Guidance. **Teach me . . . and I shall keep it.** In phrase after phrase, the speaker pleads for God's guidance in ordering his life and in refraining from folly.

41-48. The Courage for Witnessing. **Let thy mercies come.** This appeal for help is not selfish; it is inspired by a desire to have **wherewith to answer him that reproacheth me.** The speaker further declares that he will witness to kings without being ashamed.

NOTES

219

43 And take not the word of truth utterly out of my mouth; for I have hoped in thy judgments. 44 So shall I keep thy law continually for ever and ever. 45 And I will walk at liberty: for I seek thy precepts. 46 I will speak of thy testimonies also before kings, and will not be ashamed.

47 And I will delight myself in thy commandments, which I have loved. 48 My hands also will I lift up unto thy commandments, which I have loved; and I will meditate in thy statutes.

ZAIN

49 Remember the word unto thy servant, upon which thou hast caused me to hope. 50 This *is* my comfort in my affliction: for thy word hath quickened me. 51 The proud have had me greatly in derision: *yet* have I not declined from thy law. 52 I remembered thy judgments of old, O Lord; and have comforted myself.

53 Horror hath taken hold upon me because of the wicked that forsake thy law. 54 Thy statutes have been my songs in the house of my pilgrimage. 55 I have remembered thy name, O Lord, in the night, and have kept thy law. 56 This I had, because I kept thy precepts.

CHETH

57 *Thou art* my portion, O Lord: I have said that I would keep thy words. 58 I intreated thy favour with *my* whole heart: be merciful unto me according to thy word. 59 I thought on my ways, and turned my feet unto thy testimonies. 60 I made haste, and delayed not to keep thy commandments. 61 The bands of the wicked have robbed me: *but* I have not forgotten thy law.

62 At midnight I will rise to give thanks unto thee because of thy righteous judgments. 63 I *am* a companion of all *them* that fear thee, and of them that keep thy precepts. 64 The earth, O Lord, is full of thy mercy: teach me thy statutes.

TETH

65 Thou hast dealt well with thy servant, O Lord, according unto thy word. 66 Teach me good judgment and knowledge: for I have believed thy com-

43 May I never forget your words; for they are my only hope. 44,45,46 Therefore I will keep on obeying you forever and forever, free within the limits of your laws. I will speak to kings about their value, and they will listen with interest and respect.

47 How I love your laws! How I enjoy your commands! 48 "Come, come to me," I call to them, for I love them and will let them fill my life.

49,50 Never forget your promises to me your servant, for they are my only hope. They give me strength in all my troubles; how they refresh and revive me! 51 Proud men hold me in contempt for obedience to God, but I stand unmoved. 52 From my earliest youth I have tried to obey you; your Word has been my comfort.

53 I am very angry with those who spurn your commands. 54 For these laws of yours have been my source of joy and singing through all these years of my earthly pilgrimage. 55 I obey them even at night and keep my thoughts, O Lord, on you. 56 What a blessing this has been to me—to constantly obey.

57 Jehovah is mine! And I promise to obey! 58 With all my heart I want your blessings. Be merciful just as you promised. 59,60 I thought about the wrong direction in which I was headed, and turned around and came running back to you. 61 Evil men have tried to drag me into sin, but I am firmly anchored to your laws.

62 At midnight I will rise to give my thanks to you for your good laws. 63 Anyone is my brother who fears and trusts the Lord and obeys him. 64 O Lord, the earth is full of your lovingkindness! Teach me your good paths.

65 Lord, I am overflowing with your blessings, just as you promised. 66 Now teach me good judgment as well as knowl-

49-56. The Source of Comfort. Remember the word unto thy servant. . . . this is my comfort. In the time of affliction, God's teachings have been his stay and the songs in the house of my pilgrimage.

57-64. The Resolution of Faithfulness. I have said that I would keep thy words. Thinking upon his ways brought him to the point where he could turn his feet unto God's testimonies. His gratitude is evident in his promise to arise at midnight to thank God.

65-72. The Discipline of Affliction. It is good for me that I have been afflicted. Having gone astray before his affliction, the psalmist now sees a beneficent purpose in his suffering.

NOTES

mandments. 67 Before I was afflicted I went astray: but now have I kept thy word. 68 Thou *art* good, and doest good; teach me thy statutes.

69 The proud have forged a lie against me: *but* I will keep thy precepts with *my* whole heart. 70 Their heart is as fat as grease; *but* I delight in thy law.

71 *It is* good for me that I have been afflicted; that I might learn thy statutes. 72 The law of thy mouth *is* better unto me than thousands of gold and silver.

JOD

73 Thy hands have made me and fashioned me: give me understanding, that I may learn thy commandments. 74 They that fear thee will be glad when they see me; because I have hoped in thy word.

75 I know, O Lord, that thy judgments *are* right, and *that* thou in faithfulness hast afflicted me. 76 Let, I pray thee, thy merciful kindness be for my comfort, according to thy word unto thy servant. 77 Let thy tender mercies come unto me, that I may live: for thy law *is* my delight.

78 Let the proud be ashamed; for they dealt perversely with me without a cause: *but* I will meditate in thy precepts.

79 Let those that fear thee turn unto me, and those that have known thy testimonies. 80 Let my heart be sound in thy statutes; that I be not ashamed.

CAPH

81 My soul fainteth for thy salvation: *but* I hope in thy word. 82 Mine eyes fail for thy word, saying, When wilt thou comfort me? 83 For I am become like a bottle in the smoke; *yet* do I not forget thy statutes. 84 How many *are* the days of thy servant? when wilt thou execute judgment on them that persecute me? 85 The proud have digged pits for me, which *are* not after thy law. 86 All thy commandments *are* faithful: they persecute me wrongfully; help thou me. 87 They had almost consumed me upon earth; but I forsook not thy precepts. 88 Quicken me after thy lovingkindness; so shall I keep the testimony of thy mouth.

edge. For your laws are my guide. 67 I used to wander off until you punished me; now I closely follow all you say. 68 You are good and do only good; make me follow your lead.

69 Proud men have made up lies about me, but the truth is that I obey your laws with all my heart. 70 Their minds are dull and stupid, but I have sense enough to follow you.

71,72 The punishment you gave me was the best thing that could have happened to me, for it taught me to pay attention to your laws. They are more valuable to me than millions in silver and gold!

73 You made my body, Lord; now give me sense to heed your laws. 74 All those who fear and trust in you will welcome me because I too am trusting in your Word.

75,76,77 I know, O Lord, that your decisions are right and that your punishment was right and did me good. Now let your lovingkindness comfort me, just as you promised. Surround me with your tender mercies, that I may live. For your law is my delight.

78 Let the proud be disgraced, for they have cut me down with all their lies. But I will concentrate my thoughts upon your laws.

79 Let all others join me, who trust and fear you, and we will discuss your laws. 80 Help me to love your every wish; then I will never have to be ashamed of myself.

81 I faint for your salvation; but I expect your help, for you have promised it. 82 My eyes are straining to see your promises come true. When will you comfort me with your help? 83 I am shriveled like a wineskin in the smoke, exhausted with waiting. But still I cling to your laws and obey them. 84 How long must I wait before you punish those who persecute me? 85,86 These proud men who hate your truth and laws have dug deep pits for me to fall in. Their lies have brought me into deep trouble. Help me, for you love only truth. 87 They had almost finished me off, yet I refused to yield and disobey your laws. 88 In your kindness, spare my life; then I can continue to obey you.

73-80. The Justice of Retribution. **Let the proud be ashamed.** After voicing again his desire for understanding, he pleads for God's blessings upon himself and shame upon his enemies. His end desire is that he may strengthen the faith of others.

81-88. The Hope in Darkness. **My soul fainteth . . . I hope in thy word.** In a succession of sobs, he expresses his hope and determination in his darkest hour. With each plea for comfort he reiterates his desire to be faithful.

NOTES

LAMED

89 For ever, O Lord, thy word is settled in heaven. 90 Thy faithfulness *is* unto all generations: thou hast established the earth, and it abideth. 91 They continue this day according to thine ordinances: for all *are* thy servants.

92 Unless thy law *had been* my delights, I should then have perished in mine affliction. 93 I will never forget thy precepts: for with them thou hast quickened me. 94 I *am* thine, save me; for I have sought thy precepts. 95 The wicked have waited for me to destroy me: *but* I will consider thy testimonies. 96 I have seen an end of all perfection: *but* thy commandment *is* exceeding broad.

MEM

97 O how love I thy law! it *is* my meditation all the day. 98 Thou through thy commandments hast made me wiser than mine enemies: for they *are* ever with me. 99 I have more understanding than all my teachers: for thy testimonies *are* my meditation. 100 I understand more than the ancients, because I keep thy precepts.

101 I have refrained my feet from every evil way, that I might keep thy word. 102 I have not departed from thy judgments: for thou hast taught me. 103 How sweet are thy words unto my taste! *yea, sweeter* than honey to my mouth! 104 Through thy precepts I get understanding: therefore I hate every false way.

NUN

105 Thy word *is* a lamp unto my feet, and a light unto my path. 106 I have sworn, and I will perform *it,* that I will keep thy righteous judgments.
107 I am afflicted very much: quicken me, O Lord, according unto thy word. 108 Accept, I beseech thee, the freewill offerings of my mouth, O Lord, and teach me thy judgments. 109 My soul *is* continually in my hand: yet do I not forget thy law. 110 The wicked have laid a snare for me: yet I erred not from thy precepts. 111 Thy testimonies have I taken as an heritage for ever: for they *are* the rejoicing of my heart. 112 I have inclined mine heart to perform thy statutes alway, *even unto* the end.

89 Forever, O Lord, your Word stands firm in heaven. 90,91 Your faithfulness extends to every generation, like the earth you created; it endures by your decree, for everything serves your plans.

92 I would have despaired and perished unless your laws had been my deepest delight. 93 I will never lay aside your laws, for you have used them to restore my joy and health. 94 I am yours! Save me! For I have tried to live according to your desires. 95 Though the wicked hide along the way to kill me, I will quietly keep my mind upon your promises.

96 Nothing is perfect except your words. 97 Oh, how I love them. I think about them all day long. 98 They make me wiser than my enemies, because they are my constant guide. 99 Yes, wiser than my teachers, for I am ever thinking of your rules. 100 They make me even wiser than the aged.

101 I have refused to walk the paths of evil for I will remain obedient to your Word. 102,103 No, I haven't turned away from what you taught me; your words are sweeter than honey. 104 And since only your rules can give me wisdom and understanding, no wonder I hate every false teaching.

105 Your words are a flashlight to light the path ahead of me, and keep me from stumbling. 106 I've said it once and I'll say it again and again: I will obey these wonderful laws of yours.

107 I am close to death at the hands of my enemies; oh, give me back my life again, just as you promised me. 108 Accept my grateful thanks and teach me your desires. 109 My life hangs in the balance, but I will not give up obedience to your laws. 110 The wicked have set their traps for me along your path, but I will not turn aside. 111 Your laws are my joyous treasure forever. 112 I am determined to obey you until I die.

89-96. The Triumph of Faith. Unless thy law [had been] my delights, I should then have perished (v. 92). The hope of the preceding strophe becomes an assured victory here. He affirms that he will never forget God's precepts since **with them thou hast quickened me.**

97-104. The Rapture of Enlightenment. **O how love I thy law!** Without the usual petitions, the psalmist describes how his study of the divine law has made him wiser and more understanding than his enemies, his teachers, and the aged. The emphasis is here upon the law itself, the source of knowledge rather than on native intelligence.

105-112. The Light of Life. **Thy word is a lamp . . . a light.** His pilgrimage through life is under the guidance of God's teachings. He thus vows to follow the light wherever it may lead and whatever dangers may be involved.

SAMECH

113 I hate *vain* thoughts: but thy law do I love. 114 Thou *art* my hiding place and my shield: I hope in thy word. 115 Depart from me, ye evildoers: for I will keep the commandments of my God. 116 Uphold me according unto thy word, that I may live: and let me not be ashamed of my hope. 117 Hold thou me up, and I shall be safe: and I will have respect unto thy statutes continually.

118 Thou hast trodden down all them that err from thy statutes: for their deceit *is* falsehood. 119 Thou puttest away all the wicked of the earth *like* dross: therefore I love thy testimonies. 120 My flesh trembleth for fear of thee; and I am afraid of thy judgments.

AIN

121 I have done judgment and justice: leave me not to mine oppressors. 122 Be surety for thy servant for good: let not the proud oppress me. 123 Mine eyes fail for thy salvation, and for the word of thy righteousness. 124 Deal with thy servant according unto thy mercy, and teach me thy statutes. 125 I *am* thy servant; give me understanding, that I may know thy testimonies.

126 *It is* time for *thee,* Lord, to work: *for* they have made void thy law. 127 Therefore I love thy commandments above gold; yea, above fine gold. 128 Therefore I esteem all *thy* precepts *concerning* all *things to be* right; *and* I hate every false way.

PE

129 Thy testimonies *are* wonderful: therefore doth my soul keep them. 130 The entrance of thy words giveth light; it giveth understanding unto the simple. 131 I opened my mouth, and panted: for I longed for thy commandments.

132 Look thou upon me, and be merciful unto me, as thou usest to do unto those that love thy name. 133 Order my steps in thy word: and let not any iniquity have dominion over me. 134 Deliver me from the oppression of man: so will I keep thy precepts. 135 Make thy face to shine upon thy servant; and teach me thy statutes. 136 Rivers of

113 I hate those who are undecided whether or not to obey you; but my choice is clear—I love your law. 114 You are my refuge and my shield, and your promises are my only source of hope. 115 Begone, you evil-minded men. Don't try to stop me from obeying God's commands. 116 Lord, you promised to let me live! Never let it be said that God failed me. 117 Hold me safe above the heads of all my enemies; then I can continue to obey your laws.

118 But you have rejected all who reject your laws. They are only fooling themselves. 119 The wicked are the scum you skim off and throw away; no wonder I love to obey your laws! 120 I tremble in fear of you; I fear your punishments.

121 Don't leave me to the mercy of my enemies, for I have done what is right; I've been perfectly fair. 122 Commit yourself to bless me! Don't let the proud oppress me! 123 My eyes grow dim with longing for you to fulfill your wonderful promise to rescue me. 124 Lord, deal with me in lovingkindness, and teach me, your servant, to obey; 125 for I am your servant; therefore give me common sense to apply your rules to everything I do.

126 Lord, it is time for you to act. For these evil men have violated your laws, 127 while I love your commandments more than the finest gold. 128 Every law of God is right, whatever it concerns. I hate every other way.

129 Your laws are wonderful; no wonder I obey them. 130 As your plan unfolds, even the simple can understand it. 131 No wonder I wait expectantly for each of your commands.

132 Come and have mercy on me as is your way with those who love you. 133 Guide me with your laws so that I will not be overcome by evil. 134 Rescue me from the oppression of evil men; then I can obey you. 135 Look down in love upon me and teach me all your laws. 136 I weep because your

**113-120. The Inspiration of Loyalty.
Thou art my hiding place and my shield.**
The sharp contrast drawn between faith-
less men and the psalmist emphasizes
the loyalty of the latter. This loyalty
gives him a sense of safety and the inspiration to face the future.

121-128. The Time of Intervention.
It is time for thee, Lord, to work. After
declaring that he has diligently followed
the right, the psalmist appeals for action
on God's part. So completely have his
oppressors disregarded God's law that
only divine judgment is left for them.

129-136. The Wonder of Illumination.
Thy testimonies are wonderful. The
greatest wonder is the inner light that
gives understanding even to the un-
learned man. The psalmist is brokenhearted over those who do not keep
God's law.

NOTES

waters run down mine eyes, because they keep not thy law.

TZADDI

137 Righteous *art* thou, O Lord, and upright *are* thy judgments. 138 Thy testimonies *that* thou hast commanded *are* righteous and very faithful. 139 My zeal hath consumed me, because mine enemies have forgotten thy words. 140 Thy word *is* very pure: therefore thy servant loveth it. 141 I *am* small and despised: *yet* do not I forget thy precepts.

142 Thy righteousness *is* an everlasting righteousness, and thy law *is* the truth. 143 Trouble and anguish have taken hold on me: *yet* thy commandments *are* my delights. 144 The righteousness of thy testimonies *is* everlasting: give me understanding, and I shall live.

KOPH

145 I cried with *my* whole heart; hear me, O Lord: I will keep thy statutes. 146 I cried unto thee; save me, and I shall keep thy testimonies. 147 I prevented the dawning of the morning, and cried: I hoped in thy word. 148 Mine eyes prevent the *night* watches, that I might meditate in thy word. 149 Hear my voice according unto thy lovingkindness: O Lord, quicken me according to thy judgment.

150 They draw nigh that follow after mischief: they are far from thy law. 151 Thou *art* near, O Lord; and all thy commandments *are* truth. 152 Concerning thy testimonies, I have known of old that thou hast founded them for ever.

RESH

153 Consider mine affliction, and deliver me: for I do not forget thy law. 154 Plead my cause, and deliver me: quicken me according to thy word. 155 Salvation *is* far from the wicked: for they seek not thy statutes. 156 Great *are* thy tender mercies, O Lord: quicken me according to thy judgments.

157 Many *are* my persecutors and mine enemies; *yet* do I not decline from thy testimonies. 158 I beheld the transgressors, and was grieved; because they kept not thy word. 159 Consider how I love thy precepts: quicken me, O Lord, according to thy lovingkindness. 160 Thy

laws are disobeyed.

137 O Lord, you are just and your punishments are fair. 138 Your demands are just and right. 139 I am indignant and angry because of the way my enemies have disregarded your laws. 140 I have thoroughly tested your promises and that is why I love them so much. 141 I am worthless and despised, but I don't despise your laws.

142 Your justice is eternal for your laws are perfectly fair. 143 In my distress and anguish, your commandments comfort me. 144 Your laws are always fair; help me to understand them and I shall live.

145 I am praying with great earnestness; answer me, O Lord, and I will obey your laws. 146 "Save me," I cry, "for I am obeying." 147 Early in the morning, before the sun is up, I was praying and pointing out how much I trust in you. 148 I stay awake through the night to think about your promises. 149 Because you are so loving and kind, listen to me and make me well again.

150 Here come these lawless men to attack me; 151 but you are near, O Lord; all your commandments are based on truth. 152 I have known from earliest days that your will never changes. 153 Look down upon my sorrows and rescue me, for I am obeying your commands. 154 Yes, rescue me and give me back my life again just as you have promised. 155 The wicked are far from salvation for they do not care for your laws. 156 Lord, how great is your mercy; oh, give me back my life again.

157 My enemies are so many. They try to make me disobey, but I have not swerved from your will. 158 I loathed these traitors because they care nothing for your laws. 159 Lord, see how much I really love your demands. Now give me back my life and health because you are so kind. 160 There is

137-144. The Challenge of Righteousness. **Righteous art thou, O Lord.** The concept of God's nature as righteous finds emphasis here in verses 137,138, 142, and 144. Because the Lord is righteous, his judgments and testimonies, also, are everlastingly righteous.

145-152. The Assurance from Prayer. **I cried . . . hear me, O Lord.** Recalling the many times he has prayed unceasingly for divine help, he cries again for God's quickening power. Then he reaffirms his faith in the Lord's nearness and the verity of His teaching.

153-160. The Consciousness of Need. **Consider mine affliction, and deliver me.** The severity of the speaker's affliction and his understanding of his personal need are clearly shown in the repetition of **quicken me** in verses 154,156, and 159. The enduring nature of God's righteous judgments is his hope and assurance.

NOTES

word *is* true *from* the beginning: and
every one of thy righteous judgments
endureth for ever.

SCHIN

161 Princes have persecuted me without a cause: but my heart standeth in
awe of thy word. 162 I rejoice at thy
word, as one that findeth great spoil.
163 I hate and abhor lying: *but* thy law
do I love. 164 Seven times a day do I
praise thee because of thy righteous
judgments.

165 Great peace have they which love
thy law: and nothing shall offend them.
166 Lord, I have hoped for thy salvation,
and done thy commandments. 167 My
soul hath kept thy testimonies; and I
love them exceedingly. 168 I have kept
thy precepts and thy testimonies: for all
my ways *are* before thee.

TAU

169 Let my cry come near before thee,
O Lord: give me understanding according to thy word. 170 Let my supplication
come before thee: deliver me according
to thy word. 171 My lips shall utter
praise, when thou hast taught me thy
statutes. 172 My tongue shall speak of
thy word: for all thy commandments
are righteousness. 173 Let thine hand
help me; for I have chosen thy precepts.
174 I have longed for thy salvation, O
Lord; and thy law *is* my delight. 175 Let
my soul live, and it shall praise thee;
and let thy judgments help me.

176 I have gone astray like a lost sheep;
seek thy servant; for I do not forget
thy commandments.

PSALM 120

A Song of degrees

IN my distress I cried unto the Lord,
and he heard me.

2 Deliver my soul, O Lord, from lying
lips, *and* from a deceitful tongue. 3 What
shall be given unto thee? or what shall
be done unto thee, thou false tongue?
4 Sharp arrows of the mighty, with
coals of juniper.

5 Woe is me, that I sojourn in Mesech, *that* I dwell in the tents of Ke-dar!
6 My soul hath long dwelt with him
that hateth peace. 7 I *am for* peace: but
when I speak, they *are* for war.

utter truth in all your laws; your decrees are
eternal.

161 Great men have persecuted me,
though they have no reason to, but I stand
in awe of only your words. 162 I rejoice in
your laws like one who finds a great treasure. 163 How I hate all falsehood but how I
love your laws. 164 I will praise you seven
times a day because of your wonderful laws.

165 Those who love your laws have great
peace of heart and mind and do not stumble. 166 I long for your salvation, Lord, and
so I have obeyed your laws. 167 I have looked
for your commandments and I love them
very much; 168 yes, I have searched for them.
You know this because everything I do is
known to you.

169 O Lord, listen to my prayers; give me
the common sense you promised. 170 Hear
my prayers; rescue me as you said you
would. 171 I praise you for letting me learn
your laws. 172 I will sing about their wonder,
for each of them is just. 173 Stand ready to
help me because I have chosen to follow
your will. 174 O Lord, I have longed for your
salvation, and your law is my delight. 175 If
you will let me live, I will praise you; let
your laws assist me.

176 I have wandered away like a lost
sheep; come and find me for I have not
turned away from your commandments.

120 IN MY TROUBLES I pled with God
to help me and he did!

2 Deliver me, O Lord, from liars. 3 O lying tongue, what shall be your fate? 4 You
shall be pierced with sharp arrows and
burned with glowing coals.

5,6 My troubles pile high among these
haters of the Lord, these men of Meshech
and Kedar. I am tired of being here among
these men who hate peace. 7 I am for peace,
but they are for war, and my voice goes
unheeded in their councils.

161-168. The Peace in Love. Great peace have they which love thy law. Even in the presence of potent enemies, the psalmist has an inner peace that grows out of his love for God's way. Note the absence of any petition, as in verses 97-104.

169-176. The Determination of Steadfastness. My lips shall utter praise. The psalmist sums up his message by pleading for further spiritual help, while declaring his intention to stand fast upon the foundation of God's teachings.

Psalm 120. The Sojourn of the Pilgrims

Psalm 120 begins a new collection that extends through 134. Each lyric in this group is designated by a term variously translated "A Song of Degrees" (AV), "A Song of Ascents" (ASV), and "A Pilgrim Song." Various theories as to the meaning of the term relate it to the return from Babylon, the fifteen steps from the women's court to the men's court, the climactic parallelism in these poems, and the journeys of pilgrims. The most likely theory is that this collection arose as a hymnbook for pilgrims coming up to the Temple for the great feasts. The fact that 120, 124, 125, 130, 131 are not explicitly related to a pilgrimage points to their incorporation into the collection from other sources. Most of these psalms fit into the pattern of life in post-Exilic society, although some may have first had a pre-Exilic origin.

1,2. A Cry for Deliverance. Deliver my soul, O Lord. The psalmist finds himself in the wretched plight of one who has to associate with men given to falsehood. His appeal for deliverance is based upon God's past answers to him in times of similar trouble. Many understand that there is some reference here to the slanderous opposition of Sanballat and Tobiah to Nehemiah's rebuilding the walls of Jerusalem (Neh 4; 6).

3,4. A Plea for Retribution. What shall be given unto thee? The deceitful tongue and its owner are singled out for judgment. The answer to the rhetorical questions is based upon the nature of the alleged offense. Sharp arrows and hot coals will provide fitting retribution.

5-7. A Lament for Peace. Woe is me . . . I am for peace. The poet's basic complaint is that he finds it necessary to sojourn among bloodthirsty and barbaric enemies. **Mesech** in Asia Minor and **Kedar** in the north Arabian desert south of Damascus are used symbolically to represent barbaric powers.

NOTES

PSALM 121

A Song of degrees

I WILL lift up mine eyes unto the hills, from whence cometh my help. ² My help *cometh* from the Lord, which made heaven and earth. ³ He will not suffer thy foot to be moved: he that keepeth thee will not slumber. ⁴ Behold, he that keepeth Israel shall neither slumber nor sleep.

⁵ The Lord *is* thy keeper: the Lord *is* thy shade upon thy right hand. ⁶ The sun shall not smite thee by day, nor the moon by night. ⁷ The Lord shall preserve thee from all evil: he shall preserve thy soul. ⁸ The Lord shall preserve thy going out and thy coming in from this time forth, and even for evermore.

121 SHALL I LOOK to the mountain gods for help? ² No! My help is from Jehovah who made the mountains! And the heavens too! ³,⁴ He will never let me stumble, slip or fall. For he is always watching, never sleeping.

⁵ Jehovah himself is caring for you! He is your defender. ⁶ He protects you day and night. ⁷ He keeps you from all evil, and preserves your life. ⁸ He keeps his eye upon you as you come and go, and always guards you.

PSALM 122

A Song of degrees of David

I WAS glad when they said unto me, Let us go into the house of the Lord. ² Our feet shall stand within thy gates, O Jerusalem. ³ Jerusalem is builded as a city that is compact together: ⁴ Whither the tribes go up, the tribes of the Lord, unto the testimony of Israel, to give thanks unto the name of the Lord. ⁵ For there are set thrones of judgment, the thrones of the house of David.

⁶ Pray for the peace of Jerusalem: they shall prosper that love thee. ⁷ Peace be within thy walls, *and* prosperity within thy palaces. ⁸ For my brethren and companions' sake, I will now say, Peace *be* within thee. ⁹ Because of the house of the Lord our God I will seek thy good.

122 I WAS GLAD for the suggestion of going to Jerusalem, to the Temple of the Lord. ²,³ Now we are standing here inside the crowded city. ⁴ All Israel—Jehovah's people—have come to worship as the law requires, to thank and praise the Lord. ⁵ Look! There are the judges holding court beside the city gates, deciding all the people's arguments.

⁶ Pray for the peace of Jerusalem. May all who love this city prosper. ⁷ O Jerusalem, may there be peace within your walls and prosperity in your palaces. ⁸ This I ask for the sake of all my brothers and my friends who live here; ⁹ and may there be peace as a protection to the Temple of the Lord.

Psalm 121. The Helper of the Pilgrims

The intense assurance of those journeying up to Zion is reflected in this pilgrim song. They here express a deep sense of trust in God without a murmur of complaint or word of petition. The song was probably used as an antiphonal hymn, although the exact voices or parts used cannot be identified with certainty.

1,2. The Source of Help. From whence cometh my help? Looking up to the hills around Zion, one of the pilgrims voices a question which sets the mood for all that follows. The question does not express doubt but introduces the affirmation that contains the theme of the psalm, namely, that his helper is Jehovah the Creator.

3-8. The Promise of Protection. The Lord is thy keeper. All verses except verse 6 employ the Hebrew word *shāmar* to emphasize this idea of God's guardianship. Unlike the sentry who occasionally slumbers, or Baal, who has to be awakened (cf. I Kgs 18:27), the Lord never slumbers or sleeps. The psalmist employs climactic parallelism throughout, building up each new phrase from the thought in the preceding phrase. Note that the conclusion applies to the pilgrims in that God preserves them in every phase of their journey, seeing them safely home.

Psalm 122. The City of the Pilgrims

This poem is oriented around the visit of a pilgrim to Jerusalem. By indicating that the journey is accomplished, it acts as a sequel to the two preceding psalms. Some interpreters hold that the speaker has returned home and is reminiscing about his recent pilgrimage. Although this is possible, it is more likely that he is still in Jerusalem, about to leave for home.

1,2. Joy in Pilgrimage. I was glad when they said . . . let us go. The psalmist recalls with what joy he responded to the invitation to join a group of pilgrims. Now the journey is complete and he can say, **Our feet have stood within thy gates, O Jerusalem.** The future tense of the AV is not appropriate in the light of the following verses.

3-5. Impressions of Jerusalem. Jerusalem . . . compact together. While the city undoubtedly was fully built up within massive walls, the emphasis here seems to be upon its function in unifying the people. The verb *hābar*, translated "compact," refers primarily to close human associations. The going up of the tribes accentuates this togetherness and the attendant sense of fellowship.

6-9. Prayer for Jerusalem. Pray for the peace of Jerusalem. Before leaving, the pilgrim exhorts his companions to pray for the prosperity and peace of the city, because here is the house of the Lord. There is an excellent play on words in the Hebrew, not evident in any English translation.

NOTES

GOD'S GUARDIANSHIP

(GO TO SLEEP IN PEACE. GOD IS AWAKE!)

PSALM 123

A Song of degrees

Unto thee lift I up mine eyes, O thou that dwellest in the heavens.

2 Behold, as the eyes of servants *look* unto the hand of their masters, *and* as the eyes of a maiden unto the hand of her mistress; so our eyes *wait* upon the Lord our God, until that he have mercy upon us.

3 Have mercy upon us, O Lord, have mercy upon us: for we are exceedingly filled with contempt. 4 Our soul is exceedingly filled with the scorning of those that are at ease, *and* with the contempt of the proud.

PSALM 124

A Song of degrees of David

If *it had not been* the Lord who was on our side, now may Israel say; 2 If *it had not been* the Lord who was on our side, when men rose up against us: 3 Then they had swallowed us up quick, when their wrath was kindled against us: 4 Then the waters had overwhelmed us, the stream had gone over our soul: 5 Then the proud waters had gone over our soul.

6 Blessed *be* the Lord, who hath not given us *as* a prey to their teeth. 7 Our soul is escaped as a bird out of the snare of the fowlers: the snare is broken, and we are escaped.

8 Our help *is* in the name of the Lord, who made heaven and earth.

PSALM 125

A Song of degrees

They that trust in the Lord *shall be* as mount Zion *which* cannot be removed, *but* abideth for ever.

2 *As* the mountains *are* round about Jerusalem, so the Lord *is* round about his people from henceforth even for ever. 3 For the rod of the wicked shall not rest upon the lot of the righteous; lest the righteous put forth their hands

123 O GOD ENTHRONED in heaven, I lift my eyes to you.

2 We look to Jehovah our God for his mercy and kindness just as a servant keeps his eyes upon his master or a slave girl watches her mistress for the slightest signal.

3,4 Have mercy on us, Lord, have mercy. For we have had our fill of contempt and of the scoffing of the rich and proud.

124 IF THE LORD had not been on our side (let all Israel admit it), if the Lord had not been on our side, 2,3 we would have been swallowed alive by our enemies, destroyed by their anger. 4,5 We would have drowned beneath the flood of these men's fury and pride.

6 Blessed be Jehovah who has not let them devour us. 7 We have escaped with our lives as a bird from a hunter's snare. The snare is broken and we are free!

8 Our help is from the Lord who made heaven and earth.

125 THOSE WHO TRUST in the Lord are steady as Mount Zion, unmoved by any circumstance.

2 Just as the mountains surround and protect Jerusalem, so the Lord surrounds and protects his people. 3 For the wicked shall not rule the godly, lest the godly be

Psalm 123. The Plea of the Pilgrims

This is an intense lament by an individual who speaks for his people. The change from the singular to the plural pronoun at the end of verse 1 suggests an antiphonal arrangement in actual use as a pilgrim song.

1,2. The Eye of Hope Unto thee lift I up mine eyes. The psalmist refers to eyes four times in these verses, in order to emphasize the fact that the pilgrims are seeking God's favor. Just as the servant and the maiden look to their superiors for favor, so those in the band of pilgrims wait for God's mercy.

3,4. The Plea for Mercy. Have mercy upon us, O Lord. The measure of their need is indicated by the reiteration of this cry for mercy. The previous mention of servants and masters, coupled with the contempt for **those that are at ease,** suggests either the widespread servitude of Israel during the Exile or the dispersion during post-Exilic days.

Psalm 124. The Deliverer of the Pilgrims

Here the community at large expresses thanksgiving. While the original purpose was undoubtedly to praise God for a particular act of deliverance, the place of the poem in this pilgrim collection indicates a general use as well. Because travelers were constantly subject to danger, the words of this psalm would have given them assurance and strengthened their trust.

1-5. Deliverance by God. If it had not been the Lord. The repetition in verses 1 and 2 is liturgical; the congregation (later the pilgrims) repeated the words of the leader. Note that the effective use of conditional clauses as a triple apodosis (vv. 3-5) completes the double protasis (vv. 1,2). **If** it had not been for the Lord, **then** the end would have been certain and complete.

6-8. Thanksgiving to God. Blessed be the Lord. The psalmist further employs figures of speech to describe the narrow escape and to heighten the expression of gratitude. The last verse refers to the act of calling upon **the name of the Lord** in prayer, recognizing him as the source of help.

Psalm 125. The Security of the Pilgrims

This song of trust emphasizes the confidence of the faithful in Israel. Like the preceding psalm, this one was not designed as a pilgrim song but has been included in the collection. The actual use in pilgrimages can be envisioned from the references to the mountains round about Jerusalem, which come into view after a long and arduous journey.

1-3. A Statement of Confidence. They that trust . . . as Mount Zion. . . . As the mountains . . . so the Lord. Not only is God's presence symbolized by the hills around Jerusalem, but also those who trust in the Lord are immovable like the rock of Zion. If foreign rule did remain permanently, a general departure from the faith would occur, even among the righteous. The danger of apostasy is too great even for the righteous to bear.

NOTES

unto iniquity. 4 Do good, O Lord, unto *those that be* good, and to *them that are* upright in their hearts. 5 As for such as turn aside unto their crooked ways, the Lord shall lead them forth with the workers of iniquity: *but* peace *shall be* upon Israel.

forced to do wrong. 4 O Lord, do good to those who are good, whose hearts are right with the Lord; 5 but lead evil men to execution. And let Israel have quietness and peace.

PSALM 126

A Song of degrees
WHEN the Lord turned again the captivity of Zion, we were like them that dream. 2 Then was our mouth filled with laughter, and our tongue with singing: then said they among the heathen, The Lord hath done great things for them.

3 The Lord hath done great things for us; *whereof* we are glad. 4 Turn again our captivity, O Lord, as the streams in the south.

5 They that sow in tears shall reap in joy. 6 He that goeth forth and weepeth, bearing precious seed, shall doubtless come again with rejoicing, bringing his sheaves *with him*.

126 WHEN JEHOVAH BROUGHT back his exiles to Jerusalem, it was like a dream! 2 How we laughed and sang for joy. And the other nations said, "What amazing things the Lord has done for them."

3 Yes, glorious things! What wonder! What joy! 4 May we be refreshed as by streams in the desert.

5 Those who sow tears shall reap joy. 6 Yes, they go out weeping, carrying seed for sowing, and return singing, carrying their sheaves.

PSALM 127

A Song of degrees for Solomon
EXCEPT the Lord build the house, they labour in vain that build it: except the Lord keep the city, the watchman waketh *but* in vain. 2 *It is* vain for you to rise up early, to sit up late, to eat the bread of sorrows: *for* so he giveth his beloved sleep.

3 Lo, children *are* an heritage of the Lord: *and* the fruit of the womb *is his* reward. 4 As arrows *are* in the hand of a mighty man; so *are* children of the youth. 5 Happy *is* the man that hath his quiver full of them: they shall not be ashamed, but they shall speak with the enemies in the gate.

127 UNLESS THE LORD builds a house, the builders' work is useless. Unless the Lord protects a city, sentries do no good. 2 It is senseless for you to work so hard from early morning until late at night, fearing you will starve to death; for God wants his loved ones to get their proper rest.

3 Children are a gift from God; they are his reward. 4 Children born to a young man are like sharp arrows to defend him. 5 Happy is the man who has his quiver full of them. That man shall have the help he needs when arguing with his enemies.

4,5. A Prayer for Favor. Do good, O Lord. The psalmist prays for God's favor upon the faithful, whom he identifies as the **good** and **upright.** In contrast to these individuals, the unfaithful renegades are abandoned to their just fate. The psalm closes with the simple prayer, **Peace upon Israel.**

Psalm 126. The Restoration of the Pilgrims

Psalm 126 is the lament of the community over disappointed hopes past and present. Although there is an obvious reference here to the return from the Exile, the conditions are not those pictured in early post-Exilic society. The psalmist deals with the ideal conditions expected and with the disillusionment experienced for many years.

1-3. The Ideal of Restoration. We were like them in a dream. The hope of a glorious restoration was idealized to the point of being too good to be true. The phrase, **turned again the captivity,** may be translated *restored the fortunes.* However, the context seems to demand a picture within the Exile. There was singing and laughter — like that on V-Day — when the Edict of Cyrus was made known. The exiles joined in a chorus of praise reiterating the words of the observers from other nations.

4-6. The Plea for Fulfillment. Turn again our captivity, O Lord. The beautiful ideal of restoration envisioned by the prophets and sung about by the exiles was not fully realized by those who returned to the homeland. Conditions were anything but glorious and ideal (cf. Hag 1:10,11; 2:19). Therefore, the plea is now made for completion of the ideal. Even as the farmer sows in anxiety and reaps in joyful singing, Israel will realize the restoration ideal. Christian workers have often made an application of verses 5 and 6 to the ministry of soul winning.

Psalm 127. The Dependence of the Pilgrims

The didacticism of this psalm is characteristic of the teachings of Wisdom literature. Here the emphasis is placed upon the futility of human effort without God's help. Although the original didactic purpose was general, this psalm found special application as a folk song of the pilgrims.

1,2. A Dependence upon the Lord. Except the Lord build . . . keep. Man's utter dependence on God is illustrated by reference to basic human endeavors. Building a house and watching over a city cannot succeed (according to divine standards of success) if God is not included in man's plans and efforts. Even the diligent man who works from early morning until late evening cannot hope for success without God's blessings and sanction.

3-5. A Heritage from the Lord. Lo, children are an heritage of the Lord. The concept of the necessity of dependence upon God is carried over into the building of a family (cf. Gen 30:2). A recognition that children are God's gift is the basis for building a successful home. Joy and protection are pictured as the results of fruitfulness in the bearing and rearing of children. Especially important are the sons of a man's youth, who can protect him and plead his cause, in his old age, against his adversaries in the local court of justice inside the city gate.

NOTES

HE RESTORETH MY SOUL !

237

PSALM 128

A Song of degrees

BLESSED *is* every one that feareth the Lord; that walketh in his ways. ² For thou shalt eat the labour of thine hands: happy *shalt* thou *be,* and *it shall be* well with thee. ³ Thy wife *shall be* as a fruitful vine by the sides of thine house: thy children like olive plants round about thy table. ⁴ Behold, that thus shall the man be blessed that feareth the Lord.

⁵ The Lord shall bless thee out of Zion: and thou shalt see the good of Jerusalem all the days of thy life. ⁶ Yea, thou shalt see thy children's children, *and* peace upon Israel.

128 BLESSINGS ON ALL who reverence and trust the Lord—on all who obey him!

² Their reward shall be prosperity and happiness. ³ Your wife shall be contented in your home. And look at all those children! There they sit around the dinner table as vigorous and healthy as young olive trees. ⁴ That is God's reward to those who reverence and trust him.

⁵ May the Lord continually bless you with heaven's blessings as well as with human joys. ⁶ May you live to enjoy your grandchildren! And may God bless Israel!

PSALM 129

A Song of degrees

MANY a time have they afflicted me from my youth, may Israel now say: ² Many a time have they afflicted me from my youth: yet they have not prevailed against me.

³ The plowers plowed upon my back: they made long their furrows. ⁴ The Lord *is* righteous: he hath cut asunder the cords of the wicked.

⁵ Let them all be confounded and turned back that hate Zion. ⁶ Let them be as the grass *upon* the housetops, which withereth afore it groweth up: ⁷ Wherewith the mower filleth not his hand; nor he that bindeth sheaves his bosom. ⁸ Neither do they which go by say, The blessing of the Lord *be* upon you: we bless you in the name of the Lord.

129 PERSECUTED FROM MY earliest youth (Israel is speaking), ² and faced with never-ending discrimination— but not destroyed! My enemies have never been able to finish me off!

³,⁴ Though my back is cut to ribbons with their whips, the Lord is good. For he has snapped the chains that evil men had bound me with.

⁵ May all who hate the Jews be brought to ignominious defeat. ⁶,⁷ May they be as grass in shallow soil, turning sere and yellow when half grown, ignored by the reaper, despised by the binder. ⁸ And may those passing by refuse to bless them by saying, "Jehovah's blessings be upon you; we bless you in Jehovah's name."

Psalm 128. The Home Life of the Pilgrims

Like the preceding psalm, this one is didactic in character, and thus vitally connected with Wisdom literature. The basic Wisdom teaching, "the fear of the Lord is the beginning of wisdom," is the starting point for the psalmist. He then applies this truth to the ideal home situation. Although not designed as a song for pilgrims, the psalm probably found its way into the collection as a folk song which met the needs of all pilgrims.

1-4. Blessings upon the Home. Blessed is every one that feareth the Lord. The psalmist begins by stating that happiness is the lot of the one who has learned to fear the Lord and walk in His ways. It is well with him because he eats the products of his labor rather than losing them in the time of drought or sharing them with oppressive overlords. His wife is likened to a fruitful vine, while his children are compared to the tender shoots of the olive tree. This picture of contentment, joy, prosperity, and fruitfulness illustrates how the God-fearer finds perfect happiness.

5,6. Blessings upon the Community. Thou shall see the good of Jerusalem. A vital part of the blessing enjoyed by one who fears God comes from beyond the limits of his home — out of Zion. The corporate nature of Israel's society is seen in the adaptation of this psalm for public worship. Like Psalm 125, this one closes with the brief prayer, **Peace upon Israel.**

Psalm 129. The Plea of Suffering Israel

This is a lament of the community, with overtones of confidence and trust. The characteristics of a song of trust are present, but they are overshadowed by the complaint and appeal of the lament. Reviewing past troubles brings the psalmist confidence, while his appeals regarding the future result give him assurance of relief.

1-4. Israel's Past Afflictions. Many a time have they afflicted me. The long history of Israel's troubles is compressed by the psalmist into one statement. From the time of the Exodus (Israel's **youth**) onward, the nation had suffered severe affliction from numerous foes. Two metaphors are used to illustrate this affliction: the marks of a whip upon their backs are likened to the furrows made by a plow; and the cords of their oppressors are likened to the ropes used to harness oxen. However, the Lord manifested his righteousness by cutting the cords and delivering his people.

5-8. Israel's Future Hope. Let them all be confounded. In an imprecation upon those that hate Zion, the speaker expresses the desire that the enemy may be put to shame and turn homeward. Then a lengthy simile is employed to request that the evil plans of the enemy be thwarted. The grass which grew on the dirt rooftops withered quickly because the soil was too shallow for its roots. It could not be grasped by the reaper nor bound into sheaves. It was not even worth the customary greeting of those passing by.

NOTES

PSALM 130

A Song of degrees

OUT of the depths have I cried unto thee, O Lord. ² Lord, hear my voice: let thine ears be attentive to the voice of my supplications.

³ If thou, Lord, shouldest mark iniquities, O Lord, who shall stand? ⁴ But *there is* forgiveness with thee, that thou mayest be feared. ⁵ I wait for the Lord, my soul doth wait, and in his word do I hope. ⁶ My soul *waiteth* for the Lord more than they that watch for the morning: *I say, more than* they that watch for the morning.

⁷ Let Israel hope in the Lord: for with the Lord *there is* mercy, and with him *is* plenteous redemption. ⁸ And he shall redeem Israel from all his iniquities.

PSALM 131

A Song of degrees of David

LORD, my heart is not haughty, nor mine eyes lofty: neither do I exercise myself in great matters, or in things too high for me. ² Surely I have behaved and quieted myself, as a child that is weaned of his mother: my soul *is* even as a weaned child.

³ Let Israel hope in the Lord from henceforth and for ever.

130 O LORD, FROM the depths of despair I cry for your help: ² "Hear me! Answer! Help me!"

³,⁴ Lord, if you keep in mind our sins then who can ever get an answer to his prayers? But you forgive! What an awesome thing this is! ⁵ That is why I wait expectantly, trusting God to help, for he has promised. ⁶ I long for him more than sentinels long for the dawn.

⁷ O Israel, hope in the Lord; for he is loving and kind, and comes to us with armloads of salvation. ⁸ He himself shall ransom Israel from her slavery to sin.

131 LORD, I AM not proud and haughty. I don't think myself better than others. I don't pretend to "know it all." ² I am quiet now before the Lord, just as a child who is weaned from the breast. Yes, my begging has been stilled.

³ O Israel, you too should quietly trust in the Lord—now, and always.

Psalm 130. The Redeemer of the Pilgrims

Here an individual voices a penitential prayer as his personal plea for forgiveness. The closing plea for others in the household of Israel does not make the entire psalm corporate, but rather emphasizes the personal nature of the speaker's appeal. However, since the psalmist's troubles and despair were shared by the nation, the psalm became appropriate for the bands of pilgrims in post-Exilic society.

1,2. The Cry of the Penitent. Out of the depths have I cried. The speaker is more probably using a present tense here, as the remainder of the prayer shows. He is still calling **out of the depths** when the psalm closes, but has clearly expressed his assurance and hope.

3,4. The Assurance of Forgiveness. But there is forgiveness with thee. The universality of sin is forcefully presented in the statement that no one could be justified if God marked down every sin rather than blotting sins out. The only hope comes in God's forgiveness, which in turn quickens the feeling of awe in the forgiven sinner.

5,6. The Expectancy in Hope. I wait for the Lord . . . and in his word do I hope. The sense of expectancy is strongly emphasized by the repetition of phrases. The speaker's whole being (his **soul**) is engaged in diligent waiting. He waits for the Lord even as the sentinel on the walls awaits the relief of the morning change of watch.

7,8. The Application to Israel. Let Israel hope in the Lord. The psalmist's thoughts turn to others who need to share his enthusiastic confidence. In view of the loving-kindness and abundant redemption of the Lord, he can assert that God will redeem Israel **from all his iniquities.**

Psalm 131. The Composure of the Pilgrims

Though essentially a song of trust, this beautiful literary composition reads like a confession. The picture of humble resignation to God's leading exemplifies a deep sense of personal discipline. While some interpreters treat this psalm as a corporate expression, the final plea for Israel suggests that an individual voice speaks consistently throughout. It was only natural that a beautiful expression of humility like this should become a folk song of the pilgrims.

1,2. A Spirit of Humility. Lord, my heart is not haughty. After a long struggle, the psalmist has been weaned from his presumptuous desires and his excessive pride. He can now declare himself free of the former attitudes of haughtiness and unbridled ambition. He has calmed or composed his soul or inner self so that he is now like a weaned child upon his mother's lap, no longer fretting after her milk.

3. A Desire for Israel. Let Israel hope in the Lord. As in the preceding psalm, here the writer expresses his desire that others in Israel may come to know his inner peace.

NOTES

PSALM 132

A Song of degrees

LORD, remember David, *and* all his afflictions: ² How he sware unto the Lord, *and* vowed unto the mighty *God* of Jacob; ³ Surely I will not come into the tabernacle of my house, nor go up into my bed; ⁴ I will not give sleep to mine eyes, *or* slumber to mine eyelids, ⁵ Until I find out a place for the Lord, an habitation for the mighty *God* of Jacob.

⁶ Lo, we heard of it at Eph-ra-tah: we found it in the fields of the wood. ⁷ We will go into his tabernacles: we will worship at his footstool. ⁸ Arise, O Lord, into thy rest; thou, and the ark of thy strength.

⁹ Let thy priests be clothed with righteousness; and let thy saints shout for joy.

¹⁰ For thy servant David's sake turn not away the face of thine anointed. ¹¹ The Lord hath sworn *in* truth unto David; he will not turn from it; Of the fruit of thy body will I set upon thy throne. ¹² If thy children will keep my covenant and my testimony that I shall teach them, their children shall also sit upon thy throne for evermore.

¹³ For the Lord hath chosen Zion; he hath desired *it* for his habitation. ¹⁴ This *is* my rest for ever: here will I dwell; for I have desired it. ¹⁵ I will abundantly bless her provision: I will satisfy her poor with bread. ¹⁶ I will also clothe her priests with salvation: and her saints shall shout aloud for joy. ¹⁷ There will I make the horn of David to bud: I have ordained a lamp for mine anointed. ¹⁸ His enemies will I clothe with shame: but upon himself shall his crown flourish.

PSALM 133

A Song of degrees of David

BEHOLD, how good and how pleasant *it is* for brethren to dwell together in unity! ² *It is* like the precious ointment upon the head, that ran down upon the beard, *even* Aaron's beard: that went down to the skirts of his garments; ³ As the dew of Her-mon, *and as the dew* that descended upon the mountains of Zion: for there the Lord commanded the blessing, *even* life for evermore.

132 LORD, DO YOU remember that time when my heart was so filled with turmoil? ²⁻⁵ I couldn't rest, I couldn't sleep, thinking how I ought to build a permanent home for the Ark of the Lord, a Temple for the mighty one of Israel. Then I vowed that I would do it; I made a solemn promise to the Lord.

⁶ First the Ark was in Ephrathah, then in the distant countryside of Jaar. ⁷ But now it will be settled in the Temple, in God's permanent home here on earth. That is where we will go to worship him. ⁸ Arise, O Lord, and enter your Temple with the Ark, the symbol of your power.

⁹ We will clothe the priests in white, the symbol of all purity. May our nation shout for joy.

¹⁰ Do not reject your servant David—the king you chose for your people. ¹¹ For you promised me that my son would sit on my throne and succeed me. And surely you will never go back on a promise! ¹² You also promised that if my descendants will obey the terms of your contract with me, then the dynasty of David shall never end.

¹³ O Lord, you have chosen Jerusalem as your home: ¹⁴ "This is my permanent home where I shall live," you said, "for I have always wanted it this way. ¹⁵ I will make this city prosperous and satisfy her poor with food. ¹⁶ I will clothe her priests with salvation; her saints shall shout for joy. ¹⁷ David's power shall grow, for I have decreed for him a mighty Son. ¹⁸ I'll clothe his enemies with shame, but he shall be a glorious King."

133 HOW WONDERFUL IT is, how pleasant, when brothers live in harmony! ² For harmony is as precious as the fragrant anointing oil that was poured over Aaron's head, and ran down onto his beard, and onto the border of his robe. ³ Harmony is as refreshing as the dew on Mount Hermon, on the mountains of Israel. And God has pronounced this eternal blessing on Jerusalem, even life forevermore.

Psalm 132. The Assurance of the Pilgrims

Unique among the songs in the pilgrim collection, this one appears to have been included because of its nature as a processional hymn, which may well have been rendered antiphonally. It is basically a song of Zion, connected in thought with David's bringing the ark of the covenant to Jerusalem.

1-10. The Prayer of the Congregation. Lord, remember David. Although David's afflictions are mentioned first, the emphasis of this prayer is upon his intention to find a suitable place for the ark. Since the historical narratives mention no oath in this connection, the psalmist may be drawing from an independent tradition. Verses 6,7 were probably rendered by a group of pilgrims as they re-enacted the search for the ark, its discovery in Kirjath-jearim (the fields of the wood), and its entrance into Jerusalem. The prayer is concluded in verse 10 with a plea for God to show favor to each successive king in the line of David.

11-18. The Response of the Lord. The Lord hath sworn. . . . hath chosen. These verses act as a liturgical response quoting from two separate oracles of the Lord. The first oracle (vv. 11,12) is the promise to David that his royal line will continue as long as his descendants are faithful (cf. II Sam 7:12-16). The second oracle (vv. 14-18) is introduced by the statement in verse 13 that the Lord has chosen Zion. Because of this divine choice, there will be spiritual and material blessings for Zion and the line of David, while there will be shame upon Israel's enemies. Since, when a man died without children, his family line was stopped, his lamp was said to be put out; therefore a lamp symbolized offspring. Thus God ordained a series of descendants of David, to culminate in Messiah the Light of the world (cf. I Kgs 11:36; 15:4).

Psalm 133. The Brotherhood of the Pilgrims

In this short didactic poem we have a beautiful expression of family solidarity, in keeping with the emphasis of the Wisdom writers. The suggestion of many commentators that the psalm mirrors Nehemiah's efforts to increase the population of Jerusalem is intriguing. However, the psalm must have more significant connection with the spirit of fellowship and brotherly harmony at the great feasts.

1. The Premise Stated. Behold, how good and how pleasant. The writer begins with a proverbial statement concerning the benefits of brotherly solidarity. The emphasis is upon the pattern of ancient Hebrew life, in which married sons, with their children, continued to live with their parents. A wider application, however, is evident in the family and tribal reunions on the feast occasions.

2,3. The Principle Illustrated. Like the precious ointment . . . as the dew. The psalmist employs two comparisons to illustrate the principle embodied in his basic premise. Even as the anointing oil upon the high priest's head symbolized his consecration, so this spirit of brotherly love permeated the nation and symbolized its consecration. Even as dew upon vegetation symbolizes fertility and growth, the sense of true brotherhood revived and quickened the devotion of the nation as a whole.

NOTES

243

PSALM 134

A Song of degrees

BEHOLD, bless ye the Lord, all *ye* servants of the Lord, which by night stand in the house of the Lord. ² Lift up your hands *in* the sanctuary, and bless the Lord.
³ The Lord that made heaven and earth bless thee out of Zion.

134 OH, BLESS THE Lord, you who serve him as watchmen in the Temple every night. ² Lift your hands in holiness and bless the Lord.
³ The Lord bless you from Zion—the Lord who made heaven and earth.

PSALM 135

PRAISE ye the Lord. Praise ye the name of the Lord; praise *him,* O ye servants of the Lord. ² Ye that stand in the house of the Lord, in the courts of the house of our God, ³ Praise the Lord; for the Lord *is* good: sing praises unto his name; for *it is* pleasant. ⁴ For the Lord hath chosen Jacob unto himself, *and* Israel for his peculiar treasure.
⁵ For I know that the Lord *is* great, and *that* our Lord *is* above all gods. ⁶ Whatsoever the Lord pleased, *that* did he in heaven, and in earth, in the seas, and all deep places. ⁷ He causeth the vapours to ascend from the ends of the earth; he maketh lightnings for the rain; he bringeth the wind out of his treasuries. ⁸ Who smote the firstborn of Egypt, both of man and beast. ⁹ *Who* sent tokens and wonders into the midst of thee, O Egypt, upon Pharaoh, and upon all his servants. ¹⁰ Who smote great nations, and slew mighty kings; ¹¹ Sihon king of the Amorites, and Og king of Ba-shan, and all the kingdoms of Canaan: ¹² And gave their land *for* an heritage, an heritage unto Israel his people.
¹³ Thy name, O Lord, *endureth* for ever; *and* thy memorial, O Lord, throughout all generations. ¹⁴ For the Lord will judge his people, and he will repent himself concerning his servants.
¹⁵ The idols of the heathen *are* silver and gold, the work of men's hands. ¹⁶ They have mouths, but they speak not; eyes have they, but they see not; ¹⁷ They have ears, but they hear not; neither is there *any* breath in their mouths. ¹⁸ They that make them are like unto them: *so is* everyone that trusteth in them.

135 HALLELUJAH! YES, LET his people praise him as they stand in his Temple courts. ³ Praise the Lord because he is so good; sing to his wonderful name. ⁴ For the Lord has chosen Israel as his personal possession.
⁵ I know the greatness of the Lord—that he is greater far than any other god. ⁶ He does whatever pleases him throughout all of heaven and earth, and in the deepest seas. ⁷ He makes mists rise throughout the earth and sends the lightning to bring down the rain; and sends the winds from his treasuries. ⁸ He destroyed the eldest child in each Egyptian home, along with the firstborn of the flocks. ⁹ He did great miracles in Egypt before Pharaoh and all his people. ¹⁰ He smote great nations, slaying mighty kings— ¹¹ Sihon, king of Amorites; and Og, the king of Bashan; and the kings of Canaan— ¹² and gave their land as an eternal gift to his people Israel.
¹³ O Jehovah, your name endures forever; your fame is known to every generation. ¹⁴ For Jehovah will vindicate his people, and have compassion on his servants.
¹⁵ The heathen worship idols of gold and silver, made by men— ¹⁶ idols with speechless mouths and sightless eyes ¹⁷ and ears that cannot hear; they cannot even breathe. ¹⁸ Those who make them become like them! And so do all who trust in them!

Psalm 134. The Benediction upon the Pilgrims

Here is a fitting conclusion for the collection of folk songs used by the pilgrims. In its benedictory nature this psalm corresponds to the benediction at the end of each book within the Psalter. The position of the song in the collection and the reference to night service suggest that it was sung at the close of evening worship. The Feast of Tabernacles is the most likely occasion.

1,2. The Call to the Priests and Levites. Behold, bless ye the Lord, all ye servants. That the regular ministers of the Temple are addressed is generally recognized. However, the voice of the call is variously ascribed to the high priest, a Levitical choir, or the gathered pilgrims. The last explanation gives more reason for inclusion of the psalm in the collection, since the pilgrims actively participate. The temple ministrants are called to lift up their hands in an attitude of prayer and bless the Lord.

3. The Response by the Priests. The Lord . . . bless thee. The answer to the call is given in a shortened form of the priestly blessing found in Num 6:22-26. The people are reminded that God is Creator and that his blessings flow forth **out of Zion.** This may well have been used as the final act before the pilgrims returned to their homes.

Psalm 135. A Mosaic of God's Works

This hymn of praise is a mosaic of quotations from other psalms and various books of the OT. The main emphasis is upon those works of God which illustrate his power in nature and history. That the psalm was designed for temple worship in an antiphonal pattern is evident from its structure. However, there is no unanimity in the division into voices. Undoubtedly, there were solo parts, Levitical choruses, and congregational responses.

1-4. The Initial Call to Praise. Praise ye the Lord. Similar phrases are repeated as an emphatic liturgical call to praise. As in the preceding psalm, those who **stand in the house of the Lord** are undoubtedly the priests and Levites. The Lord's goodness and his choice of Israel are given as initial reasons for praise.

5-14. The Greatness of Yahweh. For I know that the Lord is great . . . above all gods. The I is emphatic, indicating personal knowledge, and possibly the shift to a solo voice in actual temple use. The use of the name *Yahweh* is here important, because it is Israel's covenant God who is contrasted with the gods of the heathen. He is described as the God of Nature (vv. 5-7), doing whatsoever he pleases in heaven, in earth, in the seas, and in all deep places. He is further described as the God of History (vv. 8-14), leading his chosen people out of Egypt and through the conquest of Canaan.

15-18. The Impotency of Idols. The idols of the heathen. This section is quoted almost verbatim from Ps 115:4-8. However, the words are especially appropriate here to set in sharp contrast the omnipotence of the Lord and the uselessness of all idols.

NOTES

245

¹⁹ Bless the Lord, O house of Israel: bless the Lord, O house of Aaron: ²⁰ Bless the Lord, O house of Levi: ye that fear the Lord, bless the Lord. ²¹ Blessed be the Lord out of Zion, which dwelleth at Jerusalem. Praise ye the Lord.

¹⁹ O Israel, bless Jehovah! High priests of Aaron, bless his name. ²⁰ O Levite priests, bless the Lord Jehovah! Oh, bless his name, all of you who trust and reverence him. ²¹ All people of Jerusalem, praise the Lord, for he lives here in Jerusalem. Hallelujah!

PSALM 136

O GIVE thanks unto the Lord; for *he is* good: for his mercy *endureth* for ever.

² O give thanks unto the God of gods: for his mercy *endureth* for ever. ³ O give thanks to the Lord of lords: for his mercy *endureth* for ever. ⁴ To him who alone doeth great wonders: for his mercy *endureth* for ever. ⁵ To him that by wisdom made the heavens: for his mercy *endureth* for ever. ⁶ To him that stretched out the earth above the waters: for his mercy *endureth* for ever. ⁷ To him that made great lights: for his mercy *endureth* for ever: ⁸ The sun to rule by day: for his mercy *endureth* for ever: ⁹ The moon and stars to rule by night: for his mercy *endureth* for ever. ¹⁰ To him that smote Egypt in their firstborn: for his mercy *endureth* for ever: ¹¹ And brought out Israel from among them: for his mercy *endureth* for ever: ¹² With a strong hand, and with a stretched out arm: for his mercy *endureth* for ever. ¹³ To him which divided the Red sea into parts: for his mercy *endureth* for ever: ¹⁴ And made Israel to pass through the midst of it: for his mercy *endureth* for ever: ¹⁵ But overthrew Pharaoh and his host in the Red sea: for his mercy *endureth* for ever.

¹⁶ To him which led his people through the wilderness: for his mercy *endureth* for ever. ¹⁷ To him which smote great kings: for his mercy *endureth* for ever: ¹⁸ And slew famous kings: for his mercy *endureth* for ever: ¹⁹ Sihon king of the Amorites: for his mercy *endureth* for ever: ²⁰ And Og the king of Ba-shan: for his mercy *endureth* for ever: ²¹ And gave their land for an heritage: for his mercy *endureth* for ever: ²² *Even* an heritage unto Israel his servant: for his mercy *endureth* for ever.

136 OH, GIVE THANKS to the Lord, for he is good; his lovingkindness continues forever.

² Give thanks to the God of gods, for his lovingkindness continues forever. ³ Give thanks to the Lord of lords, for his lovingkindness continues forever. ⁴ Praise him who alone does mighty miracles, for his lovingkindness continues forever. ⁵ Praise him who made the heavens, for his lovingkindness continues forever. ⁶ Praise him who planted the water within the earth, for his lovingkindness continues forever. ⁷ Praise him who made the heavenly lights, for his lovingkindness continues forever: ⁸ the sun to rule the day, for his lovingkindness continues forever; ⁹ and the moon and stars at night, for his lovingkindness continues forever. ¹⁰ Praise the God who smote the firstborn of Egypt, for his lovingkindness to Israel continues forever. ¹¹,¹² He brought them out with mighty power and upraised fist to strike their enemies, for his lovingkindness to Israel continues forever. ¹³ Praise the Lord who opened the Red Sea to make a path before them, for his lovingkindness continues forever, ¹⁴ and led them safely through, for his lovingkindness continues forever— ¹⁵ but drowned Pharaoh's army in the sea, for his lovingkindness to Israel continues forever.

¹⁶ Praise him who led his people through the wilderness, for his lovingkindness continues forever. ¹⁷ Praise him who saved his people from the power of mighty kings, for his lovingkindness continues forever, ¹⁸ and killed famous kings who were their enemies, for his lovingkindness to Israel continues forever: ¹⁹ Sihon, king of Amorites—for God's lovingkindness to Israel continues forever— ²⁰ and Og, king of Bashan—for his lovingkindness to Israel continues forever. ²¹ God gave the land of these kings to Israel as a gift forever, for his lovingkindness to Israel continues forever; ²² yes, a permanent gift to his servant Israel, for his lovingkindness continues forever.

19-21. The Final Call to Praise. Bless the Lord. The call to praise in Psalms 115 and 118 is expanded by the addition of **O house of Levi** and a concluding verse. The nation as a whole, the priests, the Levites, and the God-fearing worshipers may all have had their own antiphonal parts, but ended the psalm in chorus.

Psalm 136. God's Enduring Mercy

This hymn of thanksgiving greatly resembles Psalm 135 in content. It is, however, much more liturgical, having an antiphonal refrain that appears in every verse. The fact that the psalm is easier to read and understand without the refrain suggests that it originally stood without this repetition in verses 4-25. Yet the refrain gave it a distinctive character and a prominent place in Jewish worship. In the Rabbinical writings, it was designated as "the Great Hallel" (sometimes in conjunction with Ps 135). The term **Hallelujah** at the end of the preceding psalm probably should stand at the beginning of this psalm, as evidenced by the LXX.

1-3. The Call to Thanksgiving. O give thanks unto the Lord. The psalm opens with a threefold invitation to join in thanking God for his goodness and mercy. It is addressed by the leader or choir to the congregation. The refrain was probably sung throughout by the entire group of worshipers. The brevity of the refrain is especially evident in the three words of the Hebrew *(for forever his lovingkindness).* The three terms for God — **Yahweh, God of gods,** and **Lord of lords** — are interesting in light of the emphasis in the preceding psalm on the impotency of idols and the omnipotence of God.

4-9. The God of Creation. Wonders ... heavens ... earth ... lights. In concise statements the wonders of creation are made to testify to God's loving-kindness and goodness. Each time **to him** is used, it is the object of **O give thanks.**

10-25. The God of History. To him that smote Egypt. Each event, from Egypt to Canaan, witnesses to the way God manifests his loving-kindness within the scope of Israel's history.

NOTES

²³ Who remembered us in our low estate: for his mercy *endureth* for ever: ²⁴ And hath redeemed us from our enemies: for his mercy *endureth* for ever.

²⁵ Who giveth food to all flesh: for his mercy *endureth* for ever. ²⁶ O give thanks unto the God of heaven: for his mercy *endureth* for ever.

²³ He remembered our utter weakness, for his lovingkindness continues forever. ²⁴ And saved us from our foes, for his lovingkindness continues forever. ²⁵ He gives food to every living thing, for his lovingkindness continues forever. ²⁶ Oh, give thanks to the God of heaven, for his lovingkindness continues forever.

PSALM 137

BY the rivers of Babylon, there we sat down, yea, we wept, when we remembered Zion. ² We hanged our harps upon the willows in the midst thereof. ³ For there they that carried us away captive required of us a song; and they that wasted us *required of us* mirth, *saying,* Sing us *one* of the songs of Zion. ⁴ How shall we sing the Lord's song in a strange land? ⁵ If I forget thee, O Jerusalem, let my right hand forget *her cunning.* ⁶ If I do not remember thee, let my tongue cleave to the roof of my mouth; if I prefer not Jerusalem above my chief joy.

⁷ Remember, O Lord, the children of Edom in the day of Jerusalem; who said, Rase *it,* rase *it, even* to the foundation thereof. ⁸ O daughter of Babylon, who art to be destroyed; happy *shall he be,* that rewardeth thee as thou hast served us. ⁹ Happy *shall he be,* that taketh and dasheth thy little ones against the stones.

137 WEEPING, WE SAT beside the rivers of Babylon thinking of Jerusalem. ² We have put away our lyres, hanging them upon the branches of the willow trees, ^{3,4} for how can we sing? Yet our captors, our tormentors, demand that we sing for them the happy songs of Zion! ^{5,6} If I forget you, O Jerusalem, let my right hand forget its skill upon the harp. If I fail to love her more than my highest joy, let me never sing again.

⁷ O Jehovah, do not forget what these Edomites did on that day when the armies of Babylon captured Jerusalem. "Raze her to the ground!" they yelled. ⁸ O Babylon, evil beast, you shall be destroyed. Blessed is the man who destroys you as you have destroyed us. ⁹ Blessed is the man who takes your babies and smashes them against the rocks!

PSALM 138

A Psalm *of David*

I WILL praise thee with my whole heart: before the gods will I sing praise unto thee. ² I will worship toward thy holy temple, and praise thy name for thy lovingkindness and for thy truth: for thou hast magnified thy word above all thy name. ³ In the day when I cried thou answeredst me, *and* strengthenedst me *with* strength in my soul.

138 LORD, WITH ALL my heart I thank you. I will sing your praises before the armies of angels in heaven. ² I face your Temple as I worship, giving thanks to you for all your lovingkindness and your faithfulness, for your promises are backed by all the honor of your name. ³ When I pray, you answer me, and encourage me by giving me the strength I need.

26. The Doxology of Thanksgiving. **O give thanks unto the God of heaven.** The opening call is here repeated but with a different term for God. This term would be especially fitting if the emphasis were first on the creative wonders of God alone.

Psalm 137. The Song of the Exiles

A deep spirit of revenge is clearly evident in this community lament. The opening verses evoke a deep sympathy for the captives, while the final verses give vent to their indignation experienced when they witnessed the desolation of their land. While it is not certain where the psalmist was when he wrote this song, he appears to have been one of the exiles who returned to Jerusalem in 538 B.C. His first view of Jerusalem may well have prompted his imprecations against Edom and Babylonia.

1-3. Sorrows of the Exile. **By the rivers of Babylon . . . we wept.** The voice of the psalmist sobs with pathos as he describes the heartbreak of captivity. The exiles undoubtedly had special places along the Euphrates or its canal system where they would mourn their condition. When asked to sing for the amusement of their captors, they would answer by hanging their lyres on the willows that lined the river banks.

4-6. Love for Jerusalem. **How shall we sing the Lord's song.** After all, how could they sing the sacred songs of the temple services for the amusement of those in a foreign land? That would have been to desecrate holy things and to commit treason against Zion. The psalmist would rather have lost his ability to play the lyre and sing than to have forgotten the sanctity of Jerusalem.

7-9. Hatred Toward Enemies. **Children of Edom. . . . daughter of Babylon.** The intensity of the psalmist's emotions is seen in his hatred toward his enemies as well as in his love for Jerusalem. He singles out Edom for her conduct in aiding the enemy against Jerusalem (cf. Ezk 25:12-14; 35; Ob 10-14). Then Babylon becomes the object of the psalmist's impassioned imprecation. Although such ruthless slaughter as depicted in verse 9 usually was practiced in sacking ancient cities (Isa 13:16; Nah 3:10) and was used against Israel (II Kgs 8:12; Hos 13:16), we can hardly justify these words.

Psalm 138. Wholehearted Thanksgiving

This piece begins as a hymn of thanksgiving but later becomes a song of trust. Even though the speaker is in the midst of troubles, he begins not with a lament but with grateful acknowledgment of God's blessings. Many of the ideas and phrases of this piece are reminiscent of other sections of Scripture, especially Isa 40—66. Several manuscripts of the LXX connect this psalm with the time of Haggai and Zechariah.

1-3. Praise for Strength. **I will praise thee with my whole heart.** The psalmist has experienced a recent answer to his prayers for help. Because of God's gift of spiritual strength, he engages in wholehearted worship. The phrase, **before the gods,** has been variously interpreted,

NOTES

4 All the kings of the earth shall praise thee, O Lord, when they hear the words of thy mouth. 5 Yea, they shall sing in the ways of the Lord: for great *is* the glory of the Lord. 6 Though the Lord *be* high, yet hath he respect unto the lowly: but the proud he knoweth afar off. 7 Though I walk in the midst of trouble, thou wilt revive me: thou shalt stretch forth thine hand against the wrath of mine enemies, and thy right hand shall save me. 8 The Lord will perfect *that which* concerneth me: thy mercy, O Lord, *endureth* for ever: forsake not the works of thine own hands.

4 Every king in all the earth shall give you thanks, O Lord, for all of them shall hear your voice. 5 Yes, they shall sing about Jehovah's glorious ways, for his glory is very great. 6 Yet though he is so great, he respects the humble, but proud men must keep their distance. 7 Though I am surrounded by troubles, you will bring me safely through them. You will clench your fist against my angry enemies! Your power will save me. 8 The Lord will work out his plans for my life—for your lovingkindness, Lord, continues forever. Don't abandon me—for you made me.

PSALM 139

To the chief Musician, A Psalm of David

O LORD, thou hast searched me, and known *me*. 2 Thou knowest my downsitting and mine uprising, thou understandest my thought afar off. 3 Thou compassest my path and my lying down, and art acquainted *with* all my ways. 4 For *there is* not a word in my tongue, *but,* lo, O Lord, thou knowest it altogether. 5 Thou hast beset me behind and before, and laid thine hand upon me.

6 *Such* knowledge *is* too wonderful for me; it is high, I cannot *attain* unto it. 7 Whither shall I go from thy spirit? or whither shall I flee from thy presence? 8 If I ascend up into heaven, thou *art* there: if I make my bed in hell, behold, thou *art there.* 9 *If* I take the wings of the morning, *and* dwell in the uttermost parts of the sea; 10 Even there shall thy hand lead me, and thy right hand shall hold me. 11 If I say, Surely the darkness shall cover me; even the night shall be light about me. 12 Yea, the darkness hideth not from thee; but the night shineth as the day: the darkness and the light *are* both alike *to thee.*

139 O LORD, YOU have examined my heart and know everything about me. 2 You know when I sit or stand. When far away you know my every thought. 3 You chart the path ahead of me, and tell me where to stop and rest. Every moment, you know where I am. 4 You know what I am going to say before I even say it. 5 You both precede and follow me, and place your hand of blessing on my head.

6 This is too glorious, too wonderful to believe! 7 I can *never* be lost to your Spirit! I can *never* get away from my God! 8 If I go up to heaven, you are there; if I go down to the place of the dead, you are there. 9 If I ride the morning winds to the farthest oceans, 10 even there your hand will guide me, your strength will support me. 11 If I try to hide in the darkness, the night becomes light around me. 12 For even darkness cannot hide from God; to you the night shines as bright as day. Darkness and light are both alike to you.

because the LXX uses *angels* and the Targum has *judges*. However, **gods** seems to be the best translation because of the subsequent reference to **the kings of the earth.** Since they now serve their various gods but will in future worship the true God, the psalmist challenges the power of these "gods" (cf. Ps 95:3; 96:4,5; 97:7).

4-6. Worship by Kings. **All the kings of the earth shall praise thee.** The praise of the individual is envisioned as ultimately becoming universal. There is a striking relation here to the Edict of Cyrus, in which the conquering king praises Yahweh (along with the gods of the other displaced peoples). Note that God's glory is especially revealed in his condescension toward the lowly.

7,8. Assurance of Deliverance. **Though I walk in . . . trouble, thou wilt revive me.** The speaker expresses a deep confidence that God will fulfill his promises and complete the deliverance of Israel. Although the whole psalm is spoken by an individual in a very personal manner, he is voicing thanksgiving and assurance for his nation as well.

Psalm 139. The Personal Concern of God

Here an individual who has had an intimate knowledge of and experience with God offers his personal prayer. From the standpoint of OT theology, this is the climax of thought in the Psalter on God's personal relationship to the individual. The psalmist does not engage in abstract philosophy or speculative meditation; he merely describes his humble walk with God and shares his experiential knowledge of the Lord.

1-6. The Omniscience of God. **O Lord, thou hast searched me, and known me.** The psalmist is convinced by experience that God knows everything about him. He realizes that God's perfect knowledge goes behind his individual acts to his motives and purposes. While he stands in awe at his own understanding of divine omniscience, he knows that full comprehension is beyond human understanding.

7-12. The Omnipresence of God. **Whither shall I go from thy spirit?** By means of two rhetorical questions, the psalmist shows that he can never move beyond the reach of God's personal concern. He does not contemplate trying to do so, but uses this method of presenting his thoughts. The four suppositions which follow express the extremes of the universe and reinforce his basic premise.

13 For thou hast possessed my reins: thou hast covered me in my mother's womb. 14 I will praise thee; for I am fearfully *and* wonderfully made: marvellous *are* thy works; and *that* my soul knoweth right well. 15 My substance was not hid from thee, when I was made in secret, *and* curiously wrought in the lowest parts of the earth. 16 Thine eyes did see my substance, yet being unperfect; and in thy book all *my members* were written, *which* in continuance were fashioned, when *as yet there was* none of them.

17 How precious also are thy thoughts unto me, O God! how great is the sum of them! 18 *If* I should count them, they are more in number than the sand: when I awake, I am still with thee.

19 Surely thou wilt slay the wicked, O God: depart from me therefore, ye bloody men. 20 For they speak against thee wickedly, *and* thine enemies take *thy name* in vain. 21 Do not I hate them, O Lord, that hate thee? and am not I grieved with those that rise up against thee? 22 I hate them with perfect hatred: I count them mine enemies.

23 Search me, O God, and know my heart: try me, and know my thoughts: 24 And see if *there be any* wicked way in me, and lead me in the way everlasting.

PSALM 140

To the chief Musician, A Psalm of David

DELIVER me, O Lord, from the evil man: preserve me from the violent man; 2 Which imagine mischiefs in *their* heart; continually are they gathered together *for* war. 3 They have sharpened their tongues like a serpent; adders' poison *is* under their lips. Se-lah. 4 Keep me, O Lord, from the hands of the wicked; preserve me from the violent man; who have purposed to overthrow my goings. 5 The proud have hid a snare for me, and cords; they have spread a net by the wayside; they have set gins for me. Se-lah.

6 I said unto the Lord, Thou *art* my God: hear the voice of my supplications, O Lord. 7 O God the Lord, the strength of my salvation, thou hast cov-

13 You made all the delicate, inner parts of my body, and knit them together in my mother's womb. 14 Thank you for making me so wonderfully complex! It is amazing to think about. Your workmanship is marvelous—and how well I know it. 15 You were there while I was being formed in utter seclusion! 16 You saw me before I was born and scheduled each day of my life before I began to breathe. Every day was recorded in your Book!

17,18 How precious it is, Lord, to realize that you are thinking about me constantly! I can't even count how many times a day your thoughts turn towards me. And when I waken in the morning, you are still thinking of me!

19 Surely you will slay the wicked, Lord! Away, bloodthirsty men! Begone! 20 They blaspheme your name and stand in arrogance against you—how silly can they be? 21 O Lord, shouldn't I hate those who hate you? Shouldn't I be grieved with them? 22 Yes, I hate them, for your enemies are my enemies too.

23 Search me, O God, and know my heart; test my thoughts. 24 Point out anything you find in me that makes you sad, and lead me along the path of everlasting life.

140 O LORD, DELIVER me from evil men. Preserve me from the violent, 2 who plot and stir up trouble all day long. 3 Their words sting like poisonous snakes. 4 Keep me out of their power. Preserve me from their violence, for they are plotting against me. 5 These proud men have set a trap to catch me, a noose to yank me up and leave me dangling in the air; they wait in ambush with a net to throw over and hold me helpless in its meshes.

6,7,8 O Jehovah, my Lord and Savior, my God and my shield—hear me as I pray!

13-18. The Foreknowledge of God. My substance was not hid from thee. Two ideas are involved in the psalmist's thought here: the wondrous way in which he was created, and the way God knew all that was going on in the process. He seems to emphasize the latter as he sees the hand of God ordering his entire life. This is actually another glimpse of the omniscience of God in the marvelous processes of creation and procreation. Again the speaker stands in awe at the incomprehensible nature of God's thoughts.

19-24. The Problem of Evil. Surely thou wilt slay the wicked. This surprising change of tone and outlook is regarded by some interpreters as a later addition. However, the intensity of conviction apparent in the earlier verses is seen again here. God, who has such minute knowledge of man, cannot overlook flagrant sinners. The psalmist closes with the personal plea that God will **search, try, know, see,** and **lead** him. His goal is the **way everlasting,** the way of life and peace, as compared with the way of ruin and destruction for the wicked.

Psalm 140. A Plea for Preservation

An individual who has suffered bitter persecution from the ungodly within Israel utters this lament. It is closely related to Psalms 141—143, reflecting the same general conditions and employing similar language, form, and thought patterns. And it may possibly reflect the beginnings of party strife in Israel, although the groups cannot now be identified by name.

1-8. His Appeal for Help. Deliver me, O Lord. Through three stanzas (vv. 1-3; 4,5; 6-8) the psalmist makes his appeal for God's help. He pleads: **deliver me, preserve me, keep me, grant not . . . the desires of the wicked.** He uses very descriptive terms to describe these enemies in order to portray vividly his own danger. The singular designations are to be understood collectively, as shown in the use of plural verbs. The four traps which the enemies set are probably to be interpreted in a figurative sense here.

ered my head in the day of battle. ⁸ Grant not, O Lord, the desires of the wicked: further not his wicked device; *lest* they exalt themselves. Se-lah. ⁹ *As for* the head of those that compass me about, let the mischief of their own lips cover them. ¹⁰ Let burning coals fall upon them: let them be cast into the fire; into deep pits, that they rise not up again.

¹¹ Let not an evil speaker be established in the earth: evil shall hunt the violent man to overthrow *him*. ¹² I know that the Lord will maintain the cause of the afflicted, *and* the right of the poor. ¹³ Surely the righteous shall give thanks unto thy name: the upright shall dwell in thy presence.

Don't let these wicked men succeed; don't let them prosper and be proud. ⁹ Let their plots boomerang! Let them be destroyed by the very evil they have planned for me. ¹⁰ Let burning coals fall down upon their heads, or throw them into the fire, or into deep pits from which they can't escape.

¹¹ Don't let liars prosper here in our land; quickly punish them. ¹² But the Lord will surely help those they persecute; he will maintain the rights of the poor. ¹³ Surely the godly are thanking you, for they shall live in your presence.

PSALM 141

A Psalm of David

Lord, I cry unto thee: make haste unto me; give ear unto my voice, when I cry unto thee. ² Let my prayer be set forth before thee *as* incense; *and* the lifting up of my hands *as* the evening sacrifice.

³ Set a watch, O Lord, before my mouth; keep the door of my lips. ⁴ Incline not my heart to *any* evil thing, to practise wicked works with men that work iniquity: and let me not eat of their dainties. ⁵ Let the righteous smite me; *it shall be* a kindness: and let him reprove me; *it shall be* an excellent oil, *which* shall not break my head: for yet my prayer also *shall be* in their calamities. ⁶ When their judges are overthrown in stony places, they shall hear my words; for they are sweet. ⁷ Our bones are scattered at the grave's mouth, as when one cutteth and cleaveth *wood* upon the earth.

⁸ But mine eyes *are* unto thee, O God the Lord: in thee is my trust; leave not my soul destitute. ⁹ Keep me from the snares *which* they have laid for me, and the gins of the workers of iniquity. ¹⁰ Let the wicked fall into their own nets, whilst that I withal escape.

141 QUICK, LORD, ANSWER me—for I have prayed. Listen when I cry to you for help! ² Regard my prayer as my evening sacrifice and as incense wafting up to you.

³ Help me, Lord, to keep my mouth shut and my lips sealed. ⁴ Take away my lust for evil things; don't let me want to be with sinners, doing what they do, sharing their dainties. ⁵ Let the godly smite me! It will be a kindness! If they reprove me, it is medicine! Don't let me refuse it. But I am in constant prayer against the wicked and their deeds. ^{6,7} When their leaders are condemned, and their bones are strewn across the ground, then these men will finally listen to me and know that I am trying to help them.

⁸ I look to you for help, O Lord God. You are my refuge. Don't let them slay me. ⁹ Keep me out of their traps. ¹⁰ Let them fall into their own snares, while I escape.

9-11. His Desire for Retribution. Let the mischief of their own lips cover them. The deep bitterness of the psalmist becomes more apparent in these verses. While he employs figurative language in expressing his desires regarding his enemies, it is clear that he wants all of their evil plans to turn upon them. He will not be satisfied with less than their complete destruction.

12,13. His Confidence in the Lord. I know that the Lord will maintain the cause of the afflicted. The psalmist is convinced that the righteous, in contrast to the wicked, shall have cause for rejoicing, because God champions those who, like the psalmist, are oppressed.

Psalm 141. A Cry for Protection

This psalm is another lament by an individual who has suffered at the hands of the powerful ungodly in Israel. His prayer is not the usual form of lament, where deliverance from enemies is sought. It is more spiritual in that he seeks God's help to overcome the temptations about him.

1,2. His Appeal for an Answer. Lord, I cry . . . make haste . . . give ear. The psalmist begins with an urgent plea for God to hear and answer his prayer. The reference to **incense** and **evening sacrifice** suggests the meal (AV "meat") offering, which was accompanied by prayer and presented both morning and evening.

3-5. His Prayer for Strength. Set a watch, O Lord, before my mouth. Passing over the circumstances of his complaint, the psalmist prays for strength to overcome temptation. He seeks power to guard his speech, keep his heart pure, avoid the practices of the wicked, refrain from sharing in their luxurious indulgences, and welcome reproof from the righteous.

6-10. His Confidence in Retribution. When their judges are overthrown. The historical circumstances behind verses 6,7 are taken for granted. It appears that the speaker expects to be proven right when these judges are punished. Verse 7 either refers to a slaughter of the psalmist's friends or should be translated *their bones* rather than **our bones.** Whatever the original meaning behind these verses, the psalmist is looking to God to continue to strengthen him, while he is certain that the wicked man will receive retributive justice by falling into his own trap.

PSALM 142

Maschil of David; A Prayer when he was in the cave

I CRIED unto the Lord with my voice; with my voice unto the Lord did I make my supplication. ² I poured out my complaint before him; I shewed before him my trouble. ³ When my spirit was overwhelmed within me, then thou knewest my path. In the way wherein I walked have they privily laid a snare for me. ⁴ I looked on *my* right hand, and beheld, but *there was* no man that would know me: refuge failed me; no man cared for my soul. ⁵ I cried unto thee, O Lord: I said, Thou *art* my refuge *and* my portion in the land of the living.

⁶ Attend unto my cry; for I am brought very low: deliver me from my persecutors; for they are stronger than I. ⁷ Bring my soul out of prison, that I may praise thy name: the righteous shall compass me about; for thou shalt deal bountifully with me.

PSALM 143

A Psalm of David

HEAR my prayer, O Lord, give ear to my supplications: in thy faithfulness answer me, *and* in thy righteousness. ² And enter not into judgment with thy servant: for in thy sight shall no man living be justified.

³ For the enemy hath persecuted my soul; he hath smitten my life down to the ground; he hath made me to dwell in darkness, as those that have been long dead. ⁴ Therefore is my spirit overwhelmed within me; my heart within me is desolate.

⁵ I remember the days of old; I meditate on all thy works; I muse on the work of thy hands. ⁶ I stretch forth my hands unto thee: my soul *thirsteth* after thee, as a thirsty land. Se-lah. ⁷ Hear me speedily, O Lord: my spirit faileth: hide not thy face from me, lest I be like unto them that go down into the pit. ⁸ Cause me to hear thy lovingkindness in the morning; for in thee do I trust: cause me to know the way wherein I should walk; for I lift up my soul unto

142 HOW I PLEAD with God, how I implore his mercy, pouring out my troubles before him. ³ For I am overwhelmed and desperate, and you alone know which way I ought to turn to miss the traps my enemies have set for me. ⁴ (There's one—just over there to the right!) No one gives me a passing thought. No one will help me; no one cares a bit what happens to me. ⁵ Then I prayed to Jehovah. "Lord," I pled, "you are my only place of refuge. Only you can keep me safe.

⁶ "Hear my cry, for I am very low. Rescue me from my persecutors, for they are too strong for me. ⁷ Bring me out of prison, so that I can thank you. The godly will rejoice with me for all your help."

143 HEAR MY PRAYER, O Lord; answer my plea, because you are faithful to your promises. ² Don't bring me to trial! For as compared with you, no one is perfect.

³ My enemies chased and caught me. They have knocked me to the ground. They force me to live in the darkness like those in the grave. ⁴ I am losing all hope; I am paralyzed with fear.

⁵ I remember the glorious miracles you did in days of long ago. ⁶ I reach out for you. I thirst for you as parched land thirsts for rain. ⁷ Come quickly, Lord, and answer me, for my depression deepens; don't turn away from me or I shall die. ⁸ Let me see your kindness to me in the morning, for I am trusting you. Show me where to walk, for

Psalm 142. A Supplication for Deliverance

Here is the prayer of a devout individual who is facing intense persecution. It follows the normal pattern of a personal lament. The psalmist voices his appeal, makes his complaint, states his petition, and closes with a note of confidence. In this fervent prayer, he makes no appeals for revenge and voices no vindictive imprecations.

1,2. The Appeal. I cried unto the Lord with my voice. The verbs in verses 1-5 should be translated as present tense, since the context shows that the psalmist is not recounting a previous appeal. His great need is made obvious by the terms **cry** and **pour out**, as well as by his emphasis upon crying aloud with his voice.

3,4. The Complaint. They privily laid a snare for me. . . . no man cared for me. The psalmist realizes that God has known his condition from the beginning. For this reason, he merely states the fact of his trouble and describes his sense of dejection.

5-7. The Petition. Deliver me. . . . Bring my soul out of prison. Appealing again for attention to his needs, the psalmist declares that God is now his only refuge. The reference to a **prison** may represent an actual confinement or a state of distress. Vowing to praise God for his deliverance leads him to express his confidence that others will join him in this thanksgiving.

Psalm 143. A Prayer for Guidance and Deliverance

Again an individual in dire trouble utters this very personal prayer. His persecutors have all but taken his life. While seeking deliverance, his greatest desire is for God's direction and guidance. Since he comes as a repentant sinner, this psalm is classed as one of the Penitentials (cf. Ps 6, 32, 38, 51, 102, 130).

1-6. The Appeal of the Penitent. Hear my prayer . . . and enter not into judgment. After pleading for attention, the psalmist implies his guilt in God's sight. He does not plead innocence but casts himself on the mercy of God. His complaint, tersely stated, as in the preceding psalm, indicates a bitter persecution. He has been pursued, crushed, and made to dwell in darkness like unto death. However, remembering God's mighty works of the past gives him courage to appeal for further manifestations of power.

7-12. The Plea for Action. Hear me speedily, O Lord. In rapid-fire petitions, the psalmist expresses the urgency of his need for help. He seeks a speedy answer, an expression of God's loving-kindness, direction for life, deliverance from his persecutors, instruction in God's will, and destruction of his enemies. As a penitent servant, he feels certain that retribution will be accomplished.

NOTES

thee. ⁹ Deliver me, O Lord, from mine enemies: I flee unto thee to hide me. ¹⁰ Teach me to do thy will; for thou *art* my God: thy spirit *is* good; lead me into the land of uprightness.

¹¹ Quicken me, O Lord, for thy name's sake: for thy righteousness' sake bring my soul out of trouble. ¹² And of thy mercy cut off mine enemies, and destroy all them that afflict my soul: for I *am* thy servant.

PSALM 144

A Psalm *of David*

BLESSED *be* the Lord my strength, which teacheth my hands to war, *and* my fingers to fight: ² My goodness, and my fortress; my high tower, and my deliverer; my shield, and *he* in whom I trust; who subdueth my people under me.

³ Lord, what *is* man, that thou takest knowledge of him! *or* the son of man, that thou makest account of him! ⁴ Man is like to vanity: his days *are* as a shadow that passeth away.

⁵ Bow thy heavens, O Lord, and come down: touch the mountains, and they shall smoke. ⁶ Cast forth lightning, and scatter them: shoot out thine arrows, and destroy them.

⁷ Send thine hand from above; rid me, and deliver me out of great waters, from the hand of strange children; ⁸ Whose mouth speaketh vanity, and their right hand *is* a right hand of falsehood.

⁹ I will sing a new song unto thee, O God: upon a psaltery *and* an instrument of ten strings will I sing praises unto thee. ¹⁰ *It is he* that giveth salvation unto kings: who delivereth David his servant from the hurtful sword. ¹¹ Rid me, and deliver me from the hand of strange children, whose mouth speaketh vanity, and their right hand *is* a right hand of falsehood:

¹² That our sons *may be* as plants grown up in their youth; *that* our daughters *may be* as corner stones, polished *after* the similitude of a palace: ¹³ *That* our garners *may be* full, affording all manner of store: *that* our sheep may bring forth thousands and ten thousands

my prayer is sincere. ⁹ Save me from my enemies, O Lord, I run to you to hide me. ¹⁰ Help me to do your will, for you are my God. Lead me in good paths, for your Spirit is good.

¹¹ Lord, saving me will bring glory to your name. Bring me out of all this trouble because you are true to your promises. ¹² And because you are loving and kind to me, cut off all my enemies and destroy those who are trying to harm me; for I am your servant.

144 BLESS THE LORD who is my immovable Rock. He gives me strength and skill in battle. ² He is always kind and loving to me; he is my fortress, my tower of strength and safety, my deliverer. He stands before me as a shield. He subdues my people under me.

³ O Lord, what is man that you even notice him? Why bother at all with the human race? ⁴ For man is but a breath; his days are like a passing shadow.

⁵ Bend down the heavens, Lord, and come. The mountains smoke beneath your touch. ⁶ Let loose your lightning bolts, your arrows, Lord, upon your enemies, and scatter them.

⁷ Reach down from heaven and rescue me; deliver me from deep waters, from the power of my enemies. ⁸ Their mouths are filled with lies; they swear to the truth of what is false.

⁹ I will sing you a new song, O God, with a ten-stringed harp. ¹⁰ For you grant victory to kings! You are the one who will rescue your servant David from the fatal sword. ¹¹ Save me! Deliver me from these enemies, these liars, these treacherous men.

¹²⁻¹⁵ Here is my description of a truly happy land where Jehovah is God:

Sons vigorous and tall as growing plants.
Daughters of graceful beauty like the pillars of a palace wall.
Barns full to the brim with crops of every kind.
Sheep by the thousands out in our fields.

Psalm 144. Triumph in War and Peace

Beginning as a hymn of praise, this psalm shifts to the lament pattern after verse 4. Many commentators have raised serious questions as to its unity. Verses 12-15 appear to have once been a part of an unknown psalm. In fact, the entire psalm is a compilation of citations from other psalms (cf. Ps 8, 18, 33, 39, 104).

1-4. Past Blessings Acknowledged. Blessed be the Lord my strength. The psalmist opens with a hymn of praise for God's aid to him as a warrior. He has come to know the Lord personally, for he calls him **my rock, my lovingkindness, my fortress, my refuge, my deliverer,** and **my shield.** The contrast between God's greatness and man's insignificance impresses the psalmist. Using the familiar words from Psalm 8, he confesses humility before introducing his petition for help.

5-8. Present Deliverance Sought. Bow thy heavens, O Lord, and come down. This prayer for a manifestation of God's power in the form of a theophany is drawn from several verses in Psalms 18 and 104. The psalmist is requesting that God intervene in the struggles with his enemies, because they are guilty of false charges and breaking of treaties.

9-11. Future Praise Vowed. I will sing a new song unto thee, O God. Following many quotations from old songs, the psalmist vows to give thanksgiving in a new form when the victory is won. After making this vow and expressing himself as confident of victory, he repeats the appeal of verses 7,8.

12-15. Peace and Prosperity Pictured. Sons as plants . . . daughters as cornerstones. As indicated above, this appears to be quoted from an unknown psalm. The picture is an idealized view of family life in a community **whose God is the Lord.** The sons are vigorous as young plants; the daughters are tall and stately; the barns are full; the flocks are prolific; and the oxen are strong. Such are material blessings expected in such an ideal society.

NOTES

in our streets: **14** *That* our oxen *may be* strong to labour; *that there be* no breaking in, nor going out; that *there be* no complaining in our streets. **15** Happy *is that* people, that is in such a case: *yea,* happy *is that* people, whose God *is* the Lord.

PSALM 145

David's Psalm *of Praise*

I WILL extol thee, my God, O king; and I will bless thy name for ever and ever. **2** Every day will I bless thee; and I will praise thy name for ever and ever.

3 Great *is* the Lord, and greatly to be praised; and his greatness *is* unsearchable. **4** One generation shall praise thy works to another, and shall declare thy mighty acts. **5** I will speak of the glorious honour of thy majesty, and of thy wondrous works. **6** And *men* shall speak of the might of thy terrible acts: and I will declare thy greatness. **7** They shall abundantly utter the memory of thy great goodness, and shall sing of thy righteousness.

8 The Lord *is* gracious, and full of compassion; slow to anger, and of great mercy. **9** The Lord *is* good to all: and his tender mercies *are* over all his works. **10** All thy works shall praise thee, O Lord; and thy saints shall bless thee. **11** They shall speak of the glory of thy kingdom, and talk of thy power; **12** To make known to the sons of men his mighty acts, and the glorious majesty of his kingdom. **13** Thy kingdom *is* an everlasting kingdom, and thy dominion *endureth* throughout all generations.

14 The Lord upholdeth all that fall, and raiseth up all *those that be* bowed down. **15** The eyes of all wait upon thee; and thou givest them their meat in due season. **16** Thou openest thine hand, and satisfiest the desire of every living thing.

17 The Lord *is* righteous in all his ways, and holy in all his works. **18** The Lord *is* nigh unto all them that call upon him, to all that call upon him in truth. **19** He will fulfil the desire of them that fear him: he also will hear their cry, and will save them. **20** The Lord preserveth all them that love him: but all the wicked will he destroy.

Oxen loaded down with produce.
No enemy attacking the walls, but peace everywhere.
No crime in our streets.
Yes, happy are those whose God is Jehovah.

145 I WILL PRAISE you, my God and King, and bless your name each day and forever.

3 Great is Jehovah! Greatly praise him! His greatness is beyond discovery! **4** Let each generation tell its children what glorious things he does. **5** I will meditate about your glory, splendor, majesty and miracles. **6** Your awe-inspiring deeds shall be on every tongue; I will proclaim your greatness. **7** Everyone will tell about how good you are, and sing about your righteousness.

8 Jehovah is kind and merciful, slow to get angry, full of love. **9** He is good to everyone, and his compassion is intertwined with everything he does. **10** All living things shall thank you, Lord, and your people will bless you. **11** They will talk together about the glory of your kingdom and mention examples of your power. **12** They will tell about your miracles and about the majesty and glory of your reign. **13** For your kingdom never ends. You rule generation after generation.

14 The Lord lifts the fallen and those bent beneath their loads. **15** The eyes of all mankind look up to you for help; you give them their food as they need it. **16** You constantly satisfy the hunger and thirst of every living thing.

17 The Lord is fair in everything he does, and full of kindness. **18** He is close to all who call on him sincerely. **19** He fulfills the desires of those who reverence and trust him; he hears their cries for help and rescues them. **20** He protects all those who love him, but destroys the wicked.

Psalm 145. Praise for God's Greatness

This hymn of praise is both a triumphant expression of faith by an individual and a call to men to glorify the greatness of God. It carries a note of universal appeal too seldom present in expressions of the faith of Israel. The psalmist uses an acrostic framework, beginning each verse with a letter of the Hebrew alphabet. Only one letter is missing, the *nun*, which should come between verses 13 and 14. The psalm serves as an introduction to the final collection of praises (Ps 145–150).

1,2. The Promise of Praise. I will extol . . . bless . . . praise. The purpose of the psalmist is clearly shown in his promise to praise God **every day,** yea, **for ever and ever.** His personal relationship and his universal outlook are seen in his initial address to **my God, O king.**

3-20. The Greatness of God. Great is the Lord, and greatly to be praised. Verse 3 is the theme of his praise. Although this greatness is unsearchable, the psalmist does an admirable job of illustrating it. His hope is constantly that others will bear witness to God's greatness. In the verses that follow he emphasizes God's greatness in terms of his mighty works, his glory and splendor, his great goodness, his gracious compassion, his tender mercies, his glorious and everlasting kingdom, his providential care, his righteousness, his holiness, and his availability for those who call upon him in truth and with fear. This understanding of God's nature is a high-water mark in the Psalter.

NOTES

21 My mouth shall speak the praise of the Lord: and let all flesh bless his holy name for ever and ever.

PSALM 146

PRAISE ye the Lord. Praise the Lord, O my soul. 2 While I live will I praise the Lord: I will sing praises unto my God while I have any being.

3 Put not your trust in princes, *nor* in the son of man, in whom *there is* no help. 4 His breath goeth forth, he returneth to his earth; in that very day his thoughts perish. 5 Happy *is he* that *hath* the God of Jacob for his help, whose hope *is* in the Lord his God: 6 Which made heaven, and earth, the sea, and all that therein *is:* which keepeth truth for ever: 7 Which executeth judgment for the oppressed: which giveth food to the hungry. The Lord looseth the prisoners: 8 The Lord openeth *the eyes of* the blind: the Lord raiseth them that are bowed down: the Lord loveth the righteous: 9 The Lord preserveth the strangers; he relieveth the fatherless and widow: but the way of the wicked he turneth upside down.

10 The Lord shall reign for ever, *even* thy God, O Zion, unto all generations. Praise ye the Lord.

PSALM 147

PRAISE ye the Lord: for *it is* good to sing praises unto our God; for *it is* pleasant; *and* praise is comely.

2 The Lord doth build up Jerusalem: he gathereth together the outcasts of Israel. 3 He healeth the broken in heart, and bindeth up their wounds. 4 He telleth the number of the stars; he calleth them all by *their* names. 5 Great *is* our Lord, and of great power: his understanding *is* infinite. 6 The Lord lifteth up the meek: he casteth the wicked

146 PRAISE THE LORD! Yes, really praise him! 2 I will praise him as long as I live, yes, even with my dying breath.

3 Don't look to men for help; their greatest leaders fail; 4 for every man must die. His breathing stops, life ends, and in a moment all he planned for himself is ended. 5 But happy is the man who has the God of Jacob as his helper, whose hope is in the Lord his God— 6 the God who made both earth and heaven, the seas and everything in them. He is the God who keeps every promise, 7 and gives justice to the poor and oppressed, and food to the hungry. He frees the prisoners, 8 and opens the eyes of the blind; he lifts the burdens from those bent down beneath their loads. For the Lord loves good men. 9 He protects the immigrants, and cares for the orphans and widows. But he turns topsyturvy the plans of the wicked.

10 The Lord will reign forever. O Jerusalem, your God is King in every generation! Hallelujah! Praise the Lord!

147 HALLELUJAH! YES, PRAISE the Lord! How good it is to sing his praises! How delightful, and how right!

2 He is rebuilding Jerusalem and bringing back the exiles. 3 He heals the brokenhearted, binding up their wounds. 4 He counts the stars and calls them all by name. 5 How great he is! His power is absolute! His understanding is unlimited. 6 The Lord supports the humble, but brings the wicked into

21. The Doxology of Praise. Let all flesh bless his holy name for ever and ever. After repeating his promise of personal praise, the speaker opens the invitation to all flesh. His desire includes all mankind and extends as long as the world endures.

Psalm 146. Praise for God's Help

This is the first of five similar hymns of praise, all beginning and ending with *Hallelujah*. This small collection has served as a short hymnal to be used daily in the worship of the Synagogue. Like most of the psalms in this final Book, the present form of these psalms reflects post-Exilic circumstances, thought, and language.

1,2. The Vow of Praise. While I live will I praise the Lord. In language similar to that of the preceding psalm, the vow of praise is set forth in absolute terms.

3,4. The Powerlessness of Man. Put not your trust in princes. Because of his own experiences, the psalmist pleads with men not to depend on the favors of noblemen (cf. Prov 19:6). He realizes that no lasting help can come from one whose breath and thoughts vanish while his body goes back to dust. The exact circumstance to which the psalmist refers cannot be identified. However, such a conclusion could be drawn from any time in Israel's history.

5-10. The Power of God. Happy is he . . . whose hope is in the Lord. The one who has the Lord as his helper and his hope is truly blessed. This hope is based upon God's creation of the universe, his loving care of man, and his everlasting reign. The special emphasis upon God as the champion of the needy and the oppressed suggests that the psalmist was a member of such a group within the society of his day. Note the fivefold emphasis placed upon the name Yahweh in verses 7-10.

Psalm 147. Praise for God's Providence

The outpouring of gratitude, as in this psalm, has always been a vital part of Israel's worship. This is truly a hymn of praise from beginning to end without a word of complaint or a single petition. A logical development is difficult to discover because three psalms are here compressed into one (vv. 1-6, 7-11, 12-20). These separate elements are partly evident in the LXX, where verses 12-20 are listed as a different psalm.

1-6. His Goodness to Israel. The Lord doth build up . . . he gathereth together. After a brief call to praise, the psalmist declares how good the Lord has been to his people. Verses 2,3 undoubtedly refer to the restoration following the Exile. Each thing that God has done is linked up with his greatness, his power, and his understanding.

NOTES

down to the ground. 7 Sing unto the Lord with thanksgiving; sing praise upon the harp unto our God: 8 Who covereth the heaven with clouds, who prepareth rain for the earth, who maketh grass to grow upon the mountains. 9 He giveth to the beast his food, *and* to the young ravens which cry. 10 He delighteth not in the strength of the horse: he taketh not pleasure in the legs of a man. 11 The Lord taketh pleasure in them that fear him, in those that hope in his mercy.

12 Praise the Lord, O Jerusalem; praise thy God, O Zion. 13 For he hath strengthened the bars of thy gates; he hath blessed thy children within thee. 14 He maketh peace *in* thy borders, *and* filleth thee with the finest of the wheat. 15 He sendeth forth his commandment *upon* earth: his word runneth very swiftly. 16 He giveth snow like wool: he scattereth the hoarfrost like ashes. 17 He casteth forth his ice like morsels: who can stand before his cold? 18 He sendeth out his word, and melteth them: he causeth his wind to blow, *and* the waters flow. 19 He sheweth his word unto Jacob, his statutes and his judgments unto Israel. 20 He hath not dealt so with any nation: and *as for his* judgments, they have not known them. Praise ye the Lord.

PSALM 148

Praise ye the Lord. Praise ye the Lord from the heavens: praise him in the heights. 2 Praise ye him, all his angels: praise ye him, all his hosts. 3 Praise ye him, sun and moon: praise him, all ye stars of light. 4 Praise him, ye heavens of heavens, and ye waters that *be* above the heavens.

5 Let them praise the name of the Lord: for he commanded, and they were created. 6 He hath also stablished them for ever and ever: he hath made a decree which shall not pass.

7 Praise the Lord from the earth, ye dragons, and all deeps: 8 Fire, and hail; snow, and vapours; stormy wind fulfilling his word: 9 Mountains, and all hills; fruitful trees, and all cedars: 10 Beasts, and all cattle; creeping things,

the dust. 7 Sing out your thanks to him; sing praises to our God, accompanied by harps. 8 He covers the heavens with clouds, sends down the showers and makes the green grass grow in mountain pastures. 9 He feeds the wild animals and the young ravens cry to him for food. 10 The speed of a horse is nothing to him. How puny in his sight is the strength of a man. 11 But his joy is in those who reverence him, those who expect him to be loving and kind.

12 Praise him, O Jerusalem! Praise your God, O Zion! 13 For he has fortified your gates against all enemies, and blessed your children. 14 He sends peace across your nation, and fills your barns with plenty of the finest wheat. 15 He sends his orders to the world. How swiftly his word flies. 16 He sends the snow in all its lovely whiteness, and scatters the frost upon the ground, 17 and hurls the hail upon the earth. Who can stand before his freezing cold? 18 But then he calls for warmer weather, and the spring winds blow and all the river ice is broken. 19 He has made known his laws and ceremonies of worship to Israel— 20 something he has not done with any other nation; they have not known his commands.

Hallelujah! Yes, praise the Lord!

148 PRAISE THE LORD, O heavens! Praise him from the skies! 2 Praise him, all his angels, all the armies of heaven. 3 Praise him, sun and moon, and all you twinkling stars. 4 Praise him, skies above. Praise him, vapors high above the clouds.

5 Let everything he has made give praise to him. For he issued his command, and they came into being; 6 he established them forever and forever. His orders will never be revoked.

7 And praise him down here on earth, you creatures of the ocean depths. 8 Let fire and hail, snow, rain, wind and weather, all obey. 9 Let the mountains and hills, the fruit trees and cedars, 10 the wild animals and

7-11. His Providence over Nature. Who covereth the heaven with clouds. The thought is extended beyond the borders of Israel to encompass all creatures. The Lord's provision of rain and food is especially important in a land where skies are cloudless from April to October. The psalmist realizes that God's favor is not based upon physical strength in man or beast.

12-20. His Care for Jerusalem. For he hath strengthened the bars of thy gates. Jerusalem and Zion are used as parallel terms in descriptive personification, symbolizing God's people who dwell and worship within. The blessings of protection, peace, and prosperity are set forth as present realities. The psalm closes with a reference to Israel's unique relationship to God as his Chosen People.

Psalm 148. Praise by All Creation

The third hymn of praise in the closing collection is a call for a universal chorus of praise by everything in heaven and on earth. The closing verse undoubtedly refers to the return from exile and indicates the reason and occasion for such world-shaking praise.

1-6. The Call to the Heavens. From the heavens . . . in the heights. Using the language of the ancient Near-Eastern cosmology, the psalmist seeks praise from the heavenly beings and the heavenly phenomena. Verses 5,6 are a response or a refrain which was probably sung by a choir in an antiphonal manner. God's creation of the heavenly objects and his sustaining of them are reason enough for praise.

7-12. The Call to the Earth. From the earth. The psalmist begins with the depths of the earth and refers to all forms of life, inanimate and animate. Note that man, as the crown of creation, is reserved until the last. Verses 13,14 act as a second response, signifying the basic reasons for this praise. God's glory and the redeeming of his Chosen People are judged to be sufficient reasons.

NOTES

and flying fowl: ¹¹ Kings of the earth, and all people; princes, and all judges of the earth: ¹² Both young men, and maidens; old men, and children: ¹³ Let them praise the name of the Lord: for his name alone is excellent; his glory *is* above the earth and heaven. ¹⁴ He also exalteth the horn of his people, the praise of all his saints; *even* of the children of Israel, a people near unto him. Praise ye the Lord.

cattle, the snakes and birds, ¹¹ the kings and all the people, with their rulers and their judges, ¹² young men and maidens, old men and children— ¹³ all praise the Lord together. For he alone is worthy. His glory is far greater than all of earth and heaven. ¹⁴ He has made his people strong, honoring his godly ones—the people of Israel, the people closest to him.

Hallelujah! Yes, praise the Lord!

PSALM 149

PRAISE ye the Lord. Sing unto the Lord a new song, *and* his praise in the congregation of saints.

² Let Israel rejoice in him that made him: let the children of Zion be joyful in their King. ³ Let them praise his name in the dance: let them sing praises unto him with the timbrel and harp.

⁴ For the Lord taketh pleasure in his people: he will beautify the meek with salvation. ⁵ Let the saints be joyful in glory: let them sing aloud upon their beds.

⁶ *Let* the high *praises* of God *be* in their mouth, and a two-edged sword in their hand; ⁷ To execute vengeance upon the heathen, *and* punishments upon the people; ⁸ To bind their kings with chains, and their nobles with fetters of iron; ⁹ To execute upon them the judgment written: this honour have all his saints. Praise ye the Lord.

149 HALLELUJAH! YES, PRAISE the Lord! Sing him a new song. Sing his praises, all his people.

² O Israel, rejoice in your Maker. O people of Jerusalem, exult in your King. ³ Praise his name with dancing, accompanied by drums and lyre.

^{4,5} For Jehovah enjoys his people; he will save the humble. Let his people rejoice in this honor. Let them sing for joy as they lie upon their beds.

^{6,7} Adore him, O his people! And take a double-edged sword to execute his punishment upon the nations. ⁸ Bind their kings and leaders with iron chains, ⁹ and execute their sentences.

He is the glory of his people. Hallelujah! Praise him!

PSALM 150

PRAISE ye the Lord. Praise God in his sanctuary: praise him in the firmament of his power. ² Praise him for his mighty acts: praise him according to his excellent greatness. ³ Praise him with the sound of the trumpet: praise him with the psaltery and harp. ⁴ Praise him with the timbrel and dance: praise him with stringed instruments and organs. ⁵ Praise him upon the loud cymbals: praise him upon the high sounding cymbals.

⁶ Let every thing that hath breath praise the LORD. Praise ye the LORD.

150 HALLELUJAH! YES, PRAISE the Lord!

Praise him in his Temple, and in the heavens he made with mighty power. ² Praise him for his mighty works. Praise his unequaled greatness. ³ Praise him with the trumpet and with lute and harp. ⁴ Praise him with the tambourines and processional. Praise him with stringed instruments and horns. ⁵ Praise him with the cymbals, yes, loud clanging cymbals.

⁶ Let everything alive give praises to the Lord! *You* praise him!

Hallelujah!

Psalm 149. Praise for God's Triumph

This hymn of praise makes special reference to the celebration of a recent victory. Many interpreters understand the closing verses to be eschatological rather than historical. However, the first four verses are clearly related to a present reality of God's deliverance. Although the event cannot be identified precisely, the purpose of the original composition is evidently to thank God for victory at the time of the warriors' return.

1-4. The Summons to Praise. Sing unto the Lord a new song. The scene is a great assembly of the **saints** or godly ones at the Temple. The importance of the occasion is seen in the need for a new song to celebrate the new victory of their armies. Verse 3 with its mention of dancing brings out clearly the spirit of rejoicing and joy requested in verse 2. The victory itself is an indication that God's favor and salvation have been poured out on his oppressed people.

5-9. The Song of Victory. Let the saints be joyful . . . let them sing aloud. The pious ones are pictured as rejoicing in triumph and singing on their beds because safety is now their reward. The picture of the warriors praising God with "two-mouthed" (AV, *two-edged*) swords in their hands is symbolic of the victories achieved in his name. Figuratively, God's saints today are to wield the sword of the Spirit, which is the word of God (Eph 6:17; Heb 4:12).

Psalm 150. Praise in Its Universal Climax

This final hymn of praise measures up to its position of honor as the doxology for the whole Psalter. Every phrase in the psalm seems to build upon the preceding thought in preparation for the climax, which comes suddenly as an outburst of mighty praise from the host of heaven and earth.

1. The Place Specified. In his sanctuary . . . in the firmament. The sanctuary may have reference to God's heavenly habitation or the earthly Temple. While the former meaning is parallel to **the firmament,** the latter idea would have much more significance for the assembled worshipers.

2. The Reasons Advanced. His mighty acts . . . his excellent greatness. His mighty acts in creation and history have been the theme of many psalms. His greatness has been a recurring theme in these final hymns of praise (cf. Ps 145, 147).

3-5. The Instruments Enumerated. With the sound of . . . The psalmist seems to have arranged these instruments in random order. It is likely that each was sounded when it was mentioned and continued to play through the end of the Hallelujah (cf. W. O. E. Oesterley, *The Psalms*, p. 589 ff., for a description of the instruments involved).

6. The Choir Assembled. Let everything that hath breath. Not merely the priests and Levites nor merely the congregation, but all the creatures of time and space which have breath are included in this choir of choirs. The Psalter ends, but the melody lingers on as the worshipers continue to chant, *Hallelujah,* **Praise ye the Lord.**

NOTES

BIBLIOGRAPHY

ALEXANDER, JOSEPH A. *The Psalms Translated and Explained.* 2 vols. 6th ed. New York: Scribner, Armstrong & Co., 1873.

BRIGGS, CHARLES A., and BRIGGS, EMILIE G. *The Book of Psalms (International Critical Commentary).* 2 vols. Edinburgh: T. & T. Clark, 1907.

CHEYNE, T. K. *The Book of Psalms.* London: Kegan Paul, Trench, Trubner & Co., 1904.

CLARKE, ARTHUR G. *Analytical Studies in the Psalms.* Kilmarnock: John Ritchie, Ltd., 1949.

COHEN, A. *The Psalms* (The Soncino Books of the Bible). Hindhead, Surrey: The Soncino Press, 1945.

DAVIES, T. WITTON. *The Psalms, LXXIII–CL (The Century Bible).* Edinburgh: T. C. & E. C. Jack, 1906.

DAVISON, W. T. *The Psalms I–LXXII (The Century Bible).* Edinburgh: T. C. & E. C. Jack, n.d.

DELITZSCH, FRANZ. *Biblical Commentary on the Psalms.* Translated by Francis Bolton. 3 vols. Grand Rapids: Wm. B. Eerdmans Publishing Co., Reprint, 1949.

EISELEN, FREDERICK C. *The Psalms and Other Sacred Writings.* New York: The Methodist Book Concern, 1918.

GUNKEL, HERMANN. *Die Psalmen.* Göttingen: Vanderhoeck and Ruprecht, 1926.

JAMES, FLEMING. *Thirty Psalmists.* New York: G. P. Putnam's Sons, 1938.

KIRKPATRICK, A. F. *The Book of Psalms.* 3 vols. *(The Cambridge Bible for Schools and Colleges.)* Cambridge: The University Press, 1902.

LESLIE, E. A. *The Psalms.* New York: Abingdon Cokesbury, 1949.

LESLIE, E. A., and SHELTON, W. A. "Psalms," *Abingdon Bible Commentary.* New York: Abingdon Cokesbury, 1929.

MACLAREN, ALEXANDER. *The Psalms.* New York: Funk & Wagnalls Co., 1908.

McCULLOUGH, W. STEWART, and TAYLOR, WILLIAM R. "The Book of Psalms," *The Interpreter's Bible.* Vol. 4. New York: Abingdon Press, 1955.

McFADYEN, JOHN E. *The Psalms in Modern Speech and Rhythmical Form.* London: James Clarke & Co., 1926.

MORGAN, G. CAMPBELL. *Notes on the Psalms.* New York: Fleming H. Revell Co., 1947.

MOWINCKEL, SIGMUND. *Psalmenstudien.* 6 vols. Kristiania: Dybwad, 1921–1924.

OESTERLEY, W. O. E. *A Fresh Approach to the Psalms.* New York: Charles Scribner's Sons, 1937.

——. *The Psalms.* London: Society for the Promoting of Christian Knowledge, 1939.

PATTERSON, JOHN. *The Praises of Israel.* New York: Charles Scribner's Sons, 1950.

PATTON, JOHN H. *Canaanite Parallels in the Book of Psalms.* Baltimore: Johns Hopkins University Press, 1944.

PEROWNE, J. J. STEWART. *The Book of Psalms.* 2 vols. London: G. Bell & Sons, 1892.

PETERS, JOHN D. *The Psalms as Liturgies.* New York: G. P. Putnam's Sons, 1922.

ROBINSON, THEODORE H. *The Poetry of the Old Testament.* London: Gerald Duckworth, 1947.

SIMPSON, DAVID C. *The Psalmists.* London: Oxford University Press, 1926.

SNAITH, NORMAN H. "The Psalms," *Twentieth Century Bible Commentary.* New York: Harper & Brothers, 1955.

——. *Studies in the Psalter.* London: Epworth Press, 1926.

TERRIEN, SAMUEL. *The Psalms and Their Meaning for Today.* New York: The Bobbs-Merrill Company, 1952.

WALKER, ROLLIN H. *The Modern Message of the Psalms.* New York: Abingdon Cokesbury, 1938.

PROVERBS

INTRODUCTION

The Teaching of Proverbs. The essence of the Book of Proverbs is the teaching of moral and ethical principles. The peculiarity of this book is that it is largely given over to teaching by contrasts. Especially noteworthy are chapters 10—15, where almost every verse is divided by the word "but."

In the first section, chapters 1–9, there is also a use of contrast—between good and evil. The good in this section is denominated by several words—wisdom, instruction, understanding, justice, judgment, equity, knowledge, discretion, learning, counsels—but especially wisdom, which occurs seventeen times in this portion and twenty-two times in the rest of the book. What amounts to a text for the book is the well-known statement of 1:7, "The fear of the Lord is the beginning of wisdom," which is repeated near the end of the section (9:10). This statement reappears verbatim (with the clauses reversed) in the alphabetical Psalm 111:10, and in almost identical form as the climax of chapter 28 of Job, which describes in highly poetic form the search for wisdom.

Peculiar to this section of Proverbs is the personification of wisdom as a woman. This is first seen in 3:15. Actually, in 3:15-18 the pronouns referring to wisdom could be translated "it" as well as "she," but the personification is accepted because of later references. Proverbs 7:4 opens the way for the personification, "Say unto wisdom, Thou art my sister." It is complete in chapters 8 and 9, where Wisdom invites fools to partake of her feast. Only in Proverbs and only in this first part is wisdom thus personified.

It is essential to the understanding of this first part to recognize this personification. Since "wisdom" in Hebrew is a feminine noun, it therefore is naturally and readily personified as a woman. More important, the author here is contrasting "wisdom," the virtuous woman, with the harlot, the strange woman. And just as wisdom stands for all virtue, so probably the strange woman typifies and includes all sin.

The contrast is a studied and artistic one. Wisdom cries in the streets (8:3). Her invitation is, "Whoso is simple, let him turn in hither" (9:4). In contrast, the foolish woman, who invites to stolen waters and whose guests are in the depths of hell (9:17,18), issues the identical invitation, "Whoso is simple, let him turn in hither" (9:16). Wisdom calls the simple to forsake sin; the harlot calls him to its indulgence.

This section, Proverbs 1 to 9, therefore contrasts sin and righteousness. The words "wisdom," "instruction," "understanding," etc., used throughout this passage, do not mean merely human intelligence and skill; but rather they are contrasted with that which is evil. Wisdom as here used is therefore a moral quality. It should be observed that this is a special usage. In most of the Old Testament, wisdom is mere skill or sagacity. Even in Ecclesiastes, where wisdom is also emphasized, it is merely human intelligence and therefore is included with folly as vanity (Eccl 2:12-15). Only in Job 28 and in certain psalms (37:30; 51:6; 90:12; 111:10) is the Proverbs concept of wisdom noticeable. Even the wisdom for which Solomon was famed in the historical books is not exactly this wisdom. He was famous for his skill in natural science (I Kgs 4:33) and jurisprudence (I Kgs 3:16-28) and for his high intelligence (I Kgs 10:1-9). Proverbs adds to the concept of mental acumen the moral rectitude that alone makes intelligence worth while.

In the second section, the Proverbs of Solomon, 10:1—22:16, the teaching is presented almost exclusively by the single verse treatment. Through chapter 15, the teaching is by contrast, indicated by a "but" in the middle of nearly every verse. Thereafter there are parallels of thought more often than contrasts.

This section covers a wide range of subjects and defies outline. The viewpoint, however, is fairly consistent. Solomon is contrasting wisdom and folly. And, as in Section I, this is not intelligence versus stupidity; it is moral wisdom versus sin. In this section wisdom is never personified, but the same synonyms for it as occur in Section I are used here—understanding, righteousness, instruction.

The fool also has his parallels: the scorner, the slothful, the froward. The following sections (see Outline) continue in this vein. As Toy points out (Crawford H. Toy, ICC on *Proverbs*, p. xi), the ethics of the book are very high. Honesty, truthfulness, respect for life and property are insisted upon. Men are urged to extend justice, love, mercy to others. A good family life, with careful training of children and high status of women, is reflected.

As to religious outlook, the Lord is understood to be the author of morality and justice, and monotheism is presupposed. The references to the Law and prophecy (29:18), priesthood and sacrifices (15:8; 21:3,27) are scarce, however. The author speaks in his own right, inculcating principles of right conduct as from the Lord.

Authorship. The name of Solomon occurs in three parts of the book—1:1; 10:1; and 25:1. There is thus a claim of Solomonic authorship for the major sections, indeed for all sections except Parts III, 22:17—24:22; IV, 24:23-34; and VI, 30:1—31:31. This claim is disputed by critical scholars. Toy (*op. cit.* p. xix), who denies the Mosaic authorship of the Pentateuch and holds that Isaiah and the prophets did not write the books attributed to them, rather naturally gives no credit to Solomon here. On the grounds of many internal indications, he assigns the book a post-Exilic date. Driver (S. R. Driver, *Introduction to the Literature of the Old Testament*, 4th ed., pp. 381ff.) holds that parts of the book are pre-Exilic, but little if any of it is by Solomon. Pfeiffer (Robert H. Pfeiffer, *Introduction to the Old Testament*, pp. 649-659) goes over the internal characteristics of Proverbs thinking to date various strata. Because Wisdom literature in Egypt about 1700–1500 B.C. was purely secular, he concludes that the religious strata in Proverbs must derive form the fourth century B.C. After reconstructing to his own satisfaction the history of thought in Israel, he dates Proverbs relative to that development. His conclusion is that the book was finished after 400 B.C. and sometime before the end of the third century.

W. F. Albright ("Some Canaanite-Phoenician Sources of Hebrew Wisdom" in *Wisdom in Israel and the Ancient Near East*, ed. by M. Noth and D. W. Thomas, p. 13) studies the similarity of the language to Ugaritic, and argues that the book in "its entire content" is probably pre-Exilic, but that much of it was orally transmitted until the fifth century. He holds that a Solomonic nucleus is probable. See also an article by one of Albright's students, Cullen I. K. Story, "The Book of Proverbs and Northwest Semitic Literature," JBL, LXIV (1945), 319-337. Charles T. Fritsch (*The Book of Proverbs*, IB, Vol. IV, p. 775) on like grounds holds a very similar opinion. Oesterley (W. O. E. Oesterley, *The Book of Proverbs*, p. xxvi) would place most of the book in pre-Exilic times, but dates Section I, 1:1—9:18, and Section VI, 30:1—31:31, in the third century "and quite possibly later still."

The fact is that the closest attention to these internal evidences can not date the book or its collections. Granted that secular proverbs may have preceded religious, or single-line aphorisms the more developed varieties, still the development to the complex and religious may well have been full-blown already before Solomon's day. Granted that Jeremiah opposed wise men in his day (Jer 18:18), this proves nothing about dating. He also opposed priests and prophets and kings, but that does not prove these offices to be post-Exilic! The most promising approach on dating by internal criteria is that of Albright in his comparison of Ugaritic words and forms.

Our external evidence is not so complete as we might wish it to be, but it should not be totally dismissed. Proverbs 15:8, for example, is quoted with the formula, "It is written," in the Zadokite Document (col. XI. line 20; .C. Rabin, *The Zadokite Documents*, p. 58). This shows that the book was regarded as canonical in the second century B.C. Solomon's production of "proverbs and parables" is referred to in Ecclesiasticus 48:17, dated about 180 B.C. There is as yet no external evidence previous to this. Oesterley claims a case of borrowing from Proverbs by the *Story of Ahikar* in the fifth century (see the Commentary at 23:14). One's opinion of the dating of the book will be heavily weighted by the view he holds of other books. If one holds that the Pentateuch was not written until 400 B.C. and the prophets were largely post-Exilic, he will deny that Solomon wrote Proverbs. If, however, the pre-Exilic dating of Pentateuch, Psalms and Prophets be allowed (as by this author), there seems to be no valid reason to deny the traditional ascription to Solomon of the sections that bear his name.

Fritsch (op. cit., p. 770) objects to the traditional glorifying of Solomon's wisdom when "he made so many foolish mistakes throughout his life in every realm." This seems to be a harsh judgment upon Israel's most brilliant king. That he made mistakes in his long reign of forty years is clear; but archaeology testifies to Solomon's skills in architecture, ability in administration, and discoveries in engineering in connection with his copper foundry at Ezion-geber. True, in his old age he became oppressive (I Kgs 12:10), but his later decline should not blind us to his early brilliance. More critics object to Solomon's character because of his many wives. Close attention to the texts, however, (and they are our only sources) shows that they do not picture Solomon as a creature of lust. As an important king over an area that included many petty kings of city states, Solomon doubtless concluded numerous treaties. Surely in many cases such treaties were sealed by Solomon's marrying the petty king's daughter, as was the ancient custom and as was the case in the alliance with Egypt (I Kgs 9:16,17). Solomon's marriages were doubtless largely political arrangements. His error lay not so much in lust as in allowing his politically important wives to bring their heathen worship into the city of God (I Kgs 11:7-9).

The authors of the other sections of Proverbs (III, 22:17–24:22; IV, 24:23-34; VI, 30:1–31:31) are totally unknown to us. See remarks in the Commentary. We can not, therefore, be dogmatic as to their dates except to say that there is no need to place the final editing of the book after the traditional close of the Biblical period—about 400 B.C.

Collections in Proverbs. Toy (op. cit., pp. vii, viii), and others following him, have argued that the appearance of the same line or verse in various parts of the book shows different authorship for those parts. Toy lists over fifty correspondences, some, however, not very close. He inadvertently omits 15:13 and 17:22. Most of these parallels are noted in the Commentary section of this treatment. Toy has not given sufficient attention to the obvious fact that in many cases a portion of a verse is repeated with varia-

tions that likely are significant. Such repetitions prove nothing as to collections of proverbs of different authorship. Sometimes, also, the repetition comes within a section held by Toy to be a unified collection, as 14:12 and 16:25. Here Toy is forced to suggest the existence of sub-collections. Furthermore, there is a similar repetition in an Egyptian work held to be of unified authorship (cf. Commentary on 22:28). Apparently Toy's contention is based on a fallacious assumption. It is clear that there are several distinct collections in Proverbs, as the titles show; but the internal evidence of these parallels is insufficient to disprove Solomon's authorship of those portions ascribed to him.

Proverbs and other Wisdom Literature. Just as the writing of poetry in ancient times was not limited to the Hebrews, so the literary form of Proverbs is not uniquely Hebrew. It should not surprise us to discover that there were collections of proverbs in ancient Egypt and Mesopotamia. Several such pieces may be named, but two are of special importance—the *Story of Ahikar* and the *Wisdom of Amen-em-Opet,* which must be considered below in some detail.

One of the oldest of these Wisdom pieces is the *Instruction of Ptah-Hotep,* of about 2450 B.C. in Egypt. Few parallels to it in the Book of Proverbs are alleged, but the style of writing is proverbial and the thoughts are similar in some cases. For instance, it commands obedience of . sons, humility, justice, caution at the table of a noble, listening rather than speaking, etc. Obviously such pious advice is old and was the common property of the East. Parallels between such materials and Proverbs prove nothing as to the origin of our book. Similar observations apply to the *Instruction of Ani* and other early Egyptian literature. Some pieces of Mesopotamian literature may be mentioned. The so-called Babylonian Job, entitled *I Will Praise the Lord of Wisdom,* reminds us somewhat of the Biblical Job in its story of a man in great sickness who is cured by the gods. There is also a *Dialogue about Human Misery,* sometimes called the Babylonian Ecclesiastes. The similarity of the words to the Biblical Ecclesiastes is quite minor, but it includes a few proverbial sayings.

Various Babylonian tablets from the eighth century or before include proverbs counseling one to recompense good for evil, not to speak hastily, not to enter into another's quarrel, etc. Again, since these principles of morality are very general, their presence in these tablets proves nothing about the origin of the Book of Proverbs, except that it should naturally be considered against its background. Just as Moses could draw on the laws of Hammurabi, and David used some of the forms of Canaanite poetry, so Solomon and his successors had a wealth of background material for illustrative purposes. In all these cases, however, the common ancient material was molded by the Hebrew author, who was inspired by the Spirit of God to write His revelation for His people. (All of these writings can be conveniently seen in the collection edited by James B. Pritchard, *Ancient Near Eastern Texts Relating to the Old Testament,* 2nd. ed.)

Of more consequence for our study is the *Story of Ahikar,* a tale from Mesopotamia embellished with many proverbs. The story has long been known, as portions of it occur in early Christian authors. But in 1906 eleven papyrus sheets containing the story were turned up in excavations of the Jewish colony at Elephantine, Egypt. This copy is from about 400 B.C. Ahikar was a counselor of the kings Sennacherib and Esarhaddon in Assyria, about 700 B.C. He adopted his nephew, who by deceit persuaded the king to execute Ahikar. But the official executioners, being friendly to the doomed man, hid Ahikar a while, then reinstated him when the king's wrath cooled off. Two-thirds of the booklet is composed of Ahikar's sayings, which present a number of parallels with Proverbs. W. O. E. Oesterley in his *The Book of Proverbs* (pp. xxxvii-liii) lists thirty-three parallels, which is probably a somewhat exaggerated number. Story (*op. cit.,* pp. 329-336) also presents important comparisons. For the most part these parallels are general. For instance, Ahikar cautions men against looking at a bedizened and painted woman or lusting after her in their hearts, as this is a sin against God (cf. Prov 6:25, etc.). Also he urges a father to subdue his son while he is young, else he will rebel when he is stronger (cf. Prov 19:18). It is doubtful, however, that there is any direct connection between the proverbs of Ahikar and those of the Bible. Furthermore, the proverbs of Ahikar lack the moral tone of the Book of Proverbs. They do not have the contrast of the wise man versus the sinner which is so characteristic of Proverbs. They are more secular. The Book of Proverbs, however, does occasionally use this secular backdrop to develop its moral teaching. Actually it is quite difficult to be sure—if there is dependence —which piece is the debtor. The *Story of Ahikar,* though the scene is laid in Assyria, was current among the Jews and later among the Christians. Our best copy is from a Jewish source. The proverbs of *Ahikar* could as easily have been influenced by the Book of Proverbs or by the general Jewish reservoir of proverbs as the other way around (see the Commentary on 23:14 for a probable case of borrowing by *Ahikar* from Proverbs).

Some feel that the case is different with the Egyptian *Wisdom of Amen-em-Opet.* This remarkable collection of proverbs has even more parallels to the Biblical book than does *Ahikar.* Its date is uncertain. The papyrus is later than the composition, but is itself not datable. F. Ll. Griffith did the principal work on the translation of the Egyptian. Oesterley reports Griffith's date for the book as seventh to sixth century B.C. and H. O. Lange as even later. Oesterley himself assigns the work to the eighth century or later (*The Wisdom of Egypt,* pp. 9,10). Albright favors an earlier date, about 1100–1000 B.C. (*op. cit.,* p. 6). If this date be sustained, any thought of derivation must be from an Egyptian original. John A. Wilson (ANET, p. 421), in his translation of the work, does not commit himself in regard to the date.

The nature of the parallels is to be observed. Oesterley, in his discerning study, notices that the *Wisdom of Amen-em-Opet* is very un-Egyptian. It has high ethics and a high conception of God—pointing toward monotheism of a sort. He declares that "the like is not to be found elsewhere in Egyptian literature of pre-Christian times" (*op. cit.,* p. 24). Parallels are found by Oesterley with several Old Testament books besides Proverbs, e.g., Deut 19:14; 25:13-15; 27:18; I Sam 2:6-8; Ps 1; Jer 17:6ff. These passages are not particularly significant, however, for most of them deal with themes also appearing in Proverbs, where the parallels are numerous—over forty being listed by Oesterley (*The Book of Proverbs,* pp. xxxvii–liii). The parallels occur with various parts of

Proverbs, but are particularly striking with the portion 22:17–23:14. All but five of these verses are paralleled in *Amen-em-Opet*.

Most striking of all, the Egyptian book is divided into thirty chapters (of considerable length) and concludes with an exhortation to give heed to these thirty chapters. This section in Proverbs, expanding it to include 22:17–24:22, is said to contain thirty sayings (Oesterley, *op. cit.*, p. 192). The introductory words of this section in Proverbs are, "Have not I written unto thee *excellent things*" (22:20). This can with more justification be read with very slightly different vowels, "Have not I written unto thee *thirty*." It must be admitted that the discovery of just thirty sayings in these sixty-nine verses is a bit arbitrary. And the thirty sayings are not nearly so long as the thirty chapters of the Egyptian book. Still, the parallel is striking. Oesterley (*The Wisdom of Egypt*, p. 105) points out the curious fact that the section Prov 22:17–23:12 has parallels to all but three verses in scattered parts of the Egyptian work. But the other parts of Proverbs, which have fewer parallels, have them in general with chapters X and XXI of *Amen-em-Opet*. He argues quite plausibly from this that the usage as regards borrowing differs in the different sections of the two books. Neither work borrowed directly from the other. In some sections, both borrowed from a common reservoir of proverbial sayings. But from the peculiar character of the Egyptian work, he argues that the fountain of both lay in the background of Hebrew wisdom and theology.

We can perhaps go a little further. Much has been made of the reading, "Have not I written to thee *thirty* things."

It is clear that the thirty sayings in this section of Proverbs are not copied from the Egyptian thirty. Actually, the last half of the section in Proverbs has no parallels at all with the Egyptian book. The "thirty" of Proverbs may have been modeled after the Egyptian "thirty," but in any case, it was not slavishly borrowed. Rather, we should see here another example of the characteristic use of numbers in Wisdom literature. Well-known examples are the climactic references to "three things . . . yea, four" too difficult to understand (Prov 30:18ff.) or "six things . . . yea, seven" (6:16-19). Such references can be matched in the Ugaritic literature. Baal is said to hate two sacrifices, yea, three (C. H. Gordon, *Ugaritic Literature*, p. 30). Baal captures sixty-six towns, yea, seventy-seven cities (*ibid.*, p. 36). Later, seventy-seven brothers, yea, eighty-eight are mentioned (*ibid.*, p 55). Many other examples could be given. Apparently in the sayings of *Amen-em-Opet* and in Proverbs 22:20 we have two examples of a literary use of the numeral thirty that probably could be multiplied if our sources of ancient Egyptian and Hebrew Wisdom were more complete. As to the detailed comparisons of Proverbs with the Egyptian sayings, see notes on the verses in the Commentary.

We should also mention the two apocryphal books, Ecclesiasticus of about 180 B.C., and the Wisdom of Solomon, likely a bit later. These books, of great interest in themselves, are modeled in some ways after Proverbs. But they are later, and show a further development in the personification of wisdom and in other matters. They borrow from our Book of Proverbs, not vice versa, and therefore extensive reference to them is not necessary for our present purposes.

OUTLINE

I. Solomon's tribute to wisdom, the fear of the Lord. 1:1–9:18.
    A. Introduction. 1:1-7.
    B. The righteous woman, Wisdom, versus the evil woman. 1:8–9:18.
II. Solomon's miscellaneous single-verse proverbs. 10:1–22:16.
    A. Contrasting proverbs. 10:1–15:33.
    B. Proverbs largely parallel. 16:1–22:16.
III. The Words of the Wise, thirty sayings. 22:17–24:22.
    A. Sayings paralleled in Egyptian Wisdom. 22:17–23:12.
    B. Sayings with no parallel in Egyptian. 23:13–24:22.
IV. The Words of the Wise, Appendix. 24:23-34.
V. Proverbs of Solomon, edited by Hezekiah's men. 25:1–29:27.
VI. Final appendices. 30:1–31:31.
    A. The Words of Agur. 30:1-33.
    B. The Words of Lemuel. 31:1-9.
    C. Alphabetical poem on the virtuous woman. 31:10-31.

THE PROVERBS

King James Version

CHAPTER 1

THE proverbs of Solomon the son of David, king of Israel;
2 To know wisdom and instruction; to perceive the words of understanding; 3 To receive the instruction of wisdom, justice, and judgment, and equity; 4 To give subtilty to the simple, to the young man knowledge and discretion. 5 A wise *man* will hear, and will increase learning; and a man of understanding shall attain unto wise counsels: 6 To understand a proverb, and the interpretation; the words of the wise, and their dark sayings.
7 The fear of the Lord *is* the beginning of knowledge: *but* fools despise wisdom and instruction. 8 My son, hear the instruction of thy father, and forsake not the law of thy mother: 9 For they *shall be* an ornament of grace unto thy head, and chains about thy neck.

Living Bible

1 THESE ARE THE proverbs of King Solomon of Israel, David's son:
2 He wrote them to teach his people how to live—how to act in every circumstance, 3 for he wanted them to be understanding, just and fair in everything they did. 4 "I want to make the simple-minded wise!" he said. "I want to warn young men about some problems they will face. 5,6 I want those already wise to become the wiser and become leaders by exploring the depths of meaning in these nuggets of truth."
7,8,9 How does a man become wise? The first step is to trust and reverence the Lord!
Only fools refuse to be taught. Listen to your father and mother. What you learn from them will stand you in good stead; it will gain you many honors.

COMMENTARY

I. Solomon's Tribute to Wisdom, the Fear of the Lord. 1:1–9:18.

A. Introduction. 1:1-7. Author and Subject. Some commentators have taken this portion to be an introduction to the entire book, but as various other sections also have author data, probably this is to be taken to refer to the first section alone.

1. The proverbs. The root from which this word comes is used both in Hebrew and in other Semitic languages to express comparison. A derivative in Akkadian means "mirror." From such usage, the word comes to include both a reproachful remark (Ps 69:11), and a prophet's message (e.g., Num 23:7,18). It is translated "parable" sixteen times in the OT. In the book of Proverbs it is used mainly in the titles (1:1,6; 10:1; 25:1) to denominate the comparisons and contrasts used to express the moral teaching of the book. **Of Solomon.** See the discussion of authorship in the Introduction to the book.

2-4. Wisdom . . . instruction, etc. There are here five synonyms for **wisdom.** These include **righteousness** (ASV) and **equity,** which are virtues rather than skills. The emphasis is upon moral wisdom or right conduct. **The simple.** This word, used fourteen times in Proverbs, four times elsewhere, designates the opposite of a moral man. It does not mean a simpleton in our sense of the term, but a sinner, a rascal. Proverbs has a message of morality for the wicked. It is not just a *Poor Richard's Almanac* of good advice for people of low intelligence or lazy habits. This introduction cautions us against taking the book in a secular sense. It is a book of Christian principles.

7. The fear of the Lord. A common expression in the Psalms and elsewhere, this phrase is used fourteen times in Proverbs. Illustrations of the usage occur in Ps 115:11 — "Ye that fear the Lord, trust in the Lord," and Isa 11:2,3, where the fear of the Lord is named as a characteristic of the Messiah. Such fear includes awe before the Almighty (Ps 2:11 — "Serve the Lord with fear and rejoice with trembling"). Job 28:28 is practically a definition — "The fear of the Lord, that is wisdom, and to depart from evil is understanding." Proverbs 8:13 is to the same effect — "The fear of the Lord is to hate evil." **The beginning of knowledge.** Not the "chief" or "sum," as the Hebrew root might suggest, for Prov 9:10 uses a word specifically meaning the "start" or "beginning." Rather, the first step in morality is our relation to God. **Fools despise wisdom.** "Fool" occurs eighteen times in Proverbs; seven times elsewhere. Also the usage differs. In Isa 35:8, "fool" obviously means "simpleton," as is true in our English usage. But in the specialized usage of Proverbs, "fool" means a sinner. Proverbs 14:9 is illustrative — "Fools make a mock at sin." The clause means that sinners deride holiness. The Greek LXX well renders **fools** by *ungodly.*

NOTES

¹⁰ My son, if sinners entice thee, consent thou not. ¹¹ If they say, Come with us, let us lay wait for blood, let us lurk privily for the innocent without cause: ¹² Let us swallow them up alive as the grave; and whole, as those that go down into the pit: ¹³ We shall find all precious substance, we shall fill our houses with spoil: ¹⁴ Cast in thy lot among us; let us all have one purse:

¹⁵ My son, walk not thou in the way with them; refrain thy foot from their path: ¹⁶ For their feet run to evil, and make haste to shed blood. ¹⁷ Surely in vain the net is spread in the sight of any bird. ¹⁸ And they lay wait for their *own* blood; they lurk privily for their *own* lives. ¹⁹ So *are* the ways of every one that is greedy of gain; *which* taketh away the life of the owners thereof.

²⁰ Wisdom crieth without; she uttereth her voice in the streets: ²¹ She crieth in the chief place of concourse, in the openings of the gates: in the city she uttereth her words, *saying,* ²² How long, ye simple ones, will ye love simplicity? and the scorners delight in their scorning, and fools hate knowledge? ²³ Turn you at my reproof: behold, I will pour out my spirit unto you, I will make known my words unto you. ²⁴ Because I have called, and ye refused; I have stretched out my hand, and no man regarded; ²⁵ But ye have set at nought all my counsel, and would none of my reproof: ²⁶ I also will laugh at your calamity; I will mock when your fear cometh; ²⁷ When your fear cometh as desolation, and your destruction cometh as a whirlwind; when distress and anguish cometh upon you. ²⁸ Then shall they call upon me, but I will not answer; they shall seek me early, but they shall not find me: ²⁹ For that they hated knowledge, and did not choose the fear of the Lord: ³⁰ They would none of my counsel: they despised all my reproof. ³¹ Therefore shall they eat of the fruit of their own way, and be filled with their own devices. ³² For the turning away of the simple shall slay them, and the prosperity of fools shall destroy them. ³³ But whoso hearkeneth unto me shall dwell safely, and shall be quiet from fear of evil.

¹⁰ If young toughs tell you, "Come and join us"—turn your back on them! ¹¹ "We'll hide and rob and kill," they say. ¹² "Good or bad, we'll treat them all alike. ¹³ And the loot we'll get! All kinds of stuff! ¹⁴ Come on, throw in your lot with us; we'll split with you in equal shares."

¹⁵ Don't do it, son! Stay far from men like that, ¹⁶ for crime is their way of life, and murder is their specialty. ¹⁷ When a bird sees a trap being set, it stays away, ¹⁸ but not these men; they trap themselves! They lay a booby trap for their own lives. ¹⁹ Such is the fate of all who live by violence and murder. They will die a violent death.

²⁰ Wisdom shouts in the streets for a hearing. ²¹ She calls out to the crowds along Main Street, and to the judges in their courts, and to everyone in all the land: ²² "You simpletons!" she cries. "How long will you go on being fools? How long will you scoff at wisdom and fight the facts? ²³ Come here and listen to me! I'll pour out the spirit of wisdom upon you, and make you wise. ²⁴ I have called you so often but still you won't come. I have pleaded, but all in vain. ²⁵ For you have spurned my counsel and reproof. ²⁶ Some day you'll be in trouble, and I'll laugh! Mock me, will you?—I'll mock you! ²⁷ When a storm of terror surrounds you, and when you are engulfed by anguish and distress, ²⁸ then I will not answer your cry for help. It will be too late though you search for me ever so anxiously.

²⁹ "For you closed your eyes to the facts and did not choose to reverence and trust the Lord, ³⁰ and you turned your back on me, spurning my advice. ³¹ That is why you must eat the bitter fruit of having your own way, and experience the full terrors of the pathway you have chosen. ³² For you turned away from me—to death; your own complacency will kill you. Fools! ³³ But all who listen to me shall live in peace and safety, unafraid."

B. The Righteous Woman, Wisdom, Versus the Evil Woman. 1:8–9:18. In this section the method of teaching by contrast is beautifully illustrated. In major sections, personified Wisdom is set off against sin (see Introd., *The Teaching of Proverbs*).

11. Lay wait for blood . . . for the innocent. The motive, it develops, is robbery, but this gang openly suggests murder for gain.

12. Alive as the grave. The expression is found in Num 16:30,33; Ps 55:15. The former passage says that Korah and his company were swallowed alive by the opening earth. The latter expresses the curse that men may go down "quick," i.e., "alive," into the grave. These men of Prov 1:11-14 would murder with dispatch. They would bring **whole,** i.e., healthy men down to death. **The grave.** Hebrew *she'ôl.* The present writer believes that this term simply means "grave." It is used nine times in Proverbs, three times to refer to the results of adultery. Cf. 5:5; 7:27; 9:18, where it is made parallel with "death" and "the dead." At least in 1:12, the emphasis is simply on murder. There is here no concern with the afterlife of the victims. This is not to deny that there was a belief in the afterlife and in resurrection among the Hebrews, but merely to say that this much discussed word may have a more simple meaning than is sometimes given it. (See R. Laird Harris, "The Meaning of Sheol in the Old Testament," *The Evangelical Theological Society Bulletin,* Vol. IV (1961), No. 4.)

16. Their feet. Identical with Isa 59:7. Possibly Isaiah quotes from this, or possibly it was a common expression. See comments on 30:5 for other quotations found in Proverbs from elsewhere in the OT.

22. Simple ones. Obviously those who are in sin. The word *scorners* is used in Ps 1:1 parallel with *ungodly* and *sinners.* Cf. commentary on 3:34. **25. But ye.** This should be *and ye.* Verses 24 and 25 give the reason as a protasis; the apodosis or conclusion is in verse 26. When we refuse the invitation of the Lord, there comes a time when the door of grace is shut. **32. The turning away.** The *waywardness* of sinners (so Berkeley Version). The word usually refers to apostasy, a turning away from God.

CHAPTER 2

MY son, if thou wilt receive my words, and hide my commandments with thee; ² So that thou incline thine ear unto wisdom, *and* apply thine heart to understanding; ³ Yea, if thou criest after knowledge, *and* liftest up thy voice for understanding; ⁴ If thou seekest her as silver, and searchest for her as *for* hid treasures; ⁵ Then shalt thou understand the fear of the Lord, and find the knowledge of God.

⁶ For the Lord giveth wisdom: out of his mouth *cometh* knowledge and understanding. ⁷ He layeth up sound wisdom for the righteous: *he is* a buckler to them that walk uprightly. ⁸ He keepeth the paths of judgment, and preserveth the way of his saints. ⁹ Then shalt thou understand righteousness, and judgment, and equity; *yea,* every good path. ¹⁰ When wisdom entereth into thine heart, and knowledge is pleasant unto thy soul; ¹¹ Discretion shall preserve thee, understanding shall keep thee: ¹² To deliver thee from the way of the evil *man,* from the man that speaketh froward things; ¹³ Who leave the paths of uprightness, to walk in the ways of darkness; ¹⁴ Who rejoice to do evil, *and* delight in the frowardness of the wicked; ¹⁵ Whose ways *are* crooked, and *they* froward in their paths:

¹⁶ To deliver thee from the strange woman, *even* from the stranger *which* flattereth with her words; ¹⁷ Which forsaketh the guide of her youth, and forgetteth the covenant of her God. ¹⁸ For her house inclineth unto death, and her paths unto the dead. ¹⁹ None that go unto her return again, neither take they hold of the paths of life.

²⁰ That thou mayest walk in the way of good *men,* and keep the paths of the righteous. ²¹ For the upright shall dwell in the land, and the perfect shall remain in it. ²² But the wicked shall be cut off from the earth, and the transgressors shall be rooted out of it.

2 EVERY YOUNG MAN who listens to me and obeys my instructions will be given wisdom and good sense. ³,⁴,⁵ Yes, if you want better insight and discernment, and are searching for them as you would for lost money or hidden treasure, then wisdom will be given you, and knowledge of God himself; you will soon learn the importance of reverence for the Lord and of trusting him.

⁶ For the Lord grants wisdom! His every word is a treasure of knowledge and understanding. ⁷,⁸ He grants good sense to the godly—his saints. He is their shield, protecting them and guarding their pathway. ⁹ He shows how to distinguish right from wrong, how to find the right decision every time. ¹⁰ For wisdom and truth will enter the very center of your being, filling your life with joy. ¹¹,¹²,¹³ You will be given the sense to stay away from evil men who want you to be their partners in crime—men who turn from God's ways to walk down dark and evil paths, ¹⁴ and exult in doing wrong, for they thoroughly enjoy their sins. ¹⁵ Everything they do is crooked and wrong.

¹⁶,¹⁷ Only wisdom from the Lord can save a man from the flattery of prostitutes; these girls have abandoned their husbands and flouted the laws of God. ¹⁸ Their houses lie along the road to death and hell. ¹⁹ The men who enter them are doomed. None of these men will ever be the same again.

²⁰ Follow the steps of the godly instead, and stay on the right path, ²¹ for only good men enjoy life to the full; ²² evil men lose the good things they might have had, and they themselves shall be destroyed.

2:1. **My son.** Thirteen times in the first seven chapters this address occurs. It assists in showing the unity of this section, 1:1—9:18. **6. The Lord giveth wisdom.** The essentially religious nature of the exhortation is here illustrated.

13. Ways of darkness. Verses 12-15 speak of evil in general. This is aptly typified by the expression, **ways of darkness.** It still is true that crime flourishes in the dark. The contrast is expressed in 4:18,19, where the path of the just is compared to light and the way of the wicked to darkness (a different Heb. word from that of 2:13, however). The ethical figure of light and darkness occurs also in Isa 5:20; Ps 43:3; and in a few other places where the contrast is less clear. It is not common in the OT, but is found in the Dead Sea Scrolls and in the NT.

16. The strange woman . . . the stranger. These two expressions obviously refer to the "loose" woman (so RSV). The words basically mean "alien" and "foreigner" (so Berkeley), but in Proverbs it is clear that immorality is implied. Elsewhere in the OT this is not so. Ruth calls herself a "stranger" (Ruth 2:10). These expressions when used in Proverbs are euphemistic for zônâ, "a harlot," a word seldom used in this book. **17. Guide of her youth.** Her husband (so Berkeley). **The covenant of her God.** Probably an interesting reference to the divine sanction of the marriage vows.

18. Her house inclineth unto death. The translation is difficult in detail, but the meaning is clear from the parallel: the wages of sin is death. The same thought in very similar words is repeated in 5:5; 7:27; 9:18. Closest is 7:27, which says that her house is the road to Sheol, going down to the chambers of death; i.e., adultery is fatal. It is difficult to take **her house** as the subject of **inclineth** in 2:18, however, as "house" is masculine and the verb shûah is feminine. Toy (*The Book of Proverbs,* ICC., *ad loc.*) therefore derives it from a similar verb with the same consonants, shāhāh, "to be bowed down." This is possibly correct. **The dead.** Hebrew, repāîm, translated by some as shades (so RSV and Berkeley). This translation is not necessary. The word cannot give us a theology of the underworld. Its etymology is uncertain. It is used several times in Ugaritic (C. H. Gordon, *Ugaritic Handbook,* glossary) and is there made parallel with "deities."

This usage is not very instructive, since it involves Ugaritic theology, which is quite different from that of the Bible. We are thrown back upon the seven other Biblical instances of the use of the word. Three times it is used as parallel to "dead men," twice to Sheol; twice it has no parallel. Instructive is Isa 26:14, 19. In the first verse the plaint is that the dead men, the repāîm, shall not live or rise; in the later verse it is promised that they will. The word simply means dead people. As to the state of the dead being shadowy, conscious, or unconscious, this word says nothing. (On this subject cf. the plain teaching of Phil 1:23; Lk 23:43; *et al.*). There is another word spelled the same way which is the name of one of the nations of Canaan, the Rephaims. That word is sometimes translated "giants," but probably not correctly so.

NOTES

CHAPTER 3

My son, forget not my law; but let thine heart keep my commandments: ² For length of days, and long life, and peace, shall they add to thee. ³ Let not mercy and truth forsake thee: bind them about thy neck; write them upon the table of thine heart: ⁴ So shalt thou find favour and good understanding in the sight of God and man. ⁵ Trust in the Lord with all thine heart; and lean not unto thine own understanding. ⁶ In all thy ways acknowledge him, and he shall direct thy paths.

⁷ Be not wise in thine own eyes: fear the Lord, and depart from evil. ⁸ It shall be health to thy navel, and marrow to thy bones.

⁹ Honour the Lord with thy substance, and with the firstfruits of all thine increase: ¹⁰ So shall thy barns be filled with plenty, and thy presses shall burst out with new wine.

¹¹ My son, despise not the chastening of the Lord; neither be weary of his correction: ¹² For whom the Lord loveth he correcteth; even as a father the son *in whom* he delighteth.

3 MY SON, NEVER forget the things I've taught you. If you want a long and satisfying life, closely follow my instructions. ³ Never forget to be truthful and kind. Hold these virtues tightly. Write them deep within your heart. ⁴˒⁵ If you want favor with both God and man, and a reputation for good judgment and common sense, then trust the Lord completely; don't ever trust yourself. ⁶ In everything you do, put God first, and he will direct you and crown your efforts with success.

⁷˒⁸ Don't be conceited, sure of your own wisdom. Instead, trust and reverence the Lord, and turn your back on evil; when you do that, then you will be given renewed health and vitality.

⁹˒¹⁰ Honor the Lord by giving him the first part of all your income, and he will fill your barns with wheat and barley and overflow your wine vats with the finest wines.

¹¹˒¹² Young man, do not resent it when God chastens and corrects you, for his punishment is proof of his love. Just as a father punishes a son he delights in to make him better, so the Lord corrects you.

NOTES

Abba – "Father" = is "Daddy"

FATHER – TEACHER "

3:1. My law. This phrase and "My commandments" (2:1) and similar words are not to be pressed to refer to the law of Moses. They are the advice of the father-teacher. It is given, however, as the Lord's word. The author implies that he is giving divine commands, as does Paul in I Cor 14:37. Though a practical end is often given in Proverbs, the author urges rectitude for its own sake, not because "honesty is the best policy." **2. Length of days.** A possible allusion to the first commandment with promise (Ex 20:12). **3. Bind them about thy neck.** A similar phrase, but not identical occurs in Deut 6:8. Closer is Prov 7:3: "Write them upon the table of thine heart." **5. With all thine heart.** This precious verse contrasts ordinary human wisdom and the divine wisdom that is the basis of the whole book. **Heart** in Hebrew is used symbolically to represent not so much the seat of the emotions as the seat of intellect and will. In other words, commit your inner self to God. Do not seek to be independent of him. **6. Direct.** Hebrew, *make straight*. The verse promises not so much guidance as enablement for us to go forward.

YOU FURNISH THE WILL . . .
GOD WILL FURNISH THE POWER!

GOD'S ENERGY – & "DRIVE"
HIS GIFT TO US.

9. Firstfruits. An interesting reference to the Levitical legislation. In general, Proverbs is silent as to the Mosaic laws (but cf. the verses mentioned in the Commentary at 15:8), although clearly these laws were in force when Proverbs was written — even according to critical opinion which would make both Proverbs and the Levitical legislation post-Exilic The silence of Proverbs in this regard simply shows again that an argument from silence is often fallacious. **10. New wine.** The Hebrew has two words for wine. *Yayin*, which means fermented wine, is used in the condemnatory passage in Prov 23:31-35. *Tîrôsh*, used here as the fresh product of the pressing, is properly "must," "grape juice." Both words are translated *oinos*, "wine," by the LXX.

11. Despise not the chastening of the Lord. Quoted from Job 5:17, except that in Job the characteristic name *Shaddai*, "Almighty," occurs. Hebrews 12:5,6 quotes verbatim from the LXX (Alexandrinus and Sinaiticus texts), as is usual in Hebrews. The LXX adequately represents the Hebrew. (For other quotations, in Proverbs from the OT, cf. 30:5.)

13 Happy *is* the man *that* findeth wisdom, and the man *that* getteth understanding. 14 For the merchandise of it *is* better than the merchandise of silver, and the gain thereof than fine gold. 15 She *is* more precious than rubies: and all the things thou canst desire are not to be compared unto her. 16 Length of days *is* in her right hand; *and* in her left hand riches and honour. 17 Her ways *are* ways of pleasantness, and all her paths *are* peace. 18 She *is* a tree of life to them that lay hold upon her: and happy *is every one* that retaineth her.
19 The Lord by wisdom hath founded the earth; by understanding hath he established the heavens. 20 By his knowledge the depths are broken up, and the clouds drop down the dew.
21 My son, let not them depart from thine eyes: keep sound wisdom and discretion: 22 So shall they be life unto thy soul, and grace to thy neck. 23 Then shalt thou walk in thy way safely, and thy foot shall not stumble. 24 When thou liest down, thou shalt not be afraid: yea, thou shalt lie down, and thy sleep shall be sweet. 25 Be not afraid of sudden fear, neither of the desolation of the wicked, when it cometh. 26 For the Lord shall be thy confidence, and shall keep thy foot from being taken.
27 Withhold not good from them to whom it is due, when it is in the power of thine hand to do *it*. 28 Say not unto thy neighbour, Go, and come again, and to morrow I will give; when thou hast it by thee. 29 Devise not evil against thy neighbour, seeing he dwelleth securely by thee. 30 Strive not with a man without cause, if he have done thee no harm. 31 Envy thou not the oppressor, and choose none of his ways. 32 For the froward *is* abomination to the Lord: but his secret *is* with the righteous.
33 The curse of the Lord *is* in the house of the wicked: but he blesseth the habitation of the just. 34 Surely he scorneth the scorners: but he giveth grace unto the lowly. 35 The wise shall inherit glory: but shame shall be the promotion of fools.

13,14,15 The man who knows right from wrong and has good judgment and common sense is happier than the man who is immensely rich! For such wisdom is far more valuable than precious jewels. Nothing else compares with it. 16,17 Wisdom gives:

A long, good life
Riches
Honor
Pleasure
Peace

18 Wisdom is a tree of life to those who eat her fruit; happy is the man who keeps on eating it.
19 The Lord's wisdom founded the earth; his understanding established all the universe and space. 20 The deep fountains of the earth were broken open by his knowledge, and the skies poured down rain.
21 Have two goals: wisdom—that is, knowing and doing right—and common sense. Don't let them slip away, 22 for they fill you with living energy, and are a feather in your cap. 23 They keep you safe from defeat and disaster and from stumbling off the trail. 24,25,26 With them on guard you can sleep without fear; you need not be afraid of disaster or the plots of wicked men, for the Lord is with you; he protects you.
27,28 Don't withhold repayment of your debts. Don't say "some other time," if you can pay now. 29 Don't plot against your neighbor; he is trusting you. 30 Don't get into needless fights. 31 Don't envy violent men. Don't copy their ways. 32 For such men are an abomination to the Lord, but he gives his friendship to the godly.
33 The curse of God is on the wicked, but his blessing is on the upright. 34 The Lord mocks at mockers, but helps the humble. 35 The wise are promoted to honor, but fools are promoted to shame!

NOTES

14. **Merchandise.** "Profit," or possibly, "value." 15. **Than rubies.** Cf. Job 28:18; Prov 8:11; 31:10. 18. **Tree of life.** The phrase occurs also in Gen 2:9; 3:22-24; Prov 11:30; 13:12; 15:4; Rev 2:7; 22:2. Genesis is the only satisfactory source for the reference in Proverbs. We should therefore conclude that, as in the Revelation, these verses in Proverbs relate to the narrative of the Fall. There is no evidence for a "primitive sacred tree of life," as Toy supposes. Revelation 22:2 also has reference to a tree of healing by the river of the sanctuary (cf. Ezk 47:12; Zech 14:8). Famous trees in the garden of God, Eden, are mentioned in Ezk 31:8-16. All of these references presume acquaintance with the Genesis narrative. 19. **By wisdom . . . founded the earth.** Cf. 8:25-31. The "wisdom" of Proverbs is basically an attribute of God, and is not to be equated with mere earthly maxims of a clever teacher. This wisdom is God's law. In Prov 8, wisdom is personified and called eternal, as God is eternal. Many have found here an adumbration of Christ, which is a possible interpretation, but not sure.

27. **Withhold not.** Pay wages and pay on time, i.e., treat the laborer honestly and fairly (cf. Lev 19:13; Mal 3:5). Others would broaden the injunction to include all charity. 32. **The froward.** The root meaning apparently is *to depart*. This form is used only in Prov 2:15; 3:32; 14:2; Isa 30:12. Its parallel is "crooked." The LXX says *transgressors*. Perhaps "transgressor" or "apostate" gives the meaning best. 34. **He scorneth the scorners.** The same root, *lis̩*, is used in both the noun and the verb. But the meanings probably are a shade different. The verb has the meaning "to deride" (cf. Ps 119:51). The LXX, which is quoted verbatim in Jas 4:6; I Pet 5:5, uses *resist* as a free translation. The noun, however, is limited to Proverbs, Ps 1:1, and Isa 29:20. It is one of the many synonyms for a wicked man. The Greek uses the word *arrogant*, which is a fair representation. Its opposite is *humble* (AV, *lowly)* in the last half of the verse. But there is wide variety in the Greek translation of this root. It evidently has many overtones of wickedness.

CHAPTER 4

HEAR, ye children, the instruction of a father, and attend to know understanding. ² For I give you good doctrine, forsake ye not my law. ³ For I was my father's son, tender and only *beloved* in the sight of my mother. ⁴ He taught me also, and said unto me, Let thine heart retain my words: keep my commandments, and live. ⁵ Get wisdom, get understanding: forget *it* not; neither decline from the words of my mouth. ⁶ Forsake her not, and she shall preserve thee: love her, and she shall keep thee.

⁷ Wisdom *is* the principal thing; *therefore* get wisdom: and with all thy getting get understanding. ⁸ Exalt her, and she shall promote thee: she shall bring thee to honour, when thou dost embrace her. ⁹ She shall give to thine head an ornament of grace: a crown of glory shall she deliver to thee. ¹⁰ Hear, O my son, and receive my sayings; and the years of thy life shall be many.

¹¹ I have taught thee in the way of wisdom; I have led thee in right paths. ¹² When thou goest, thy steps shall not be straitened; and when thou runnest, thou shalt not stumble. ¹³ Take fast hold of instruction; let *her* not go: keep her; for she *is* thy life.

¹⁴ Enter not into the path of the wicked, and go not in the way of evil *men*. ¹⁵ Avoid it, pass not by it, turn from it, and pass away. ¹⁶ For they sleep not, except they have done mischief; and their sleep is taken away, unless they cause *some* to fall. ¹⁷ For they eat the bread of wickedness, and drink the wine of violence.

¹⁸ But the path of the just *is* as the shining light, that shineth more and more unto the perfect day. ¹⁹ The way of the wicked *is* as darkness: they know not at what they stumble.

²⁰ My son, attend to my words; incline thine ear unto my sayings. ²¹ Let them not depart from thine eyes; keep them in the midst of thine heart. ²² For they *are* life unto those that find them, and health to all their flesh.

²³ Keep thy heart with all diligence; for out of it *are* the issues of life. ²⁴ Put away from thee a froward mouth, and

4 YOUNG MEN, LISTEN to me as you would to your father. Listen, and grow wise, for I speak the truth—don't turn away. ³ For I, too, was once a son, tenderly loved by my mother as an only child; and the companion of my father. ⁴ He told me never to forget his words. "If you follow them," he said, "you will have a long and happy life. ⁵ *Learn to be wise,* "he said, *"and develop good judgment and common sense! I cannot overemphasize this point."* ⁶ Cling to wisdom—she will protect you. Love her—she will guard you.

⁷ Determination to be wise is the first step toward becoming wise! And with your wisdom, develop common sense and good judgment. ⁸,⁹ If you exalt wisdom, she will exalt you. Hold her fast and she will lead you to great honor; she will place a beautiful crown upon your head. ¹⁰ My son, listen to me and do as I say, and you will have a long, good life.

¹¹ I would have you learn this great fact: that a life of doing right is the wisest life there is. ¹² If you live that kind of life, you'll not limp or stumble as you run. ¹³ Carry out my instructions; don't forget them, for they will lead you to real living.

¹⁴ Don't do as the wicked do. ¹⁵ Avoid their haunts—turn away, go somewhere else, ¹⁶ for evil men don't sleep until they've done their evil deed for the day. They can't rest unless they cause someone to stumble and fall. ¹⁷ They eat and drink wickedness and violence!

¹⁸ But the good man walks along in the ever-brightening light of God's favor; the dawn gives way to morning splendor, ¹⁹ while the evil man gropes and stumbles in the dark.

²⁰ Listen, son of mine, to what I say. Listen carefully. ²¹ Keep these thoughts ever in mind; let them penetrate deep within your heart, ²² for they will mean real life for you, and radiant health.

²³ *Above all else, guard your affections.* For they influence everything else in your life. ²⁴ Spurn the careless kiss of a prosti-

4:3,4. My father's son. These verses give an interesting touch. The teacher-father declares that his doctrine is not new. There is no reason why we may not see here the solicitous care of David and Bathsheba for their son Solomon. **7. Wisdom is the principal thing.** The RSV and Berkeley insist on reading here a genitive — *The beginning of wisdom is: Get wisdom.* So also Toy and Delitzsch *(The Proverbs of Solomon,* KD. Reprinted.). But this seems unnecessary. Oesterley *(op. cit.)* and Fritsch *(op. cit.)* would drop the verse, since it is not in the LXX. The same form *beginning* is used four times not in the genitive. The meaning of "chief" or "principal" is well attested. The AV translation can be defended. *The beginning of wisdom is: get wisdom* violates the thought of 1:7 and seems unsuitable. **With all thy getting.** Better, *in all that thou hast acquired.* <u>Get understanding.</u> There is not here a progress — Don't stop at wisdom; get real understanding. Rather, as is usual in Proverbs, wisdom and understanding are synonymous. **9. Crown of glory.** The expression is also used in 16:31; Isa 62:3. **12. Not . . . straitened.** The old English *strait* does not mean "straight," but rather, "strict," "narrow" (cf. Mt 7:14). Your steps will be *unimpeded* (Toy).

14. Enter not. Verses 14-27 represent the advice of wisdom — namely, Turn from evil (cf. Job 28:28). **18. The path of the just.** Note the emphatic contrast with "the way of the wicked" (v. 19). **The perfect day.** The precise meaning is debatable. Rashi and many others say *noon* (cited in Julius H. Greenstone, *Proverbs with Commentary).* The general meaning is clear: the just walk in increasing light; the wicked, in darkness (cf. comment on 2:13).

22. Life . . . and health. Cf. 3:8. **23. Keep thy heart,** i.e., the mind which should seek right conduct (cf. 23:26). **Out of it.** Grammatically this could be "out of the heart"; but more likely, "out of keeping the heart in wisdom" is life.

perverse lips put far from thee. ²⁵ Let thine eyes look right on, and let thine eyelids look straight before thee. ²⁶ Ponder the path of thy feet, and let all thy ways be established. ²⁷ Turn not to the right hand nor to the left: remove thy foot from evil.

CHAPTER 5

My son, attend unto my wisdom, *and* bow thine ear to my understanding: ² That thou mayest regard discretion, and *that* thy lips may keep knowledge. ³ For the lips of a strange woman drop *as* an honeycomb, and her mouth *is* smoother than oil: ⁴ But her end is bitter as wormwood, sharp as a two-edged sword. ⁵ Her feet go down to death; her steps take hold on hell. ⁶ Lest thou shouldest ponder the path of life, her ways are moveable, *that* thou canst not know *them*.

⁷ Hear me now therefore, O ye children, and depart not from the words of my mouth. ⁸ Remove thy way far from her, and come not nigh the door of her house: ⁹ Lest thou give thine honour unto others, and thy years unto the cruel: ¹⁰ Lest strangers be filled with thy wealth; and thy labours *be* in the house of a stranger; ¹¹ And thou mourn at the last, when thy flesh and thy body are consumed, ¹² And say, How have I hated instruction, and my heart despised reproof; ¹³ And have not obeyed the voice of my teachers, nor inclined mine ear to them that instructed me! ¹⁴ I was almost in all evil in the midst of the congregation and assembly.

¹⁵ Drink waters out of thine own cistern, and running waters out of thine own well. ¹⁶ Let thy fountains be dispersed abroad, *and* rivers of waters in the streets. ¹⁷ Let them be only thine own, and not strangers' with thee. ¹⁸ Let thy fountain be blessed: and rejoice with the wife of thy youth. ¹⁹ *Let her be as* the loving hind and pleasant roe; let her breasts satisfy thee at all times; and be thou ravished always with her love. ²⁰ And why wilt thou, my son, be ravished with a strange woman, and embrace the bosom of a stranger? ²¹ For the ways of man *are* before the eyes of the Lord, and he pondereth all his goings.

tute. Stay far from her. ²⁵ Look straight ahead; don't even turn your head to look. ²⁶ Watch your step. Stick to the path and be safe. ²⁷ Don't sidetrack; pull back your foot from danger.

5 LISTEN TO ME, my son! I know what I am saying; *listen!* ² Watch yourself, lest you be indiscreet and betray some vital information. ³ For the lips of a prostitute are as sweet as honey, and smooth flattery is her stock in trade. ⁴ But afterwards only a bitter conscience is left to you, sharp as a double-edged sword. ⁵ She leads you down to death and hell. ⁶ For she does not know the path to life. She staggers down a crooked trail, and doesn't even realize where it leads.

⁷ Young men, listen to me, and never forget what I'm about to say: ⁸ *Run from her! Don't go near her house,* ⁹ lest you fall to her temptation and lose your honor, and give the remainder of your life to the cruel and merciless; ¹⁰ lest strangers obtain your wealth, and you become a slave of foreigners. ¹¹ Lest afterwards you groan in anguish and in shame, when syphilis consumes your body, ¹² and you say, "Oh, if only I had listened! If only I had not demanded my own way! ¹³ Oh, why wouldn't I take advice? Why was I so stupid? ¹⁴ For now I must face public disgrace."

¹⁵ Drink from your own well, my son—be faithful and true to your wife. ¹⁶ Why should you beget children with women of the street? ¹⁷ Why share your children with those outside your home? ¹⁸ Let your manhood be a blessing; rejoice in the wife of your youth. ¹⁹ Let her charms and tender embrace satisfy you. Let her love alone fill you with delight. ²⁰ Why delight yourself with prostitutes, embracing what isn't yours? ²¹ *For God is closely watching you,* and he weighs carefully everything you do.

5:3. For the lips. As a honeycomb drops honey, so the strange woman speaks honeyed words; her speech (lit., *palate,* as organ of speech) is, we would say, 'slick.' **Strange woman.** See comment on 2:16. **4. Wormwood.** The Greek translates *gall* as the height of bitterness. The Hebrew *la'ănâ* appears to be a shrub of bitter taste used in the preparation of absinthe and traditionally used as medicine for deworming. **5. To death.** See comments on 2:18. **6. Lest** is difficult and is rendered by the LXX, Delitzsch, and others as a negative. **Ponder** means "weigh" or "make level." The subject could be "thou" or "she." Read, *She does not weigh (or consider) the path of life.* The last half can be translated, *Her ways wander* (so RSV). The last verb again could have as its subject "thou" or "she." *She knows it not* (Berkeley and similarly RSV). Jones and Walls ("The Proverbs," *The New Bible Commentary*) favor a slightly attested meaning of the verb, *She is not at rest.* **9. Thine honour unto others.** Proverbs 5:9-14 is aptly called "Rake's Progress" by Jones and Walls.

15. Thine own cistern. Verses 15-17 are highly poetic and beautiful exhortations to fidelity, while 16,17 probably refer to children. In any event, the blessing of marital fidelity is beautifully presented. **19. Let her breasts satisfy thee.** This Hebrew word *dad,* translated "breasts" in the AV, does not bear the connotation expected in this verse as another word, *shad,* would. Certain copies of the LXX and the parallel in Prov 7:18 argue that the word here should be read with another vowel, *dōd,* and translated *Let her love satisfy thee* (so Greenstone and RSV). **21. Before . . . the Lord.** Contrary to Toy, who usually finds in Proverbs the concept of temporal blessings as the incentive for morality, this verse shows that the outlook of the author includes the higher reference to God's

NOTES

22 His own iniquities shall take the wicked himself, and he shall be holden with the cords of his sins. 23 He shall die without instruction; and in the greatness of his folly he shall go astray.

CHAPTER 6

My son, if thou be surety for thy friend, *if* thou hast stricken thy hand with a stranger, 2 Thou art snared with the words of thy mouth, thou art taken with the words of thy mouth. 3 Do this now, my son, and deliver thyself, when thou art come into the hand of thy friend; go, humble thyself, and make sure thy friend. 4 Give not sleep to thine eyes, nor slumber to thine eyelids. 5 Deliver thyself as a roe from the hand *of the hunter,* and as a bird from the hand of the fowler.

22 The wicked man is doomed by his own sins; they are ropes that catch and hold him. 23 He shall die because he will not listen to the truth; he has let himself be led away into incredible folly.

6 SON, IF YOU endorse a note for someone you hardly know, guaranteeing his debt, you are in serious trouble. 2 You may have trapped yourself by your agreement. 3 Quick! Get out of it if you possibly can! Swallow your pride; don't let embarrassment stand in the way. Go and beg to have your name erased. 4 Don't put it off. Do it now. Don't rest until you do. 5 If you can get out of this trap you have saved yourself like a deer that escapes from a hunter, or a bird from the net.

holiness as the reason for rectitude. **23. Without instruction.** The Hebrew says, *with no instruction.* Doubtless "for lack of discipline" is meant (so RSV, BV, Jones and Walls, etc.).

6:1. If thou be surety. The practices in regard to lending among the Jews in antiquity are not fully known. Toy imagines that there was no suretyship in the "commercially simple" pre-Exilic life. It would seem, however, that the far-flung enterprises of Solomon, now illustrated by archaeology, and the increase of wealth pictured by Amos and others must have given ample opportunity for making loans and taking surety; although we do not have examples of just this thing in other Scriptures. The rabbinic attitudes are discussed by Greenstone, who remarks that the Hebrew word for "surety" here was used by the Phoenician traders and entered Latin as *arrabo.* He might have added that it is also in Greek *arrabōn* (Eph 1:14. Cf. Zellig S. Harris, *Grammar of the Phoenician Language,* "American Oriental Series," Vol. VIII; Glossary). In brief, the Levitical law forbade lending on interest to poor Israelites (Lev 25:35-37). The idea was that for a poor fellow Israelite, a man should give the needed money outright. The Law required that if a man did lend and take a pledge for collateral, he might not enter his debtor's house to remove the collateral by force. And if a poor man gave his garment as collateral, the lender must restore it to him the same day (Deut 24:10-12). These provisions answer to our minimum personal exemptions. Lending to non-Israelites was permitted, and probably commercial loans were arranged. The author of the article "Usury," in ISBE, remarks that the Pentateuchal regulations do not cover commercial loans; but perhaps he goes too far in saying that commercial loans were practically unknown. Rather, it is probable that the practice of making commercial loans gave rise to the injustices in II Kgs 4:1; Neh 5:1-12. At the year of release all Israelites' debts were remitted (Deut 15:2). This argues for commercial loans being permitted, for other loans were prohibited.

Rates of interest, if we may judge by Neh 5:11, were commonly 1 per cent per month, although they doubtless varied. Charging such high interest was usury, and those who required it of fellow Jews were condemned. The prophet Jeremiah protests (Jer 15:10) that he has not en-gaged in such ventures, yet all men hate him — presumably as they hated usurers. The word is translated *extortioner* in Ps 109:11. The very word for "usury," *neshek* (Prov 28:8), implies "bite" or "devour," though milder words are also used. Not to practice usury is an element of righteousness in Ps 15:5; Ezk 18:8, 13,17; 22:12. The practice of a creditor is illustrated in II Kgs 4:1. We can reasonably fill in the details that the husband had a commercial loan which his widow could not pay; or possibly some usurer had loaned to a widow in violation of Lev 25:35-37. The BV and the RSV translate these words by *interest.* It would seem better to translate by "usury," as apparently it is the excesses that are condemned. Because of these excesses, Solomon cautions against becoming surety for "another." He urges one to escape speedily the possibilities of ruin. Sureties are recommended in the post-biblical book, Ecclesiasticus 29:14. When they developed or what form they took, we do not know. It is probable that in the time of Solomon their abuses were such as to call forth the rebuke here recorded (see also Prov 11:15; 20:16; 27:13 — the last two verses practically identical).

NOTES

⁶ Go to the ant, thou sluggard; consider her ways, and be wise: ⁷ Which having no guide, overseer, or ruler, ⁸ Provideth her meat in the summer, *and* gathereth her food in the harvest. ⁹ How long wilt thou sleep, O sluggard? when wilt thou arise out of thy sleep? ¹⁰ *Yet* a little sleep, a little slumber, a little folding of the hands to sleep: ¹¹ So shall thy poverty come as one that travelleth, and thy want as an armed man.

¹² A naughty person, a wicked man, walketh with a froward mouth. ¹³ He winketh with his eyes, he speaketh with his feet, he teacheth with his fingers; ¹⁴ Frowardness *is* in his heart, he deviseth mischief continually; he soweth discord. ¹⁵ Therefore shall his calamity come suddenly; suddenly shall he be broken without remedy.

⁶ Take a lesson from the ants, you lazy fellow. Learn from their ways and be wise! ⁷ For though they have no king to make them work, ⁸ yet they labor hard all summer, gathering food for the winter. ⁹ But you—all you do is sleep. When will you wake up? ¹⁰ "Let me sleep a little longer!" Sure, just a little more! ¹¹ And as you sleep, poverty creeps upon you like a robber and destroys you; want attacks you in full armor.

¹²,¹³ Let me describe for you a worthless and a wicked man; first, he is a constant liar; he signals his true intentions to his friends with eyes and feet and fingers. ¹⁴ Next, his heart is full of rebellion. And he spends his time thinking of all the evil he can do, and stirring up discontent. ¹⁵ But he will be destroyed suddenly, broken beyond hope of healing.

6. The ant. Mentioned in the Bible only here and in Prov 30:25, though there probably is no question about the translation. Formerly there was a problem raised about ants storing food (see Toy). A type of ant found in the Near East, however, does this. Ants have social organization, but no ruler corresponding to a queen bee. **Thou sluggard.** This noun is found fourteen times in Proverbs and nowhere else. It is usually defined as "a lazy person." Though the word includes this idea, it may well have other overtones, such as our "ne'er-do-well," which does not mean merely a "failure." The usage in Proverbs argues that "lazy" is not the total connotation. In 15:19, the contrast is an *upright man* — not just a "worker." In 19:15 the parallel is with *remîyyâ*, which is usually rendered *deceit* in the AV and the RSV, but rendered by them *idle* in this place. In Prov 21:25,26 the contrast evidently is a *righteous man* (so AV and Berkeley). The RSV separates the two verses and supplies an extra thought in verse 26. In 26:12-16 there are several verses on the sluggard. Verse 13 is similar to 22:13. Verse 15 is from 19:24. But 26:16, as a final, perhaps climactic verse, says a "sluggard" is wise in his own eyes. We must note that this section of Proverbs 26 was introduced by verse 12, which declares that one wise in his own eyes is worse than a "fool." It is clear that the author is reproaching a "sluggard" not merely with idleness, but with associated sins. We hope to show by many examples that the word "fool" means not a "moron" but a "sinner." So the author of Proverbs here is not merely recommending thrift and diligence; he is apparently condemning a characteristic that combines shiftlessness with shiftiness! **10. A little sleep.** Verses 10 and 11 are exactly paralleled in 24:33,34, except for a couple of vowels (cf. Introd.). In this case both contexts speak of a shiftless man, using different comparisons, but the same conclusion. The saying may have been a well-known epigram. The LXX translates it a bit differently in the two places. The Syriac also differs, but not in the same way as the LXX.

12. A naughty person. Hebrew, *a man of Belial.* **Froward.** Hebrew, *crooked.* **13. Speaketh with his feet.** LXX, *makes a sign with his feet.* The Hebrew *mālal* can mean "speak," "rub," "scrape," "languish," or "wither" (BDB). The meaning "scrape" is poorly attested. The idiom may well refer to some low gesture, like our thumbing the nose. **Teacheth with his fingers.** The word probably means "point," but the connotation is difficult. Possibly another low gesture typical of the wicked man. **14. Frowardness.** A different word from that in verse 12. It is used nine times in Proverbs, elsewhere only in Deut 32:20. The root means *overturn.* It is clear that it refers to some kind of evil, but it is hard to catch the exact intent. The LXX reads *perverted* (so Fritsch). Delitzsch says *malice;* Toy: *evil.* In 8:13 "a perverse mouth" is paralleled with pride and arrogancy. In 23:33 a drunk man is pictured as speaking "perverse things," using this word. **Soweth discord.** Literally, *lets loose strife.* The LXX translation, *causes trouble to a city,* arose from confusing the word with a later derivative. The root is *dîn,* "to judge, whence *mādôn,* "strife." This word, **discord,** with variants, is found twenty-seven times in Proverbs and three times elsewhere. It is part of the peculiar moral vocabulary of the book. The wording of 16:28, a "perverse man lets loose strife," is very similar to that of this verse.

NOTES

"GOD MAKES NO PROVISION FOR IDLENESS"...

16 These six *things* doth the Lord hate: yea, seven *are* an abomination unto him: 17 A proud look, a lying tongue, and hands that shed innocent blood, 18 An heart that deviseth wicked imaginations, feet that be swift in running to mischief, 19 A false witness *that* speaketh lies, and he that soweth discord among brethren.

20 My son, keep thy father's commandment, and forsake not the law of thy mother: 21 Bind them continually upon thine heart, *and* tie them about thy neck. 22 When thou goest, it shall lead thee; when thou sleepest, it shall keep thee; and *when* thou awakest, it shall talk with thee. 23 For the commandment *is* a lamp; and the law *is* light; and reproofs of instruction *are* the way of life: 24 To keep thee from the evil woman, from the flattery of the tongue of a strange woman.

25 Lust not after her beauty in thine heart; neither let her take thee with her eyelids. 26 For by means of a whorish woman *a man is brought* to a piece of bread: and the adulteress will hunt for the precious life. 27 Can a man take fire in his bosom, and his clothes not be burned? 28 Can one go upon hot coals, and his feet not be burned? 29 So he that goeth in to his neighbour's wife; whosoever toucheth her shall not be innocent. 30 *Men* do not despise a thief, if he steal to satisfy his soul when he is hungry; 31 But *if* he be found, he shall restore sevenfold; he shall give all the substance of his house.

32 *But* whoso committeth adultery with a woman lacketh understanding: he *that* doeth it destroyeth his own soul. 33 A wound and dishonour shall he get; and his reproach shall not be wiped away. 34 For jealousy *is* the rage of a man: therefore he will not spare in the day of vengeance. 35 He will not regard any ransom; neither will he rest content, though thou givest many gifts.

CHAPTER 7

My son, keep my words, and lay up my commandments with thee. 2 Keep my commandments, and live; and my

16-19 For there are six things the Lord hates—no, seven:
Haughtiness
Lying
Murdering
Plotting evil
Eagerness to do wrong
A false witness
Sowing discord among brothers

20 Young man, obey your father and your mother. 21 Tie their instructions around your finger so you won't forget. Take to heart all of their advice. 22 Every day and all night long their counsel will lead you and save you from harm; when you wake up in the morning, let their instructions guide you into the new day. 23 For their advice is a beam of light directed into the dark corners of your mind to warn you of danger and to give you a good life. 24 Their counsel will keep you far away from prostitutes with all their flatteries.

25 Don't lust for their beauty. Don't let their coyness seduce you. 26 For a prostitute will bring a man to poverty, and an adulteress may cost him his very life. 27 Can a man hold fire against his chest and not be burned? 28 Can he walk on hot coals and not blister his feet? 29 So it is with the man who commits adultery with another's wife. He shall not go unpunished for this sin. 30 Excuses might even be found for a thief, if he steals when he is starving! 31 But even so, he is fined seven times as much as he stole, though it may mean selling everything in his house to pay it back.

32 But the man who commits adultery is an utter fool, for he destroys his own soul. 33 Wounds and constant disgrace are his lot, 34 for the woman's husband will be furious in his jealousy, and he will have no mercy on you in his day of vengeance. 35 You won't be able to buy him off no matter what you offer.

7 FOLLOW MY ADVICE, my son; always keep it in mind and stick to it. 2 Obey me and live! Guard my words as your most

16. Six things . . . yea, seven. These are not seven cardinal sins (Greenstone and Jones and Walls) nor an indefinite six or seven (Toy). Delitzsch strikes it right in saying that the proverb is climactic. The six items are background for the seventh, which receives the emphasis (cf. Job 5:19; Prov 30:18,19). The statement emphatically concludes with what verse 14 had introduced — "letting loose strife."

21. Bind them . . . upon thy heart. Cf. 3:3. **23. Commandment . . . law.** Jones and Walls well remark that this is parental instruction, but that such instruction consisted of the divine law (Deut 6:6,7). **25. In thine heart.** Note well that the OT commandments reach to the internal attitudes of man. Christ's teaching that inner lust was already inner adultery (Mt 5:28) is not an advance upon the OT teaching so much as a rescuing of the OT doctrine from the Pharisaic traditional comments (cf. R. Laird Harris, *Inspiration and Canonicity of the Bible,* p. 53). **30. A thief.** The thought is that there may be mitigating circumstances for thievery, and even restitution greatly assists in removing the blot. But for adultery there is no excuse. It brings a train of evil consequences. No restitution is possible.

35. Ransom. A good example of the meaning of *kōper,* "a payment to pacify." The root is said to mean *cover* (BDB), but it is not so used in the OT, and it is a dubious inference from the Arabic. From the noun for **ransom** a denominative verb, *kipper,* is formed, logically meaning "to give a ransom." This is the verb many times translated "to make an atonement." From this verb a second noun is formed, *kappōret,* "place of atonement." This is the word for the top of the ark called "the mercy seat" in the AV, or *hilastērion* in the LXX. Christ is called our *hilastērion,* or "propitiation," in Rom 3:25.

7:2. Apple of thine eye. *Center of the eye;* therefore the pupil, a symbol of a most precious thing. **5. Flattereth.** Not so much to "flatter" as to use smooth words, i.e., agreeable, seductive words (so Delitzsch and RSV).

law as the apple of thine eye. ³ Bind them upon thy fingers, write them upon the table of thine heart. ⁴ Say unto wisdom, Thou *art* my sister; and call understanding *thy* kinswoman: ⁵ That they may keep thee from the strange woman, from the stranger *which* flattereth with her words.

⁶ For at the window of my house I looked through my casement, ⁷ And beheld among the simple ones, I discerned among the youths, a young man void of understanding, ⁸ Passing through the street near her corner; and he went the way to her house, ⁹ In the twilight, in the evening, in the black and dark night: ¹⁰ And, behold, there met him a woman *with* the attire of an harlot, and subtil of heart. ¹¹ (She *is* loud and stubborn; her feet abide not in her house: ¹² Now *is she* without, now in the streets, and lieth in wait at every corner.)

¹³ So she caught him, and kissed him, *and* with an impudent face said unto him, ¹⁴ *I have* peace offerings with me; this day have I payed my vows. ¹⁵ Therefore came I forth to meet thee, diligently to seek thy face, and I have found thee. ¹⁶ I have decked my bed with coverings of tapestry, with carved *works*, with fine linen of Egypt. ¹⁷ I have perfumed my bed with myrrh, aloes, and cinnamon. ¹⁸ Come, let us take our fill of love until the morning: let us solace ourselves with loves. ¹⁹ For the goodman *is* not at home, he is gone a long journey: ²⁰ He hath taken a bag of money with him, *and* will come home at the day appointed.

²¹ With her much fair speech she caused him to yield, with the flattering of her lips she forced him. ²² He goeth after her straightway, as an ox goeth to the slaughter, or as a fool to the correction of the stocks; ²³ Till a dart strike through his liver; as a bird hasteth to the snare, and knoweth not that it *is* for his life.

²⁴ Hearken unto me now therefore, O ye children, and attend to the words of my mouth. ²⁵ Let not thine heart decline to her ways, go not astray in her paths. ²⁶ For she hath cast down many wounded: yea, many strong *men* have been slain by her. ²⁷ Her house *is* the way to hell, going down to the chambers of death.

precious possession. ³ Write them down, and also keep them deep within your heart. ⁴ Love wisdom like a sweetheart; make her a beloved member of your family. ⁵ Let her hold you back from visiting a prostitute, from listening to her flattery.

⁶ I was looking out the window of my house one day, ⁷ and saw a simple-minded lad, a young man lacking common sense, ⁸,⁹ walking at twilight down the street to the house of this wayward girl, a prostitute. ¹⁰ She approached him, saucy and pert, and dressed seductively. ¹¹,¹² She was the brash, coarse type, seen often in the streets and markets, soliciting at every corner for men to be her lovers.

¹³ She put her arms around him and kissed him, and with a saucy look she said, ¹⁴ "I've decided to forget our quarrel! ¹⁵ I was just coming to look for you and here you are! ¹⁶,¹⁷ My bed is spread with lovely, colored sheets of finest linen imported from Egypt, perfumed with myrrh, aloes and cinnamon. ¹⁸ Come on, let's take our fill of love until morning, ¹⁹ for my husband is away on a long trip. ²⁰ He has taken a wallet full of money with him, and won't return for several days."

²¹ So she seduced him with her pretty speech, her coaxing and her wheedling, until he yielded to her. He couldn't resist her flattery. ²² He followed her as an ox going to the butcher, or as a stag that is trapped, ²³ waiting to be killed with an arrow through its heart. He was as a bird flying into a snare, not knowing the fate awaiting it there.

²⁴ Listen to me, young men, and not only listen but obey; ²⁵ don't let your desires get out of hand; don't let yourself think about her. Don't go near her; stay away from where she walks, lest she tempt you and seduce you. ²⁶ For she has been the ruin of multitudes—a vast host of men have been her victims. ²⁷ If you want to find the road to hell, look for her house.

7. Among the simple. The silly, the morally unstable. See comment at 1:4 and cf. 9:4 and 16. **10. Subtil.** The Hebrew apparently means "guarded of heart," i.e., secretive, wily (so Delitzsch). The description of the following scene is a classic. As Delitzsch says, "like meets like," the seduction is complete, the excuses are given. But the inspired author gives tersely enough the end product of evil. **11. Loud and stubborn.** Better, *tumultuous and rebellious.* The rebellion is obviously a refusal of God's law and the obligations of morality. **14. I have peace offerings.** The peace offerings were eaten in part by the worshiper. Therefore, at national feasts with thousands present, peace offerings were given by the thousands. The woman does not mean to claim that she has recently worshiped. She is, rather, alluring the young man with the announcement that her refrigerator is full, as we would say. "My husband is away," she says; "the coast is clear. We can have our fling, and no one will know." No one but God! **20. Day appointed.** A rare word. The LXX and Syriac give the sense, *after many days.* Probably the meaning is "at full moon," which was presumably some days off.

22. Straightway. Better, *all at once* (RSV). The man's resistance to sin at last gives way, and his doom is sealed. **Stocks.** The sense is plain, but again the details are difficult. The Hebrew seems to say, "like fetters unto correction a fool (goes)." The word "fetter," however, is rare and elsewhere means anklets. The LXX translates the word for "stocks" by "dog," apparently reading a different text —"like a dog (goes) to bonds." The word "bonds" in the LXX arises from the Hebrew word for "correction," using different vowels. Then the LXX ends the verse with this clause—"as a dog goes to bonds." The word "fool" is understood with different vowels, and it is transferred to the following verse, which reads in the LXX—"A deer shot in the liver with an arrow." The LXX reading of the whole passage differs from the Hebrew only in two words. It is supported by the Syriac and Targum, and should perhaps be adopted.

27. Sheol. See comments for 1:12 and 2:18. We should not lose the solemn thrust of this passage in the details of the exposition. Sin cannot be indulged with impunity; its wages is death. The deceitfulness of sin is an old story, but the ancient Hebrew author here beauti-fully unmasks its deceit and gives the unvarnished truth. But he does not stop there. There is a cure for sin—it is the voice of Wisdom of chapter 8.

NOTES

CHAPTER 8

DOTH not wisdom cry? and understanding put forth her voice? ² She standeth in the top of high places, by the way in the places of the paths. ³ She crieth at the gates, at the entry of the city, at the coming in at the doors. ⁴ Unto you, O men, I call; and my voice *is* to the sons of man. ⁵ O ye simple, understand wisdom: and, ye fools, be ye of an understanding heart. ⁶ Hear; for I will speak of excellent things; and the opening of my lips *shall be* right things. ⁷ For my mouth shall speak truth; and wickedness *is* an abomination to my lips. ⁸ All the words of my mouth *are* in righteousness; *there is* nothing froward or perverse in them. ⁹ They *are* all plain to him that understandeth, and right to them that find knowledge. ¹⁰ Receive my instruction, and not silver; and knowledge rather than choice gold.

¹¹ For wisdom *is* better than rubies; and all the things that may be desired are not to be compared to it. ¹² I wisdom dwell with prudence, and find out knowledge of witty inventions. ¹³ The fear of the Lord *is* to hate evil: pride, and arrogancy, and the evil way, and the froward mouth, do I hate.

¹⁴ Counsel *is* mine, and sound wisdom: I *am* understanding; I have strength. ¹⁵ By me kings reign, and princes decree justice. ¹⁶ By me princes rule, and nobles, *even* all the judges of the earth. ¹⁷ I love them that love me; and those that seek me early shall find me. ¹⁸ Riches and honour *are* with me: *yea,* durable riches and righteousness. ¹⁹ My fruit *is* better than gold, yea, than fine gold; and my revenue than choice silver. ²⁰ I lead in the way of righteousness, in the midst of the paths of judgment: ²¹ That I may cause those that love me to inherit substance; and I will

8 CAN'T YOU HEAR the voice of wisdom? She is standing at the city gates and at every fork in the road, and at the door of every house. Listen to what she says: ⁴˒⁵ "Listen, men!" she calls. "How foolish and naive you are! Let me give you understanding. O foolish ones, let me show you common sense! ⁶˒⁷ Listen to me! For I have important information for you. Everything I say is right and true, for I hate lies and every kind of deception. ⁸ My advice is wholesome and good. There is nothing of evil in it. ⁹ My words are plain and clear to anyone with half a mind—if it is only open! ¹⁰ My instruction is far more valuable than silver or gold."

¹¹ For the value of wisdom is far above rubies; nothing can be compared with it. ¹² Wisdom and good judgment live together, for wisdom knows where to discover knowledge and understanding. ¹³ If anyone respects and fears God, he will hate evil. For wisdom hates pride, arrogance, corruption and deceit of every kind.

¹⁴˒¹⁵ "I, Wisdom, give good advice and common sense. Because of my strength, kings reign in power. I show the judges who is right and who is wrong. ¹⁶ Rulers rule well with my help. ¹⁷ I love all who love me. Those who search for me shall surely find me. ¹⁸ Unending riches, honor, justice and righteousness are mine to distribute. ¹⁹ My gifts are better than the purest gold or sterling silver! ²⁰ My paths are those of justice and right. ²¹ Those who love and follow me are indeed wealthy. I fill their treasuries.

8:1. Doth not wisdom cry? Greenstone well remarks that we have here not just a discourse on the beauties of family life or on chastity, else the contrast to the harlot would be a dutiful wife. But Greenstone does not follow up his suggestion to show that the contrast is really the basic one of sin versus godliness. It is for this reason that wisdom is personified and so closely paralleled with God himself. Proverbs 8:1-13 gives the exhortation of wisdom; 8:14-31 describes the exalted status of wisdom; 8:32–9:11 presents the invitation of wisdom to profit by her instruction.

5. Simple . . . fools. These are not mental fools, but, as much of the preceding shows, sinners. For **simple,** see comments on 1:4. The word $k^e sîl$, "fool," is used forty-nine times in Proverbs, eighteen in Ecclesiastes, three times elsewhere. It is obvious that it is part of what we have called the moral vocabulary of Proverbs. Its use in Ecclesiastes is somewhat different, even as its counterpart, "wisdom," is used differently there. In Ecclesiastes, wisdom is inventive genius, mental ability; folly is pleasure—even noble pleasure in works like architecture, gardening, etc. Both are alike condemned as fruitless. In Proverbs, both wisdom and folly are of a moral sort. Examples of the usage of $(k^e sîl)$ are: (1) in connection with *'iwwelet,* "folly" of the sinful sort, 12:23; 13:16; 14:8; 15:14; 17:12; etc.; this root is not found in Ecclesiastes. (2) The "fool" $(k^e sîl)$ is contrasted with the wise man or with wisdom in Prov 3:35; 10:1, 23; 13:20; 14:16; 29:11. (3) The word "fool" is paralleled with "simple" *(petî)* in 1:22; with "scorner" *(lêṣ)* in 19:29; and associated with "evil" *(ra')* in 13:19. This word "fool," or "folly," *'iwwelet,* in Proverbs, obviously connotes moral badness. This must be understood if we are to hold the teaching of Proverbs in focus. It is not a book on intelligence so much as on integrity (see Introd., *The Teaching of Proverbs*).

8. Froward. Not the word used in 2:12 and elsewhere. This root, *pātal,* means "twisted"; therefore it is used for "string," "tie," "wrestle," etc. Here it means morally twisted, the opposite of righteous. **Perverse.** Crooked. **10. My instruction.** The translation of the AV is satisfactory. The Hebrew strictly says, *Receive my instruction and do not (receive) silver.* It is a comparative negative (cf. 9:8; 31:6; and, for another famous example, see Hos 6:6). **11. Than rubies.** Cf. 3:15; 8:10; 16:16; 31:10. **12. Prudence.** Hebrew *'ormâ.* The root means "be wise," and is used in a good sense, as here, and also in a bad sense (Gen 3:1). **Inventions.** This also is used elsewhere in a bad sense (Prov 12:2). Here it is good. **13. To hate evil.** Verses amplifying the concept of "the fear of the Lord" are: 1:7,29; 2:5; 8:13; 9:10; 10:27; 14:27; 16:6; 19:23. Job 28:28, like Prov 16:6, emphasizes departing from evil. Prov 8:13 warns us that true godliness is not all positive. The teaching that sin is hateful is a wonderful and vital truth. In ancient times, as now, only the Biblical revelation stressed this truth.

NOTES

22. The Lord possessed me. A famous verse. The LXX translates, *The Lord created me;* as does the Syriac. The clear personification of these verses led most of the early Church Fathers to find here a prophecy of Christ. The Arian heretics of the fourth century therefore made much of this verse, speaking of wisdom as a created being. The orthodox party repelled this idea, as Jones and Walls say, "on other grounds." It is curious that the controversy was carried out on the basis of the LXX text. There was little recourse to the Hebrew. The Hebrew uses the word *qānâ.* This verb is used many times in the sense of "buy," "possess," "acquire." Its derivative means "cattle," or practically, "wealth." Only in Gen 14:22 would "make" be a reasonable translation. The RSV has *maker* in Gen 14:22 and *created* here. The BV has *possessor* in Gen 14:22 and *made* here. Albright holds that Ugaritic similarities with Proverbs 8 and 9 are striking, and argues for "create" on that basis (*op. cit.,* p. 7). The deeper question is, What function is here ascribed to wisdom? It seems clear that she is pictured as eternal —having existed even before God created the world. She was not active in creation, but was with God while he created. If wisdom is personified righteousness, then the eternal nature of God is righteous. **The Lord possessed me** simply means, "I was the Lord's." The verbal similarity to John 1:1 has led many to think of an adumbration of Christ. We should compare with Proverbs 8 the teaching of Ecclesiasticus 24, coming from about 180 B.C., and the Wisdom of Solomon 7. Ecclesiasticus is high in his praise of wisdom, but makes her to reside in Israel and equates her with Moses' law. The Wisdom of Solomon also appears to be an extravagant development from the teaching of Proverbs. There seems to be no clear indication that we should find Christ revealed in Proverbs 8. Nor need we be troubled about the translation, *The Lord created me.* Delitzsch remarks, "Wisdom is not God, but is God's; she . . . is not herself the Logos."

23. From everlasting. In several expressions wisdom is said to be eternal: "at the beginning of his way" (v. 22); "when there were no seas" (v. 24); "before the mountains were founded" (v. 25); i.e., before anything was created, there was wisdom. True, wisdom is said to be **brought forth** in this beginning (v. 24). But as this is highly figurative language,

there is no reason why verse 22 cannot also, in figurative language, refer to wisdom's creation. It is a poetic declaration of the eternity of wisdom. See Delitzsch for the Nicene interpretations.

24. No depths. Toy makes much of the Hebrews' conception of the world as suggested in 8:24-29. He claims that the Hebrews, like the Babylonians, thought

NOTES

27 When he prepared the heavens, I *was* there: when he set a compass upon the face of the depth: 28 When he established the clouds above: when he strengthened the fountains of the deep: 29 When he gave to the sea his decree, that the waters should not pass his commandment: when he appointed the foundations of the earth: 30 Then I was by him, *as* one brought up *with him:* and I was daily *his* delight, rejoicing always before him; 31 Rejoicing in the habitable part of his earth; and my delights *were* with the sons of men. 32 Now therefore hearken unto me, O ye children: for blessed *are they that* keep my ways.

33 Hear instruction, and be wise, and refuse it not. 34 Blessed *is* the man that heareth me, watching daily at my gates, waiting at the posts of my doors. 35 For whoso findeth me findeth life, and shall obtain favour of the Lord. 36 But he that sinneth against me wrongeth his own soul: all they that hate me love death.

27,28,29 "I was there when he established the heavens and formed the great springs in the depths of the oceans. I was there when he set the limits of the seas and gave them his instructions not to spread beyond their boundaries. I was there when he made the blueprint for the earth and oceans. 30 I was always at his side like a little child. I was his constant delight, laughing and playing in his presence. 31 And how happy I was with what he created—his wide world and all his family of mankind! 32 And so, young men, listen to me, for how happy are all who follow my instructions.

33 "Listen to my counsel—oh, don't refuse it—and be wise. 34 Happy is the man who is so anxious to be with me that he watches for me daily at my gates, or waits for me outside my home! 35 For whoever finds me finds life and wins approval from the Lord. 36 But the one who misses me has injured himself irreparably. Those who refuse me show that they love death."

Finished
12/5/82

300

of a subterranean ocean (the **depths**)
from which springs arose and in which
the **foundations** of the earth were laid.
The sky was a solid dome supported on
pillars, and rain came through it when
the "windows of heaven" were opened
(Gen 7:11). All this is an imaginary
construction by modern authors who take
literally the poetic expressions of various
passages and, putting them together,
build a crude cosmology which the Bible
does not teach. Toy argues that the Hebrews believed rain came through these
windows when they were opened. He
forgets that windows in an ancient Hebrew house did not close as ours do but
were mere slits in the walls. To open a
window in a house likely meant to cut
out a window. Also, the "windows of
heaven" could let down barley and flour
(II Kgs 7:2) or other blessings (Mal
3:10). It is obviously a figurative expression which Toy has forced into a crude
literalism. Also the assertion that the Hebrews thought of subterranean waters is
quite incorrect. The word here used
for "depths," *tᵉhôm*, is many times used
simply of the sea where Jonah sank (Jon
2:5), or where ships are tossed (Ps
107:26). Also the "waters under the
earth," of the second commandment, can
not be some unseen subterranean ocean.
They are simply the water below shore
line. As the Hebrews were forbidden to
make images of birds and stars in the
sky or animals on land, so they were forbidden to make images of anything in the
waters under the earth, i.e., fish living
in seas, lakes, and rivers (cf. Deut 4:18).
The Bible speaks of no subterranean
waters, and the assumed Hebrew cosmology of modern writers is mostly fic-
tion.

27. Set a compass. That is, marked out
the circle of the horizon (cf. 26:10;
22:14; Isa 40:22). These verses probably
all refer to the circle of the horizon.
The use of this phrase should teach
us that the other expressions, "the four
corners of the earth," the "ends of the
earth," were not meant to imply that the
earth is square.

30. One brought up. This Hebrew
word is used only here and in Jer 52:15.
The LXX says: *I was arranging.* The
meaning *master workman* (RSV and
Berkeley) may be the best. It is based
on a tablet found at Taanach which has
the root as "wizard," or "craftsman" (W.
F. Albright, "A Prince of Taanach in the
Fifteenth Century," BASOR, No. 94,
(April, 1944), p. 18).

CHAPTER 9

WISDOM hath builded her house, she hath hewn out her seven pillars: ² She hath killed her beasts; she hath mingled her wine; she hath also furnished her table. ³ She hath sent forth her maidens: she crieth upon the highest places of the city, ⁴ Whoso *is* simple, let him turn in hither: *as for* him that wanteth understanding, she saith to him, ⁵ Come, eat of my bread, and drink of the wine *which* I have mingled. ⁶ Forsake the foolish, and live; and go in the way of understanding.

⁷ He that reproveth a scorner getteth to himself shame: and he that rebuketh a wicked *man getteth* himself a blot. ⁸ Reprove not a scorner, lest he hate thee: rebuke a wise man, and he will love thee. ⁹ Give *instruction* to a wise *man,* and he will be yet wiser: teach a just *man,* and he will increase in learning. ¹⁰ The fear of the Lord *is* the beginning of wisdom: and the knowledge of the holy *is* understanding. ¹¹ For by me thy days shall be multiplied, and the years of thy life shall be increased. ¹² If thou be wise, thou shalt be wise for thyself: but *if* thou scornest, thou alone shalt bear *it.*

¹³ A foolish woman *is* clamorous: *she is* simple, and knoweth nothing. ¹⁴ For she sitteth at the door of her house, on a seat in the high places of the city, ¹⁵ To call passengers who go right on their ways: ¹⁶ Whoso *is* simple, let him turn in hither: and *as for* him that wanteth understanding, she saith to him, ¹⁷ Stolen waters are sweet, and bread *eaten* in secret is pleasant. ¹⁸ But he knoweth not that the dead *are* there; *and that* her guests *are* in the depths of hell.

9 WISDOM HAS BUILT a palace supported on seven pillars, ² and has prepared a great banquet, and mixed the wines, ³ and sent out her maidens inviting all to come. She calls from the busiest intersections in the city, ⁴ "Come, you simple ones without good judgment; ⁵ come to wisdom's banquet and drink the wines that I have mixed. ⁶ Leave behind your foolishness and begin to live; learn how to be wise."

⁷,⁸ If you rebuke a mocker, you will only get a smart retort; yes, he will snarl at you. So don't bother with him; he will only hate you for trying to help him. But a wise man, when rebuked, will love you all the more. ⁹ Teach a wise man, and he will be the wiser; teach a good man, and he will learn more. ¹⁰ *For the reverence and fear of God are basic to all wisdom. Knowing God results in every other kind of understanding.* ¹¹ "I, Wisdom, will make the hours of your day more profitable and the years of your life more fruitful." ¹² Wisdom is its own reward, and if you scorn her, you hurt only yourself.

¹³ A prostitute is loud and brash, and never has enough of lust and shame. ¹⁴ She sits at the door of her house or stands at the street corners of the city, ¹⁵ whispering to men going by, and to those minding their own business. ¹⁶ "Come home with me," she urges simpletons. ¹⁷ "Stolen melons are the sweetest; stolen apples taste the best!" ¹⁸ But they don't realize that her former guests are now citizens of hell.

9:1. Wisdom. Here, as in Prov 1:20, the noun is feminine plural, yet used with a feminine singular verb. This usage is well attested from Ugaritic grammar, as Albright has pointed out ("Some Canaanite—Phoenician Sources of Hebrew Wisdom," *Wisdom in Israel and the Ancient Near East,* ed. by M. Noth and D. W. Thomas, p. 9). **Seven pillars.** This has been variously interpreted as a feature of architecture, the liberal arts, seven sacraments, etc. (see Toy). It was even used by T. E. Lawrence as the (irrelevant) title of his book on the Arabian campaign in World War I! Probably it is a round number of perfection, suggesting that Wisdom is fully prepared to satisfy. **2. Mingled her wine.** Just what practice is meant is not clear. The Greeks mingled wine with water in a bowl called a *kratēr,* and the LXX translates, *she has mingled her wine in a bowl.* Revelation 14:10 declares that the wicked will drink the wine of God's wrath unmixed, i.e., undiluted. The apocryphal book II Maccabees 15:39 declares that wine undiluted with water was thought distasteful. The rabbis held that the Passover wine should be diluted with three parts of water (Art. "wine," ISBE; The Mishnah, Berakoth 7:5). Obviously, not all the wine of antiquity was thus diluted or it would all have been nonintoxicating. Wine was also mixed with spices (Isa 5:22). Wisdom's wine is at all events symbolic. **5. Come, eat.** The blessed call often appears as an invitation to a banquet; cf. Isa 55:1; Jn 6:35; Rev 22:17. **Of.** This is a good example of the Ugaritic usage of the preposition *b,* meaning "from" (Story, *op. cit.,* p. 329).

7. A scorner. See notes on 1:22 and 3:34. Here **scorner** parallels "sinner." **8. Reprove not a scorner.** The negative is comparative. It does not treat some men as incorrigible (as Toy), but warns of the rebuff to be expected from a sinner. See 8:10 for another comparative negative. **10. Fear of the Lord.** See comments on 1:7. **The holy.** Better, *the Holy One* (RSV) or *Most Holy* (Berkeley). The noun is plural, but is evidently a plural of majesty (see above, 9:1) and is parallel with **Lord.**

13. Foolish. The feminine abstract form of the noun "fool," which is frequent in Proverbs for the folly of sin (see comments on 8:5). **Clamorous.** See also 7:11, where the word occurs in a similar context. It means "loud," probably with immoral overtones. **18. The dead.** Not the *shades* (RSV) or *ghosts* (BV). The Hebrew word is simply a poetic parallel for the dead. See comments on 2:18. On the whole picture of the harlot, see 7:5-27; 5:3-13, etc. Here the major contrast of wisdom versus sin in the first portion of the book finds its conclusion.

NOTES

CHAPTER 10

THE proverbs of Solomon. A wise son maketh a glad father: but a foolish son *is* the heaviness of his mother.

2 Treasures of wickedness profit nothing: but righteousness delivereth from death.

3 The Lord will not suffer the soul of the righteous to famish: but he casteth away the substance of the wicked.

4 He becometh poor that dealeth *with* a slack hand: but the hand of the diligent maketh rich.

These are the proverbs of Solomon:

10 HAPPY IS THE man with a level-headed son; sad the mother of a rebel.

2 Ill-gotten gain brings no lasting happiness; right living does.

3 The Lord will not let a good man starve to death, nor will he let the wicked man's riches continue forever.

4 Lazy men are soon poor; hard workers get rich.

II. Miscellaneous Proverbs of Solomon. 10:1–22:16.

It is our contention that in Proverbs the inspired Word of God is given in a special literary form. Just as David used the vehicle of poetry, so Solomon used the vehicle of Wisdom literature, which teaches largely by contrast. In the first major section (I) the contrast is maintained throughout long passages—e.g., the evil woman is set over against wisdom. In Section II the contrast is expressed in short one-verse units. The great majority of verses in this section have a "but" in the middle of the verse.

The exposition is made more difficult by the isolated nature of these proverbs. There is no immediate context to guide us. Some commentators have concluded that the proverbs follow no plan, but are a motley collection (Greenstone). Toy calls them "detached aphorisms." Delitzsch declares that there is a grouping according to thought, not in a comprehensive plan, but in a "progressive unfolding" that "continuously wells forth." There is a kind of unity in this section, but it comes rather from the language and subject than from the arrangement. A proverb is annunciated, then repeated elsewhere with variations which add to the meaning. The first instance may contrast parts *a* and *b*; the second, *a* and *c*. Even a third may occur, comparing *a* with *d*. Putting all three instances together, we get a fuller definition of the thought expressed in *a*. We would feel it easier if these thoughts were grouped together. The ancients evidently found it more interesting to have these thoughts separated and somewhat concealed. Also, as we have seen, there is a certain unity in the moral vocabulary used. So, many proverbs concern the righteous, the wise, the upright versus the cruel, the foolish, the perverse. Adequate study of one verse may involve concordance study of the whole book—but better, not mere mechanical concordance study so much as a thoughtful musing over the whole outlook of the author. For by repetition, contrast, distinctive vocabulary, and varied consideration of the theme, God, through this author, teaches us that righteousness exalteth anyone, but sin is always a reproach. Again we must insist that this is not a *Poor Richard's Almanac* of pithy, common sense sayings bearing on life's problems; this is a divine collection of sayings pointing out the way of holiness.

A. Contrasting Proverbs. 10:1–15:33.

10:1. The proverbs of Solomon. See Introduction, *Authorship*. A wise son. This phrase is used again in 13:1; 15:20. In the latter, 20a is identical with 10:1a. The contrast in 13:1 is with a "scorner" (see comments on 1:22). In 15:20 the contrast is with a "fool" (see notes on 8:5). **2. Treasures of wickedness,** i.e., ill-gotten gain. Verse 10:2 b parallels 11:4 b. **3. Soul of the righteous.** Here, as often, soul is used for the whole person (cf. Ps 37:3,25). **4. A slack hand.** At first sight, in the English translations, this appears to be merely a recommendation of thrift. But the word **slack** usually means *deceitful*. The difficulty is that its root, *rāmâ*, may mean either "deceive" or "grow loose," though the latter meaning is not well attested. We find the contrast with "diligent" at 12:24 and 12:27. "Slack" is paralleled with "sluggard" in 19:15, which is contrasted with "diligent" in 13:4. "Sluggard" has moral connotations, as we have shown at 6:6. We may therefore conclude that 10:4 means, "The one working with a deceitful hand becomes poor; but the upright hand makes

NOTES

305

⁵ He that gathereth in summer *is* a wise son: *but* he that sleepeth in harvest *is* a son that causeth shame.

⁶ Blessings *are* upon the head of the just: but violence covereth the mouth of the wicked.

⁷ The memory of the just *is* blessed: but the name of the wicked shall rot.

⁸ The wise in heart will receive commandments: but a prating fool shall fall.

⁹ He that walketh uprightly walketh surely: but he that perverteth his ways shall be known.

¹⁰ He that winketh with the eye causeth sorrow: but a prating fool shall fall.

¹¹ The mouth of a righteous *man is* a well of life: but violence covereth the mouth of the wicked.

¹² Hatred stirreth up strifes: but love covereth all sins.

¹³ In the lips of him that hath understanding wisdom is found: but a rod *is* for the back of him that is void of understanding.

¹⁴ Wise *men* lay up knowledge: but the mouth of the foolish *is* near destruction.

¹⁵ The rich man's wealth *is* his strong city: the destruction of the poor *is* their poverty.

¹⁶ The labour of the righteous *tendeth* to life: the fruit of the wicked to sin.

¹⁷ He *is in* the way of life that keepeth instruction: but he that refuseth reproof erreth.

¹⁸ He that hideth hatred *with* lying lips, and he that uttereth a slander, *is* a fool.

¹⁹ In the multitude of words there wanteth not sin: but he that refraineth his lips *is* wise.

²⁰ The tongue of the just *is as* choice silver: the heart of the wicked *is* little worth.

²¹ The lips of the righteous feed many: but fools die for want of wisdom.

²² The blessing of the Lord, it maketh rich, and he addeth no sorrow with it.

²³ *It is* as sport to a fool to do mischief: but a man of understanding hath wisdom.

²⁴ The fear of the wicked, it shall come upon him: but the desire of the righteous shall be granted.

⁵ A wise youth makes hay while the sun shines, but what a shame to see a lad who sleeps away his hour of opportunity.

⁶ The good man is covered with blessings from head to foot, but an evil man inwardly curses his luck.

⁷ We all have happy memories of good men gone to their reward, but the names of wicked men stink after them.

⁸ The wise man is glad to be instructed, but a self-sufficient fool falls flat on his face.

⁹ A good man has firm footing, but a crook will slip and fall.

¹⁰ Winking at sin leads to sorrow; bold reproof leads to peace.

¹¹ There is living truth in what a good man says, but the mouth of the evil man is filled with curses.

¹² Hatred stirs old quarrels, but love overlooks insults.

¹³ Men with common sense are admired as counselors; those without it are beaten as servants.

¹⁴ A wise man holds his tongue. Only a fool blurts out everything he knows; that only leads to sorrow and trouble.

¹⁵ The rich man's wealth is his only strength. The poor man's poverty is his only curse.

¹⁶ The good man's earnings advance the cause of righteousness. The evil man squanders his on sin.

¹⁷ Anyone willing to be corrected is on the pathway to life. Anyone refusing has lost his chance.

¹⁸ To hate is to be a liar; to slander is to be a fool.

¹⁹ Don't talk so much. You keep putting your foot in your mouth. Be sensible and turn off the flow!

²⁰ When a good man speaks, he is worth listening to, but the words of fools are a dime a dozen.

²¹ A godly man gives good advice, but a rebel is destroyed by lack of common sense.

²² The Lord's blessing is our greatest wealth. All our work adds nothing to it!

²³ A fool's fun is being bad; a wise man's fun is being wise!

²⁴ The wicked man's fears will all come true, and so will the good man's hopes.

rich." **5. A wise son.** In the English translations this is a proverb opposing laziness. Toy, however, remarks that the verse could as well be reversed—"A wise son gathers in summer," etc. This is the order of the Greek. According to this view, we have here one characteristic of a good man—he is provident—rather than a suggestion that to be provident makes one good!

6. Violence covereth. It is better to turn the phrase around, as do the RSV and the Berkeley. The contrast is better seen in 10:11, where 11 b is identical with 6 b: the mouth of the wicked "conceals violence." **7. The memory of the just is blessed.** This phrase is famous as being used by Jews after mentioning a good man deceased. It is a Hebrew *requiescat in pace,* usually abbreviated to *z s l (zēker saddiq libᵉrākâ).* **8. A prating fool.** The word **fool** ("always morally bad," BDB) and its feminine parallel,"foolishness," are used fifty times in the OT, and forty-one of these occurrences of *'ĕwîl* are in Proverbs. The translation **fool** is misleading in modern English. Some such word as "rascal" would be better. Verse 8 b is repeated in 10 b.

10. Winketh. See comments on 6:13. **11. Violence.** See Verse 6. **12. Love covereth.** Observe the connection between this verse and 17:9; 16:28. In 17:9 the opposite of the man who covers a transgression is the man who magnifies another's fault. Such a man in 16:28 "soweth strife." To stir up strife is the characteristic of hate in 10:12. There are verbal similarities between this passage and 6:14-19, which see. Obviously the meaning here, and in the allusions in I Pet 4:8 and Jas 5:20, is not that if we love others, our love will atone for our sins; but if we truly love others, we will minimize their faults.

14. The fool is near destruction. Jones and Walls nicely remark that **destruction** in this proverb furnishes a catchword for the next verse. Often this happens, and the catchword offers a connection between the proverbs that is totally missed in English. **15. The rich.** This verse alone would be misleading. Neither riches nor poverty is a sacrament in Proverbs. Comparison with 18:11 shows that the rich man *thinks* in his own conceit (or imagination) that his riches are his strength. **19. Multitude of words.** Probably verses 18-21 go together, as 20 and 21 show that it is not loquacity that is condemned, but evil speech.

23. Fool. The remainder of the chapter gives a series of terse contrasts between the wicked and the godly. **Mischief.** Only three places in the AV is *zimmâ* so translated. Elsewhere it is "wickedness," "lewdness," "crime." A

NOTES

²⁵ As the whirlwind passeth, so *is* the wicked no *more:* but the righteous *is* an everlasting foundation.

²⁶ As vinegar to the teeth, and as smoke to the eyes, so *is* the sluggard to them that send him.

²⁷ The fear of the Lord prolongeth days: but the years of the wicked shall be shortened.

²⁸ The hope of the righteous *shall be* gladness: but the expectation of the wicked shall perish.

²⁹ The way of the Lord *is* strength to the upright: but destruction *shall be* to the workers of iniquity.

³⁰ The righteous shall never be removed: but the wicked shall not inhabit the earth.

³¹ The mouth of the just bringeth forth wisdom: but the froward tongue shall be cut out.

³² The lips of the righteous know what is acceptable: but the mouth of the wicked *speaketh* frowardness.

²⁵ Disaster strikes like a cyclone and the wicked are whirled away. But the good man has a strong anchor.

²⁶ A lazy fellow is a pain to his employers—like smoke in their eyes or vinegar that sets the teeth on edge.

²⁷ Reverence for God adds hours to each day; so how can the wicked expect a long, good life?

²⁸ The hope of good men is eternal happiness; the hopes of evil men are all in vain.

²⁹ God protects the upright but destroys the wicked.

³⁰ The good shall never lose God's blessings, but the wicked shall lose everything.

³¹ The good man gives wise advice, but the liar's counsel is shunned.

³² The upright speak what is helpful; the wicked speak rebellion.

CHAPTER 11

A FALSE balance *is* abomination to the Lord: but a just weight *is* his delight.

² *When* pride cometh, then cometh shame: but with the lowly *is* wisdom.

³ The integrity of the upright shall guide them: but the perverseness of transgressors shall destroy them.

⁴ Riches profit not in the day of wrath: but righteousness delivereth from death.

⁵ The righteousness of the perfect shall direct his way: but the wicked shall fall by his own wickedness.

⁶ The righteousness of the upright shall deliver them: but transgressors shall be taken in *their own* naughtiness.

⁷ When a wicked man dieth, *his* expectation shall perish: and the hope of unjust *men* perisheth.

⁸ The righteous is delivered out of trouble, and the wicked cometh in his stead.

⁹ An hypocrite with *his* mouth destroyeth his neighbour: but through knowledge shall the just be delivered.

¹⁰ When it goeth well with the righteous, the city rejoiceth: and when the wicked perish, *there is* shouting.

11 THE LORD HATES cheating and delights in honesty.

² Proud men end in shame, but the meek become wise.

³ A good man is guided by his honesty; the evil man is destroyed by his dishonesty.

⁴ Your riches won't help you on Judgment Day; only righteousness counts then.

⁵ The upright are directed by their honesty; the wicked shall fall beneath their load of sins.

⁶ The good man's goodness delivers him; the evil man's treachery is his undoing.

⁷ When an evil man dies, his hopes all perish, for they are based upon this earthly life.

⁸ God rescues good men from danger while letting the wicked fall into it.

⁹ Evil words destroy. Godly skill rebuilds.

¹⁰ The whole city celebrates a good man's success—and also the godless man's death.

rascal thinks sin is fun. **31. Froward.** Here and in verse 32 *perverse* is better.

11:1. A false balance. The same thought is in 16:11. In 20:10 differing weights and measures are called an "abomination to the Lord," and in 20:23 a "false balance" is again condemned. There were various methods of commercial thievery. One was to have a falsely graduated balance. Another was to have shekel weights of varying weight to be used in buying or selling to one's own advantage. These were the "diverse weights." **A just weight.** Hebrew, *a perfect stone.* Stones were used for weights, and it was all too easy to grind them off or chip them down. The law of Moses forbade all such dishonesty (Lev 19:36; Deut 25:15; cf. Ezk 45:10; Amos 8:5, *et al.*). Our governments today have bureaus of weights and measures to maintain standards. In the theocracy of Israel, establishing of such standards fell often to the priests. Therefore we find references to the "shekel of the sanctuary" (Ex 38:26). Weights were especially important, for in the absence of coinage in the early days, silver and gold were weighed for payments. Many shekel weights have been discovered. They average about 11.4 grams for the normal shekel (R. B. Y. Scott, "Weights and Measures of the Bible," BA, XXII (1959), 32-40).

2. Pride. In the Hebrew there is alliteration between **pride,** *zādôn,* and **shame,** *qālôn.* **7. The expectation of the wicked.** Verse 7a is parallel to 10:28b. See also 11:23. In Job the term *expectation* (AV, *hope,* Job 14:7) is used of the afterlife (cf. Job 14:7-15). If the wicked man has no hope after death, if his expectation is wrath, whereas the expectation of the righteous is joy, then the author here by faith looks beyond the grave as did Job, David, Daniel, and others.

NOTES

11 By the blessing of the upright the city is exalted: but it is overthrown by the mouth of the wicked.

12 He that is void of wisdom despiseth his neighbour: but a man of understanding holdeth his peace.

13 A talebearer revealeth secrets: but he that is of a faithful spirit concealeth the matter.

14 Where no counsel *is,* the people fall: but in the multitude of counsellors *there is* safety.

15 He that is surety for a stranger shall smart *for it:* and he that hateth suretiship is sure.

16 A gracious woman retaineth honour: and strong *men* retain riches.

17 The merciful man doeth good to his own soul: but *he that is* cruel troubleth his own flesh.

18 The wicked worketh a deceitful work: but to him that soweth righteousness *shall be* a sure reward.

19 As righteousness *tendeth* to life: so he that pursueth evil *pursueth it* to his own death.

20 They that are of a froward heart *are* abomination to the Lord: but *such as are* upright in *their* way *are* his delight.

21 *Though* hand *join* in hand, the wicked shall not be unpunished: but the seed of the righteous shall be delivered.

22 *As* a jewel of gold in a swine's snout, *so is* a fair woman which is without discretion.

23 The desire of the righteous *is* only good: *but* the expectation of the wicked *is* wrath.

24 There is that scattereth, and yet increaseth; and *there is* that withholdeth more than is meet, but *it tendeth* to poverty. 25 The liberal soul shall be made fat: and he that watereth shall be watered also himself.

26 He that withholdeth corn, the people shall curse him: but blessing *shall be* upon the head of him that selleth *it.*

27 He that diligently seeketh good procureth favour: but he that seeketh mischief, it shall come unto him.

28 He that trusteth in his riches shall fall; but the righteous shall flourish as a branch.

29 He that troubleth his own house shall inherit the wind: and the fool *shall be* servant to the wise of heart.

11 The good influence of godly citizens causes a city to prosper, but the moral decay of the wicked drives it downhill.

12 To quarrel with a neighbor is foolish; a man with good sense holds his tongue.

13 A gossip goes around spreading rumors, while a trustworthy man tries to quiet them.

14 Without wise leadership, a nation is in trouble; but with good counselors there is safety.

15 Be sure you know a person well before you vouch for his credit! Better refuse than suffer later.

16 Honor goes to kind and gracious women, mere money to cruel men.

17 Your own soul is nourished when you are kind; it is destroyed when you are cruel.

18 The evil man gets rich for the moment, but the good man's reward lasts forever.

19 The good man finds life; the evil man, death.

20 The Lord hates the stubborn but delights in those who are good.

21 You can be very sure that the evil man will not go unpunished forever. And you can also be very sure that God will rescue the children of the godly.

22 A beautiful woman lacking discretion and modesty is like a fine gold ring in a pig's snout.

23 The good man can look forward to happiness, while the wicked can expect only wrath.

24,25 It is possible to give away and become richer! It is also possible to hold on too tightly and lose everything. Yes, the liberal man shall be rich! By watering others, he waters himself.

26 People curse the man who holds his grain for higher prices, but they bless the man who sells it to them in their time of need.

27 If you search for good you will find God's favor; if you search for evil you will find his curse.

28 Trust in your money and down you go! Trust in God and flourish as a tree!

29 The fool who provokes his family to anger and resentment will finally have nothing worthwhile left. He shall be the servant of a wiser man.

13. A talebearer. Hebrew, *rākîl*, "slanderer." The statement in 13 a parallels that in 20:19a, which see. **Concealeth.** See also 10:12, where the same word is used. **14. Multitude of counsellors.** Cf. 24:6 for the same expression. **15. Surety.** See comments on 6:1.

16. A gracious woman. Not in the modern sense of gracious, i.e., cultured and kindly, but literally *a woman of grace.* Possibly verse 16 b is not a mere added statement, but a well-known comparison—"A gracious woman retaineth honor as surely as a ruthless man gets wealth." **17. The merciful man.** Probably a parallel to the "woman of grace" in verse 16. **His soul . . . his flesh;** i.e., himself. There is a reward to goodness. **18. Deceitful . . . reward.** An alliteration, *sheqer* versus *seker.* Such alliterations, catchwords, and repetitions are some of the style features of Proverbs that sometimes explain the order of the material, but are lost in translation. **20. Froward.** *Crooked.* **Upright.** *Perfect, complete* (morally).

22. Jewel of gold. The nose ring often worn by an Oriental woman. How incongruous in the nose of so unclean an animal! But not more so than a woman having beauty without character. **Discretion.** This is doubtless moral perception, as in Ps 119:66. The *good taste* of the Berkeley Version is far too colorless.

24. There is that scattereth. Verses 24-29 may be taken together as treating of liberality—"Give and it shall be given unto you again." This person gives from a heart of blessing (v. 25). The opposite hoards corn—and we may suppose there were many black marketeers in times of siege and famine—and gets a curse for a blessing. The error lies not in *having* riches but in *trusting* in them (v. 2).

25-31. The righteous will flourish (cf. Ps 1:3; 52:7,8; 92:12-14; Jer 17:8). This thought occurs frequently in Proverbs.

30 The fruit of the righteous *is* a tree of life; and he that winneth souls *is* wise.

31 Behold, the righteous shall be recompensed in the earth: much more the wicked and the sinner.

CHAPTER 12

WHOSO loveth instruction loveth knowledge: but he that hateth reproof *is* brutish.

2 A good *man* obtaineth favour of the Lord: but a man of wicked devices will he condemn.

3 A man shall not be established by wickedness: but the root of the righteous shall not be moved.

4 A virtuous woman *is* a crown to her husband: but she that maketh ashamed *is* as rottenness in his bones.

5 The thoughts of the righteous *are* right: *but* the counsels of the wicked *are* deceit.

6 The words of the wicked *are* to lie in wait for blood: but the mouth of the upright shall deliver them.

7 The wicked are overthrown, and *are* not: but the house of the righteous shall stand.

8 A man shall be commended according to his wisdom: but he that is of a perverse heart shall be despised.

9 *He that is* despised, and hath a servant, *is* better than he that honoureth himself, and lacketh bread.

10 A righteous *man* regardeth the life of his beast: but the tender mercies of the wicked *are* cruel.

11 He that tilleth his land shall be satisfied with bread: but he that followeth vain *persons is* void of understanding.

12 The wicked desireth the net of evil *men:* but the root of the righteous yieldeth *fruit.*

13 The wicked is snared by the transgression of *his* lips: but the just shall come out of trouble.

14 A man shall be satisfied with good by the fruit of *his* mouth: and the recompence of a man's hands shall be rendered unto him.

15 The way of a fool *is* right in his own eyes: but he that hearkeneth unto counsel *is* wise.

30 Godly men are growing a tree that bears life-giving fruit, and all who win souls are wise.

31 Even the godly shall be rewarded here on earth; how much more the wicked!

12 TO LEARN, YOU must want to be taught. To refuse reproof is stupid.

2 The Lord blesses good men and condemns the wicked.

3 Wickedness never brings real success; only the godly have that.

4 A worthy wife is her husband's joy and crown; the other kind corrodes his strength and tears down everything he does.

5 A good man's mind is filled with honest thoughts; an evil man's mind is crammed with lies.

6 The wicked accuse; the godly defend.

7 The wicked shall perish; the godly shall stand.

8 Everyone admires a man with good sense, but a man with a warped mind is despised.

9 It is better to get your hands dirty —and eat, than to be too proud to work —and starve.

10 A good man is concerned for the welfare of his animals, but even the kindness of godless men is cruel.

11 Hard work means prosperity; only a fool idles away his time.

12 Crooks are jealous of each other's loot, while good men long to help each other.

13 Lies will get any man into trouble, but honesty is its own defense.

14 Telling the truth gives a man great satisfaction, and hard work returns many blessings to him.

15 A fool thinks he needs no advice, but a wise man listens to others.

30. Tree of life. See comment on 3:18.
Winneth souls. The idiom is not clear.
Literally it is, *the one who takes souls*
(persons) *is wise.* Some interpret, "the wise
man wins friends" (Berkeley). Fritsch
says *take* means "to destroy." The RSV
gives an unnecessary conjecture that law-
lessness takes many lives (changing
hākām to *hāmās).* Delitzsch supports the
AV, which is satisfactory, though it may
include more than fishing for men. **31.**
The righteous. The LXX interprets it that
the righteous will be punished for their
sin; much more the wicked. This is quoted verbatim in I Pet 4:18. However,
the Hebrew can also be understood to
mean that the righteous will get a blessing, while the wicked will receive judgment. The Syriac agrees with the LXX,
and this interpretation can be accepted.
   12:4. Virtuous woman. The phrase is
used again in 31:10. The word *hayil,*
when relating to men, especially soldiers,
means "strength." Referring to a wife, it
designates the womanly virtues, perhaps
"nobility." Proverbs 11:16 speaks of a
woman of *grace;* 19:14 refers to a *wise*
woman. All of these terms in the context
of Proverbs speak of a *good* woman under various aspects. **8. Wisdom.** The word
sēkel is here contrasted with a "perverse"
or "twisted" heart. Elsewhere it is contrasted with "deceiving" (13:15), "sinful
folly" (16:22; 23:9). Delitzsch, Toy, and
others seem quite wrong in calling it
only "intelligence." Moral wisdom or
goodness surely is intended.
   11. Vain persons. This proverb is repeated almost verbatim in 28:19. The
RSV, Berkeley, and Delitzsch translate
as *vain pursuits.* But the word is not so
used elsewhere. In Jud 9:4; 11:3; II Sam
6:20 it refers to vain persons, rascals.
The LXX says *vanities,* perhaps referring
to idols. **12. Net of evil.** The word **net** is
difficult. The LXX omits it. The Syriac
translates it, *to do evil.* It can mean
strong tower (RSV), hardly *booty* (Berkeley). The root is *to hunt.* Possibly the
Syriac gives a clue for a helpful reading
—"the desire of the wicked is to hunt

NOTES

¹⁶ A fool's wrath is presently known: but a prudent *man* covereth shame.

¹⁷ *He that* speaketh truth sheweth forth righteousness: but a false witness deceit.

¹⁸ There is that speaketh like the piercings of a sword: but the tongue of the wise *is* health.

¹⁹ The lip of truth shall be established for ever: but a lying tongue *is* but for a moment.

²⁰ Deceit *is* in the heart of them that imagine evil: but to the counsellors of peace *is* joy.

²¹ There shall no evil happen to the just: but the wicked shall be filled with mischief.

²² Lying lips *are* abomination to the Lord: but they that deal truly *are* his delight.

²³ A prudent man concealeth knowledge: but the heart of fools proclaimeth foolishness.

²⁴ The hand of the diligent shall bear rule: but the slothful shall be under tribute.

²⁵ Heaviness in the heart of man maketh it stoop: but a good word maketh it glad.

²⁶ The righteous *is* more excellent than his neighbour: but the way of the wicked seduceth them.

²⁷ The slothful *man* roasteth not that which he took in hunting: but the substance of a diligent man *is* precious.

²⁸ In the way of righteousness *is* life: and *in* the pathway *thereof there is* no death.

¹⁶ A fool is quick-tempered; a wise man stays cool when insulted.

¹⁷ A good man is known by his truthfulness; a false man by deceit and lies.

¹⁸ Some people like to make cutting remarks, but the words of the wise soothe and heal.

¹⁹ Truth stands the test of time; lies are soon exposed.

²⁰ Deceit fills hearts that are plotting for evil; joy fills hearts that are planning for good!

²¹ No real harm befalls the good, but there is constant trouble for the wicked.

²² God delights in those who keep their promises, and abhors those who don't.

²³ A wise man doesn't display his knowledge, but a fool displays his foolishness.

²⁴ Work hard and become a leader; be lazy and never succeed.

²⁵ Anxious hearts are very heavy but a word of encouragement does wonders!

²⁶ The good man asks advice from friends; the wicked plunge ahead—and fall.

²⁷ A lazy man won't even dress the game he gets while hunting, but the diligent man makes good use of everything he finds.

²⁸ The path of the godly leads to life. So why fear death?

CHAPTER 13

A WISE son *heareth* his father's instruction: but a scorner heareth not rebuke.

² A man shall eat good by the fruit of *his* mouth: but the soul of the transgressors *shall eat* violence.

³ He that keepeth his mouth keepeth his life: *but* he that openeth wide his lips shall have destruction.

⁴ The soul of the sluggard desireth, and *hath* nothing: but the soul of the diligent shall be made fat.

⁵ A righteous *man* hateth lying: but a wicked *man* is loathsome, and cometh to shame.

13 A WISE YOUTH accepts his father's rebuke; a young mocker doesn't.

² The good man wins his case by careful argument; the evil-minded only wants to fight.

³ Self-control means controlling the tongue! A quick retort can ruin everything.

⁴ Lazy people want much but get little, while the diligent are prospering.

⁵ A good man hates lies; wicked men lie constantly and come to shame.

evil, taking it in an Aramaic form. **18. There is that speaketh.** Several proverbs begin with this special construction, "There is that . . . " Verses 18-23 have to do with evil speech.

28. No death. Not the usual negative for this Hebrew construction, but it is used similarly in 31:4. The LXX and Syriac make 28 b a contrast to 28 a, "the ways of the wicked are unto death," which is adopted by the RSV, Fritsch, Toy, and others. The reading of the AV, the BV, Delitzsch, Greenstone, and others refers the verse to immortality. But the note in Berkeley that there are "few assertions of immortality in the Old Testament" is unfortunate. Many positive references to resurrection and the future life exist in the Psalms and Prophets, though most are debated by 'liberal' scholars. Cf. Job 19:25-27; Ps 16:10; 17:15; Isa 25:8; 26:19; Ezk 37:10; Dan 12:2; and others.

13:1. A wise son. See comments on 10:1. The verb "heareth" is to be supplied in the first half as in the AV, the LXX, and the Syriac. **4. The soul of the sluggard. Soul** simply means the individual, the sluggard himself. On **sluggard** as a moral term, see notes on 6:6.

NOTES

315

6 Righteousness keepeth *him that is* upright in the way: but wickedness overthroweth the sinner.

7 There is that maketh himself rich, yet *hath* nothing: *there is* that maketh himself poor, yet *hath* great riches.

8 The ransom of a man's life *are* his riches· but the poor heareth not rebuke.

9 The light of the righteous rejoiceth: but the lamp of the wicked shall be put out.

10 Only by pride cometh contention: but with the well advised *is* wisdom.

11 Wealth *gotten* by vanity shall be diminished: but he that gathereth by labour shall increase.

12 Hope deferred maketh the heart sick: but *when* the desire cometh, *it is* a tree of life.

13 Whoso despiseth the word shall be destroyed: but he that feareth the commandment shall be rewarded.

14 The law of the wise *is* a fountain of life, to depart from the snares of death.

15 Good understanding giveth favour: but the way of transgressors *is* hard.

16 Every prudent *man* dealeth with knowledge: but a fool layeth open *his* folly.

17 A wicked messenger falleth into mischief: but a faithful ambassador *is* health.

18 Poverty and shame *shall be to* him that refuseth instruction: but he that regardeth reproof shall be honoured.

19 The desire accomplished is sweet to the soul: but *it is* abomination to fools to depart from evil.

20 He that walketh with wise *men* shall be wise: but a companion of fools shall be destroyed.

21 Evil pursueth sinners: but to the righteous good shall be repayed.

22 A good *man* leaveth an inheritance to his children's children: and the wealth of the sinner *is* laid up for the just.

23 Much food *is in* the tillage of the poor: but there is *that is* destroyed for want of judgment.

24 He that spareth his rod hateth his son: but he that loveth him chasteneth him betimes.

25 The righteous eateth to the satisfying of his soul: but the belly of the wicked shall want.

6 A man's goodness helps him all through life, while evil men are being destroyed by their wickedness.

7 Some rich people are poor, and some poor people have great wealth!

8 Being kidnapped and held for ransom never worries the poor man!

9 The good man's life is full of light. The sinner's road is dark and gloomy.

10 Pride leads to arguments; be humble, take advice and become wise.

11 Wealth from gambling quickly disappears; wealth from hard work grows.

12 Hope deferred makes the heart sick; but when dreams come true at last, there is life and joy.

13 Despise God's Word and find yourself in trouble. Obey it and succeed.

14 The advice of a wise man refreshes like water from a mountain spring. Those accepting it become aware of the pitfalls on ahead.

15 A man with good sense is appreciated. A treacherous man must walk a rocky road.

16 A wise man thinks ahead; a fool doesn't, and even brags about it!

17 An unreliable messenger can cause a lot of trouble. Reliable communication permits progress.

18 If you refuse criticism you will end in poverty and disgrace; if you accept criticism you are on the road to fame.

19 It is pleasant to see plans develop. That is why fools refuse to give them up even when they are wrong.

20 Be with wise men and become wise. Be with evil men and become evil.

21 Curses chase sinners, while blessings chase the righteous!

22 When a good man dies, he leaves an inheritance to his grandchildren; but when a sinner dies, his wealth is stored up for the godly.

23 A poor man's farm may have good soil, but injustice robs him of its riches.

24 If you refuse to discipline your son, it proves you don't love him; for if you love him you will be prompt to punish him.

25 The good man eats to live, while the evil man lives to eat.

8. Ransom . . . are his riches. The thought is that a rich man attacked or kidnapped can ransom himself. Under Hebrew law a man could not buy his freedom from judgment. **The poor heareth not rebuke.** Cf. 1 b, "The scorner heareth not rebuke." To "hear not rebuke" is characteristic of an evil man. Why say it about the poor? The LXX and Syriac follow the Hebrew. The RSV emends drastically. Possibly we should read *rāsh,* "poor," as *rō'sh,* "chief," and make it parallel to verse 8 a. The "chief" ("bigshot," as we say) hears no rebuke; he can always buy his way out of a tight spot. **9. The lamp of the wicked.** See also 20:20; 24:20; Job 18:5; 21:17. It was a popular metaphor. **12. Tree of life.** See comment on 3:18.

14. The law of the wise. The preceding verse mentions the "word" and the "commandment." **Law,** therefore, is the meaning here rather than *teaching* (RSV, Berkeley). This verse is like 14:27 with the "law of the wise" replaced by the "fear of the Lord." It is surely purposive that the author thus recurs to a similar thought with variations. **15. Good understanding giveth favour.** Very similar to 3:4. *Ḥēn,* **favour** and sēkel, **understanding,** are here so clearly moral terms, coming as the result of God's commandments, that it is difficult to see how Delitzsch can call *sēkel* "fine culture." The BV has, *Ideal understanding lends attractiveness.* The RSV speaks of *good sense.* These translations miss the meaning that contrasts goodness with transgression. **16. Prudent man.** Cf. 8:12. A wise man, an opposite to *kesîl,* "knave." **20. Companion of fools shall be destroyed.** A play on words. In the Hebrew, **companion** and **destroyed** are similar words.

24. Spareth his rod. On the rod of correction, see also 19:18; 22:15; 23:13, 14. "Spare the rod and spoil the child," has become a common saying. We should remember, however, that Proverbs does not recommend brutal beatings. Nor is physical chastisement the only instrument of child training mentioned (cf. 22:6). Indeed, instruction in righteousness and in the fear of the Lord is that without which mere whipping will fail.

NOTES

CHAPTER 14

EVERY wise woman buildeth her house: but the foolish plucketh it down with her hands.

2 He that walketh in his uprightness feareth the Lord: but *he that is* perverse in his ways despiseth him.

3 In the mouth of the foolish *is* a rod of pride: but the lips of the wise shall preserve them.

4 Where no oxen *are,* the crib *is* clean: but much increase *is* by the strength of the ox.

5 A faithful witness will not lie: but a false witness will utter lies.

6 A scorner seeketh wisdom, and *findeth it* not: but knowledge *is* easy unto him that understandeth.

7 Go from the presence of a foolish man, when thou perceivest not *in him* the lips of knowledge.

8 The wisdom of the prudent is to understand his way: but the folly of fools *is* deceit.

9 Fools make a mock at sin: but among the righteous *there is* favour.

10 The heart knoweth his own bitterness; and a stranger doth not intermeddle with his joy.

11 The house of the wicked shall be overthrown: but the tabernacle of the upright shall flourish.

12 There is a way which seemeth right unto a man, but the end thereof *are* the ways of death.

13 Even in laughter the heart is sorrowful; and the end of that mirth *is* heaviness.

14 The backslider in heart shall be filled with his own ways: and a good man *shall be satisfied* from himself.

15 The simple believeth every word: but the prudent *man* looketh well to his going.

16 A wise *man* feareth, and departeth from evil: but the fool rageth, and is confident.

17 *He that is* soon angry dealeth foolishly: and a man of wicked devices is hated.

18 The simple inherit folly: but the prudent are crowned with knowledge.

19 The evil bow before the good; and the wicked at the gates of the righteous.

20 The poor is hated even of his own neighbour: but the rich *hath* many friends.

14 A WISE WOMAN builds her house, while a foolish woman tears hers down by her own efforts.

2 To do right honors God; to sin is to despise him.

3 A rebel's foolish talk should prick his own pride! But the wise man's speech is respected.

4 An empty stable stays clean—but there is no income from an empty stable.

5 A truthful witness never lies; a false witness always lies.

6 A mocker never finds the wisdom he claims he is looking for, yet it comes easily to the man with common sense.

7 If you are looking for advice, stay away from fools.

8 The wise man looks ahead. The fool attempts to fool himself and won't face facts.

9 The common bond of rebels is their guilt. The common bond of godly people is good will.

10 Only the person involved can know his own bitterness or joy—no one else can really share it.

11 The work of the wicked will perish; the work of the godly will flourish.

12 Before every man there lies a wide and pleasant road that seems right but ends in death.

13 Laughter cannot mask a heavy heart. When the laughter ends, the grief remains.

14 The backslider gets bored with himself; the godly man's life is exciting.

15 Only a simpleton believes what he is told! A prudent man checks to see where he is going.

16 A wise man is cautious and avoids danger; a fool plunges ahead with great confidence.

17 A short-tempered man is a fool. He hates the man who is patient.

18 The simpleton is crowned with folly; the wise man is crowned with knowledge.

19 Evil men shall bow before the godly.

20 Even his own neighbors despise the poor man, while the rich have many "friends."

14:1. Every wise woman. Not quite the same wording as in 9:1, but here and in 14:2 the mention of the one "fearing the Lord" is doubtless a reference to the first section of the book, 1:I—9:18.

5. A false witness. Repeated with interesting variations in 19:5,9 and 21:28. The wording is close to that of the ninth commandment, but not identical with it.

9. Fools . . . mock at sin. The first half of this verse is difficult, largely because **mock** is used as a finite verb only six times in the OT. Its meaning is not clear. Close to 14:9 is 19:28—"An ungodly witness *mocks* at justice" (RSV). It seems that there is equal reason to translate here with the AV, **fools mock at sin. 12. A way which seemeth right.** This verse is repeated verbatim in 16:25. (On these repetitions cf. Introd., *Collections in Proverbs*). In this case, there is a catchword in verse 12, "its end," which ties it to verse 13. **13. Even in laughter.** Rather than understand this verse to show a pessimism not common in Proverbs, the verse can be joined to the preceding, and read—"The end of the way that seems right to a man is sorrowful and heavy."

20. The poor is despised of his neighbor. This verse does not merely state a common truth, much less approve it. The

NOTES

21 He that despiseth his neighbour sinneth: but he that hath mercy on the poor, happy *is* he.

22 Do they not err that devise evil? but mercy and truth *shall be* to them that devise good.

23 In all labour there is profit: but the talk of the lips *tendeth* only to penury.

24 The crown of the wise *is* their riches: *but* the foolishness of fools *is* folly.

25 A true witness delivereth souls: but a deceitful *witness* speaketh lies.

26 In the fear of the Lord *is* strong confidence: and his children shall have a place of refuge.

27 The fear of the Lord *is* a fountain of life, to depart from the snares of death.

28 In the multitude of people *is* the king's honour: but in the want of people *is* the destruction of the prince.

29 *He that is* slow to wrath *is* of great understanding: but *he that is* hasty of spirit exalteth folly.

30 A sound heart *is* the life of the flesh: but envy the rottenness of the bones.

31 He that oppresseth the poor reproacheth his Maker: but he that honoureth him hath mercy on the poor.

32 The wicked is driven away in his wickedness: but the righteous hath hope in his death.

33 Wisdom resteth in the heart of him that hath understanding: but *that which is* in the midst of fools is made known.

34 Righteousness exalteth a nation: but sin *is* a reproach to any people.

35 The king's favour *is* toward a wise servant: but his wrath *is against* him that causeth shame.

CHAPTER 15

A SOFT answer turneth away wrath: but grievous words stir up anger.

2 The tongue of the wise useth knowledge aright: but the mouth of fools poureth out foolishness.

3 The eyes of the Lord *are* in every place, beholding the evil and the good.

4 A wholesome tongue *is* a tree of life: but perverseness therein *is* a breach in the spirit.

21 To despise the poor is to sin. Blessed are those who pity them.

22 Those who plot evil shall wander away and be lost, but those who plan good shall be granted mercy and quietness.

23 Work brings profit; talk brings poverty!

24 Wise men are praised for their wisdom; fools are despised for their folly.

25 A witness who tells the truth saves good men from being sentenced to death, but a false witness is a traitor.

26 Reverence for God gives a man deep strength; his children have a place of refuge and security.

27 Reverence for the Lord is a fountain of life; its waters keep a man from death.

28 A growing population is a king's glory; a dwindling nation is his doom.

29 A wise man controls his temper. He knows that anger causes mistakes.

30 A relaxed attitude lengthens a man's life; jealousy rots it away.

31 Anyone who oppresses the poor is insulting God who made them. To help the poor is to honor God.

32 The godly have a refuge when they die, but the wicked are crushed by their sins.

33 Wisdom is enshrined in the hearts of men of common sense, but it must shout loudly before fools will hear it.

34 Godliness exalts a nation, but sin is a reproach to any people.

35 A king rejoices in servants who know what they are doing; he is angry with those who cause trouble.

15 A SOFT ANSWER turns away wrath, but harsh words cause quarrels.

2 A wise teacher makes learning a joy; a rebellious teacher spouts foolishness.

3 The Lord is watching everywhere and keeps his eye on both the evil and the good.

4 Gentle words cause life and health; griping brings discouragement.

catchword **his neighbor** in verse 21 shows that to despise one's neighbor thus is sin. **24. Their riches.** The Greek, reading one letter differently, has *The crown of the wise is their prudence* (so also the RSV).

27. The fear of the Lord. This goes with verse 26, as the repetition of "the fear of the Lord" shows. Otherwise the verse is a parallel to 13:14. **31. He that honoreth him.** See comments on 19:17, and compare 17:5. **32. Hope in his death.** As it stands, a real witness to hope in eternity. For **in his death** the LXX and Syriac have *bᵉtummô, in his integrity,* reading the *m* and *t* reversed. This is strong witness against the Hebrew text, and it is adopted in the RSV. Toy argues for it because, he says, the author had no hope in a future life. It is dangerous thus to prejudge a question. See comment on 12:28. But the text *in his integrity* has good support.

15:4. Tree of life. See notes on 3:18.

⁵ A fool despiseth his father's instruction: but he that regardeth reproof is prudent.

⁶ In the house of the righteous *is* much treasure: but in the revenues of the wicked is trouble.

⁷ The lips of the wise disperse knowledge: but the heart of the foolish *doeth* not so.

⁸ The sacrifice of the wicked *is* an abomination to the Lord: but the prayer of the upright *is* his delight.

⁹ The way of the wicked *is* an abomination unto the Lord: but he loveth him that followeth after righteousness.

¹⁰ Correction *is* grievous unto him that forsaketh the way: *and* he that hateth reproof shall die.

¹¹ Hell and destruction *are* before the Lord: how much more then the hearts of the children of men?

¹² A scorner loveth not one that reproveth him: neither will he go unto the wise.

¹³ A merry heart maketh a cheerful countenance: but by sorrow of the heart the spirit is broken.

¹⁴ The heart of him that hath understanding seeketh knowledge: but the mouth of fools feedeth on foolishness.

¹⁵ All the days of the afflicted *are* evil: but he that is of a merry heart hath a continual feast.

¹⁶ Better *is* little with the fear of the Lord than great treasure and trouble therewith.

¹⁷ Better *is* a dinner of herbs where love is, than a stalled ox and hatred therewith.

¹⁸ A wrathful man stirreth up strife: but *he that is* slow to anger appeaseth strife.

¹⁹ The way of the slothful *man is* as an hedge of thorns: but the way of the righteous *is* made plain.

²⁰ A wise son maketh a glad father: but a foolish man despiseth his mother.

²¹ Folly *is* joy to *him that is* destitute of wisdom: but a man of understanding walketh uprightly.

²² Without counsel purposes are disappointed: but in the multitude of counsellors they are established.

²³ A man hath joy by the answer of his mouth: and a word *spoken* in due season, how good *is it!*

⁵ Only a fool despises his father's advice; a wise son considers each suggestion.

⁶ There is treasure in being good, but trouble dogs the wicked.

⁷ Only the good can give good advice. Rebels can't.

⁸ The Lord hates the gifts of the wicked, but delights in the prayers of his people.

⁹,¹⁰ The Lord despises the deeds of the wicked, but loves those who try to be good. If they stop trying, the Lord will punish them; if they rebel against that punishment, they will die.

¹¹ The depths of hell are open to God's knowledge. How much more the hearts of all mankind!

¹² A mocker stays away from wise men because he hates to be scolded.

¹³ A happy face means a glad heart; a sad face means a breaking heart.

¹⁴ A wise man is hungry for truth, while the mocker feeds on trash.

¹⁵ When a man is gloomy, everything seems to go wrong; when he is cheerful, everything seems right!

¹⁶ Better a little with reverence for God, than great treasure and trouble with it.

¹⁷ It is better to eat soup with someone you love than steak with someone you hate.

¹⁸ A quick-tempered man starts fights; a cool-tempered man tries to stop them.

¹⁹ A lazy fellow has trouble all through life; the good man's path is easy!

²⁰ A sensible son gladdens his father. A rebellious son saddens his mother.

²¹ If a man enjoys folly, something is wrong! The sensible stay on the pathways of right.

²² Plans go wrong with too few counselors; many counselors bring success.

²³ Everyone enjoys giving good advice, and how wonderful it is to be able to say the right thing at the right time!

8. The sacrifice of the wicked is an abomination. The phrase, **abomination to the Lord,** ties together verses 8 and 9. A number of verses are thus associated in the Hebrew. Proverbs 15:8 a is repeated in 21:27 a, where it is added that such sacrifice comes from a wicked heart. This verse is quoted in the Zadokite Documents of the age of the Dead Sea literature (see Introd. under *Authorship*). Toy, representing the older 'liberals,' remarks that sacrifices are mentioned in Proverbs only here and in 7:14; 17:1; 21:3,27, and always with disapprobation (but see also 3:9). He sees here a contrast between the prophetic religion, which called for morality, and the priestly emphasis on ritual. He cites the Sermon on the Mount as part of the prophetic movement, which he sees also in Amos 5:22; Isa 1:11; Jer 7:22; I Sam 15:22; and others. Happily, this one-sided reconstruction of Israel's religion, with its perversion of such texts, is no longer fashionable. Of course the prophets opposed idolatrous sacrifices (Jer 7:18; Amos 4:4, 5; and others) and sacrifice offered in disobedience; but they did not oppose true sacrifice. Indeed, Isaiah calls the coming suffering Servant a "sin offering" (Isa 53:10). Unfortunately the newer 'liberalism' of the so-called Swedish school goes off on another tangent: It indeed unites the prophets and priests, but makes them together the devotees of the Babylonian New Year cult.

11. Hell and destruction are before the Lord. Observe how this verse is connected with, "The eyes of the Lord are in every place" (15:3) and "The ways of man are before the eyes of the Lord" (5:21). **Destruction** *(Abaddon)* is paralleled with *Sheol* here and in 27:20 and Job 26:6. It is paralleled with "death" in Job 28:22 and with "grave" in Ps 88:11. Elsewhere it is used only in Job 31:12 and Rev 9:11. Its root means *perish, die* (BDB). Delitzsch falls prey to the common tendency of scholars to interpret *Sheol* and *Abaddon* by the Greek *Tartarus* and *Hades*. This is fallacious, for the Greek and Hebrew conceptions of the afterlife were as different as their deities. These words do not designate the realm of the dead nor place it in a subterranean cavern. They are simply poetic words for the grave, which, of course, is underground. For *Sheol,* see notes on 1:12 and 2:18.

12. Scorner. A sinner. See notes on 1:22. **13. A merry heart.** A happy heart. Similar to 17:22. This is a secular prov-

erb used apparently as a foil for the next one, regarding "an understanding heart," i.e., a heart of integrity (cf. 12:25). **17. A stalled ox.** An ox in his stall, a fattened ox (RSV, Berkeley). Verses 16 to 18 go together as proverbs against anger. Verse 18 a parallels 29:22 a.

20. A wise son. See comments on 10:1.

NOTES

²⁴ The way of life *is* above to the wise, that he may depart from hell beneath.

²⁵ The Lord will destroy the house of the proud: but he will establish the border of the widow.

²⁶ The thoughts of the wicked *are* an abomination to the Lord: but *the words* of the pure *are* pleasant words.

²⁷ He that is greedy of gain troubleth his own house; but he that hateth gifts shall live.

²⁸ The heart of the righteous studieth to answer: but the mouth of the wicked poureth out evil things.

²⁹ The Lord *is* far from the wicked: but he heareth the prayer of the righteous.

³⁰ The light of the eyes rejoiceth the heart: *and* a good report maketh the bones fat.

³¹ The ear that heareth the reproof of life abideth among the wise. ³² He that refuseth instruction despiseth his own soul: but he that heareth reproof getteth understanding.

³³ The fear of the Lord *is* the instruction of wisdom; and before honour *is* humility.

²⁴ The road of the godly leads upward, leaving hell behind.

²⁵ The Lord destroys the possessions of the proud but cares for widows.

²⁶ The Lord hates the thoughts of the wicked but delights in kind words.

²⁷ Dishonest money brings grief to all the family, but hating bribes brings happiness.

²⁸ A good man thinks before he speaks; the evil man pours out his evil words without a thought.

²⁹ The Lord is far from the wicked, but he hears the prayers of the righteous.

³⁰ Pleasant sights and good reports give happiness and health.

³¹,³² If you profit from constructive criticism you will be elected to the wise men's hall of fame. But to reject criticism is to harm yourself and your own best interests.

³³ Humility and reverence for the Lord will make you both wise and honored.

CHAPTER 16

THE preparations of the heart in man, and the answer of the tongue, *is* from the Lord.

² All the ways of a man *are* clean in his own eyes; but the Lord weigheth the spirits.

³ Commit thy works unto the Lord, and thy thoughts shall be established.

⁴ The Lord hath made all *things* for himself: yea, even the wicked for the day of evil.

⁵ Every one *that is* proud in heart *is* an abomination to the Lord: *though* hand *join* in hand, he shall not be unpunished.

⁶ By mercy and truth iniquity is purged: and by the fear of the Lord *men* depart from evil.

⁷ When a man's ways please the Lord, he maketh even his enemies to be at peace with him.

⁸ Better *is* a little with righteousness than great revenues without right.

⁹ A man's heart deviseth his way: but the Lord directeth his steps.

16 WE CAN MAKE our plans, but the final outcome is in God's hands.

² We can always "prove" that we are right, but is the Lord convinced?

³ Commit your work to the Lord, then it will succeed.

⁴ The Lord has made everything for his own purposes—even the wicked, for punishment.

⁵ Pride disgusts the Lord. Take my word for it—*proud men shall be punished.*

⁶ Iniquity is atoned for by mercy and truth; evil is avoided by reverence for God.

⁷ When a man is trying to please God, God makes even his worst enemies to be at peace with him.

⁸ A little, gained honestly, is better than great wealth gotten by dishonest means.

⁹ We should make plans—counting on God to direct us.

24. Hell beneath. For Sheol, see notes on 1:12 and 2:18. The blessing of the good man saves from premature death. Toy takes it that the wise man is preserved from premature descent to the under- world. Delitzsch makes it a contrast be- tween heaven above and Sheol for the ungodly, in a development of the doc- trine of the future life. It is simpler to take it as life versus death.

B. Proverbs Largely Parallel. 16:1— 22:16.

16:2. Clean in his own eyes. The same thought appears in 14:12 and 16:25. This verse makes it more explicit that the Lord is the true Judge. The same, with vari- ations, occurs in 21:2. **3. Commit thy works.** This wording is very similar to that of Ps 37:5. And Ps 37:1 is distinctly parallel with Prov 24:19.

4. Even the wicked for the day of evil. This verse has been appealed to in sup- port of an extreme Calvinism. Delitzsch comments that "the wickedness of free agents is contemplated in this plan," but he does not take the verse in the sense of a predestination to evil, which careful Calvinists do not hold. Calvin himself, according to Delitzsch, asserted that pre- destination to evil would be a "horrible dogma." But in the Bible divine sover- eignty is taught side by side with free agency. The celebrated verse, "I make peace and create evil" (Isa 45:7), clearly does not mean moral evil, but calamity. **5. Proud in heart.** Note the intercon- nection of verses against pride: the haughty spirit and pride before destruc- tion (16:18); pride before destruction, and before honor, humility (18:12); be- fore honor, humility (15:33); all pride is an abomination to the Lord (16:5; cf. also 11:20 a).

8. A little with righteousness. See 15:16, 17 for similar wording.

¹⁰ A divine sentence *is* in the lips of the king: his mouth transgresseth not in judgment.

¹¹ A just weight and balance *are* the Lord's: all the weights of the bag *are* his work.

¹² *It is* an abomination to kings to commit wickedness: for the throne is established by righteousness.

¹³ Righteous lips *are* the delight of kings; and they love him that speaketh right.

¹⁴ The wrath of a king *is as* messengers of death: but a wise man will pacify it.

¹⁵ In the light of the king's countenance *is* life; and his favour *is* as a cloud of the latter rain.

¹⁶ How much better *is it* to get wisdom than gold! and to get understanding rather to be chosen than silver!

¹⁷ The highway of the upright *is* to depart from evil: he that keepeth his way preserveth his soul.

¹⁸ Pride *goeth* before destruction, and an haughty spirit before a fall.

¹⁹ Better *it is to be* of an humble spirit with the lowly, than to divide the spoil with the proud.

²⁰ He that handleth a matter wisely shall find good: and whoso trusteth in the Lord, happy *is* he.

²¹ The wise in heart shall be called prudent: and the sweetness of the lips increaseth learning.

²² Understanding *is* a wellspring of life unto him that hath it: but the instruction of fools *is* folly.

²³ The heart of the wise teacheth his mouth, and addeth learning to his lips.

²⁴ Pleasant words *are as* an honeycomb, sweet to the soul, and health to the bones.

²⁵ There is a way that seemeth right unto a man, but the end thereof *are* the ways of death.

²⁶ He that laboureth laboureth for himself; for his mouth craveth it of him.

²⁷ An ungodly man diggeth up evil: and in his lips *there is* as a burning fire.

²⁸ A froward man soweth strife: and a whisper separateth chief friends.

²⁹ A violent man enticeth his neighbour, and leadeth him into the way *that is* not good.

¹⁰ God will help the king to judge the people fairly; there need be no mistakes.

¹¹ The Lord demands fairness in every business deal. He established this principle.

¹² It is a horrible thing for a king to do evil. His right to rule depends upon his fairness.

¹³ The king rejoices when his people are truthful and fair.

¹⁴ The anger of the king is a messenger of death and a wise man will appease it.

¹⁵ Many favors are showered on those who please the king.

¹⁶ How much better is wisdom than gold, and understanding than silver!

¹⁷ The path of the godly leads away from evil; he who follows that path is safe.

¹⁸ Pride goes before destruction and haughtiness before a fall.

¹⁹ Better poor and humble than proud and rich.

²⁰ God blesses those who obey him; happy the man who puts his trust in the Lord.

²¹ The wise man is known by his common sense, and a pleasant teacher is the best.

²² Wisdom is a fountain of life to those possessing it, but a fool's burden is his folly.

²³ From a wise mind comes careful and persuasive speech.

²⁴ Kind words are like honey—enjoyable and healthful.

²⁵ Before every man there lies a wide and pleasant road he thinks is right, but it ends in death.

²⁶ Hunger is good—if it makes you work to satisfy it!

²⁷ Idle hands are the devil's workshop; idle lips are his mouthpiece.

²⁸ An evil man sows strife; gossip separates the best of friends.

²⁹ Wickedness loves company—and leads others into sin.

10. A divine sentence. Verses 10-15 point out various duties and functions of kings (Greenstone). The passage begins with an interesting verse that must have pleased King James I in 1611! But the word *qesem*, **divine sentence,** is nowhere else used in a good sense! It means basically *divination,* or *oracle* (LXX). *Inspired decisions* (RSV) and *godly* decision (Berkeley) are too grandiose to fit the Hebrew. Delitzsch reminds us that Israel never thought her kings infallible. The proverb of verse 10 means that true judgment is the duty of kings. That duty is specified and limited in 16:12,13. **11. A just weight.** See exegesis of 11:1. **15. His favour.** The word carries on the idea of 16:13, where the king's delight (the same word) is said to be righteous lips.

16. Better . . . than gold. Cf. 8:10, 11. **18. Pride . . . before destruction.** See note on verse 5.

21. Increaseth learning. Verse 21 b is parallel to 23 b in a conscious association. Evidently the Hebrew sages loved this repetition with artistic variation. **22. Wellspring of life.** For 22 a, cf. 10:11; 13:14; 14:27. For 22b, cf. 14:24.

25. A way that seemeth right. Verbatim with 14:12. Cf. 16:2. **28. A whisperer.** Compare 17:9; 18:8 (which is the same as 26:22). On talebearing, see exegesis of 20:19. As 16:28 a shows, a **whisperer** is not merely one who whispers secrets but a "perverse" man (RSV and Berkeley) who "sows discord" (cf. 6:14,19).

NOTES

³⁰ He shutteth his eyes to devise froward things: moving his lips he bringeth evil to pass.

³¹ The hoary head *is* a crown of glory, *if* it be found in the way of righteousness.

³² *He that is* slow to anger *is* better than the mighty; and he that ruleth his spirit than he that taketh a city.

³³ The lot is cast into the lap; but the whole disposing thereof *is* of the Lord.

CHAPTER 17

BETTER *is* a dry morsel, and quietness therewith, than an house full of sacrifices *with* strife.

² A wise servant shall have rule over a son that causeth shame, and shall have part of the inheritance among the brethren.

³ The fining pot *is* for silver, and the furnace for gold: but the Lord trieth the hearts.

⁴ A wicked doer giveth heed to false lips; *and* a liar giveth ear to a naughty tongue.

⁵ Whoso mocketh the poor reproacheth his Maker: *and* he that is glad at calamities shall not be unpunished.

⁶ Children's children *are* the crown of old men; and the glory of children *are* their fathers.

⁷ Excellent speech becometh not a fool: much less do lying lips a prince.

⁸ A gift *is as* a precious stone in the eyes of him that hath it: whithersoever it turneth, it prospereth.

⁹ He that covereth a transgression seeketh love; but he that repeateth a matter separateth *very* friends.

¹⁰ A reproof entereth more into a wise man than an hundred stripes into a fool.

¹¹ An evil *man* seeketh only rebellion: therefore a cruel messenger shall be sent against him.

¹² Let a bear robbed of her whelps meet a man, rather than a fool in his folly.

¹³ Whoso rewardeth evil for good, evil shall not depart from his house.

¹⁴ The beginning of strife *is as* when one letteth out water: therefore leave off contention, before it be meddled with.

³⁰ The wicked man stares into space with pursed lips, deep in thought, planning his evil deeds.

³¹ White hair is a crown of glory and is seen most among the godly.

³² It is better to be slow-tempered than famous; it is better to have self-control than to control an army.

³³ We toss the coin, but it is the Lord who controls its decision.

17 A DRY CRUST eaten in peace is better than steak every day along with argument and strife.

² A wise slave will rule his master's wicked sons and share their estate.

³ Silver and gold are purified by fire, but God purifies hearts.

⁴ The wicked enjoy fellowship with others who are wicked; liars enjoy liars.

⁵ Mocking the poor is mocking the God who made them. He will punish those who rejoice at others' misfortunes.

⁶ An old man's grandchildren are his crowning glory. A child's glory is his father.

⁷ Truth from a rebel or lies from a king are both unexpected.

⁸ A bribe works like magic. Whoever uses it will prosper!

⁹ Love forgets mistakes; nagging about them parts the best of friends.

¹⁰ A rebuke to a man of common sense is more effective than a hundred lashes on the back of a rebel.

¹¹ The wicked live for rebellion; they shall be severely punished.

¹² It is safer to meet a bear robbed of her cubs than a fool caught in his folly.

¹³ If you repay evil for good, a curse is upon your home.

¹⁴ It is hard to stop a quarrel once it starts, so don't let it begin.

31. Crown of glory. The young have strength for their glory (20:29), and the aged have gray hairs. But this verse makes explicit the condition for the glory of the aged—righteousness. **33. The lot is cast.** Greenstone rightly concludes (versus Toy and Delitzsch) that this is not a special sanction of lots to determine matters, much less to determine the divine will. It is merely a declaration that the lot—the most capricious of human acts—is controlled by the all-powerful God.

17:1. A house full of sacrifices. Plenty to eat. A large part of the peace offering was eaten by the worshiper. See notes on 7:14. **2. A son that causeth shame.** See also 19:26; 29:15. A wise servant, i.e., an upright one, will dispossess a wicked son. Toy interprets this in a purely secular way, entitling it, "Cleverness succeeds"!

3. The fining pot. The crucible used in refining. **5. Whoso mocketh the poor.** Compare 14:31 a, which is very similar, and notes on 19:17. **6. The crown of old men.** See notes on 16:31.

8. A gift. Hebrew, *a bribe.* That bribes are effective is here given as common knowledge (cf. 18:16; 21:14). But the author does not stop there; he condemns their use (17:23). **9. Covereth a transgression.** For a truth similar to this, see 10:12. See 16:28 and the exegesis of 20:19 for the truth of 9 b. A good example of the interlocking of distant verses in Proverbs.

12. A bear robbed of her whelps. The same figure is used in Hos 13:8. In Proverbs there are not as many illustrations from nature as we might expect. **13. Evil for good.** Most commentators take this as showing that Proverbs warns merely against ingratitude. But even evil for evil is also condemned (see 20:22;

329

15 He that justifieth the wicked, and he that condemneth the just, even they both *are* abomination to the Lord.

16 Wherefore *is there* a price in the hand of a fool to get wisdom, seeing *he hath* no heart *to it?*

17 A friend loveth at all times, and a brother is born for adversity.

18 A man void of understanding striketh hands, *and* becometh surety in the presence of his friend.

19 He loveth transgression that loveth strife: *and* he that exalteth his gate seeketh destruction.

20 He that hath a froward heart findeth no good: and he that hath a perverse tongue falleth into mischief.

21 He that begetteth a fool *doeth it* to his sorrow: and the father of a fool hath no joy.

22 A merry heart doeth good *like* a medicine: but a broken spirit drieth the bones.

23 A wicked *man* taketh a gift out of the bosom to pervert the ways of judgment.

24 Wisdom *is* before him that hath understanding; but the eyes of a fool *are* in the ends of the earth.

25 A foolish son *is* a grief to his father, and bitterness to her that bare him.

26 Also to punish the just *is* not good, *nor* to strike princes for equity.

27 He that hath knowledge spareth his words: *and* a man of understanding is of an excellent spirit. 28 Even a fool, when he holdeth his peace, is counted wise: *and* he that shutteth his lips *is* esteemed a man of understanding.

15 The Lord despises those who say that bad is good, and good is bad.

16 It is senseless to pay tuition to educate a rebel who has no heart for truth.

17 A true friend is always loyal, and a brother is born to help in time of need.

18 It is poor judgment to countersign another's note, to become responsible for his debts.

19 Sinners love to fight; boasting is looking for trouble.

20 An evil man is suspicious of everyone and tumbles into constant trouble.

21 It's no fun to be a rebel's father.

22 A cheerful heart does good like medicine, but a broken spirit makes one sick.

23 It is wrong to accept a bribe to twist justice.

24 Wisdom is the main pursuit of sensible men, but a fool's goals are at the ends of the earth!

25 A rebellious son is a grief to his father and a bitter blow to his mother.

26 How short-sighted to fine the godly for being good! And to punish nobles for being honest!

27,28 The man of few words and settled mind is wise; therefore, even a fool is thought to be wise when he is silent. It pays him to keep his mouth shut.

CHAPTER 18

THROUGH desire a man, having separated himself, seeketh *and* intermeddleth with all wisdom.

2 A fool hath no delight in understanding, but that his heart may discover itself.

3 When the wicked cometh, *then* cometh also contempt, and with ignominy reproach.

4 The words of a man's mouth *are as* deep waters, *and* the wellspring of wisdom *as* a flowing brook.

18 THE SELFISH MAN quarrels against every sound principle of conduct by demanding his own way.

2 A rebel doesn't care about the facts. All he wants to do is yell.

3 Sin brings disgrace.

4 A wise man's words express deep streams of thought.

25:21,22, quoted in Rom 12:20). **18. Becometh surety.** See exegesis of 6:1. **21. The father of a fool.** See exegesis of 10:1 and compare 17:25 for this word "fool" (Heb. *nābāl;* hence Nabal, I Sam 25:25). In Proverbs it is found only here and in 17:7; 30:22. It is one of the many synonyms for "fool." As in Ps 14:1, it does not mean mere stupidity. Psalm 14:1 means, "The rascal hath said in his heart, 'There is no God.'" **22. A merry heart.** Note similarity to 15:13. In this verse also there is a catchword, similar to one in the preceding verse. **23. A gift.** That is, a bribe (cf. v. 8). **25. A foolish son.** Cf. 17:21 and see notes on 10:1. Verses 21, 25 both use the word *kesîl*, "fool," in their first part, but show artistic variation in the second half. **27. Excellent spirit.** Better, *calm spirit* (Berkeley and Delitzsch). We may question Toy's dictum that 17:27,28 merely teaches the "value of silence." Rather, as Delitzsch shows and the words **understanding** and **fool** (*'ewîl,* "rascal") emphasize, the teaching is against angry talk. **18:1. Separated.** This verse is somewhat difficult to understand in detail. Hence, it has been given some strained interpretations. Delitzsch takes the first part of the verse as a condemnation of the "schismatic and the sectary," i.e., of dissenting churchmen, in the modern sense of the term. Hillel, also, according to Greenstone, took it to condemn religious separatism. But this interpretation is unnecessary and disagrees with other Scripture. Paul separated himself from the Pharisees (Acts 19:9) in a way that was surely justified. Obviously, this verse has nothing to do with such questions. The **separated** is the one wrongfully separated from God, seeking his own desire, not the Lord's. Such a man is a sinner. **4. Deep waters.** For 4 a, compare

⁵ *It is* not good to accept the person of the wicked, to overthrow the righteous in judgment.

⁶ A fool's lips enter into contention, and his mouth calleth for strokes. ⁷ A fool's mouth *is* his destruction, and his lips *are* the snare of his soul.

⁸ The words of a talebearer *are* as wounds, and they go down into the innermost parts of the belly.

⁹ He also that is slothful in his work is brother to him that is a great waster.

¹⁰ The name of the Lord *is* a strong tower: the righteous runneth into it, and is safe.

¹¹ The rich man's wealth *is* his strong city, and as an high wall in his own conceit.

¹² Before destruction the heart of man is haughty, and before honour *is* humility.

¹³ He that answereth a matter before he heareth *it,* it *is* folly and shame unto him.

¹⁴ The spirit of a man will sustain his infirmity; but a wounded spirit who can bear?

¹⁵ The heart of the prudent getteth knowledge; and the ear of the wise seeketh knowledge.

¹⁶ A man's gift maketh room for him, and bringeth him before great men.

¹⁷ *He that is* first in his own cause *seemeth* just; but his neighbour cometh and searcheth him.

¹⁸ The lot causeth contentions to cease, and parteth between the mighty.

¹⁹ A brother offended *is harder to be won* than a strong city: and *their* contentions *are* like the bars of a castle.

²⁰ A man's belly shall be satisfied with the fruit of his mouth; *and* with the increase of his lips shall he be filled.

²¹ Death and life *are* in the power of the tongue: and they that love it shall eat the fruit thereof.

²² *Whoso* findeth a wife findeth a good *thing,* and obtaineth favour of the Lord.

²³ The poor useth intreaties; but the rich answereth roughly.

²⁴ A man *that hath* friends must shew himself friendly: and there is a friend *that* sticketh closer than a brother.

⁵ It is wrong for a judge to favor the wicked and condemn the innocent.

⁶,⁷ A fool gets into constant fights. His mouth is his undoing! His words endanger him.

⁸ What dainty morsels rumors are. They are eaten with great relish!

⁹ A lazy man is brother to the saboteur.

¹⁰ The Lord is a strong fortress. The godly run to him and are safe.

¹¹ The rich man thinks of his wealth as an impregnable defense, a high wall of safety. What a dreamer!

¹² Pride ends in destruction; humility ends in honor.

¹³ What a shame—yes, how stupid!—to decide before knowing the facts!

¹⁴ A man's courage can sustain his broken body, but when courage dies, what hope is left?

¹⁵ The intelligent man is always open to new ideas. In fact, he looks for them.

¹⁶ A bribe does wonders; it will bring you before men of importance!

¹⁷ Any story sounds true until someone tells the other side and sets the record straight.

¹⁸ A coin toss ends arguments and settles disputes between powerful opponents.

¹⁹ It is harder to win back the friendship of an offended brother than to capture a fortified city. His anger shuts you out like iron bars.

²⁰ Ability to give wise advice satisfies like a good meal!

²¹ Those who love to talk will suffer the consequences. Men have died for saying the wrong thing!

²² The man who finds a wife finds a good thing; she is a blessing to him from the Lord.

²³ The poor man pleads and the rich man answers with insults.

²⁴ There are "friends" who pretend to be friends, but there is a friend who sticks closer than a brother.

20:5 a. **5. To accept the person of the wicked.** To show partiality in judgment. Cf. 17:15,16; 24:23; 28:21; Deut 1:17; 16:19; *et al.* **8. Talebearer.** Parallel to 26:22. See note on 20:19. **Wounds.** Used only in these verses. Most modern versions say *dainty morsels,* but the evidence for the reading is slight.

11. A high wall. This term is from the same root as for "safe" in verse 10. This proverb offers a contrast to that in 10, which gives the secret of true safety. A rich man is safe only "in his own imagination." The RSV derives its reading from a different root and thus misses the connection with 18:10. Verse 11 a is parallel to 10:15 a. **12. Before destruction.** Note the similarity between 18:12 a and 16:18 a; between 18:12 b and 15:33 b. See notes on 16:5. **20. The fruit of his mouth.** This verse speaks not of food, but of speech, and warns about what Jones and Walls call the "lethal power of the tongue"!

22. A wife. The LXX supplies a *good* wife, which is understood from 12:4 and 31:10, but need not be expressed.

CHAPTER 19

BETTER *is* the poor that walketh in his integrity, than *he that is* perverse in his lips, and is a fool.

2 Also, *that* the soul *be* without knowledge, *it is* not good; and he that hasteth with *his* feet sinneth.

3 The foolishness of man perverteth his way: and his heart fretteth against the Lord.

4 Wealth maketh many friends; but the poor is separated from his neighbour.

5 A false witness shall not be unpunished, and *he that* speaketh lies shall not escape.

6 Many will intreat the favour of the prince: and every man *is* a friend to him that giveth gifts.

7 All the brethren of the poor do hate him: how much more do his friends go far from him? he pursueth *them with* words, *yet* they *are* wanting *to him*.

8 He that getteth wisdom loveth his own soul: he that keepeth understanding shall find good.

9 A false witness shall not be unpunished, and *he that* speaketh lies shall perish.

10 Delight is not seemly for a fool; much less for a servant to have rule over princes.

11 The discretion of a man deferreth his anger; and *it is* his glory to pass over a transgression.

12 The king's wrath *is* as the roaring of a lion; but his favour *is* as dew upon the grass.

13 A foolish son *is* the calamity of his father: and the contentions of a wife *are* a continual dropping.

14 House and riches *are* the inheritance of fathers: and a prudent wife *is* from the Lord.

15 Slothfulness casteth into a deep sleep; and an idle soul shall suffer hunger.

16 He that keepeth the commandment keepeth his own soul; *but* he that despiseth his ways shall die.

17 He that hath pity upon the poor lendeth unto the Lord; and that which he hath given will he pay him again.

18 Chasten thy son while there is hope, and let not thy soul spare for his crying.

19 BETTER BE POOR and honest than rich and dishonest.

2 It is dangerous and sinful to rush into the unknown.

3 A man may ruin his chances by his own foolishness and then blame it on the Lord!

4 A wealthy man has many "friends"; the poor man has none left.

5 Punish false witnesses. Track down liars.

6 Many beg favors from a man who is generous; everyone is his friend!

7 A poor man's own brothers turn away from him in embarrassment; how much more his friends! He calls after them, but they are gone.

8 He who loves wisdom loves his own best interest and will be a success.

9 A false witness shall be punished and a liar shall be caught.

10 It doesn't seem right for a fool to succeed or for a slave to rule over princes!

11 A wise man restrains his anger and overlooks insults. This is to his credit.

12 The king's anger is as dangerous as a lion's. But his approval is as refreshing as the dew on grass.

13 A rebellious son is a calamity to his father, and a nagging wife annoys like constant dripping.

14 A father can give his sons homes and riches, but only the Lord can give them understanding wives.

15 A lazy man sleeps soundly—and goes hungry!

16 Keep the commandments and keep your life; despising them means death.

17 When you help the poor you are lending to the Lord—and he pays wonderful interest on your loan!

18 Discipline your son in his early years while there is hope. If you don't you will ruin his life.

19:1. Better is the poor. Observe that 19:1a is identical with 28:6a. The contrast in 19:1 is with a perverse man, a fool. In 28:6, the contrast is with a perverse rich man. Not riches per se are condemned, but riches with wickedness. **3. Fretteth against the Lord.** The Hebrew verb means *be angry* or *vexed*. Berkeley *resentful* is good. The LXX says *blames God.* **4. Wealth maketh many friends.** Note the similarity to 14:20. Here the thought is elaborated in 19:6,7. See comments on 17:8,23. The fact of the influence of wealth is stated here, but not approved of; elsewhere the evil use of gifts is condemned. **5. A lying witness.** Almost identical with 19:9.

10. Delight. Better *luxury* (as in most versions). **11. Discretion.** The word *sēkel* refers to wisdom, but that moral wisdom which Proverbs commends. *Prudent* (Berkeley) is better than *good sense* (RSV). **Deferreth . . . anger.** The phrase means to restrain anger, be slow to anger. The noun in Ex 34:6 is "longsuffering."

13. The contentions of a wife. Such proverbs on the contentious woman sometimes evoke humor. The verses of similar wording are 21:19; 25:24; and 27:15. The AV gives the impression that the continual drip of a leaky roof is like a nagging woman. But the Hebrew word for **contentions** does not mean nagging. The sin objected to is clearly anger. The same root is used for "discord" (cf. 6:14, 19). Much is said against anger in men. These verses protest against the same vice in women. **14. Prudent.** Same root as "delight" in 19:10. **15. Slothfulness.** See notes on 6:6.

17. He that hath pity upon the poor. He that is charitable. Proverbs 14:31 a is similar. Charity for the poor is earnestly enjoined in Hebrew law (Deut 15:7 ff.). Many verses in Proverbs recommend this liberality (21:13; 22:9,16; 28:3,8,27; 29:7). The usurer, on the other hand, is condemned because he oppresses the poor (cf. on 6:1).

18. Chasten thy son. See comments on 13:24; 23:13,14. The word **his crying** is derived from the root *hāmâ*, to "murmur," "roar." The word can also be read as from the root *mût*, "to kill." Toy translates, *Set not thy heart on his destruction,* and is followed by Greenstone, the RSV, Berkeley, and others. Delitzsch is similar. The Hebrew literally is *unto his crying* (or *his death*) *do not lift up thy soul.* The AV translation still seems closer than the others to the Hebrew wording and

context. But as the parallel in 23:14 speaks of chastisement as saving the child from death, so perhaps, in compressed expression, this proverb means the same: "Don't avoid chastening and [thus] bring on his death."

NOTES

¹⁹ A man of great wrath shall suffer punishment: for if thou deliver *him,* yet thou must do it again.

²⁰ Hear counsel, and receive instruction, that thou mayest be wise in thy latter end.

²¹ *There are* many devices in a man's heart; nevertheless the counsel of the Lord, that shall stand.

²² The desire of a man *is* his kindness: and a poor man *is* better than a liar.

²³ The fear of the Lord *tendeth* to life: and *he that hath it* shall abide satisfied; he shall not be visited with evil.

²⁴ A slothful *man* hideth his hand in *his* bosom, and will not so much as bring it to his mouth again.

²⁵ Smite a scorner, and the simple will beware: and reprove one that hath understanding, *and* he will understand knowledge.

²⁶ He that wasteth *his* father, *and* chaseth away *his* mother, *is* a son that causeth shame, and bringeth reproach.

²⁷ Cease, my son, to hear the instruction *that causeth* to err from the words of knowledge.

²⁸ An ungodly witness scorneth judgment: and the mouth of the wicked devoureth iniquity.

²⁹ Judgments are prepared for scorners, and stripes for the back of fools.

¹⁹ A short-tempered man must bear his own penalty; you can't do much to help him. If you try once you must try a dozen times!

²⁰ Get all the advice you can and be wise the rest of your life.

²¹ Man proposes, but God disposes.

²² Kindness makes a man attractive. And it is better to be poor than dishonest.

²³ Reverence for God gives life, happiness, and protection from harm.

²⁴ Some men are so lazy they won't even feed themselves!

²⁵ Punish a mocker and others will learn from his example. Reprove a wise man and he will be the wiser.

²⁶ A son who mistreats his father or mother is a public disgrace.

²⁷ Stop listening to teaching that contradicts what you know is right.

²⁸ A worthless witness cares nothing for truth—he enjoys his sinning too much.

²⁹ Mockers and rebels shall be severely punished.

CHAPTER 20

WINE *is* a mocker, strong drink *is* raging: and whosoever is deceived thereby is not wise.

² The fear of a king *is* as the roaring of a lion: *whoso* provoketh him to anger sinneth *against* his own soul.

³ *It is* an honour for a man to cease from strife: but every fool will be meddling.

⁴ The sluggard will not plow by reason of the cold; *therefore* shall he beg in harvest, and *have* nothing.

⁵ Counsel in the heart of man *is like* deep water; but a man of understanding will draw it out.

⁶ Most men will proclaim every one his own goodness: but a faithful man who can find?

⁷ The just *man* walketh in his integrity: his children *are* blessed after him.

20 WINE GIVES FALSE courage; hard liquor leads to brawls; what fools men are to let it master them, making them reel drunkenly down the street!

² The king's fury is like that of a roaring lion; to rouse his anger is to risk your life.

³ It is an honor for a man to stay out of a fight. Only fools insist on quarreling.

⁴ If you won't plow in the cold, you won't eat at the harvest.

⁵ Though good advice lies deep within a counselor's heart, the wise man will draw it out.

⁶ Most people will tell you what loyal friends they are, but are they telling the truth?

⁷ It is a wonderful heritage to have an honest father.

24. **A slothful man.** The proverb of 24 a is repeated in 26:15 in a series dealing with sloth. 26. **A son that causeth shame.** See notes on 10:1, and compare 29:15, which repeats this phrase. 27. **Instruction that causeth to err.** The words that causeth are not in the Hebrew, and Proverbs does not use this word *instruction* of false teaching. Therefore the RSV and the Berkeley correctly take the proverb to mean hearing instruction "only to stray" from it.

20:1. **Wine is a mocker.** See the commentary on 3:10 on wine. **Strong drink.** Hebrew, *shēkār.* The exact meaning is uncertain. It was not strong drink in our sense of the word; for before distillation was invented by the Arabs, no drink was stronger than about 7-10 per cent. It was intoxicating, as the Scriptural context frequently shows. Toy and Berkeley (footnote) suggest that it may have been a drink fermented from fruit juices. The writer of the article on "drink" in ISBE argues that *shēkār* is the term comprehending all such beverages, including wine. This is argued from Num 28:7,14. The term may at least have included beer. We know that beer was made and used in Palestine, for pottery used for straining beer has been found. No word in Hebrew appears to refer to beer specifically. Wine was forbidden to ministering priests (Lev 10:9) and Nazarites (Num 6:3). It was used as a drink offering, but this was not drunk. "Libation offering" would be more accurate. The word for **mocker** is *lēṣ,* "scorner." As Delitzsch says, the wine is condemned with its effects. We may notice that the condemnation is rather severe. **Deceived thereby.** The word usually means "err" or "lead astray." The BDB argues that it means also "reel" in drunkenness. However, the only evidence for that is Isa 28:7, where the word is used in reference to "erring" through wine and also "erring" in vision. It should not be limited to getting drunk, as Berkeley implies. The passage concerns *any* use of wine, because of its final effects. The LXX says, *But every fool is entangled with them.* See comments on 23:29 ff.

2. **The fear of a king.** On kings, see 16:10 ff. and 20:8.

4. **By reason of the cold.** The word does not mean "cold" so much as "fall" or "winter." He does not plow in plowing season. Cf. 10:5. Diligence is a virtue. Note the apostolic rule in II Thess 3:10.

5. **Deep water.** Compare the similar verse,

18:4. 6. **His own goodness.** The word *hesed* means "goodness," "kindness" (BDB), not "loyalty" (RSV). The BV here and the RSV often elsewhere have "steadfast love," which is more curious and strange than wrong. The word includes love, but the steadfastness found in some contexts is due to the steadfastness of the God who loves.

NOTES

⁸ A king that sitteth in the throne of judgment scattereth away all evil with his eyes.

⁹ Who can say, I have made my heart clean, I am pure from my sin?

¹⁰ Divers weights, *and* divers measures, both of them *are* alike abomination to the Lord.

¹¹ Even a child is known by his doings, whether his work *be* pure, and whether *it be* right.

¹² The hearing ear, and the seeing eye, the Lord hath made even both of them.

¹³ Love not sleep, lest thou come to poverty; open thine eyes, *and* thou shalt be satisfied with bread.

¹⁴ *It is* naught, *it is* naught, saith the buyer: but when he is gone his way, then he boasteth.

¹⁵ There is gold, and a multitude of rubies: but the lips of knowledge *are* a precious jewel.

¹⁶ Take his garment that is surety *for* a stranger: and take a pledge of him for a strange woman.

¹⁷ Bread of deceit *is* sweet to a man; but afterwards his mouth shall be filled with gravel.

¹⁸ *Every* purpose is established by counsel: and with good advice make war.

¹⁹ He that goeth about *as* a talebearer revealeth secrets: therefore meddle not with him that flattereth with his lips.

²⁰ Whoso curseth his father or his mother, his lamp shall be put out in obscure darkness.

²¹ An inheritance *may be* gotten hastily at the beginning; but the end thereof shall not be blessed.

²² Say not thou, I will recompense evil; *but* wait on the Lord, and he shall save thee.

²³ Divers weights are an abomination unto the Lord; and a false balance *is* not good.

²⁴ Man's goings *are* of the Lord; how can a man then understand his own way?

²⁵ *It is* a snare to the man *who* devoureth *that which is* holy, and after vows to make enquiry.

²⁶ A wise king scattereth the wicked, and bringeth the wheel over them.

⁸ A king sitting as judge weighs all the evidence carefully, distinguishing the true from false.

⁹ Who can ever say, "I have cleansed my heart; I am sinless"?

¹⁰ The Lord despises every kind of cheating.

¹¹ The character of even a child can be known by the way he acts—whether what he does is pure and right.

¹² If you have good eyesight and good hearing, thank God who gave them to you.

¹³ If you love sleep, you will end in poverty. Stay awake, work hard, and there will be plenty to eat!

¹⁴ "Utterly worthless!" says the buyer as he haggles over the price. But afterwards he brags about his bargain!

¹⁵ Good sense is far more valuable than gold or precious jewels.

¹⁶ It is risky to make loans to strangers!

¹⁷ Some men enjoy cheating, but the cake they buy with such ill-gotten gain will turn to gravel in their mouths.

¹⁸ Don't go ahead with your plans without the advice of others; don't go to war until they agree.

¹⁹ Don't tell your secrets to a gossip unless you want them broadcast to the world.

²⁰ God puts out the light of the man who curses his father or mother.

²¹ A fortune can be made from cheating, but there is a curse that goes with it.

²² Don't repay evil for evil. Wait for the Lord to handle the matter.

²³ The Lord loathes all cheating and dishonesty.

²⁴ Since the Lord is directing our steps, why try to understand everything that happens along the way?

²⁵ It is foolish and rash to make a promise to the Lord before counting the cost.

²⁶ A wise king stamps out crime by severe punishment.

8. A king. See 20:2.
10. Divers weights. Diverse, differing weights. See notes on 11:1. **13. Love not sleep.** On industry, see 6:9-11. **16. Surety.** This verse is identical with 27:13. On sureties, see notes on 6:1.
19. A talebearer. Hebrew, *rākîl*. Proverbs 20:19a parallels 11:13a. Proverbs 20:19 b explains the meaning: "Do not go with one of deceiving lips" (read "deceive," not "flatter," for the Hebrew *pātâ*). *Rākîl* elsewhere is translated *slander*. Leviticus 19:16 condemns it. But a **talebearer** is not what children call a "tattletale." Another word, *nirgān*, is used in 16:28; 18:8 (which parallels 26:22); 26:20. Here, too, the emphasis is not on tattling, but on spreading slander and discord. **20. Curseth his father.** A capital offense (Ex 21:17; Lev 20:9). Varying degrees of cursing and filial rebellion were recognized. Doubtless capital punishment was exacted only in extreme cases. But the divine attitude toward the offense is given here and in 30:11 (note context). **Obscure darkness.** The word means *pupil of the eye,* as a symbol for blackness or for the middle of the night. **22. Recompense evil.** The principle set forth here is reinforced in 25:21,22, quoted in Rom 12:20. **23. Divers weights.** Compare verse 10 and see notes on 11:1.
24. Man's goings are of the Lord. The first part of 20:24 is identical with the first part of the more famous verse, Ps 37:23. As Ps 37:1 is also echoed in Prov 24:19, we need not hesitate to call these proverbs quotations (note other quotations in 30:5,6). **26. Scattereth the wicked.** Note the similarity to 20:8 b. Literally, *winnows* the wicked. **Bringeth the wheel over them.** The word **wheel** is often used elsewhere, but its use in punishment is unknown. It may be figurative here. Just as a man winnows grain and brings the threshing wheel over it, so a

27 The spirit of man *is* the candle of the Lord, searching all the inward parts of the belly.

28 Mercy and truth preserve the king: and his throne is upholden by mercy.

29 The glory of young men *is* their strength: and the beauty of old men *is* the grey head.

30 The blueness of a wound cleanseth away evil: so *do* stripes the inward parts of the belly.

CHAPTER 21

THE king's heart *is* in the hand of the Lord, *as* the rivers of water: he turneth it whithersoever he will.

2 Every way of a man *is* right in his own eyes: but the Lord pondereth the hearts.

3 To do justice and judgment *is* more acceptable to the Lord than sacrifice.

4 An high look, and a proud heart, *and* the plowing of the wicked, *is* sin.

5 The thoughts of the diligent *tend* only to plenteousness; but of every one *that is* hasty only to want.

6 The getting of treasures by a lying tongue *is* a vanity tossed to and fro of them that seek death.

7 The robbery of the wicked shall destroy them; because they refuse to do judgment.

8 The way of man *is* froward and strange: but *as for* the pure, his work *is* right.

9 *It is* better to dwell in a corner of the housetop, than with a brawling woman in a wide house.

10 The soul of the wicked desireth evil: his neighbour findeth no favour in his eyes.

11 When the scorner is punished, the simple is made wise: and when the wise is instructed, he receiveth knowledge.

12 The righteous *man* wisely considereth the house of the wicked: *but God* overthroweth the wicked for *their* wickedness.

13 Whoso stoppeth his ears at the cry of the poor, he also shall cry himself, but shall not be heard.

14 A gift in secret pacifieth anger: and a reward in the bosom strong wrath.

27 A man's conscience is the Lord's searchlight exposing his hidden motives.

28 If a king is kind, honest and fair, his kingdom stands secure.

29 The glory of young men is their strength; of old men, their experience.

30 Punishment that hurts chases evil from the heart.

21 JUST AS WATER is turned into irrigation ditches, so the Lord directs the king's thoughts. He turns them wherever he wants to.

2 We can justify our every deed but God looks at our motives.

3 God is more pleased when we are just and fair than when we give him gifts.

4 Pride, lust, and evil actions are all sin.

5 Steady plodding brings prosperity; hasty speculation brings poverty.

6 Dishonest gain will never last, so why take the risk?

7 Because the wicked are unfair, their violence boomerangs and destroys them.

8 A man is known by his actions. An evil man lives an evil life; a good man lives a godly life.

9 It is better to live in the corner of an attic than with a crabby woman in a lovely home.

10 An evil man loves to harm others; being a good neighbor is out of his line.

11 The wise man learns by listening; the simpleton can learn only by seeing scorners punished.

12 The godly learn by watching ruin overtake the wicked.

13 He who shuts his ears to the cries of the poor will be ignored in his own time of need.

14 An angry man is silenced by giving him a gift!

PRAY FOR THOSE IN AUTHORITY

king punishes evil. **29. The grey head.**
See exegesis of 16:31. **30. The blueness
of a wound.** Better, *blows of bruising,*
i.e., that bruise. These cure a man of evil.
Stripes . . . the inward parts. It is not that
stripes reach the inward parts (Berkeley). Rather, the stripes, like the blows,
cleanse the inner man (same phrase as
in 27 b).

21:2. Right in his own eyes. Almost
identical with 16:2. **3. More acceptable
. . . than sacrifice.** The thought is that of
I Sam 15:22, but the wording varies
somewhat. On sacrifices, see Prov 15:8.
9. Brawling woman. Parallel to 25:24.
Actually, anger is the sin condemned.
A wide house. Apparently a storehouse or
granary according to Ugaritic evidence
(Story, *op. cit.*, p. 325). **10. The wicked.**
There is a play on words. In Hebrew,
"wicked" and "neighbor" sound alike. **12.
Wisely considereth.** A verse difficult in
detail. The AV supplies "God" as subject of the second half. The BV makes
the second half passive. Neither treatment is fully justified by the text. Perhaps it would help to divide the verse
differently: "The righteous act wisely at
home; wickedness overthrows the wicked in ruin." This involves adding a vowel
for "wickedness."

13. The cry of the poor. See exegesis
of 19:17. **14. A reward in the bosom.** A

NOTES

¹⁵ *It is* joy to the just to do judgment: but destruction *shall be* to the workers of iniquity.

¹⁶ The man that wandereth out of the way of understanding shall remain in the congregation of the dead.

¹⁷ He that loveth pleasure *shall be* a poor man: he that loveth wine and oil shall not be rich.

¹⁸ The wicked *shall be* a ransom for the righteous, and the transgressor for the upright.

¹⁹ *It is* better to dwell in the wilderness, than with a contentious and an angry woman.

²⁰ *There is* treasure to be desired and oil in the dwelling of the wise; but a foolish man spendeth it up.

²¹ He that followeth after righteousness and mercy findeth life, righteousness, and honour.

²² A wise *man* scaleth the city of the mighty, and casteth down the strength of the confidence thereof.

²³ Whoso keepeth his mouth and his tongue keepeth his soul from troubles.

²⁴ Proud *and* haughty scorner *is* his name, who dealeth in proud wrath.

²⁵ The desire of the slothful killeth him; for his hands refuse to labour.

²⁶ He coveteth greedily all the day long: but the righteous giveth and spareth not.

²⁷ The sacrifice of the wicked *is* abomination: how much more, *when* he bringeth it with a wicked mind?

²⁸ A false witness shall perish: but the man that heareth speaketh constantly.

²⁹ A wicked man hardeneth his face: but *as for* the upright, he directeth his way.

³⁰ *There is* no wisdom nor understanding nor counsel against the Lord.

³¹ The horse *is* prepared against the day of battle: but safety *is* of the Lord.

CHAPTER 22

A *good* name *is* rather to be chosen than great riches, *and* loving favour rather than silver and gold.

² The rich and poor meet together: the Lord *is* the maker of them all.

³ A prudent *man* foreseeth the evil, and hideth himself: but the simple pass on, and are punished.

---

¹⁵ A good man loves justice, but it is a calamity to evil-doers.

¹⁶ The man who strays away from common sense will end up dead!

¹⁷ A man who loves pleasure becomes poor; wine and luxury are not the way to riches!

¹⁸ The wicked will finally lose; the righteous will finally win.

¹⁹ Better to live in the desert than with a quarrelsome, complaining woman.

²⁰ The wise man saves for the future, but the foolish man spends whatever he gets.

²¹ The man who tries to be good, loving and kind finds life, righteousness and honor.

²² The wise man conquers the strong man and levels his defenses.

²³ Keep your mouth closed and you'll stay out of trouble.

²⁴ Mockers are proud, haughty and arrogant.

²⁵,²⁶ The lazy man longs for many things but his hands refuse to work. He is greedy to get, while the godly love to give!

²⁷ God loathes the gifts of evil men, especially if they are trying to bribe him!

²⁸ A false witness must be punished; an honest witness is safe.

²⁹ An evil man is stubborn, but a godly man will reconsider.

³⁰ No one, regardless of how shrewd or well-advised he is, can stand against the Lord.

³¹ Go ahead and prepare for the conflict, but victory comes from God.

22 IF YOU MUST choose, take a good name rather than great riches; for to be held in loving esteem is better than silver and gold.

² The rich and the poor are alike before the Lord who made them all.

³ A prudent man foresees the difficulties ahead and prepares for them; the simpleton goes blindly on and suffers the consequences.

bribe. See notes on 17:8. **16. The congregation of the dead.** The word is *repā'im*, "shades," according to Toy (also Berkeley, n.). The idea is certainly not that the wicked "find rest" (Berkeley), but that they "dwell" or "lie down" (Delitzsch). The phrase, *assembly of the dead*, says nothing of the state of existence of their souls. It refers merely to their lying in the grave. See exegesis of 2:18.

18. A ransom for the righteous. An unusual thought and unusual use of **ransom**. The LXX has *offscouring*, evidently interpreting the verse to mean that the wicked are but refuse in contrast to the righteous. The general sense of the verse is that the bad and not the good suffer judgment (Toy). In Isa 43:3,4 the word is used of God's judgment on Egypt in order to deliver Israel.

19. A contentious . . . woman. See comments on 19:13. **27. The sacrifice of the wicked.** Verse 27 a is parallel with 15:8 a, which see. **28. A false witness.** Parallel to 19:9 b.

22:1. A good name. Not just reputation in our sense of good name, but good character. **3. A prudent man.** This

⁴ By humility *and* the fear of the Lord *are* riches, and honour, and life.

⁵ Thorns *and* snares *are* in the way of the froward: he that doth keep his soul shall be far from them.

⁶ Train up a child in the way he should go: and when he is old, he will not depart from it.

⁷ The rich ruleth over the poor, and the borrower *is* servant to the lender.

⁸ He that soweth iniquity shall reap vanity: and the rod of his anger shall fail.

⁹ He that hath a bountiful eye shall be blessed; for he giveth of his bread to the poor.

¹⁰ Cast out the scorner, and contention shall go out; yea, strife and reproach shall cease.

¹¹ He that loveth pureness of heart, *for* the grace of his lips the king *shall be* his friend.

¹² The eyes of the Lord preserve knowledge, and he overthroweth the words of the transgressor.

¹³ The slothful *man* saith, *There is* a lion without, I shall be slain in the streets.

¹⁴ The mouth of strange women *is* a deep pit: he that is abhorred of the Lord shall fall therein.

¹⁵ Foolishness *is* bound in the heart of a child; *but* the rod of correction shall drive it far from him.

¹⁶ He that oppresseth the poor to increase his *riches, and* he that giveth to the rich, *shall* surely *come* to want.

¹⁷ Bow down thine ear, and hear the words of the wise, and apply thine heart unto my knowledge. ¹⁸ For *it is* a pleasant thing if thou keep them within thee; they shall withal be fitted in thy lips. ¹⁹ That thy trust may be in the Lord, I have made known to thee this day, even to thee.

⁴ True humility and respect for the Lord lead a man to riches, honor and long life.

⁵ The rebel walks a thorny, treacherous road; the man who values his soul will stay away.

⁶ Teach a child to choose the right path, and when he is older he will remain upon it.

⁷ Just as the rich rule the poor, so the borrower is servant to the lender.

⁸ The unjust tyrant will reap disaster and his reign of terror shall end.

⁹ Happy is the generous man, the one who feeds the poor.

¹⁰ Throw out the mocker, and you will be rid of tension, fighting and quarrels.

¹¹ He who values grace and truth is the king's friend.

¹² The Lord preserves the upright but ruins the plans of the wicked.

¹³ The lazy man is full of excuses. "I can't go to work!" he says. "If I go outside I might meet a lion in the street and be killed!"

¹⁴ A prostitute is a dangerous trap; those cursed of God are caught in it.

¹⁵ A youngster's heart is filled with rebellion, but punishment will drive it out of him.

¹⁶ He who gains by oppressing the poor or by bribing the rich shall end in poverty.

¹⁷,¹⁸,¹⁹ Listen to this wise advice; follow it closely, for it will do you good, and you can pass it on to others: *Trust in the Lord.*

verse is identical with 27:12. **4. By humility.** That is, the consequence of humility and the fear of the Lord. Cf. the triad in 21:21.

5. The froward. The crooked, perverse. **6. Train up a child.** Not a common word for "educate," but the meaning is clear and the promise a rich one.

7. The rich ruleth over the poor. With 22:1,2 in mind, we see that this clause states a fact, but does not approve of it. Possibly the verse is another warning against borrowing with usury: "As surely as the rich rule over the poor, so the borrower is servant . . ." See exegesis of 6:1, on usury. **8. The rod of his anger shall fail.** The LXX here adds a couplet, "God blesses a cheerful and liberal man, but the folly·of his works he shall punish." Possibly II Cor 9:7 alludes to the first half of this verse, but of that we cannot be sure. We need not suppose a different Hebrew text, though that would not be impossible.

14. Strange women. The parallel verse, 23:27, shows that loose women are meant (so RSV).

15. Folly . . . in the heart of a child. As we have seen, folly is not just "stupid· tricks, silly sport" (Delitzsch), for which indeed we should not whip our children. Nor does the verse say they are "morally immature" (Toy). It says they are sinners and need punishment. The current theories that children are not naturally bad, but only maladjusted, and that education should lead them to self-expression, find no support in Proverbs.

16. He that giveth to the rich. Giving bribes or gifts is condemned (see notes on 17:8,23). Oppressing the poor is often condemned in Scripture, but giving to the poor is commended in 28:27.

III. The Words of the Wise, Thirty Sayings. 22:17–24:22.

The previous section, 10:1–22:16, had the heading, "The Proverbs of Solomon." It was composed almost exclusively of two-part verses. The present section is composed of longer units, often four-part stanzas, or "tetrastichs" (e.g., vv. 23,23). It is not accurate to say, with Oesterley and Fritsch, that at 22:17 the LXX has the heading, "The Words of the Wise," for in the Greek, "Words" is in the dative case, whereas in a heading it would be in the nominative case. The LXX translation is a bit free, but is substantially like the

Hebrew except that it includes two words of verse 18 in 17. The phrase, "Words of the Wise," found in both Greek and Hebrew, does, however, suitably chracterize this section.

A. Sayings Paralleled in Egyptian Wisdom. 22:17–23:12. The parallels in this section to the *Wisdom of Amen-em-Opet* are taken from ANET and may conveniently be located by reference to the table at the bottom of p. 424 in that work. (For a discussion of these parallels and their significance, see Introd., *Proverbs and Other Wisdom Literature.*)

17. Bow down thine ear. The similarity between this verse and the introduction of the Egyptian composition has been much emphasized. But the expressions, "Give ear," "Listen to the words of wisdom," are quite general and are found elsewhere in Psalms and Proverbs.

18. They shall withal be fitted in thy lips. Oesterley and Fritsch hold that the word *withal,* or *altogether,* does not make sense. They suggest the translation, *peg,* because the Egyptian parallel in *Amen-em-Opet* has an obscure word which may mean that. But the word "peg" hardly fits better than "altogether." There is no good reason for alteration. The LXX has *hama,* "together." **19. Even to thee.** Toy and Oesterley object to these words as redundant. But we must not judge the Hebrew by our ideas of redundancy. Greenstone quotes Prov 23: 15 and I Kgs 21:19 for very similar phraseology.

NOTES

20 Have not I written to thee excellent things in counsels and knowledge, 21 That I might make thee know the certainty of the words of truth; that thou mightest answer the words of truth to them that send unto thee?

22 Rob not the poor, because he *is* poor: neither oppress the afflicted in the gate: 23 For the Lord will plead their cause, and spoil the soul of those that spoiled them.

24 Make no friendship with an angry man; and with a furious man thou shalt not go: 25 Lest thou learn his ways, and get a snare to thy soul.

26 Be not thou *one* of them that strike hands, *or* of them that are sureties for debts. 27 If thou hast nothing to pay, why should he take away thy bed from under thee?

28 Remove not the ancient landmark, which thy fathers have set.

29 Seest thou a man diligent in his business? he shall stand before kings; he shall not stand before mean *men*.

20,21 In the past, haven't I been right? Then believe what I am telling you now, and share it with others.

22,23 Don't rob the poor and sick! For the Lord is their defender. If you injure them he will punish you.

24,25 Keep away from angry, short-tempered men, lest you learn to be like them and endanger your soul.

26,27 Unless you have the extra cash on hand, don't countersign a note. Why risk everything you own? They'll even take your bed!

28 Do not move the ancient boundary marks. That is stealing.

29 Do you know a hard-working man? He shall be successful and stand before kings!

20. Excellent things. Older commentators and BDB struggled with this word, which comes from a root for *three*. It is used elsewhere only in the phrase, *yesterday three days*, meaning "formerly." The slight alteration of the vowels suggested by the Egyptian evidence (see Introd., *Proverbs and Other Wisdom Literature*) to read *thirty* is a happy solution. The word, then, is used to refer to the thirty proverbs following in this section. Toy suggests that the mention of writing in this verse is unusual in Proverbs and points toward a late date. Oesterley, arguing for dependence on the Egyptian writing, concludes the opposite! **21. That thou mightest answer the words of truth.** Oesterley compares this with the Egyptian, "to direct a report to one who has sent him," referring it to the proper delivery of a message. But the following verses are not instructions for messenger boys! Indeed, even the Egyptian is obviously of deeper meaning, for it goes on: "in order to direct him to the ways of life." The Hebrew uses a plural—"to the ones sending thee." The LXX probably has the right meaning: "Answer words of truth to them that question thee" (cf. I Pet 3:15).

23. The Lord will plead their cause. This has no parallel in *Amen-em-Opet*. The Egyptian, after all, gives only common sense dicta of morality. Proverbs absorbs these dicta from many sources and makes them the background of its divine instruction.

24. An angry man . . . a furious man. Literally, an *owner of anger . . . a man of wrath*. In 29:22 the phraseology is similar, but reversed: "A man of anger . . . an owner of wrath." The Egyptian parallel is: "Do not associate to thyself the heated man nor visit him for conversation." Several times *Amen-em-Opet* contrasts the "heated" man with the "silent" man; i.e., the impulsive versus the humbly pious (ANET, p. 422, n. 7).
25. Lest thou learn his ways. The alleged Egyptian parallel, "Lest a terror carry thee off," is not impressive.
26. That strike hands. No parallel is alleged for 22:26,27. On the dangers of suretyship, see notes on 6:1.
28. Remove not the ancient landmark. The Egyptian says, "Do not carry off the landmark at the boundaries of the arable land . . . nor encroach upon the boundaries of a widow." Removing landmarks meant falsifying the survey and stealing land (cf. Deut 19:14 and 27:

17). This verse does not teach veneration for historical markers, but respect of property rights. The Egyptian proverb is similar but peculiarly adapted to the Nile Valley. Some have argued (Toy, pp. viii) that repetition of a proverb argues for two collections, since one author would not repeat himself. However, in this collection of the "thirty" this proverb occurs a second time, but with a variant ending (23:10). Interestingly, *Amen-em-Opet* (in the English) also has a repetition of three lines of text (ANET, p. 422, col. 2; p. 423, col. 2). Since such repetition was apparently purposive, it cannot be used to prove that there were two authors. Cf. Introd., *Collections in Proverbs*.

29. A man diligent in his business. Because the Egyptian says, "The scribe who is experienced in his office, he will find himself worthy to be a courtier," and because the word **diligent** is sometimes associated in the OT with scribes, Oesterley and Fritsch assume that a scribe is meant here. But there is no warrant for this limitation. The Egyptians in *Amen-em-Opet* and elsewhere ("In Praise of Learned Scribes," ANET, pp. 432, 434) glorified the work of scribes as a profession superior to all others. The Hebrew exalts diligence in any work.

NOTES

CHAPTER 23

WHEN thou sittest to eat with a ruler, consider diligently what *is* before thee: ² And put a knife to thy throat, if thou *be* a man given to appetite. ³ Be not desirous of his dainties: for they *are* deceitful meat.

⁴ Labour not to be rich: cease from thine own wisdom. ⁵ Wilt thou set thine eyes upon that which is not? for *riches* certainly make themselves wings; they fly away as an eagle toward heaven.

⁶ Eat thou not the bread of *him that hath* an evil eye, neither desire thou his dainty meats: ⁷ For as he thinketh in his heart, so *is* he: Eat and drink, saith he to thee; but his heart *is* not with thee. ⁸ The morsel *which* thou hast eaten shalt thou vomit up, and lose thy sweet words.

⁹ Speak not in the ears of a fool: for he will despise the wisdom of thy words.

¹⁰ Remove not the old landmark; and enter not into the fields of the fatherless: ¹¹ For their redeemer *is* mighty; he shall plead their cause with thee.

¹² Apply thine heart unto instruction, and thine ears to the words of knowledge.

¹³ Withhold not correction from the child: for *if* thou beatest him with the rod, he shall not die. ¹⁴ Thou shalt beat him with the rod, and shalt deliver his soul from hell.

23 WHEN DINING WITH a rich man, be on your guard and don't stuff yourself, though it all tastes so good; for he is trying to bribe you, and no good is going to come of his invitation.

⁴,⁵ Don't weary yourself trying to get rich. Why waste your time? For riches can disappear as though they had the wings of a bird!

⁶,⁷,⁸ Don't associate with evil men; don't long for their favors and gifts. Their kindness is a trick; they want to use you as their pawn. The delicious food they serve will turn sour in your stomach and you will vomit it, and have to take back your words of appreciation for their "kindness."

⁹ Don't waste your breath on a rebel. He will despise the wisest advice.

¹⁰,¹¹ Don't steal the land of defenseless orphans by moving their ancient boundary marks, for their Redeemer is strong; he himself will accuse you.

¹² Don't refuse to accept criticism; get all the help you can.

¹³,¹⁴ Don't fail to correct your children; discipline won't hurt them! They won't die if you use a stick on them! Punishment will keep them out of hell.

23:1. To eat with a ruler. It seems superficial to say, with Fritsch and Oesterley, that this concerns good table manners. Rather, it concerns one's relation to royalty. It enjoins fear and caution before a king. The point is that the king's table is not for mere surfeiting, but for conference. We get a picture of a king's feast accompanied by discussion in the *Letter of Aristeas,* lines 236-274 (R. H. Charles, *The Apocrypha and Pseudepigrapha of the Old Testament,* II, 117, 118), where the Jewish envoys to Ptolemy are tested with questions by the king at table. The parallel from *Amen-em-Opet* reads, "Eat not bread in the presence of a ruler . . . look upon the dish that is before thee." The differences are as great as the similarity. In Proverbs the attitude toward the king (cf. also 25:6,7) is the backdrop for the warning of 23:4,5 against seeking uncertain riches, power, or advancement. **2. Knife to thy throat.** Threaten your appetite with death. **5. Set thine eyes.** Literally, *if you make your eyes fly* after riches, they in turn fly away. The alleged Egyptian parallel refers to riches acquired by robbery.

6. An evil eye. Not an eye of evil enchantment as used in superstition. The LXX already erred in this fashion. The phrase occurs in 28:22, which does not greatly clarify, but Greenstone, Toy, and Delitzsch compare 23:6 with 22:9, where the "good of eye" refers to a bountiful man. So here the RSV is correct, *the stingy man.* The Egyptian parallel is only approximate. **Do not desire his dainties.** Repeated from 23:3. It should be cut out from verse 3, say Toy and Oesterley, but there is no warrant for its excision. **8. Lose thy sweet words.** Cf. verse 9. The "fool" will despise the wisdom of thy words. This parallel assists in identifying the "fool" of 23:9 with the stingy man of verses 6,7.

10. The old landmark. See 22:28. Here end the parallels to *Amen-em-Opet.*

B. Sayings with No Parallel in Egyptian. 23:13—24:22. Curiously the alleged parallels with the Egyptian stop suddenly, and the last two-thirds of this section of the "thirty" has but one alleged parallel with the thirty chapters of the Egyptian work. **12. Apply thine heart.** A new subdivision of the "thirty" is hinted at by these words (cf. the heading of 22:17). **13. Withhold not correction.** On the use of the rod, see exegesis of 13:24. **14.**

Deliver his soul from hell. This translation of the AV is too specific. The word **soul** very often means simply the person (cf. Ps 107:9 and many other instances in concordances). The word Sheol may mean and often does mean simply the grave (see Gen 42:38; Isa 14:11; and comment on Prov 1:12; 2:18). The parallel expression of 23:13 is "he shall not die." The verse likely does not mean that beating will save the child's soul (Greenstone), but that it will be spiritually beneficial and save him from untimely death (Delitzsch, Toy). Oesterley makes the very interesting observation that this proverb has a parallel in the sayings of Ahikar. But in form, the saying is more like 23:14 in the Elephantine copy of *Ahikar* than in other copies, which presumably give Babylonian originals. He concludes that the Jews in Egypt modeled their *Ahikar* after this verse in Proverbs. This section of Proverbs therefore goes back farther than the fifth century (cf. Introd., *Proverbs and Other Wisdom Literature).*

NOTES

15 My son, if thine heart be wise, my heart shall rejoice, even mine. 16 Yea, my reins shall rejoice, when thy lips speak right things.

17 Let not thine heart envy sinners: but *be thou* in the fear of the Lord all the day long. 18 For surely there is an end; and thine expectation shall not be cut off.

19 Hear thou, my son, and be wise, and guide thine heart in the way. 20 Be not among winebibbers; among riotous eaters of flesh: 21 For the drunkard and the glutton shall come to poverty: and drowsiness shall clothe *a man* with rags. 22 Hearken unto thy father that begat thee, and despise not thy mother when she is old. 23 Buy the truth, and sell *it* not; *also* wisdom, and instruction, and understanding. 24 The father of the righteous shall greatly rejoice: and he that begetteth a wise *child* shall have joy of him. 25 Thy father and thy mother shall be glad, and she that bare thee shall rejoice.

26 My son, give me thine heart, and let thine eyes observe my ways. 27 For a whore *is* a deep ditch; and a strange woman *is* a narrow pit. 28 She also lieth in wait as *for* a prey, and increaseth the transgressors among men.

29 Who hath woe? who hath sorrow? who hath contentions? who hath babbling? who hath wounds without cause? who hath redness of eyes? 30 They that tarry long at the wine; they that go to seek mixed wine. 31 Look not thou upon the wine when it is red, when it giveth his colour in the cup, *when* it moveth itself aright. 32 At the last it biteth like a serpent, and stingeth like an adder. 33 Thine eyes shall behold strange women, and thine heart shall utter perverse things. 34 Yea, thou shalt be as he that lieth down in the midst of the sea, or as he that lieth upon the top of a mast. 35 They have stricken me, *shalt thou say, and* I was not sick; they have beaten me, *and* I felt *it* not: when shall I awake? I will seek it yet again.

15,16 My son, how I will rejoice if you become a man of common sense. Yes, my heart will thrill to your thoughtful, wise words.

17,18 Don't envy evil men but continue to reverence the Lord all the time, for surely you have a wonderful future ahead of you. There is hope for you yet!

19,20,21 O my son, be wise and stay in God's paths; don't carouse with drunkards and gluttons, for they are on their way to poverty. And remember that too much sleep clothes a man with rags. 22 Listen to your father's advice and don't despise an old mother's experience. 23 Get the facts at any price, and hold on tightly to all the good sense you can get. 24,25 The father of a godly man has cause for joy—what pleasure a wise son is! So give your parents joy!

26,27,28 O my son, trust my advice—stay away from prostitutes. For a prostitute is a deep and narrow grave. Like a robber, she waits for her victims as one after another become unfaithful to their wives.

29,30 Whose heart is filled with anguish and sorrow? Who is always fighting and quarreling? Who is the man with bloodshot eyes and many wounds? It is the one who spends long hours in the taverns, trying out new mixtures. 31 Don't let the sparkle and the smooth taste of strong wine deceive you. 32 For in the end it bites like a poisonous serpent; it stings like an adder. 33 You will see hallucinations and have delirium tremens, and you will say foolish, silly things that would embarrass you no end when sober. 34 You will stagger like a sailor tossed at sea, clinging to a swaying mast. 35 And afterwards you will say, "I didn't even know it when they beat me up . . . . Let's go and have another drink!"

15. My son. A new subsection characterized by longer treatment of topics. **16. My reins.** Literally, *kidneys.* The Hebrew language used the kidneys and liver as psychological terms very much as we use the "heart." The Hebrew "heart" more closely approximates our word "mind."

20. Be not among winebibbers. The word *sābā'* occurs only here and in Deut 21:20; Isa 56:12; Nah 1:10. **Winebibber** is not an exact rendering. The word refers not so much to a man's drinking habitually, as to his drinking strong drink (Isa 56:12). Delitzsch defines as "to drink wine or other intoxicating drinks."
21. Glutton. There seems to be no justification for this translation. The word is used elsewhere in Deut 21:20; Prov 23:20; 28:7; Lam 1:8,11; Jer 15:19; and a derivative is used in Ps 12:8. In five of these cases eating of food is not even suggested by the context. The basic meaning is to be "light," "worthless." It refers more to the riotous nature of a feast than to overeating (cf. Prov 23:20). Apparently overeating per se is not condemned at all.
26-28. My son, give me thine heart. A solemn call to the attention of the hearer. Cf. Prov 5; 7; 9 for condemnation of adultery.
29. Who hath woe . . . sorrow? This section seems to be not just a condemnation of excessive drinking, but an exhortation to avoid drink because of its final fatal consequences. Cf. commentary on 3:10, where a nonintoxicating drink is mentioned. **30. Tarry long.** One word, actually, derived from the common preposition "after." It means "remain behind." It is used in Ps 127:2 to mean "stay up late" in anxiety. It is used in Isa 5:11 in a passage similar to ours to refer to staying up late at night to drink. What an old and common tragedy! **Mixed wine.** See notes on 9:2. **31. Giveth his colour in the cup.** Emphasis upon the allurements of the drink. Literally, *gives its eye.* RSV, *sparkles.* **Moveth itself aright.** Literally, *goes straight.* RSV, *goes down smoothly.*
32. At the last. Emphatic condemnation. "Look not" (v. 31), because of the eventual consequences. You will not slide downhill if you never start down the grade! How forceful is the comparison to a serpent's venom, and how apt! Does the author appear to imply that a little is all right, but you must not go too far? That is not our attitude toward a serpent's venom. **Stingeth.** The meaning of the Hebrew word is uncertain, but the translation "sting" is not appropriate to a snake's bite. This same word is used of a snake's bite in Ugaritic (Story, *op. cit.*, p. 326).

33. Strange women. Not *strange things,* as in the RSV. The word is used in Prov 2:16; 5:3,20; 7:5; 22:14, always of harlots. We have the tragic accompaniments and consequences of drink—immorality, insensibility, irresponsibility. It is not importing extraneous thoughts to remark that not a word is said here of allowance of moderate drinking. Nor can the words from Prov 31:4-7 be fairly alleged for this. That passage mentions excessive drinking to drug the deeply unfortunate. It probably does not excuse such conduct, but only contrasts the situation of a king with that of a criminal: "Others do this; you can not afford to."

If this is the conclusion of Proverbs, how much more careful should we be in our day. The wine and strong drink of Biblical times were more like our light

NOTES

RE *Planning*

CHAPTER 24

BE not thou envious against evil men, neither desire to be with them. ² For their heart studieth destruction, and their lips talk of mischief.

³ Through wisdom is an house builded; and by understanding it is established: ⁴ And by knowledge shall the chambers be filled with all precious and pleasant riches.

⁵ A wise man *is* strong; yea, a man of knowledge increaseth strength.

⁶ For by wise counsel thou shalt make thy war: and in multitude of counsellors *there is* safety.

⁷ Wisdom *is* too high for a fool: he openeth not his mouth in the gate.

⁸ He that deviseth to do evil shall be called a mischievous person.

⁹ The thought of foolishness *is* sin: and the scorner *is* an abomination to men.

¹⁰ *If* thou faint in the day of adversity, thy strength *is* small.

¹¹ If thou forbear to deliver *them that are* drawn unto death, and *those that are* ready to be slain; ¹² If thou sayest, Behold, we knew it not; doth not he that pondereth the heart consider *it?* and he that keepeth thy soul, doth *not* he know *it?* and shall *not* he render to *every* man according to his works?

¹³ My son, eat thou honey, because *it is* good; and the honeycomb, *which is* sweet to thy taste: ¹⁴ So *shall* the knowledge of wisdom *be* unto thy soul: when thou hast found *it,* then there shall be a reward, and thy expectation shall not be cut off.

¹⁵ Lay not wait, O wicked *man,* against the dwelling of the righteous; spoil not his resting place: ¹⁶ For a just *man* falleth seven times, and riseth up again: but the wicked shall fall into mischief.

¹⁷ Rejoice not when thine enemy falleth, and let not thine heart be glad when he stumbleth: ¹⁸ Lest the Lord see *it,* and it displease him, and he turn away his wrath from him.

¹⁹ Fret not thyself because of evil *men,* neither be thou envious at the wicked; ²⁰ For there shall be no reward to the evil *man;* the candle of the wicked shall be put out.

24 DON'T ENVY GODLESS men; don't even enjoy their company. ² For they spend their days plotting violence and cheating.

³,⁴ Any enterprise is built by wise planning, becomes strong through common sense, and profits wonderfully by keeping abreast of the facts.

⁵ A wise man is mightier than a strong man. Wisdom is mightier than strength.

⁶ Don't go to war without wise guidance; there is safety in many counselors.

⁷ Wisdom is too much for a rebel. He'll not be chosen as a counselor!

⁸ To plan evil is as wrong as doing it.

⁹ The rebel's schemes are sinful, and the mocker is the scourge of all mankind.

¹⁰ You are a poor specimen if you can't stand the pressure of adversity.

¹¹,¹² Rescue those who are unjustly sentenced to death; don't stand back and let them die. Don't try to disclaim responsibility by saying you didn't know about it. For God, who knows all hearts, knows yours, and he knows you knew! And he will reward everyone according to his deeds.

¹³,¹⁴ My son, honey whets the appetite, and so does wisdom! When you enjoy becoming wise, there is hope for you! A bright future lies ahead!

¹⁵,¹⁶ O evil man, leave the upright man alone, and quit trying to cheat him out of his rights. Don't you know that this good man, though you trip him up seven times, will each time rise again? But one calamity is enough to lay you low.

¹⁷ Do not rejoice when your enemy meets trouble. Let there be no gladness when he falls— ¹⁸ for the Lord may be displeased with you and stop punishing him!

¹⁹,²⁰ Don't envy the wicked. Don't covet his riches. For the evil man has no future; his light will be snuffed out.

wines and beer. The people had no distillation and so could not make strong liquors. In our day, social drinking much more easily turns into alcoholism. Also, in a mechanized age a single drink can have far worse consequences for others than 23:35 suggests. Why, therefore, should so many cling to a practice that rapidly enslaves and so frequently degrades? Why can not drinking be just as sociable with soft drinks? Or, if the escape provided by alcohol constitutes the value of the social glass, is not the desire to "escape" already the incipient drunkenness against which our author contends? Ecclesiasticus, one of the apocryphal books accepted by Roman Catholics, but not by Protestants, has a differing treatment denouncing drunkenness, but expressly allowing moderate drinking (Ecclesiasticus 31:25-30).

24:1-3. Through wisdom is an house builded. In this portion and the verses following, the thoughts are similar to some in the first section, 1:1–9:18. This may indicate some dependence (cf. 9:1). **5. A wise man is strong.** The LXX, Syriac, and Targum say *is better than a strong man,* which is smoother (RSV reading is similar). **7. Too high for a fool.** In 24:7-9 folly and sin appear again as the standard proverbial contrast to wisdom.

10. Thy strength is small. This involves a play on the words *ṣārâ,* "adversity," and *ṣar,* "small," "compressed." **12. Doth not he know.** Probably this verse joins with the preceding and exposes the flimsy excuses of mortals. The verses insist that we are our brother's keepers. **Shall not he render.** The thought resembles that of Ps 62:12, but the wording is not identical. It reappears in Mt 16:27.

13. My son. Another subsection of this division of the "thirty." **14. Thy expectation.** Cf. 23:18.

17. When thine enemy falleth. The same thought as in 17:5. Oesterley and Fritsch object to the last thought of 24:18 —that if we rejoice not, the Lord will continue to punish our enemies; otherwise he will spare them! Toy, Delitzsch, and Greenstone do not take so strict a view. A similarly strict treatment of Rom 12:20 (quoted from Prov 25:21,22) would have us feed our enemies in order to condemn them more severely! Rather, these expressions give results in such matters, not purposes. **19. Fret not thyself.** This verse is identical with Ps 37:1 except for the last word. For other quotations, see 30:5.

21 My son, fear thou the Lord and the king: *and* meddle not with them that are given to change: 22 For their calamity shall rise suddenly; and who knoweth the ruin of them both?

23 These *things* also *belong* to the wise. *It is* not good to have respect of persons in judgment. 24 He that saith unto the wicked, Thou *art* righteous; him shall the people curse, nations shall abhor him: 25 But to them that rebuke *him* shall be delight, and a good blessing shall come upon them.

26 *Every man* shall kiss *his* lips that giveth a right answer.

27 Prepare thy work without, and make it fit for thyself in the field; and afterwards build thine house.

28 Be not a witness against thy neighbour without cause; and deceive *not* with thy lips. 29 Say not, I will do so to him as he hath done to me: I will render to the man according to his work.

30 I went by the field of the slothful, and by the vineyard of the man void of understanding; 31 And, lo, it was all grown over with thorns, *and* nettles had covered the face thereof, and the stone wall thereof was broken down. 32 Then I saw, *and* considered *it* well: I looked upon *it, and* received instruction. 33 *Yet* a little sleep, a little slumber, a little folding of the hands to sleep: 34 So shall thy poverty come *as* one that travelleth; and thy want as an armed man.

21,22 My son, watch your step before the Lord and the king, and don't associate with radicals. For you will go down with them to sudden disaster, and who knows where it all will end?

Here are some additional proverbs:

23 It is wrong to sentence the poor, and let the rich go free. 24 He who says to the wicked, "You are innocent," shall be cursed by many people of many nations; 25 but blessings shall be showered on those who rebuke sin fearlessly.

26 It is an honor to receive a frank reply. 27 Develop your business first before building your house.

28,29 Don't testify spitefully against an innocent neighbor. Why lie about him? Don't say, "Now I can pay him back for all his meanness to me!"

30,31 I walked by the field of a certain lazy fellow and saw that it was overgrown with thorns, and covered with weeds; and its walls were broken down. 32,33 Then, as I looked, I learned this lesson:

"A little extra sleep,
A little more slumber,
A little folding of the hands to rest"

34 means that poverty will break in upon you suddenly like a robber, and violently like a bandit.

CHAPTER 25

THESE *are* also proverbs of Solomon, which the men of Hez-e-ki-ah king of Judah copied out.

2 *It is* the glory of God to conceal a thing: but the honour of kings *is* to search out a matter. 3 The heaven for height, and the earth for depth, and the heart of kings *is* unsearchable.

4 Take away the dross from the silver, and there shall come forth a vessel for the finer. 5 Take away the wicked *from* before the king, and his throne shall be established in righteousness.

6 Put not forth thyself in the presence of the king, and stand not in the place

25 THESE PROVERBS OF Solomon were discovered and copied by the aides of King Hezekiah of Judah:

2,3 It is God's privilege to conceal things, and the king's privilege to discover and invent. You cannot understand the height of heaven, the size of the earth, or all that goes on in the king's mind!

4,5 When you remove dross from silver, you have sterling ready for the silversmith. When you remove corrupt men from the king's court, his reign will be just and fair.

6,7 Don't demand an audience with the king as though you were some powerful

IV. The Words of the Wise, Appendix. 24:23-34.

The main reason for calling this a separate section is that with 24:22, the "thirty sayings" come to an end. Toy and Delitzsch, who wrote before the section of the "thirty" was suggested, speak of this section as an appendix or supplement to that portion, as indeed it probably is. The material is not greatly different. The LXX inserts 30:1-14 before this section.

23. Respect of persons. Cf. 18:5.

26. Kiss his lips. Fritsch, Oesterley, and others remark that kissing the lips is not elsewhere mentioned in the OT. Toy thought the custom came from the Persians. Another argument from silence! It is definitely mentioned in Ugaritic (C. H. Gordon, *Ugaritic Literature*, p. 60).

29. As he hath done to me. This is really a statement of the golden rule (Lk 6:31). It is finely expressed here, but also elsewhere (20:22; 17:13; 25:21, 22). This high ethical principle is not opposed to the Mosaic legislation of an "eye for [an] eye" (Ex 21:24; Lev 24:20; Deut 19:21). This particular Mosaic law was for judges, and it required that the penalty fit the crime. It was probably not intended to be executed literally, and we have no cases of its literal application in the OT. It was and is a principle of justice. Christ (in Mt 5:38) did not contradict this principle of OT law, but did object to the Pharisaic interpretation which allowed a vengeful attitude (see the author's *Inspiration and Canonicity of the Bible*, pp. 50-52). There are parallels to this 24:29 in the Babylonian *Counsels of Wisdom* (ANET, p. 427). After all, it is not the ethics of Christianity that is unique—God has given all men consciences. The ethics of Christianity is the highest, but the unique element is redemption.

30-34. The field of the slothful. See comment on 6:6-11. The last verses of the two sections are practically identical.

V. Proverbs of Solomon, Edited by Hezekiah's Men. 25:1–29:27.

The LXX inserts 30:15–31:9 before this section. **1.** The meaning of the heading is obscure. It begins like the headings in 1:1; 10:1, except that **these also** reminds us of 24:23. But what did the **men of Hezekiah** do? Collect, or edit, or recopy? The verb "to copy out" means "to be old" or "to remove." Oesterley and Fritsch claim that the meaning "copy out" is very late. True, it is used in post-biblical times, but our evidence regarding literary activity is not full enough to deny it to earlier times as well. Toy says the reference to Hezekiah has no more value than the titles of the Psalms or headings of the prophetical books! We may add, no less value either. Oesterley quotes the Talmudic tradition that Hezekiah edited Proverbs and Ecclesiastes. He explains away the tradition by asserting that it arose because Hezekiah had a prominent scribe, Shebna, at court! (Isa 37:2) Oesterley forgets that other kings—likely all kings—had scribes (II Sam 8:17; I Kgs 4:3) whose duties were apparently military more than literary. They mustered the army. It is safer just to take this heading at its face value. It appears in the LXX and therefore is older, at least, than 200 B.C.

2-7. Honour of kings. A short section on kings. Note in verses 2 and 3 the repetition of the catchwords translated **search out** and **unsearchable.** Also in verses 4 and 5 the secular proverb on refining is tied with moral maxim by the repetition of **take away.** The ideal king is established in righteousness. Fritsch remarks that the reference to kings argues for a pre-Exilic date.

NOTES

of great *men:* 7 For better *it is* that it be said unto thee, Come up hither; than that thou shouldest be put lower in the presence of the prince whom thine eyes have seen.

8 Go not forth hastily to strive, lest *thou know not* what to do in the end thereof, when thy neighbour hath put thee to shame. 9 Debate thy cause with thy neighbour *himself;* and discover not a secret to another: 10 Lest he that heareth *it* put thee to shame, and thine infamy turn not away.

11 A word fitly spoken *is like* apples of gold in pictures of silver.

12 *As* an earring of gold, and an ornament of fine gold, *so is* a wise reprover upon an obedient ear.

13 As the cold of snow in the time of harvest, *so is* a faithful messenger to them that send him: for he refresheth the soul of his masters.

14 Whoso boasteth himself of a false gift *is like* clouds and wind without rain.

15 By long forbearing is a prince persuaded, and a soft tongue breaketh the bone.

16 Hast thou found honey? eat so much as is sufficient for thee, lest thou be filled therewith, and vomit it.

17 Withdraw thy foot from thy neighbour's house; lest he be weary of thee, and *so* hate thee.

18 A man that beareth false witness against his neighbour *is* a maul, and a sword, and a sharp arrow.

19 Confidence in an unfaithful man in time of trouble *is like* a broken tooth, and a foot out of joint.

20 *As* he that taketh away a garment in cold weather, *and as* vinegar upon nitre, so *is* he that singeth songs to an heavy heart.

21 If thine enemy be hungry, give him bread to eat; and if he be thirsty, give him water to drink: 22 For thou shalt heap coals of fire upon his head, and the Lord shall reward thee.

23 The north wind driveth away rain: so *doth* an angry countenance a backbiting tongue.

24 *It is* better to dwell in the corner of the housetop, than with a brawling woman and in a wide house.

25 *As* cold waters to a thirsty soul, so *is* good news from a far country.

prince. It is better to wait for an invitation rather than to be sent back to the end of the line, publicly disgraced!

8,9,10 Don't be hot-headed and rush to court! You may start something you can't finish and go down before your neighbor in shameful defeat. So discuss the matter with him privately. Don't tell anyone else, lest he accuse you of slander and you can't withdraw what you said.

11 Timely advice is as lovely as golden apples in a silver basket.

12 It is a badge of honor to accept valid criticism.

13 A faithful employee is as refreshing as a cool day in the hot summertime.

14 One who doesn't give the gift he promised is like a cloud blowing over a desert without dropping any rain.

15 Be patient and you will finally win, for a soft tongue can break hard bones.

16 Do you like honey? Don't eat too much of it, or it will make you sick!

17 Don't visit your neighbor too often, or you will outwear your welcome!

18 Telling lies about someone is as harmful as hitting him with an axe, or wounding him with a sword, or shooting him with a sharp arrow.

19 Putting confidence in an unreliable man is like chewing with a sore tooth, or trying to run on a broken foot.

20 Being happy-go-lucky around a person whose heart is heavy is as bad as stealing his jacket in cold weather, or rubbing salt in his wounds.

21,22 If your enemy is hungry, give him food! If he is thirsty, give him something to drink! This will make him feel ashamed of himself, and God will reward you.

23 As surely as a wind from the north brings cold, just as surely a retort causes anger!

24 It is better to live in a corner of an attic than in a beautiful home with a cranky, quarrelsome woman.

25 Good news from far away is like cold water to the thirsty.

11,12. A word fitly spoken. The figure of speech is difficult to interpret because our vocabulary of Hebrew fruits is not extensive. Delitzsch says **apples of gold** are oranges; Toy says quinces. More important, the **word fitly spoken** of verse 11 is equal to the **wise reprover** of verse 12. **13. As the cold of snow.** Another beautiful comparison. But it does not mean a snowfall in harvest (Mar.–Sept.), which did not happen and would have been disastrous. It refers to a cool drink from the snowy mountains or a cooling trip to them.

15. Breaketh the bone. Softness accomplishes hard things if you have patience.

16,17. From thy neighbor's house. Verse 16 serves as a backdrop to 17. The two verses are tied together by the verbs **be filled** and **be weary,** which in Hebrew are the same. **18. False witness.** The words of 18 a quote the ninth commandment. For other quotations, see 30:5.

20. Vinegar upon nitre. The chemistry is simple and interesting. **Nitre** is the old English for "soda," which was collected from the alkali lakes of Egypt. It was called "natron" in Egyptian. The reaction causes carbon dioxide gas to bubble up violently. The simile does not emphasize "cheering," as Oesterley says, but rather violence. The RSV follows the LXX "wound," but likely the LXX misunderstood the chemistry. The RSV footnote strangely says, "Heb. *lye.*" This would fit neither the chemistry nor the vocabulary. Egyptian natron was a prominent source of soda until Napoleon, noting its value in his Egyptian campaign, offered a prize for its industrial synthesis. **21,22. Thine enemy.** See notes on 24:17. Quoted in Rom 12:20 in the LXX form, which closely follows the Hebrew.

24. Brawling woman. Parallel to 21:9. A woman of discord. See notes on 19:13.

26 A righteous man falling down before the wicked *is as* a troubled fountain, and a corrupt spring.

27 *It is* not good to eat much honey: so *for men* to search their own glory *is not* glory.

28 He that *hath* no rule over his own spirit *is like* a city *that is* broken down, *and* without walls.

CHAPTER 26

As snow in summer, and as rain in harvest, so honour is not seemly for a fool.

2 As the bird by wandering, as the swallow by flying, so the curse causeless shall not come.

3 A whip for the horse, a bridle for the ass, and a rod for the fool's back.

4 Answer not a fool according to his folly, lest thou also be like unto him.

5 Answer a fool according to his folly, lest he be wise in his own conceit.

6 He that sendeth a message by the hand of a fool cutteth off the feet, *and* drinketh damage.

7 The legs of the lame are not equal: so *is* a parable in the mouth of fools.

8 As he that bindeth a stone in a sling, so *is* he that giveth honour to a fool.

9 *As* the thorn goeth up into the hand of a drunkard, so *is* a parable in the mouth of fools.

10 The great *God* that formed all *things* both rewardeth the fool, and rewardeth transgressors.

11 As a dog returneth to his vomit, *so* a fool returneth to his folly.

12 Seest thou a man wise in his own conceit? *there is* more hope of a fool than of him.

13 The slothful *man* saith, *There is* a lion in the way; a lion *is* in the streets.

14 *As* the door turneth upon his hinges, so *doth* the slothful upon his bed. 15 The slothful hideth his hand in *his* bosom; it grieveth him to bring it again to his mouth. 16 The sluggard *is* wiser in his own conceit than seven men that can render a reason.

17 He that passeth by, *and* meddleth with strife *belonging* not to him, *is like* one that taketh a dog by the ears.

26 If a godly man compromises with the wicked, it is like polluting a fountain or muddying a spring.

27 Just as it is harmful to eat too much honey, so also it is bad for men to think about all the honors they deserve!

28 A man without self-control is as defenseless as a city with broken-down walls.

26 HONOR DOESN'T GO with fools any more than snow with summertime or rain with harvest time!

2 An undeserved curse has no effect. Its intended victim will be no more harmed by it than by a sparrow or swallow flitting through the sky.

3 Guide a horse with a whip, a donkey with a bridle, and a rebel with a rod to his back!

4,5 When arguing with a rebel, don't use foolish arguments as he does, or you will become as foolish as he is! Prick his conceit with silly replies!

6 To trust a rebel to convey a message is as foolish as cutting off your feet and drinking poison!

7 In the mouth of a fool a proverb becomes as useless as a paralyzed leg.

8 Honoring a rebel will backfire like a stone tied to a slingshot!

9 A rebel will misapply an illustration so that its point will no more be felt than a thorn in the hand of a drunkard.

10 The master may get better work from an untrained apprentice than from a skilled rebel!

11 As a dog returns to his vomit, so a fool repeats his folly.

12 There is one thing worse than a fool, and that is a man who is conceited.

13 The lazy man won't go out and work. "There might be a lion outside!" he says. 14 He sticks to his bed like a door to its hinges! 15 He is too tired even to lift his food from his dish to his mouth! 16 Yet in his own opinion he is smarter than seven wise men.

17 Yanking a dog's ears is no more foolish than interfering in an argument that isn't any of your business.

26. Righteous man falling. The Hebrew verb means *to be moved.* Delitzsch, Oesterley, and Fritsch rightly take it to refer to moral defection.

27. To search their own glory. The verse is hard to understand, though the words as they stand are not difficult. Most writers say the verse is hopelessly corrupt and makes no sense (Fritsch, Oesterley, and Toy). It is about as logical to say that there is an idiom concealed in the compressed expression which escapes us. Greenstone follows the AV. Delitzsch changes some vowels to get, *to search difficult things is honour.* **28. No rule over his own spirit.** Very similar to 16:32.

26:1. A fool. Verses 1-12 constitute a subsection on the subject of fools. See exegesis of 10:8. Moral folly is intended. **4,5. Answer not a fool.** A famous case of apparent contradiction, not real. The balance is due to the artistic contrast of proverbs, not to a mistake. In one sense you should answer a rascal; in another sense, not. These verses caused some early Jewish rabbis to question the canonicity of Proverbs! More sober minds saw through the difficulty. **7. Not equal.** Better, *hang down, be useless.* **8. A sling.** Not the usual word for "sling." Perhaps: "like one who puts stones in a heap."

10. The great God that formed all. All commentaries admit the difficulty of this verse. The LXX departs widely. "God" is not in the Hebrew. **Formed** can have several meanings, among which a common one is "pierce." **The great** is read *archer* by the RSV, which is possible, but *arrow* is equally possible (cf. Job 16:13). A possibility is, "An arrow pierces all; so is one who rewards a fool and a transgressor." **11. As a dog returneth to his vomit.** Quoted in II Pet 2:22. **12. A man wise in his own eyes.** This attitude of pride is repeatedly denominated sin (3:7; 26:5,16; 28:11). It is even possible that this is a climax line after the whole discussion of a fool; i.e., a man of pride is worse.

13-16. The slothful man. See comments on 6:6. **15. Hideth his hand.** Practically identical with 19:24.

17. Meddleth with strife. The Hebrew text has *'ōbēr mit'abbēr,* "passing by and vexing oneself." The AV, following the Syriac and Vulgate, reads as if the word were *mit'āreb.* Likely Delitzsch is right in making the "passing by" refer to the dog (so also Oesterley). "Like one taking a passing dog by the ears" is one who vexes himself in another's lawsuit.

NOTES

18 As a mad *man* who casteth firebrands, arrows, and death, 19 So *is* the man *that* deceiveth his neighbour, and saith, Am not I in sport?

20 Where no wood is, *there* the fire goeth out: so where *there is* no talebearer, the strife ceaseth.

21 *As* coals *are* to burning coals, and wood to fire; so *is* a contentious man to kindle strife.

22 The words of a talebearer *are* as wounds, and they go down into the innermost parts of the belly.

23 Burning lips and a wicked heart *are like* a potsherd covered with silver dross.

24 He that hateth dissembleth with his lips, and layeth up deceit within him; 25 When he speaketh fair, believe him not: for *there are* seven abominations in his heart. 26 *Whose* hatred is covered by deceit, his wickedness shall be shewed before the *whole* congregation.

27 Whoso diggeth a pit shall fall therein: and he that rolleth a stone, it will return upon him.

28 A lying tongue hateth *those that are* afflicted by it; and a flattering mouth worketh ruin.

CHAPTER 27

BOAST not thyself of to morrow; for thou knowest not what a day may bring forth.

2 Let another man praise thee, and not thine own mouth; a stranger, and not thine own lips.

3 A stone *is* heavy, and the sand weighty; but a fool's wrath *is* heavier than them both.

4 Wrath *is* cruel, and anger *is* outrageous; but who *is* able to stand before envy?

5 Open rebuke *is* better than secret love.

6 Faithful *are* the wounds of a friend; but the kisses of an enemy *are* deceitful.

7 The full soul loatheth an honeycomb; but to the hungry soul every bitter thing is sweet.

8 As a bird that wandereth from her nest, so *is* a man that wandereth from his place.

18,19 A man who is caught lying to his neighbor and says, "I was just fooling," is like a madman throwing around firebrands, arrows and death!

20 Fire goes out for lack of fuel, and tensions disappear when gossip stops.

21 A quarrelsome man starts fights as easily as a match sets fire to paper.

22 Gossip is a dainty morsel eaten with great relish.

23 Pretty words may hide a wicked heart, just as a pretty glaze covers a common clay pot.

24,25,26 A man with hate in his heart may sound pleasant enough, but don't believe him; for he is cursing you in his heart. Though he pretends to be so kind, his hatred will finally come to light for all to see.

27 The man who sets a trap for others will get caught in it himself. Roll a boulder down on someone, and it will roll back and crush you.

28 Flattery is a form of hatred and wounds cruelly.

27 DON'T BRAG ABOUT your plans for tomorrow—wait and see what happens.

2 Don't praise yourself; let others do it!

3 A rebel's frustrations are heavier than sand and rocks.

4 Jealousy is more dangerous and cruel than anger.

5 Open rebuke is better than hidden love!

6 Wounds from a friend are better than kisses from an enemy!

7 Even honey seems tasteless to a man who is full; but if he is hungry, he'll eat anything!

8 A man who strays from home is like a bird that wanders from its nest.

22. Talebearer. This verse is like 18:8.
See comments on 20:19. **23. Silver dross.**
A new word for pottery glaze found in
the Ugaritic literature explains this verse.
The two words "silver dross," *kesep
sigim* should be one word, "like glaze,"
with the consonants *kspsg* (cf. H. L.
Ginsberg, "The North Canaanite Myth of
Anath and Aqhat," BASOR, No. 98
(April, 1945), p. 21, and W. F. Albright,
"A New Hebrew Word for Glaze in
Proverbs 26:23," *ibid.*, pp. 24,25). **24.
He that hateth.** Repeated in 26:26 as a
catchword expanding the thought.

27:1. Boast not thyself of tomorrow. A
common, but solemn, thought. Oesterley
gives a parallel from the *Wisdom of
Amen-em-Opet* differing somewhat from
the quotation in ANET, p. 423 (ch.
XIX. 12.13). The general parallel may be
allowed, however. **2. Let another man
praise thee. Praise** is the same Hebrew
word as "boast" in verse 1.

NOTES

⁹ Ointment and perfume rejoice the heart: so *doth* the sweetness of a man's friend by hearty counsel.

¹⁰ Thine own friend, and thy father's friend, forsake not; neither go into thy brother's house in the day of thy calamity: *for* better *is* a neighbour *that is* near than a brother far off.

¹¹ My son, be wise, and make my heart glad, that I may answer him that reproacheth me.

¹² A prudent *man* foreseeth the evil, *and* hideth himself; *but* the simple pass on, *and* are punished.

¹³ Take his garment that is surety for a stranger, and take a pledge of him for a strange woman.

¹⁴ He that blesseth his friend with a loud voice, rising early in the morning, it shall be counted a curse to him.

¹⁵ A continual dropping in a very rainy day and a contentious woman are alike. ¹⁶ Whosoever hideth her hideth the wind, and the ointment of his right hand, *which* bewrayeth *itself*.

¹⁷ Iron sharpeneth iron; so a man sharpeneth the countenance of his friend.

¹⁸ Whoso keepeth the fig tree shall eat the fruit thereof: so he that waiteth on his master shall be honoured.

¹⁹ As in water face *answereth* to face, so the heart of man to man.

²⁰ Hell and destruction are never full; so the eyes of man are never satisfied.

²¹ *As* the fining pot for silver, and the furnace for gold; so *is* a man to his praise.

²² Though thou shouldest bray a fool in a mortar among wheat with a pestle, *yet* will not his foolishness depart from him.

²³ Be thou diligent to know the state of thy flocks, *and* look well to thy herds.

²⁴ For riches *are* not for ever: and doth the crown *endure* to every generation?

²⁵ The hay appeareth, and the tender grass sheweth itself, and herbs of the mountains are gathered. ²⁶ The lambs *are* for thy clothing, and the goats *are* the price of the field. ²⁷ And *thou shalt have* goats' milk enough for thy food, for the food of thy household, and *for* the maintenance for thy maidens.

⁹ Friendly suggestions are as pleasant as perfume.

¹⁰ Never abandon a friend—either yours or your father's. Then you won't need to go to a distant relative for help in your time of need.

¹¹ My son, how happy I will be if you turn out to be sensible! It will be a public honor to me.

¹² A sensible man watches for problems ahead and prepares to meet them. The simpleton never looks, and suffers the consequences.

¹³ The world's poorest credit risk is the man who agrees to pay a stranger's debts.

¹⁴ If you shout a pleasant greeting to a friend too early in the morning, he will count it as a curse!

¹⁵ A constant dripping on a rainy day and a cranky woman are much alike! ¹⁶ You can no more stop her complaints than you can stop the wind or hold onto anything with oil-slick hands.

¹⁷ A friendly discussion is as stimulating as the sparks that fly when iron strikes iron.

¹⁸ A workman may eat from the orchard he tends; anyone should be rewarded who protects another's interests.

¹⁹ A mirror reflects a man's face, but what he is really like is shown by the kind of friends he chooses.

²⁰ Ambition and death are alike in this: neither is ever satisfied.

²¹ The purity of silver and gold can be tested in a crucible, but a man is tested by his reaction to men's praise.

²² You can't separate a rebel from his foolishness though you crush him to powder.

²³,²⁴ Riches can disappear fast. And the king's crown doesn't stay in his family forever—so watch your business interests closely. Know the state of your flocks and your herds; ²⁵,²⁶,²⁷ then there will be lamb's wool enough for clothing, and goat's milk enough for food for all your household after the hay is harvested, and the new crop appears, and the mountain grasses are gathered in.

12. **The simple.** The verse is parallel to 22:3. 13. **Take his garment.** Parallel to 20:16. 14. **Blessing his friend.** Most writers say this insincere, overly loud blessing is a curse. Possibly also we have here a contrary use of "bless," meaning "curse" (see the lexicons). A morning curse will come home at night!

15. **A continual dropping.** Very similar to 19:13. 16. **Hideth the wind.** The thought is of something impossible. Better, *Whoso treasures her, treasures up wind,* i.e., she is worthless. Toy and Oesterley declare the last of the verse impossible. The Delitzsch reading seems all right, *oil meets his right hand,* i.e., he grasps nothing.

17. **Iron sharpeneth iron.** The significance of this proverb is well known in education. But it illustrates the fact that the similes chosen in Proverbs may be obscure. 19. **As in water.** Probably this refers to reflections in water.

20. **Hell and destruction.** Hebrew *Sheol* and *Abaddon.* On Sheol, see 1:12; 2:18. Sheol often means merely the grave, here called insatiable. 21. **Fining pot.** Refining pot. 22. **Bray a fool.** Pound him as when pounding grain in a mortar to grind it.

363

CHAPTER 28

THE wicked flee when no man pursueth: but the righteous are bold as a lion.

² For the transgression of a land many *are* the princes thereof: but by a man of understanding *and* knowledge the state *thereof* shall be prolonged.

³ A poor man that oppresseth the poor *is like* a sweeping rain which leaveth no food.

⁴ They that forsake the law praise the wicked: but such as keep the law contend with them.

⁵ Evil men understand not judgment: but they that seek the Lord understand all *things*.

⁶ Better *is* the poor that walketh in his uprightness, than *he that is* perverse *in his* ways, though he *be* rich.

⁷ Whoso keepeth the law *is* a wise son: but he that is a companion of riotous *men* shameth his father.

⁸ He that by usury and unjust gain increaseth his substance, he shall gather it for him that will pity the poor.

⁹ He that turneth away his ear from hearing the law, even his prayer *shall be* abomination.

¹⁰ Whoso causeth the righteous to go astray in an evil way, he shall fall himself into his own pit: but the upright shall have good *things* in possession.

¹¹ The rich man *is* wise in his own conceit; but the poor that hath understanding searcheth him out.

¹² When righteous *men* do rejoice, *there is* great glory: but when the wicked rise, a man is hidden.

¹³ He that covereth his sins shall not prosper: but whoso confesseth and forsaketh *them* shall have mercy.

¹⁴ Happy *is* the man that feareth alway: but he that hardeneth his heart shall fall into mischief.

¹⁵ *As* a roaring lion, and a ranging bear; *so is* a wicked ruler over the poor people.

¹⁶ The prince that wanteth understanding *is* also a great oppressor: *but* he that hateth covetousness shall prolong *his* days.

¹⁷ A man that doeth violence to the blood of *any* person shall flee to the pit; let no man stay him.

28 THE WICKED FLEE when no one is chasing them! But the godly are bold as lions!

² When there is moral rot within a nation, its government topples easily; but with honest, sensible leaders there is stability.

³ When a poor man oppresses those even poorer, he is like an unexpected flood sweeping away their last hope.

⁴ To complain about the law is to praise wickedness. To obey the law is to fight evil.

⁵ Evil men don't understand the importance of justice, but those who follow the Lord are much concerned about it.

⁶ Better to be poor and honest than rich and a cheater.

⁷ Young men who are wise obey the law; a son who is a member of a lawless gang is a shame to his father.

⁸ Income from exploiting the poor will end up in the hands of someone who pities them.

⁹ God doesn't listen to the prayers of men who flout the law.

¹⁰ A curse on those who lead astray the godly. But men who encourage the upright to do good shall be given a worthwhile reward.

¹¹ Rich men are conceited, but their real poverty is evident to the poor.

¹² When the godly are successful, everyone is glad. When the wicked succeed, everyone is sad.

¹³ A man who refuses to admit his mistakes can never be successful. But if he confesses and forsakes them, he gets another chance.

¹⁴ Blessed is the man who reveres God, but the man who doesn't care is headed for serious trouble.

¹⁵ A wicked ruler is as dangerous to the poor as a lion or bear attacking them.

¹⁶ Only a stupid prince will oppress his people, but a king will have a long reign if he hates dishonesty and bribes.

¹⁷ A murderer's conscience will drive him into hell. Don't stop him!

28:1. The wicked. Though there is no heading here, most writers understand a new subsection. The proverbs in chapters 28; 29 remind us of those in the second section (10:1–22:16), with their frequent contrasts of good and evil.

2. Many are the princes. Their reigns are brief and troubled. **4. Forsake the law.** Toy is right in pointing out that the words imply a codified law, like the law of Moses. He concludes that therefore the verse is late. We could as well argue that the Law is early! **Contend.** They oppose the wicked. Oesterley remarks that "forsaking the law" concords best with the Greek period. As if God's people at other periods were always faithful! **8. Usury.** See notes on 6:1. **9. His prayer shall be abomination.** Because insincere (cf. 20:4).

13. Whoso confesseth. Oesterley argues that this is a late usage of the word (though it occurs in David's psalm of penitence, 32). Toy and Fritsch observe that here forgiveness depends not on sacrifice, but on ethics. This is a good case of arguing from silence. Psalm 32 also omits mention of sacrifice. But David's other psalm of penitence, 51, does enjoin sacrifice in verses 16-19. These verses are cut off by W. R. Taylor (IB, *ad loc.*) as a later appendix. The fact is that God requires both contrition and sacrifice. **14. Mischief.** Trouble, *calamity* (RSV).

17. That doeth violence. Toy, Oesterley, and Fritsch declare the Hebrew impossible. But Greenstone relates the verse to homicide. The root *'shq* appears in Syriac, and clearly means "accuse." A man accused of the blood of a person shall flee unto the pit (or grave). Let them not support him. The verb *'āshaq* is perhaps chosen to contrast with *'āqash* of verse 18.

¹⁸ Whoso walketh uprightly shall be saved: but *he that is* perverse *in his* ways shall fall at once.

¹⁹ He that tilleth his land shall have plenty of bread: but he that followeth after vain *persons* shall have poverty enough.

²⁰ A faithful man shall abound with blessings: but he that maketh haste to be rich shall not be innocent.

²¹ To have respect of persons *is* not good: for for a piece of bread *that* man will transgress.

²² He that hasteth to be rich *hath* an evil eye, and considereth not that poverty shall come upon him.

²³ He that rebuketh a man afterwards shall find more favour than he that flattereth with the tongue.

²⁴ Whoso robbeth his father or his mother, and saith, *It is* no transgression; the same *is* the companion of a destroyer.

²⁵ He that is of a proud heart stirreth up strife: but he that putteth his trust in the Lord shall be made fat.

²⁶ He that trusteth in his own heart is a fool: but whoso walketh wisely, he shall be delivered.

²⁷ He that giveth unto the poor shall not lack: but he that hideth his eyes shall have many a curse.

²⁸ When the wicked rise, men hide themselves: but when they perish, the righteous increase.

CHAPTER 29

He, that being often reproved hardeneth *his* neck, shall suddenly be destroyed, and that without remedy.

² When the righteous are in authority, the people rejoice: but when the wicked beareth rule, the people mourn.

³ Whoso loveth wisdom rejoiceth his father: but he that keepeth company with harlots spendeth *his* substance.

⁴ The king by judgment establisheth the land: but he that receiveth gifts overthroweth it.

⁵ A man that flattereth his neighbour spreadeth a net for his feet. ⁶ In the transgression of an evil man *there is* a snare: but the righteous doth sing and rejoice.

¹⁸ Good men will be rescued from harm, but cheaters will be destroyed.

¹⁹ Hard work brings prosperity; playing around brings poverty.

²⁰ The man who wants to do right will get a rich reward. But the man who wants to get rich quick will quickly fail.

²¹ Giving preferred treatment to rich people is a clear case of selling one's soul for a piece of bread.

²² Trying to get rich quick is evil and leads to poverty.

²³ In the end, people appreciate frankness more than flattery.

²⁴ A man who robs his parents and says, "What's wrong with that?" is no better than a murderer.

²⁵ Greed causes fighting; trusting God leads to prosperity.

²⁶ A man is a fool to trust himself! But those who use God's wisdom are safe.

²⁷ If you give to the poor, your needs will be supplied! But a curse upon those who close their eyes to poverty.

²⁸ When the wicked prosper, good men go away; when the wicked meet disaster, good men return.

29 THE MAN WHO is often reproved but refuses to accept criticism will suddenly be broken and never have another chance.

² With good men in authority, the people rejoice; but with the wicked in power, they groan.

³ A wise son makes his father happy, but a lad who hangs around with prostitutes disgraces him.

⁴ A just king gives stability to his nation, but one who demands bribes destroys it.

⁵,⁶ Flattery is a trap; evil men are caught in it, but good men stay away and sing for joy.

21. Respect of persons. Cf. 18:5 for similar references. **22. An evil eye.** Cf. 23:6. **23. Afterward.** Literally, *after me.* Toy, Oesterley, and Fritsch urge its deletion. A simple change of vowel would make it read easily, "A man rebuking another."

25. A proud heart. A similar phrase occurs in 21:4. **26. Trusteth in his own heart.** A conscious contrast to verse 25, "one trusting in the Lord." **28. When the wicked rise.** Parallel to 28:12, with slight variations.

29:4. He that receiveth gifts. The word **gifts** usually refers to the heave offering of the Temple. But it clearly refers to taxes in Ezk 45:13,16; so here it should be taken as taxes that are too heavy, or gifts that are in effect bribes. It is not the usual word for "bribes." **5. A man**

NOTES

7 The righteous considereth the cause of the poor: *but* the wicked regardeth not to know *it*.

8 Scornful men bring a city into a snare: but wise *men* turn away wrath.

9 *If* a wise man contendeth with a foolish man, whether he rage or laugh, *there is* no rest.

10 The bloodthirsty hate the upright: but the just seek his soul.

11 A fool uttereth all his mind: but a wise *man* keepeth it in till afterwards.

12 If a ruler hearken to lies, all his servants *are* wicked.

13 The poor and the deceitful man meet together: the Lord lighteneth both their eyes.

14 The king that faithfully judgeth the poor, his throne shall be established for ever.

15 The rod and reproof give wisdom: but a child left *to himself* bringeth his mother to shame.

16 When the wicked are multiplied, transgression increaseth: but the righteous shall see their fall.

17 Correct thy son, and he shall give thee rest; yea, he shall give delight unto thy soul.

18 Where *there is* no vision, the people perish: but he that keepeth the law, happy *is* he.

19 A servant will not be corrected by words: for though he understand he will not answer.

20 Seest thou a man *that is* hasty in his words? *there is* more hope of a fool than of him.

21 He that delicately bringeth up his servant from a child shall have him become *his* son at the length.

22 An angry man stirreth up strife, and a furious man aboundeth in transgression.

23 A man's pride shall bring him low: but honour shall uphold the humble in spirit.

24 Whoso is partner with a thief hateth his own soul: he heareth cursing, and bewrayeth *it* not.

25 The fear of man bringeth a snare: but whoso putteth his trust in the Lord shall be safe.

26 Many seek the ruler's favour; but *every* man's judgment *cometh* from the Lord.

7 The good man knows the poor man's rights; the godless don't care.

8 Fools start fights everywhere while wise men try to keep peace.

9 There's no use arguing with a fool. He only rages and scoffs, and tempers flare.

10 The godly pray for those who long to kill them.

11 A rebel shouts in anger; a wise man holds his temper in and cools it.

12 A wicked ruler will have wicked aides on his staff.

13 Rich and poor are alike in this: each depends on God for light.

14 A king who is fair to the poor shall have a long reign.

15 Scolding and spanking a child helps him to learn. Left to himself, he brings shame to his mother.

16 When rulers are wicked, their people are too; but good men will live to see the tyrant's downfall.

17 Discipline your son and he will give you happiness and peace of mind.

18 Where there is ignorance of God, the people run wild; but what a wonderful thing it is for a nation to know and keep his laws!

19 Sometimes mere words are not enough—discipline is needed. For the words may not be heeded.

20 There is more hope for a fool than for a man of quick temper.

21 Pamper a servant from childhood, and he will expect you to treat him as a son!

22 A hot-tempered man starts fights and gets into all kinds of trouble.

23 Pride ends in a fall, while humility brings honor.

24 A man who assists a thief must really hate himself! For he knows the consequence but does it anyway.

25 Fear of man is a dangerous trap, but to trust in God means safety.

26 Do you want justice? Don't fawn on the judge, but ask the Lord for it!

that flatters. Cf. 26:28; 28:23. **8. Into a snare.** Better, *Set a city aflame* (so RSV).

10. The just seek his soul. The usage of **seek** does not seem to admit of "seek to help." Therefore, Oesterley and Fritsch call the second line impossible. Delitzsch and Greenstone solve it satisfactorily by making the "they" refer to the wicked— *they attempt the life of the upright.* **11. Uttereth all his mind.** Not so much **mind** as *anger* (so Delitzsch, Oesterley, RSV).

15. Bringeth his mother to shame. Note the parallel in 19:26.

16. When the wicked are multiplied. Multiplied is the same word as is translated "authority" in verse 2, but it is here applied to the wicked. Oesterley remarks, "See note on verse 2, where the same slight corruption of the text occurs." We would rather say, "See verse 2, where Oesterley again slightly forces the text!" It is not logical to assume the same corruption in two verses without good reason.

18. Where there is no vision. This famous verse has often been misquoted because the word **vision** has taken on new meaning since A.D. 1611. The Hebrew (and originally the AV) means "where there is no prophetic vision, the people perish." The RSV is right, *Where there is no prophecy.* The proverb does not refer to the need for high idealism, as it is often taken to do. There is no warrant for Fritsch's comment here and at 13:13 that the Prophets of the OT were already canonized and the Writings were not. (The author's *Inspiration and Canonicity of the Bible,* pp. 138-148, gives the evidence on the canonization of the Writings.) **Perish.** Better, *cast off* restraint (ASV).

22. An angry man. Similar wording in 15:18; 22:24.

24. Bewrayeth. An old English word for "betray," "divulge." Cf. Lev 5:1, which requires confession from partners in guilt.

25,26. The fear of man and of rulers is overcome by the fear of God (cf. 18:10).

27 An unjust man *is* an abomination to the just: and *he that is* upright in the way *is* abomination to the wicked.

CHAPTER 30

THE words of A-gur the son of Ja-keh, *even* the prophecy: the man spake unto Ith-i-el, even unto Ith-i-el and U-cal,

2 Surely I *am* more brutish than *any* man, and have not the understanding of a man. 3 I neither learned wisdom, nor have the knowledge of the holy. 4 Who hath ascended up into heaven, or descended? who hath gathered the wind in his fists? who hath bound the waters in a garment? who hath established all the ends of the earth? what *is* his name, and what *is* his son's name, if thou canst tell?

5 Every word of God *is* pure: he *is* a shield unto them that put their trust in him. 6 Add thou not unto his words, lest he reprove thee, and thou be found a liar.

27 The good hate the badness of the wicked. The wicked hate the goodness of the good.

30 *These are the messages of Agur, son of Jakeh, from Massa, addressed to Ithiel and Ucal:*
2 I am tired out, O God, and ready to die. I am too stupid even to call myself a human being! 3 I cannot understand man, let alone God. 4 Who else but God goes back and forth to heaven? Who else holds the wind in his fists, and wraps up the oceans in his cloak? Who but God has created the world? If there is any other, what is his name—and his son's name—if you know it?

5 Every word of God proves true. He defends all who come to him for protection. 6 Do not add to his words, lest he rebuke you, and you be found a liar.

VI. Final Appendices. 30:1–31:31.

A. The Words of Agur. 30:1-33. The LXX divides these last chapters into four parts: 30:1-9 is located after 24:22; 30:10-33 and 31:1-9 are found after 24:34; 31:10-31 is at the end of the book. The reference to Agur is difficult to understand. Of Agur, Jakeh, Ithiel, and Ucal (v.1), we know nothing. Furthermore, the time and location of the author are equally obscure. In view of the difficulties of the text, Toy and Oesterley call it hopelessly corrupt. Agur and the other proper names do not occur in the LXX, which begins: "My son, reverence my words, and receive them and repent. Thus saith the man to them that believe in God, and I cease." In this version, the Hebrew words sometimes translated Ithiel and Ucal are probably rendered as common nouns or verbs. The Syriac translates the name Ucal as *prevail* and renders Ithiel only once. The vowels of our present Hebrew text were inserted in late times and apparently served to confuse this section. The original consonants, however, seem to have been very close to what is represented both in the LXX and the Syriac, and in our modern Hebrew.

1. There is no reason to emend the first verse to read — **The words of Agur the son of Jakeh, the oracle which the man saith.** The names **Ithiel** and **Ucal** present more of a problem. The most unusual explanation suggested is that given by Charles C. Torrey ("Proverbs, Chapter 30," JBL, LXXIII (1954), 93-96). He argues that these words are not names but an Aramaic phrase. The letters as they stand in the original, with slightly different vowels, can be translated, "I am not God." They then form a contrast to verse 2, "For I am more brutish than a man." In favor of Torrey's suggestion is the well-known fact that in 31:2 the Aramaic word for "son" is used three times.

4. **What is his name, and what is his son's name?** The speaker seeks the answer to the riddle of the universe in words reminiscent of God's challenge to Job in Job 38:4-9. He seeks for God. The question about God's **son** is peculiar. Greenstone denies that the name applies to Israel or Moses or the Logos, but gives no positive suggestion to explain it. Delitzsch suggests that it refers to the mediator in creation, revealed at last as God's Son. He well remarks, "He would not

have ventured this question if he did not suppose that God was not a unity who was without manifoldness in Himself."

5. **Every word of God is tried.** This verse is quoted verbatim from Ps 18:30, substituting the Aramaic form of **God** for "Lord." The idea is that the answer to his search is in God's Word. Cf. other quotations from the OT in 1:16; 3:11; 20:24; 24:19; 25:18; 30:5. 6. **Add thou not.** From Deut 4:2. Oesterley and Fritsch are right in calling this a reference to Scripture. Oesterley, however, says much that cannot be supported about the third division of the OT not being complete until Christian times. The Dead Sea scrolls show the OT canon to have been complete in the second century B.C. at least. See exegesis of 29:18.

NOTES

⁷ Two *things* have I required of thee; deny me *them* not before I die: ⁸ Remove far from me vanity and lies: give me neither poverty nor riches; feed me with food convenient for me: ⁹ Lest I be full, and deny *thee,* and say, Who *is* the Lord? or lest I be poor, and steal, and take the name of my God *in vain.*

¹⁰ Accuse not a servant unto his master, lest he curse thee, and thou be found guilty.

¹¹ *There is* a generation *that* curseth their father, and doth not bless their mother. ¹² *There is* a generation *that are* pure in their own eyes, and *yet* is not washed from their filthiness. ¹³ *There is* a generation, O how lofty are their eyes! and their eyelids are lifted up. ¹⁴ *There is* a generation, whose teeth *are as* swords, and their jaw teeth *as* knives, to devour the poor from off the earth, and the needy from *among* men.

¹⁵ The horseleach hath two daughters, *crying,* Give, give. There are three *things that* are never satisfied, *yea,* four *things* say not, *It is* enough: ¹⁶ The grave; and the barren womb; the earth *that* is not filled with water; and the fire *that* saith not, *It is* enough.

¹⁷ The eye *that* mocketh at *his* father, and despiseth to obey *his* mother, the ravens of the valley shall pick it out, and the young eagles shall eat it.

¹⁸ There be three *things which* are too wonderful for me, yea, four which I know not: ¹⁹ The way of an eagle in the air; the way of a serpent upon a rock; the way of a ship in the midst of the sea; and the way of a man with a maid. ²⁰ Such *is* the way of an adulterous woman; she eateth, and wipeth her mouth, and saith, I have done no wickedness.

⁷ O God, I beg two favors from you before I die: ⁸ First, help me never to tell a lie. Second, give me neither poverty nor riches! Give me just enough to satisfy my needs! ⁹ For if I grow rich, I may become content without God. And if I am too poor, I may steal, and thus insult God's holy name.

¹⁰ Never falsely accuse a man to his employer, lest he curse you for your sin.

¹¹,¹² There are those who curse their father and mother, and feel themselves faultless despite their many sins. ¹³,¹⁴ They are proud beyond description, arrogant, disdainful. They devour the poor with teeth as sharp as knives!

¹⁵,¹⁶ There are two things never satisfied, like a leech forever craving more: no, three things! no, four!

> Hell
> The barren womb
> A barren desert
> Fire

¹⁷ A man who mocks his father and despises his mother shall have his eye plucked out by ravens and eaten by vultures.

¹⁸,¹⁹ There are three things too wonderful for me to understand—no, four!

> How an eagle glides through the sky.
> How a serpent crawls upon a rock.
> How a ship finds its way across the heaving ocean.
> The growth of love between a man and a girl.

²⁰ There is another thing too: how a prostitute can sin and then say, "What's wrong with that?"

7-33. Numerical proverbs (cf. Introd., *Proverbs and Other Wisdom Literature*). In these sequences of three things, yea, four, it is probably the climactic fourth that is emphasized. It is the author's contention that in the Beatitudes, also, there is this climactic teaching in the two sets of four blessings: Mt 5:3-6; 7-10; see also Lk 6:20-23,24-26. Jesus' teaching in the Jewish proverbial and climactic method emphasizes the fourth item.

8. Feed me with food convenient for me. The Hebrew is, *appointed for me.*

10. Do not accuse. *Calumniate* (Delitzsch). This proverb is the only one in this section standing alone, says Oesterley. Toy thinks it out of place. But likely, as in 6:14-19, the numerical proverb begins with a thought that is reiterated in the concluding statement. "Do not slander a servant," says verse 10. The climactic item mentioned in verse 14 speaks of one with "teeth as knives."

15. The horseleech. This proverb has occasioned much comment because of the obscurity of the point. Toy and Oesterley conclude that the text is corrupt. Delitzsch repeats in the middle of verse 15 the reference to the grave and barren womb from 16. The LXX assigns three daughters to the leech. Our trouble is in seeking too much. For the numerical proverb, all that is required is a backdrop to set off the climax. Verse 7 refers to two things; cf. notes on verse 17. The two insatiate daughters of the leech in verse 15 simply form a background for the 3 and 4 of 15 and 16. The sage could count!

17. Mocketh at his father. An isolated verse, out of place, say Oesterley and Fritsch. As noted above, it is part of a regular sequence—2 plus 3, yea 4. Mocking the father and despising the mother are the backdrop to the **three** and **four** of verses 18-20.

19. The way of a man with a maid. This **maid** is the famous word *'almâ*, "maiden," used in Isa 7:14; Gen 24:43 (of Rebecca); Ex 2:8 (of Miriam); Ps 68:25; and Song 1:3; 6:8 (where the "virgins" are distinguished from queens and concubines). The word nowhere refers to a married woman. In the case of the girl Miriam, it could hardly refer to a marriageable girl. It means a virgin and a young virgin. The root means "conceal." Probably the word refers to a maiden still kept in her father's house. Toy, Oesterley, Fritsch, and Greenstone take the point of our verse to be not the

marvels of courtship, but the mysteries of procreation. But Delitzsch points out that there are other words—"male and female," or "man and wife"—to express this. Here the words are literally, *strong man* and *maiden.* Delitzsch takes the proverb as a reference to sin, immorality concealed. However, the "virgin" seems to be contrasted with the adulteress of verse 20. And adultery as it is repeatedly pictured in Proverbs is never represented as **wonderful** or "past knowledge." There seems to be no good reason why the more romantic view cannot still be held: Wonderful is the way of courtship, issuing at last in the mysteries of love and life begotten.

NOTES

²¹ For three *things* the earth is disquieted, and for four *which* it cannot bear: ²² For a servant when he reigneth; and a fool when he is filled with meat; ²³ For an odious *woman* when she is married; and an handmaid that is heir to her mistress.

²⁴ There be four *things which are* little upon the earth, but they *are* exceeding wise: ²⁵ The ants *are* a people not strong, yet they prepare their meat in the summer; ²⁶ The conies *are but* a feeble folk, yet make they their houses in the rocks; ²⁷ The locusts have no king, yet go they forth all of them by bands; ²⁸ The spider taketh hold with her hands, and is in kings' palaces.

²⁹ There be three *things* which go well, yea, four are comely in going: ³⁰ A lion *which is* strongest among beasts, and turneth not away for any; ³¹ A greyhound; an he goat also; and a king, against whom *there is* no rising up.

³² If thou hast done foolishly in lifting up thyself, or if thou hast thought evil, *lay* thine hand upon thy mouth.

³³ Surely the churning of milk bringeth forth butter, and the wringing of the nose bringeth forth blood: so the forcing of wrath bringeth forth strife.

CHAPTER 31

THE words of king Lem-u-el, the prophecy that his mother taught him. ² What, my son? and what, the son of my womb? and what, the son of my vows? ³ Give not thy strength unto women, nor thy ways to that which destroyeth kings.

⁴ *It is* not for kings, O Lem-u-el, *it is* not for kings to drink wine; nor for princes strong drink: ⁵ Lest they drink, and forget the law, and pervert the judgment of any of the afflicted. ⁶ Give strong drink unto him that is ready to perish, and wine unto those that be of heavy hearts. ⁷ Let him drink, and forget his poverty, and remember his misery no more.

²¹,²²,²³ There are three things that make the earth tremble—no, four it cannot stand:

A slave who becomes a king.

A rebel who prospers.

A bitter woman when she finally marries.

A servant girl who marries her mistress' husband.

²⁴⁻²⁸ There are four things that are small but unusually wise:

Ants: they aren't strong, but store up food for the winter.

Cliff badgers: delicate little animals who protect themselves by living among the rocks.

The locusts: though they have no leader, they stay together in swarms.

The lizards: they are easy to catch and kill, yet are found even in king's palaces!

²⁹,³⁰,³¹ There are three stately monarchs in the earth—no, four:

The lion, king of the animals. He won't turn aside for anyone.

The peacock.

The he-goat.

A king as he leads his army.

³² If you have been a fool by being proud or plotting evil, don't brag about it—cover your mouth with your hand in shame.

³³ As the churning of cream yields butter, and a blow to the nose causes bleeding, so anger causes quarrels.

31 *These are the wise sayings of King Lemuel of Massa, taught to him at his mother's knee:*

² O my son, whom I have dedicated to the Lord, ³ do not spend your time with women—the royal pathway to destruction.

⁴ And it is not for kings, O Lemuel, to drink wine and whiskey. ⁵ For if they drink they may forget their duties and be unable to give justice to those who are oppressed. ⁶,⁷ Hard liquor is for sick men at the brink of death, and wine for those in deep depression. Let them drink to forget their poverty and misery.

21-31. Three sets of proverbs on authority and kingship. The point of the first two is not clear, yet each of the three has some reference to the king. Perhaps the first two especially set off the last one. **23. An handmaid that is heir.** An upside down situation, like a servant's being king. **25. The ants.** See comment on 6:6-8. **26. The conies.** Not rabbits, which do not live in the rocks, but apparently cliff badgers, peculiar little animals, distantly related to the rhinoceros (ISBE, article, "coney"). Conies are classed as unclean in the Mosaic law (Lev 11:5; Deut 14:7), because they chew the cud. Some have objected that conies are not ruminants and only seem to chew the cud. The description in Leviticus, however, is probably not intended to be a scientific description of ruminants, but only a classification based on the easily observed chewing habits of these cliff badgers. The Hebrew may mean no more than that. **27. Locusts.** Not the cicada or seventeen-year locust, but a type of grasshopper. **28. Spider.** Opinions differ regarding the translation of this word, but Delitzsch gives good argument for the meaning "lizard"—a small animal which you can take in your hands (RSV), and which invades king's palaces.

31. Greyhound. The meaning of the Hebrew word is uncertain. The RSV says *strutting cock,* but Delitzsch's arguments for **greyhound** are reasonable. **Rising up.** The Hebrew word is unknown. The LXX *speaking publicly before his nation* is as good a reading as we can get.

B. The Words of Lemuel. 31:1-9. The LXX omits the name of Lemuel in 1 and 4. The Syriac renders it Muel.

1. Prophecy. This is the word for a prophetic oracle. But it could be the name of a place (RSV, *Lemuel, king of Massa).* It is difficult to account for the absence of the article with "king," but there are no articles in this section, perhaps because of Aramaic influence. It seems easiest to translate the first part as a title: "The words of King Lemuel, a prophecy, the words which his mother taught him."

2. What, my son? Three times the word "son" is used in the Aramaic form *bar,* as in Ps 2:12. **3. Kings.** Again, an Aramaic form. **4. It is not for kings.** The choice of the negative is peculiar, as in 12:28. The LXX follows a different text,

but the Hebrew seems preferable. Delitzsch suggests the translation, "Let it not be . . . ." It is the more difficult reading, and, as is generally agreed, the harder reading is usually preferred.

6. Give strong drink. As mentioned at 23:31, this is not an allowance of moderate drinking, as Fritsch suggests, nor cynical advice (Oesterley). It may recommend alcohol as a drug (Toy). Delitzsch mentions the wine offered at executions by the noble women at Jerusalem on the basis of this verse (cf. Mk 15:23). More likely, however, the verse is a comparative negative (cf. 8:10): Regardless of others, you should not take it. Wine, women, and song are the old debasing trio. A king has a higher responsibility, for which see verses 8,9.

NOTES

10 - 31

8 Open thy mouth for the dumb in the cause of all such as are appointed to destruction. 9 Open thy mouth, judge righteously, and plead the cause of the poor and needy.

10 Who can find a virtuous woman? for her price *is* far above rubies. 11 The heart of her husband doth safely trust in her, so that he shall have no need of spoil. 12 She will do him good and not evil all the days of her life. 13 She seeketh wool, and flax, and worketh willingly with her hands. 14 She is like the merchants' ships; she bringeth her food from afar. 15 She riseth also while it is yet night, and giveth meat to her household, and a portion to her maidens. 16 She considereth a field, and buyeth it: with the fruit of her hands she planteth a vineyard. 17 She girdeth her loins with strength, and strengtheneth her arms. 18 She perceiveth that her merchandise *is* good: her candle goeth not out by night.

19 She layeth her hands to the spindle, and her hands hold the distaff. 20 She stretcheth out her hand to the poor; yea, she reacheth forth her hands to the needy. 21 She is not afraid of the snow for her household: for all her household *are* clothed with scarlet. 22 She maketh herself coverings of tapestry; her clothing *is* silk and purple. 23 Her husband is known in the gates, when he sitteth among the elders of the land. 24 She maketh fine linen, and selleth *it;* and delivereth girdles unto the merchant.

25 Strength and honour *are* her clothing; and she shall rejoice in time to come. 26 She openeth her mouth with wisdom; and in her tongue *is* the law of kindness. 27 She looketh well to the ways of her household, and eateth not the bread of idleness. 28 Her children arise up, and call her blessed; her husband *also,* and he praiseth her. 29 Many daughters have done virtuously, but thou excellest them all.

30 Favour *is* deceitful, and beauty *is* vain: *but* a woman *that* feareth the Lord, she shall be praised. 31 Give her of the fruit of her hands; and let her own works praise her in the gates.

8 You should defend those who cannot help themselves. 9 Yes, speak up for the poor and needy and see that they get justice.

10 If you can find a truly good wife, she is worth more than precious gems! 11 Her husband can trust her, and she will richly satisfy his needs. 12 She will not hinder him, but help him all her life. 13 She finds wool and flax and busily spins it. 14 She buys imported foods, brought by ship from distant ports. 15 She gets up before dawn to prepare breakfast for her household, and plans the day's work for her servant girls. 16 She goes out to inspect a field, and buys it; with her own hands she plants a vineyard. 17 She is energetic, a hard worker, 18 and watches for bargains. She works far into the night!

19,20 She sews for the poor, and generously gives to the needy. 21 She has no fear of winter for her household, for she has made warm clothes for all of them. 22 She also upholsters with finest tapestry; her own clothing is beautifully made—a purple gown of pure linen. 23 Her husband is well known, for he sits in the council chamber with the other civic leaders. 24 She makes belted linen garments to sell to the merchants.

25 She is a woman of strength and dignity, and has no fear of old age. 26 When she speaks, her words are wise, and kindness is the rule for everything she says. 27 She watches carefully all that goes on throughout her household, and is never lazy. 28 Her children stand and bless her; so does her husband. He praises her with these words: 29 "There are many fine women in the world, but you are the best of them all!"

30 Charm can be deceptive and beauty doesn't last, but a woman who fears and reverences God shall be greatly praised. 31 Praise her for the many fine things she does. These good deeds of hers shall bring her honor and recognition from even the leaders of the nations.

C. Alphabetical Poem on the Virtuous Woman. 31:10-31. The alphabet in this piece is regular, as in Lamentations 1 and Psalm 119. (Lamentations 2; 3; 4 have the letters *Ayin* and *Pe* reversed. Some of the alphabetical psalms have minor irregularities). Since an alphabet was discovered in Ugarit dating from the fifteenth century, alphabetical pieces need no longer be thought of as late.

10. A virtuous woman. Literally, *a noble wife*. The same phrase as in 12:4. Fritsch remarks on the high status of women shown in 12:4; 18:22; 19:14; and other places.

15. Meat to her household. The Hebrew words for **food** and **portion** are unusual, but used in a very similar sense in 30:8. **16. She considereth a field.** Oesterley remarks that this is exaggeration, since "these things were wholly outside a woman's sphere." Can we really be so sure? Do we not tend to judge ancient Israel by modern Arabia? **18. Candle.** The oil lamp of ancient times. Does this refer to a custom of burning lamps all night? The meaning is, she has plenty of oil. Contrast Mt 25:8.

19. Spindle . . . distaff. The RSV reverses these. The word for "spindle" is used only here. "Distaff" in one other case seems to mean "staff." The Hebrew women had no spinning wheel, but rotated doughnut-shaped weights on sticks to form thread. This was their **spindle.** The word now is found in Ugaritic as a woman's instrument, but the context adds little of detail (Story, *op. cit.*, p. 329). **21. Scarlet.** The LXX says *double,* using different vowels. This would fit well because of the mention of cold, but the change is not necessary. The word means good clothing.

26. Wisdom. Her virtues are not mere industry. Wisdom and kindness and nobility are hers—not the characteristics of a sluggard. These virtues, typical of the Book of Proverbs, are capped by the fact that she "feareth the Lord" (v. 30; cf. 1:7).

The book ends as it begins, with that wisdom which is the fear of the Lord.

BIBLIOGRAPHY

DELITZSCH, FRANZ. *The Proverbs of Solomon.* Grand Rapids: William B. Eerdmans Publishing Company, reprinted, 1950.

DRIVER, S. R. *Introduction to the Literature of the Old Testament,* 4th ed. New York: Scribners, 1893.

FRITSCH, CHARLES T. "The Book of Proverbs, Introduction and Exegesis," *Interpreter's Bible.* Vol. IV. New York and Nashville: Abingdon, 1955.

GORDON, CYRUS H. *Ugaritic Handbook.* Rome: Pontifical Biblical Institute, 1947.

————. *Ugaritic Literature.* Rome: Pontifical Biblical Institute, 1949.

GREENSTONE, JULIUS H. *Proverbs with Commentary.* Philadelphia: Jewish Publication Society of America, 1950.

HARRIS, R. LAIRD. *Inspiration and the Canonicity of the Bible.* Grand Rapids: Zondervan Publishing House, 1957.

JONES, W. A. REES and WALLS, ANDREW F. "The Proverbs," *The New Bible Commentary.* Edited by F. Davidson, A. M. Stibbs, and E. F. Kevan. London: Inter-Varsity Press, 1953.

NOTH, M. and THOMAS, D. W. (eds.). *Wisdom in Israel and the Ancient Near East.* Leiden: Brill, 1955.

OESTERLEY, W. O. E. *The Book of Proverbs.* New York: Dutton, 1929.

————. *The Wisdom of Egypt and the Old Testament.* London: Society for the Promotion of Christian Knowledge, 1927.

PFEIFFER, ROBERT H. *Introduction to the Old Testament.* New York: Harper & Brothers, 1948.

PRITCHARD, JAMES B. (ed.). *Ancient Near Eastern Texts Relating To the Old Testament.* Princeton, Princeton University Press, 1955.

STORY, CULLEN I. K. "The Book of Proverbs and Northwest Semitic Literature," *Journal of Biblical Literature,* LXIV (1945), 319-337.

TORREY, CHARLES C. "Proverbs, Chapter 30," *Journal of Biblical Literature,* LXXIII (1954), 93-96.

TOY, CRAWFORD H. *The Book of Proverbs. (The International Critical Commentary.)* Edinburgh: T. & T. Clark, 1899.

YOUNG, EDWARD J. *An Introduction to the Old Testament.* Grand Rapids: William B. Eerdmans Publishing Company, 1949.